Donated to
Augustana University College
by

Mark Lede

93/94 ANNUAL FUND

A . M . K L E I N

AN ANNOTATED BIBLIOGRAPHY

A.M. Klein

AN ANNOTATED BIBLIOGRAPHY

*Zailig Pollock, Usher Caplan,
and Linda Rozmovits*

ECW PRESS

1993

CANADIAN CATALOGUING IN PUBLICATION DATA

Pollock, Zailig, 1948–
A.M. Klein: an annotated bibliography

Includes indexes.
ISBN 1-55022-095-0

1. Klein, A.M. (Abraham Moses), 1909–1972 –
Bibliography.   I. Caplan, Usher, 1947– .   II. Rozmovits, Linda, 1959–
III. Title.

1993
REF   PS8521.L43Z991016.811′52C92-094268-7
z8466.55C36 1993

74262

This book has been published with the assistance of a grant from the
Canadian Federation for the Humanities, using funds provided
by the Social Sciences and Humanities Research Council of Canada.
Additional grants have been provided by the
Ontario Arts Council and The Canada Council.

Design and imaging by ECW Type & Art, Oakville, Ontario.
Distributed by General Publishing Co. Limited, Don Mills, Ontario.

Published by ECW PRESS,
1980 Queen Street East, Toronto, Ontario M4L 1J2

TABLE OF CONTENTS

INTRODUCTION

A.M. KLEIN has long been recognized as the most gifted Canadian poet of his generation and, many would add, the most gifted poet Canada has yet produced. This note is first sounded by Leon Edel, in the earliest recorded appreciation of Klein, and it has been echoed throughout the years by a wide variety of critics and poets, English, French, and Yiddish (see, for example, comments by Munroe Beattie, E.K. Brown, H.M. Caiserman-Vital, Northrop Frye, Jacob Glatstein, Irving Layton, Seymour Mayne, T.A. Marshall, Robert Melançon, A.J.M. Smith, and William Walsh). But, although recognition of Klein's outstanding gifts has been widespread, there has been less agreement concerning the extent to which Klein's potential found fulfilment in the course of his career. Two issues arise repeatedly in discussions of this question. The first is the brutal abruptness with which Klein's career came to its end, when he was still apparently at the height of his powers. The second issue is Klein's relationship with his community, a relationship which clearly enriched his art in many ways, but which may have seriously constrained it as well. These two issues are not unconnected, for there is much to suggest that Klein's often troubled relationship with his community played at least some role in precipitating his final breakdown.

Klein was born in 1909, in Ratno, Ukraine, and was brought to Montreal the next year where he grew up in a vital Jewish milieu. This milieu shaped Klein's perceptions of and attitudes to the world, even after it had ceased to exist in the form in which he first knew it, and even when it no longer formed the immediate subject matter of his verse. It was a milieu in which Yiddish culture was still vigorous and in which the poet and man of letters still had a role to play in relation to his community, as spokesman, advocate, mediator, a role which had no real parallel anywhere else in Canada at this period. Throughout his career Klein never abandoned his vision of the poet's social role, and from this perspective his years as editor of the *Canadian Jewish Chronicle* and as speech writer for Samuel Bronfman can be at least partly understood as an extension, rather than a contradiction, of his poetic vocation.

Klein was not unattracted by the modernist vision of art as a means of transcending the demands and responsibilities of the social world, as seen, for example, in Rainer Maria Rilke or Wallace Stevens, but he could never fully accept the possibility of existing as a poet apart from a sustaining community. In his early poetry, dating from the late 1920s and early 1930s, Klein consciously set himself the task of giving voice to his immediate Jewish community and its traditions. By the time *The Rocking Chair and Other Poems* was published in 1948, his constituency had enlarged to include the Québécois and, by implication, all humanity, but the role remained essentially the same. And it is a source of great poignance in his most important poem, "Portrait of the Poet as Landscape," that, although the poet is forced to acknowledge that his role has been usurped and perverted by impostors, he refuses, in the end, to abandon it, even in the face of almost overwhelming despair.

Klein's conception of the poet's social role gives his poetry, at its best, a broad human dimension lacking in the work of many of his contemporaries. But this conception is not without its dangers as well. The early Jewish poetry, in particular, has been criticized for being limited by its essentially uncritical celebratory spirit, which can sometimes lead to a romanticized simplification of experience. Related charges have been brought against the darker poems of the late 1930s and early 1940s — the political satires, *The Hitleriad* (1944), and *Poems* (1944) — in which Klein presents himself as spokesman for speechless victims, first of the Depression and then of Hitler. These works have been seen by critics such as Randall Jarrell (in his unjust but not imperceptive review of *Poems*) and John Sutherland as essentially public rhetoric that substitutes for the genuine private voice of poetry responding to the complexities of experience. It is not to deny the many fine successes in *Hath Not a Jew . . .* (1940) and *Poems*, as well as in isolated passages of the political satires and *The Hitleriad*, to admit that there is some truth in these charges.

The Rocking Chair and Other Poems, however, is another matter. In this collection, Klein still retains his social role as advocate of greater understanding and sympathy among human communities, but his purpose is more implicit and more subtly conveyed than before. The Québécois community he portrays in *The Rocking Chair and Other Poems* is one that he understands because of its parallels with his own, but he can view it with a greater sense of ironic distance, and hence with a greater freedom, than was ever possible to him in his specifically Jewish poems. Klein was a great admirer of James Joyce (whose *Ulysses* became the subject of a massive unfinished commentary that dominated the last years of his career), and he was perhaps inspired by the boldness of the Catholic Joyce, in entering the mind of the Jew Leopold Bloom, to attempt the reverse himself. Klein's portrayal of the Catholic milieu of Quebec — its mixture of irony and of sympathy, of deep attraction and perhaps equally deep suspicion — is the closest he ever got to the spirit of Joyce.

More obviously Joycean in form — with its multilayered language and mythic substructure — is Klein's last published work, the novel *The Second Scroll* (1951). But the book differs greatly from the works of Joyce as well as from *The Rocking Chair and Other Poems* in spirit, more specifically in the distance it takes on its subject: in one way it is less distanced, in another more so. It is less distanced in that Klein is once more in a very explicit way the spokesman for his people, an advocate for a cause, totally unironic in his commitment to it. But it is more distanced as well, since what he responds to in Israel is essentially foreign to his own experience as a Jew of the Diaspora. The founding of the Israeli state moves Klein profoundly, but in a real sense it calls his very existence as a Jew and as a poet into question, and his palpable excitement is not untinged with anxiety. *The Second Scroll* was, on the whole, well received, but it has always been a much more controversial achievement than *The Rocking Chair and Other Poems*, and rightly so. It contains some of Klein's finest writing, but many passages appear worked up, overwrought. If, in *The Rocking Chair and Other Poems*, Klein achieved a near perfect balance between his private voice and his public role, in *The Second Scroll* there is a sense of tension rather than balance, a sense that, in hindsight, perhaps forebodes Klein's final collapse.

Just as controversial as Klein's vision of the poet's role has been the language through which he expresses this vision, and for similar reasons: Klein's sense of himself as part of a sustaining community extends to his sense of language as well. Few other writers (an obvious exception is his master, Joyce) have drawn so lavishly on the wealth of vocabulary, idiom, and poetic expression accumulated by the vast community of English speakers from Chaucer's day to our own. Klein also makes his own contributions to this wealth from Yiddish, Hebrew, Latin, and French (to name only the languages most important to him). Clearly, this approach to language is an expression of Klein's sense of himself as part of a larger sustaining community, which he sustains in return. If Klein's writing is sometimes overblown and self-indulgent, as Louis Dudek charges, at its frequent best it is not. Even when Klein's ambitions fail they "are not mean ambitions. It is something / merely to entertain them" ("Portrait of the Poet as Landscape").

At the time of his breakdown in the early 1950s, Klein was engaged on a number of works, mostly in prose. Much of this material is of great psychological interest and some (for example, the unfinished novel, "The Golem") suggests that Klein's best work, in prose at least, may still have lain ahead of him. After his death in 1972, Klein's papers were deposited in the National Archives of Canada, where they were catalogued and made available on microfilm. The availability of this material, as well as the appearance of most of Klein's previously published poetry in *The Collected Poems of A.M. Klein*, compiled by Miriam Waddington, helped fuel new interest in Klein, and more has been written on him in the last two decades than ever before. The most important development in Klein studies in recent years is the publication of his collected works, of which four volumes have already appeared: *Beyond Sambation: Selected Essays and Editorials, 1928–1955*, *The Short Stories of A.M. Klein*, *Literary Essays and Reviews*, and *The Complete Poems of A.M. Klein*. Future volumes will include previously unpublished prose, letters, and *The Second Scroll*.

Part I of this bibliography is based on the bibliography prepared by Usher Caplan and included in his dissertation on Klein [C247], an earlier version of which was published in the *A.M. Klein Symposium* [C5]. The current version contains one major addition, an annotated, indexed bibliography of Klein's journalism, prepared by Zailig Pollock and Linda Rozmovits. This replaces the selective section on the journalism in Caplan's bibliography. Apart from this major addition, the current version contains a number of minor corrections and additions.

Under "Books," Klein's three poetry pamphlets have been included. Prose pamphlets, which are best seen as an extension of Klein's journalism, are listed under "Essays, Articles, and Reviews."

"Essays, Articles, and Reviews" consists of an annotated list of Klein's journalism, mostly material Klein wrote for various Jewish periodicals from the late 1920s to the mid-1950s. Klein edited the monthly *Judaean* (Montreal) from October 1928 to June 1932, the monthly *Canadian Zionist* from September 1936 to June 1937, and the weekly *Canadian Jewish Chronicle* from November 1938 to June 1955. He also wrote editorials for the *Chronicle* for several weeks each summer during the early and middle 1930s, and a column for the daily *Keneder Adler* (also called *Canadian Jewish Eagle*, *Jewish Daily Eagle*, and *The Eagle*), from December 1938 to September 1941. Much of the material from this column was reprinted in the *Canadian Jewish Chronicle*.

With the exceptions noted below, the items in "Essays, Articles, and Reviews" are listed chronologically, each one preceded by a seven-character code indicating year, month, day, and distinguishing between items appearing on the same day. Thus, 40.08.30E means the fifth item listed for 30 August 1940. The index to this material is keyed to these codes.

Since Klein's titles are often cryptic, each item is annotated: the title is followed by a brief summary, in brackets. When an item has been reprinted, the annotation is given for the first printing; reprintings are cross-listed to the earliest version. The one exception is items that first appeared in the *Keneder Adler* and were reprinted in the *Canadian Jewish Chronicle*. Since the *Canadian Jewish Chronicle* is much more accessible than the *Keneder Adler*, the *Chronicle* versions have been annotated and the *Adler* versions cross-listed. In any case, when a piece in the *Adler* was reprinted in the *Chronicle* the delay was never more than a few days. When unpublished or undated versions of an item exist (the latter generally mimeographed pamphlets issued by the Hadassah Organization), they are noted after the main entry.

Each item is identified as signed [s], initialled [i], or unsigned [u]. In attributing unsigned material to Klein, we have chosen to err on the side of caution. In the case of material appearing in journals other than the *Canadian Jewish Chronicle*, only those items that are explicitly attributed to Klein have been listed. The items from the *Canadian Jewish Chronicle* present a more complex case. As far as we are able to judge, Klein indicated whenever a particular item was not written by him, at least until the final years of his editorship. It is in the final years that genuine difficulties of attribution arise. In the early 1950s, Klein began to show the first signs of his eventual collapse; he continued as editor of the *Canadian Jewish Chronicle* until June of 1955, but his contributions to it became increasingly intermittent in the period leading up to his resignation. In the case of material from this period, only those items have been included which all three editors of this bibliography are convinced, on the basis of style and subject matter, are by Klein. There are, no doubt, a number of items by Klein that we have omitted. However, we are reasonably confident that all the items included are by Klein.

Certain items have been listed separately from the main list. These include the three articles on Joyce, which are qualitatively different from Klein's journalism. We felt that inclusion of these items in the main list would serve little purpose and would, in fact, make them less accessible. Three undated mimeographed pamphlets have also been listed separately.

All of Klein's anonymous work for Samuel Bronfman, head of Seagram's and president of the Canadian Jewish Congress from 1939 to 1959, has been omitted. A large amount of this material (in the form of drafts and carbon copies) is included in the Klein papers.

No reference has been made to very fragmentary manuscripts, miscellaneous notes, and notebooks (including some short diaries).

Part II of the bibliography was prepared by Zailig Pollock. It is possible to state with some confidence that all the major Canadian writings on Klein have been included, but a substantial amount has been written on Klein in Jewish books and periodicals throughout the world and some items of this sort may have been missed.

— Zailig Pollock

ACKNOWLEDGEMENTS

Most of the research for this bibliography was done at the following institutions: the National Archives of Canada, the National Library of Canada, the Jewish Public Library of Montreal, the New York Public Library, McGill University's McLennan Library, the University of Toronto's Robarts Library, the Trent University Library, and the archives of the Canadian Jewish Congress in Montreal.

We would like to thank John Pollock and Didi Pollock for providing translations of the Yiddish items in Part II. We would also like to thank the following individuals for valuable assistance of various kinds: Adam Fuerstenberg, Seymour Mayne, Judith Nefsky, Michael Peterman, David Rome, and Francis Zichy.

The preparation of the annotated, indexed bibliography of Klein's journalism was made possible through two grants awarded by the Strategic Grants Division of the Social Sciences and Humanities Research Council of Canada, under the Canadian Studies Research Tools program.

I

Works by A.M. Klein

A   Books (Poetry, Prose Fiction, Translations [Prose], Posthumous Collections) and Manuscripts

Poetry

A1   *Hath Not a Jew* . . . . New York: Behrman's Jewish Book House, 1940. 116 pp.

A2   *The Hitleriad.* New York: New Directions, 1944. 31 pp.

A3   *Poems.* Philadelphia: Jewish Publication Society of America, 1944. 82 pp. Reprint ed., New York: Arno, 1975.

A4   *Poems of French Canada.* [Montreal: Canadian Jewish Congress, 1947.] 8 pp.

A5   *Seven Poems.* [Montreal: Canadian Jewish Congress, 1948.] 8 pp.

A6   *Huit poèmes canadiens* (en anglais). Montreal: [Canadian Jewish Congress, 1948.] 16 pp.

A7   *The Rocking Chair and Other Poems.* Toronto: Ryerson, 1948. Reprinted with drawings by Thoreau MacDonald, 1951, 1966. 56 pp.

Prose Fiction

A8   *The Second Scroll.* New York: Knopf, 1951. Second printing, 1952. 198 pp.

_____. Introd. M.W. Steinberg. New Canadian Library, No. 22. Toronto: McClelland and Stewart, 1957. 142 pp.

_____. Introd. Sidney Feshbach. Marlboro, Vt.: Marlboro, 1985. 198 pp. [A photographic reprint of the Knopf edition.]

_____. *Le Second Rouleau*. Trans. by Charlotte and Robert Melançon. Montreal: Boréal, 1990. 217 pp.

Translations [Prose]

A9 *Journey of My Life*. [H. Wolofsky.] Montreal: Eagle, 1945. 181 pp.

A10 *From Palestine to Israel*. [Moishe Dickstein.] Montreal: Eagle, 1951. 108 pp.

A11 *Of Jewish Music, Ancient and Modern*. [Israel Rabinovitch.] Montreal: Book Centre, 1952. 321 pp.

Posthumous Collections

A12 *The Collected Poems of A.M. Klein*. Compiled with an Introd. by Miriam Waddington. Toronto: McGraw-Hill Ryerson, 1974. 373 pp.

A13 *Beyond Sambation: Selected Essays and Editorials 1928–1955*. Ed. by M.W. Steinberg and Usher Caplan, with an Introd. by M.W. Steinberg. Toronto: Univ. of Toronto Press, 1982. 541 pp.

A14 *The Short Stories of A.M. Klein*. Ed. with an Introd. by M.W. Steinberg. Toronto: Univ. of Toronto Press, 1983. 338 pp.

A15 *A.M. Klein: Poesie*. Selected and translated, with an afterword by Mariantonietta di Stefano. Rome: Bulzoni, 1984. 213 pp.

A16 *Literary Essays and Reviews*. Ed. by Usher Caplan and M.W. Steinberg, with an Introd. by Usher Caplan. Toronto: Univ. of Toronto Press, 1987. 424 pp.

A17 *A.M. Klein: The Complete Poems*. Ed. with an Introd. by Zailig Pollock. 2 vols. Toronto: Univ. of Toronto Press, 1990. 1115 pp.

A18 *Doctor Dwarf & Other Poems for Children*. Ed. Mary Alice Downie and Barbara Robertson. Illus. by Gail Gertner. Kingston, Ont.: Quarry, 1990. n.p.

Manuscripts

A19 A.M. Klein Papers
National Archives of Canada
Ottawa, Ontario

The National Archives of Canada acquired A.M. Klein's personal papers from his heirs in 1973. In the interest of conservation, access to the original papers is restricted, but microfilms of the collection are available at the Archives and, for limited periods, through interlibrary loans. A small number of items have been added to the collection since 1973. The Klein collection also includes photographs in the National Photography Collection and sound recordings of material by and about Klein in the Sound Archives [see B537 and C260–C264]. The following general outline lists the material by volumes. For a more detailed listing, see Finding Aid No. 3 at the National Archives.

Vols. 1–3 Correspondence; two fragmentary diaries.

Vols. 3–11 Literary manuscripts — poetry, fiction, drama, criticism, and translations; copies of Klein's own books, with his revisions.

Vols. 11–14 Speeches and lectures on general and Jewish topics; notes for readings; McGill lecture notes; pocket notebooks, assorted notes, and fragments; edited material.

Vol. 15 Personal records and memorabilia, including manuscripts by Leo Kennedy.

Vols. 16–18 Election campaign, 1944–49.

Vols. 19–28 Samuel Bronfman material, including work done for the Canadian Jewish Congress and for Seagram's.

Vols. 29–31 Clippings of works by and about Klein, and about James Joyce.

Vols. 31–34 Printed material, including Klein's copies of *Ulysses*.

Vol. 35 Additional material, including correspondence, manuscripts, and clippings.

Apart from its Klein collection, the National Archives of Canada has Klein's correspondence with Ellsworth Mason dealing with *Ulysses*, and letters and manuscripts in the Lavy Becker Papers, the Rose Carlofsky Papers, the Joseph Frank Papers, and the David Lewis Papers.

The Usher Caplan collection of research material relating to Klein contains photocopies of some privately held letters.

A20 Archives
    American Jewish Historical Society
    Waltham, Massachusetts

A letter to Stephen S. Wise.

A21 Archives
    Canadian Jewish Congress
    Montreal, Quebec

Letters to H.M. Caiserman and Oscar Cohen; a collection of research materials, mostly from the internal files of the Canadian Jewish Congress.

A22 University of Chicago Library
University of Chicago
Chicago, Illinois

Poetry manuscripts and letters to *Poetry* [Chicago] magazine.

A23 Archives
Concordia University
Montreal, Quebec

Letters to Irving Layton and John Sutherland.

A24 Jewish Public Library
Montreal, Quebec

An extensive research collection on Klein, including a small number of manuscripts and letters, some originals and some photocopies. Included are letters to Isidore Goldstick and Melech Ravitch.

A25 Philadelphia Jewish Archives Centre
Philadelphia, Pennsylvania

Letters to the Jewish Publication Society.

A26 Archives
Queen's University
Kingston, Ontario

Letters to Alan Crawley, Lorne Pierce, and the Ryerson Press.

A27 University of Saskatchewan
Saskatoon, Saskatchewan

Letters to Ralph Gustafson.

A28 Humanities Research Center
University of Texas
Austin, Texas

Letters to Alfred A. Knopf, Inc., and copies of other related letters concerning *The Second Scroll*.

A29   Thomas Fisher Rare Book Library
University of Toronto
Toronto, Ontario

Letters to Earle Birney and A.J.M. Smith.

A30   Archives
YIVO Institute
New York, New York

Letters to Jacob Gladstone [sic; Glatstein] and Shmuel Niger.

A31   Private collections of letters include those of Samuel Abramson, Ephraim Broido, Leon Edel, Frank Flemington, Leo Kennedy, James Laughlin (New Directions Press), David Lewis, Shonie Levi, Guy Sylvestre, and Meyer Weisgal.

B   Individual Items (Poetry, Fiction, Drama, Translations [Poetry], Translations [Prose], Edited Material, Audio-Visual Material, Reprinted Anthology Contributions: A Selection, and Essays, Articles, and Reviews).

Note: When an item appears in one of Klein's books or pamphlets, in one of his manuscript volumes, or in a newspaper or periodical, this fact is noted in the entry through one of the following abbreviations:

BOOKS AND PAMPHLETS

Hath Not a Jew	*HNJ*
Huit poèmes canadiens (en anglais)	*HPC*
Poems	*P*
Poems of French Canada	*PFC*
The Rocking Chair and Other Poems	*RC*
The Second Scroll [page references to Knopf edition]	*SS*
Seven Poems	*SVP*

MANUSCRIPT VOLUMES

"XXII Sonnets" (1931)	22S
"Gestures Hebraic" (1932)	GH
"Gestures Hebraic and Poems" (1932)	GHP
"Poems" (1932)	P32
"Poems" (1934)	P34
"Selected Poems" (1954–55)	SP

PERIODICALS

Canadian Forum	*CF*
Canadian Jewish Chronicle	*CJC*
Canadian Zionist	*CZ*
Keneder Adler	*KA*
Menorah Journal	*MJ*

Poetry

B1 "Accept, my dear, these jewels which I bring." MS 20410.

B2 "Actuarial Report." *Preview* 12 (Mar. 1943), 7–8; *CF* XXIII (June 1943), 60; *CJC*, 17 Apr. 1953, p. 4; SP 2103–04; MS 2117–19.

B3 "Address to the Choirboys." *Opinion* XIV, 7 (May 1944), 5; *CJC*, 18 Aug. 1944, p. 9; MS 2120–23; MS 2353–55 ["Instruction for the Choirboys"].

B4 "Advice to the Young." P32 1718; GHP 1940.

B5 "Advice to Young Virgins." P32 1652; GHP 1882.

B6 "Against Mammon, a Murmuring." GH 1589 ["Rather than have my brethern (sic) bend the knee"]; GHP 1839 ["Rather than have my brethern (sic) bend the knee"]; SP 2062; MS 2124; MS 2580–85 ["A psalm for the sons of Korah"].

B7 "Age draws his fingernail across my brow." 22S 1476; P32 1608; GHP 1848; MS 2125.

B8 "Air-Map." *Poetry* LXX (July 1947), 178; *PFC*, p. 5; *SVP*, p. 5; *HPC*, p. 10; *RC*, p. 19; *Poetry* archives, University of Chicago Library.

¶ "Amo . . . amas . . . et cetera." See: "Love."

B9 "And in that drowning instant." *Opinion* XIII, 12 (Oct. 1943), 17; *SS*, pp. 195–97; MS 2127–28; MS 2600 ["A psalm of that which is remembered at the moment of drowning"].

B10 "Anguish." *McGilliad* II, 5 (April 1931), 102; *CF* xiii (April 1933), 257; P32 1662; GHP 1890.

B11 "Annual Banquet: Chambre de Commerce." *RC*, p. 49.

B12 "Apologia." MS 2276.

B13 "April Disappointments." P32 1676; GHP 1902.

B14 "April Fool." P32 1675; GHP 1901.

B15 "April Fulfilment." P32 1677; GHP 1903.

B16 "Arabian Love Song." *Opinion* II, 9 (1 Aug. 1932), 8; GH 1513; GHP 1752.

B17 "Arbiter Bibendi." P32 1732; GHP 1953.

B18 "Arithmetic." *Judaean* VI, 9 (June 1933), 71; *Opinion* IV, 4 (Feb. 1934), 19; P34 1992.

B19 "Assurance." P32 1649; GHP 1879.

B20 "Astrologer." P32 1727; GHP 1949.

B21 "At Home." MS 2129–30.

B22 "Autobiographical." *CF* XXIII (Aug. 1943), 106 ["Autobiography"]; Smith, *The Book of Canadian Poetry* (1943), pp. 398–400; *Chicago Jewish Forum* III (Winter 1944–45), 102–03; *SS*, pp. 123–26; SP 2113–16; MS 2131–44.

¶ "Autobiography." See: "Autobiographical."

B23 "Auto-da-fé." MS 1304–66; untitled MS in possession of estate of Mrs. S. Lewis [photocopy of Lewis MS in Vol. 35 of Klein papers].

B24 "Autumn." *Harp* IV, 3 (Sept.–Oct. 1928), 16; P32 1664; GHP 1892.

B25 "Autumn Night." P32 1664; GHP 1892.

B26 "Ave atque Vale." *MJ* XXIII, 1 (Spring 1935), 44–45 ["Heirlooms"]; *HNJ*, pp. 3–5; GH 1590–92; GHP 1840–42; MS 2145–55, 2744 (pp. 3–5).

B27 "Baal Shem Tov." *Judaean* VIII, 1 (Oct. 1934), 4; *Opinion* V, 6 (April 1935), 15; *HNJ*, p. 108; P34 2003; MS 2744 (p. 108).

B28 "Baldhead Elisha." *Opinion* V, 6 (April 1935), 14–15; P34 1971; MS 2586 ["A psalm in Elisha's despite"].

B29 "Ballad for Unfortunate Ones." *HNJ*, pp. 102–03; P34 2024–25; MS 2744 (pp. 102–03).

B30 "Ballad of Quislings." *Saturday Night* LVI (30 Aug. 1941), 25; *CJC*, 17 April 1953, p. 4; MS 2156–59.

B31 "Ballad of Signs and Wonders." *CJC*, 13 April 1928, p. 9; GH 1548–51; GHP 1789–92; MS 2160.

B32 "Ballad of the Dancing Bear." *Centennial Jubilee Edition of the Jewish Daily Eagle*, 8 July 1932, pp. 43–44; *HNJ*, pp. 88–101; GH 1540–47; GHP 1781–88; P34 2029–40.

B33 "Ballad of the Days of the Messiah." *Hebrew Union College Monthly* XXIX, 1 (Nov. 1941), 13; *CJC*, 5 Dec. 1941, p. 12; *P*, pp. 61–62; MS 2161–66.

B34 "Ballad of the dream that was not dreamed." MS 2167–68.

B35 "Ballad of the Evil Eye." MS 2169–72.

B36 "Ballad of the Nuremberg Tower Clock." *Saturday Night* LVII (8 Nov. 1941), 10; *CJC*, 24 March 1944, p. 4; MS 2173–81.

B37 "Ballad of the Nursery Rhymes." *CF* XXI (Nov. 1941), 244; *CJC*, 24 March 1944, p. 4; *CJC*, 24 Oct. 1952, p. 4; MS 2182–84.

B38 "Ballad of the Thwarted Axe." *CF* XXI (Oct. 1941), 212; *CJC*, 24 March 1944, p. 4; *P*, pp. 59–60; MS 2185–90.

B39 "Ballad of the Werewolves." MS 2191–94.

B40 "Bandit." *Judaean* VI, 3 (Dec. 1932), 22 ["A Jewish Bandit"]; *HNJ*, pp. 84–85; *CJC*, 12 Dec. 1952, p. 4; P34 1983.

B41 "Barricade Smith: His Speeches." *CF* XVIII (Aug. 1938), 147–48; (Sept. 1938), 173; (Oct. 1938), 210; (Nov. 1938), 242–43; MS 2195–2212; MS 2498–99 [part only: "Of the Lily Which Toils Not"].

B42 "Basic English." *CF* XXIV (Sept. 1944), 138; SP 2065–67; MS 2213–28.

B43 "Beaver." *CJC*, 21 Nov. 1952, p. 4; MS 2229–30.

B44 "A benediction." *Opinion* I, 5 (4 Jan. 1932), 14 ["Benediction"]; *P*, p. 24; GH 1503–04 ["Benediction"]; SP 2059; MS 2231–32.

B45 "A benediction for the new moon." *P*, p. 26; MS 2233–34.

B46 "Benedictions." *SS*, p. 190.

B47 "Bestiary." *Judaean* VIII, 9 (June 1935), 70; *HNJ*, pp. 78–79; Smith, *The Book of Canadian Poetry* (1943), pp. 397–98; Klinck and Watters, *Canadian Anthology* (1955), p. 382; P34 1975–76; SP 2052–53; MS 2235–39; 2744 (pp. 78–79).

B48 "Betray me not. Treat me as scurvily." 22S 1474; P32 1606; GHP 1847.

B49 "Biography." *Opinion* V, 6 (April 1935), 14; *HNJ*, p. 85; P34 1973.

B50 "Bion in His Old Age." P32 1723; GHP 1945.

B51 "Birthday Sonnet." MS 20415.

B52 "Blind Girl's Song." P32 1715; GHP 1937.

B53 "Blue Print for a Monument of War." *CF* XVII (Sept. 1937), 208–09.

B54 "Boredom." *McGill Daily*, 10 Dec. 1927, p. 2; P32 1711; GHP 1933.

B55 "Bounty Royal." GH 1517; P32 1636; GHP 1868.

B56 "Bread." *Preview* 19 (March 1944), 1; *Contemporary Poetry* V, 1 (Spring 1945), 3 ["A psalm for the breaking of bread"]; *Canadian Review*, undated tearsheet (see MS 24812); *RC*, p. 14; SP 2051; MS 2240–41.

B57 "The Break-up." *Poetry* LXX (July 1947), 179; *PFC*, p. 6; *SVP*, p. 6; *HPC*, p. 11; *RC*, p. 25; *Poetry* archives, University of Chicago Archives.

¶ "The Bride." See: "For the bride, a song, to be sung by virgins."

¶ "Bring on the rich, the golden-dotted soup." See: "A psalm of Abraham which he made at the feast."

B58 "Business." *CF* IX (Aug. 1929), 379; P32 1625; GHP 1858.

¶ "Calendar." See: "A psalm, with trumpets for the months."

B59 "Calvary." *CF* XII (Nov. 1931), 58.

B60 "Cantabile." *Northern Review* II, 3 (Sept.–Oct. 1948), 30–31.

B61 "Cantor." *HNJ*, pp. 110–12; P34 2014–15.

B62 "Captain Scuttle." P34 2008–13; MS 2242–47.

¶ "Cargo." See: "A song that the ships of Jaffa did sing in the night."

¶ "Cavalcade." See: "A psalm of horses and their riders."

¶ "Chad Gadyah." See: "Haggadah."

¶ "Chatzkel the Hunter." See: "A psalm of a mighty hunter before the Lord."

B63 "Childe Harold's Pilgrimage." *Opinion* VIII, 8 (Sept. 1938), 15–16; *CJC*, 18 Nov. 1938, p. 6; *Judaean Annual* X, 8 (June 1939), 7–10; *HNJ*, pp. 6–13; MS 2248–51, 2744 (pp. 6–13).

B64 "Christian Poet and Hebrew Maid." *McGilliad* II, 2 (Dec. 1930), 13; P32 1698–99; GHP 1921–22; MS in possession of Leo Kennedy ["Prothalamium"].

B65 "A Coloured Gentleman." P32 1722; GHP 1944.

B66 "Come Two, Like Shadows." *Poetry* LXI (Feb. 1943), 595; SP 2093; MS 2252–55, 3473–74; *Poetry* archives, University of Chicago Library.

B67 "Commercial Bank." *Preview* 19 (March 1944), 1; *RC*, p. 26; MS 2256.

B68 "Composition." P32 1705; GHP 1927.

B69 "Concerning a Strange King." P34 2006–07 ["The Mad Monarch"]; MS 2257–58.

B70 "Concerning Four Strange Sons." *Canadian Zionist* IV, 10 (March 1937), 103; *CJC*, 31 March 1939, p. 3; P34 1982.

B71 "Conjectures." *Poetry Yearbook* 1927–28 (Canadian Authors Association), pp. 21–22.

B72 "Consider, then, the miracle you wrought." 22S 1484; P32 1616; GHP 1852.

B73 "Counting Out Rhyme." *Opinion* III, 6 (April 1933), 22; *HNJ*, p. 76; P34 1994.

B74 "Coward in Consolation." P32 1634; GHP 1867.

B75 "The Cripples." *Poetry* LXX (July 1947), 177–78; *PFC*, p. 3; *SVP*, p. 4; *HPC*, p. 9; *RC*, p. 4; *Poetry* archives, University of Chicago Library.

B76 "Dance Chassidic." *Jewish Standard*, 10 Oct. 1930, p. 442; *HNJ*, pp. 61–62; GH 1567–68; GHP 1810–11; MS 2744 (pp. 61–62).

B77 "Dark Cleopatra on a Gilded Couch." P32 1627; GHP 1860.

B78 "A Deed of Daring." *HNJ*, p. 85; P34 1970.

B79 "Dentist." *Preview* 20 (May 1944), 12; MS 2259–68, 2486–89.

B80 "Desiderata." *CF* XII (Sept. 1932), 459; P32 1712; GHP 1934.

B81 "Desideratum." *Contemporary Verse* 8 (June 1943), 3; *New Directions* 8 (1944), 194–95; SP 2063–64; MS 2269–74.

B82 "Design for Mediaeval Tapestry." *American Caravan* IV (1931), 351–57; *HNJ*, pp. 42–51; *CJC*, 7 Nov. 1947, pp. 8–9; GH 1520–27; GHP 1757–65; MS 2744 (pp. 42–51).

B83 "Dial B and L." MS 2275.

B84 "Dialogue." *YMHA Beacon* V, 14 (18 April 1930), 7; *Opinion* II, 12 (22 Aug. 1932), 12; GH 1552; GHP 1793.

B85 "Diary of Abraham Segal, Poet." *CF* XII (May 1932), 297–300; GHP 1829–38.

¶ "Direction to the Scribe." See: "To the chief scribe, a psalm of Abraham, in the day of the gladness of his heart."

B86 "Discord of the Crow." P32 1665; GHP 1893.

B87 "Discovery of Spring." P32 1678–79; GHP 1904–05; Rose Carlofsky papers, National Archives of Canada.

B88 "Dissolution." P32 1716; GHP 1938; Rose Carlofsky papers, National Archives of Canada ["Sonnet"].

B89 "Divine Titillation." *CF* XIII (June 1933), 331; P32 1712; GHP 1934.

¶ "The Dock at Nuernberg." See: *The Hitleriad.*

B90 "Doctor Drummond." *CF* XXVI (Sept. 1946), 136; MS 2278–81.

B91 "Doctor Dwarf." *HNJ*, pp. 86–87; P34 1966–67.

B92 "Dominion Square." MS 2282.

B93 "Dress Manufacturer: Fisherman." *Contemporary Verse* 22 (Fall 1947), 3–4; *RC*, pp. 20–21.

B94 "Earthquake." *CF* XII (Feb. 1932), 173.

B95 "Ecclesiastes 13." *Opinion* II, 17–18 (26 Sept. 1932), 12; GH 1579; P32 1719; GHP 1820, 1941.

B96 "Elegy." P32 1712; GHP 1934.

B97 "Elegy." *New Palestine*, 4 April 1947, pp. 106–07; *CJC*, 25 April 1947, pp. 8–9; *SS*, pp. 127–34; MS 2283–84.

B98 "Elijah." *Judaean* V, 1 (Oct. 1931), 8; *Judaean* V, 3 (Dec. 1931), 16; *Opinion* V, 4 (Feb. 1935), 17; *HNJ*, pp. 109–10; P34 1988–89.

B99 [Epigrams] MS 7325, 7345, 7353–61.

¶ "Epistle to Be Left on the Tomb of Rashi." See: "A psalm of Abraham, to be written down and left on the tomb of Rashi."

B100 "Epitaph." *YMHA Beacon* V, 14 (18 April 1930), 18.

B101 "Epitaph." MS 2285–86.

B102 "Epitaph Forensic." *McGill Daily*, 12 Nov. 1927, p. 2.

B103 "Escape." MS 1367–1463.

B104 "Et j'ai lu tous les livres." MS 2287, 3464.

B105 "Exorcism Vain." *McGilliad* II, 5 (April 1931), 98–99; GH 1573; MS 2578–79 ["A psalm for them that utter dark sayings"].

B106 "Fable." P32 1663; GHP 1891.

B107 "Fairy Tale." P34 1979–81.

B108 "Falstaff." *McGilliad* I, 1 (March 1930), 7; P32 1700; GHP 1923.

B109 "February Morning." P32 1673; GHP 1900.

B110 "Festival." *Opinion* I, 16 (21 March 1932), 11; *CJC*, 3 March 1950, p. 7; MS 2288–90.

B111 "Figure." P32 1663; GHP 1891.

B112 "Filling Station." *RC*, p. 48.

B113 "Finis." P32 1642; GHP 1873.

B114 "Five Characters." *MJ* XIII, 5 (Nov. 1927), 497–98; *CJC*, 2 Dec. 1927, p. 4; *Judaean* III, 6 (March 1930), 7 [one section only: "Mordecai"]; *Judaean* IX, 6 (March 1936), 45.

B115 "Five Weapons Against Death." *MJ* XVI, 1 (Jan. 1929), 49–51; P32 1629–32; GHP 1862–65.

B116 "Fixity." *Canadian Mercury* I, 5–6 (April–May 1929), 110; P32 1669; GHP 1897.

B117 "For Minda on her 21st birthday." MS 20416–17.

B118 "For the bride, a song to be sung by virgins." *Opinion* I, 8 (25 Jan. 1932), 13 ["The Bride"]; *P*, p. 23; GH 1503 ["With Clean Lips"].

B119 "For the bridegroom coming out of his chamber, a song." *Opinion* I, 5 (4 Jan. 1932), 14 ["Song for Canopies"]; *P*, p. 22; GH 1502–03 ["Song for Canopies"].

B120 "For the chief physician: A song for hunters." *Opinion* XI, 12 (Oct. 1941), 28; *P*, p. 9.

B121 "For the Sisters of the Hôtel Dieu." *Poetry* LXX (July 1947), 178; *PFC*, p. 4; *SVP*, p. 5; *HPC*, p. 10; *RC*, p. 6; SP 2070; MS 2291; *Poetry* archives, University of Chicago Library.

B122 "Fragment on the Death of Shelley." P32 1721; GHP 1943.

B123 "Frankly." P32 1641; GHP 1872.

B124 "Frigidaire." *Poetry* LXX (July 1947), 180–81; *PFC*, p. 8; *SVP*, p. 8; *HPC*, p. 13; *RC*, p. 18; SP 2074; MS 2292; *Poetry* archives, University of Chicago Library.

B125 "From beautiful dreams I rise; I rise from dreams." 22S 1486; P32 1618; GHP 1853.

B126 "Funeral in April." *YMHA Beacon*, April 1931 [unverified, but identified in Klein's scrapbook of clippings]; P32 1650; GHP 1880.

B127 "Gargoyle." P32 1624; GHP 1857.

⁋ "Genesis." See: "A psalm touching genealogy."

B128 "Getzel Gelt." *Judaean* VIII, 9 (June 1935), 70; P34 1997–98.

B129 "Gift." *Opinion* V, 6 (April 1935), 14; *HNJ*, pp. 80–81; P34 1977.

B130 "Girlie Show." MS 2294–97, 3489, 3491–92.

B131 "The Golem." *Opinion* XV, 7 (June 1945), 8; *CJC*, 13 July 1945, p. 9; MS 2298.

B132 "Grace Before Poison." *Poetry* LVIII (April 1941), 6–7 ["To the Chief Musician Upon Shoshannim, A Song of Loves"]; *New Directions* 8 (1944), 197 ["To the Chief Musician Upon Shoshannim. A Song of Loves"]; *CJC*, 24 Oct. 1947, p. 6 ["To the Chief Musician Upon Shoshannim. A Song of Loves"]; *SS*, pp. 190–91; MS 2691–92 ["To the Chief Musician Upon Shoshannim. A Song of Loves"].

B133 "Grain Elevator." *Poetry* LXX (July 1947), 175–76; *PFC*, p. 2; *SVP*, p. 3; *HPC*, p. 8; *RC*, p. 7; *Poetry* archives, University of Chicago Library.

B134 "The Green Old Age." *Preview* 22 (Dec. 1944), 10–11; *Accent* V, 4 (Summer 1945), 197; *RC*, p. 24; MS 2299–2300.

B135 "Greeting on This Day." *MJ* XVIII, 1 (Jan. 1930), 1–4; *HNJ*, pp. 22–28; Klinck and Watters, *Canadian Anthology* (1955), p. 382; GH 1495–1501; GHP 1739–44; MS 2301–02, 2744 (pp. 22–28).

B136 "Haggadah." *CJC*, 24 April 1929, p. 18; *Judaean* II, 7 (April 1929), 5 [part only: "Chad Gadyah"]; *Jewish Standard*, 27 March 1931, p. 341 [part only: "Etching," "Once in a Year," "The Still Small Voice"]; *Judaean* VI, 7 (April 1933), 55 [part only: "Etching," "Once in a Year," "The Still Small Voice"]; *Canadian Zionist* I, 2 (April 1934), 12; Schwarz, *A Golden Treasury of Jewish Literature* (1937), pp. 649–51; *CJC*, 7 April 1939, p. 4; *HNJ*, pp. 52–56; GH 1563–66; GHP 1805–09.

B137 "Haunted House." *Canadian Mercury* I, 2 (Jan. 1929), 35; P32 1644–48; GHP 1875–78.

B138 "Heirloom." *Opinion* V, 6 (April 1935), 14; *HNJ*, pp. 77–78; Smith, *The Book of Canadian Poetry* (1943), p. 397; P34 1958; MS 2303–04, 2744 (pp. 77–78).

  ¶ "Heirlooms." See: "Ave atque Vale."

B139 "Here they are — all those sunny April days." Handwritten inscription to Bessie Kozlov, in copy of *Poems* by Edna St. Vincent Millay, signed "Abbie," Oct. 1931. In Klein's personal library, owned by his heirs.

B140 "Heroic." *Opinion* I, 19 (11 April 1932), 14; GH 1560; GHP 1803.

B141 "Hibernation." Rose Carlofsky papers, National Archives of Canada.

B142 "Histrionic Sonnet." P32 1626; GHP 1859.

B143 *The Hitleriad. First Statement* II, 1 (Aug. 1943), ii–3 [sections I–IV]; *First*

Statement II, 3 (Oct. 1943), 4–7 [sections XIIÄXV]; *The Hitleriad* (1944); *CJC*, 4 Oct. 1946, pp. 6–7 [selections: "The Dock at Nuernberg"]; MS 6017–25 [selections]; Lavy Becker papers, National Archives of Canada.

B144 "Homage." P32 1623; GHP 1856.

B145 "Hommage." MS 2276.

B146 "Hormisdas Arcand." *RC*, p. 46; MS 2305.

¶ "Incognito." See: "Lamed Vav: A psalm to utter in memory of great goodness."

B147 "Indian Reservation: Caughnawaga." *Poetry* LXVI (Sept. 1945), 318–19; *RC*, pp. 11–12; MS 2306–07; *Poetry* archives, University of Chicago Library.

B148 "In Memoriam: Arthur Ellis." *Circle* VIIÄVIII (1946), 54–60; SP 2100–02; MS 2308–44.

B149 "In Memoriam: Lillian Freiman." *CJC*, 8 Nov. 1940, p. 3.

B150 "*In Re* Solomon Warshawer." *CJC*, 19 April 1940, p. 3 [section]; *MJ* XXVIII, 2 (Summer 1940), 138–42; Smith, *The Book of Canadian Poetry* (1943), pp. 391–95; *P*, pp. 49–55; *CJC*, 27 Feb. 1953, p. 4 [section]; Klinck and Watters, *Canadian Anthology* (1955), pp. 385–389; SP 2082–89; MS 2345–52, 2745 (pp. 49–55), 2746 (pp. 49–55); Smith, *The Book of Canadian Poetry*, 3rd ed. (1957); galleys for *MJ*, in the possession of Leo Kennedy.

¶ "Instruction for the Choirboys." See: "Address to the Choirboys."

B151 "Into the Town of Chelm." *Judaean* VI, 9 (June 1933), 71; *Opinion* VI, 1 (Nov. 1935), 19; *HNJ*, pp. 82–83; *CJC*, 15 Feb. 1946, p. 8; P34 1961; MS 5131–32.

B152 "Invitation." P32 1655; GHP 1884.

B153 "Invocation to Death." *Opinion* II, 1 (6 June 1932), 11; GH 1518; GHP 1755.

B154 "I shall not bear much burden when I cross." *Opinion* II, 8 (25 July 1932), 16; *HNJ*, p. 70; Klinck and Watters, *Canadian Anthology* (1955), p. 383; 22S 1488; P32 1620; GHP 1854; MS 2356, 2744 (p. 70).

¶ "A Jewish Bandit." See: "Bandit."

B155 "Jonah." *Opinion* III, 6 (April 1933), 22; P34 1968–69; MS 2576–77 ["A Psalm for Jonah within the fish's belly"].

B156 "Jonah Katz." *Judaean* VIII, 9 (June 1935), 70; *HNJ*, pp. 83–84; P34 1965.

B157 "Joseph." *Judaean* I, 9 (June 1928), 1; GH 1578; GHP 1819.

¶ "Kaddish." See: "A psalm, forbidden to Cohanim."

B158 "Kalman Rhapsodizes." *Opinion* III, 4 (Feb. 1933), 29; GH 1519; GHP 1756; MS 2601 ["A psalm of the heavenly minister"].

B159 "King Dalfin." *HNJ*, pp. 105–06; P34 2026–27.

B160 "King Elimelech." *Judaean* IV, 12 (Sept. 1931); *Opinion* V, 7 (May 1935), 25; *HNJ*, pp. 103–04; P34 2016–17.

B161 "A Kiss." MS 2362–63.

B162 "Koheleth." *Judaean* II, 8 (May 1929), 7; GH 1554–55; GHP 1795–97.

B163 "Krieghoff: Calligrammes." *RC*, p. 13.

B164 "La Belle Dame Sans Merci." *McGill Daily*, 19 Nov. 1927, p. 2 [by A.M. Keats].

B165 "Lamed Vav: A psalm to utter in memory of great goodness." *Reconstructionist* II, 12 (16 Oct. 1936), 13 ["Incognito"]; *P*, p. 14; GH 1576 ["Incognito"].

B166 "Last Will and Testament." P32 1656; GHP 1885; Rose Carlofsky papers, National Archives of Canada.

B167 "The Lay of the Lady." *McGill Daily*, 3 Dec. 1927, p. 2 [by Mak].

B168 "Legend of Lebanon." *Jewish Standard*, 14 April 1933, pp. 172, 200–202; MS 2364–80.

B169 "Les Filles Majeures." *RC*, p. 47.

B170 "Les Vespasiennes." SP 2107–08; MS 2381–86.

B171 "Letters to One Absent." P32 1653–54; GHP 1883.

B172 "Let them pronounce me sentimental. I." 22S 1485; P32 1617; GHP 1852.

B173 "Librairie Delorme." *RC*, p. 44.

B174 "The Library." *Preview* 22 (Dec. 1944), 10; *CJC*, 21 Nov. 1952, p. 4; SP 2096–97; MS 2387–2401.

B175 "Life and Eternity." MS 2672; original manuscript in Jewish Public Library of Montreal.

B176 "Litany." *Opinion* II, 17–18 (26 Sept. 1932), 12; GH 1514; P32 1622; GHP 1855.

B177 "Lone Bather." *RC*, pp. 37–38.

B178 "Lookout: Mount Royal." *RC*, pp. 33–34; MS 2402–04.

B179 "Loosen the drawbridge, men! I am pursued." 22S 1480; P32 1612; GHP 1850.

B180 "Lost Fame." GH 1516; GHP 1753.

B181 "Lothario." P32 1708; GHP 1930.

B182 "Love." *New Directions* 8 (1944), 199; MS 2126 ["Amo . . . amas . . . et cetera"]; MS 2405–09.

¶ "Lowell Levi." See: "Portrait, and Commentary."

B183 "Lullaby for a Hawker's Child." P34 1978.

B184 "Mâ aleyk — No Evil Befall You." MS 2275.

B185 "Madman's Song." P34 2021.

¶ "The Mad Monarch." See: "Concerning a Strange King."

B186 "Mais, c'est pas de mes oignons, ça!" MS 2276.

B187 "Manuscript: Thirteenth Century." *CF* XIV (Sept. 1934), 474–76; P32 1681–95; GHP 1906–19; MS 2412–21.

B188 "Market Song." *McGilliad* II, 4 (Feb.–March 1931), 64; *HNJ*, pp. 74–75; P32 1702–03; GHP 1925; P34 1996; SP 2055; MS 2422, 2744 (pp. 74–75).

B189 "Maschil of Abraham: A prayer when he was in the cave." *Reconstructionist* VI, 18 (10 Jan. 1941), 12; *P*, pp. 2–3; MS 2745 (pp. 2–3), 2746 (pp. 2–3).

B190 "Mattathias." *CJC*, 14 Dec. 1928, p. 22.

B191 "M. Bertrand." *Poetry* LXX (July 1947), 179–80; *PFC*, p. 7; *SVP*, p. 7; *HPC*, p. 12; *RC*, p. 41; MS 2436; *Poetry* archives, University of Chicago Library.

B192 "Meditation Upon Survival." *Contemporary Verse* 32 (Summer 1950), 9–10; MS 2423–34.

B193 "Messiah." *Judaean* V, 8 (May 1932), 7; *Opinion* III, 6 (April 1933), 23; P34 1990–91.

B194 "Midnight Awakening." Rose Carlofsky papers, National Archives of Canada.

B195 "M. le juge Dupré." MS 2305, 2435.

B196 "Momus." P32 1706; GHP 1928.

B197 "The Monkey." *McGill Daily*, 5 Nov. 1927, p. 2 [by MAK].

B198 "Monsieur Gaston." *Contemporary Verse* 22 (Fall 1947), 5; *RC*, p. 43; SP 2075; MS 2437–38.

B199 "Montreal." *Preview* 21 (Sept. 1944), 3–5; *RC*, pp. 29–31; SP 2071–73; MS 2439–41.

¶ "Mordecai." See: "Five Characters."

B200 "The Mountain." *RC*, pp. 35–36.

B201 "Mourners." *Judaean* VI, 9 (June 1933), 71; *Opinion* VII, 2 (Dec. 1936), 20; *HNJ*, pp. 79–80; P34 1959; MS 2744 (pp. 79–80).

B202 "Murals for a House of God." *Opinion* III, 9 (July 1933), 18–21; *P*, pp. 56–58 [one section only: "Rabbi Yom-Tob of Mayence Petitions His God"]; MS 2442–85.

B203 "My dear plutophilanthropist." MS 3475–76.

B204 "My literati friends in restaurants." *Opinion* II, 8 (25 July 1932), 16; 22S 1487; P32 1619; GHP 1853.

B205 "Nehemiah." *Opinion* II, 3 (20 June 1932), 11; GH 1572; GHP 1816.

B206 "Ni la mort ni le soleil." *Contemporary Poetry* V, 1 (Spring 1945), 3; *CJC*, 24 Oct. 1952, p. 4; SP 2095; MS 2486; A.J.M. Smith papers, University of Toronto Library.

B207 "Nocturne." P32 1662; GHP 1889.

B208 "Nose Aristocratic." P34 1999.

B209 "Not All the Perfumes of Arabia." *Contemporary Verse* 8 (June 1943), 4–5; *Opinion* XIV, 2 (Dec. 1943), 13; *CJC*, 21 Nov. 1952, p. 4; MS 2487–89.

B210 "The Notary." *RC*, p. 42; MS 2490–91.

B211 "Not from a hermit's grotto, nor monk's cell." 22S 1478; P32 1610; GHP 1849.

B212 "Now we will suffer loss of memory." *Opinion* I, 19 (11 April 1932), 14 ["Satirical"]; *HNJ*, pp. 70–71; Klinck and Watters, *Canadian Anthology* (1955), p. 383; GH 1561 ["Satirical"]; GHP 1803–04 ["Satirical"]; MS 2492, 2744 (pp. 70–71).

B213 "Obituary Notices." *McGill Daily*, 17 Dec. 1927, p. 8.

B214 "October Heresy." *Alarm Clock* II, 1 (Nov. 1933), 3; P32 1666; GHP 1894.

⁋ "Of Castles in Spain" [group of 3 poems] See: "To One Gone to the Wars"; "Toreador"; "Sonnet Without Music."

B215 "Of Daumiers a Portfolio." *New Frontier* II, 4 (Sept. 1937), 10–11; MS 24643–44.

B216 "Of Remembrance." *CJC*, 24 Oct. 1947, p. 6 ["To the chief musician, a psalm of the Bratzlaver, a psalm of the beginning of things"]; *SS*, pp. 191–93; MS 2679–82 ["To the chief musician, a psalm of the Bratzlaver, a psalm of the beginning of things"].

B217 "Of the Friendly Silence of the Moon." MS 2493–97.

⁋ "Of the Lily Which Toils Not" [part of a group]. See: "Barricade Smith: His Speeches."

B218 "Of the Making of Gragers." *CJC*, 3 March 1950, p. 7; MS 2500.

B219 "Of Tradition." MS 2501.

B220 "O God! O Montreal." *Contemporary Verse* 22 (Fall 1947), 4; MS 2502.

B221 "An Old Dame Prates in Galilee." P32 1714; GHP 1936.

B222 "Old Maids." GH 1505; MS 2503.

B223 "Old Maid's Wedding." *CF* XII (Nov. 1931), 58; P32 1663; GHP 1890.

B224 "Only the voice of the sea can tell my love." MS 20409.

¶ "On Man, on the Rainbow." See: "Spinoza: On Man, on the Rainbow."

B225 "On the Road to Palestine." *Judaean* V, 3 (Dec. 1931), 6; P34 1995.

B226 "Oracles of the Clock." P32 1725–26; GHP 1947–48.

B227 "Orders." *McGilliad* I, 1 (March 1930), 7; *HNJ*, p. 116; P32 1701; GHP 1924; P34 2028.

B228 "Oriental Garden." GH 1571; GHP 1815.

B229 "Out of a Pit of Perpendiculars." P32 1728–31; GHP 1950–52.

B230 "Out of the Pulver and the Polished Lens." *CF* XI (Sept. 1931), 453–54; *Opinion* III, 1 (Nov. 1932), 16–17; *New Provinces*, pp. 29–34; *HNJ*, pp. 30–36; GH 1506–12; GHP 1746–51; MS 2653 [section V only: "Spinoza: More Geometrico Demonstratae"]; MS 2703 [section VI only], 2744 (pp. 30–36).

B231 "Palmam qui meruit." MS 2276–77.

B232 "Parade of St. Jean Baptiste." *CF* XXVII (Feb. 1948), 258–59; *HPC*, pp. 14–16; MS 2504–10.

¶ "Paradise." See: "Psalm of the fruitful field."

B233 "Pastoral of the City Streets." *RC*, pp. 39–40; MS 2511–12.

B234 "Pathetic Fallacy." P32 1643; GHP 1874.

B235 "Pawnshop." *First Statement* II, 12 (April–May 1945), 26–28; *Accent* V, 4 (Summer 1945), 195–96; *RC*, pp. 22–23; MS 2513–16, 3492–94.

B236 "Penultimate Chapter." *CF* XXIII (May 1943), 36; *CJC*, 17 April 1953, p. 4; SP 2098–99; MS 2517–21.

B237 "Petition for that my father's soul should enter into heaven." MS 2522–27.

B238 "Philosopher's Stone." *CF* XII (Feb. 1932), 173.

B239 "Phyllis O'Fee." MS 2528–32.

B240 "Pigeons." P34 2023.

B241 "Plumaged Proxy." *Opinion* I, 23 (9 May 1932), 11; *HNJ*, p. 60; GH 1569; GHP 1812; SP 2054; MS 2533, 2744 (p. 60).

B242 "The Poet to the Big Business Man." P32 1710; GHP 1932.

B243 "Polish Village." *Saturday Night* LVII (31 Jan. 1942), 3; MS 2534–35.

B244 "Political Meeting." *CF* XXVI (Sept. 1946), 136; *RC*, pp. 15–16; SP 2078–79.

B245 "Portrait." GH 1574; GHP 1817.

B246 "Portrait, and Commentary." MS 2410 ["Lowell Levi"]; MS 2536–45.

¶ "Portrait of the Poet as a Nobody." See: "Portrait of the Poet as Landscape."

B247 "Portrait of the Poet as Landscape." *First Statement* III, 1 (June–July 1945), 3–8 ["Portrait of the Poet as a Nobody"]; *RC*, pp. 50–56; SP 2044–50; MS 2546–61.

B248 "Portraits of a Minyan." *MJ* XVII, 1 (Oct. 1929), 86–88; *HNJ*, pp. 14–21; GH 1528–33; GHP 1766–73; SP 2057 [one section only: "Sophist"]; MS 2651 [one section only: "Sophist"]; MS 2744 (pp. 18–19, 21).

B249 "Post-War Planning." MS 2562–64.

B250 "Prayer." P32 1635; MS 2565 ["A prayer against the witnessing of grief"].

¶ "A prayer against the witnessing of grief." See: "Prayer."

B251 "A prayer of Abraham, against madness." *Jewish Frontier* IX, 4 (March 1942), 8 ["A Psalm of Abraham on Madness"]; *P*, pp. 27–28; MS 2745 (pp. 27–28).

B252 "A prayer of Abraham that he be forgiven for blasphemy." *MJ* XXIX (Autumn 1941), 280; MS 2566.

B253 "A Prayer of the afflicted when he is overwhelmed." *Opinion* XI, 12 (Oct. 1941), 28; MS 2567.

B254 "Preacher." *YMHA Beacon* V, 14 (18 April 1930), 2; *Reconstructionist* II, 12 (16 Oct. 1936), 13; *HNJ*, pp. 63–64; GH 1538–39; GHP 1779–80; MS 2744 (pp. 63–64).

B255 "Preface." P32 1697; GHP 1920.

B256 "The prince to the princess in the fairy-tale." 22S 1469; P32 1601; GHP 1844–45.

B257 "Probabilities." P32 1713; GHP 1935.

B258 "Protest." MS 1395, 1450; P32 1704; GHP 1926.

¶ "Prothalamium." See: "A psalm of Abraham touching the crown with which he was crowned on the day of his espousals."

B259 "The Provinces." *Northern Review* I, 1 (Dec. 1945–Jan. 1946), 27–28; *RC*, pp. 2–3; MS 2568–70.

¶ "The Prowler." See: "A psalm of Abraham of that which is visited upon him."

¶ "Psalm." See: "A psalm of Abraham, when he hearkened to a voice, and there was none." See: "A psalm or prayer — praying his portion with beasts."

¶ "Psalm 151." See: "A psalm of Abraham, touching his green pastures."

B260 "A psalm, forbidden to Cohanim." *Opinion* II, 10 (8 Aug. 1932), 8 ["Kaddish"]; *P*, p. 41; GH 1553 ["Kaddish"]; GHP 1794 ["Kaddish"]; MS 2357 ["Kaddish"].

B261 "A psalm for five holy pilgrims, yea, six on the King's highway." *MJ* XXIX (Autumn 1941), 280–81; *P*, p. 19.

    ❡ "A psalm for Jonah within the fish's belly." See: "Jonah."

    ❡ "A psalm for them that utter dark sayings." See: "Exorcism Vain."

    ❡ "A psalm for the sons of Korah." See: "Against Mammon, a Murmuring."

    ❡ "A psalm in Elisha's despite." See: "Baldhead Elisha."

B262 "A psalm of Abraham, concerning that which he beheld upon the heavenly scarp." *Poetry* LIX (March 1942), 315–16 ["Upon the Heavenly Scarp"]; Smith, *The Book of Canadian Poetry* (1943), p. 396 ["Upon the Heavenly Scarp"]; *New Directions* 8 (1944), 196 ["Upon the Heavenly Scarp"]; *P*, pp. 7–8; Klinck and Watters, *Canadian Anthology* (1955), p. 384; SP 2080–81; MS 2587–91, 2745 (pp. 7–8), 2746 (pp. 7–8); *Poetry* archives, University of Chicago Library; Klein papers, Canadian Jewish Congress Archives.

B263 "A psalm of Abraham concerning the arrogance of the son of man." *MJ* XXIX (Autumn 1941), 283; MS 2592–93.

B264 "A psalm of Abraham of that which is visited upon him." *MJ* XXIX (Autumn 1941), 284; *CJC*, 21 Nov. 1952, p. 4; SP 2092 ["The Prowler"]; MS 2571 ["The Prowler"]; MS 2594–96.

    ❡ "A psalm of Abraham on Madness." See: "A prayer of Abraham, against madness."

B265 "A psalm of Abraham, praying a green old age." *MJ* XXIX (Autumn 1941), 283–84; MS 2597.

B266 "A psalm of Abraham, to be written down and left on the tomb of Rashi." *Opinion* X, 7 (May 1940), 10 ["Epistle to be left on the Tomb of Rashi"]; *P*, pp. 42–43; *CJC*, 10 April 1953, p. 10; SP 2110–11; MS 2745 (pp. 42–43).

B267 "A psalm of Abraham, touching his green pastures." *Poetry* LVIII (April 1941), 6 ["Psalm 151"]; *P*, p. 5; *Poetry* archives, University of Chicago Library.

B268 "A psalm of Abraham, touching the crown with which he was crowned on the day of his espousals." *Opinion* I, 5 (4 Jan. 1932), 14 ["Prothalamium"]; *Reconstructionist* II, 12 (16 Oct. 1936), 13 ["Prothalamium"]; *P*, p. 20; GH 1515 ["Prothalamium"].

B269 "A psalm of Abraham, when he hearkened to a voice, and there was none." *First Statement* I, 14 [1943], 2; *P*, p. 1; SP 2112 ["Psalm"]; MS 2572 ["Psalm"]; MS 2598, 2745 (p. 1), 2746 (p. 1).

B270 "A Psalm of Abraham, when he was sore pressed." *Opinion* XI, 12 (Oct. 1941), 28; *P*, p. 4.

B271 "A psalm of Abraham, which he made at the feast." *Opinion* I, 8 (25 Jan. 1932), 13 ["The Wedding Feast"]; *P*, p. 25; GH 1504–05 ["Bring on the rich, the golden-dotted soup"].

B272 "A psalm of Abraham, which he made because of fear in the night." *MJ* XXIX (Autumn 1941), 281–82; *First Statement* I, 14 [1943], 1; *P*, pp. 44–45; MS 2745 (pp. 44–45).

B273 "A psalm of a mighty hunter before the Lord." *P*, pp. 15–16; P34 2000–01 ["Chatzkel the Hunter"].

B274 "A psalm of horses and their riders." *CJC*, 24 Oct. 1947, p. 6; P34 2022 ["Cavalcade"].

❡ "Psalm of Justice." See: "A psalm of justice and its scales."

B275 "A psalm of justice and its scales." *MJ* XXIX (Autumn 1941), 282; *P*, p. 29; SP 2091 ["Psalm of Justice"]; MS 2599 ["Psalm of Justice"]; MS 2745, p. 29.

B276 "A psalm of resignation." *MJ* XXIX (Autumn 1941), 285; *CJC*, 10 April 1953, p. 10.

❡ "A psalm of that which is remembered at the moment of drowning." See: "And in that drowning instant."

B277 "Psalm of the fruitful field." *Opinion* IV, 6 (April 1934), 23 ["Paradise"]; *P*, pp. 10–11; P34 1985–86 ["Paradise"].

❡ "A psalm of the heavenly minister." See: "Kalman Rhapsodizes."

B278 "A psalm of time and the firmament." MS 2602.

B279 "A psalm or prayer — praying his portion with beasts." *Hebrew Union College Monthly* XXIX, 4 (April 1942), 15 ["Psalm"]; *First Statement* I, 14 [1943], 2; *P*, p. 34; MS 2573–75 ["Psalm"].

B280 "A psalm, to be preserved against two wicked words." *P*, pp. 12–13; MS 2603–04; 2745 (pp. 12–13), 2746 (pp. 12–13).

B281 "A psalm to teach humility." *MJ* XXIX (Autumn 1941), 284–85; *P*, p. 33; SP 2056.

B282 "A Psalm touching genealogy." *P*, p. 46; *Chicago Jewish Forum* III (Spring 1945), 162; MS 2293 ["Genesis"]; MS 2605.

B283 "A psalm, with trumpets for the months." *Judaean* VIII, 9 (June 1935), 70 ["Calendar"]; *CJC*, 24 Oct. 1947, p. 6; P34 2002 ["Calendar"].

❡ "Quebec Liquor Commission." See: Quebec Liquor Commission Store."

B284 "Quebec Liquor Commission Store." *Canadian Poetry Magazine* X, 2

(Dec. 1946), 19–20 ["Quebec Liquor Commission"]; *RC*, pp. 27–28; Earle Birney Papers, University of Toronto Library.

¶ "Rabbi Yom-Tob of Mayence Petitions His God." *P*, pp. 56–58. See: "Murals for a House of God."

¶ "Rather than have my brethern [sic] bend the knee." See: "Against Mammon, a Murmuring."

B285 "Reb Levi Yitschok Talks to God." *Opinion* I, 10 (Feb. 1932), 16; Program of the Ninth National Judaean Convention (1932); *Judaean* IX, 9 (June 1936), 70; *HNJ*, pp. 57–59; GH 1586–88; GHP 1826–28; MS 2744 (pp. 57–59).

B286 "Reply Courteous." GH 1570; GHP 1813–14.

B287 "Request." P32 1724; GHP 1946.

B288 "Ressurection [sic]." P32 1651, 1717; GHP 1881, 1939.

B289 "Reveille in Winter." P32 1673; GHP 1899.

B290 "Rev Owl." *Opinion* V, 6 (April 1935), 15; *HNJ*, p. 115; P34 2020.

B291 "Riddle." P34 1974.

B292 "Ritual." MS 2276–77.

B293 "The Rocking Chair." *Nation* CLXI (6 Oct. 1945), 341; *RC*, p. 1; SP 2068–69; MS 2606–11.

B294 "Sacred Enough You Are." *HNJ*, p. 67; P32 1599; GHP 1843.

B295 "Saga the First." MS 2612.

¶ "Satirical." See: "Now we will suffer loss of memory."

B296 "Saturday Night." *Haboneh*, Dec. 1931 [unverified, but identified in Klein's scrapbook of clippings]; GH 1575; GHP 1818; MS 3391.

B297 "Scholar." *Opinion* III, 6 (April 1933), 22–23; *Judaean* VI, 9 (June 1933), 71; *HNJ*, pp. 112–13; P34 1962.

B298 "Scribe." *Jewish Standard*, 30 Oct. 1931, p. 360; *HNJ*, pp. 65–66; GH 1556–57; GHP 1798–99.

B299 "Seasons." *Dalhousie Review* XII, 2 (July 1932), 209–10; P32 1658–61 ["Words in their Season"]; GHP 1886–88 ["Words in their Season"]; Rose Carlofsky papers, National Archives of Canada [Winter section only, titled "Hibernation"].

B300 "Sennet from Gheel." *Poetry* LIX (March 1942), 316–17; *New Directions* 8 (1944), 195; MS 2613–16; *Poetry* archives, University of Chicago Library.

B301 "Sentimental." *Opinion* I, 19 (11 April 1932), 14; GH 1562; GHP 1804.

B302 "A Sequence of Songs." *Poetry* XXXV (Oct. 1929), 22–24; P32 1637–40; GHP 1869–71.

B303 "Sestina on the Dialectic." SP 2105–06; MS 2617–33.

B304 "Seventy regal moons, with clouds as train." 22S 1471; P32 1603; GHP 1845–46.

B305 "The Shechinah of Shadows." MS 2634–36.

B306 "Shelley." P32 1720; GHP 1942.

B307 "Shiggaion of Abraham which he sang unto the Lord." *Opinion* XI, 12 (Oct. 1941), 28; *P*, p. 30.

B308 "A Silver Sonnet." MS 20411.

B309 "Sincere, laborious for the common weal." *CJC*, 7 March 1941, p. 3; MS 20495–96; MS 20499; MS 20506.

B310 "Sire Alexandre Grandmaison." *RC*, p. 45; MS 2637–38.

B311 "Sleep Walking Scene." P32 1670; GHP 1897.

B312 "The Snowshoers." *Queen's Quarterly* LIV (Winter 1947–48), 412; *RC*, p. 5; SP 2076–77; MS 2639.

B313 "So having praised the laurelled and the crowned." MS 20421.

B314 "Soirée of Velvel Kleinburger." *CF* XII (Aug. 1932), 424–25; *New Provinces*, pp. 35–38; GH 1581–85; GHP 1821–25; MS 2740–43.

B315 "Song." P32 1672; GHP 1898.

❡ "Song." See: "Song to be sung at dawn."

B316 "Song Before Winter." P32 1671; GHP 1898.

❡ "Song for Canopies." See: "For the bridegroom coming out of his chamber, a song."

B317 "A song for wanderers." *P*, p. 18.

B318 "A song of degrees." *Reconstructionist* VII, 3 (21 March 1941), 6; *P*, p. 6; MS 2745 (p. 6).

B319 "Song of Exclamations." *Opinion* III, 6 (April 1933), 23; *HNJ*, p. 73; P34 1987.

B320 "Song of Innocence." SP 2090; MS 2640–42.

B321 "Song of Sweet Dishes." *Judaean* VIII, 1 (Oct. 1934), 4; *Judaean* VIII, 9 (June 1935), 70; *CJC*, 7 June 1940, p. 4; P34 1972.

B322 "Song of Toys and Trinkets." *Opinion* III, 6 (April 1933), 22 ["Toys"]; *HNJ*, pp. 72–73; P34 1984 ["Toys"].

B323 "A song that the ships of Jaffa did sing in the night." *Judaean* II, 4 (Jan. 1929), 8 ["Cargo"]; *CJC*, 1 Feb. 1929, p. 19 ["Cargo"]; *P*, p. 40; GH 1580 ["Cargo"]; MS 2643.

B324 "Song to be sung at dawn." *Judaean* VI, 9 (June 1933), 71 ["Song"]; *HNJ*, p. 74; P34 1993 ["Song"].

B325 "Song without music." MS 2644–45.

B326 "Sonnet in Time of Affliction." *Judaean* III, 1 (Oct. 1929), 6; *Avukah Annual* 1925–30, p. 103; *HNJ*, p. 29; MS 2646.

B327 "Sonnet of the Starving One." P34 2004.

¶ "Sonnet Semitic." See: "Would that three centuries past had seen us born."

B328 "Sonnet Unrhymed." *Accent* V, 4 (Summer 1945), 197; SP 2094; MS 2647–50.

B329 "Sonnet Without Music." *CF* XVIII (June 1938), 79; Joseph N. Frank papers, National Archives of Canada.

¶ "Sophist." See: "Portrait of a Minyan."

B330 "Soror Addita Musis." P32 1707; GHP 1929.

B331 "Speak me no deaths. Prevent that word from me." 22S 1475; P32 1607; GHP 1847; MS 2652.

B332 "The Spinning Wheel." *Canadian Poetry Magazine* X, 2 (Dec. 1946), 20–21; *RC*, p. 17; Earle Birney papers, University of Toronto Library.

¶ "Spinoza: More Geometrico Demonstratae." See: "Out of the Pulver and the Polished Lens."

B333 "Spinoza: On Man, on the Rainbow." SP 2109; MS 2744 (p. 34 and flyleaf).

B334 "Spring Exhibit." *New Directions* 8 (1944), 195; MS 2654–55.

B335 "Stance of the Amidah." *SS*, pp. 193–95; MS 2656–57.

B336 "The Sugaring." *RC*, p. 10; MS 2658–59.

B337 "Sybarite though I be." P32 1628; GHP 1861.

¶ "Syllogism." See: "Talisman in Seven Shreds."

B338 "Symbols." P32 1709; GHP 1931.

B339 "Symbols." Rose Carlofsky papers, National Archives of Canada.

B340 "Tailpiece to an Anthology." MS 2660.

B341 "Talisman in Seven Shreds." *MJ* XX, 8 (Summer 1932), 148–50; *HNJ*, pp. 37–41; GH 1534–37; GHP 1774–78; SP 2060–61 ["Tetragrammaton"; "Syllogism"]; MS 2661–67 ["Syllogism"; "Embryo of Dusts"; "Tetragrammaton"; "Fons Vitae"]; 2744 (pp. 37–41).

¶ "Tetragrammaton." See: "Talisman in Seven Shreds."

B342 "That Legendary Eagle, Death." *CF* XXIII (Sept. 1943), 127; *CJC*, 17 April 1953, p. 4; MS 2668–69.

B343 "These Candle Lights." *Judaean* II, 3 (Dec. 1928), 8 [titled in Hebrew letters, "Ha-nerot ha-lalu"]; *CJC*, 14 Dec. 1928, p. 22; *CZ* III, 6 (Nov. 1936), 40; GH 1577; MS 2670.

B344 "These northern stars are scarabs in my eyes." *HNJ*, pp. 68–69; 22S 1479; P32 1611; GHP 1849.

B345 "Think not, my dear, because I do not call." 22S 1470; P32 1602; GHP 1845; MS 2671; hand-written in gift copy to Bessie Kozlov of *Poems* by Edna St. Vincent Millay, inscribed by Klein Oct. 1931. In Klein's personal library, owned by his heirs.

B346 "This is no myth." P32 1623; GHP 1856.

B347 "This is too terrible a season! Worms." 22S 1472; P32 1604; GHP 1846.

B348 "Threnody." *McGill Daily*, 17 Dec. 1927, p. 8.

B349 "Thus does our life, moving on tranquil seas." MS 20414.

B350 " 'Tis very well to parrot the nightingale." 22S 1477; P32 1609; GHP 1848.

B351 "To Keats." MS 2672; original manuscript in Jewish Public Library of Montreal.

B352 "To Michael Hirsch." MS 20419–20.

B353 "To One Gone to the Wars." *CF* XVIII (June 1938), 79; Joseph N. Frank papers, National Archives of Canada.

B354 "Toreador." *CF* XVIII (June 1938), 79; Joseph N. Frank papers, National Archives of Canada.

B355 "To the chief bailiff, a psalm of the King's writ." *MJ* XXIX (Autumn 1941), 282–83; MS 2673–74.

B356 "To the Chief Musician, Al-Taschith, Michtam of Abraham; When one sent, and they watched the house to kill him." *Poetry* LVIII (April 1941), 7–8; *New Directions* 8 (1944), 198–99; MS 2675–76; *Poetry* archives, University of Chicago Library.

B357 "To the chief Musician, a Psalm of Israel, to bring to remembrance." *Opinion* XI, 12 (Oct. 1941), 26; *P*, p. 32.

B358 "To the chief musician, a psalm of the Bratzlaver, a parable." *New Directions* 8 (1944), 198; *P*, p. 35; MS 2677–78.

¶ "To the chief musician, a psalm of the Bratzlaver, a psalm of the beginning of things." See: "Of Remembrance."

B359 "To the chief musician: a Psalm of the Bratzlaver, touching a good gardener." *P*, pp. 37–39; MS 2683–84.

B360 "To the chief musician, a Psalm of the Bratzlaver, when he considered how the pious are overwhelmed." MS 2685–89.

B361 "To the chief musician, a Psalm of the Bratzlaver, which he wrote down as the stammerer spoke." *CJC*, 8 Nov. 1940, p. 3 [section]; *P*, p. 36; MS 2690.

❡ "To the Chief Musician upon Shoshannim, A song of Loves." See: "Grace Before Poison."

B362 "To the chief musician, who played for the dancers." *P*, p. 17; MS 2693.

B363 "To the chief scribe, a psalm of Abraham, in the day of the gladness of his heart." *Opinion* I, 5 (4 Jan. 1932), 14 ["Direction to the Scribe"]; *P*, p. 21; GH 1502 ["Direction to the Scribe"].

B364 "To the Jewish Poet." *CJC*, 6 July 1928, p. 21.

B365 "To the Lady who wrote about Herzl." MS 2694–96.

B366 "To the prophets, minor and major, a Psalm or Song." *Opinion* XI, 12 (Oct. 1941), 28; *P*, p. 31.

B367 "Town Fool's Song." P34 1960.

❡ "Toys." See: "Song of Toys and Trinkets."

B368 "Tribute to the Ballet Master." MS 2698–2700.

B369 "Université de Montréal — Faculté de Droit." *RC*, pp. 8–9; MS 2701–02.

❡ "Unto the crown of bone and regnant brain." See: "Out of the Pulver and the Polished Lens."

B370 "Upon a time there lived a dwarf, a Jew." *Opinion* II, 8 (25 July 1932), 16; *HNJ*, p. 69; 22S 1481; P32 1613; GHP 1850.

❡ "Upon the Heavenly Scarp." See: "A psalm of Abraham, concerning that which he beheld upon the heavenly scarp."

B371 "Variation of a Theme." *Preview* 5 (July 1942), 1–2 ["Variation on a Theme"] *New Directions* 8 (1944), 193–94; MS 2704–05 ["Variation on a Theme"].

❡ "Variation on a Theme." See: "Variation of a Theme."

B372 "The Venerable Bee." *Judaean* VIII, 1 (Oct. 1934), 4; *Opinion* V, 6 (April 1935), 14; *HNJ*, pp. 114–15; P34 2005.

B373 "Wandering Beggar." *HNJ*, pp. 106–07; P34 2018–19.

❡ "The Wedding Feast." See: "A psalm of Abraham, which he made at the feast."

B374 "The Well-Chanted Grace." MS 20418.

B375 "Were I to talk until the crack o' doom." *Opinion* II, 8 (25 July 1932), 16; 22S 1489; P32 1621; GHP 1854.

B376 "What Winter Has Said, Is Said." P32 1674; GHP 1899.

B377 "Where Shall I Find Choice Words." *Opinion* III, 7 (May 1933), 22; P32 1633; GHP 1866.

B378 "The White Old Lady." *CF* XXVI (Sept. 1946), 136; MS 2706.

B379 "Who Hast Fashioned." *SS*, pp. 189–90.

B380 "Why do you love me as you say you do." 22S 1468; P32 1600; GHP 1844; MS 2707.

B381 "Winter Night: Mount Royal." *RC*, p. 32.

B382 "Wishing to embarass me, but politely." MS 2410.

¶ "With Clean Lips." See: "For the bride, a song to be sung by virgins."

B383 "Within my iron days, my nights of stone." 22S 1482; P32 1614; GHP 1851.

B384 "Without your love, without your love for me." 22S 1483; P32 1615; GHP 1851; MS 2708.

B385 "Wood Notes Wild." *CF* XIII (Nov. 1932), 60; P32 1667–69; GHP 1895–96.

B386 "The Words of Plauni-Ben-Plauni to Job." *Jewish Tribune*, 7 Feb. 1930, p. 9; GH 1558–59; GHP 1800–02.

B387 "Would that three centuries past had seen us born." *HNJ*, p. 68; Klinck and Watters, *Canadian Anthology* (1955), p. 383; 22S 1473; P32 1605; GHP 1846; SP 2058 ["Sonnet Semitic"]; MS 2709–10, 2744 (p. 68).

B388 "Wrestling Ring." MS 2411, 2711.

B389 "Yehuda Halevi, His Pilgrimage." *CJC*, 19 Sept. 1941, pp. 9–12; *P*, pp. 65–82; MS 2712–38.

B390 "Yossel Letz." *Judaean* V, 7 (April 1932), 7; program of the Ninth National Judaean Convention (1932); *Opinion* III, 6 (April 1933), 23; P34 1963–64.

Fiction

B391 "Adloyada." MS 4473–78 [chapter from unfinished novel].

B392 ". . . And It Shall Come to Pass." *CJC*, 29 Oct. 1948, p. 4; MS 2747–50.

B393 "And the Mome Raths Outgrabe." *Here and Now* II, 4 (June 1949), 31–37; MS 2751–2801.

B394 "The Anti-Hill." *CJC*, 9 Sept. 1932, pp. 7–8 [by Aben Kandel, possibly Klein].

B395 "The Bald-Headed Monarch." *Judaean* IV, 8 (May 1931), 7–8 [by Ben Kalonymus].

B396 "Beggars I Have Known." *CF* XVI (June 1936), 19–20; MS 2802–07.

B397 "The Beggars of Baghdad." MS 2808–26 [notes only].

B398 "The Bells of Sobor Spasitula." MS 2827–2972.

¶ "The Biography of a Dictator — A Fable for Our Times." See: "Blood and Iron."

B399 "Blood and Iron." *Jewish Standard*, Jan. 1936, pp. 5, 14–15; *CJC*, 4 Aug. 1944, pp. 4, 8 ["The Biography of a Dictator — A Fable for Our Times"].

B400 "By the Profit of a Beard." *Judaean* III, 9 (June 1930), 7–8 [by Ben Kalonymus].

B401 "The Chanukah Dreidel." *Judaean* IV, 3 (Dec. 1930), 7–8 [by Ben-Kalonymos]; *CJC*, 23 Dec. 1938, pp. 7, 23 [by Ben Kalonymus].

¶ *Comes the Revolution*. See: *That Walks Like a Man*.

B402 "Conversations Celestial." *Judaean* II, 6 (March 1929), 2 [by A.M.].

B403 "Epistle Theological." *Reflex* IV, 1 (Jan. 1929), 68–74.

B404 "Friends, Romans, Hungrymen." *New Frontier* I, 1 (April 1936), 16, 18.

¶ "From Whose Bourne . . ." See: "No Traveller Returns."

B405 "The Golem." MS 2986–3331 [unfinished].

B406 "Hapaxlegomenon." MS 4458–72 [chapter from unfinished novel].

B407 "The Inverted Tree." MS 3526–49 [unfinished].

B408 "Kapusitchka." *CJC*, 15 Oct. 1948, p. 4.

B409 "Letter from Afar." MS 3332–52.

B410 "The Lingo." MS 3353–75 [unfinished].

B411 "The Lost Twins." *Judaean* IV, 1 (Oct. 1930), 7 [by Ben-Kalonymus].

B412 "Master of the Horn." *CJC*, 30 Sept. 1932, pp. 14, 67–69; MS 3376–83.

B413 "The Meed of the Minnesinger." *Jewish Tribune*, 5 Dec. 1930, pp. 10–11, 31; *Jewish Standard*, 30 March 1934, pp. 16, 75–78.

B414 "Memoirs of a Campaigner." *CZ* V, 2 (May 1937), 21, 25.

B415 "A Myriad-Minded Man." MS 3384–3415.

B416 "No Traveller Returns . . ." *CJC*, 30 June 1944, pp. 4, 16 [by Arthur Haktani]; MS 2973–85 ["From Whose Bourne . . ." by Marco Kirkham].

B417 "Once Upon a Time . . ." *Judaean* V, 7 (April 1932), 5, 7 [by Ben Kalonymus].

B418 "One More Utopia." *CJC*, 7 Sept. 1945, pp. 5, 87–88; MS 3416–25.

B419 "The Parliament of Fowles." *McGilliad* II, 1 (Nov. 1930), 9–11.

B420 "The Parrot and the Goat." *Judaean* IV, 6 (March 1931), 7–8 [by Ben Kalonymus].

B421 "Portrait of an Executioner." MS 3441–54 [by Marco Kirkham].

B422 "Prophet in Our Midst." *Judaean* III, 7 (April 1930), 8 [by Ben Kalonymus].

B423 "Raw Material." MS 3454–3558 [collection of diaries and prose fragments].

B424 "The Responsa." MS 3559–86 [unfinished].

B425 "Rite of Abraham." MS 3587–96 [notes only].

B426 *The Second Scroll* [See A8]. MS 3597–3610 [Chapter II only].

B427 "The Seventh Scroll." *Jewish Standard*, 22 Sept. 1933, pp. 119, 163–67; *CJC*, 12 Sept. 1947, pp. 4–7; 19 Sept. 1947, pp. 9, 15; MS 3680–98.

B428 "Shmelka." MS 3699–3714.

B429 "Stranger and Afraid." MS 3715–79 [unfinished].

B430 "Synopsis." MS 3780–3801.

B431 "The Tale of the Marvellous Parrot." *CZ* IV, 10 (March 1937), 106, 108; *CJC*, 11 April 1941, p. 5.

B432 *That Walks Like a Man.* MS 3802–4441 [by Dan Mosher, originally titled *Comes the Revolution*].

B433 "Too Many Princes . . ." *Judaean* V, 2 (Nov. 1931), 7–8 [by Ben Kalonymus].

B434 "The Trail of the Clupea Harengus." *CJC*, 28 June 1946, pp. 9–13.

B435 "The Triumph of Zalman Tiktiner." *Judaean* IV, 2 (Nov. 1930), 8 [by Ben Kalonymus].

B436 "We Who Are About to be Born." *CJC*, 2 June 1944, p. 4; MS 3155, 4479.

B437 "Whom God Hath Joined." MS 4480–4504.

B438 "Yclept a Pip." MS 4505–16 [by Marco Kirkham].

Drama

B439 *Conscience.* MS 4525–4632 [parts by Klein; adapted from *The Hands of Euridice* by Pedro Bloch].

B440 "Death of the Golem." MS 4517–24 [notes only].

B441 *Hershel of Ostropol.* *CJC*, 31 March 1939, pp. 19–27; 13 Sept. 1939, pp. 19–26; MS 4633–88.

B442 "The Icepick." MS 4689–4772 [unfinished].

B443 "O Canada." MS 4773–98 [unfinished].

B444 "The Three Judgements." *SS*, pp. 151–88 (114–35).

B445 *Worse Visitors We Shouldn't Have.* MS 4799–5007.

Translations [Poetry]

B446 "And This I Know." [J.I. Segal] Leftwich, *The Golden Peacock* (1939), p. 403; *Canadian Jewish Yearbook* (1940–41), p. 145; MS 5431–32.

B447 "Autobiographical." [J.I. Segal] Leftwich, *The Golden Peacock* (1939), p. 404; *Canadian Jewish Yearbook* (1940–41), p. 144; MS 5429–30.

B448 "Awakening." [Robert Choquette] Glassco, *The Poetry of French Canada in Translation*, p. 92. (Translated with Regina Shoolman.)

B449 "Bear Thou, O Wind, My Love." [Yehuda Halevi] Handwritten in copy of *Selected Poems of Jehudah Halevi*, dated 1936. In Jewish Public Library of Montreal.

B450 "Behold." [Abraham Shlonsky] *Judaean* IV, 4 (Jan. 1931), 6; *CJC*, 6 Feb. 1931, p. 22; *Opinion* I, 7 (18 Jan. 1932), 13; Schwarz, *A Golden Treasury of Jewish Literature* (1937), pp. 643–44; *CJC*, 9 Aug. 1946, p. 7.

B451 "Beneath the Burden." [Chaim Nachman Bialik] *Judaean* IX, 8 (May 1936), 61; *Opinion* VI, 9 (July 1936), 17 *Jewish Frontier* X, 8 (Aug. 1943), 22; *Chaim Nachman Bialik*, mimeographed pamphlet issued by Hadassah Organization of Canada, n.d. [p. 8]; MS 5333–34.

B452 "Be There No Altar." [Judah Carni] *Judaean* IV, 4 (Jan. 1931), 6; *CJC*, 6 Feb. 1931, p. 22; *Opinion* I, 7 (18 Jan. 1932), 10.

B453 "Canticum Canticorum." [M.L. Halpern] *CJC*, 9 Sept. 1932, p. 5.

B454 [Chassidic Folk Songs] MS 5519–50.

B455 "The Chastisement of God." [Chaim Nachman Bialik] *CZ* III, 4 (Sept. 1936), 7; *Jewish Frontier* IX, 5 (May 1942), 12; *Chaim Nachman Bialik*, mimeographed pamphlet issued by Hadassah Organization of Canada, n.d. [pp. 11–12]; MS 5335–38; *Herzl-Bialik Memorial Book*, issued by Zionist Organization of Canada, June 1945, pp. 36–37.

B456 "The Childless One." [Rachel] *Jewish Standard*, May 1937, p. 4; Schwarz, *A Golden Treasury of Jewish Literature* (1937), p. 646; *CJC*, 9 Aug. 1946, p. 7.

    ¶ "The City of Slaughter." See: "In the City of Slaughter."

B457 "Come, Gird Ye Your Loins." [Chaim Nachman Bialik] *CZ* v, 1 (April 1937), 5; *CJC*, 18 July 1941, p. 8; *Chaim Nachman Bialik*, mimeographed pamphlet issued by Hadassah Organization of Canada, n.d. [p. 17].

B458 "Conceit Curious." [M.L. Halpern] *CJC*, 9 Sept. 1932, p. 5.

B459 "Confession." [J.I. Segal] *CJC*, 23 Oct. 1940, p. 4; *CJC*, 12 March 1954, p. 3; MS 5433.

B460 "The Dance of Despair." [Chaim Nachman Bialik] *CZ* v, 3 (June 1937), 38; *CJC*, 19 April 1940, p. 6; *Jewish Frontier* IX, 9 (Sept. 1942), 21; *CJC*, 7 April 1944, p. 6; Efros, *Selected Poems of H.N. Bialik* (1948), pp. 214–17; *CJC*, 24 April 1953, p. 4; *Chaim Nachman Bialik*, mimeographed pamphlet issued by Hadassah Organization of Canada, n.d. [pp. 15–17].

B461 "Dawn." [Rachel] *Jewish Standard*, May 1937, p. 4; Schwarz, *A Golden Treasury of Jewish Literature* (1937), pp. 645–46; *CJC*, 9 Aug. 1946, p. 7.

B462 "The Eleventh: In Memory of Isaac, son of the tailor." [Jacob Gladstone] *CJC*, 7 Feb. 1947, p. 7.

B463 "The Gifted One." [Jacob Gladstone] *CJC*, 7 Feb. 1947, p. 7.

B464 "The Glory of the Homeland." [David Simonovitch] *Jewish Standard*, 11 Sept. 1931, pp. 152, 154; *Opinion* I, 24 (16 May 1932), 15; *Judaean* VII, 7 (April 1934), 56.

B465 "Goats." [J.I. Segal] MS 5427.

B466 "God Grant My Part and Portion Be." [Chaim Nachman Bialik] *Judaean* IX, 8 (May 1936), 61; *Opinion* VI, 9 (July 1936), 17; *Jewish Frontier* X, 6 (June 1943), 20–21; *Chaim Nachman Bialik*, mimeographed pamphlet issued by Hadassah Organization of Canada, n.d. [pp. 7–8]; MS 5339–40.

B467 "The Golden Parrot." [M.L. Halpern] *CJC*, 9 Sept. 1932, p. 5.

B468 "In the City of Slaughter." [Chaim Nachman Bialik] *CJC*, 2 Oct. 1940, pp. 9–11; *Jewish Frontier* IX, 8 (Aug. 1942), 16–19 ["The City of Slaughter"]; Efros, *Selected Poems of H.N. Bialik* (1948), pp. 114–28 ["The City of Slaughter"]; *CJC*, 1 May 1953, p. 4; MS 5341–89.

¶ "Jerusalem." See: "Mother Jerusalem."

B469 "The Kaddish (An experiment in translation)." [Jewish liturgy] *CJC*, 24 Oct. 1952, p. 4; MS 2358–61.

B470 "Ki-Ki." [M.L. Halpern] *CJC*, 9 Sept. 1932, p. 5.

B471 "A King." [J.I. Segal] Leftwich, *The Golden Peacock* (1939), pp. 405–06; MS 5425–26.

B472 "King Rufus." [J.I. Segal] *YMHA Beacon* VI, 14 (1 May 1931), 37;

Leftwich, *The Golden Peacock* (1939), pp. 404–05; MS 5428.

B473 "Kings of the Emek." [Uri Zvi Greenberg] *Judaean* IV, 4 (Jan. 1931), 6; *CJC*, 6 Feb. 1931, p. 22; Schwarz, *A Golden Treasury of Jewish Literature* (1937), pp. 642–43; *CJC*, 9 Aug. 1946, p. 7.

B474 "Kinnereth." [Rachel] *Jewish Standard*, May 1937, p. 4; Schwarz, *A Golden Treasury of Jewish Literature* (1937), p. 645; *CJC*, 9 Aug. 1946, p. 7; *SS*, p. 98 (78).

B475 "The Last Song." [M.L. Halpern] *CJC*, 9 Sept. 1932, p. 5; *Jewish Observer* IV, 1 (Dec. 1945), 93.

B476 "Last Will and Testament." [M.L. Halpern] *CJC*, 9 Sept. 1932, p. 5.

B477 "The Lord Has Not Revealed." [Chaim Nachman Bialik] *CZ* III, 4 (Sept. 1936), 7; *Jewish Frontier* IX, 4 (April 1942), 10; *Chaim Nachman Bialik*, mimeographed pamphlet issued by Hadassah Organization of Canada, n.d. [pp. 10–11]; MS 5338, 5390–92.

B478 "Lord, Hele Me, Y-wis I Shal be Heled." [Yehuda Halevi] MS 5405.

B479 "Make Blind O Sun of Jerusalem." [Judah Carni] *Judaean* IV, 4 (Jan. 1931), 6; *CJC*, 6 Feb. 1931, p. 22; *Opinion* I, 7 (18 Jan. 1932), 10.

B480 "Mother Jerusalem." [Uri Zvi Greenberg] *Judaean* IV, 6 (March 1931), 8 ["Jerusalem"]; *Jewish Standard* 11 Sept. 1931, p. 154; *CJC*, 11 Oct. 1940, p. 7.

B481 "No More Tears." [H. Leivick] *Jewish Observer* IV, 1 (Dec. 1945), 93.

B482 "Now Such Am I . . ." [Rachel] *Jewish Standard*, May 1937, p. 4; Schwarz, *A Golden Treasury of Jewish Literature* (1937), pp. 644–45; *CJC*, 9 Aug. 1946, p. 7.

B483 "Ode to Zion." [Yehuda Halevi] *CJC*, 19 Sept. 1941, pp. 11–12 [as part of: "Yehuda Halevi, His Pilgrimage"]; *P*, pp. 78–81 [as part of: "Yehuda Halevi, His Pilgrimage"]; *CJC*, 12 Dec. 1947, p. 4; *CJC*, 20 Aug. 1948, p. 4; MS 5408–13, 5979–80.

B484 "O Dove Beside the Water." [Yehuda Halevi] Handwritten in copy of *Selected Poems of Jehudah Halevi*, dated 1936. In Jewish Public Library of Montreal.

B485 "Of the ancient house of the Clinii . . ." [Horace] MS 5416–20.

B486 "O Heighte Sovereign, O Worldes Prys." [Yehuda Halevi] MS 5406–07.

B487 "Old Gold." [J.I. Segal] *CJC*, 23 Oct. 1940, p. 4; *CJC*, 12 March 1954, p. 3; MS 5433.

B488 "On My Returning." [Chaim Nachman Bialik] *CZ* III, 9 (Feb. 1937), 93; *Chaim Nachman Bialik*, mimeographed pamphlet issued by Hadassah Organization of Canada, n.d. [p. 9].

B489 "O Site Most Kingly, O Royal Sanctum." [Solomon ben Moses ha-Levi Alkabez] *CJC*, 7 Oct. 1949, p. 8; *SS*, p. 117 (90); MS 5979.

B490 "Portrait of the Artist." [M.L. Halpern] *CJC*, 9 Sept. 1932, p. 5.

B491 "The Prayer of a Physician." [Mordechai Etziony] *Canadian Medical Association Journal* 56 (1947), 100–01.

B492 "The Prescription." [Immanuel of Rome] MS 2987–88.

B493 "Rachel." [Rachel] *Jewish Standard*, May 1937, p. 4; Schwarz, *A Golden Treasury of Jewish Literature* (1937), p. 645; *CJC*, 9 Aug. 1946, p. 7.

B494 "Reb Zorach." [J.I. Segal] *CJC*, 23 Oct. 1940, p. 4.

B495 "Rubaiyat of Yehuda Halevi." [Yehuda Halevi] *Reconstructionist* III, 20 (11 Feb. 1938), 10–11; *CJC*, 16 Aug. 1946, p. 8.

B496 "Sabbath." [Abraham Shlonsky] *Jewish Standard*, 11 Sept. 1931, p. 152.

B497 "Seer, begone." [Chaim Nachman Bialik] MS 5393, 5395.

B498 "Smoke." [Jacob Gladstone] *CJC*, 7 Feb. 1947, p. 7.

B499 "Song." [J.I. Segal] *CJC*, 23 Oct. 1940, p. 4; *CJC*, 12 March 1954, p. 6; MS 5433.

B500 "Speak to your people, therefore, in this wise." [J.I. Segal] *CJC*, 2 Nov. 1945, p. 16.

B501 "A spirit passed before me." [Chaim Nachman Bialik] MS 5396–5400.

B502 "Stars flicker and fall." [Chaim Nachman Bialik] MS 5401.

B503 "Sunset." [Mani Leib] *Jewish Observer* I, 3 (Jan. 1944), 21.

B504 "To Jerusalem the Holy." [Yehuda Halevi] *CZ* III, 5 (Oct. 1936), 23 [tr. Ben Kalonymos]; *Reconstructionist* IV, 9 (17 June 1938), 16; *CJC*, 20 Aug. 1948, p. 4; *SS*, pp. 93–94 (75) [last four lines]; MS 5842; MS 5846–47.

B505 "To Leuconoe." [Horace] MS 5422.

B506 "To L. Munatius Plancus." [Horace] MS 5423–24.

B507 "To Lydia." [Horace] MS 5421.

B508 "Unfavored." [Mordecai Temkin] *Jewish Standard*, 11 Sept. 1931, p. 152.

B509 "Upon the Highway." [A. Broides] *Jewish Standard*, 11 Sept. 1931, p. 154.

B510 "Upon the Slaughter." [Chaim Nachman Bialik] Efros, *Selected Poems of H.N. Bialik* (1948), pp. 112–13.

B511 "War." [J.I. Segal] *CJC*, 23 Oct. 1940, p. 4; *CJC*, 12 March 1954, p. 3.

B512 "We are a generation heaven-doomed." [Leib Jaffe] *CJC*, 26 May 1933, p. 8.

B513 "When the Days Shall Grow Long." [Chaim Nachman Bialik] *CZ* IV, 10 (March 1937), 103; *CJC*, 27 Dec. 1940, p. 13; *Jewish Frontier* X, 6 (June 1943), 20; Efros, *Selected Poems of H.N. Bialik* (1948), pp. 206–08; *Chaim Nachman Bialik*, mimeographed pamphlet issued by Hadassah Organization of Canada, n.d. [pp. 13–14]; MS 5402–03.

B514 "The Windows are Grated." [H. Leivick] *Jewish Observer* IV, 1 (Dec. 1945), 93.

B515 "Wine." [Micah Joseph Lebensohn] Schwarz, *A Golden Treasury of Jewish Literature* (1937), pp. 598–99.

B516 "With Every Stone." [Judah Carni] *Jewish Standard*, 11 Sept. 1931, p. 154; *Opinion* I, 11 (15 Feb. 1932), 7; *Judaean* VII, 7 (April 1934), 56.

B517 "The Word." [Chaim Nachman Bialik] MS 5394.

B518 [Yiddish Folk Songs] *Judaean* III, 3 (Dec. 1929), 8; *CJC*, 10 Jan. 1930, p. 22; *Jewish Standard*, 15 April 1932, p. 103; 22 April 1932, p. 127; *Judaean* V, 9 (June 1932), pp. 2, 5–6; *CJC*, 2 Sept. 1932, pp. 6–7; *Canadian Zionist* III, 4 (Sept. 1936), p. 3; *CJC*, 31 March 1939, pp. 19–27; *CJC*, 13 Sept. 1939, pp. 19–26; *CJC*, 7 April 1944, pp. 9–10; *CJC*, 31 May 1946, p. 8; MS 4033–88, 4799–5007, 5434–5518, 5551–94.

B519 "You walk upon your sunlit roads." [Leib Jaffe] *CJC*, 26 May 1933, p. 8.

Translations [Prose]

B520 "Abou-el-Calb." [Moses Smelyansky] *Judaean* IV, 4 (Jan. 1931), 8 [tr. Ben-Kalonymus].

B521 ". . . And on Purim Sober." [J.L. Peretz] *Judaean* III, 6 (March 1930), 8 [tr. Ben-Kalonymos].

B522 "Atallah." [Moses Smelyansky] *Judaean* III, 1 (Oct. 1929), 7–8 [tr. Ben-Kalonymos].

B523 "Atonement." [J.L. Peretz] *Judaean* II, 8 (May 1929), 8 [tr. Ben-Kalonymos].

B524 "A Beautiful Tale Touching My Prayerbook." [S.Y. Agnon] *CJC*, 3 April 1953, p. 6; *Jewish Spectator* XVIII, 7 (Sept. 1953) 14–15 ["My New Prayerbook"].

B525 *The Book of Aggadah* [Bialik and Ravnitsky] *CJC*, 1947: 21 Feb., pp. 8, 16; 28 Feb., pp. 8, 13; 7 March, pp. 8, 13; 14 March, p. 8; 21 March, pp. 9, 15; 28 March, pp. 6, 14; 4 April, p. 6; 10 April, p. 6; 9 May, p. 4; 20 June, p. 6; 27 June, pp. 6, 15; *CJC*, 1948: 26 March, pp. 8, 13; 2 April, p. 8; 9 April, p. 8; 23 April, pp. 6–7; 29 April, p. 5; 7 May, p. 5; 21 May, p. 8; 28 May, pp. 8, 13; 4 June, pp. 8, 16;

3 Sept., p. 8; *CJC*, 1951: 2 Nov., p. 9; 9 Nov., p. 10; 16 Nov., p. 10; 23 Nov., p. 10; 30 Nov., p. 10; 7 Dec., p. 10; 21 Dec., p. 34; 28 Dec., p. 10; *CJC*, 1952: 4 Jan., p. 10; 11 Jan., p. 10; 18 Jan., p. 10; 25 Jan., p. 10; 1 Feb., p. 10; 15 Feb., p. 12; 22 Feb., p. 12; 29 Feb., p. 12; 7 March, p. 10; 14 March, p. 10; 21 March, p. 10; 28 March, p. 10; 9 April, p. 14; 18 April, p. 10; 25 April, p. 8; 2 May, p. 8; 9 May, p. 4; 16 May, p. 4; 23 May, p. 4; 29 May, p. 4; 6 June, p. 4; 13 June, p. 4; 20 June, p. 4; 27 June, p. 4; 4 July, p. 4; 11 July, p. 4; 18 July, p. 4; 25 July, p. 4; 1 Aug., p. 4; 8 Aug., p. 4; 15 Aug., p. 4; 22 Aug., p. 4; 29 Aug., p. 4; 5 Sept., pp. 4, 12; 12 Sept., p. 4; 3 Oct., p. 4; 17 Oct., p. 4; 31 Oct., p. 4; 7 Nov., p. 4; MS 5595–5685.

B526 "The Culture of Israel." [Chaim Nachman Bialik] *CJC*, 1949: 25 March, p. 4; 1 April, p. 4; 27 May, p. 4; 2 June, p. 6; 10 June, p. 4; 17 June, pp. 4, 9; 24 June, p. 4; 1 July, p. 4; 8 July, p. 4; 15 July, p. 8; 22 July, p. 8; 29 July, p. 8; 5 Aug., p. 8; 12 Aug., pp. 8, 13.

B527 "Desecrated Graveyard." [Yehoash] *Judaean* III, 2 (Nov. 1929), 7–8.

B528 "In Memoriam: Theodor Herzl." [Nahum Sokolow] *CZ* V, 3 (June 1937), 40 [tr. Avigdor Kaufman].

B529 "The Last Hour." [David Frishman] *Judaean* II, 3 (Dec. 1928), 7–8; *CJC*, 14 Dec. 1928, p. 22.

B530 "Mani Lieb — A Self Portrait." [Mani Lieb] *CJC*, 11 Nov. 1932, pp. 7, 14; *Judaean* VI, 3 (Dec. 1932), 21.

¶ "My New Prayerbook." See: "A Beautiful Tale Touching My Prayerbook."

B531 "Nasal Remarks." [David Frishman] Judaean II, 5 (Feb. 1929), 7.

B532 "Ne'ilah in Gehenna." [I.L. Peretz] *Commentary* XVII, 1 (Jan. 1954), 68–71; Howe and Greenberg, *A Treasury of Yiddish Stories* (1953), pp. 213–19; MS 5686–94.

B533 "A Night of Horror." [Avigdor Hameiri] *Jewish Standard*, 22 April 1932, pp. 130, 176–78, 180.

B534 "The Tale of the Wonderful Goat" [S.Y. Agnon] *CZ* III, 7 (Dec. 1936), 57.

Edited Material

B535 "Jewish Themes in English Writing." *CJC*, 1953: 29 May, p. 4; 5 June, p. 4; 12 June, p. 4; 19 June, p. 4; 26 June, p. 4; 3 July, p. 4; 10 July, p. 4; 17 July, p. 4; 24 July, p. 4; 31 July, p. 4; 7 Aug., pp. 8–9; 14 Aug., p. 4; 21 Aug., p. 4; *CJC*, 1954: 21 May, p. 4; 28 May, p. 4; MS 7790–7876.

B536 "Weizmann's Wit and Wisdom." *CJC*, 14 Nov. 1952, p. 4.

Audio-Visual Material

B537 National Archives of Canada
Sound Archives Ottawa, Ontario

A.M. KLEIN COLLECTION (ACC. 1973–81)

Speech by Klein delivered at the 8th Plenary Session of the Canadian Jewish Congress in Toronto, 24 Oct. 1949 [29 mins.].

Reading from *The Second Scroll* by Harry Goldstein, delivered at the Warsaw Ghetto Memorial Meeting in Detroit, 6 April 1952 [14 mins.].

Part of speech by Klein entitled "Martyrs and Heroes," delivered at the Warsaw Ghetto Memorial Meeting in Detroit, 6 April 1952 [38 mins.].

Part of radio play *The Second Scroll*, broadcast by CBC as part of CBC *Wednesday Night*, 7 May 1952 [58 mins.]

Reading of his poems by Klein to the Canadian Authors' Association, at McGill, 22 Nov. 1955 [50 mins.].

Reading of his poems by Klein, with comments by Patrick Waddington, broadcast by CBC International Service, Sept. 1957 [13 mins.].

B538 *Six Montreal Poets*. Folkways Records, 1957. Reading of his poems by Klein.

B539 "Autobiographical." NFB, 1965.
A black and white film interpretation of Klein's poem, "Autobiographical." [10 min. 14 sc.].

B540 "La Cité de Memoire." The French version of the above.

Reprinted Anthology Contributions: A Selection

B541 "Out of the Pulver and the Polished Lens," "Soirée of Velvel Kleinburger." In *New Provinces: Poems of Several Authors*. Toronto: Macmillan, 1936, pp. 29–38.

B542 "Heirloom," "The Still Small Voice." In *A Little Anthology of Canadian Poets*. The Poets of the Year. Ed. Ralph Gustafson. Norfolk, Conn.: New Directions, 1943, n.p.

B543 "Autobiographical," "Bestiary," "Heirloom," "*In Re* Solomon Warshawer," "A Psalm of Abraham, Concerning that which He Beheld upon the Heavenly Scarp." In *The Book of Canadian Poetry: A Critical and Historical Anthology*. Ed. A.J.M. Smith, Chicago: University of Chicago Press, 1943, pp. 391–400.

B544 "Autobiographical," "Bestiary," "For the Sisters of the Hôtel Dieu," *from*

36

"Greeting on This Day," "Indian Reservation: Caughnawaga," "*In Re* Solomon Warshawer," "I Shall Not Bear Much Burden When I Cross," "Librairie Delorme," "Lone Bather," "Monsieur Gaston," "Now We will Suffer Loss of Memory," "Pastoral of the City Streets," "Political Meeting," "Portrait of the Poet as Landscape," "A Psalm of Abraham, Concerning that which He Beheld upon the Heavenly Scarp," "The Rocking Chair," "The Snowshoers," "Would that Three Centuries Past had Seen Us Born!" In *Canadian Anthology*. Eds. C.F. Klinck and R.E. Watters. Toronto: W.J. Gage Ltd., 1955, pp. 382–402.

B545 "Bread," "Heirloom," "A Psalm of Abraham, Concerning that which He Beheld upon the Heavenly Scarp," "The Rocking Chair," "The Still Small Voice," "To the Chief Musician, who Played for the Dancers." In *The Penguin Book of Canadian Verse*. Ed. Ralph Gustafson. Harmondsworth: Penguin, 1958, pp. 158–162.

B546 "Bestiary," "Heirloom," "Indian Reservation: Caughnawaga," "Montreal," "Political Meeting," "Quebec Liquor Commission Store," "The Still Small Voice," "The Sugaring." In *The Oxford Book of Canadian Verse in English and French*. Ed. A.J.M. Smith. Toronto: Oxford University Press, 1960, pp. 252–63.

B547 "Autobiographical," "*In Re* Solomon Warshawer," "Monsieur Gaston," "Montreal," "Political Meeting." In *Modern Canadian Verse in English and French*. Ed. A.J.M. Smith. Toronto: Oxford University Press, 1967, pp. 90–104.

B548 "Ballad of the Days of the Messiah," "The Cripples," "Design for Mediaeval Tapestry," "Elijah," "Frigidaire," "Grain Elevator,", *from* "Greeting on this Day," *from The Hitleriad*, "Krieghoff: Calligrammes," "Lone Bather," "Monsieur Gaston," "Montreal," "Of Kith and Kin," "Out of the Pulver and the Polished Lens," "Political Meeting," "Portrait of the Poet as Landscape," "A Psalm of Abraham, Touching His Green Pastures," "A Psalm of Abraham, which He Made Because of Fear in the Night," "A Psalm or Prayer — Praying His Portion with Beasts," "A Psalm to Teach Humility," "A Song that the Ships of Jaffa Did Sing in the Night," "Sonnet in Time of Affliction," "The Still Small Voice," "The Sugaring," "These Northern Stars are Scarabs in My Eyes," "To the Chief Musician, Who Played for the Dancers." In *Poets Between the Wars*. Ed. Milton Wilson. New Canadian Library, No. 5. Toronto: McClelland and Stewart, 1967, pp. 156–94.

B549 "Autobiographical," "The Cripples," "Grain Elevator," *from The Hitleriad*, "Lookout: Mount Royal," "Portrait of the Poet as Landscape," "A Psalm of Abraham, Concerning that which He Beheld upon the Heavenly Scarp," "A Psalm Touching Genealogy," "The Rocking Chair," "Sonnet in Time of Affliction." In *Literature in Canada*. Eds. Douglas Daymond and Leslie

Monkman. Toronto: Gage, 1978, II. 205–19.

B550 "Autobiographical," "Genesis" [Chapter One of *The Second Scroll*], "Now We Will Suffer Loss of Memory," "Once in a Year," " A Psalm Touching Genealogy." In *The Spice Box: An Anthology of Jewish Canadian Writing*. Eds. Gerri Sinclair and Morris Wolfe. Toronto: Lester and Orpen Dennys, 1981, pp. 31–44.

B551 "The Break-Up," "Heirloom," "Indian Reservation: Caughnawaga," "Portrait of the Poet as Landscape." In *The New Oxford Book of Canadian Verse in English*. Ed. Margaret Atwood. Toronto: Oxford University Press, 1982, pp. 127–33.

B552 "Autobiographical," "For the Bridegroom Coming out of His Chamber," "Heirloom," "Political Meeting," "Portrait of the Poet as Landscape," "A Prayer of Abraham, Against Madness," "A Psalm of Abraham, Concerning that Which He Beheld Upon the Heavenly Scarp," "A Psalm Touching Genealogy," "Reb Levi Yitschok Talks to God," "The Rocking Chair." In *An Anthology of Canadian Literature in English*. Eds. Russell Brown and Donna Bennett, Toronto: Oxford University Press, 1982, I. 494–509.

B553 "Autobiographical," "Heirloom," "Montreal," "Out of the Pulver and the Polished Lens," "Political Meeting," "Portrait of the Poet as Landscape," "A Psalm to Teach Humility," "The Rocking Chair," "Sestina on the Dialectic." In *Canadian Poetry*. Eds. Jack David and Robert Lecker. Toronto: General Publishing and Downsview: ECW PRESS, 1982, pp. 194–215.

Essays, Articles, and Reviews

ARTICLES ON JOYCE

B554 "The Oxen of the Sun." *Here and Now* I, 3 (Jan. 1949), 28–48.

B555 "The Black Panther: A Study in Technique." *Accent* X, 3 (Spring 1950), 139–55. See also MS 5142–62 [notes].

B556 "A Shout in the Street." *New Directions* 13 (1951), 327–45.

UNDATED PAMPHLETS

B557 "Brief History of the Jews in Poland." Mimeographed pamphlet, 5 pp.

B558 "The Jews of Germany." Mimeographed pamphlet issued by the Hadassah Organization of Canada, 8 pp.

B559 "Latter-day Heptateuch." [Review of *A Golden Treasury of Jewish Literature*, ed. Leo W. Schwartz]. Mimeographed pamphlet labelled "Hadassah Study Paper," 5 pp.

NOTE: Each item is identified as signed [s], initialled [i], or unsigned [u].

27.10.13A "Ave Atque Vale." [University education]. *McGill Daily*, 13 Oct. 1927, p. 2 [s] (Appius M. Klandius).

27.10.21A "The Intellectual." [Presenting oneself as an intellectual]. *McGill Daily*, 21 Oct. 1927, p. 2 [i].

27.10.29A "Worse Verse." [Free verse]. *McGill Daily*, 29 Oct. 1927, p. 2 [i].

27.11.05A "G.K. Chesterton." [G.K. Chesterton]. *McGill Daily*, 5 Nov. 1927, p. 2 [i].

27.11.12A "Verbum Sat." [Apology for his own verbosity]. *McGill Daily*, 12 Nov. 1927, p. 2 [i].

27.11.19A "The Treason of Tradition." [Attacking the influence of tradition in modern society]. *McGill Daily*, 19 Nov. 1927, p. 2 [i].

27.11.26A "Of Course 13." [Apology for the tone of the *McGilliad*]. *McGill Daily*, 26 Nov. 1927, p. 2 [i].

27.12.03A "Cubism." [Cubism]. *McGill Daily*, 3 Dec. 1927, p. 2 [i].

27.12.10A "Wanderlust [*sic, should be* Wonderlust]." [Poetic vision]. *McGill Daily*, 10 Dec. 1927, p. 2 [i].

27.12.17A "Finis Coronat Opus." ["Obituary" for the *McGilliad*]. *McGill Daily*, 17 Dec. 1927, p. 8 [i].

28.10.00A "5688 — A Retrospect." [A review of the past year]. *Judaean* 2, 1 (Oct. 1928), pp. 2, 4 [i].

28.11.00A "Notes on Cultural Zionism." [Cultural Zionism]. *Judaean* 2, 2 (Nov. 1928), p. 3 [i].

29.02.00A "The Bible." [A review of the Jewish Publication Society edition of the Bible]. *Judaean* 2, 5 (1929), pp. 4, 5 [i].

29.03.00A "The Hebrew University." [Hebrew University]. *Judaean* 2, 6 (Mar. 1929), pp. 1, 5 [u].

29.04.00A "A Ghetto Purim." [Description of a Purim celebration]. *Judaean* 3, 6 (Apr. 1929), pp. 3–5 [i].

29.04.00B "The Chosen People." [Review of *The Chosen People* by Jean and Jerome Tharaud]. *Canadian Mercury* 1, 5–6 (Apr.–May 1929), p. 117 [i].

29.05.00A "Koheleth — A Review of Rabbi Zlotnik's Book." [Review of *Koheleth* by Rabbi J. L. Zlotnik]. *Judaean* 2, 9 (May 1929), pp. 3, 6 [s].

29.11.00A "Our Language." [Importance of Hebrew language]. *Judaean* 3, 2 (Nov. 1929), p. 1 [u].

29.12.00A "The Modern Maccabee." [Pacifism and Jewish history]. *Judaean*, 3, 3 (Dec. 1929), p. 1 [u].

30.01.00A "Messiah in Our Days." [Messianism and Jewish history]. *Judaean* 3, 4 (Jan. 1930), p. 1 [u].

30.01.24A "Danger To Canadian Jewish Youth." [Excerpt from an address]. *CJC*, 24 Jan. 1930, p. 9 [s].

30.04.00A "The Student Looks at the Professor." [University professors]. *McGilliad* 1, 2 (Apr. 1930), 4–5 [s].

30.04.18A "A Curse on Columbus." [Review of *Jews Without Money* by Michael Gold]. YMHA *Beacon* 5, 14 (18 Apr. 1930), 18 [s].

30.09.19A "Canadian Jewish Youth — Whither?" [Importance of Zionist activism among Canadian Jewish youth]. *CJC*, 19 Sept. 1930, pp. 19, 31 [s].

30.11.14A "Baal Shem in Modern Dress." [Review of *Lyric* by J.I. Segal]. *CJC*, 14 Nov. 1930, pp. 14, 18 [s].

31.00.00A "Aims and Ideals of Young Judaea." [Jewish history and the future of the Jews]. *Yearbook of Young Judaea*, 1931, pp. 7–11 [s].

31.01.00A "Novel in Four Dimensions." [Review of *Success* by Lion Feuchtwanger]. *McGilliad* 2, 3 (Jan. 1931), 17–18 [s].

31.02.00A "Professor Walter's Mendelssohn." [Review of *Moses Mendelssohn* by Dr. Hermann Walter]. *McGilliad* 1, 4 (Feb.–Mar. 1931), 86–87 [s].

31.06.00A "Theodor Herzl." [Theodor Herzl]. *Judaean* 4, 7 (June 1931), pp. 3–4, 7 [u]. *See also* MS 7450 [fragment].

31.11.00A "The Chovevei Zion." [History of Chovevei Zion]. *Judaean* 5, 2 (Nov. 1931), pp. 2, 8 [s].

31.12.00A "Benjamin Disraeli." [Benjamin Disraeli]. *Judaean* 5, 3 (Dec. 1931), p. 5 [s].

32.03.00A "The Jew in English Poetry." [The Jew in English poetry]. *Judaean* 5, 6 (Mar. 1932), pp. 5, 8 [s]. *See also* "The Jews of England," mimeographed pamphlet issued by Hadassah Organization of Canada, n.d., part 2 [pp. 1–5].

32.05.00A "Zionism — Our National Will-to-Live" [Zionism]. *Judaean* 5, 8 (May 1932), pp. 5, 8 [s].

32.06.00B "Jewish Folk Songs." [Jewish Folk Songs]. *Judaean* 5, 9 (June 1932), pp. 2, 5, 6 [s].

32.06.10A "The Jew in English Poetry." [*See* 32.03.00A]. *Jewish Standard*, 10 June 1932, pp. 297, 305–6 [s].

32.07.08A "The Twin Racketeers of Journalism." [Adrien Arcand and Joseph Ménard]. *CJC*, 8 July 1932, pp. 3–4 [u].

32.07.08B "A French-Canadian Speaks." [French Canadian cleric speaks out against racism]. *CJC*, 8 July 1932, p. 4 [u].

32.07.08C "German Inconsistency." [Nazis confiscate Jewish property]. *CJC*, 8 July 1932, p. 4 [u].

32.07.08D "Latinizing Hebrew." [Suggestion to latinize the Hebrew alphabet]. *CJC*, 8 July 1932, pp. 4–5 [u].

32.07.08E "Jewish Hitlerism." [Jew fends off Nazi attack]. *CJC*, 8 July 1932, p. 5 [u].

32.07.08F "Jewish Unity." [Need for Jewish unity]. *CJC*, 8 July 1932, p. 5 [u].

32.07.08G "Physical Judaism." [Judaism and athletics]. *CJC*, 8 July 1932, p. 5 [u].

32.07.08H "Lord Passfield Becomes a Hero." [Lord Passfield is warmly received in Moscow]. *CJC*, 8 July 1932, p. 5 [u].

32.07.08I "Soldiers and Statesmen." [Arthur Wauchope becomes High Commissioner for Palestine]. *CJC*, 8 July 1932, p. 5 [u].

32.07.08J "La Cause des Juifs." [Anti-Semitism]. *KA Centennial Jubilee Edition*, 8 July 1932, pp. 66–7 [s].

32.07.15A "A French-Canadian Editor Speaks." [French-Jewish relations in Quebec]. *CJC*, 15 July 1932, p. 3 [u].

32.07.15B "The Philadelphia Convention." [35th Annual Convention of the Zionist Organization of America]. *CJC*, 15 July 1932, pp. 3, 5 [u].

32.07.15C "The Ottawa Conference." [British foreign policy on Palestine and the Palestine economy]. *CJC*, 15 July 1932, p. 5 [u].

32.07.15D "Frisco Takes the Cake." [San Francisco synagogue publishes a cookbook]. *CJC*, 15 July 1932, p. 5 [u].

32.07.15E "Beards and the Man." [Beards]. *CJC*, 15 July 1932, p. 5 [u].

32.07.22A "A Challenge to Justice." [Injunction against anti-Semitic publications]. *CJC*, 22 July 1932, p. 3 [u].

32.07.22B "The Twentieth of Tammuz." [Anniversary of the death of Theodor Herzl]. *CJC*, 22 July 1932, p. 3 [u].

32.07.22C "Divided Unions." [Labour unrest in Montreal]. *CJC*, 22 July 1932, pp. 3, 4 [u].

32.07.22D "Lord Plumer." [Death of Lord Plumer]. *CJC*, 22 July 1932, p. 4 [u].

32.07.22E "Boston Beans and Felix Frankfurter." [Felix Frankfurter refuses position in Massachusetts State Supreme Court]. *CJC*, 22 July 1932, p. 4 [u].

32.07.22F "Victorious Circulars." [Controversy over Hebrew education in Montreal]. *CJC*, 22 July 1932, p. 4 [u].

32.07.29A "The Deputy-Speaker: Full of Sound and Fury." [Anti-Semitism of Armand Lavergne]. *CJC*, 29 July 1932, p. 3 [u].

32.07.29B "Dictatorship in Germany." [Nazis stage a virtual coup d'état]. *CJC*, 29 July 1932, pp. 3–4 [u].

32.07.29C "The European Cockpit." [First International Disarmament Conference]. *CJC*, 29 July 1932, pp. 4, 16 [u].

32.07.29D "The 'Third Degree'." [Police brutality in U.S.]. *CJC*, 29 July 1932, p. 4 [u].

32.08.05A " 'Mushroom' Synagogues." [Use of temporary synagogues during High Holidays]. *CJC*, 5 Aug. 1932, p. 3 [u].

32.08.05B "The German Elections." [German elections]. *CJC*, 5 Aug. 1932, pp. 3–4 [u].

32.08.05C "Mussolini and His Cabinet." [Government of Benito Mussolini]. *CJC*, 5 Aug. 1932, p. 4 [u].

32.08.05D "The Song of the Shirt." [Survey of international situation]. *CJC*, 5 Aug. 1932, p. 4 [u].

32.08.05E "Proletarian Poetry." [Writers under Joseph Stalin]. *CJC*, 5 Aug. 1932, p. 4 [u].

32.08.12A "Is the Jew Dishonest?" [Anti-Semitism]. *CJC*, 12 Aug. 1932, p. 3 [u].

32.08.12B "Yiddish Encyclopedia." [Criticism of new Yiddish encyclopedia]. *CJC*, 12 Aug. 1932, pp. 3, 4 [u].

32.08.12C "The Spanish Enigma." [Uncertain position of Jews in Spain]. *CJC*, 12 Aug. 1932, p. 4 [u].

32.08.12D "What Shall We Wear?" [Debate over proper synagogue attire]. *CJC*, 12 Aug. 1932, p. 4 [u].

32.08.12E "Poland Defends the Jews." [Pole attacks German anti-Semitism]. *CJC*, 12 Aug. 1932, p. 4 [u].

32.08.12F "A Decline and A Rise." [Decline of Yiddish and the rise of Hebrew]. *CJC*, 12 Aug. 1932, pp. 4, 16 [u].

32.08.12G "The Holy See Versus Armand Lavergne." [Armand Lavergne accuses Jews of committing ritual sacrifices]. *CJC*, 12 Aug. 1932, pp. 5, 17 [s].

32.08.26A "St. Armand de Montmagny, Martyr." [Anti-Semitism of Armand Lavergne]. *CJC*, 26 Aug. 1932, pp. 5, 17 [s].

32.09.23A "The Jew and His Proverb." [Jewish proverbs]. *CJC*, 23 Sept. 1932, pp. 5, 16 [s].

32.10.07A "White Magic." [Review of *The Zohar* by Ariel Bension]. *CJC*, 7 Oct. 1932, pp. 5, 16 [s].

32.10.14A "If . . . ?" [Speculations on the course of history]. *CJC*, 14 Oct. 1932, pp. 6, 7 [s].

32.10.21A "Science in The Talmud." [Science in the Talmud]. *CJC*, 21 Oct. 1932, pp. 5, 17 [s].

32.10.28A "Riddle Me This Riddle." [Jewish riddles]. *CJC*, 28 Oct. 1932, pp. 5, 17 [s].

32.11.00A "Riddle Me This Riddle." [*See* 32.10.28A]. *Judaean* 6, 2 (Nov. 1932), p. 11 [s].

32.11.04A "What Price Judaism?" [Importance of Vaad Ha'ir]. *CJC*, 4 Nov. 1932, pp. 8, 17 [s].

33.01.00A "Max Nordau 1879–1923." [Max Nordau]. *Judaean* 7, 4 (Jan. 1933), pp. 30–1 [s].

34.01.00A "The Jew and His Proverb." [*See* 32.09.23A]. *Judaean* 7, 4 (Jan. 1934), pp. 28–9 [s].

34.01.05A "Mortal Coils." [Review of *The Shrouding* by Leo Kennedy]. *CJC*, 4 Jan. 1934, p. 9 [s].

34.02.00A "Jewish Humour." [Jewish humour]. *Judaean* 7, 5 (Feb. 1934), pp. 36, 39 [s]. *See also* MS 5133–37.

34.05.00A "Within Zionism." [Reply to anti-Zionist article by William Zuckerman]. *CZ*, 1, 3 (May 1934), pp. 5, 8 [s].

34.10.00A "Presidential Message." [Need for Zionist activity in view of growing anti-Semitism]. *Judaean* 8, 1 (Oct. 1934), p. 1 [s].

34.12.00A "An Open Letter to the Jewish Youth of Canada." [Need for Zionist activity in Canada]. *Judaean* 8, 3 (Dec. 1934), p. 17 [s].

34.12.00B "Palestine Note Book." [News from Palestine]. *CZ*, 1, 8 (Dec. 1934), p. 6 [s].

34.12.00C "History of Palestine." [Review of *History of Palestine* by Jacob de Haas]. *Judaean* 8, 3 (Dec. 1934), p. 23 [s].

34.12.00D "History of Palestine." [*See* 34.12.00C]. *CZ* 1, 8 (Dec. 1934), p. 8 [s].

35.02.00A "If." [*See* 32.10.14A]. *Judaean* 8, 5 (Feb. 1935), pp. 35, 40 [s].

35.05.00A "Science in the Talmud." [*See* 32.10.21A]. *Judaean* 8, 8 (May 1935), pp. 59, 64 [s].

35.07.19A "The Vatican vs. The Brown House." [Catholic Church condemns Nazism]. *CJC*, 19 July 1935, p. 3 [u].

35.07.19B "Alfred Dreyfus." [Death of Alfred Dreyfus]. *CJC*, 19 July 1935, p. 3 [u].

35.07.19C "Blackskins and Blackshirts." [Italy prepares to invade Abyssinia]. *CJC*, 19 July 1935, p. 4 [u].

35.07.19D "Einstein Among The Stars." [Albert Einstein has a new theory of space]. *CJC*, 19 July 1935, p. 4 [u].

35.07.19E "Shaw on Intermarriage." [George Bernard Shaw suggests compulsory intermarriage of gentiles and Jews]. *CJC*, 19 July 1935, p. 4 [u].

35.07.26A "Hitler Bares His Teeth." [Persecution of Jews and Catholics in Nazi Germany]. *CJC*, 26 July 1935, p. 4 [u].

35.07.26B "The Codex Sinaiticus." [Codex Sinaiticus to be bound in pig skin]. *CJC*, 26 July 1935, p. 4 [u].

35.08.02A "Hatikvah in Government House." [Hatikvah played at an official reception in Palestine]. *CJC*, 2 Aug. 1935, p. 3 [u].

35.08.02B "Orchids for Laguardia." [Fiorello La Guardia refuses German application for a massage licence]. *CJC*, 2 Aug. 1935, p. 3 [u].

35.08.02C "Val David and Goliath." [Torah scroll stolen from the Val David synagogue]. *CJC*, 2 Aug. 1935, p. 3 [u].

35.08.02D "The Mosquito and the Lion." [Italo-Abyssinian War]. *CJC*, 2 Aug. 1935, p. 4 [u].

35.08.02E "Rhubarb and Lemons." [Germans move against import of lemons from Italy]. *CJC*, 2 Aug. 1935, p. 4 [u].

35.08.02F "Poesy in the Reich." [Nazism and Christianity]. *CJC*, 2 Aug. 1935, p. 4 [u].

35.08.09A "Krolestvo Cyganskie." [Konrad Bercovici]. *CJC*, 9 Aug. 1935, p. 3 [u].

35.08.09B "The 'Christian Century' In a Pagan Era." [American Protestant Publication condemns Nazism]. *CJC*, 9 Aug. 1935, p. 4 [u].

35.08.09C "Welcome David Lewis." [David Lewis returns to Montreal]. *CJC*, 9 Aug. 1935, p. 4 [u].

35.08.09D "Infant Industries." [Zionist flags are imported from Japan]. *CJC*, 9 Aug. 1935, p. 4 [u].

35.08.09E "Editors Please Copy." [Poet attacks editor of the *Yiddishe Presse*]. *CJC*, 9 Aug. 1935, p. 4 [u].

35.08.09F "The Shadow of God." [Suicide of Abdul Kerem Effendi]. *CJC*, 9 Aug. 1935, p. 4 [u].

35.08.09G "Ghandi [*sic*] and Nudism." [Mahatma Gandhi declares himself to be against nudism]. *CJC*, 9 Aug. 1935, p. 4 [u].

35.11.00A "Zionism — Redefined for Judaeans." [*See* 32.05.00A]. *Judaean* 9, 2 (Nov. 1935), pp. 9, 15–16 [s].

35.11.00B "Of Hebrew Humor." [Hebrew humour]. Opinion 6, 1 (Nov. 1935), 15–19 [s]. *See also* MS 5107–32.

36.09.00A "Knight of The Road." [Yishuv ideology]. *CZ* 3, 4 (Sept. 1936), p. 3 [u].

36.10.00A "The Strike Ended." [End of Arab strike in Palestine]. *CZ*, 3, 5 (Oct. 1936), p. 19 [u].

36.10.00B "Hadassah to The Fore." [Work of Hadassah in Canada]. *CZ*, 3, 5 (Oct. 1936), p. 19 [u].

36.10.00C "Ontario Zionists Meet in Toronto." [Zionist activity in Ontario]. *CZ*, 3, 5 (Oct. 1936), p. 19 [u].

36.10.00D "The Man of Many Dreams." [Meier Dizengoff]. *CZ*, 3, 5 (Oct. 1936), pp. 21, 24–5, 29 [s].

36.10.00E "News, Views and Jews." [Humorous Jewish news]. *CZ*, 3, 5 (Oct. 1936), pp. 23–4 [s] (Ben-Kalonymus).

36.10.00F "A Year Book." [Review of *The American Jewish Yearbook*, vol. 38]. *CZ*, 5, 5 (Oct. 1936), p. 25 [u].

36.10.00G "The Book of The Year." [Review of *The Jews of Germany* by Marvin Lowenthal]. *CZ*, 3, 5 (Oct. 1936), p. 25 [u].

36.11.00A "Cantonization." [Proposed partition of Palestine]. *CZ*, 3, 6 (Nov. 1936), p. 35 [u].

36.11.00B "New, Views and Jews." [Humorous Jewish news]. *CZ*, 3, 6 (Nov. 1936), pp. 39, 47 [s] (Ben-Kalonymous).

36.12.00A "National Young Judaea Day." [National Young Judaea Day]. *CZ*, 3, 7 (Dec. 1936), p. 51 [u].

36.12.00B "Evacuation." [Relocation of Polish Jews]. *CZ*, 3, 7 (Dec. 1936), p. 51 [u].

36.12.00C "The Royal Commission." [Chaim Weizmann represents Zionist position to Peel Commission]. *CZ*, 3, 7 (Dec. 1936), p. 51 [u].

36.12.00D [Untitled]. [Review of *I Sang My Song of Zion: Poems* by Leib Jaffe, translated by Sylvia Satten]. *CZ* 3, 7 (Dec. 1936), p. 54 [i].

36.12.00E [Untitled]. [Review of *Hebrew Origins* by T.J. Meek]. *CZ*, 3, 7 (Dec. 1936), pp. 54, 64 [u].

36.12.00F "News, Views and Jews." [Humorous Jewish news]. *CZ* 3, 7 (Dec. 1936), pp. 55, 61 [s] (Ben-Kalonymus).

37.01.00A "The Shekel." [The shekel]. *CZ*, 3, 8 (Jan. 1937), [u].

37.01.00B "The Daughters of Music." [Arturo Toscanini conducts in Palestine]. *CZ*, 3, 8 (Jan. 1937), pp. 67, 70 [u].

37.01.00C [Untitled]. [Review of *Palestine on the Eve* by Ladislas Farago and *Some of My Best Friends are Jews* by Robert Gessner]. *CZ*, 3, 8 (Jan. 1937), p. 68 [u].

37.01.00D "Jerusalem Calling." [Radio broadcasts in Palestine]. *CZ*, 3, 8 (Jan. 1937), pp. 69–70, 75 [s] (Avigdor Kaufman).

37.02.00A "The Blessed Isles." [Need for a Jewish homeland in Palestine]. *CZ*, 3, 9 (Feb. 1937), p. 83 [u].

37.02.00B "The Man Without A Country." [Leon Trotsky on Zionism]. *CZ*, 3, 9 (Feb. 1937), p. 83 [u].

37.02.00C "Viton's Vital Statistics." [Journalism of Albert Viton on Palestine]. *CZ*, 3, 9 (Feb. 1937), p. 83 [u].

37.02.00D "News, Views and Jews." [Humorous Jewish news]. *CZ*, 3, 9 (Feb. 1937), pp. 85, 90 [s] (Ben-Kalonymus).

37.03.00A "And It Was At Midnight." [*See* 41.04.11A]. *CZ*, 4, 10 (Mar. 1937), p. 99 [u].

37.03.00B "The Ten Plagues." [Nazi Germany]. *CZ*, 4, 10 (Mar. 1937), p. 103 [s] (Ben-Kalonymos).

37.04.00A "The United Palestine Appeal." [United Palestine Appeal]. *CZ*, 4, 1 (Apr. 1937), p. 3 [u].

37.04.00B "Jacob de Haas." [Death of Jacob de Haas]. *CZ*, 5, 1 (Apr. 1937), p. 3 [u].

37.04.00C "Did You Know? . . ." [Facts about Palestine]. *CZ*, 5, 1 (Apr. 1937), p. 7 [s] (Ben-Kalonymos).

37.05.00A "The Cant of Cantonization." [Proposed partition of Palestine]. *CZ*, 5, 2 (May 1937), p. 19 [u].

37.05.00B "The Letter Must Be Stamped." [Issue of commemorative postage stamps]. *CZ*, 5, 2 (May 1937), p. 20 [s] (Avigdor Kaufman).

37.05.00C "News, Views and Jews." [Humorous Jewish news]. *CZ*, 5, 3 (May 1937), p. 23 [s] (Ben-Kalonymus).

37.05.00D "Laughter Holding Both His Sides." [Review of *Fun'm Yiddishn Kval* by Salem Miller]. *CZ*, 5, 2 (May 1937), pp. 24–5 [i].

37.06.00A "Chaim Nachman Bialik 1873–1934." [Chaim Nachman Bialik]. *CZ*, 5, 3 (June 1937), pp. 35–36, 43 [s]. *See also* "Chaim Nachman Bialik," mimeographed pamphlet issued by Hadassah Organization of Canada, n.d. [pp. 1–6].

37.06.00B "The Sinking of the Titanic." [Review of *Titans of Hebrew Verse* by Harry H. Fein]. *CZ*, 5, 3 (June 1937), p. 37 [u].

37.06.00C "News, Views and Jews." [Humorous Jewish news]. *CZ*, 5, 3 (June 1937), p. 48 [s] (Ben-Kalonymos).

37.07.09A "Balfour! Thou Shouldst Be Living at This Hour." [British foreign policy on Palestine]. *CJC*, 9 July 1937, pp. 3–4 [s].

37.07.09B "Census of Jewish Education." [Census of Jewish education in Montreal]. *CJC*, 9 July 1937, p. 4 [u].

37.07.16A "Coal From the Pits of Germany." [Boycotting German coal]. *CJC*, 16 July 1937, p. 4 [u].

37.07.16B "Talking With Hands." [Columbia University study refutes stereotype of Jews gesturing while they talk]. *CJC*, 16 July 1937, p. 4 [u].

37.07.23A "Lloyd George and the Royal Commission Report." [David Lloyd George defends Jewish interests]. *CJC*, 23 July 1937, p. 3 [u].

37.07.23B "Non-Intervention." [Non-intervention in view of the rise of fascism]. *CJC*, 23 July 1937, p. 3 [u].

37.07.23C "It Is Your Problem!" [Debate over partition of Palestine]. *CJC*, 23 July 1937, p. 4 [u].

37.07.23D "The Late Dr. Coralnik." [Death of Abraham Coralnik]. *CJC*, 23 July 1937, p. 4 [u].

37.07.23E "A Dog's Life." [Dognapping in Los Angeles]. *CJC*, 23 July 1937, p. 4 [u].

37.07.23F "A Semitic Paragraph." [Germans in Palestine]. *CJC*, 23 July 1937, p. 4 [u].

37.07.30A "Parliament and Partition." [British parliamentary debate on partition of Palestine]. *CJC*, 30 July 1937, p. 3 [u].

37.07.30B "The Book of Jubilee." [Jewish journalist hails Peel Commission Report as salvation of the Jews]. *CJC*, 30 July 1937, p. 3 [u].

37.07.30C "Dictatorship and the Fourth Estate." [Fate of the press in Soviet Union and Italy]. *CJC*, 30 July 1937, p. 4 [u].

37.07.30D "The Book of Revelations." [Colonial secretary claims Balfour Declaration was not written by Balfour]. *CJC*, 30 July 1937, p. 4 [u].

37.07.30E "The Book of Samuel." [Anti-Zionism of Samuel Shulman]. *CJC*, 30 July 1937, p. 4 [u].

37.08.06A "Zurich . . ." [Twentieth World Zionist Congress in Zurich]. *CJC*, 6 Aug. 1937, p. 3 [u].

37.08.06B ". . . And Geneva." [League of Nations, Permanent Mandates Commission debates Peel Commission report]. *CJC*, 6 Aug. 1937, p. 3 [u].

37.08.06C "Mountain Gangsterism." [Jewish homes and stores attacked in Ste. Adèle, Quebec]. *CJC*, 6 Aug. 1937, p. 4 [u].

37.08.06D "Poisoned at the Well." [Journalism used as propaganda]. *CJC*, 6 Aug. 1937, p. 4 [u].

37.08.06E "The Belfast Outrage." [Irish nationalists terrorize visit of British Royalty to Ireland]. *CJC*, 6 Aug. 1937, p. 4 [u].

37.08.06F "The Morning Post Changes." [*London Morning Post*'s stance on Zionism]. *CJC*, 6 Aug. 1937, p. 4 [u].

37.08.06G " 'Pro' or 'Anti'." [Paul Gouin on French Canadian Nationalism]. *CJC*, 6 Aug. 1937, p. 4 [u].

38.01.00A "Thirty Plots and Holy Writ." [*See* 38.04.15A]. *KA*, Jan. 1938, pp. 95–96 [s].

38.04.15A "Thirty Plots and Holy Writ." [The Bible contains all basic literary plots]. *CJC*, 15 Apr. 1938, pp. 35–8 [s]. *See also* MS 5045–53.

38.11.11A "The Jewish Federation Campaign." [Fundraising for the Federation of Jewish Charities]. *CJC*, 11 Nov. 1938, p. 3 [u].

38.11.11B "The Palestine Partition Commission." [Peel Commission report on proposed partitioning of Palestine]. *CJC*, 11 Nov. 1938, p. 3 [u].

38.11.11C "Bercovitch by Acclamation." [Peter Bercovitch fills seat for Cartier riding]. *CJC*, 11 Nov. 1938, p. 3 [u].

38.11.11D "Footnote to Conquest." [Persecution of Jews in Nazi occupied Czechoslavakia]. *CJC*, 11 Nov. 1938, p. 3 [u].

38.11.11E "Ersatz" [Explaining ersatz]. *CJC*, 11 Nov. 1938, p. 4 [u].

38.11.11F "Fiat Lux." [Libya seeks to increase its birthrate]. *CJC*, 11 Nov. 1938, p. 4 [u].

38.11.11G "Jews' Aire." [Jews are held in camps in Palestine]. *CJC*, 11 Nov. 1938, p. 4 [u].

38.11.11H "Script For a Scenario." [Charlie Chaplin's *The Great Dictator*]. *CJC*, 11 Nov. 1938, p. 4 [u].

38.11.11I "Chamberlain In Paris." [Neville Chamberlain goes to Paris]. *CJC*, 11 Nov. 1938, p. 4 [u].

38.11.18A "Vandal and Victim." [Kristallnacht]. *CJC*, 18 Nov. 1938, p. 3 [i].

38.11.18B "Coughlin's Protocols." [Anti-Semitism of Charles Coughlin]. *CJC*, 18 Nov. 1938, pp. 3, 4 [i].

38.11.18C "Kemal Ataturk." [Death of Kemal Ataturk]. *CJC*, 18 Nov. 1938, p. 4 [i].

38.11.18D " 'La Nation' and the Jewish Problem." [*La Nation* adopts a more sympathetic position toward Jews]. *CJC*, 18 Nov. 1938, p. 4 [i].

38.11.18E "The Fall of Jericho." [British take Jericho from Arabs]. *CJC*, 18 Nov. 1938, p. 4 [i].

38.11.18F "Twenty years of War Undeclared." [Irony of armistice celebration in light of militarism in Europe]. *CJC*, 18 Nov. 1938, p. 4 [i].

38.11.25A "Mussolini and Mickey Mouse." [Cartoons banned in Italy]. *CJC*, 25 Nov. 1938, p. 4 [i].

38.11.25B "The Spirit of St. Louis." [Charles Lindbergh takes up residence in Germany]. *CJC*, 25 Nov. 1938, p. 4 [i].

38.11.25C "Lo the Poor Indian." [Joseph Goebbels warns Canada to stay out of German affairs]. *CJC*, 25 Nov. 1938, p. 4 [i].

38.11.25D "Jehova in Exile." [Name of Jehova is banned in Germany]. *CJC*, 25 Nov. 1938, p. 4 [i].

38.11.25E "A Premature Map." [Germans publish an atlas listing British territories as German]. *CJC*, 25 Nov. 1938, p. 4 [i].

38.11.25F "The Nobel Peace Prize." [Nobel Peace Prize awarded to the Nansen office]. *CJC*, 25 Nov. 1938, p. 4 [i].

38.12.02A "Le Devoir Sees Its Duty." [Anti-Semitic journalism in Quebec]. *CJC*, 2 Dec. 1938, p. 3 [i].

38.12.02B "The Ten Commandments: Nazi Version." [Religion in Nazi Germany]. *CJC*, 2 Dec. 1938, pp. 3–4 [i].

38.12.02C "Chamberlain's Socks." [Foreign policy of Neville Chamberlain]. *CJC*, 2 Dec. 1938, p. 4 [i].

38.12.02D "Cultural Arguments." [Cultural exchanges between Germany, Italy and Japan]. *CJC*, 2 Dec. 1938, p. 4 [i].

38.12.02E "Devil's Island." [Appeasement policy of Edouard Daladier]. *CJC*, 2 Dec. 1938, p. 4 [i].

38.12.02F "Hitler: Contributing Editor." [Excerpts from speeches of Adolf Hitler on his peaceful intentions]. *CJC*, 2 Dec. 1938, p. 4 [i].

38.12.09A "The J.D.C. and ORT Compaign." [Fundraising campaign for the Joint Distribution Committee and ORT (acronym for Russian "Society for Manual Work")]. *CJC*, 9 Dec. 1938, p. 3 [i].

38.12.09B "Municipal Elections." [Jewish participation in Montreal civic affairs]. *CJC*, 9 Dec. 1938, p. 3 [i].

38.12.09C "Obituary." [Death of Corneliu Codreanu]. *CJC*, 9 Dec. 1938, p. 3 [i].

38.12.09D "Of Spontainety [*sic*]." [Rise of fascism is claimed to be spontaneous]. *CJC*, 9 Dec. 1938, pp. 3, 4 [i].

38.12.09E "Cities of Refuge." [Obscure locations proposed as refuge for Jews]. *CJC*, 9 Dec. 1938, p. 4 [i].

38.12.09F "Purge No. 77." [Shortage of diapers in the Soviet Union]. *CJC*, 9 Dec. 1938, p. 4 [i].

38.12.09G "The Pope and Democracy." [Anti-Semitism in Quebec]. *CJC*, 9 Dec. 1938, p. 4 [i].

38.12.09H "Ford — 1938 Model." [Henry Ford changes his attitude towards Jews]. *CJC*, 9 Dec. 1938, p. 4 [i].

38.12.16A "The Law of the Swiss." [Switzerland passes anti-racist human rights legislation]. *CJC*, 16 Dec. 1938, p. 3 [i].

38.12.16B "The Pan-American Conference." [U.S. foreign policy on the Americas]. *CJC*, 16 Dec. 1938, p. 3 [i].

38.12.16C "Of Palestine Products." [Consumer league founded to support Palestine's economy]. *CJC*, 16 Dec. 1938, p. 3 [i].

38.12.16D "The Required Encyclical." [Nazi threat to Roman Catholicism]. *CJC*, 16 Dec. 1938, p. 4 [i].

38.12.16E "Stage Directions." [Appeasement policy of Neville Chamberlain]. *CJC*, 16 Dec. 1938, p. 4 [i].

38.12.16F "The Quakers and the Quack." [Quakers propose a pilgrimage to convert Adolf Hitler]. *CJC*, 16 Dec. 1938, p. 4 [i].

38.12.16G "The Mahatma and the Jewish Question." [Mahatma Gandhi]. *CJC*, 16 Dec. 1938, p. 4 [i].

38.12.18A "What's In a Name!" [Klein names his column in the *Keneder Adler*]. *KA*, 18 Dec. 1938, p. 8 [s].

38.12.19A "Mr. H. G. Wells: Crystal-gazer." [*See* 38.12.23B]. *KA*, 19 Dec. 1938, p. 6 [s].

38.12.20A "Ecrasez L'Infame." [*See* 38.12.23C]. *KA*, 20 Dec. 1938, p. 6 [s].

38.12.20B "Hjalmar Pharaoh Schacht." [*See* 38.12.23D]. *KA*, 20 Dec. 1938, p. 6 [s].

38.12.21A "The School Report." [*See* 38.12.23E]. *KA*, 21 Dec. 1938, p. 6 [s].

38.12.21B "Face the Musicas!" [*See* 38.12.23F]. *KA*, 21 Dec. 1938, p. 6 [s].

38.12.22A "Conquest a La Carte." [*See* 38.12.30E]. *KA*, 22 Dec. 1938, p. 6 [s].

38.12.23A "The Feast of Lights." [Chanukah]. *CJC*, 23 Dec. 1938, p. 3 [i].

38.12.23B "Mr. H.G. Wells: Crystal-Gazer." [Anti-Semitic writings of H.G. Wells]. *CJC*, 23 Dec. 1938, p. 3 [i].

38.12.23C "Ecrasez L'Infame." [Election rigging in Quebec]. *CJC*, 23 Dec. 1938, p. 4 [i].

38.12.23D "Hjalmar Pharaoh Schacht." [Proposed scheme to ransom Jews]. *CJC*, 23 Dec. 1938, p. 4 [i].

38.12.23E "The School Report." [Education in Quebec]. *CJC*, 23 Dec. 1938, p. 4 [i].

38.12.23F "Face the Musicas!" [McKesson and Robbins scandal]. *CJC*, 23 Dec. 1938, p. 4 [i].

38.12.23G "Hens in Goose-Step." [German hens are expected to increase egg production]. *CJC*, 23 Dec. 1938, p. 4 [i].

38.12.23H "Hens in Goose-Step." [*See* 38.12.23G]. *KA*, 23 Dec. 1938, p. 8 [s].

38.12.23I "Semitic Antisemites." [*See* 38.12.30D]. *KA*, 23 Dec. 1938, p. 8 [s].

38.12.25A "Peace On Earth." [*See* 38.12.30A]. *KA*, 25 Dec. 1938, p. 6 [s].

38.12.25B "And Good Will Towards Men." [*See* 38.12.30B]. *KA*, 25 Dec. 1938, p. 6 [s].

38.12.26A "Season's Gift." [*See* 38.12.30G]. *KA*, 26 Dec. 1938, p. 6 [s].

38.12.26B "Echo of the Boycott." [Jewish boycott of German products]. *KA*, 26 Dec. 1938, p. 6 [s].

38.12.27A "Insurgency Among The Insurgents." [*See* 38.12.30F]. *KA*, 27 Dec. 1938, p. 6 [s].

38.12.27B "The Kettle and the Pot." [Germans protest remarks of Harold Ickes]. *KA*, 27 Dec. 1938, p. 6 [s].

38.12.28A "Liberty In A Teapot." [*See* 38.12.30H]. *KA*, 28 Dec. 1938, p. 6 [s].

38.12.28B "Children Refugees." [*See* 38.12.30C]. *KA*, 28 Dec. 1938, p. 6 [s].

38.12.29A "A Good Deed In a Naughty World." [Bolivia offers sanctuary to Jewish refugees]. *KA*, 29 Dec. 1938, p. 6 [s].

38.12.29B "Kirche, Kuche and Kinder." [*See* 39.01.13G]. *KA*, 29 Dec. 1938, p. 6 [s].

38.12.29C "Herzl's Bones." [*See* 39.01.06C]. *KA*, 29 Dec. 1938, p. 6 [s].

38.12.30A "Peace on Earth." [Growing conflict on eve of New Year]. *CJC*, 30 Dec. 1938, p. 3 [i].

38.12.30B "And Good Will Towards Wen [*sic*]." [Growing anti-Semitism in Europe]. *CJC*, 30 Dec. 1938, p. 3 [i].

38.12.30C "Children Refugees." [Fundraising campaign for Youth Aliyah]. *CJC*, 30 Dec. 1938, p. 3 [i].

38.12.30D "Semitic Antisemites." [Arab-Jewish relations in Palestine]. *CJC*, 30 Dec. 1938, p. 3 [i].

38.12.30E "Conquest a la Carte." [Nazi aggression in Europe]. *CJC*, 30 Dec. 1938, p. 4 [i].

38.12.30F Insurgency Among the Insurgents [Opposition to Italian involvement in Spanish Civil War]. *CJC*, 30 Dec. 1938, p. 4 [i].

38.12.30G "Season's Gift." [Proposed gifts for world leaders]. *CJC*, 30 Dec. 1938, p. 4 [i].

38.12.30H "Liberty in a Teapot." [British politics]. *CJC*, 30 Dec. 1938, p. 4 [i].

38.12.30I "Kindliness Towards Kine." [*See* 39.01.06H]. *KA*, 30 Dec. 1938, p. 6 [s].

38.12.30J "Ah, Bitter Chill It Was!" [*See* 39.01.06B]. *KA*, 30 Dec. 1938, p. 6 [s].

38.12.30K "Scientific Discovery." [*See* 39.01.06E]. *KA*, 30 Dec. 1938, p. 6 [s].

38.12.30L "Under the Rome-Berlin Axis." [Introduction of anti-Semitic laws in Czechoslovakia]. *KA*, 30 Dec. 1938, p. 6 [s].

39.01.01A "Resolutions, Astrology, and Gematria." [*See* 39.01.06A]. *KA*, 1 Jan. 1939, p. 8 [s].

39.01.02A "Music and The Savage Breast." [*See* 39.01.06F]. *KA*, 2 Jan. 1938, p. 6 [s].

39.01.02B "Add Musical Note." [Adolf Hitler wants the German anthem played more slowly]. *KA*, 2 Jan. 1939, p. 6 [s].

39.01.02C "The Lima Declarations." [*See* 39.01.06G]. *KA*, 2 Jan. 1939, p. 6 [s].

39.01.03A "Goebbels Whipped." [*See* 39.01.06D]. *KA*, 3 Jan. 1939, p. 6 [s].

39.01.04A "Karel Capek." [Death of Karel Čapek]. *KA*, 4 Jan. 1939, p. 6 [s].

39.01.04B "Fiat Lux." [Quebec government policy on its universities]. *KA*, 4 Jan. 1939, p. 6 [s].

39.01.04C "Education Survey." [Need for improved Jewish education in North America]. *KA*, 4 Jan. 1939, p. 6 [s].

39.01.05A "O Gentle Reader!" [Klein comments on readers' responses to his column]. *KA*, 5 Jan. 1939, p. 6 [s].

39.01.06A "Resolutions, Astrology, and Gematria." [Looking back at 1938 and ahead to 1939]. *CJC*, 6 Jan. 1939, p. 3 [i].

39.01.06B "Ah, Bitter Chill It Was!" [Pan-American Conference at Lima]. *CJC*, 6 Jan. 1939, p. 3 [i].

39.01.06C "Herzl's Bones." [Nazi's deface the tomb of Theodor Herzl]. *CJC*, 6 Jan. 1939, p. 3 [i].

39.01.06D "Goebbels Whipped." [Joseph Goebbels is beaten by friends of Gustav Froelich]. *CJC*, 6 Jan. 1939, p. 4 [i].

39.01.06E "Scientific Discovery." [Totalitarian dictatorships]. *CJC*, 6 Jan. 1939, p. 4 [i].

39.01.06F "Music and the Savage Breast." [Erich Kleiber refuses to conduct at La Scala]. *CJC*, 6 Jan. 1939, p. 4 [i].

39.01.06G "The Lima Declarations." [Conference at Lima]. *CJC*, 6 Jan. 1939, p. 4 [i].

39.01.06H "Kindliness Towards Kine." [Lithuanian government makes "shechita" illegal]. *CJC*, 6 Jan. 1939, p. 4 [i].

39.01.06I "The Nazi Radiorator." [*See* 39.01.13E]. *KA*, 6 Jan. 1939, p. 6 [s].

39.01.06J "Norman And Teuton." [*See* 39.01.13F]. *KA*, 6 Jan. 1939, p. 6 [s].

39.01.08A "Anti-Semitism on the March." [Anti-Semitism in New York City]. *KA*, 8 Jan. 1939, p. 8 [s].

39.01.10A "Prof. Felix Frankfurter." [*See* 39.01.13C]. *KA*, 10 Jan. 1939, p. 6 [s].

39.01.10B "Wells Takes Them For a Ride." [*See* 39.01.13D]. *KA*, 10 Jan. 1939, p. 6 [s].

39.01.11A "The Golem of Prague." [*See* 39.01.20D]. *KA*, 11 Jan. 1939, p. 6 [s].

39.01.11B "Mooney Freed." [*See* 39.01.20E]. *KA*, 11 Jan. 1939, p. 6 [s].

39.01.13A "The Talmud Torah Campaign." [Need for Jewish education to combat growing anti-Semitism]. *CJC*, 13 Jan. 1939, p. 3 [i].

39.01.13B "Roosevelt's Momentous Address." [Franklin Delano Roosevelt delivers an anti-isolationist address]. *CJC*, 13 Jan. 1939, p. 3 [i].

39.01.13C "Prof. Felix Frankfurter." [Felix Frankfurter is appointed to U.S. Supreme Court]. *CJC*, 13 Jan. 1939, p. 4 [i].

39.01.13D "Wells Takes Them for a Ride." [H. G. Wells suggests a way of ridding the world of certain world leaders]. *CJC*, 13 Jan. 1939, p. 4 [i].

39.01.13E "The Nazi Radiorator." [Pro-Nazi message broadcast on the CBC]. *CJC*, 13 Jan. 1939, p. 4 [i].

39.01.13F "Norman and Teuton." [Meeting between Montague Norman and Hjalmar Schacht]. *CJC*, 13 Jan. 1939, p. 4 [i].

39.01.13G "Kirche, Kuche, and Kinder." [Women in Nazi Germany]. *CJC*, 13 Jan. 1939, p. 4 [i].

39.01.13H "The Ominous Prologue." [Confiscation of art treasures from Churches in Germany]. *KA*, 13 Jan. 1939, p. 6 [s].

39.01.13I "Not Enough Stones, and Too Much Bread!" [*See* 39.01.20F]. *KA*, 13 Jan. 1939, p. 6 [s].

39.01.15A "A Dutch Treat." [*See* 39.01.20G]. *KA*, 15 Jan. 1939, p. 8 [s].

39.01.15B "Musical Notes." [Anecdotes about propaganda]. *KA*, 15 Jan. 1939, p. 8 [s].

39.01.17A "Tale of a Slingshot." [Dutch boy breaks German consulate window with slingshot]. *KA*, 17 Jan. 1939, p. 6 [s].

39.01.18A "No Pact at Rome." [*See* 39.01.27F]. *KA*, 18 Jan. 1939, p. 6 [s].

39.01.18B "That Way Madness Lies." [*See* 39.01.27G]. *KA*, 18 Jan. 1939, p. 6 [s].

39.01.19A "Suffering Unlimited." [Jewish refugees and the international refugee commission]. *KA*, 19 Feb. 1939, p. 8 [s].

39.01.20A "The Canadian Jewish Congress." [Canadian Jewish Congress meets in Toronto]. *CJC*, 20 Jan. 1939, p. 3 [i].

39.01.20B "Mr. Louis Fitch at the Legislative Assembly." [Louis Fitch addresses the Quebec Legislative Assembly]. *CJC*, 20 Jan. 1939, p. 3 [i].

39.01.20C "The Montreal Daily Star." [Seventieth birthday of the *Montreal Daily Star*]. *CJC*, 20 Jan. 1939, p. 3 [i].

39.01.20D "The Golem of Prague." [Rising anti-Semitism in Czechoslovakia]. *CJC*, 20 Jan. 1939, p. 4 [i].

39.01.20E "Mooney Freed." [Tom Mooney is freed after twenty years in San Quentin]. *CJC*, 20 Jan. 1939, p. 4 [i].

39.01.20F "Not Enough Stones, and Too Much Bread!" [World economics]. *CJC*, 20 Jan. 1939, p. 4 [i].

39.01.20G "A Dutch Treat." [Social problems in Nazi Germany]. *CJC*, 20 Jan. 1939, p. 4 [i].

39.01.20H "Nazi Propaganda: Canadian Department." [*See* 39.01.27E]. *KA*, 20 Jan. 1939, p. 8 [s].

39.01.22A "Life of The Bee." [Nazis try to improve honey production]. *KA*, 22 Jan. 1939, p. 8 [s].

39.01.22B "Library Note." [New edition of *Mein Kampf* to be published in U.S.]. *KA*, 22 Jan. 1939, p. 8 [s].

39.01.22C "The Sequel: Mein Sieg." [*See* 39.01.27H]. *KA*, 22 Jan. 1939, p. 8 [s].

39.01.22D "Gandhi and Nazism." [Ineffectuality of passive resistance]. *KA*, 22 Jan. 1939, p. 8 [s].

39.01.24A "March of Time." [Newsreel on refugees]. *KA*, 24 Jan. 1939, p. 6 [s].

39.01.24B "The Round Table: A Square Deal?" [*See* 39.02.03F]. *KA*, 24 Jan. 1939, p. 6 [s].

39.01.25A "Spain at the Eleventh Hour." [*See* 39.02.03G]. *KA*, 25 Jan. 1939, p. 6 [s].

39.01.25B "A New German Custom." [*See* 39.02.03E]. *KA*, 25 Jan. 1939, p. 6 [s].

39.01.25C "Nostrum Mare." [International struggle for control of the Mediterranean]. *KA*, 25 Jan. 1939, p. 6 [s].

39.01.27A "Mr. Samuel Bronfman, President of Canadian Jewish Congress." [Samuel Bronfman is elected president of the Canadian Jewish Congress]. *CJC*, 27 Jan. 1939, p. 3 [i].

39.01.27B "Jan Masaryk." [Jan Masaryk addresses the Canadian Jewish Congress]. *CJC*, 27 Jan. 1939, p. 3 [i].

39.01.27C "Bnai Brith Membership Campaign." [B'nai Brith membership campaign]. *CJC*, 27 Jan. 1939, p. 3 [i].

39.01.27D "They Shall Not Pass." [Anti-Semitism in Quebec]. *CJC*, 27 Jan. 1939, p. 3 [i].

39.01.27E "Nazi Propaganda: Canadian Department." [German Consul General to Ottawa urges banning of a Soviet anti-German film]. *CJC*, 27 Jan. 1939, p. 4 [i].

39.01.27F "No Pact at Rome." [Neville Chamberlain returns from talks with Benito Mussolini]. *CJC*, 27 Jan. 1939, p. 4 [i].

39.01.27G "That Way Madness Lies." [Psychologist declares U.S. on verge of nervous collapse]. *CJC*, 27 Jan. 1939, p. 4 [i].

39.01.27H "The Sequel; Mein Sieg." [German policy toward France]. *CJC*, 27 Jan. 1939, p. 4 [i].

39.01.27I "Of 'Pins And Needles'." [*See* 39.02.03H]. *KA*, 27 Jan. 1939, p. 6 [s].

39.01.29A "Refugees: The Scorned and The Rejected." [*See* 39.02.03D]. *KA*, 29 Jan. 1939, p. 8 [s].

39.01.31A "A Bible Translation." [*See* 39.02.10C]. *KA*, 31 Jan. 1939, p. 6 [s].

39.02.01A "Alarm-Clocks in Europe." [*See* 39.02.10G]. *KA*, 1 Feb. 1939, p. 6 [s].

39.02.01B "Suits, By Hitler." [*See* 39.02.10D]. *KA*, 1 Feb. 1939, p. 6 [s].

39.02.01C "Jewry's New Saviour." [*See* 39.02.10E]. *KA*, 1 Feb. 1939, p. 6 [s].

39.02.03A "The Call of the Histadrut." [Fundraising campaign for the Histadrut]. *CJC*, 3 Feb. 1939, p. 3 [i].

39.02.03B "The Land of the Cactus." [Anti-Semitism in Mexico]. *CJC*, 3 Feb. 1939, p. 3 [i].

39.02.03C "Hitler the Peacemaker." [Speech of Adolf Hitler]. *CJC*, 3 Feb. 1939, p. 3 [i].

39.02.03D "Refugees: The Scorned and the Rejected." [Anti-Semites oppose the admission of Jewish refugees to Canada]. *CJC*, 3 Feb. 1939, p. 4 [i].

39.02.03E "A New German Custom." [Jews flee Nazi Germany]. *CJC*, 3 Feb. 1939, p. 4 [i].

39.02.03F "The Round Table: A Square Deal." [The Mufti boycotts Arab-Jewish talks]. *CJC*, 3 Feb. 1939, p. 4 [i].

39.02.03G "Spain at the Eleventh Hour." [Spanish Civil War]. *CJC*, 3 Feb. 1939, p. 4 [i].

39.02.03H "Pins and Needles." [Review of *Pins and Needles*, a musical review]. *CJC*, 3 Feb. 1939, p. 12 [s].

39.02.03I "Note on Dictator's Economics." [Economics and fascist dictatorships]. *KA*, 3 Feb. 1939, p. 6 [s].

39.02.05A "Some Haman-Taschen." [Purim story and contemporary events]. *KA*, 5 Mar. 1939, p. 8 [s].

39.02.05B "The Rhine and the Potomac." [Franklin Delano Roosevelt announces policy of direct aid to democracies threatened by dictatorships]. *KA*, 5 Feb. 1939, p. 8 [s].

39.02.05C "War: The Evolution of a Menagerie." [*See* 39.02.10F]. *KA*, 5 Feb. 1939, p. 8 [s].

39.02.07A "I'd Rather Be Right . . ." [Franklin Delano Roosevelt denies announcement of direct aid to democracies threatened by dictatorship]. *KA*, 7 Feb. 1939, p. 6 [s].

39.02.07B "Municipal Civil Service." [Montreal alderman recommends institution of a municipal civil service]. *KA*, 7 Feb. 1939, p. 6 [s].

39.02.08A "The Five Who Laughed." [*See* 39.02.24E]. *KA*, 8 Feb. 1939, p. 6 [s].

39.02.10A "The Round Table Conference." [Arab-Jewish Conference in London]. *CJC*, 10 Feb. 1939, p. 3 [i].

39.02.10B "Arcand Rides Again." [Fascism and anti-Semitism in Quebec]. *CJC*, 10 Feb. 1939, p. 3 [i].

39.02.10C "A Bible Translation." [Modern translation of the Bible]. *CJC*, 10 Feb. 1939, p. 4 [i].

39.02.10D "Suits by Hitler." [Economics in Nazi Germany]. *CJC*, 10 Feb. 1939, p. 4 [i].

39.02.10E "Jewry's New Saviour." [Adolf Hitler and the Jews of Europe]. *CJC*, 10 Feb. 1939, p. 4 [i].

39.02.10F "War: The Evolution of a Menagerie." [Development of military technology]. *CJC*, 10 Feb. 1939, p. 4 [i].

39.02.10G "Alarm Clocks in Europe." [Rise of fascism in Europe]. *CJC*, 10 Feb. 1939, p. 4 [i].

39.02.10H "Little Red Riding Houde." [*See* 39.02.24F]. *KA*, 10 Feb. 1939, p. 6 [s].

39.02.12A "Rosenberg's Reservations." [*See* 39.02.17F]. *KA*, 12 Feb. 1939, p. 8 [s].

39.02.14A "Pope Pius XI." [*See* 39.02.17D]. *KA*, 14 Feb. 1939, p. 6 [s].

39.02.14B "The MacDonald Question." [*See* 39.02.17E]. *KA*, 14 Feb. 1939, p. 6 [s].

39.02.17A "Dr. Weizmann's Address." [Chaim Weizmann's speech to the Arab-Jewish Conference]. *CJC*, 17 Feb. 1939, p. 3 [i].

39.02.17B "Justice Brandeis Resigns." [Louis Brandeis resigns from U.S. Supreme Court]. *CJC*, 17 Feb. 1939, p. 3 [i].

39.02.17C "Good Will and Bad Eggs." [Central and South America reject Italian aid]. *CJC*, 17 Feb. 1939, p. 3 [i].

39.02.17D "Pope Pius XI." [Death of Pope Pius XI]. *CJC*, 17 Feb. 1939, p. 4 [i].

39.02.17E "The MacDonald Question." [Malcolm Macdonald at the Arab-Jewish Conference]. *CJC*, 17 Feb. 1939, p. 4 [i].

39.02.17F "Rosenberg's Reservations." [Alfred Rosenberg proposes a solution to the Jewish problem]. *CJC*, 17 Feb. 1939, p. 4 [i].

39.02.17G "The Mac-Pap's Arrive." [Mackenzie-Papineau Battalion returns to Canada]. *CJC*, 17 Feb. 1939, p. 4 [i].

39.02.17H "I Can Tell You, Bela! Bela!" [*See* 39.02.24G]. *KA*, 17 Feb. 1939, p. 6 [s].

39.02.17I "The Father of International Law." [Irony of honouring father of international law in light of world events]. *KA*, 17 Feb. 1939, p. 6 [s].

39.02.19A "Suffering Unlimited." [Jewish refugees and the international refugee commission]. *KA*, 19 Feb. 1939, p. 8 [s].

39.02.21A "Imitative Poland." [Poland seeks to rid itself of Jews]. *KA*, 21 Feb. 1939, p. 6 [s].

39.02.21B "The Fascist Temperament." [*See* 39.02.24D]. *KA*, 21 Feb. 1939, p. 6 [s].

39.02.21C "French Somaliland." [France occupies Somaliland]. *KA*, 21 Feb. 1939, p. 6 [s].

39.02.21D "Canadian Immigration." [Ernest Stapleford urges open immigration policy for Canada]. *KA*, 21 Feb. 1939, p. 6 [s].

39.02.22A "The Circus at Madison Square Garden." [*See* 39.03.03B]. *KA*, 22 Feb. 1939, p. 6 [s].

39.02.24A "Revolt in Syria." [Anti-French revolt in Syria]. *CJC*, 24 Feb. 1939, p. 3 [i].

39.02.24B "The Soviet Union: Breaker of the Boycott." [Soviet Union breaks boycott of fascist states]. *CJC*, 24 Feb. 1939, p. 3 [i].

39.02.24C "Quacks in the Reich." [Shortage of doctors in Nazi Germany]. *CJC*, 24 Feb. 1939, p. 3 [i].

39.02.24D "The Fascist Temperament." [Fascism in Spain]. *CJC*, 24 Feb. 1939, p. 3 [i].

39.02.24E "The Five Who Laughed." [Five comic actors are banned from performing in Nazi Germany]. *CJC*, 24 Feb. 1939, p. 4 [i].

39.02.24F "Little Red Riding Houde." [Camillien Houde and fascism in Quebec]. *CJC*, 24 Feb. 1939, p. 4 [i].

39.02.24G "I Can Tell You, Bela! Bela!" [Resignation of Bela Imredy as prime minister of Hungary]. *CJC*, 24 Feb. 1939, p. 4 [i].

39.02.24H "Adder's Tongue and Crocodile Tears." [Suggestion to extend Rome-Berlin axis to the Vatican]. *KA*, 24 Feb. 1939, p. 8 [s].

39.02.24I "Swastika Over Canada." [*See* 39.03.10F]. *KA*, 24 Feb. 1939, p. 8 [s].

39.02.24J "The Silence Strike." [Arabs at Round Table Conference refuse to speak]. *KA*, 24 Feb. 1939, p. 8 [s].

39.02.26A "Of Him Whom We Envy." [*See* 39.03.10D]. *KA*, 26 Feb. 1939, p. 6 [s].

39.02.28A "Gigli Water." [*See* 39.03.10E]. *KA*, 28 Feb. 1939, p. 6 [s].

39.02.28B "Hines's 13 Varieties." [Conviction of Jimmy Hines]. *KA*, 28 Feb. 1939, p. 6 [s].

39.03.01A "Les Demi Civilizes." [*See* 39.03.03C]. *KA*, 1 Mar. 1939, p. 6 [s].

39.03.03A "The Munich of Zionism?" [British foreign policy on Palestine]. *CJC*, 3 Mar. 1939, p. 3 [i].

39.03.03B "The Circus at Madison Square Garden." [Nazi rally at Madison Square Gardens]. *CJC*, 3 Mar. 1939, p. 4 [i].

39.03.03C "Les Demi Civilizes." [Anti-Semitism in Quebec]. *CJC*, 3 Mar. 1939, p. 4 [i].

39.03.03D "Balaam-Franco." [Fascism of Francisco Franco]. *KA*, 3 Mar. 1939, p. 8 [s].

39.03.03E "Non-innocents Abroad." [German interference in British and Canadian affairs]. *KA*, 3 Mar. 1939, p. 8 [s].

39.03.05A "Some Haman-Taschen." [Purim story and contemporary events]. *KA*, 5 Mar. 1939, p. 8 [s].

39.03.07A "Pope Pius XII." [*See* 39.03.10A]. *KA*, 7 Mar. 1939, p. 6 [s].

39.03.07B "The MacMahon Letters." [*See* 39.03.10G]. *KA*, 7 Mar. 1939, p. 6 [s].

39.03.08A "Wishful Biography." [*See* 39.03.17C]. *KA*, 8 Mar. 1939, p. 6 [s].

39.03.10A "Pope Pius XII." [Election of Pope Pius XII]. *CJC*, 10 Mar. 1939, p. 3 [u].

39.03.10B "Principle Verboten." [Jewish forced labour in Nazi Germany]. *CJC*, 10 Mar. 1939, p. 3 [u].

39.03.10C "The Pan-Arab Chimera." [Arab Palestine]. *CJC*, 10 Mar. 1939, p. 3 [u].

39.03.10D "Of Him Whom We Envy." [Faith vs. rationalism]. *CJC*, 10 Mar. 1939, p. 4 [i].

39.03.10E "Gigli Water." [Anti-Semitic comments of Benjamin Gigli]. *CJC*, 10 Mar. 1939, p. 4 [i].

39.03.10F "Swastika Over Canada." [Fascism in Canada]. *CJC*, 10 Mar. 1939, p. 4 [i].

39.03.10G "The MacMahon Letters." [Publication of the letters of Sir Henry MacMahon]. *CJC*, 10 Mar. 1939, p. 4 [i].

39.03.10H "Humor in the Reich." [Jokes about Nazi Germany]. *KA*, 10 Mar. 1939, p. 8 [s].

39.03.14A "Stalin the Man of Flexible Steel." [*See* 39.03.17B]. *KA*, 14 Mar. 1939, p. 6 [s].

39.03.15A "The Ides of March." [Jews are expelled from Italy]. *KA*, 15 Mar. 1939, p. 6 [s].

39.03.15B "La Chamberlaine." [*See* 39.03.17D]. *KA*, 15 Mar. 1939, p. 6 [s].

39.03.15C "The Most Powerful Man In The World." [Mahatma Gandhi]. *KA*, 15 Mar. 1939, p. 6 [s].

39.03.17A "Czechoslovakia, Going, Going, Gone!" [Germany takes over Czechoslovakia]. *CJC*, 17 Mar. 1939, p. 3 [i].

39.03.17B "Stalin: The Man of Flexible Steel." [German-Soviet Non-aggression Pact]. *CJC*, 17 Mar. 1939, p. 4 [i].

39.03.17C "Wishful Biography." [Rumours of Adolf Hitler's death]. *CJC*, 17 Mar. 1939, p. 4 [i].

39.03.17D "La Chamberlaine." [Satire on Neville Chamberlain's policy of appeasement]. *CJC*, 17 Mar. 1939, p. 4 [i].

39.03.17E "The Final Plan." [*See* 39.03.24E]. *KA*, 17 Mar. 1939, p. 6 [s].

39.03.19A "The European Nightmare." [*See* 39.03.24F]. *KA*, 19 Mar. 1939, p. 8 [s].

39.03.21A "It Ain't Gonna Rain No More." [*See* 39.03.24G]. *KA*, 21 Mar. 1939, p. 6 [s].

39.03.21B "From the Frying Pan." [Edouard Daladier comes to power in France]. *KA*, 21 Mar. 1939, p. 6 [s].

39.03.22A "A Good Deed In a Naughty World." [*See* 39.03.31G]. *KA*, 22 Mar. 1939, p. 6 [s].

39.03.22B "Canada Condemms Hitler." [*See* 39.03 31F]. *KA*, 22 Mar. 1939, p. 6 [s].

39.03.24A "And Now Memel." [Nazi aggression in Europe]. *CJC*, 24 Mar. 1939, p. 3 [i].

39.03.24B "The Canadian Jewish Congress." [Resolutions of the Canadian Jewish Congress]. *CJC*, 24 Mar. 1939, p. 3 [i].

39.03.24C "Building the World of Tomorrow." [Need for a Jewish homeland]. *CJC*, 24 Mar. 1939, p. 3 [i].

39.03.24D "A Study in Contrasts." [Albert Einstein on democracy, Joseph Goebbels on Nazism]. *CJC*, 24 Mar. 1939, p. 3 [i].

39.03.24E "The Final Plan." [Malcolm MacDonald announces his plan for Palestine]. *CJC*, 24 Mar. 1939, p. 4 [i].

39.03.24F "The European Nightmare." [Nazi aggression in Europe]. *CJC*, 24 Mar. 1939, p. 4 [i].

39.03.24G "It Ain't Gonna Rain No More." [Neville Chamberlain's policy of appeasement]. *CJC*, 24 Mar. 1939, p. 4 [i].

39.03.24H "The Plucky Czech Consuls." [*See* 39.03.31E]. *KA*, 24 Mar. 1939, p. 8 [s].

39.03.24I "Hot and Cold." [Adolf Hitler wants to establish an air base in Iceland]. *KA*, 24 Mar. 1939, p. 8 [s].

39.03.26A "If I Were Chief Rabbi of Palestine." [*See* 39.03.31D]. *KA*, 26 Mar. 1939, p. 6 [s].

39.03.28A "Duce Wild." [Speech of Benito Mussolini]. *KA*, 28 Mar. 1939, p. 6 [s].

39.03.28B "Preliminary Motion." [Communist purge trials]. *KA*, 28 Mar. 1939, p. 6 [s].

39.03.29A "The 'Stop Hitler' Farce." [British appeasement]. *KA*, 29 Mar. 1939, p. 6, [s].

39.03.31A "Our Haggadah." [Passover and Jewish history]. *CJC*, 31 Mar. 1939, p. 3 [i].

39.03.31B "The Four Questions." [Jewish history and the rise of Nazism]. *CJC*, 31 Mar. 1939, p. 3 [i].

39.03.31C "The Ten Plagues." [Nazi aggression in Europe]. *CJC*, 31 Mar. 1939, p. 3 [i].

39.03.31D "If I Were Chief Rabbi of Palestine." [Need for greater Jewish population in Palestine]. *CJC*, 31 Mar. 1939, p. 63 [i].

39.03.31E "The Plucky Czech Consuls." [Czech diplomats refuse to turn their consulates over to Germany]. *CJC*, 31 Mar. 1939, p. 63 [i].

39.03.31F "Canada Condemns Hitler." [Adolf Hitler is condemned in the House of Commons]. *CJC*, 31 Mar. 1939, p. 63 [i].

39.03.31G "A Good Deed in a Naughty World." [Voters of Zurich unseat six anti-Semitic politicians]. *CJC*, 31 Mar. 1939, p. 63 [i].

39.03.31H "Defeatism or Rose-Coloured Glasses?" [*See* 39.04.07D]. *KA*, 31 Mar. 1939, p. 6 [s].

39.04.07A "The Axis, the Triangle, the Circle." [Growth of the fascist alliance]. *CJC*, 7 Apr. 1939, p. 3 [i].

39.04.07B "Arms Across the Sea." [Nazism in Argentina]. *CJC*, 7 Apr. 1939, p. 3 [i].

39.04.07C "Belgian and Dane." [Fascism in Belgium and Denmark]. *CJC*, 7 Apr. 1939, p. 3 [i].

39.04.07D "Defeatism or Rose Colored Glasses?" [Reply to Israel Rabinovitch on Nazi aggression in Europe]. *CJC*, 7 Apr. 1939, p. 4 [i].

39.04.07E "Tempest in a Teapot." [British preparedness in case of war]. *KA*, 7 Apr. 1939, p. 8 [s].

39.04.07F "Wuthering Heights." [*See* 39.04.14F]. *KA*, 7 Apr. 1939, p. 8 [s].

39.04.09A "The Hebrew Free Loan Association." [*See* 39.04.14C]. *KA*, 9 Apr. 1939, p. 8 [s].

39.04.12A "Mr. Woodsworth and Peace." [*See* 39.04.14D]. *KA*, 12 Apr. 1939, p. 6 [s].

39.04.12B "The Might of Rome." [*See* 39.04.14E]. *KA*, 12 Apr. 1939, p. 6 [s].

39.04.14A "The United Palestine Appeal." [United Palestine Appeal]. *CJC*, 14 Apr. 1939, p. 3 [i].

39.04.14B "The Protector of Islam." [Benito Mussolini and the Islamic nations]. *CJC*, 14 Apr. 1939, p. 3 [i].

39.04.14C "The Hebrew Free Loan Association." [Hebrew Free Loan Association]. *CJC*, 14 Apr. 1939, p. 4 [i].

39.04.14D "Mr. Woodsworth and Peace." [J. S. Woodsworth advocates a pacifist approach to fascism]. *CJC*, 14 Apr. 1939, p. 4 [i].

39.04.14E "The Might of Rome." [Italian annexation of Albania]. *CJC*, 14 Apr. 1939, p. 4 [i].

39.04.14F "Wuthering Heights." [Censoring of film version of *Wuthering Heights* in Quebec]. *CJC*, 14 Apr. 1939, p. 4 [i].

39.04.14G "Jurisprudence." [*See* 39.04.21E]. *KA*, 14 Apr. 1939, p. 8 [s].

39.04.14H "Mercy Killing For The Poor." [*See* 39.04.21D]. *KA*, 14 Apr. 1939, p. 8 [s].

39.04.16A "Two Plays." [Review of productions of *Awake and Sing* and *Who is Who*]. *KA*, 16 Apr. 1939, p. 8 [s].

39.04.18A "Roosevelt the Peacemaker." [*See* 39.04.21F]. *KA*, 18 Apr. 1939, p. 6 [s].

39.04.19A "Murder in the Consulate." [*See* 39.04.21G]. *KA*, 19 Apr. 1939, p. 6 [s].

39.04.19B "Apartments Wanted." [League of Nations will have to leave Swiss headquarters in the event of war]. *KA*, 19 Apr. 1939, p. 6 [s].

39.04.21A "Demagogues and Refugees." [Anti-Semitism in Quebec]. *CJC*, 21 Apr. 1939, p. 3 [i].

39.04.21B "Deportation of Nazis." [Canada amends its Espionage Act]. *CJC*, 21 Apr. 1939, p. 3 [i].

39.04.21C "Word from Palestine." [British foreign policy on Palestine]. *CJC*, 21 Apr. 1939, p. 3 [i].

39.04.21D "Mercy Killing for the Poor." [Edward Dyer advocates euthanasia of the aged poor]. *CJC*, 21 Apr. 1939, p. 4 [i].

39.04.21E "Jurisprudence." [Mental cruelty suit in U.S.]. *CJC*, 21 Apr. 1939, p. 4 [i].

39.04.21F "Roosevelt the Peacemaker." [Franklin Delano Roosevelt's open letter to Adolf Hitler]. *CJC*, 21 Apr. 1939, p. 4 [i].

39.04.21G "Murder in the Consulate." [Assassination of the British consul in Iraq]. *CJC*, 21 Apr. 1939, p. 4 [i].

39.04.21H "Song of Love." [*See* 39.04.28F]. *KA*, 21 Apr. 1939, p. 6 [s].

39.04.21I "Hitler's Birthday." [*See* 39.04.28G]. *KA*, 21 Apr. 1939, p. 6 [s].

39.04.21J "And Two Birthday Presents." [*See* 39.04.28H]. *KA*, 21 Apr. 1939, p. 6 [s].

39.04.25A "Police Circular." [*See* 39.04.28E]. *KA*, 25 Apr. 1939, p. 6 [s].

39.04.26A "The Most Unkindest Cut." [British foreign policy on Palestine]. *KA*, 26 Apr. 1939, p. 6 [s].

39.04.28A "Conscription in Britain." [Conscription in Britain]. *CJC*, 28 Apr. 1939, p. 3 [i].

39.04.28B "The Fourth Estate in France." [Prosecution of anti-Semites in France]. *CJC*, 28 Apr. 1939, p. 3 [i].

39.04.28C "The Beth David Synagogue." [Fiftieth anniversary of the Beth David Synagogue]. *CJC*, 28 Apr. 1939, p. 3 [i].

39.04.28D "Welcome to Leivick." [Leivick Halpern]. *CJC*, 28 Apr. 1939, p. 4 [i].

39.04.28E "Police Circular." [Police circular for Adolf Hitler]. *CJC*, 28 Apr. 1939, p. 4 [i].

39.04.28F "Song of Love." [Nazi propaganda aimed at Arab world]. *CJC*, 28 Apr. 1939, p. 4 [i].

39.04.28G "Hitler's Birthday." [Adolf Hitler's Birthday]. *CJC*, 28 Apr. 1939, p. 4 [i].

39.04.28H "And a Birthday Present." [Edouard Beneš establishes a committee for Czech independence]. *CJC*, 28 Apr. 1939, p. 4 [i].

39.04.28I " 'Gott Strafe England'." [German hatred for England]. *KA*, 28 Apr. 1939, p. 8 [s].

39.04.28J "Revelations in a Court Room." [Fascist activity in Canada]. *KA*, 28 Apr. 1939, p. 8 [s].

39.04.28K "Lest They Forget." [Fascist contempt for Britain]. *KA*, 28 Apr. 1939, p. 8 [s].

39.04.28L "Tarboush of Truce." [*See* 39.05.05H]. *KA*, 28 Apr. 1939, p. 8 [s].

39.04.30A "Hitler's Speech." [*See* 39.05.05B]. *KA*, 30 Apr. 1939, p. 8 [s].

39.05.02A "Life Under The Dictators." [*See* 39.05.05D]. *KA*, 2 May 1939, p. 6 [s].

39.05.02B "Floral Greeting." [*See* 39.05.05E]. *KA*, 2 May 1939, p. 6 [s].

39.05.02C "A Penny Serenade." [*See* 39.05.05F]. *KA*, 2 May 1939, p. 6 [s].

39.05.02D "Daylight Saving Time." [*See* 39.05.05G]. *KA*, 2 May 1939, p. 6 [s].

39.05.03A "Hitler and the Refugees." [Adolf Hitler speaks on Jewish threat]. *KA*, 3 May 1939, p. 6 [s].

39.05.03B "St. Louis Division." [Quebec government re-zones St. Louis riding]. *KA*, 3 May 1939, p. 6 [s].

39.05.05A "Revelations in the House." [Louis Fitch speaks out against fascism in Quebec]. *CJC*, 5 May 1939, p. 3 [i].

39.05.05B "Hitler's Speech: Its Content." [Analysis of a speech by Adolf Hitler]. *CJC*, 5 May 1939, p. 4 [i].

39.05.05C "It's Technique." [Analysis of Adolf Hitler's oratorical style]. *CJC*, 5 May 1939, p. 4 [i].

39.05.05D "Life Under the Dictators." [Life in totalitarian dictatorships]. *CJC*, 5 May 1939, p. 4 [i].

39.05.05E "Floral Greetings." [Czechs protest Nazi occupation]. *CJC*, 5 May 1939, p. 4 [i].

39.05.05F "A Penny Serenade." [Blackshirts misunderstand fascist ideology]. *CJC*, 5 May 1939, p. 4 [i].

39.05.05G "Daylight Saving Time." [Daylight Saving Time]. *CJC*, 5 May 1939, p. 4 [i].

39.05.05H "Tarboush of Truce." [The Mufti loses support in Palestine]. *CJC*, 5 May 1939, p. 4 [i].

39.05.05I "An Apt Retort." [*See* 39.05.12F]. *KA*, 5 May 1939, p. 6 [s].

39.05.05J "Neutrality Lane." [Adolf Hitler tries to form alliances in Scandinavia]. *KA*, 5 May 1939, p. 6 [s].

39.05.05K "Off With Litvinoff." [Maxim Litvinoff resigns as Commissar of External Affairs for the Soviet Union]. *KA*, 5 May 1939, p. 6 [s].

39.05.07A "Discord in 'Harmonia'." [*See* 39.05.12D]. *KA*, 7 May 1939, p. 8 [s].

39.05.07B "Another Speech." [*See* 39.05.12E]. *KA*, 7 May 1939, p. 8 [s].

39.05.09A "Hitler Psycho-analyzed." [Psychiatric appraisals of Adolf Hitler]. *KA*, 9 May 1939, p. 6 [s].

39.05.10A "A Fountain and a Shrine." [*See* 39.05.12B]. *KA*, 10 May 1939, p. 6 [s].

39.05.10B "The Play's the Thing." [*See* 39.05.12C]. *KA*, 10 May 1939, p. 6 [s].

39.05.12A "Welcome to their Majesties." [Visit of King George and Queen Elizabeth to Canada]. *CJC*, 12 May 1939, p. 3 [u].

39.05.12B "A Fountain and a Shrine." [In memory of Louis Rubenstein]. *CJC*, 12 May 1939, p. 4 [i].

39.05.12C "The Play's the Thing." [Establishment of a Jewish Theatre School in Montreal]. *CJC*, 12 May 1939, p. 4 [i].

39.05.12D "Discord In 'Harmonia'." [Quebec police seize a Nazi propaganda film]. *CJC*, 12 May 1939, p. 4 [i].

39.05.12E "Another Speech." [Beck declares his intention to defend Danzig from Nazi aggression]. *CJC*, 12 May 1939, p. 4 [i].

39.05.12F "An Apt Report [*sic, should* be Retort]." [U.S. plan to sell arms to Britain and France]. *CJC*, 12 May 1939, p. 4 [i].

39.05.12G "Racial Science." [Anthropologist argues for Jewish superiority]. *KA*, 12 May 1939, p. 8 [s].

39.05.14A "Suggestions for Editors." [*See* 39.05.19D]. *KA*, 14 May 1939, p. 8 [s].

39.05.14B "A Real Headline." [*See* 39.05.19E]. *KA*, 14 May 1939, p. 8 [s].

39.05.16A "Persuasion By Kidnap." [*See* 39.05.19F]. *KA*, 16 May 1939, p. 6 [s].

39.05.16B "A Touch From Franco." [*See* 39.05.26C]. *KA*, 16 May 1939, p. 6 [s].

39.05.16C "Soldiers in Diapers." [*See* 39.05.26D]. *KA*, 16 May 1939, p. 6 [s].

39.05.16D "How to Reduce." [Hermann Goering loses weight]. *KA*, 16 May 1939, p. 6 [s].

39.05.17A "Mussolini's Speech." [*See* 39.05.19G]. *KA*, 17 May 1939, p. 6 [s].

39.05.18A "Welcome To Their Majesties." [*See* 39.05.12A]. *KA*, 18 May 1939, p. 1 [u].

39.05.19A "Jewish General Hospital Maintenance Campaign." [Jewish General Hospital Maintenance Campaign]. *CJC*, 19 May 1939, p. 3 [i].

39.05.19B "The Feast of Weeks." [Shavuoth]. *CJC*, 19 May 1939, p. 3 [i].

39.05.19C "Mr. B.G. Sack." [Fiftieth birthday of B.G. Sack]. *CJC*, 19 May 1939, p. 3 [i].

39.05.19D "Suggestions for Editors." [Newspaper coverage of fascist advance in Europe]. *CJC*, 19 May 1939, p. 4 [i].

39.05.19E "A Real Headline." [Announcement that Russian women are getting heavier]. *CJC*, 19 May 1939, p. 4 [i].

39.05.19F "Persuasion By Kidnap." [Kidnapping of George Palmer Putnam]. *CJC*, 19 May 1939, p. 4 [i].

39.05.19G "Mussolini's Speech." [Oratorical style of Benito Mussolini]. *CJC*, 19 May 1939, p. 4 [i].

39.05.21A "Rejoice, Ye Bulls of Bashan." [*See* 39.05.26B]. *KA*, 21 May 1939, p. 8 [s].

39.05.26A "The White Paper." [MacDonald white paper on Palestine]. *CJC*, 26 May 1939, p. 3 [i].

39.05.26B "Rejoice, Ye Bulls of Bashan." [Spain under Francisco Franco]. *CJC*, 26 May 1939, p. 4 [i].

39.05.26c "A Touch From Franco." [Francisco Franco negotiates a $100,000,000 loan]. *CJC*, 26 May 1939, p. 4 [i].

39.05.26d "Soldiers in Diapers." [Children may be drafted in Rumania]. *CJC*, 26 May 1939, p. 4 [i].

39.05.26e "The World Trembles." [Review of *The Yiddish Troupers of Poland*, a theatrical revue]. *CJC*, 26 May 1939, p. 4 [i].

39.05.30a " 'Life' And 'Time' of American Journalism." [*See* 39.06.02d]. *KA*, 30 May 1939, p. 6 [s].

39.05.30b "Pledges and Relativity." [*See* 39.06.02f]. *KA*, 30 May 1939, p. 6 [s].

39.05.31a "Situations Wanted." [*See* 39.06.02e]. *KA*, 31 May 1939, p. 6 [s].

39.05.31b "Unanimity at the City Hall." [*See* 39.06.02c]. *KA*, 31 May 1939, p. 6 [s].

39.06.02a "Hitler and The Church." [Religious persecution in Nazi Germany]. *CJC*, 2 June 1939, p. 3 [u].

39.06.02b "The Pope and Racism." [Pope elevates two blacks to the Episcopate]. *CJC*, 2 June 1939, p. 3 [u].

39.06.02c "Unanimity at the City Hall." [Congratulating Montreal police for handling of royal visit]. *CJC*, 2 June 1939, p. 4 [i].

39.06.02d " 'Life' and 'Time' of American Journalism." [False reporting of royal visit to Quebec]. *CJC*, 2 June 1939, p. 4 [i].

39.06.02e "Situations Wanted." [King Zog of Albania seeks a new post]. *CJC*, 2 June 1939, p. 4 [i].

39.06.02f "Pledges and Relativity." [Albert Einstein's address at the World's Fair, Palestine Pavilion]. *CJC*, 2 June 1939, p. 4 [i].

39.06.02g "Statesmen! Smartest Little [*sic*]." [Jews and Czechs fight Nazism]. *CJC*, 2 June 1939, p. 4 [i].

39.06.02h "Treatise on Treaties." [British foreign policy on Palestine]. *CJC*, 2 June 1939, p. 4 [i].

39.06.02i "A German Menu." [*See* 39.06.09c]. *KA*, 2 June 1939, p. 8 [s].

39.06.04a " 'Luftmenschen' and 'Wassermenschen'." [*See* 39.06.09d]. *KA*, 4 June 1939, p. 8 [s].

39.06.06a "The Bald-Head Club." [Club for bald men]. *KA*, 6 June 1939, p. 6 [s].

39.06.06b "Of Refugees." [*See* 39.06.09e]. *KA*, 6 June 1939, p. 6 [s].

39.06.07A "Hitler, Art Critic." [Adolf Hitler's views on art]. *KA*, 7 June 1939, p. 6 [s].

39.06.09A " 'The National Unity Party'." [Fascism in Quebec]. *CJC*, 9 June 1939, p. 3 [u].

39.06.09B "Modern Marranos." [German Jewish refugees convert to Christianity in Bolivia]. *CJC*, 9 June 1939, p. 3 [u].

39.06.09C "A German Menu." [Food shortages in Nazi Germany]. *CJC*, 9 June 1939, p. 4 [i].

39.06.09D " 'Luftmenschen' and 'Wassermenschen'." [Plight of Jewish refugees]. *CJC*, 9 June 1939, p. 4 [i].

39.06.09E "Of Refugees." [Admission of refugees to Canada]. *CJC*, 9 June 1939, p. 4 [i].

39.06.09F "A Seven Per Cent Jew." [Lord Samuel's views on Palestine]. *CJC*, 9 June 1939, p. 4 [i].

39.06.09G "Postscript to Non-Intervention." [*See* 39.06.23H]. *KA*, 9 June 1939, p. 8 [s].

39.06.09H "Why Hitler Helped Spain." [*See* 39.06.16F]. *KA*, 9 June 1939, p. 8 [s].

39.06.11A "Uniforms and Humans." [*See* 39.06.16D]. *KA*, 11 June 1939, p. 8 [s].

39.06.11B "Moses and Freud." [*See* 39.06.16E]. *KA*, 11 June 1939, p. 8 [s].

39.06.13A "The Modern Mariners." [*See* 39.06.16G]. *KA*, 13 June 1939, p. 8 [s].

39.06.14A "The Bear Dance." [*See* 39.06.23F]. *KA*, 14 June 1939, p. 6 [s].

39.06.14B "Footnotes to the White Paper." [*See* 39.06.23G]. *KA*, 14 June 1939, p. 6 [s].

39.06.14C "Quiz." [*See* 39.07.14G]. *KA*, 14 June 1939, p. 6 [s].

39.06.16A "The Old World and the New." [Four European countries offer temporary asylum to Jewish refugees]. *CJC*, 16 June 1939, p. 3 [i].

39.06.16B "Extra-curricular High School Activities." [Anti-Semitism in U.S.]. *CJC*, 16 June 1939, p. 3 [u].

39.06.16C "Living Space for the Jews." [Spread of Nazism in Europe]. *CJC*, 16 June 1939, p. 3 [u].

39.06.16D "Uniforms and Humans." [German youth immune from punishment for crimes committed in uniform]. *CJC*, 16 June 1939, p. 4 [i].

39.06.16E "Moses and Freud." [Sigmund Freud claims that Moses was an Egyptian]. *CJC*, 16 June 1939, p. 4 [i].

39.06.16F "Why Hitler Helped Spain." [German involvement in the Spanish Civil War]. *CJC*, 16 June 1939, p. 4 [i].

39.06.16G "The Modern Mariners." [Jewish refugees aboard the *S.S. St. Louis*]. *CJC*, 16 June 1939, p. 4 [i].

39.06.16H " 'Stop Thief'." [Nazi propaganda]. *KA*, 16 June 1939, p. 8 [s].

39.06.16I "Ambassadorial Duties." [German ambassador to Britain engages in espionage]. *KA*, 16 June 1939, p. 8 [s].

39.06.18A "Memorandum to the League." [Chaim Weizmann's memorandum to the League of Nations on the British white paper on Palestine]. *KA*, 18 June 1939, p. 8 [s].

39.06.20A "Underwater, Underground." [*See* 39.06.23D]. *KA*, 20 June 1939, p. 6 [s].

39.06.20B "Design in Yellow." [Japanese blockade of British Settlement at Tientsin]. *KA*, 20 June 1939, p. 6 [s].

39.06.20C " 'We Trustfully Place Our Faith'." [*See* 39.06.23E]. *KA*, 20 June 1939, p. 6 [s].

39.06.21A "Ship A-Hoy!" [*See* 39.06.30D]. *KA*, 21 June 1939, p. 6 [s].

39.06.23A "MacDonald's Apologia." [Malcolm MacDonald defends the British white paper on Palestine]. *CJC*, 23 June 1939, p. 3 [i].

39.06.23B "What, No National Unity?" [Adrien Arcand and the Union Nationale in Quebec]. *CJC*, 23 June 1939, p. 3 [u].

39.06.23C "History Outlives Policy." [Cyrus Adler on international fascism]. *CJC*, 23 June 1939, p. 3 [u].

39.06.23D "Underwater, Underground." [Sinking of three submarines]. *CJC*, 23 June 1939, p. 4 [i].

39.06.23E " 'We Trustfully Place Our Faith'." [Nazi-occupied Czechoslovakia]. *CJC*, 23 June 1939, p. 4 [i].

39.06.23F "The Bear Dance." [Expulsion of Jews from Poland]. *CJC*, 23 June 1939, p. 4 [i].

39.06.23G "Footnotes to the White Paper." [British foreign policy on Palestine]. *CJC*, 23 June 1939, p. 4 [i].

39.06.23H "Postscript to Non-Intervention." [German and Italian involvement in the Spanish Civil War]. *CJC*, 23 June 1939, p. 4 [i].

39.06.23I "A Cycle of Cathay." [*See* 39.06.30C]. *KA*, 23 June 1939, p. 8 [s].

39.06.25A "Free for All?" [*See* 39.06.30E]. *KA*, 25 June 1939, p. 8 [s].

39.06.25B "The Burgler's Plans." [Confiscation of Jewish property]. *KA*, 25 June 1939, p. 8 [s].

39.06.25C "Some Statistics." [World distribution of Jews]. *KA*, 25 June 1939, p. 8 [s].

39.06.27A "Twisting the Lion's Tail." [Japanese harrassment of British]. *KA*, 27 June 1939, p. 6 [s].

39.06.27B "The Chinese B.V.D.'s." [Japanese blockade at Tientsin]. *KA*, 27 June 1939, p. 6 [s].

39.06.28A "Almanac de Chamberlain." [*See* 39.07.07B]. *KA*, 28 June 1939, p. 6 [s].

39.06.30A "The Reversal of Versailles." [Treaty of Versailles]. *CJC*, 30 June 1939, p. 3 [u].

39.06.30B "The Late Maxwell Goldstein." [Death of Maxwell Goldstein]. *CJC*, 30 June 1939, p. 3 [u].

39.06.30C "A Cycle of Cathay." [China is suggested as a Jewish homeland]. *CJC*, 30 June 1939, p. 4 [i].

39.06.30D "Ship A-Hoy!" [Palestine Maritime Lloyd Ltd.]. *CJC*, 30 June 1939, p. 4 [i].

39.06.30E "Free For All?" [Egypt and Turkey bid to assume the British Mandate over Palestine]. *CJC*, 30 June 1939, p. 4 [i].

39.06.30F "What's in a Name?" [*See* 39.07.07C]. *KA*, 30 June 1939, p. 6 [s].

39.07.02A "Oh Splendid Harvest Moon!" [*See* 39.07.07D]. *KA*, 2 July 1939, p. 8 [s].

39.07.04A "Nazis Learn Yiddish." [Nazis learn Yiddish]. *KA*, 4 July 1939, p. 6 [s].

39.07.04B "Marked Money." [*See* 39.07.21H]. *KA*, 4 July 1939, p. 6 [s].

39.07.05A "Words In Their Season." [*See* 39.07.14F]. *KA*, 5 July 1939, p. 6 [s].

39.07.05B "The Case of Myrna Loy." [U.S. authorities reject Myrna Loy's submitted passport photo]. *KA*, 5 July 1939, p. 6 [s].

39.07.07A "Chaim Nachman Bialik 1873–1934." [*See* 37.06.00A]. *CJC*, 7 July 1939, pp. 3, 14–15 [s].

39.07.07B "Almanac de Chamberlain." [Neville Chamberlain's foreign policy]. *CJC*, 7 July 1939, p. 4 [i].

39.07.07C "What's In A Name." [*Le Devoir* challenges the practice of legal name changing]. *CJC*, 7 July 1939, p. 4 [i].

39.07.07D "O Splendid Harvest Moon." [Imminence of war]. *CJC*, 7 July 1939, p. 4 [i].

39.07.07E "A Peculiar Request." [*See* 39.07.14D]. *KA*, 7 July 1939, p. 6 [s].

39.07.09A "A Modest Proposal." [*See* 39.07.14E]. *KA*, 9 July 1939, p. 8 [s].

39.07.11A " 'A Nazi Screen'." [Quebec government charges Harmonia Club for showing fascist film]. *KA*, 11 July 1939, p. 6 [s].

39.07.12A "The Canadian Messiah." [*See* 39.07.21G]. *KA*, 12 July 1939, p. 6 [s].

39.07.14A "The Reich's 'Union of Jews'." [Establishment of the Union of German Jews]. *CJC*, 14 July 1939, p. 3 [u].

39.07.14B "An Arab Who's Who." [Arab nationalism]. *CJC*, 14 July 1939, p. 3 [u].

39.07.14C "After Conversion — What?" [Conversion of Jews in Italy]. *CJC*, 14 July 1939, p. 3 [u].

39.07.14D "A Peculiar Request." [Malcolm MacDonald requests other nations to hinder the entry of illegal immigrants to Palestine]. *CJC*, 14 July 1939, p. 4 [i].

39.07.14E "A Modest Proposal." [Satirical alternative to a Jewish homeland]. *CJC*, 14 July 1939, p. 4 [i].

39.07.14F "Words In Their Season." [Accidents on summer holidays]. *CJC*, 14 July 1939, p. 4 [i].

39.07.14G "Quiz." [Satire on Neville Chamberlain]. *CJC*, 14 July 1939, p. 4 [i].

39.07.14H "What Every Dictator Should Own." [Remorselessness of fascist dictators]. *KA*, 14 July 1939, p. 8 [s].

39.07.14I "More Vandalism." [Nazis vandalize statue of Thomas Masaryk]. *KA*, 14 July 1939, p. 8 [s].

39.07.16A "Hitler's Humanitarianism." [*See* 39.07.28F]. *KA*, 16 July 1939, p. 8 [s].

39.07.16B "Mysterious Hollywood." [MGM abandons proposed production of *It Can't Happen Here*]. *KA*, 16 July 1939, p. 8 [s].

39.07.18A "The Borne to Which no Traveller Returns." [*See* 39.07.21E]. *KA*, 18 July 1939, p. 6 [s].

39.07.18B "Plane Talk." [*See* 39.07.21F]. *KA*, 18 July 1939, p. 6 [s].

39.07.19A "Nazi Truth." [*See* 39.07.28D]. *KA*, 19 July 1939, p. 6 [s].

39.07.19B "The Saviour of the British Empire." [*See* 39.07.28G]. *KA*, 19 July 1939, p. 6 [s].

39.07.21A "McDonald on McDonald." [British foreign policy on Palestine]. *CJC*, 21 July 1939, p. 3 [u].

39.07.21B "Espionage and Propaganda." [Espionage through journalism]. *CJC*, 21 July 1939, p. 3 [u].

39.07.21C "Silver Tongued Coughlin." [Elliot Roosevelt speaks out against Charles Coughlin]. *CJC*, 21 July 1939, p. 3 [u].

39.07.21D "Ninth of Ab." [Tisha B'Av]. *CJC*, 21 July 1939, p. 3 [u].

39.07.21E "The Borne to Which No Traveller Returns." [Mayor Lucien Borne of Quebec City forbids meetings to incite race hatred]. *CJC*, 21 July 1939, p. 4 [i].

39.07.21F "Plane Talk." [Show of Strength by the R.A.F.]. *CJC*, 21 July 1939, p. 4 [i].

39.07.21G "The Canadian Messiah." [Adrien Arcand]. *CJC*, 21 July 1939, p. 4 [i].

39.07.21H "Marked Money." [Italy finances Arab terrorism]. *CJC*, 21 July 1939, p. 4 [i].

39.07.21I [Untitled]. [Overeating in Germany]. *KA*, 21 July 1939, p. 6 [s].

39.07.21J "The Fuehrer Has a Date." [*See* 39.07.28E]. *KA*, 21 July 1939, p. 6 [s].

39.07.25A "German Generosity." [*See* 39.07.28H]. *KA*, 25 July 1939, p. 6 [s].

39.07.25B " 'By Their Leaders Shall You Know Them?' " [Arrest of Fritz Kuhn]. *KA*, 25 July 1939, p. 6 [s].

39.07.26A "Mass Weddings." [Mass wedding in Quebec]. *KA*, 26 July 1939, p. 6 [s].

39.07.26B " 'Say it With Music'." [*See* 39.08.11F]. *KA*, 26 July 1939, p. 6 [s].

39.07.28A "The Mad Man of Gotham." [Fascism in U.S.]. *CJC*, 28 July 1939, p. 3 [u].

39.07.28B "Yodelling in Harmony." [Germans in the Italian Tyrol Region return to Germany]. *CJC*, 28 July 1939, p. 3 [u].

39.07.28C "Farewell, A Long Farewell." [Pro-Nazi Germans leave Canada]. *CJC*, 28 July 1939, p. 3 [u].

39.07.28D "Nazi Truth." [Nazi journalistic propaganda]. *CJC*, 28 July 1939, p. 4 [i].

39.07.28E "The Fuehrer Has a Date." [Adolf Hitler is jilted by a dancer]. *CJC*, 28 July 1939, p. 4 [i].

39.07.28F "Hitler's Humanitarianism." [Son of Kurt Schuschnigg is subjected to Nazi indoctrination]. *CJC*, 28 July 1939, p. 4 [i].

39.07.28G "The Saviour of the British Empire." [Oswald Mosley]. *CJC*, 28 July 1939, p. 4 [i].

39.07.28H "German Generosity." [Germans offer to allow one hundred Jews to attend fourth World Zionist Congress]. *CJC*, 28 July 1939, p. 4 [i].

39.07.28I "A Summer Idyll, or Love in the Mountains." [Anti-Semitism in Quebec]. *KA*, 28 July 1939, p. 6 [s].

39.07.30A "Arab Ransom Schemes." [*See* 30.08.04E]. *KA*, 30 July 1939, p. 8 [s].

39.07.30B " 'Don't Excite Yourself Dear'." [*See* 39.08.04F]. *KA*, 30 July 1939, p. 8 [s].

39.08.01A "Incident in Vienna." [*See* 39.08.04B]. *KA*, 1 Aug. 1939, p. 6 [s].

39.08.01B "Goebbels Has Another Bad Dream." [*See* 39.08.04C]. *KA*, 1 Aug. 1939, p. 6 [s].

39.08.01C "French Measure; Somewhat Belated." [*See* 39.08.04D]. *KA*, 1 Aug. 1939, p. 6 [s].

39.08.04A "Mountain Music: Discord in the Laurentians." [Anti-Semitism in Quebec]. *CJC*, 4 Aug. 1939, p. 3 [u].

39.08.04B "Incident in Vienna." [Anti-Nazi forces vandalize a Nazi statue]. *CJC*, 4 Aug. 1939, p. 4 [i].

39.08.04C "Goebbels Has Another Bad Dream." [Joseph Goebbels' anti-Semitic journalism]. *CJC*, 4 Aug. 1939, p. 4 [i].

39.08.04D "French Measure; Somewhat Belated." [French government introduces measures to increase population]. *CJC*, 4 Aug. 1939, p. 4 [i].

39.08.04E "Arab Ransom Schemes." [Arab terrorism]. *CJC*, 4 Aug. 1939, p. 4 [i].

39.08.04F " 'Don't Excite Yourself, Dear'." [Isolationism]. *CJC*, 4 Aug. 1939, p. 4 [i].

39.08.04G "Reichstag Fire and Danzig Dynamite." [Nazi propaganda plots]. *CJC*, 4 Aug. 1939, p. 4 [i].

39.08.04H "Higher Wages for MP's." [English member of parliament complains about low wages]. *CJC*, 4 Aug. 1939, p. 4 [i].

39.08.04I "Twenty-five Years After." [Armistice Day]. *KA*, 4 Aug. 1939, p. 6 [s].

39.08.04J "Noble Heroism." [British scientist wants to test efficacy of bomb shelters]. *KA*, 4 Aug. 1939, p. 6 [s].

39.08.06A "Incendiary Speech and Arsonist Act." [Anti-Semitism in Quebec]. *KA*, 6 Aug. 1939, p. 8 [s].

39.08.08A "Dr. Schmidt on Religious Freedom." [*See* 39.08.11D]. *KA*, 8 Aug. 1939, p. 6 [s].

39.08.09A "The Suicide Club." [*See* 39.08.11E]. *KA*, 9 Aug. 1939, p. 6 [s].

39.08.11A "Words in Their Season: Mr. Samuel Bronfman's Congress Address." [Samuel Bronfman's address to the Canadian Jewish Congress Western Conference]. *CJC*, 11 Aug. 1939, p. 3 [u].

39.08.11B "The Missing Link." [Fascism in England]. *CJC*, 11 Aug. 1939, p. 3 [i].

39.08.11C "Appeasement for Palestine." [British foreign policy on Palestine]. *CJC*, 11 Aug. 1939, p. 3 [u].

39.08.11D "Dr. Schmidt on Religious Freedom." [Religion in Nazi Germany]. *CJC*, 11 Aug. 1939, p. 4 [i].

39.08.11E "The Suicide Club." [Refugees prefer suicide to deportation to Germany]. *CJC*, 11 Aug. 1939, p. 4 [i].

39.08.11F "Say it With Music." [Labour relations and music]. *CJC*, 11 Aug. 1939, p. 4 [i].

39.08.11G "Churchill on The State of the World." [*See* 39.08.18F]. *KA*, 11 Aug. 1939, p. 6 [s].

39.08.13A "The Mushroom Synagogue." [*See* 39.08.18G]. *KA*, 13 Aug. 1939, p. 8 [s].

39.08.13B "A False Report." [Benito Mussolini attends opera to dispell false rumour of heart attack]. *KA*, 13 Aug. 1939, p. 8 [s].

39.08.13C "The Axis." [The Berlin-Rome Axis]. *KA*, 13 Aug. 1939, p. 8 [s].

39.08.13D "Benevolent Neutrality." [Yugoslavia repudiates Axis suggestion that it remain neutral in case of war]. *KA*, 13 Aug. 1939, p. 8 [s].

39.08.15A "The Deadline Approaches." [*See* 39.08.18E]. *KA*, 15 Aug. 1939, p. 6 [s].

39.08.15B "Footnote to Ethiopia." [Italians plan to send Jewish refugees to Ethiopia]. *KA*, 15 Aug. 1939, p. 6 [s].

39.08.16A "Le Devoir Stands on Guard." [*See* 39.08.18H]. *KA*, 16 Aug. 1939, p. 6 [s].

39.08.18A "The Twenty-First Zionist Congress." [The twenty-first Zionist Congress]. *CJC*, 18 Aug. 1939, p. 3 [u].

39.08.18B "Pogroms in Slovakia." [Pogroms in Nazi puppet state of Slovakia]. *CJC*, 18 Aug. 1939, p. 3 [u].

39.08.18C "Mechanized Anti-Semitism." [Anti-Semitism in Quebec]. *CJC*, 18 Aug. 1939, p. 3 [u].

39.08.18D "The Moral of Syria." [France suspends the Syrian constitution]. *CJC*, 18 Aug. 1939, p. 3 [u].

39.08.18E "The Deadline Approaches." [Talks on the future of Danzig]. *CJC*, 18 Aug. 1939, p. 4 [i].

39.08.18F "Churchill on the State of the World." [Winston Churchill's address on the state of the world]. *CJC*, 18 Aug. 1939, p. 4 [i].

39.08.18G "The Mushroom Synagogue." [Use of temporary synagogues during High Holidays]. *CJC*, 18 Aug. 1939, p. 4 [i].

39.08.18H "Le Devoir Stands on Guard." [*Le Devoir* on the admission of refugees to Canada]. *CJC*, 18 Aug. 1939, p. 6 [s].

39.08.18I "Illegal Immigration." [*See* 39.08.25E]. *KA*, 18 Aug. 1939, p. 8 [s].

39.08.20A [Untitled]. [Permanent Mandates Commission of the League of Nations repudiates British white paper on Palestine]. *KA*, 20 Aug. 1939, p. 8 [s].

39.08.22A "Mysterious Week-Ends." [Journalistic confusion in reporting world events]. *KA*, 22 Aug. 1939, p. 6 [s].

39.08.22B "Ben-Gurion's Speech." [*See* 39.09.01G]. *KA*, 22 Aug. 1939, p. 6 [s].

39.08.23A "We Know You, Al!" [*See* 39.08.25C]. *KA*, 23 Aug. 1939, p. 6 [s].

39.08.25A "Comrade Hitler and Fuehrer Stalin: Heil Tovarisch." [Berlin-Moscow Axis]. *CJC*, 25 Aug. 1939, p. 3 [i].

39.08.25B "Congress Fiddles While . . ." [Internal dissent within the World Zionist Organization]. *CJC*, 25 Aug. 1939, p. 3 [u].

39.08.25C "We Know You, Al!" [Reply to anti-Zionist article of Al Segal]. *CJC*, 25 Aug. 1939, p. 4 [i].

39.08.25D "White Paper Repudiated." [League of Nations repudiates British white paper on Palestine]. *CJC*, 25 Aug. 1939, p. 4 [i].

39.08.25E "Illegal Immigration." [Agriculture in Palestine]. *CJC*, 25 Aug. 1939, p. 4 [i].

39.08.27A "Habonim Convention." [*See* 39.09.01B]. *KA*, 27 Aug. 1939, p. 8 [s].

39.08.27B "The New Katzenjammer Kids." [Tongue-in-cheek remarks about world figures]. *KA*, 27 Aug. 1939, p. 8 [s].

39.08.29A "The Futility of News Comments." [*See* 39.09.01D]. *KA*, 29 Aug. 1939, p. 8 [s].

39.08.29B "Totalitarian War Objectives." [*See* 39.09.01E]. *KA*, 29 Aug. 1939, p. 8 [s].

39.09.01A "Jewry and the Recent Crises." [Fate of European Jews]. *CJC*, 1 Sept. 1939, p. 3 [u].

39.09.01B "The Habonim Convention." [Habonim convention]. *CJC*, 1 Sept. 1939, p. 3 [u].

39.09.01C " 'Revolution of Nihilism'." [Motivation for Nazism]. *CJC*, 1 Sept. 1939, p. 3 [u].

39.09.01D "On the Futility of News-Comments." [Futility of reporting on continually changing world situation]. *CJC*, 1 Sept. 1939, p. 4 [i].

39.09.01E "Totalitarian War Objectives." [Germany's war objectives]. *CJC*, 1 Sept. 1939, p. 4 [i].

39.09.01F "The Russo-German Pact." [German-Soviet Non-aggression pact]. *CJC*, 1 Sept. 1939, p. 4 [i].

39.09.01G "Ben-Gurion's Speech." [David Ben Gurion on British white paper on Palestine]. *CJC*, 1 Sept. 1939, p. 4 [i].

39.09.01H "Refugees and the Crises." [Refugees in wartime]. *CJC*, 1 Sept. 1939, p. 4 [i].

39.09.01I "Arcand Weeps for Polish Jewry." [*See* 39.09.13C]. *KA*, 1 Sept. 1939, p. 8 [s].

39.09.04A "The Issue is Clear!" [*See* 39.09.08E]. *KA*, 4 Sept. 1939, p. 6 [s].

39.09.06A "War Profiteering." [Canadian government takes action against war profiteering]. *KA*, 6 Sept. 1939, p. 6 [s].

39.09.06B "Arcand Takes on the Vow of Silence." [Adrien Arcand ceases his activities]. *KA*, 6 Sept. 1939, p. 6 [s].

39.09.07A "International Crises." [War activity in Europe and the Middle East]. *KA*, 7 Sept. 1939, p. 6 [s].

39.09.08A "The War Guilt." [German invasion of Poland]. *CJC*, 8 Sept. 1939, p. 3 [u].

39.09.08B "President Roosevelt's Speech." [Franklin Delano Roosevelt's "neutrality" speech]. *CJC*, 8 Sept. 1939, p. 3 [u].

39.09.08C "Hitler and God." [Adolf Hitler declares God to be with Nazis]. *CJC*, 8 Sept. 1939, p. 3 [u].

39.09.08D "The Forum To-Day." [Need for Jewish public affairs forums]. *CJC*, 8 Sept. 1939, p. 3 [u].

39.09.08E "The Issue is Clear!" [WWII begins]. *CJC*, 8 Sept. 1939, p. 4 [s].

39.09.08F "Hitler in Chelm." [Adolf Hitler passes through Chelm]. *KA*, 8 Sept. 1939, p. 8 [s].

39.09.08G "Six Million Pamphlets." [British drop pamphlets on Germany]. *KA*, 8 Sept. 1939, p. 8 [s].

39.09.10A "Note Without Comment." [Anti-Semitism in Quebec]. *KA*, 10 Sept. 1939, p. 8 [s].

39.09.10B "The Defence of England." [Book on the defence of England]. *KA*, 10 Sept. 1939, p. 8 [s].

39.09.12A "German Shrecklichkeit [*sic*]." [German offensive in Poland]. *KA*, 12 Sept. 1939, p. 6 [s].

39.09.12B "Ideology in a Vacuum." [*See* 39.09.13D]. *KA*, 12 Sept. 1939, p. 6 [s].

39.09.13A "The New Year." [The Jewish New Year on the eve of WWII]. *CJC*, 13 Sept. 1939, p. 3 [u].

39.09.13B "Polish Jewry." [Need for aid for Polish Jews]. *CJC*, 13 Sept. 1939, p. 3 [u].

39.09.13C "Arcand Weeps for Polish Jewry." [Adrien Arcand on Jews in Poland]. *CJC*, 13 Sept. 1939, p. 118 [i].

39.09.13D "Ideology in a Vacuum." [J.S. Woodsworth on Canada's stand against Nazism]. *CJC*, 13 Sept. 1939, p. 122 [i].

39.09.13E "Flowers for Hitler." [Adolf Hitler orders that he be given flowers in Poland]. *KA*, 13 Sept. 1939, p. 22 [s].

39.09.13F "Peace Proposals." [Hermann Goering suggests that the war is limited to Poland]. *KA*, 13 Sept. 1939, p. 22 [s].

39.09.13G "On the Western Front." [War with France]. *KA*, 13 Sept. 1939, p. 22 [s].

39.09.13H "Soviet Mobilization." [Soviet mobilization]. *KA*, 13 Sept. 1939, p. 22 [s].

39.09.13I "Neutrality." [Neutrality during WWII]. *KA*, 13 Sept. 1939, p. 22 [s].

39.09.13J "New Year Greetings." [Wish for defeat of Adolf Hitler in coming year]. *KA*, 13 Sept. 1939, p. 22 [s].

39.09.17A "The Pace of the Russian Bear." [Speculation on Soviet war activity]. *KA*, 17 Sept. 1939, p. 8 [s].

39.09.17B "War Talk." [*See* 39.09.22D]. *KA*, 17 Sept. 1939, p. 8 [s].

39.09.19A [Untitled]. [Soviet collaboration with Germany in Poland]. *KA*, 19 Sept. 1939, p. 6 [s].

39.09.20A [Untitled]. [Isolationism of Charles Lindbergh]. *KA*, 20 Sept. 1939, p. 6 [s].

39.09.22A "A Bluffer State?" [Soviet Union proposes a Jewish state in part of occupied Poland]. *CJC*, 22 Sept. 1939, p. 3 [u].

39.09.22B "The Fuehrer's Fury." [Speech of Adolf Hitler]. *CJC*, 22 Sept. 1939, p. 3 [i].

39.09.22C "Among the Missing." [Reported arrests of Julius Streicher and Joseph Goebbels]. *CJC*, 22 Sept. 1939, p. 3 [u].

39.09.22D "War-Talk." [War vocabulary appears in advertising]. *CJC*, 22 Sept. 1939, p. 4 [i].

39.09.22E "Molotoff Speaks." [Vyacheslav Molotov on Poland]. *CJC*, 22 Sept. 1939, p. 4 [i].

39.09.22F "Col. Lindbergh Flies Again." [Isolationism of Charles Lindbergh]. *CJC*, 22 Sept. 1939, p. 4 [i].

39.09.22G "The Division of the Booty." [Germany and Soviet Union discuss partition of Poland]. *KA*, 22 Sept. 1939, p. 8 [s].

39.09.22H "Another Lie Exploded." [*See* 39.09.27F]. *KA*, 22 Sept. 1939, p. 8 [s].

39.09.24A "And Money in the Bank." [*See* 39.09.27E]. *KA*, 24 Sept. 1939, p. 6 [s].

39.09.27A "The Feast of Tabernacles." [Succoth]. *CJC*, 27 Sept. 1939, p. 3 [u].

39.09.27B "A Jewish Branch of the Canadian Red Cross." [Organization of a Jewish branch of the Canadian Red Cross]. *CJC*, 27 Sept. 1939, p. 3 [u].

39.09.27C "Sigmund Freud." [Death of Sigmund Freud]. *CJC*, 27 Sept. 1939, p. 3 [u].

39.09.27D "Social Note." [German-Soviet relations]. *CJC*, 27 Sept. 1939, p. 3 [u].

39.09.27E "And Money in the Bank." [Top Nazis keep private fortunes in secret foreign accounts]. *CJC*, 27 Sept. 1939, p. 4 [i].

39.09.27F "Another Lie Exploded." [German-Soviet relations]. *CJC*, 27 Sept. 1939, p. 4 [i].

39.09.27G "Of Peace and War." [Nazi aggression in Europe]. *CJC*, 27 Sept. 1939, p. 4 [i].

39.09.27H "Mussolini the Faded." [Compromised position of Benito Musso-lini in the Berlin-Rome Axis]. *CJC*, 27 Sept. 1939, p. 4 [i].

39.09.27I "The Blue Book." [British book documenting events leading up to wwii]. *KA*, 27 Sept. 1939, p. 8 [s].

39.09.27J "German Generals Do Not Die in Bed." [Death of Werner von Fritsch]. *KA*, 27 Sept. 1939, p. 8 [s].

39.10.01A "The Kneeling Lady of the Baltic." [*See* 39.10.06F]. *KA*, 1 Oct. 1939, p. 8 [s].

39.10.01B "We Face the Facts." [*See* 39.10.06G]. *KA*, 1 Oct. 1939, p. 8 [s].

39.10.03A "The Double Dealers." [*See* 39.10.06D]. *KA*, 3 Oct. 1939, p. 6 [s].

39.10.03B "War Technique." [*See* 39.10.06E]. *KA*, 3 Oct. 1939, p. 6 [s].

39.10.04A "Obituary on Poland." [Fate of Poland]. *KA*, 4 Oct. 1939, p. 8 [s].

39.10.04B "Will Hitler Abdicate?" [Rumours that Adolf Hitler will abdicate]. *KA*, 4 Oct. 1939, p. 8 [s].

39.10.06A "The Fate of Polish Jewry." [Fate of Jews in occupied Poland]. *CJC*, 6 Oct. 1939, p. 3 [u].

39.10.06B "Canadian Young Judaea Convention." [Thirteenth Young Judaea Convention]. *CJC*, 6 Oct. 1939, p. 3 [u].

39.10.06C "The Disadvantage of a Democracy at War." [British cabinet is indecisive on the eve of war]. *CJC*, 6 Oct. 1939, p. 3 [u].

39.10.06D "The Double-Dealers." [Berlin-Moscow Axis]. *CJC*, 6 Oct. 1939, p. 4 [i].

39.10.06E "War Technique." [U-boat warfare against the British navy]. *CJC*, 6 Oct. 1939, p. 4 [i].

39.10.06F "The Kneeling Lady of the Baltic." [Soviet aggression in the Baltic]. *CJC*, 6 Oct. 1939, p. 4 [i].

39.10.06G "We Face the Facts." [German-Soviet Non-aggression pact]. *CJC*, 6 Oct. 1939, p. 4 [i].

39.10.08A "Peace, Peace, But There Is No Peace!" [*See* 39.10.13E]. *KA*, 8 Oct. 1939, p. 8 [s].

39.10.10A "Hitler's Judenstaat." [*See* 39.10.13D]. *KA*, 10 Oct. 1939, p. 6 [s].

39.10.11A "A Matter of Taste." [*See* 39.10.13F]. *KA*, 11 Oct. 1939, p. 6 [s].

39.10.13A "Our War Aims." [Allied objectives for entering into wwii]. *CJC*, 13 Oct. 1939, p. 3 [u].

39.10.13B "Private David Croll." [David Croll volunteers for military service]. *CJC*, 13 Oct. 1939, p. 3 [u].

39.10.13C "Hitler's Choice." [Possibility of a German Western offensive]. *CJC*, 13 Oct. 1939, p. 3 [u].

39.10.13D "Hitler's Judenstaat." [Adolf Hitler proposes a Jewish state in Europe]. *CJC*, 13 Oct. 1939, p. 4 [i].

39.10.13E "Peace, Peace, But There is No Peace!" [Speech of Adolf Hitler]. *CJC*, 13 Oct. 1939, p. 4 [i].

39.10.13F "A Matter of Taste." [Soviet propaganda justifies alliance with fascism]. *CJC*, 13 Oct. 1939, p. 4 [i].

39.10.13G "The Shocking Shaw." [*See* 39.10.27H]. *KA*, 13 Oct. 1939, p. 8 [s].

39.10.13H "Lithuania's Jerusalem." [Negotiations between Soviet Union and Lithuania]. *KA*, 13 Oct. 1939, p. 8 [s].

39.10.15A "The Offensive Peace Offensive." [Adolf Hitler's professed pacifism]. *KA*, 15 Oct. 1939, p. 8 [s].

39.10.15B "Where's Joe." [*See* 39.10.20F]. *KA*, 15 Oct. 1939, p. 6 [s].

39.10.17A "The Heart that Beats in a Bottle." [*See* 39.10.20G]. *KA*, 17 Oct. 1939, p. 6 [s].

39.10.18A "No Concealed Assets." [*See* 39.10.20H]. *KA*, 18 Oct. 1939, p. 6 [s].

39.10.18B " 'He Sent A Letter to His Lover!' " [*See* 39.10.20E]. *KA*, 18 Oct. 1939, p. 6 [s].

39.10.20A "Peacemakers and Warmongers." [Nazi view of pacifists and aggressors]. *CJC*, 20 Oct. 1939, p. 3 [u].

39.10.20B "Albert R. Carmen." [Death of Albert Carmen]. *CJC*, 20 Oct. 1939, p. 3 [u].

39.10.20C "The New Monroe Doctrine." [American isolationism]. *CJC*, 20 Oct. 1939, p. 3 [u].

39.10.20D "Y.M.H.A. Membership Appeal." [Y.M.H.A. membership appeal]. *CJC*, 20 Oct. 1939, p. 3 [u].

39.10.20E " 'He Sent a Letter to His Lover'." [Berlin-Moscow Axis]. *CJC*, 20 Oct. 1939, p. 4 [i].

39.10.20F "Where's Joe." [Benito Mussolini and the Berlin-Rome axis]. *CJC*, 20 Oct. 1939, p. 4 [i].

39.10.20G "The Heart That Beats in a Bottle." [Charles Lindbergh and U.S. isolationism]. *CJC*, 20 Oct. 1939, p. 4 [i].

39.10.20H "No Concealed Assets." [Sally Rand's bankruptcy]. *CJC*, 20 Oct. 1939, p. 4 [i].

39.10.20I "The Bankruptcy of Nazi Ideology." [Nazi ideology]. *KA*, 20 Oct. 1939, p. 8 [s].

39.10.22A "The Mufti Moves." [*See* 39.10.27F]. *KA*, 22 Oct. 1939, p. 10 [s].

39.10.22B "A Turkish Delight." [*See* 39.10.27G]. *KA*, 22 Oct. 1939, p. 10 [s].

39.10.24A "The Ghastly White Paper Laid." [*See* 39.10.27D]. *KA*, 24 Oct. 1939, p. 8 [s].

39.10.24B ". . . And Nowhere To Go!" [*See* 39.10.27E]. *KA*, 24 Oct. 1939, p. 8 [s].

39.10.25A "Hurrah For A Mother-In-Law." [*See* 39.11.03E]. *KA*, 25 Oct. 1939, p. 6 [s].

39.10.25B "Methinks The Lady Doth Protest Too Much." [Adolf Hitler's activities]. *KA*, 25 Oct. 1939, p. 6 [s].

39.10.27A " 'We Must Carry On!' " [Federation of Jewish Philanthropies campaign]. *CJC*, 27 Oct. 1939, p. 3 [u].

39.10.27B "The Quebec Elections." [Defeat of the Duplessis government]. *CJC*, 27 Oct. 1939, p. 3 [u].

39.10.27C "A Contrite Italy." [Anti-Semitism in Italy]. *CJC*, 27 Oct. 1939, p. 3 [u].

39.10.27D "The Ghastly White Paper Laid." [Elihu Stone and Stephen Wise on British white paper on Palestine]. *CJC*, 27 Oct. 1939, p. 4 [i].

39.10.27E "And Nowhere to Go!" [Need for a Jewish homeland]. *CJC*, 27 Oct. 1939, p. 4 [i].

39.10.27F "The Mufti Moves." [The Mufti leaves Syria]. *CJC*, 27 Oct. 1939, p. 4 [i].

39.10.27G "A Turkish Delight." [Franco-British Turkish Treaty of Mutual Assistance]. *CJC*, 27 Oct. 1939, p. 4 [i].

39.10.27H "The Shocking Shaw." [George Bernard Shaw on WWII]. *CJC*, 27 Oct. 1939, p. 4 [i].

39.10.27I "A Polish Emissary." [Jozef Haller visits U.S.]. *KA*, 27 Oct. 1939, p. 8 [s].

39.10.27J "Roosevelt and Refugees." [*See* 39.11.03G]. *KA*, 27 Oct. 1939, p. 8 [s].

39.10.29A "Fire From Flint." [*See* 39.11.03F]. *KA*, 29 Oct. 1939, p. 8 [s].

39.10.29B "Required Reading." [*Mein Kampf* and *Das Kapital* are recommended reading for British soldiers]. *KA*, 29 Oct. 1939, p. 8 [s].

39.10.31A "Embargo Lifted; Nazism Dropped." [*See* 39.11.03C]. *KA*, 31 Oct. 1939, p. 6 [s].

39.10.31B "Love's Bitter Path." [*See* 39.11.03D]. *KA*, 31 Oct. 1939, p. 6 [s].

39.11.01A "German Atrocity." [British report on German concentration camps]. *KA*, 1 Nov. 1939, p. 6 [s].

39.11.01B "Jewish Colonization?" [*See* 39.12.08H]. *KA*, 1 Nov. 1939, p. 6 [s].

39.11.03A "Polish Jewry." [Jews in Poland]. *CJC*, 3 Nov. 1939, p. 3 [i].

39.11.03B "Molotov and His Marionettes." [Soviet foreign policy]. *CJC*, 3 Nov. 1939, p. 3 [u].

39.11.03C "Embargo Lifted; Nazism Dropped." [U.S. sale of arms during WWII]. *CJC*, 3 Nov. 1939, p. 4 [i].

39.11.03D "Love's Bitter Path." [Attempted suicide of Unity Freeman-Mitford]. *CJC*, 3 Nov. 1939, p. 4 [i].

39.11.03E "Hurrah for a Mother-in-Law." [Charles Lindbergh is publicly criticized by his mother-in-law]. *CJC*, 3 Nov. 1939, p. 4 [i].

39.11.03F "Fire from Flint." [Germans capture a neutral ship]. *CJC*, 3 Nov. 1939, p. 4 [i].

39.11.03G "Roosevelt and Refugees." [U.S. policy on refugees]. *CJC*, 3 Nov. 1939, p. 4 [i].

39.11.03H "Mussolini's New Cabinet." [Benito Mussolini makes changes in his cabinet]. *KA*, 3 Nov. 1939, p. 6 [s].

39.11.03I "Et Tu, Brute!" [*See* 39.11.10F]. *KA*, 3 Nov. 1939, p. 6 [s].

39.11.05A "The War Objectives." [Allied war objectives]. *KA*, 5 Nov. 1939, p. 10 [s].

39.11.07A "The Slave State." [*See* 39.11.10H]. *KA*, 7 Nov. 1939, p. 6 [s].

39.11.07B "The Lifted Embargo." [*See* 39.11.10G]. *KA*, 7 Nov. 1939, p. 6 [s].

39.11.08A "On-and-Off Molotoff." [*See* 39.11.10C]. *KA*, 8 Nov. 1939, p. 6 [s].

39.11.08B " 'Jewish Influence'." [*See* 39.11.10D]. *KA*, 8 Nov. 1939, p. 6 [s].

39.11.08C "Moseley [*sic*] Unmasked." [*See* 39.11.10E]. *KA*, 8 Nov. 1939, p. 6 [s].

39.11.10A "November Tenth and Eleventh." [Remembrance of Kristallnacht]. *CJC*, 10 Nov. 1939, p. 3 [u].

39.11.10B "The Canadian Red Cross." [Fundraising for the Canadian Red Cross]. *CJC*, 10 Nov. 1939, p. 3 [u].

39.11.10C "On-and-Off-Molotoff." [Soviet foreign policy]. *CJC*, 10 Nov. 1939, p. 4 [i].

39.11.10D " 'Jewish Influence.' " [Influence of Jews in U.S.]. *CJC*, 10 Nov. 1939, p. 4 [i].

39.11.10E "Moseley [*sic*] Unmasked." [Condemnation of Oswald Mosley]. *CJC*, 10 Nov. 1939, p. 4 [i].

39.11.10F "Et Tu, Brute!" [Polish anti-Semitism]. *CJC*, 10 Nov. 1939, p. 4 [i].

39.11.10G "The Lifted Embargo." [U.S. sale of arms during WWII]. *CJC*, 10 Nov. 1939, p. 4 [i].

39.11.10H "The Slave State." [Adolf Hitler proposes to establish a Jewish state in Poland]. *CJC*, 10 Nov. 1939, p. 4 [i].

39.11.10I "The Time Bomb." [Assassination attempt on Adolf Hitler]. *KA*, 10 Nov. 1939, p. 8 [s].

39.11.12A "Fritz Kuhn and His Jury." [Fritz Kuhn on trial]. *KA*, 12 Nov. 1939, p. 8 [s].

39.11.12B "Monkeyshines in Munich." [*See* 39.11.17E]. *KA*, 12 Nov. 1939, p. 8 [s].

39.11.14A "Craft and Statecraft." [*See* 39.11.17D]. *KA*, 14 Nov. 1939, p. 8 [s].

39.11.15A "The Great Lover." [*See* 39.11.17F]. *KA*, 15 Nov. 1939, p. 6 [s].

39.11.15B "Colonel Lindbergh Again." [*See* 39.11.17G]. *KA*, 15 Nov. 1939, p. 6 [s].

39.11.17A "Nazi Atrocity." [Nazis hinder work of the Red Cross in Poland]. *CJC*, 17 Nov. 1939, p. 3 [u].

39.11.17B "The New Polish Cabinet." [Anti-Semitism in the Polish government]. *CJC*, 17 Nov. 1939, p. 3 [u].

39.11.17C "An International Whodunit." [Assassination attempt on Adolf Hitler]. *CJC*, 17 Nov. 1939, p. 3 [u].

39.11.17D "Craft and Statecraft." [Plan to establish a Jewish state in Ethiopia]. *CJC*, 17 Nov. 1939, p. 4 [i].

39.11.17E "Monkeyshines in Munich." [Staged assassination attempt on Adolf Hitler]. *CJC*, 17 Nov. 1939, p. 4 [i].

39.11.17F "The Great Lover." [Fritz Kuhn charges personal telegraphs to the Reich]. *CJC*, 17 Nov. 1939, p. 4 [i].

39.11.17G "Colonel Lindbergh Again." [Racism of Charles Lindbergh]. *CJC*, 17 Nov. 1939, p. 4 [i].

39.12.08H "Jewish Colonization?" [Adolf Hitler's Jewish colonies in Poland]. *CJC*, 8 Dec. 1939, p. 4 [i].

39.12.08I "Twenty-Five Years of J.D.C." [*See* 39.12.15E]. *KA*, 8 Dec. 1939, p. 8 [s].

39.12.08J "The Finnish Resistance." [*See* 39.12.15F]. *KA*, 8 Dec. 1939, p. 8 [s].

39.12.12A " 'Protective Custody'." [*See* 39.12.15G]. *KA*, 12 Dec. 1939, p. 6 [s].

39.12.12B "A False Passport." [*See* 39.12.15H]. *KA*, 12 Dec. 1939, p. 6 [s].

39.12.13A "Militant Molotov." [War between Soviet Union and Finland]. *KA*, 13 Dec. 1939, p. 6 [s].

39.12.13B " 'The Greatest Living Person'." [*See* 39.12.15I]. *KA*, 13 Dec. 1939, p. 6 [s].

39.12.15A "War and Price Control." [Canada takes steps to prevent war profiteering]. *CJC*, 15 Dec. 1939, p. 3 [u].

39.12.15B "Dr. Manion Looks Into the Future." [Robert James Manion on Canada after WWII]. *CJC*, 15 Dec. 1939, p. 3 [u].

39.12.15C "Shaw is Also Among the Prophets." [George Bernard Shaw on world affairs]. *CJC*, 15 Dec. 1939, p. 3 [u].

39.12.15D "Cuba Victimizes Refugees." [Refugees in Cuba]. *CJC*, 15 Dec. 1939, p. 3 [u].

39.12.15E "Twenty-Five Years of J.D.C." [Joint Distribution Committee]. *CJC*, 15 Dec. 1939, p. 4 [i].

39.12.15F "The Finnish Resistance." [The Finns resist Soviet attack]. *CJC*, 15 Dec. 1939, p. 4 [i].

39.12.15G " 'Protective Custody'." [Fritz Kuhn is sent to Sing-Sing]. *CJC*, 15 Dec. 1939, p. 4 [i].

39.12.15H "A False Passport." [Earl Browder and communism in U.S.]. *CJC*, 15 Dec. 1939, p. 4 [i].

39.12.15I " 'The Greatest Living Person'." [Princeton students declare Adolf Hitler the greatest living person]. *CJC*, 15 Dec. 1939, p. 4 [i].

39.12.15J "Words in Their Season." [*See* 39.12.22E]. *KA*, 15 Dec. 1939, p. 8 [s].

39.12.15K "The Olympic Games." [1940 Olympic games to be held in Finland]. *KA*, 15 Dec. 1939, p. 8 [s].

39.12.17A "The Bremen, and Davy Jones' Locker." [Allied submarine refrains from sinking a German ship]. *KA*, 17 Dec. 1939, p. 8 [s].

39.12.17B "Poetic Justice." [*See* 39.12.22C]. *KA*, 17 Dec. 1939, p. 8 [s].

39.12.19A "Stalin's Strip Tease." [*See* 39.12.22B]. *KA*, 19 Dec. 1939, p. 6 [s].

39.12.20A "Red Star Over Poland." [*See* 39.12.22D]. *KA*, 20 Dec. 1939, p. 6 [s].

39.12.20B "The Nazi Fifth Column." [Nazi propaganda]. *KA*, 20 Dec. 1939, p. 6 [s].

39.12.22A "Goebbels, Laroche & Co.; Broadcasters." [Anti-Semitic broadcast in Quebec]. *CJC*, 22 Dec. 1939, pp. 3, 14 [u].

39.12.22B "Stalin's Strip-Tease." [Alliance of communism and fascism]. *CJC*, 22 Dec. 1939, p. 4 [i].

39.12.22C "Poetic Justice." [Confiscation of the estate of Fritz Thyssen]. *CJC*, 22 Dec. 1939, p. 4 [i].

39.12.22D "Red Star Over Poland." [Jewish communism in occupied Poland]. *CJC*, 22 Dec. 1939, p. 4 [i].

39.12.22E "Words in Their Season." [Lord Milne on Nazism]. *CJC*, 22 Dec. 1939, p. 4 [i].

39.12.22F "Professor Selig Brodetsky." [Selig Brodetsky is elected president of the Board of Jewish Deputies in England]. *KA*, 22 Dec. 1939, p. 8 [s].

39.12.22G "Suicide; Nazi-Maritime Policy." [Nazi losses at sea]. *KA*, 22 Dec. 1939, p. 8 [s].

39.12.24A "Returns of the Day." [*See* 39.12.29G]. *KA*, 24 Dec. 1939, p. 8 [s].

39.12.26A "Baedeker for Law." [*See* 39.12.29F]. *KA*, 26 Dec. 1939, p. 6 [s].

39.12.27A "Nazi Heroism." [*See* 39.12.29D]. *KA*, 27 Dec. 1939, p. 6 [s].

39.12.27B "Stalin and the Jews." [*See* 39.12.29E]. *KA*, 27 Dec. 1939, p. 6 [s].

39.12.27C "Hess Pinch-Hits for Hitler." [Rudolf Hess delivers Adolf Hitler's usual Christmas message]. *KA*, 27 Dec. 1939, p. 6 [s].

39.12.29A "Piecemeal Peace." [Proposal to negotiate peace with Adolf Hitler]. *CJC*, 29 Dec. 1939, p. 3 [u].

39.12.29B "A Jewish War." [Boris Smolar on Jewish casualties in WWII]. *CJC*, 29 Dec. 1939, p. 3 [u].

39.12.29C "Violation of Good Faith." [Jews in Rumania]. *CJC*, 29 Dec. 1939, p. 3 [u].

39.12.29D "Nazi Heroism." [Nazi-occupied Poland]. *CJC*, 29 Dec. 1939, p. 4 [i].

39.12.29E "Stalin and the Jews." [Jews in Soviet Union demonstrate on behalf of Jews in occupied Poland]. *CJC*, 29 Dec. 1939, p. 4 [i].

39.12.29F "Baedeker for Law." [Review of *A Short Treatise on the Practical Side of Civil Procedure* by S.M. Webber]. *CJC*, 29 Dec. 1939, p. 4 [i].

39.12.29G "Returns of the Day." [Joseph Stalin's birthday]. *CJC*, 29 Dec. 1939, p. 4 [i].

39.12.29H "Liar's Contest." [*See* 40.01.05F]. *KA*, 29 Dec. 1939, p. 6 [s].

39.12.29I "The Arabs and the Soviets." [Arab-Soviet relations]. *KA*, Dec. 29, 1939, p. 6 [s].

39.12.31A "1939–1940." [*See* 40.01.05D]. *KA*, 31 Dec. 1939, p. 8 [s].

39.12.31B "Sloppy Journalism." [*See* 40.01.05E]. *KA*, 31 Dec. 1939, p. 8 [s].

40.01.02A "The Women." [*See* 40.01.12E]. *KA*, 2 Jan. 1940, p. 8 [s].

40.01.05A "The Talmud Torah Campaign." [Importance of Jewish education to Jewish survival]. *CJC*, 5 Jan. 1940, p. 3 [u].

40.01.05B "Some Palestine Statistics." [Jewish development of Palestine]. *CJC*, 5 Jan. 1940, p. 3 [u].

40.01.05C "A Naturalization Case." [Kurt Ludecke petitions to become a naturalized American citizen]. *CJC*, 5 Jan. 1939, p. 3 [u].

40.01.05D "1939–1940." [A look back at 1939 and ahead to 1940]. *CJC*, 5 Jan. 1940, p. 4 [i].

40.01.05E "Sloppy Journalism." [*Le Canada* reports on number of Jews in British forces]. *CJC*, 5 Jan. 1940, p. 4 [i].

40.01.05F "Liar's Contest." [Propaganda of Joseph Goebbels]. *CJC*, 5 Jan. 1940, p. 4 [i].

40.01.05G "The Ten Lost Tribes." [Nazis claim the British to be one of the ten lost tribes of Israel]. *CJC*, 5 Jan. 1940, p. 4 [i].

40.01.05H "The Children of Quebec." [Quebec law prohibits children under sixteen from entering movie theatres]. *CJC*, 5 Jan. 1940, p. 4 [i].

40.01.09A "The Resignation of Hore-Belisha." [*See* 40.01.12D]. *KA*, 9 Jan. 1940, p. 6 [s].

40.01.10A "Of Army Procedure." [Military discipline]. *KA*, 10 Jan. 1940, p. 6 [s].

40.01.10B "Humbert Wolfe." [*See* 40.01.12F]. *KA*, 10 Jan. 1940, p. 6 [s].

40.01.12A "Sanity in War Financing." [Canada's economy during WWII]. *CJC*, 12 Jan. 1940, p. 3 [u].

40.01.12B "Montreal Youth Aliyah." [Montreal Youth Aliyah]. *CJC*, 12 Jan. 1940, p. 3 [u].

40.01.12C "Of King's Counsel." [Jewish lawyers awarded King's Counsel in Quebec]. *CJC*, 12 Jan. 1940, p. 3 [u].

40.01.12D "The Resignation of Hore-Belisha." [Nazi propaganda about the resignation of Leslie Hore-Belisha]. *CJC*, 12 Jan. 1940, p. 4 [i].

40.01.12E "The Women." [Wives of prominent Nazis leave Germany]. *CJC*, 12 Jan. 1940, p. 4 [i].

40.01.12F "Humbert Wolfe." [Death of Humbert Wolfe]. *CJC*, 12 Jan. 1940, p. 4 [i].

40.01.12G "Wit and Half-Wit." [*See* 40.01.19E]. *KA*, 12 Jan. 1940, p. 8 [s].

40.01.14A "M. Jean-Charles Harvey and Pan-Americanism." [*See* 40.01.19G]. *KA*, 14 Jan. 1940, p. 8 [s].

40.01.16A "The Finns Receive An Ultimatum." [Soviets deliver an ultimatum to Finland]. *KA*, 16 Jan. 1940, p. 6 [s].

40.01.17A "It Can't Happen Here?" [*See* 40.01.19F]. *KA*, 17 Jan. 1940, p. 6 [s]

40.01.19A "Until the Memoirs Are Written." [Mystery surrounding the resignation of Leslie Hore-Belisha]. *CJC*, 19 Jan. 1940, p. 3 [u].

40.01.19B "Of Jewish Humour." [Jewish humour]. *CJC*, 19 Jan. 1940, p. 3 [u].

40.01.19C "The Oneg Shabbos." [Revival of Jewish culture in Montreal]. *CJC*, 19 Jan. 1940, p. 3 [u].

40.01.19D "Stalin, Hitler, — and Trotsky." [Leon Trotsky on the Berlin-Moscow Axis]. *CJC*, 19 Jan. 1940, p. 3 [u].

40.01.19E "Wit and Half-wit." [Anti-Semitism in Quebec journalism]. *CJC*, 19 Jan. 1940, p. 4 [i].

40.01.19F "It Can't Happen Here." [FBI uncovers a plot to overthrow U.S. government]. *CJC*, 19 Jan. 1940, p. 4 [i].

40.01.19G "M. Jean-Charles Harvey and Pan-Americanism." [Jean-Charles Harvey]. *CJC*, 19 Jan. 1940, p. 4 [i].

40.01.19H "Hitler's Bawdy Guards." [*See* 40.01.26F]. *KA*, 19 Jan. 1940, p. 6 [s].

40.01.19I "Nazi Morality." [Himmler urges Germans to procreate, in or out of marriage]. *KA*, 19 Jan. 1940, p. 6 [s].

40.01.21A "Exaggerated News." [*See* 40.01.26E]. *KA*, 21 Jan. 1940, p. 8 [s].

40.01.21B "Mr. Hepburn's Private War." [*See* 40.01.26G]. *KA*, 21 Jan. 1940, p. 8 [s].

40.01.21C "A New Five-Year Plan." [Soviet Union apologizes for military action]. *KA*, 21 Jan. 1940, p. 8 [s].

40.01.23A "Coughlin Persists." [*See* 40.01.26D]. *KA*, 23 Jan. 1940, p. 6 [s].

40.01.24A "The Unhappy Neutrals." [Winston Churchill questions neutrality]. *KA*, 24 Jan. 1940, p. 6 [s].

40.01.24B "The Moscow Humorist." [*See* 40.01.26C]. *KA*, 24 Jan. 1940, p. 6 [s].

40.01.26A "To Goebbels, via Siberia." [Berlin-Moscow and Berlin-Rome Axes]. *CJC*, 26 Jan. 1940, p. 3 [u].

40.01.26B "Refugees." [Canadian immigration policy]. *CJC*, 26 Jan. 1940, p. 3 [u].

40.01.26C "The Moscow Humorist." [Soviet propaganda on the war in Finland]. *CJC*, 26 Jan. 1940, p. 3 [u].

40.01.26D "Coughlin Persists." [Fascism in U.S.]. *CJC*, 26 Jan. 1940, p. 4 [i].

40.01.26E "Exaggerated News." [Accusation that reports of events in Poland are exaggerated]. *CJC*, 26 Jan. 1940, p. 4 [i].

40.01.26F "Hitler's Bawdy Guards." [Nazis order Jews to establish houses of prostitution in Warsaw]. *CJC*, 26 Jan. 1940, p. 4 [i].

40.01.26G "Mr. Hepburn's Private War." [Mitchell Hepburn condemns Mackenzie King government's war effort]. *CJC*, 26 Jan. 1940, p. 4 [i].

40.01.26H "A Conscientious Objector." [*See* 40.02.02G]. *KA*, 26 Jan. 1940, p. 8 [s].

40.01.26I "A Discussion in Bacon." [*See* 40.02.16D]. *KA*, 26 Jan. 1940, p. 8 [s].

40.01.26J "Mussolini Gets Something." [*See* 40.02.02H]. *KA*, 26 Jan. 1940, p. 8 [s].

40.01.28A "Forthcoming Elections." [*See* 40.02.02E]. *KA*, 28 Jan. 1940, p. 8 [s].

40.01.28B "A Coughlin Investigation?" [*See* 40.02.02F]. *KA*, 28 Jan. 1940, p. 8 [s].

40.01.30A "Coals of Fire." [*See* 40.02.02C]. *KA*, 30 Jan. 1940, p. 6 [s].

40.01.30B "Will Le Devoir Print It?" [*See* 40.02.02D]. *KA*, 30 Jan. 1940, p. 6 [s].

40.01.31A "The Barbarian's Laws." [Nazi laws for forced Jewish labour]. *KA*, 31 Jan. 1940, p. 6 [s].

40.02.02A "Four Speeches." [Oratory of world leaders]. *CJC*, 2 Feb. 1940, p. 3 [u].

40.02.02B "Labor Palestine." [Campaign for Labour Palestine]. *CJC*, 2 Feb. 1940, p. 3 [u].

40.02.02C "Coals of Fire." [Bishop of Birmingham suggests relaxation of the British naval blockade of Germany]. *CJC*, 2 Feb. 1940, p. 4 [i].

40.02.02D "Will Le Devoir Print It?" [Jews in the French armed forces]. *CJC*, 2 Feb. 1940, p. 4 [i].

40.02.02E "Forthcoming Elections." [William Lyon Mackenzie King calls an election]. *CJC*, 2 Feb. 1940, p. 4 [i].

40.02.02F "A Coughlin Investigation?" [Investigation of Christian Front movement in U.S.]. *CJC*, 2 Feb. 1940, p. 4 [i].

40.02.02G "A Conscientious Objector." [A conscientious objector is exempted from military service in Britain]. *CJC*, 2 Feb. 1940, p. 4 [i].

40.02.02H "Mussolini Gets Something." [Berlin-Rome Axis]. *CJC*, 2 Feb. 1940, p. 4 [i].

40.02.02I "The Polish White Paper." [*See* 40.02.09F]. *KA*, 2 Feb. 1940, p. 8 [s].

40.02.02J "Arab-Jewish Relations." [*See* 40.02.09G]. *KA*, 2 Feb. 1940, p. 8 [s].

40.02.04A "Even Homer Nods." [Klein apologizes for errors in his column]. *KA*, 4 Feb. 1940, p. 8 [s].

40.02.06A "Stanley in Africa." [*See* 40.02.09E]. *KA*, 6 Feb. 1940, p. 6 [s].

40.02.07A "When Thieves Fall Out." [*See* 40.02.09D]. *KA*, 7 Feb. 1940, p. 6 [s].

40.02.07B " 'The Purely Objective Mind'." [Chaim Zhitlovsky defends Nazism]. *KA*, 7 Feb. 1940, p. 6 [s].

40.02.09A "Pharaoh's Blueprint." [Jews in Nazi Germany]. *CJC*, 9 Feb. 1940, p. 3 [u].

40.02.09B "A Letter to Father Coughlin." [Letter of Fred A. Stern to Charles Coughlin]. *CJC*, 9 Feb. 1940, p. 3 [u].

40.02.09C "Bird Sanctuary." [Greater concern for animal welfare than for welfare of human beings]. *CJC*, 9 Feb. 1940, p. 3 [u].

40.02.09D "When Thieves Fall Out." [Expulsion of Jews from Czechoslovakia is delayed]. *CJC*, 9 Feb. 1940, p. 4 [i].

40.02.09E "Stanley in Africa." [Policies of War Secretary Oliver Stanley]. *CJC*, 9 Feb. 1940, p. 4 [i].

40.02.09F "The Polish White Paper." [Polish government-in-exile releases a white paper on occupied Poland]. *CJC*, 9 Feb. 1940, p. 4 [i].

40.02.09G "Arab-Jewish Relations." [Improved Arab-Jewish relations in Palestine]. *CJC*, 9 Feb. 1940, p. 4 [i].

40.02.09H "Can Hitler Attack America?" [Pierre van Paassen on isolationism]. *KA*, 9 Feb. 1940, p. 8 [s].

40.02.13A "Rosita Forbes, A Lost Explorer." [*See* 40.02.16C]. *KA*, 13 Feb. 1940, p. 6 [s].

40.02.14A "Roosevelt Tells Them." [*See* 40.02.16B]. *KA*, 14 Feb. 1940, p. 6 [s].

40.02.16A "Lord Tweedsmuir." [Death of Lord Tweedsmuir]. *CJC*, 16 Feb. 1940, p. 3 [u].

40.02.16B "Roosevelt Tells Them." [Franklin Delano Roosevelt on the Soviet Union]. *CJC*, 16 Feb. 1940, p. 4 [i].

40.02.16C "Rosita Forbes, A Lost Explorer." [Rosita Forbes on Jews and the German economy]. *CJC*, 16 Feb. 1940, p. 4 [i].

40.02.16D "A Discussion in Bacon." [Jews and food rationing in England]. *CJC*, 16 Feb. 1940, p. 4 [i].

40.02.16E "Miss Rosita Forges [*sic, should be* Forbes] Explains." [*See* 40.02.23D]. *KA*, 16 Feb. 1940, p. 8 [s].

40.02.19A "Publication of Relief Lists?" [*See* 40.02.23E]. *KA*, 19 Feb. 1940, p. 6 [s].

40.02.21A "Including The Scandinavian." [*See* 40.02.23C]. *KA*, 21 Feb. 1940, p. 6 [s].

40.02.21B "Of National Characteristics." [*See* 40.02.23F]. *KA*, 21 Feb. 1940, p. 6 [s].

40.02.23A "Canadian Jewish Congress." [Canadian Jewish Congress]. *CJC*, 23 Feb. 1940, p. 3 [u].

40.02.23B "Jewish Writers in Poland." [Jewish Writers in Poland]. *CJC*, 23 Feb. 1940, p. 3 [i].

40.02.23C "Including the Scandinavian." [British naval success]. *CJC*, 23 Feb. 1940, p. 3 [u].

40.02.23D "Miss Rosita Forbes Explains." [Rosita Forbes answers charges of anti-Semitism]. *CJC*, 23 Feb. 1940, p. 4 [i].

40.02.23E "Publication of Relief Lists?" [Suggestion to publish names of relief recipients in order to reduce fraud]. *CJC*, 23 Feb. 1940, p. 4 [i].

40.02.23F "Of National Characteristics." [German national character]. *CJC*, 23 Feb. 1940, p. 4 [i].

40.02.23G "By Their Own Actions." [*See* 40.03.01D]. *KA*, 23 Feb. 1940, p. 6 [s].

40.02.23H "Mental Reservations." [*See* 40.03.01E]. *KA*, 23 Feb. 1940, p. 6 [s].

40.02.26A "What's In A Name?" [*See* 40.03.01G]. *KA*, 26 Feb. 1940, p. 6 [s].

40.02.26B "Find The Bomb." [Development of wwii]. *KA*, 26 Feb. 1940, p. 6 [s].

40.02.27A [Untitled]. [Speech of Neville Chamberlain]. *KA*, 27 Feb. 1940, p. 6 [s].

40.03.01A "Of Neutrals." [Neutral nations during wwii]. *CJC*, 1 Mar. 1940, p. 3 [u].

40.03.01B "The Anzacs in Palestine." [Jews welcome Australian soldiers to Tel Aviv]. *CJC*, 1 Mar. 1940, p. 3 [u].

40.03.01C "After Peace, What?" [Jewish rights]. *CJC*, 1 Mar. 1940, p. 3 [u].

40.03.01D "By Their Own Action." [Conviction of William Weiner]. *CJC*, 1 Mar. 1940, p. 4 [i].

40.03.01E "Mental Reservations." [Nazi detention of Jews in camps]. *CJC*, 1 Mar. 1940, p. 4 [i].

40.03.01F "Of All Things." [Allied and German war objectives]. *CJC*, 1 Mar. 1940, p. 4 [i].

40.03.01G "What's In a Name?" [Benito Mussolini decrees he must be referred to only as "Duce"]. *CJC*, 1 Mar. 1940, p. 4 [i].

40.03.01H "Mussolini's Private War." [Italy institutes anti-Jewish laws]. *KA*, 1 Mar. 1940, p. 8 [s].

40.03.01I "The Bread of Affliction." [*See* 40.03.08B]. *KA*, 1 Mar. 1940, p. 8 [s].

40.03.03A "Litterick's Love." [*See* 40.03.08C]. *KA*, 3 Mar. 1940, p. 8 [s].

40.03.03B "Adolph's Poor Almanac." [*See* 40.03.08D]. *KA*, 3 Mar. 1940, p. 8 [s].

40.03.05A "Van Gildemeister, Refugee." [Van Gildemeister suggests Ethiopia as a home for the Jews]. *KA*, 5 Mar. 1940, p. 6 [s].

40.03.05B "A Gesture From The Pope." [*See* 40.03.08E]. *KA*, 5 Mar. 1940, p. 6 [s].

40.03.06A "Hitler's Technique." [*See* 40.03.08F]. *KA*, 6 Mar. 1940, p. 6 [s].

40.03.08A "The Palestine Land Ordinance." [British restrict Jewish rights to purchase land in Palestine]. *CJC*, 8 Mar. 1940, p. 3 [u].

40.03.08B "The Bread of Affliction." [Soviet Union exports matzo to Germany]. *CJC*, 8 Mar. 1940, p. 4 [i].

40.03.08C "Litterick's Love." [Canadian communist condemns Canada's participation in wwii]. *CJC*, 8 Mar. 1940, p. 4 [i].

40.03.08D "Adolph's Poor Almanac." [Confiscation and destruction of books in Nazi Germany]. *CJC*, 8 Mar. 1940, p 4 [i].

40.03.08E "A Gesture From The Pope." [Pope defends Jews in Italy]. *CJC*, 8 Mar. 1940, p. 4 [i].

40.03.08F "Hitler's Technique." [Nazi ideology]. *CJC*, 8 Mar. 1940, p. 4 [i].

40.03.08G "Hepburn Chief Censor." [Mitchell Hepburn bans a film on Canada's war effort]. *KA*, 8 Mar. 1940, p. 8 [s].

40.03.10A "Streicher and Nero." [*See* 40.03.15F]. *KA*, 10 Mar. 1940, p. 10 [s].

40.03.10B "Welles Won't Call Again." [Sumner Welles meets with Adolf Hitler]. *KA*, 10 Mar. 1940, p. 10 [s].

40.03.12A "Crocodile Tears." [*See* 40.03.15E]. *KA*, 12 Mar. 1940, p. 6 [s].

40.03.13A "A Novel Way to Combat Anti-Semitism." [*See* 40.03.15D]. *KA*, 13 Mar. 1940, p. 6 [s].

40.03.13B "Hitler's Memorial Speech." [*See* 40.03.15G]. *KA*, 13 Mar. 1940, p. 6 [s].

40.03.15A "Peace in Finland." [Capitulation of Finland]. *CJC*, 15 Mar. 1940, p. 3 [u].

40.03.15B "Addendum To The Palestine Land Ordinance." [Bernard Rosenblatt on the Palestine Land Ordinance]. *CJC*, 15 Mar. 1940, p. 3 [u].

40.03.15C "The Federal Elections." [Cartier riding, Canadian federal election]. *CJC*, 15 Mar. 1940, p. 3 [u].

40.03.15D "A Novel Way to Combat Anti-Semitism." [Anti-Semitism in U.S.]. *CJC*, 15 Mar. 1940, p. 4 [u].

40.03.15E "Crocodile Tears." [Soviet attitude toward Jews]. *CJC*, 15 Mar. 1940, p. 4 [i].

40.03.15F "Streicher and Nero." [Julius Streicher claims Jews helped Nero burn down Rome]. *CJC*, 15 Mar. 1940, p. 4 [u].

40.03.15G "Hitler's Memorial Speech." [Speech of Adolf Hitler]. *CJC*, 15 Mar. 1940, p. 4 [u].

40.03.17A "Four Sacred Hours." [*See* 40.03.22G]. *KA*, 17 Mar. 1940, p. 8 [s].

40.03.17B "Finland Finita. [*See* 40.03.22H]. *KA*, 17 Mar. 1940, p. 8 [s].

40.03.19A "Whither Roumania." [*See* 40.03.22F]. *KA*, 19 Mar. 1940, p. 6 [s].

40.03.20A "The Brenner Rendez-Vous." [*See* 40.03.22E]. *KA*, 20 Mar. 1940, p. 6 [s].

40.03.22A "The Jewish General Hospital." [Fundraising for the Jewish General Hospital]. *CJC*, 22 Mar. 1940, p. 3 [u].

40.03.22B "Those Whom The Gods Would Destroy." [Nazi propaganda]. *CJC*, 22 Mar. 1940, p. 3 [u].

40.03.22C "Einstein's Cosmos." [Flaws in theories of Albert Einstein]. *CJC*, 22 Mar. 1940, p. 3 [u].

40.03.22D "The Repentance of Fritz Thyssen." [Fritz Thyssen criticizes Adolf Hitler]. *CJC*, 22 Mar. 1940, p. 3 [u].

40.03.22E "The Brenner Rendez-Vous." [Brenner Pass meeting between Adolf Hitler and Benito Mussolini]. *CJC*, 22 Mar. 1940, p. 4 [u].

40.03.22F "Whither Roumania." [Rumanian concessions to Germany]. *CJC*, 22 Mar. 1940, p. 4 [u].

40.03.22G "Four Sacred Hours." [Jewish workers aid refugees]. *CJC*, 22 Mar. 1940, p. 4 [u].

40.03.22H "Finland Finita." [German-Soviet relations]. *CJC*, 22 Mar. 1940, p. 4 [u].

40.03.22I "The Repentance of Fritz Thyssen." [*See* 40.03.22D]. *KA*, 22 Mar. 1940, p. 8 [s].

40.03.22J "Hepburn and the Finns." [*See* 40.03.29C]. *KA*, 22 Mar. 1940, p. 8 [s].

40.03.26A "Moseley's [*sic*] Britain." [*See* 40.03.29D]. *KA*, 26 Mar. 1940, p. 6 [s].

40.03.26B "The Alaska Bill." [*See* 40.03.29G]. *KA*, 26 Mar. 1940, p. 6 [s].

40.03.27A "The Nazis and the Church." [*See* 40.03.29F]. *KA*, 27 Mar. 1940, p. 6 [s].

40.03.29A "The Federal Elections." [Canadian Federal elections]. *CJC*, 29 Mar. 1940, p. 3 [u].

40.03.29B " 'Let My People Go!' " [Jews are not permitted to leave Poland]. *CJC*, 29 Mar. 1940, p. 3 [u].

40.03.29C "Hepburn and the Finns." [Mitchell Hepburn offers asylum to 100,000 Finnish refugees]. *CJC*, 29 Mar. 1940, p. 4 [u].

40.03.29D "Moseley's [*sic*] Britain." [Anti-Semitism of Oswald Mosley]. *CJC*, 29 Mar. 1940, p. 4 [u].

40.03.29E "The Higher Diplomacy." [U.S. diplomat declares Nazism to be a threat to democracy]. *CJC*, 29 Mar. 1940, p. 4 [u].

40.03.29F "The Nazis and the Church." [Religious persecution in Nazi Germany]. *CJC*, 29 Mar. 1940, p. 4 [u].

40.03.29G "The Alaska Bill." [Plan to use refugees to develop Alaskan territory]. *CJC*, 29 Mar. 1940, p. 4 [u].

40.03.29H "Three Portraits." [*See* 40.04.05D]. *KA*, 29 Mar. 1940, p. 8 [s].

40.04.02A "With Three Grains of Salt." [*See* 40.04.05E]. *KA*, 2 Apr. 1940, p. 6 [s].

40.04.03A "Inquisition in Modern Dress." [*See* 40.04.05C]. *KA*, 3 Apr. 1940, p. 6 [s].

40.04.03B "Bertrand Russell." [Bertrand Russell loses college position over personal conduct]. *KA*, 3 Apr. 1940, p. 6 [s].

40.04.05A "The United Palestine Appeal." [Campaign for the United Palestine Appeal]. *CJC*, 5 Apr. 1940, p. 3 [u].

40.04.05B "The Tarnished Silver Shirts." [Fascism in U.S.]. *CJC*, 5 Apr. 1940, p. 3 [u].

40.04.05C "Inquisition in Modern Dress." [Jews in fascist Spain]. *CJC*, 5 Apr. 1940, p. 4 [u].

40.04.05D "Three Portraits." [Review of *Drei Diktatoren* by Emil Ludwig]. *CJC*, 5 Apr. 1940, p. 4 [u].

40.04.05E "With Three Grains of Salt." [Nazi propaganda about foreign policy]. *CJC*, 5 Apr. 1940, p. 4 [u].

40.04.05F "Beaverbrook's Defense." [*See* 40.04.12E]. *KA*, 5 Apr. 1940, p. 8 [s].

40.04.08A " 'They Missed the Bus'." [Speech of Neville Chamberlain on Adolf Hitler]. *KA*, 8 Apr. 1940, p. 6 [s].

40.04.08B "The Spring Offensive." [Nazi offensives against Polish Jews]. *KA*, 8 Apr. 1940, p. 6 [s].

40.04.08C "Where Angels Fear To Tread." [Gordon Conant claims allies will lose without the help of U.S.]. *KA*, 8 Apr. 1940, p. 6 [s].

40.04.09A "When Will They Learn." [*See* 40.04.12F]. *KA*, 9 Apr. 1940, p. 8 [s].

40.04.09B "French War Aims." [*See* 40.04.12G]. *KA*, 9 Apr. 1940, p. 8 [s].

40.04.10A "The Battle of the Maps." [*See* 40.04.12D]. *KA*, 10 Apr. 1940, p. 6 [s].

40.04.12A "Including The Scandinavian." [War at sea off the coast of Norway]. *CJC*, 12 Apr. 1940, p. 3 [u].

40.04.12B "The Late Cyrus Adler." [Death of Cyrus Adler]. *CJC*, 12 Apr. 1940, p. 3 [u].

40.04.12C "The Guggenheim Awards." [Recipients of the Guggenheim awards]. *CJC*, 12 Apr. 1940, p. 3 [u].

40.04.12D "The Battle of the Maps." [German war aims]. *CJC*, 12 Apr. 1940, p. 4 [u].

40.04.12E "Beaverbrook's Defense." [Anti-Semitic remarks of Lord Beaverbrook]. *CJC*, 12 Apr. 1940, p. 4 [u].

40.04.12F "When Will They Learn." [Polish Anti-Semitism]. *CJC*, 12 Apr. 1940, p. 4 [u].

40.04.12G "French War Aims." [French war aims]. *CJC*, 12 Apr. 1940, p. 4 [u].

40.04.12H "Britannia Rules the Waves." [*See* 40.04.26H]. *KA*, 12 Apr. 1940, p. 10 [s].

40.04.14A "The Hebrew Free Loan Association." [*See* 40.05.03G]. *KA*, 14 Apr. 1940, p. 10 [s].

40.04.14B "Women's Rights." [Women are allowed to vote in Quebec provincial elections]. *KA*, 14 Apr. 1940, p. 10 [s].

40.04.16A "General Haller: Goodwill Emissary." [*See* 40.04.26D]. *KA*, 16 Apr. 1940, p. 6 [s].

40.04.17A "Sing a Song of Neutrals." [Neutrality during WWII]. *KA*, 17 Apr. 1940, p. 6 [s].

40.04.19A "The Eternal Passover." [Relevance of Passover to Jews in WWII]. *CJC*, 19 Apr. 1940, p. 3 [u].

40.04.19B "The Italian Fence." [*See* 40.04.26E]. *KA*, 19 Apr. 1940, p. 10 [s].

40.04.19C "A German Boner!" [*See* 40.04.26F]. *KA*, 19 Apr. 1940, p. 10 [s].

40.04.19D "The Tourist Season in Europe." [*See* 40.04.26G]. *KA*, 19 Apr. 1940, p. 10 [s].

40.04.21A "The Printing Press." [*See* 40.05.03H]. *KA*, 21 Apr. 1940, p. 10 [s].

40.04.26A "The Philosophy of the Nazis." [Nazi ideology]. *CJC*, 26 Apr. 1940, p. 3 [u].

40.04.26B "Is the Party Line Shifting?" [Changing Soviet view of the war in Scandinavia]. *CJC*, 26 Apr. 1940, p. 3 [u].

40.04.26C "Warmth in Alaska." [Harold Ickes on the admission of refugees to U.S.]. *CJC*, 26 Apr. 1940, p. 3 [u].

40.04.26D "General Haller: Goodwill Emissary." [Jozef Haller on Polish Jews]. *CJC*, 26 Apr. 1940, p. 4 [u].

40.04.26E "The Italian Fence." [Italo-British relations during WWII]. *CJC*, 26 Apr. 1940, p. 4 [u].

40.04.26F "A German Boner." [Germans repatriate Aryans from Lithuania and Estonia]. *CJC*, 26 Apr. 1940, p. 4 [u].

40.04.26G "The Tourist Season in Europe." [War in the Balkans and in Scandinavia]. *CJC*, 26 Apr. 1940, p. 4, [u].

40.04.26H "Britannia Rules the Waves." [War at sea]. *CJC*, 26 Apr. 1940, p. 4 [u].

40.04.28A "Maurice Duplessis: Libertarian." [Maurice Duplessis speaks out against censorship]. *KA*, 28 Apr. 1940, p. 10 [s].

40.04.28B "Isaiah And The Beast." [Nazis vandalize a Polish synagogue]. *KA*, 28 Apr. 1940, p. 10 [s].

40.05.01A "The Fifth Column and the Refugee." [*See* 40.05.03E]. *KA*, 1 May 1940, p. 6 [s].

40.05.01B "News From Palestine." [*See* 40.05.03F]. *KA*, 1 May 1940, p. 6 [s].

40.05.03A "An Unnecessary Reward." [Samuel Church offers a million dollars for the capture of Adolf Hitler]. *CJC*, 3 May 1940, p. 3 [u].

40.05.03B "Felicitations to Rabbi H. Cohen." [Eightieth birthday of Rabbi H. Cohen]. *CJC*, 3 May 1940, p. 3 [u].

40.05.03C "Shaare Zion Synagogue." [Sod turning for the Shaare Zion Synagogue]. *CJC*, 3 May 1940, p. 3 [u].

40.05.03D "Nostrum Mare." [Italo-British relations during WWII]. *CJC*, 3 May 1940, p. 3 [u].

40.05.03E "The Fifth Column and the Refugee." [Fifth columnists and refugees in WWII]. *CJC*, 3 May 1940, p. 4 [i].

40.05.03F "News From Palestine." [British foreign policy on Palestine]. *CJC*, 3 May 1940, p. 4 [i].

40.05.03G "The Hebrew Free Loan Association." [Hebrew Free Loan Association]. *CJC*, 3 May 1940, p. 3 [u].

40.05.03H "The Printing Press." [Five hundredth anniversary of the invention of the printing press]. *CJC*, 3 May 1940, p. 4 [i].

40.05.03I "The Duce's Dilemma." [*See* 40.05.10D]. *KA*, 3 May 1940, p. 8 [s].

40.05.05A "The Shadows Move." [*See* 40.05.10E]. *KA*, 5 May 1940, p. 8 [s].

40.05.05B "What Will the Nazis Talk About Now?" [Decreasing Jewish population of Germany]. *KA*, 5 May 1940, p. 8 [s].

40.05.07A "The Nordic Literary Men." [*See* 40.05.10F]. *KA*, 7 May 1940, p. 6 [s].

40.05.07B "Italy and The Church." [*See* 40.05.10G]. *KA*, 7 May 1940, p. 6 [s].

40.05.08A "Of Stamps." [Hundredth anniversary of the use of postage stamps]. *KA*, 8 May 1940, p. 6 [s].

40.05.08B "Thyssen's Wolf! Wolf!" [*See* 40.05.10H]. *KA*, 8 May 1940, p. 6 [s].

40.05.10A "Mr. Chamberlain's Address." [Criticism of Neville Chamberlain]. *CJC*, 10 May 1940, p. 3 [u].

40.05.10B "George Lansbury." [Death of George Lansbury]. *CJC*, 10 May 1940, p. 3 [u].

40.05.10C "The Ubiquitous Fifth Column." [Fifth column fascist infiltration]. *CJC*, 10 May 1940, p. 3 [u].

40.05.10D "The Duce's Dilemma." [Vatican opposes Italian alliance with Nazism]. *CJC*, 10 May 1940, p. 4 [i].

40.05.10E "The Shadows Move." [Jews in Poland]. *CJC*, 10 May 1940, p. 4 [i].

40.05.10F "The Nordic Literary Men." [Gerhard Hauptmann and Knut Hamsun]. *CJC*, 10 May 1940, p. 4 [i].

40.05.10G "Italy and the Church." [The Catholic Church opposes fascist government of Italy]. *CJC*, 10 May 1940, p. 4 [i].

40.05.10H "Thyssen's Wolf! Wolf!" [Fritz Thyssen condemns Adolf Hitler]. *CJC*, 10 May 1940, p. 4 [i].

40.05.10I "The Vote of Confidence." [Neville Chambelain receives a vote of confidence in the House of Commons]. *KA*, 10 May 1940, p. 8 [s].

40.05.10J "The New Ten Commandments." [*See* 40.05.17F]. *KA*, 10 May 1940, p. 8 [s].

40.05.13A "History Repeats Itself." [*See* 40.05.17G]. *KA*, 13 May 1940, p. 6 [s].

40.05.14A "Belgium and Holland." [*See* 40.05.17D]. *KA*, 14 May 1940, p. 6 [s].

40.05.14B "The New Cabinet." [*See* 40.05.17E]. *KA*, 14 May 1940, p. 6 [s].

40.05.15A "Note on the Colonial Ministry." [Malcolm MacDonald dropped from the British cabinet]. *KA*, 15 May 1940, p. 6 [s].

40.05.15B "Paris Gazette." [Novel of Lion Feuchtwanger]. *KA*, 15 May 1940, p. 6 [s].

40.05.17A "The Tragedy of Holland." [Capitulation of the Netherlands]. *CJC*, 17 May 1940, p. 3 [u].

40.05.17B "As The Battle Rages." [Need for greater Allied resistance to Adolf Hitler]. *CJC*, 17 May 1940, p. 3 [u].

40.05.17C " 'For Peace and Freedom'." [Freedom of religion]. *CJC*, 17 May 1940, p. 3 [u].

40.05.17D "Belgium and Holland." [War in Belgium and the Netherlands]. *CJC*, 17 May 1940, p. 4 [i].

40.05.17E "The New Cabinet." [Reorganization of the British cabinet]. *CJC*, 17 May 1940, p. 4 [i].

40.05.17F "The New Ten Commandments." [Soviet communism and the Berlin-Moscow Axis]. *CJC*, 17 May 1940, p. 4 [i].

40.05.17G "History Repeats Itself." [Contemporary relevance of speech of David Lloyd George on WWI]. *CJC*, 17 May 1940, p. 4 [i].

40.05.21A "The Ostrich Lifts Its Head." [*See* 40.05.24E]. *KA*, 21 May 1940, p. 6 [s].

40.05.22A "Murder and Civilization." [*See* 40.05.24F]. *KA*, 22 May 1940, p. 6 [s].

40.05.22B "The Nazis And The Bible." [*See* 40.05.24D]. *KA*, 22 May 1940, p. 6 [s].

40.05.24A "India and South Africa." [Consolidation of the British Commonwealth during WWII]. *CJC*, 24 May 1940, p. 3 [u].

40.05.24B "The Modern Sichon." [Italy refuses to allow Jewish refugees to sail from Genoa]. *CJC*, 24 May 1940, p. 3 [u].

40.05.24C "What News From Moscow?" [Berlin-Moscow Axis]. *CJC*, 24 May 1940, p. 3 [u].

40.05.24D "The Nazis and the Bible." [Nazis use proceeds from sale of Gutenberg Bible to spread propaganda]. *CJC*, 24 May 1940, p. 3 [u].

40.05.24E "The Ostrich Lifts its Head." [American isolationism]. *CJC*, 24 May 1940, p. 4 [i].

40.05.24F "Murder and Civilization." [The cost of killing in modern warfare]. *CJC*, 24 May 1940, p. 4 [i].

40.05.24G "Eagle or Vulture?" [Isolationism of Charles Lindbergh]. *CJC*, 24 May 1940, p. 4 [i].

40.05.24H "Eagle or Vulture?" [*See* 40.05.24G]. *KA*, 24 May 1940, p. 8 [s].

40.05.31A "The Quebec Quislings." [Fascism in Quebec]. *CJC*, 31 May 1940, p. 3 [u].

40.05.31B "Rabbi Johanan ben Zakkai: a Symbol." [Jewish National Fund purchases land in Yavneh]. *CJC*, 31 May 1940, p. 3 [u].

40.05.31C "Et Tu Brute!" [King Leopold orders Belgian troops to surrender]. *CJC*, 31 May 1940, p. 3 [u].

40.05.31D "The Woodchopper of Doorn." [*See* 40.06.07E]. *KA*, 31 May 1940, p. 6 [s].

40.06.02A "The Fifth Column Falls." [Arrest of Adrien Arcand]. *KA*, 2 June 1940, p. 8 [s].

40.06.04A "Retreat to Glory." [*See* 40.06.07F]. *KA*, 4 June 1940, p. 6 [s].

40.06.04B "Blackout in Jerusalem." [*See* 40.06.07G]. *KA*, 4 June 1940, p. 6 [s].

40.06.05A "Sermons in Bombs." [*See* 40.06.07C]. *KA*, 5 June 1940, p. 6 [s].

40.06.05B "Toujours La Politesse." [*See* 40.06.07D]. *KA*, 5 June 1940, p. 6 [s].

40.06.07A "Shevuoth." [The meaning of the Ten Commandments in light of wwii]. *CJC*, 7 June 1940, p. 3 [u].

40.06.07B "Churchill's Speech." [Winston Churchill's speech on the retreat from Flanders]. *CJC*, 7 June 1940, p. 3 [u].

40.06.07C "Sermons in Bombs." [German bombing of southern France]. *CJC*, 7 June 1940, p. 4 [i].

40.06.07D "Toujours La Politesse." [Anti-Semitism in Quebec]. *CJC*, 7 June 1940, p. 4 [i].

40.06.07E "The Woodchopper of Doorn." [Fate of Kaiser Wilhelm leads to speculations on fate of Adolf Hitler]. *CJC*, 7 June 1940, p. 4 [i].

40.06.07F "Retreat to Glory." [Evacuation of the British Expeditionary Forces from Belgium]. *CJC*, 7 June 1940, p. 4 [i].

40.06.07G "Blackout in Jerusalem." [Jerusalem prepares for the possibility of air-raids]. *CJC*, 7 June 1940, p. 4 [i].

40.06.07H "Preview of a Talkie: Salluste Lavery." [*See* 40.06.14H]. *KA*, 7 June 1940, p. 6 [s].

40.06.10A "Le Medecin Malgre-Lui." [*See* 40.06.14G]. *KA*, 10 June 1940, p. 6 [s].

40.06.10B "Book Note." [*Mein Kampf* is translated into Russian]. *KA*, 10 June 1940, p. 6 [s].

40.06.11A "The Last of the Pacifists." [*See* 40.06.14E]. *KA*, 11 June 1940, p. 8 [s].

40.06.11B "Daniel: Contributing Editor." [*See* 40.06.14F]. *KA*, 11 June 1940, p. 8 [s].

40.06.14A "The Hand That Held The Dagger . . ." [Italy enters WWII]. *CJC*, 14 June 1940, p. 3 [u].

40.06.14B "Jewish Airman Honoured." [William Nelson is awarded the Distinguished Flying Cross]. *CJC*, 14 June 1940, p. 3 [u].

40.06.14C "Jewish Red Cross Work." [Work of the Jewish branch of the Canadian Red Cross]. *CJC*, 14 June 1940, p. 3 [u].

40.06.14D "The Jewish People's Schools." [Graduation ceremony of the Jewish People's School]. *CJC*, 14 June 1940, p. 3 [u].

40.06.14E "The Last of the Pacifists." [Pacifism as a response to Nazism]. *CJC*, 14 June 1940, p. 4 [u].

40.06.14F "Daniel: Contributing Editor." [Relevance of Daniel 11:23 to contemporary events]. *CJC*, 14 June 1940, p. 4 [u].

40.06.14G "Le Medecin Malgre Lui." [Germany recalls Jewish doctors for war service]. *CJC*, 14 June 1940, p. 4 [u].

40.06.14H "Preview of a Talkie: Salluste Lavery." [Trial of Quebec fascists]. *CJC*, 14 June 1940, p. 4 [u].

40.06.14I "Mussolini and the Jews." [*See* 40.06.21F]. *KA*, 14 June 1940, p. 8 [s].

40.06.17A "Good Americans . . . Go to Paris." [French appeal to U.S. for military assistance]. *KA*, 17 June 1940, p. 6 [s].

40.06.18A "The Capitulation of France." [*See* 40.06.21D]. *KA*, 18 June 1940, p. 6 [s].

40.06.19A "They Want to Keep It Secret." [*See* 40.06.21E]. *KA* 19 June 1940, p. 6 [s].

40.06.21A "The Mobilization Act." [Conscription in Canada]. *CJC*, 21 June 1940, p. 3 [u].

40.06.21B "A Letter From Salluste." [Salluste Lavery demands compensation from the *Canadian Jewish Chronicle* for anti-Adrien Arcand editorial]. *CJC*, 21 June 1940, p. 3 [u].

40.06.21C "A.J. Freiman." [Sixtieth birthday of Archibald Freiman]. *CJC*, 21 June 1940, p. 3 [u].

40.06.21D "The Capitulation of France." [The capitulation of France]. *CJC*, 21 June 1940, p. 4 [i].

40.06.21E "They Want to Keep it Secret." [Adolf Hitler and Benito Mussolini meet after the capitulation of France]. *CJC*, 21 June 1940, p. 4 [i].

40.06.21F "Mussolini and the Jews." [Fate of Italian Jews]. *CJC*, 21 June 1940, p. 4 [i].

40.06.23A "Exhibits Under the Stone." [*See* 40.06.28F]. *KA*, 23 June 1940, p. 8 [s].

40.06.25A "Peace With Honour?" [*See* 40.06.28E]. *KA*, 25 June 1940, p. 6 [s].

40.06.26A "King Carol Changes His Tune." [*See* 40.06.28D]. *KA*, 26 June 1940, p. 6 [s].

40.06.26B "Some Nazi Booty." [*See* 40.07.12F]. *KA*, 26 June 1940, p. 6 [s].

40.06.28A "The Ford that Shifts into Neutral." [Isolationism of Henry Ford]. *CJC*, 28 June 1940, p. 3 [u].

40.06.28B "Arcand Interned." [Internment of Adrien Arcand]. *CJC*, 28 June 1940, p. 3 [u].

40.06.28C "Dr. A.A. Roback." [Fiftieth birthday of A.A. Roback]. *CJC*, 28 June 1940, p. 3 [u].

40.06.28D "King Carol Changes His Tune." [Policies of King Carol of Rumania]. *CJC*, 28 June 1940, p. 4 [i].

40.06.28E "Peace With Honour?" [Terms of French-German collaboration]. *CJC*, 28 June 1940, p. 4 [i].

40.06.28F "Exhibits Under the Stone." [Exhibits at the inquest into fascist activity in Quebec]. *CJC*, 28 June 1940, p. 4 [i].

40.06.30A "The Bear That Walks Like A Man." [*See* 40.07.05F]. *KA*, 30 June 1940, p. 8 [s].

40.07.03A "The Mystery of the Bearded Ace." [*See* 40.07.05E]. *KA*, 3 July 1940, p. 6 [s].

40.07.05A "Pogroms in Rumania." [Anti-Semitism in Rumania]. *CJC*, 5 July 1940, p. 3 [u].

40.07.05B "Arcand's Reward." [Adrien Arcand is interned]. *CJC*, 5 July 1940, p. 3 [u].

40.07.05C "Look! We Have Guests!" [German prisoners of war arrive in Canada]. *CJC*, 5 July 1940, p. 4 [u].

40.07.05D "Bernard Shaw, Strategist." [George Bernard Shaw opposes British war strategy]. *CJC*, 5 July 1940, p. 4 [u].

40.07.05E "The Mystery of the Bearded Ace." [Death of Italo Balbo]. *CJC*, 5 July 1940, p. 4 [u].

40.07.05F "The Bear That Walks Like A Man." [Rumania loses territory to the Soviet Union]. *CJC*, 5 July 1940, p. 4 [u].

40.07.05G "Look! We Have Guests!" [*See* 40.07.05C]. *KA*, 5 July 1940, p. 8 [s].

40.07.05H "Bernard Shaw, Strategist." [*See* 40.07.05D]. *KA*, 5 July 1940, p. 8 [s].

40.07.07A "Perfidious Petain." [*See* 40.07.12E]. *KA*, 7 July 1940, p. 8 [s].

40.07.09A "The French Devolution." [Establishment of the Vichy Government in France]. *KA*, 9 July 1940, p. 6 [s].

40.07.09B "Newspaper Headlines." [Election in Mexico; Japanese foreign policy; French bombing of ships in Gibraltar harbour]. *KA*, 9 July 1940, p. 6 [s].

40.07.10A "The Youth Congress." [*See* 40.07.12D]. *KA*, 10 July 1940, p. 6 [s].

40.07.12A "The Voice of Canadian Jewry." [Speech of Samuel Bronfman]. *CJC*, 12 July 1940, p. 3 [u].

40.07.12B "The Motion Picture Industry and the War Effort." [Canadian motion picture industry supports the War Savings Campaign]. *CJC*, 12 July 1940, p. 3 [u].

40.07.12C "Whither France?" [Anti-Semitism in Vichy France]. *CJC*, 12 July 1940, p. 3 [u].

40.07.12D "The Youth Congress." [Canadian Youth Congress in Montreal]. *CJC*, 12 July 1940, p. 4 [u].

40.07.12E "Perfidious Petain." [France turns control of its navy over to Germany]. *CJC*, 12 July 1940, p. 4 [u].

40.07.12F "Some Nazi Booty." [Intellectuals imprisoned by the Nazis]. *CJC*, 12 July 1940, p. 4 [u].

40.07.16A "The Happy Warrior." [*See* 40.07.19E]. *KA*, 16 July 1940, p. 6 [s].

40.07.17A "The Bluebirds." [*See* 40.07.26I]. *KA*, 17 July 1940, p. 6 [s].

40.07.17B "Including Purges." [*See* 40.07.19F]. *KA*, 17 July 1940, p. 6 [s].

40.07.19A "They Stand On Guard." [Italy bombs Haifa]. *CJC*, 19 July 1940, p. 3 [u].

40.07.19B "Laval's Plans." [Policies of Pierre Laval]. *CJC*, 19 July 1940, p. 3 [u].

40.07.19C "An Italian War Aim." [Italy wants possession of art treasures housed in France]. *CJC*, 19 July 1940, p. 3 [u].

40.07.19D "Bastille Day." [Vichy France]. *CJC*, 19 July 1940, p. 4 [i].

40.07.19E "The Happy Warrior." [Winston Churchill reaffirms Britain's committment to fight]. *CJC*, 19 July 1940, p. 4 [i].

40.07.19F "Including Purges." [Scapegoating of Jews and communists in Vichy France]. *CJC*, 19 July 1940, p. 4 [i].

40.07.22A "Roosevelt's Decision." [*See* 40.07.26E]. *KA*, 22 July 1940, p. 6 [s].

40.07.22B "The Rock of Gibraltar." [*See* 40.07.26G]. *KA*, 22 July 1940, p. 6 [s].

40.07.23A "Hitler's Peace Offer." [*See* 40.07.26F]. *KA*, 23 July 1940, p. 6 [s].

40.07.23B "The Rivals." [*See* 40.07.26H]. *KA*, 23 July 1940, p. 6 [s].

40.07.24A "Lord Halifax's Reply to Hitler." [Speech of Lord Halifax]. *KA*, 24 July 1940, p. 6 [s].

40.07.24B "A Jewish Press in Poland." [*See* 40.08.02F]. *KA*, 24 July 1940, p. 6 [s].

40.07.26A "Bialik Memorial." [Contemporary relevance of a poem by Chaim Nachman Bialik]. *CJC*, 26 July 1940, p. 3 [u].

40.07.26B "Madagascar Again." [Madagascar as a Jewish homeland]. *CJC*, 26 July 1940, p. 3 [u].

40.07.26C "Mahatma Gandhi." [Letter of Mahatma Gandhi to Adolf Hitler]. *CJC*, 26 July 1940, p. 3 [u].

40.07.26D "Hershel Grynspan [*sic*]." [Hershel Grynszpan is captured by the Nazis]. *CJC*, 26 July 1940, p. 3 [u].

40.07.26E "Roosevelt's Decision." [Franklin Delano Roosevelt decides to run for a third term of office]. *CJC*, 26 July 1940, p. 4 [i].

40.07.26F "Hitler's Peace Offer." [Speech of Adolf Hitler]. *CJC*, 26 July 1940, p. 4 [i].

40.07.26G "The Rock of Gilbraltar." [Francisco Franco expresses a desire to control Gibraltar]. *CJC*, 26 July 1940, p. 4 [i].

40.07.26H "The Rivals." [Maurice Thorez seeks cooperation with Adolf Hitler]. *CJC*, 26 July 1940, p. 4 [i].

40.07.26I "The Bluebirds." [Maurice Maeterlinck seeks refuge in U.S.]. *CJC*, 26 July 1940, p. 4 [i].

40.07.28A "A Farce of Justice." [*See* 40.08.02E]. *KA*, 28 July 1940, p. 8 [s].

40.07.30A "Shadow and Substance." [*See* 40.08.02D]. *KA*, 30 July 1940, p. 6 [s].

40.07.31A "On The Horns of a Dilemma." [*See* 40.08.09E]. *KA*, 31 July 1940, p. 6 [s].

40.08.02A "An Italian Tribute." [Italian view of a possible invasion of England]. *CJC*, 2 Aug. 1940, p. 3 [u].

40.08.02B "Hitler, the Strategist." [Adolf Hitler as a great strategist]. *CJC*, 2 Aug. 1940, p. 3 [u].

40.08.02c "Aliens Who Are Not Enemies." [Refugees are interned in Britain]. *CJC*, 2 Aug. 1940, p. 3 [u].

40.08.02d "Shadow and Substance." [Chaim Zhitlovsky]. *CJC*, 2 Aug. 1940, p. 4 [i].

40.08.02e "A Farce of Justice." [Trial of Edouard Daladier]. *CJC*, 2 Aug. 1940, p. 4 [i].

40.08.02f "A Jewish Press in Poland." [Jewish newspapers in occupied Poland]. *CJC*, 2 Aug. 1940, p. 4 [i].

40.08.04a " 'Full of Possibilities'." [*See* 40.08.09c]. *KA*, 4 Aug. 1940, p. 8 [s].

40.08.04b "The Base of the Fifth Column." [*See* 40.08.09d]. *KA*, 4 Aug. 1940, p. 8 [s].

40.08.06a "You Can Houdewink Some of the People . . ." [*See* 40.08.09b]. *KA*, 6 Aug. 1940, p. 6 [s].

40.08.07a "Julius Streicher." [Death of Julius Streicher]. *KA*, 7 Aug. 1940, p. 6 [s].

40.08.07b "A Contrast." [*See* 40.08.16f]. *KA*, 7 Aug. 1940, p. 6 [s].

40.08.09a "Vladimir Jabotinsky." [Vladimir Jabotinsky]. *CJC*, 9 Aug. 1940, p. 3 [i].

40.08.09b "You Can Houdewink Some of the People." [Camillien Houde]. *CJC*, 9 Aug. 1940, p. 4 [i].

40.08.09c " 'Full of Possibilities'." [Soviet foreign policy]. *CJC*, 9 Aug. 1940, p. 4 [i].

40.08.09d "The Base of the Fifth Column." [Fifth column activities in U.S.]. *CJC*, 9 Aug. 1940, p. 4 [i].

40.08.09e "On the Horns of a Dilemma." [Rumania is forced to give up territory]. *CJC*, 9 Aug. 1940, p. 4 [i].

40.08.11a "The Savage Speaks." [*See* 40.08.16g]. *KA*, 11 Aug. 1940, p. 8 [s].

40.08.11b "Lindbergh Flies a Kite: The Trojan Ass." [*See* 40.08.16h]. *KA*, 11 Aug. 1940, p. 8 [s].

40.08.13a "Anti-Semitism: The Smoke-Screen." [*See* 40.08.16d]. *KA*, 13 Aug. 1940, p. 6 [s].

40.08.13b "Ambassador Cudahy." [*See* 40.08.16e]. *KA*, 13 Aug. 1940, p. 6 [s]

40.08.14a "Laval in Trouble." [*See* 40.08.23f]. *KA*, 14 Aug. 1940, p. 6 [s].

40.08.16a "The Yellow Badge." [Christian Belgians wear yellow stars in sympathy for the Jews]. *CJC*, 16 Aug. 1940, p. 3 [u].

40.08.16B "Strictly Business." [Fascism and American business]. *CJC*, 16 Aug. 1940, p. 3 [u].

40.08.16C "Anti-Semitism in France." [Government of Vichy France does not institute anti-Semitism as official policy]. *CJC*, 16 Aug. 1940, p. 3 [u].

40.08.16D "Anti-Semitism the Smoke-Screen." [Rumanian government passes anti-Semitic laws]. *CJC*, 16 Aug. 1940, p. 4 [i].

40.08.16E "Ambassador Cudahy." [Isolationist views of U.S. ambassador to Belgium]. *CJC*, 16 Aug. 1940, p. 4 [i].

40.08.16F "A Contrast." [David Croll and Camillien Houde]. *CJC*, 16 Aug. 1940, p. 4 [i].

40.08.16G "The Savage Speaks." [Nazi ideology]. *CJC*, 16 Aug. 1940, p. 4 [i].

40.08.16H "Lindbergh Flies a Kite: The Trojan Ass." [Isolationism of Charles Lindbergh]. *CJC*, 16 Aug. 1940, p. 4 [i].

40.08.18A "The Greeks Now [*sic, should be* Know] A Word For It." [*See* 40.08.23D]. *KA*, 18 Aug. 1940, p. 8 [s].

40.08.20A "Now!" [*See* 40.08.23C]. *KA*, 20 Aug. 1940, p. 6 [s].

40.08.20B "A Meeting at Ogdensburg." [*See* 40.08.23E]. *KA*, 20 Aug. 1940, p. 6 [s].

40.08.21A "Birds of a Feather." [*See* 40.08.23G]. *KA*, 21 Aug. 1940, p. 6 [s].

40.08.21B "The Blockade." [German threat to blockade Britain]. *KA*, 21 Aug. 1940, p. 6 [s].

40.08.23A "The Road to Victory." [Speech of Winston Churchill]. *CJC*, 23 Aug. 1940, p. 3 [u].

40.08.23B "Leon Trotsky." [Assassination of Leon Trotsky]. *CJC*, 23 Aug. 1940, p. 3 [u].

40.08.23C "Now!" [U.S. ambassador to France urges American entry into WWII]. *CJC*, 23 Aug. 1940, p. 4 [i].

40.08.23D "The Greeks Know a Word For It." [Italy prepares for a campaign against Greece]. *CJC*, 23 Aug. 1940, p. 4 [i].

40.08.23E "A Meeting At Ogdensburg." [Canada-U.S. joint defense pact]. *CJC*, 23 Aug. 1940, p. 4 [i].

40.08.23F "Laval in Trouble." [Pierre Laval falls out of favour of fascist regime]. *CJC*, 23 Aug. 1940, p. 4 [i].

40.08.23G "Birds of a Feather." [Cooperation of the Ku Klux Klan and the German-American Bund]. *CJC*, 23 Aug. 1940, p. 4 [i].

40.08.25A "'Never Has So Much Been Owed to So Few'." [*See* 40.08.30G]. *KA*, 25 Aug. 1940, p. 8 [s].

40.08.25B "Another Italian Leo [*sic, should be* Hero]." [*See* 40.08.30H]. *KA*, 25 Aug. 1940, p. 8 [s].

40.08.27A "Vichy Effervesces." [*See* 40.08.30E]. *KA*, 27 Aug. 1940, p. 6 [s].

40.08.27B "Sherwood on Americanism." [*See* 40.08.30F]. *KA*, 27 Aug. 1940, p. 6 [s].

40.08.28A "Another Explanation of the Petain Pantomime." [*See* 40.08.30I]. *KA*, 28 Aug. 1940, p. 6 [s].

40.08.28B "Dies Reports." [Report on fifth column activity in U.S.]. *KA*, 28 Aug. 1940, p. 6 [s].

40.08.30A "The Balkan Pot." [Imminence of war in the Balkans]. *CJC*, 30 Aug. 1940, p. 3 [u].

40.08.30B "The Peculiar Poles." [Anti-Semitism of Poles in exile]. *CJC*, 30 Aug. 1940, p. 3 [u].

40.08.30C "The New Paganism." [Vichy government rescinds anti-racism laws]. *CJC*, 30 Aug. 1940, p. 3 [u].

40.08.30D "Willkie's Pronouncement." [Wendell Willkie refuses association with Charles Coughlin]. *CJC*, 30 Aug. 1940, p. 3 [u].

40.08.30E "Vichy Effervesces." [Anti-Semitism in Vichy France]. *CJC*, 30 Aug. 1940, p. 4 [i].

40.08.30F "Sherwood on Americanism." [Robert Sherwood on American isolationism]. *CJC*, 30 Aug. 1940, p. 4 [i].

40.08.30G "'Never Has So Much Been Owed To So Few'." [Defence of Britain by the R.A.F.]. *CJC*, 30 Aug. 1940, p. 4 [i].

40.08.30H "Another Italian Hero." [Haj Ammin al-Husseini and Benito Mussolini]. *CJC*, 30 Aug. 1940, p. 4 [i].

40.08.30I "Another Explanation of the Petain Pantomine." [Vichy France]. *CJC*, 30 Aug. 1940, p. 4 [i].

40.09.02A "Devil's Island." [*See* 40.09.06H]. *KA*, 2 Sept. 1940, p. 6 [s].

40.09.02B "Peacemeal [*sic*] Warfare." [*See* 40.09.06I]. *KA*, 2 Sept. 1940, p. 6 [s].

40.09.03A "Of Wine and Water." [*See* 40.09.06G]. *KA*, 3 Sept. 1940, p. 6 [s].

40.09.03B "A Difficult Problem." [*See* 40.09.06F]. *KA*, 3 Sept. 1940, p. 6 [s].

40.09.04A "Roosevelt Speaks." [*See* 40.09.06E]. *KA*, 4 Sept. 1940, p. 6 [s].

40.09.06A "Milton Bombed." [John Milton's statue is hit by a bomb]. *CJC*, 6 Sept. 1940, p. 3 [u].

40.09.06B "A Jewish Army." [Organization of a Jewish National Army]. *CJC*, 6 Sept. 1940, p. 3 [u].

40.09.06C "And the Palestinian Force." [WWII in the Middle East]. *CJC*, 6 Sept. 1940, p. 3 [u].

40.09.06D "Bubble, Bubble, Toil and Trouble." [Rumania in WWII]. *CJC*, 6 Sept. 1940, p. 3 [u].

40.09.06E "Roosevelt Speaks." [Franklin Delano Roosevelt urges preparedness versus isolationism]. *CJC*, 6 Sept. 1940, p. 4 [i].

40.09.06F "A Difficult Problem." [Refugees are suspected of being fifth column agents]. *CJC*, 6 Sept. 1940, p. 4 [i].

40.09.06G "Of Wine and Water." [Prohibition in Vichy France]. *CJC*, 6 Sept. 1940, p. 4 [i].

40.09.06H "Devil's Island." [Vichy France]. *CJC*, 6 Sept. 1940, p. 4 [i].

40.09.06I "Peacemeal [*sic*] Warfare." [Winston Churchill rejects Adolf Hitler's offer of peace]. *CJC*, 6 Sept. 1940, p. 4 [i].

40.09.09A "King Carol Goes." [*See* 40.09.13F]. *KA*, 9 Sept. 1940, p. 6 [s].

40.09.09B "The Immortal Profile." [*See* 40.09.13G]. *KA*, 9 Sept. 1940, p. 6 [s].

40.09.10A "German Schrecklichkeit." [*See* 40.09.13D]. *KA*, 10 Sept. 1940, p. 6 [s].

40.09.10B "No Margin For Error." [*See* 40.09.13E]. *KA*, 10 Sept. 1940, p. 6 [s].

40.09.11A "The Evolution of a Communist." [*See* 40.09.13H]. *KA*, 11 Sept. 1940, p. 6 [s].

40.09.11B "And The Kremlin, Too." [*See* 40.09.20H]. *KA*, 11 Sept. 1940, p. 6 [s].

40.09.13A "The Battle of Britain." [Bombing of London]. *CJC*, 13 Sept. 1940, p. 3 [u].

40.09.13B "The Bombing of Tel Aviv." [Italians bomb Tel Aviv]. *CJC*, 13 Sept. 1940, p. 3 [u].

40.09.13C "The Second War Loan." [Canada launches its second war loan]. *CJC*, 13 Sept. 1940, p. 3 [u].

40.09.13D "German Schrecklichkeit." [Bombing of London]. *CJC*, 13 Sept. 1940, p. 4 [i].

40.09.13E "No Margin For Error." [Claire Boothe on American isolationism]. *CJC*, 13 Sept. 1940, p. 4 [i].

40.09.13F "King Carol Goes." [King Carol leaves Rumania]. *CJC*, 13 Sept. 1940, p. 4 [i].

40.09.13G "The Immortal Profile." [John Barrymore casts his profile in cement at Grauman's Chinese Theatre]. *CJC*, 13 Sept. 1940, p. 4 [i].

40.09.13H "The Evolution of a Communist." [Jacques Doriot adopts a fascist, anti-Semitic stance]. *CJC*, 13 Sept. 1940, p. 4 [i].

40.09.16A "Einstein and God." [*See* 40.09.20F]. *KA*, 16 Sept. 1940, p. 6 [s].

40.09.16B "A False Prospectus." [*See* 40.09.20G]. *KA*, 16 Sept. 1940, p. 6 [s].

40.09.18A "Leon Blum Accused." [*See* 40.09.20D]. *KA*, 18 Sept. 1940, p. 6 [s].

40.09.18B "Mahatma Ghandi [*sic*]." [*See* 40.09.20E]. *KA*, 18 Sept. 1940, p. 6 [s].

40.09.20A "The Army of San Marino." [San Marino declares war against Britain]. *CJC*, 20 Sept. 1940, p. 3 [u].

40.09.20B "The Inscrutable Sphinx." [Italy attacks Egypt]. *CJC*, 20 Sept. 1940, p. 3 [u].

40.09.20C "Two Voices Are There." [Switzerland declares its intention to remain a democracy]. *CJC*, 20 Sept. 1940, p. 3 [u].

40.09.20D "Leon Blum Accused." [Arrest of Leon Blum]. *CJC*, 20 Sept. 1940, p. 4 [i].

40.09.20E "Mahatma Ghandi [*sic*]." [Mahatma Gandhi urges Indian co-operation with Britain]. *CJC*, 20 Sept. 1940, p. 4 [i].

40.09.20F "Einstein and God." [Albert Einstein's view of God]. *CJC*, 20 Sept. 1940, p. 4 [u].

40.09.20G "A False Prospectus." [*Globe and Mail* criticizes Jewish war effort]. *CJC*, 20 Sept. 1940, p. 4 [u].

40.09.20H "And the Kremlin Too." [Soviet press on events in Rumania]. *CJC*, 20 Sept. 1940, p. 4 [u].

40.09.22A "Wagner and Chopin." [*See* 40.09.27F]. *KA*, 22 Sept. 1940, p. 8 [s].

40.09.22B "The Blue Pencil And The Russian Bear." [*See* 40.09.27G]. *KA*, 22 Sept. 1940, p. 8 [s].

40.09.24A "The Old Stand-By." [*See* 40.09.27E]. *KA*, 24 Sept. 1940, p. 6 [s].

40.09.25A "A German Saved." [*See* 40.09.27C]. *KA*, 25 Sept. 1940, p. 6 [s].

40.09.25B "Rabbi Stephen Wise." [*See* 40.09.27D]. *KA*, 25 Sept. 1940, p. 6 [s].

40.09.27A "Sermons and Stones." [Canadian press on Jewish military participation]. *CJC*, 27 Sept. 1940, p. 3 [i].

40.09.27B "An Arab-Jewish Front." [Arab-Jewish units prepare to defend Palestine]. *CJC*, 27 Sept. 1940, p. 3 [u].

40.09.27C "A German Saved." [Canadian Jewish soldier saves a Nazi]. *CJC*, 27 Sept. 1940, p. 4 [i].

40.09.27D "Rabbi Stephen Wise." [Stephen Wise on American isolationism]. *CJC*, 27 Sept. 1940, p. 4 [i].

40.09.27E "The Old Stand-By." [Italian anti-Semitism]. *CJC*, 27 Sept. 1940, p. 4 [i].

40.09.27F "Wagner and Chopin." [Execution of Stefan Starzynski]. *CJC*, 27 Sept. 1940, p. 4 [i].

40.09.27G "The Blue Pencil and The Russian Bear." [Censorship in Soviet Union]. *CJC*, 27 Sept. 1940, p. 4 [i].

40.10.02A "The New Year." [Jewish liturgy and Jewish history]. *CJC*, 2 Oct. 1940, p. 3 [u].

40.10.02B "A Message to Jewry." [New Year's message of Samuel Bronfman]. *CJC*, 2 Oct. 1940, p. 3 [u].

40.10.08A "The Enduring Tree." [*See* 40.10.11D]. *KA*, 8 Oct. 1940, p. 6 [s].

40.10.08B "The Study of German." [*See* 40.10.11E]. *KA*, 8 Oct. 1940, p. 6 [s].

40.10.11A "The Kol Nidre Appeal." [Aid for Jews in Poland]. *CJC*, 11 Oct. 1940, p. 3 [u].

40.10.11B "Concerning Our Boys At Camp." [Military training in Canada]. *CJC*, 11 Oct. 1940, p. 3 [u].

40.10.11C "Guards For the Iron Guard." [Presence of German soldiers in Rumania]. *CJC*, 11 Oct. 1940, p. 3 [u].

40.10.11D "The Enduring Tree." [Faith in the face of despair]. *CJC*, 11 Oct. 1940, p. 4 [i].

40.10.11E "The Study of German." [Germans cannot command French horses]. *CJC*, 11 Oct. 1940, p. 4 [i].

40.10.11F "Music Hath Charm" [Review of *Jewish Music and Other Essays on Musical Topics* by Israel Rabinovitch]. *CJC*, 11 Oct. 1940, p. 6 [s].

40.10.14A "Little Man, What Now?" [*See* 40.10.16D]. *KA*, 14 Oct. 1940, p. 6 [s].

40.10.14B "The Duce Judges Others By Himself." [*See* 40.10.16E]. *KA*, 14 Oct. 1940, p. 6 [s].

40.10.16A "The Feast of Tabernacles." [Significance of Succoth in light of world events]. *CJC*, 16 Oct. 1940, p. 3 [u].

40.10.16B "Hitler In An Air Raid Shelter." [British bomb Berlin]. *CJC*, 16 Oct. 1940, p. 3 [u].

40.10.16C "The Rude Awakening." [Weakening of the Berlin-Moscow Axis]. *CJC*, 16 Oct. 1940, p. 3 [u].

40.10.16D "Little Man, What Now?" [Helplessness of the average citizen to influence world events]. *CJC*, 16 Oct. 1940, p. 4 [i].

40.10.16E "The Duce Judges Others By Himself." [Benito Mussolini tries to keep U.S. out of the war]. *CJC*, 16 Oct. 1940, p. 4 [i].

40.10.23A "The French-Canadian Press on Vichy." [Pro-Vichy views of Quebec newspapers]. *CJC*, 23 Oct. 1940, p. 3 [u].

40.10.23B "The New Order in France." [Henri Pétain on Vichy France]. *CJC*, 23 Oct. 1940, p. 3 [u].

40.10.23C "The Anti-Jewish Laws." [Anti-Semitism in Vichy France]. *CJC*, 23 Oct. 1940, p. 3 [u].

40.10.29A "Lewis by a Kayo." [*See* 40.11.01E]. *KA*, 29 Oct. 1940, p. 6 [s].

40.10.29B "Madame LaFarge [*sic, should be* Defarge] Knits at Vichy." [*See* 40.11.01F]. *KA*, 29 Oct. 1940, p. 6 [s].

40.10.30A "The Isles of Greece." [*See* 40.11.01D]. *KA*, 30 Oct. 1940, p. 6 [s].

40.11.01A "The Federation of Jewish Philanthropies." [Fundraising campaign for the Federation of Jewish Philanthropies]. *CJC*, 1 Nov. 1940, p. 3 [u].

40.11.01B "The Habonim Convention." [Habonim convention]. *CJC*, 1 Nov. 1940, p. 3 [u].

40.11.01C "A Good Amendment." [Amendment to the Defence of Canada Act]. *CJC*, 1 Nov. 1940, p. 3 [u].

40.11.01D "The Isles of Greece." [Italian offensive against Greece]. *CJC*, 1 Nov. 1940, p. 4 [i].

40.11.01E "Lewis By a Kayo." [John L. Lewis withdraws support for Franklin Delano Roosevelt]. *CJC*, 1 Nov. 1940, p. 4 [i].

40.11.01F "Madame Lafarge [*sic*] Knits at Vichy." [French collaboration in wwii]. *CJC*, 1 Nov. 1940, p. 4 [i].

40.11.05A "With Blitz and Bluff." [*See* 40.11.08B]. *KA*, 5 Nov. 1940, p. 6 [s].

40.11.05B "The Mussolini Boys." [*See* 40.11.08C]. *KA*, 5 Nov. 1940, p. 6 [s].

40.11.06A "A Celebration." [*See* 40.11.08D]. *KA*, 6 Nov. 1940, p. 6 [s].

40.11.06B "See Naples and Die." [*See* 40.11.08E]. *KA*, 6 Nov. 1940, p. 6 [s].

40.11.08A "Lillian Freiman: A Tribute." [Death of Lillian Freiman]. *CJC*, 8 Nov. 1940, p. 3 [u].

40.11.08B "With Blitz and Bluff." [Nazi propaganda aimed at Arabs]. *CJC*, 8 Nov. 1940, p. 4 [i].

40.11.08C "The Mussolini Boys." [Sons of Benito Mussolini participate in bombing of Greece]. *CJC*, 8 Nov. 1940, p. 4 [i].

40.11.08D "A Celebration." [Anniversary of the Russian Revolution]. *CJC*, 8 Nov. 1940, p. 4 [i].

40.11.08E "See Naples and Die." [Italian war effort]. *CJC*, 8 Nov. 1940, p. 4 [i].

40.11.08F "The Presidential Election." [U.S. Presidential Election]. *KA*, 8 Nov. 1940, p. 8 [s].

40.11.12A "Strange Bedfellows." [*See* 40.11.15F]. *KA*, 12 Nov. 1940, p. 6 [s].

40.11.12B "The R.A.F. Makes a Little Putsch." [*See* 40.11.15E]. *KA*, 12 Nov. 1940, p. 6 [s].

40.11.13A "Here Comes Molly." [*See* 40.11.15D]. *KA*, 13 Nov. 1940, p. 6 [s].

40.11.13B "Neville Chamberlain." [*See* 40.11.15G]. *KA*, 13 Nov. 1940, p. 6 [s].

40.11.15A "A Finger of God." [Symbolic importance of an earthquake]. *CJC*, 15 Nov. 1940, p. 3 [i].

40.11.15B "Glorious Episode." [Bay of Taranto incident]. *CJC*, 15 Nov. 1940, p. 3 [u].

40.11.15C "A Czech-Polish Federation." [Possibility of a Polish-Czech Federation after WWII]. *CJC*, 15 Nov. 1940, p. 3 [u].

40.11.15D "Here Comes Molly." [Deterioration of the Berlin-Moscow Axis]. *CJC*, 15 Nov. 1940, p. 4 [i].

40.11.15E "The R.A.F. Makes a Little Putsch." [R.A.F. bombs disrupt anniversary of the Munich Putsch]. *CJC*, 15 Nov. 1940, p. 4 [i].

40.11.15F "Strange Bedfellows." [Soviet foreign policy in WWII]. *CJC*, 15 Nov. 1940, p. 4 [i].

40.11.15G "Neville Chamberlain." [Death of Neville Chamberlain]. *CJC*, 15 Nov. 1940, p. 4 [i].

40.11.19A "The Collaboration." [*See* 40.11.22F]. *KA*, 19, Nov. 1940, p. 6 [s].

40.11.19B "The Red Ostrich." [*See* 40.11.22G]. *KA*, 19 Nov. 1940, p. 6 [s].

40.11.20A "The Balcony Warrior." [*See* 40.11.22E]. *KA*, 20 Nov. 1940, p. 6 [s].

40.II.22A "General Herzog Repents." [General Herzog breaks ties with Daniel Malan]. *CJC*, 22 [*misdated* 15] Nov. 1940, p. 3 [u].

40.II.22B "Hungary and the Axis." [Hungary joins the Axis]. *CJC*, 22 Nov. 1940, p. 3 [u].

40.II.22C "Suffer Little Children." [Nazis promote higher birthrate in Germany]. *CJC*, 22 Nov. 1940, p. 3 [u].

40.II.22D "Further Revelations by Dies." [Findings of the Dies Committee]. *CJC*, 22 Nov. 1940, p. 3 [u].

40.II.22E "The Balcony Warrior." [Benito Mussolini]. *CJC*, 22 Nov. 1944, p. 4 [i].

40.II.22F "The Collaboration." [Vichy France]. *CJC*, 22 Nov. 1940, p. 4 [i].

40.II.22G "The Red Ostrich." [American communists break ties with Stalinist Soviet Union]. *CJC*, 22 Nov. 1940, p. 4 [i].

40.II.26A "A Stupid Resolution." [*See* 40.II.29D]. *KA*, 26 Nov. 1940, p. 6 [s].

40.II.26B "The Secretary Examines His Interior." [*See* 40.II.29G]. *KA*, 26 Nov. 1940, p. 6 [s].

40.II.27A "Arms and the Corset." [*See* 40.II.29E]. *KA*, 27 Nov. 1940, p. 6 [s].

40.II.27B "The Runner Up." [*See* 40.II.29F]. *KA*, 27 Nov. 1940, p. 6 [s].

40.II.29A "Tragedy at Haifa." [Refugee ship explodes in Haifa harbour]. *CJC*, 29 Nov. 1940, p. 3 [u].

40.II.29B "The Jewish Immigrant Aid Society." [J.I.A.S. annual meeting]. *CJC*, 29 Nov. 1940, p. 3 [u].

40.II.29C "The Hadassah Bazaar." [Hadassah bazaar]. *CJC*, 29 Nov. 1940, p. 3 [u].

40.II.29D "A Stupid Resolution." [City of Hamilton bans foreign language publications]. *CJC*, 29 Nov. 1940, p. 4 [i].

40.II.29E "Arms and the Corset." [Corset manufacturers cannot obtain steel]. *CJC*, 29 Nov. 1940, p. 4 [i].

40.II.29F "The Runner Up." [Italian campaign in Greece]. *CJC*, 29 Nov. 1940, p. 4 [i].

40.II.29G "The Secretary Examines His Interior." [Outspokenness of Harold Ickes]. *CJC*, 29 Nov. 1940, p. 4 [i].

40.II.29H "Father and Son." [Speech of Randolph Churchill]. *CJC*, 29 Nov. 1940, p. 4 [i].

40.11.29I "They Mean No Peace." [Winston Churchill rejects the idea of a Christmas armistice]. *CJC*, 29 Nov. 1940, p. 4 [i].

40.11.29J "Wagner and Chopin." [*See* 40.09.27F]. *CJC*, 29 Nov. 1940, p. 4 [i].

40.12.03A "Interlude in Rumania." [*See* 40.12.06C]. *KA*, 3 Dec. 1940, p. 6 [s].

40.12.04A "Hoover's Blockade." [*See* 40.12.06B]. *KA*, 4 Dec. 1940, p. 6 [s].

40.12.06A "The United Jewish Refugee and War Relief Agencies." [The United Jewish Refugee and War Relief Agencies]. *CJC*, 6 Dec. 1940, p. 3 [u].

40.12.06B "Hoover's Blockade." [Hoover urges slackening of the British naval blockade]. *CJC*, 6 Dec. 1940, p. 4 [i].

40.12.06C "Interlude in Rumania." [Pogroms in Rumania]. *CJC*, 6 Dec. 1940, p. 4 [i].

40.12.10A "A Well-Merited Rebuke." [*See* 40.12.13E]. *KA*, 10 Dec. 1940, p. 6 [s].

40.12.11A "Elan Vital." [*See* 40.12.13C]. *KA*, 11 Dec. 1940, p. 6 [s].

40.12.13A "Full of Sound and Fuehrer." [Speech of Adolf Hitler]. *CJC*, 13 Dec. 1940, p. 3 [u].

40.12.13B "Sidi Barrani." [British capture Sidi Barrani]. *CJC*, 13 Dec. 1940, p. 3 [u].

40.12.13C "Elan Vital." [Henri Bergson refuses special treatment by Vichy government]. *CJC*, 13 Dec. 1940, p. 4 [u].

40.12.13D "Look Where He Is!" [Fritz Thyssen]. *CJC*, 13 Dec. 1940, p. 4 [u].

40.12.13E "A Well-Merited Rebuke." [J.S. Roy opposes Canada's war effort]. *CJC*, 13 Dec. 1940, p. 4 [u].

40.12.18A "The Value of Prayer." [*See* 40.12.20C]. *KA*, 18 Dec. 1940, p. 6 [s].

40.12.19A "The Disinherited One." [*See* 40.12.20D]. *KA*, 19 Dec. 1940, p. 6 [s].

40.12.19B "Some American Notes." [*See* 40.12.20E]. *KA*, 19 Dec. 1940, p. 6 [s].

40.12.20A " 'A Hose For a Neighbor'." [U.S. aid to Britain]. *CJC*, 20 Dec. 1940, p. 3 [u].

40.12.20B "The Late Moses Gelber." [Death of Moses Gelber]. *CJC*, 20 Dec. 1940, p. 3 [u].

40.12.20C "The Value of Prayer." [Professional Kaddish sayer sues for payment of fees]. *CJC*, 20 Dec. 1940, p. 4 [i].

40.12.20D "The Disinherited One." [Pierre Laval is ousted by Pierre-Etienne Flandin]. *CJC*, 20 Dec. 1940, p. 4 [i].

40.12.20E "Some American Notes." [American isolationism]. *CJC*, 20 Dec. 1940, p. 4 [i].

40.12.20F "Feuchtwanger Zionist." [Lion Feuchtwanger adopts a Zionist view]. *CJC*, 20 Dec. 1940, p. 4 [i].

40.12.27A "Chanukah." [Parallels between Chanukah story and WWII]. *CJC*, 27 Dec. 1940, p. 3 [u].

40.12.27B "The Red Martinet." [Communist newspaper at McGill]. *CJC*, 27 Dec. 1940, p. 3 [u].

40.12.31A "Thunder Over The White House." [*See* 41.01.03D]. *KA*, 31 Dec. 1940, p. 6 [s].

41.01.02A "The Doctor Looks at Yiddish Literature." [*See* 41.01.03E]. *KA*, 2 Jan. 1941, p. 6 [u].

41.01.03A "The Man of the Year." [Winston Churchill]. *CJC*, 3 Jan. 1941, p. 3 [u].

41.01.03B "The Fuehrer Sees Them Again." [Speech of Adolf Hitler]. *CJC*, 3 Jan. 1941, p. 3 [u].

41.01.03C "Jewish Youth." [Jewish press criticizes Jewish youth]. *CJC*, 3 Jan. 1941, p. 3 [u].

41.01.03D "Thunder Over the White House." [Speech of Franklin Delano Roosevelt]. *CJC*, 3 Jan. 1941, p. 4 [u].

41.01.03E "The Doctor Looks at Yiddish Literature." [Review of *The Story of Yiddish Literature* by A.A. Roback]. *CJC*, 3 Jan. 1941, pp. 4, 16 [i].

41.01.07A "A Strange Apologist." [*See* 41.01.10E]. *KA*, 7 Jan. 1941, p. 6 [s].

41.01.08A " 'The State of the Union'." [*See* 41.01.10D]. *KA*, 8 Jan. 1941, p. 6 [s].

41.01.10A "The Talmud Torah Campaign." [Fundraising campaign for the United Talmud Torahs]. *CJC*, 10 Jan. 1941, p. 3 [u].

41.01.10B "An Experiment, Not a Precedent." [British allow U.S. aid shipment to France through naval blockade]. *CJC*, 10 Jan. 1941, p. 3 [u].

41.01.10C "The Spell of the Open Road." [Hobos support the war effort]. *CJC*, 10 Jan. 1941, p. 3 [u].

41.01.10D " 'The State of the Union'." [Franklin Delano Roosevelt's State of the Union address]. *CJC*, 10 Jan. 1941, p. 4 [i].

41.01.10E "A Strange Apologist." [André Maurois on Vichy France]. *CJC*, 10 Jan. 1941, p. 4 [i].

41.01.10F "The Bard of Bardia." [Italian defeat at Bardia]. *CJC*, 10 Jan. 1941, p. 4 [i].

41.01.17A "The Canadian Zionist Convention." [Twenty-sixth Canadian Zionist convention]. *CJC*, 17 Jan. 1941, p. 3 [u].

41.01.17B "The Sirois Report." [Federal-Provincial relations in Canada]. *CJC*, 17 Jan. 1941, p. 3 [u].

41.01.17C "A Splendid Precedent." [Canadian Jewish Congress acknowledgment of Canadian Jewish cultural achievements]. *CJC*, 17 Jan. 1941, p. 4 [i].

41.01.17D "The Saturday Evening Post." [Demaree Bess on occupied Norway]. *CJC*, 17 Jan. 1941, pp. 4, 13 [i].

41.01.17E "A Splendid Precedent." [*See* 41.01.17C]. *KA*, 17 Jan. 1941, p. 8 [s].

41.01.19A "The Saturday Evening Post." [*See* 41.01.17D]. *KA*, 19 Jan. 1941, p. 8 [s].

41.01.22A "The Duce and the Fuehrer." [*See* 41.01.24C]. *KA*, 22 Jan. 1941, p. 6 [s].

41.01.24A "The Zionist and Hadassah Conventions." [Zionist Organization of Canada, 26th national convention]. *CJC*, 24 Jan. 1941, p. 3 [u].

41.01.24B "When Omer Nods." [Anti-Zionism of Omer Heroux]. *CJC*, 24 Jan. 1941, pp. 3, 15 [u].

41.01.24C "The Duce and The Fuehrer." [Strained Italian-German relations]. *CJC*, 24 Jan. 1941, p. 4 [i].

41.01.24D "The Death-Ray." [Military developments of science and technology]. *CJC*, 24 Jan. 1941, p. 4 [i].

41.01.24E "The Democratic Way." [Democracies and dictatorships]. *CJC*, 24 Jan. 1941, p. 4 [i].

41.01.28A "Mr. Butler's Message to Zionists." [*See* 41.01.31E]. *KA*, 28 Jan. 1941, p. 6 [s].

41.01.28B "Lindbergh Earns Another Medal." [*See* 41.01.31F]. *KA*, 28 Jan. 1941, p. 6 [s].

41.01.29A "A Nazi Boast." [*See* 41.01.31D]. *KA*, 29 Jan. 1941, p. 6 [s].

41.01.31A "The Geverkshaften Campaign." [Fundraising campaign for the Histadrut]. *CJC*, 31 Jan. 1941, p. 3 [u].

41.01.31B " 'To Make a Rumanian Holiday'." [Pogroms in Rumania]. *CJC*, 31 Jan. 1941, p. 3 [u].

41.01.31C "A Significant Birthday." [Birthday of Kaiser Wilhelm II]. *CJC*, 31 Jan. 1941, p. 3 [u].

41.01.31D "A Nazi Boast." [Nazi admiration for the Middle Ages]. *CJC*, 31 Jan. 1941, p. 4 [i].

41.01.31E "Mr. Butler's Message to Zionists." [Neville Butler addresses American Zionists]. *CJC*, 31 Jan. 1941, p. 4 [i].

41.01.31F "Lindbergh Earns Another Medal." [Isolationism of Charles Lindbergh]. *CJC*, 31 Jan. 1941, p. 4 [i].

41.02.05A "The Nazi Intellectual." [*See* 41.02.07D]. *KA*, 5 Feb. 1941, p. 6 [s].

41.02.07A "Canadian Young Judaea War Research Fund." [Fundraising for research institute in Palestine]. *CJC*, 7 Feb. 1941, p. 3 [u].

41.02.07B "Interned Refugees." [Internment of refugees]. *CJC*, 7 Feb. 1941, p. 3 [u].

41.02.07C "Wendell Willlkie: American." [Wendell Willkie broadcasts an anti-fascist message to Germany]. *CJC*, 7 Feb. 1941, p. 3 [u].

41.02.07D "The Nazi Intellectual." [Bronislaw Hubermann condemns cooperation of German intellectuals with Nazis]. *CJC*, 7 Feb. 1941, p. 4 [i].

41.02.07E "The Marionettes." [Vichy France]. *CJC*, 7 Feb. 1941, p. 4 [i].

41.02.07F "The Hidden Hand." [Fascism in South Africa]. *CJC*, 7 Feb. 1941, p. 4 [i].

41.02.07G "He Who Halts . . ." [Defeat of Italians in North Africa]. *CJC*, 7 Feb. 1941, p. 4 [i].

41.02.07H "The Contemporary Psalms." [Psalm 79 expresses plight of Jews]. *CJC*, 7 Feb. 1941, p. 4 [i].

41.02.12A "The Italian Empire?" [*See* 41.02.14E]. *KA*, 12 Feb. 1941, p. 6 [s].

41.02.12B "Oxidized [*sic, should be* Axidized] Rumania." [*See* 41.02.14G]. *KA*, 12 Feb. 1941, p. 6 [s].

41.02.13A "Immortal Speech." [*See* 41.02.14F]. *KA*, 13 Feb. 1941, p. 6 [s].

41.02.14A "The Jews of Benghazi." [Jews in Libya]. *CJC*, 14 Feb. 1941, p. 3 [u].

41.02.14B "It is Later Than You Think." [Wendell Willkie urges U.S. support of Britain]. *CJC*, 14 Feb. 1941, p. 3 [u].

41.02.14C "Krivitzky: Or the Case of the Unwilling Suicide." [Death of Walter Krivitsky]. *CJC*, 14 Feb. 1941, p. 3 [u].

41.02.14D "The Bulgarians." [Bulgarian neutrality in WWII]. *CJC*, 14 Feb. 1941, p. 3 [u].

41.02.14E "The Italian Empire?" [Italian defeat in North Africa]. *CJC*, 14 Feb. 1941, p. 4 [i].

41.02.14F "Immortal Speech." [Language of Winston Churchill]. *CJC*, 14 Feb. 1941, p. 4 [i].

41.02.14G "Axidized Rumania." [German presence in Rumania]. *CJC*, 14 Feb. 1941, p. 4 [i].

41.02.19A "So Sorry." [*See* 41.02.21D]. *KA*, 19 Feb. 1941, p. 6 [s].

41.02.19B "The Terrible Turk." [*See* 41.02.21E]. *KA*, 19 Feb. 1941, p. 6 [s].

41.02.21A "The Jewish General Hospital Campaign." [Fundraising for the Jewish General Hospital]. *CJC*, 21 Feb. 1941, p. 3 [u].

41.02.21B "Haile Selassie on the March." [War in Ethiopia]. *CJC*, 21 Feb. 1941, p. 3 [u].

41.02.21C "Lover's Code." [Love letters to British soldiers in Libya]. *CJC*, 21 Feb. 1941, p. 3 [u].

41.02.21D "So Sorry." [Japanese military activity in the South Pacific]. *CJC*, 21 Feb. 1941, p. 4 [i].

41.02.21E "The Terrible Turk." [Treaty between Turkey and Bulgaria]. *CJC*, 21 Feb. 1941, p. 4 [i].

41.02.21F "The Ford's Prayer." [Isolationism of Henry Ford]. *CJC*, 21 Feb. 1941, pp. 4, 16 [i].

41.02.21G "The Ford's Prayer." [*See* 41.02.21F]. *KA*, 21 Feb. 1941, p. 6 [s].

41.02.25A "Dove Conquers All." [*See* 41.02.28D]. *KA*, 25 Feb. 1941, p. 6 [s].

41.02.25B "They Got, But Not What They Wanted." [*See* 41.02.28E]. *KA*, 25 Feb. 1941, p. 6 [s].

41.02.26A "The Duce Explains." [*See* 41.02.28F]. *KA*, 26 Feb. 1941, p. 6 [s].

41.02.28A "The Late Sir Frederick Banting." [Death of Frederick Banting]. *CJC*, 28 Feb. 1941, p. 3 [u].

41.02.28B "A.B. Bennett." [Fiftieth birthday of Archibald Bennett]. *CJC*, 28 Feb. 1941, p. 3 [u].

41.02.28C "The Submarine, A Secret Weapon?" [Adolf Hitler threatens U-boat warfare]. *CJC*, 28 Feb. 1941, p. 3 [u].

41.02.28D "Dove Conquers All." [Japanese diplomacy]. *CJC*, 28 Feb. 1941, p. 4 [i].

41.02.28E "They Got, But Not What They Wanted." [Failed Nazi fifth column attack on U.S.]. *CJC*, 28 Feb. 1941, p. 4 [i].

41.02.28F "The Duce Explains." [Speech of Benito Mussolini]. *CJC*, 28 Feb. 1941, p. 4 [i].

41.03.04A "The Bulgarians Celebrate Their Independence." [*See* 41.03.07B]. *KA*, 4 Mar. 1941, p. 6 [s].

41.03.04B "Goebbels Makes a Speech." [*See* 41.03.07C]. *KA*, 4 Mar. 1941, p. 6 [s].

41.03.07A "Samuel Bronfman." [Samuel Bronfman]. *CJC*, 7 Mar. 1941, p. 3 [i].

41.03.07B "The Bulgarians Celebrate Their Independence." [Bulgaria celebrates its day of independence despite Nazi presence]. *CJC*, 7 Mar. 1941, p. 4 [i].

41.03.07C "Goebbels Makes a Speech." [Speech of Joseph Goebbels]. *CJC*, 7 Mar. 1941, p. 4 [i].

41.03.07D "Soviet Policy or Soviet Dilemma?" [German presence in Bulgaria threatens Soviet Union]. *CJC*, 7 Mar. 1941, p. 4 [i].

41.03.07E "Another Example of the New Order." [Nazis deface grave of Heinrich Heine]. *CJC*, 7 Mar. 1941, p. 4 [i].

41.03.11A "The End of Isolationism." [*See* 41.03.14B]. *KA*, 11 Mar. 1941, p. 6 [s].

41.03.11B "Ford's Latest Clarion-Call." [*See* 41.03.14C]. *KA*, 11 Mar. 1941, p. 6 [s].

41.03.13A "Purim." [*See* 41.03.14D]. *KA*, 13 Mar. 1941, p. 10 [u].

41.03.14A "The United Palestine Appeal." [Fundraising for the United Palestine Appeal]. *CJC*, 14 Mar. 1941, p. 3 [u].

41.03.14B "The End of Isolationism." [U.S. Senate approves the Lend-lease Bill]. *CJC*, 14 Mar. 1941, p. 4 [i].

41.03.14C "Ford's Latest Clarion-Call." [Henry Ford opposes trade unions]. *CJC*, 14 Mar. 1941, p. 4 [i].

41.03.14D "Purim." [Anti-Semitism through history]. *CJC*, 14 Mar. 1941, p. 4 [i].

41.03.18A "Roosevelt Addresses the World." [*See* 41.03.21F]. *KA*, 18 Mar. 1941, p. 6 [s].

41.03.21A "A Century of Anglo-Jewish Journalism." [Hundredth anniversary of the *London Jewish Chronicle*]. *CJC*, 21 Mar. 1941, p. 3 [u].

41.03.21B "And in the Spring a Young Man's Fancy . . ." [Arrival of spring in time of war]. *CJC*, 21 Mar. 1941, p. 3 [i].

41.03.21C "The Good Natured Germans." [British-French relations]. *CJC*, 21 Mar. 1941, p. 3 [u].

41.03.21D "The Fuehrer's Breath Shortens." [Adolf Hitler's oratory]. *CJC*, 21 Mar. 1941, p. 4 [i].

41.03.21E "The Battle of the Atlantic." [Speech of Winston Churchill]. *CJC*, 21 Mar. 1941, p. 4 [i].

41.03.21F "Roosevelt Addresses the World." [Speech of Franklin Delano Roosevelt]. *CJC*, 21 Mar. 1941, p. 4 [i].

41.03.28A "Blueprint of War Aims." [British war arms]. *CJC*, 28 Mar. 1941, p. 3 [u].

41.03.28B "Grynszpan's Confession." [Hershel Grynszpan]. *CJC*, 28 Mar. 1941, p. 3 [u].

41.03.28C "Germany Must Perish!" [Jew proposes sterilization of all Germans]. *CJC*, 28 Mar. 1941, p. 4 [i].

41.03.28D "The American Quisling." [Isolationism of Charles Lindbergh]. *CJC*, 28 Mar. 1941, p. 4 [i].

41.03.28E "The Stubborn Yugoslavs." [War in the Balkans]. *CJC*, 28 Mar. 1941, p. 4 [i].

41.04.04A "The Journalist in Chains." [Demaree Bess on the Warsaw Ghetto]. *CJC*, 4 Apr. 1941, p. 3 [i].

41.04.04B "A Splendid Gesture." [Interned Jewish refugees support the United Palestine Appeal]. *CJC*, 4 Apr. 1941, p. 3 [u].

41.04.04C "Whom the Gods . . ." [Vichy France]. *CJC*, 4 Apr. 1941, p. 4 [i].

41.04.04D "The Travels of Matsuoka." [Meetings between Matsuoka and other Axis leaders]. *CJC*, 4 Apr. 1941, p. 4 [i].

41.04.04E "Mussolini — On Land and Sea." [Italian defeats]. *CJC*, 4 Apr. 1941, p. 4 [i].

41.04.04F "The President As Fisherman." [Speech of Franklin Delano Roosevelt]. *CJC*, 4 Apr. 1941, p. 4 [i].

41.04.11A "And it was at Midnight." [The Passover story in modern times]. *CJC*, 11 Apr. 1941, p. 3 [u].

41.04.11B "Battle of the Balkans." [War in the Balkans]. *CJC*, 11 Apr. 1941, p. 3 [u].

41.04.11C "The Bible as Literature." [The Bible as literature]. *CJC*, 11 Apr. 1941, pp. 8–9 [s] (Ben Kalonimas). *See also* "The Bible as Literature," mimeographed pamphlet issued by Hadassah Organization of Canada, n.d.

41.04.17A "The War Outlook." [Progress of the war]. *CJC*, 17 Apr. 1941, p. 3 [i].

41.04.17B "A Jewish Chaplain." [Appointment of a Jewish chaplain to Canadian Armed Forces]. *CJC*, 17 Apr. 1941, p. 3 [u].

41.04.17C "The Jewish Incurable Hospital." [Jewish Hospital of Hope established in Montreal]. *CJC*, 17 Apr. 1941, p. 3 [u].

41.04.17D "And Yet Another Pact." [Soviet-Japanese Neutrality Pact]. *CJC*, 17 Apr. 1941, p. 4 [u].

41.04.17E "Secretary Ickes and the Nazi Fellow-Travellers . . ." [Harold Ickes speaks out against U.S. isolationism]. *CJC*, 17 Apr. 1941, p. 4 [u].

41.04.22A "The Serpent In The Garden of Eden." [*See* 41.04.25D]. *KA*, 22 Apr. 1941, p. 6 [s].

41.04.23A "Lindbergh Gets His Answer." [*See* 41.04.25E]. *KA*, 23 Apr. 1941, p. 6 [s].

41.04.23B "Calendar Note." [*See* 41.04.25F]. *KA*, 23 Apr. 1941, p. 6 [s].

41.04.25A "The Proper Perspective." [War in the Balkans]. *CJC*, 25 Apr. 1941, p. 3 [u].

41.04.25B "Pravda Boasts." [Soviet strategic position is threatened by Germany]. *CJC*, 25 Apr. 1941, p. 3 [u].

41.04.25C "Palestine Mobilization." [Mobilization of Jews in Palestine]. *CJC*, 25 Apr. 1941, p. 3 [u].

41.04.25D "The Serpent in the Garden of Eden." [The Mufti in Iraq]. *CJC*, 25 Apr. 1941, p. 4 [i].

41.04.25E "Lindbergh Gets His Answer." [Alexander de Seversky refutes Charles Lindbergh's isolationist arguments]. *CJC*, 25 Apr. 1941, p. 4 [i].

41.04.25F "Calendar Note." [Vichy government abolishes Bastille Day]. *CJC*, 25 Apr. 1941, p. 4 [i].

41.04.29A "The Honor That is Britain." [*See* 41.05.02D]. *KA*, 29 Apr. 1941, p. 6 [s].

41.05.02A "The Budget." [Canadian economy during WWII]. *CJC*, 2 May 1941, p. 3 [u].

41.05.02B "The Nazis in Greece." [War in Greece]. *CJC*, 2 May 1941, p. 3 [u].

41.05.02C "The Pravda Changes Its Tune." [Deterioration of the Berlin-Moscow Axis]. *CJC*, 2 May 1941, p. 3 [u].

41.05.02D "The Honor That is Britain." [Speech of Winston Churchill on war in Greece]. *CJC*, 2 May 1941, p. 4 [i].

41.05.02E "Lindbergh Resigns." [Charles Lindbergh resigns from U.S. Army Corps Reserve]. *CJC*, 2 May 1941, p. 4 [i].

41.05.02F "The Draft Dodger." [Draft dodgers]. *CJC*, 2 May 1941, p. 4 [i].

41.05.02G "Lindbergh Resigns." [*See* 41.05.02E]. *KA*, 2 May 1941, p. 8 [s].

41.05.02H "The Draft Dodger." [*See* 41.05.02F]. *KA*, 2 May 1941, p. 8 [s].

41.05.06A "The Son of Belial." [*See* 41.05.09B]. *KA*, 6 May 1941, p. 6 [s].

41.05.07A "Oil Upon The Waters." [*See* 41.05.09C]. *KA*, 7 May 1941, p. 6 [s].

41.05.07B "Wheeler or Roosevelt." [*See* 41.05.09D]. *KA*, 7 May 1941, p. 6 [s].

41.05.09A "Welcome to Dr. Weizmann." [Chaim Weizmann visits Canada]. *CJC*, 9 May 1941, p. 3 [u].

41.05.09B "The Son of Belial." [Adolf Hitler]. *CJC*, 9 May 1941, p. 4 [i].

41.05.09C "Oil Upon the Waters." [Disruption of oil supplies jeopardizes British strength in the Mediterannean]. *CJC*, 9 May 1941, p. 4 [i].

41.05.09D "Wheeler or Roosevelt." [Isolationism of Burton Wheeler]. *CJC*, 9 May 1941, p. 4 [i].

41.05.13A "The Russian Poo-Bah." [*See* 41.05.16D]. *KA*, 13 May 1941, p. 6 [s].

41.05.14A "Hess: Fuehrer No. 3." [*See* 41.05.16E]. *KA*, 14 May 1941, p. 6 [s].

41.05.16A "The Mother of Parliaments." [Bombing of the British House of Commons]. *CJC*, 16 May 1941, p. 3 [u].

41.05.16B "Developments At Vichy." [Collaboration of Vichy France]. *CJC*, 16 May 1941, p. 3 [u].

41.05.16C " 'An Angel of Peace'." [Rudolf Hess parachutes into Scotland]. *CJC*, 16 May 1941, p. 3 [u].

41.05.16D "The Russian Pooh-Bah." [Joseph Stalin]. *CJC*, 16 May 1941, p. 4 [i].

41.05.16E "Hess: Fuehrer No. 3." [Rudolf Hess appears in Scotland]. *CJC*, 16 May 1941, p. 4 [i].

41.05.20A "The Italian Surrender." [*See* 41.05.23D]. *KA*, 20 May 1941, p. 6 [s].

41.05.20B "Vichy Decides." [*See* 41.05.23E]. *KA*, 20 May 1941, p. 6 [s].

41.05.21A "Andre Maurois — Apologist." [*See* 41.05.23F]. *KA*, 21 May 1941, p. 6 [s].

41.05.21B "The Science of Geopolitics." [*See* 41.05.23G]. *KA*, 21 May 1941, p. 6 [s].

41.05.23A "Thirty Years of the Hebrew Free Loan Association May 28th 1911." [Thirtieth anniversary of the founding of the Hebrew Free Loan Association]. *CJC*, 23 May 1941, p. 3 [u].

41.05.23B "Some Bible Miracles." [Need for miracles to overcome Nazis]. *CJC*, 23 May 1941, p. 3 [u].

41.05.23C "Sholom Aleichem." [Sholom Aleichem]. *CJC*, 23 May 1941, p. 3 [u].

41.05.23D "The Italian Surrender." [Italian defeat in North Africa]. *CJC*, 23 May 1941, p. 4 [i].

41.05.23E "Vichy Decides." [Collaboration of Vichy France]. *CJC*, 23 May 1941, p. 4 [i].

41.05.23F "Andre Maurois — Apologist." [André Maurois on Vichy France]. *CJC*, 23 May 1941, p. 4 [i].

41.05.23G "The Science of Geopolitics." [Nazi ideology]. *CJC*, 23 May 1941, p. 4 [i].

41.05.27A "The Lesson of the Hood." [*See* 41.05.30F]. *KA*, 27 May 1941, p. 6 [s].

41.05.27B "The Darlan of the Nazis." [*See* 41.05.30G]. *KA*, 27 May 1941, p. 6 [s].

41.05.28A "The Bismarck Herring." [*See* 41.05.30D]. *KA*, 28 May 1941, p. 6 [s].

41.05.28B "The Apologia of a Traitor." [*See* 41.05.30E]. *KA*, 28 May 1941, p. 6 [s].

41.05.30A "An International Bill of Rights." [Speech of Franklin Delano Roosevelt]. *CJC*, 30 May 1941, p. 3 [u].

41.05.30B "Arms for Palestinians." [British policy on Jews in the Army in Palestine]. *CJC*, 30 May 1941, p. 3 [u].

41.05.30C "The Feast of Shavuoth." [Need for reassertion of the Ten Commandments]. *CJC*, 30 May 1941, p. 3 [u].

41.05.30D "The Bismarck Herring." [Destruction of the Bismarck]. *CJC*, 30 May 1941, p. 4 [i].

41.05.30E "The Apologia of a Traitor." [Collaboration of Pierre Laval]. *CJC*, 30 May 1941, p. 4 [i].

41.05.30F "The Lesson of the Hood." [War at sea moves closer to North America]. *CJC*, 30 May 1941, p. 4 [i].

41.05.30G "The Darlan of the Nazis." [Collaboration of Jean Darlan]. *CJC*, 30 May 1941, p. 4 [i].

41.06.04A "The War Aims." [*See* 41.06.06D]. *KA*, 4 June, 1941, p. 6 [s].

41.06.06A "The Loan and Victory!" [Canadian government launches a victory loan]. *CJC*, 6 June 1941, p. 3 [u].

41.06.06B "The Jewish People's Schools." [Jewish People's School dedicates its new location]. *CJC*, 6 June 1941, p. 3 [u].

41.06.06C "The Still Waters of Vichy." [Jean Darlan on Anglo-French relations]. *CJC*, 6 June 1941, p. 4 [i].

41.06.06D "The War Aims." [Anthony Eden describes Britain's war aims]. *CJC*, 6 June 1941, p. 4 [i].

41.06.10A "Wilhelm Hohenzollern, Deceased." [*See* 41.06.13E]. *KA*, 10 June 1941, p. 6 [s].

41.06.10B "The Pity of it, Iago." [*See* 41.06.13F]. *KA*, 10 June 1941, p. 6 [s].

41.06.11A "Strange Interlude." [*See* 41.06.13G]. *KA*, 11 June 1941, p. 6 [s].

41.06.13A "The Defence of the Defence of Crete." [Debate in British House of Commons over war strategy used in the Balkans]. *CJC*, 13 June 1941, p. 3 [u].

41.06.13B "Mussolini Whistles." [Ineffectuality of Benito Mussolini]. *CJC*, 13 June 1941, p. 3 [u].

41.06.13C "Guardian At the Perley Gates." [Anti-Semitic comments in the House of Commons]. *CJC*, 13 June 1941, p. 3 [u].

41.06.13D "Jews seek to Leave Cyprus." [Jewish refugees seek admission to Palestine]. *CJC*, 13 June 1941, p. 3 [u].

41.06.13E "Wilhelm Hohenzollern, Deceased." [Death of Kaiser Wilhelm II]. *CJC*, 13 June 1941, p. 4 [i].

41.06.13F "The Pity of it, Iago!" [Anglo-French relations during WWII]. *CJC*, 13 June 1941, p. 4 [i].

41.06.13G "Strange Interlude." [Anti-Semitism of Ernest Perley]. *CJC*, 13 June 1941, p. 4 [i].

41.06.17A "Mr. George Shaw [*sic*] And His World." [*See* 41.06.20F]. *KA*, 17 June 1941, p. 6 [s].

41.06.19A "Another Premature Obituary." [*See* 41.06.20E]. *KA*, 19 June 1941, p. 6 [s].

41.06.20A "The Closing of the Consulates." [U.S. closes all its German consulates]. *CJC*, 20 June 1941, p. 3 [u].

41.06.20B "The New Sheepskin." [Diplomas awarded in 1941 are made of inferior sheepskin]. *CJC*, 20 June 1941, p. 3 [u].

41.06.20C "Die Wacht Am Soviet." [Germans amass troops on Soviet frontiers]. *CJC*, 20 June 1941, p. 3 [u].

41.06.20D "The Closing of Parliament." [Petition in House of Commons for admission of Jewish refugees to Canada]. *CJC*, 20 June 1941, p. 3 [u].

41.06.20E "Another Premature Obituary." [Florence Friedlander Cohen dislikes Yiddish]. *CJC*, 20 June 1941, p. 4 [i].

41.06.20F "Mr. George Bernard Shaw and His World." [Political sympathies of George Bernard Shaw]. *CJC*, 20 June 1941, p. 4 [i].

41.06.24A "The End of the Honeymoon." [*See* 41.06.27D]. *KA*, 24 June 1941, p. 6 [s].

41.06.25A "Hitler's Apologia." [*See* 41.06.27E]. *KA*, 25 June 1941, p. 6 [s].

41.06.25B "The Ambiguous Allies." [*See* 41.06.27F]. *KA*, 25 June 1941, p. 6 [s].

41.06.27A "The Party Line." [Communist Party of America]. *CJC*, 27 June 1941, p. 3 [i].

41.06.27B "La Guardia's Prophecy." [Fiorello La Guardia on Adolf Hitler]. *CJC*, 27 June 1941, p. 3 [u].

41.06.27C "The Talmud Torah Graduation Exercises." [Graduation at Talmud Torah]. *CJC*, 27 June 1941, p. 3 [u].

41.06.27D "The End of the Honeymoon." [German invasion of Soviet Union]. *CJC*, 27 June 1941, p. 4 [i].

41.06.27E "Hitler's Apologia." [Adolf Hitler on war with Soviet Union]. *CJC*, 27 June 1941, p. 4 [i].

41.06.27F "The Ambiguous Allies." [Ambiguous systems of alliance during WWII]. *CJC*, 27 June 1941, p. 4 [i].

41.07.01A "Hitler: Defender of the Faith." [*See* 41.07.04F]. *KA*, 1 July 1941, p. 6 [s].

41.07.01B "Prayers in Moscow." [*See* 41.07.04C]. *KA*, 1 July 1941, p. 6 [s].

41.07.02A "The Vultures Gather." [*See* 41.07.04D]. *KA*, 2 July 1941, p. 6 [s].

41.07.02B "Vichy Breaks With Russia." [*See* 41.07.04E]. *KA*, 2 July 1941, p. 6 [s].

41.07.04A "Mr. Hoover and the War." [Herbert Hoover opposes alliance with Soviet Union]. *CJC*, 4 July 1941, p. 3 [u].

41.07.04B "The Federation of Jewish Philanthropies." [Federation of Jewish Philanthropies]. *CJC*, 4 July 1941, p. 3 [u].

41.07.04C "Prayers in Moscow." [Resurgence of religion in Soviet Union]. *CJC*, 4 July 1941, p. 4 [i].

41.07.04D "The Vultures Gather." [Soviet sympathy for Nazi anti-Semitism]. *CJC*, 4 July 1941, p. 4 [i].

41.07.04E "Vichy Breaks With Russia." [Vichy France severs relations with Soviet Union]. *CJC*, 4 July 1941, p. 4 [i].

41.07.04F "Hitler: Defender of the Faith." [Adolf Hitler claims to have attacked Soviet Union in order to defend religion]. *CJC*, 4 July 1941, p. 4 [i].

41.07.08A "The Crusader Unmasked." [*See* 41.07.11D]. *KA*, 8 July 1941, p. 6 [s].

41.07.09A "The Occupation of Iceland." [*See* 41.07.11E]. *KA*, 9 July 1941, p. 6 [s].

41.07.11A "The Vest Pocket War." [War between Ecuador and Peru]. *CJC*, 11 July 1941, p. 3 [u].

41.07.11B "The Forgotten Man." [John L. Lewis]. *CJC*, 11 July 1941, p. 3 [u].

41.07.11C "A Good Suggestion." [Suggestion to compile records of Nazi atrocities]. *CJC*, 11 July 1941, p. 3 [u].

41.07.11D "The Crusader Unmasked." [Adolf Hitler and religion]. *CJC*, 12 July 1941, p. 4 [i].

41.07.11E "The Occupation of Iceland." [U.S. forces occupy Iceland]. *CJC*, 11 July 1941, p. 4 [i].

41.07.15A "A Gentleman's Gentleman." [*See* 41.07.18D]. *KA*, 15 July 1941, p. 6 [s].

41.07.16A "Mr. Hanson's Reply." [*See* 41.07.18E]. *KA*, 16 July 1941, p. 6 [s].

41.07.18A "In Memory of Herzl." [Zionism of Theodor Herzl]. *CJC*, 18 July 1941, p. 3 [u].

41.07.18B "The Anglo-Soviet Pact." [Anglo-Soviet pact]. *CJC*, 18 July 1941, p. 3 [u].

41.07.18C " 'Do Your Worst and We Will Do Our Best.' " [Winston Churchill on the progress of the war]. *CJC*, 18 July 1941, p. 3 [u].

41.07.18D "A Gentleman's Gentleman." [P. G. Wodehouse co-operates with the Nazis]. *CJC*, 18 July 1941, p. 4 [i].

41.07.18E "Mr. Hanson's Reply." [Anti-Semitism of Ernest Perley]. *CJC*, 18 July 1941, p. 4 [i].

41.07.18F "Bastille Day." [Celebration of Bastille Day in Vichy France]. *CJC*, 18 July 1941, p. 4 [i].

41.07.23A "Lindbergh's Honor." [*See* 41.07.25B]. *KA*, 23 July 1941, p. 6 [s].

41.07.24A " 'They Missed The Boat'." [*See* 41.07.25C]. *KA*, 24 July 1941, p. 6 [s].

41.07.24B "Charlie Chaplin's Star." [*See* 41.07.25D]. *KA*, 24 July 1941, p. 6 [s].

41.07.24C "Where's Hermann?" [*See* 41.07.25E]. *KA*, 24 July 1941, p. 6 [s].

41.07.25A "The Case of Itzig Manger." [Itzig Manger]. *CJC*, 25 July 1941, p. 3 [u].

41.07.25B "Lindbergh's Honor." [Harold Ickes condemns Charles Lindbergh]. *CJC*, 25 July 1941, p. 4 [i].

41.07.25C " 'They Missed the Boat.' " [Two Nazis have difficulty getting back to Germany from U.S.]. *CJC*, 25 July 1941, p. 4 [i].

41.07.25D "Charlie Chaplin's Star." [Charlie Chaplin's *The Great Dictator* is shown in Soviet Union]. *CJC*, 25 July 1941, p. 4 [i].

41.07.25E "Where's Hermann?" [Hermann Goering disappears from the public eye]. *CJC*, 25 July 1941, p. 4 [i].

41.07.29A " 'V'." [*See* 41.08.01C]. *KA*, 29 July 1941, p. 6 [s].

41.07.30A "The Embracing Kimono." [*See* 41.08.01D]. *KA*, 30 July 1941, p. 6 [s].

41.07.30B "A German Discovery." [*See* 41.08.01E]. *KA*, 30 July 1941, p. 6 [s].

41.08.01A "The Pacific Isolationists." [American isolationism]. *CJC*, 1 Aug. 1941, p. 3 [i].

41.08.01B "Sessional Report." [Winston Churchill on the progress of the war]. *CJC*, 1 Aug. 1941, p. 3 [u].

41.08.01C " 'V'." [Resistance in WWII]. *CJC*, 1 Aug. 1941, p. 4 [i].

41.08.01D "The Embracing Kimono." [Japanese cabinet shuffle]. *CJC*, 1 Aug. 1941, p. 4 [i].

41.08.01E "A German Discovery." [Nazi propaganda]. *CJC*, 1 Aug. 1941, p. 4 [i].

41.08.07A "Dr. Weizmann's Invention." [*See* 41.08.08E]. *KA*, 7 Aug. 1941, p. 6 [s].

41.08.07B "The Son of Tolstoy." [*See* 41.08.08F]. *KA*, 7 Aug. 1941, p. 6 [s].

41.08.08A "The Fuehrer Colonizes." [Polish Jews sent to Madagascar]. *CJC*, 8 Aug. 1941, p. 3 [u].

41.08.08B "Warning to Japan." [Britain warns Japan against intervention in Thailand]. *CJC*, 8 Aug. 1941, p. 4 [i].

41.08.08C "Arma Virumque Cano." [Italian cowardice]. *CJC*, 8 Aug. 1941, p. 3 [i].

41.08.08D "The Spread of Culture." [Germans burn books in Soviet Union]. *CJC*, 8 Aug. 1941, p. 4 [i].

41.08.08E "Dr. Weizmann's Invention." [Rumor of Chaim Weizmann's having invented a new explosive]. *CJC*, 8 Aug. 1941, p. 4 [i].

41.08.08F "The Son of Tolstoy." [Lev Lvovich Tolstoy on war against fascism]. *CJC*, 8 Aug. 1941, p. 4 [i].

41.08.08G "A Cause Celebre and a Farthing Reputation." [British fascist sues the *New York Times*]. *CJC*, 8 Aug. 1941, p. 4 [i].

41.08.08H "Freedom of Religion in Russia." [Joseph Stalin allegedly promises to emancipate religion in Soviet Union]. *CJC*, 8 Aug. 1941, p. 4 [i].

41.08.12A "Letter to Benito Mussolini." [*See* 41.08.15C]. *KA*, 12 Aug. 1941, p. 6 [s].

41.08.15A "The Capitulation Complete." [Collaboration of Vichy France]. *CJC*, 15 Aug. 1941, p. 3 [u].

41.08.15B "Davis on Cudahy." [Joseph Davis on John Cudahy]. *CJC*, 15 Aug. 1941, p. 3 [u].

41.08.15C "Letter to Benito Mussolini." [Open letter to Benito Mussolini on the death of his son]. *CJC*, 15 Aug. 1941, p. 4 [i].

41.08.15D "Persian Interlude." [Nazi activity fails in Iran]. *CJC*, 15 Aug. 1941, p. 4 [i].

41.08.15E "Silk Stockings." [Silk rationing]. *CJC*, 15 Aug. 1941, p. 4 [i].

41.08.19A "The Eight Points." [*See* 41.08.22D]. *KA*, 19 July 1941, p. 6 [s].

41.08.20A "Midsummer Salesman." [*See* 41.08.22E]. *KA*, 20 Aug. 1941, p. 6 [s].

41.08.20B "Tale of a Hat." [*See* 41.08.22F]. *KA*, 20 Aug. 1941, p. 6 [s].

41.08.22A "Well Done, Kamsack Jewry." [Canadian Jewish military participation]. *CJC*, 22 Aug. 1941, p. 3 [u].

41.08.22B "Premier King Flies to Britain." [William Lyon Mackenzie King in England]. *CJC*, 22 Aug. 1941, p. 3 [u].

41.08.22C "The Howling Senators." [American isolationism]. *CJC*, 22 Aug. 1941, p. 3 [u].

41.08.22D "The Eight Points." [The Atlantic Charter]. *CJC*, 22 Aug. 1941, p. 4 [i].

41.08.22E "Midsummer Salesman." [Germans in Iran]. *CJC*, 22 Aug. 1941, p. 4 [i].

41.08.22F "Tale of a Hat." [Anglo-American relations]. *CJC*, 22 Aug. 1941, p. 4 [i].

41.08.26A "Collaboration With The New Order." [*See* 41.08.29D]. *KA*, 26 Aug. 1941, p. 6 [s].

41.08.27A "Churchill's Speech." [*See* 41.08.29E]. *KA*, 27 Aug. 1941, p. 6 [s].

41.08.29A "Philanthropies, Amalgamated." [Amalgamation of Jewish philanthropic agencies in Montreal]. *CJC*, 29 Aug. 1941, p. 3 [u].

41.08.29B "Incidents in the Ukraine." [War in Soviet Union]. *CJC*, 29 Aug. 1941, p. 3 [u].

41.08.29C "Black Sheep or Persian Lamb?" [War in Iran]. *CJC*, 29 Aug. 1941, p. 3 [u].

41.08.29D "Collaboration With The New Order." [Collaboration with or resistance to Nazism]. *CJC*, 29 Aug. 1941, p. 4 [i].

41.08.29E "Churchill's Speech." [Speech of Winston Churchill]. *CJC*, 29 Aug. 1941, p. 4 [i].

41.09.02A "The Fuehrer and the Duce." [*See* 41.09.05E]. *KA*, 2 Sept. 1941, p. 6 [s].

41.09.03A "Ibn Sheik-Al-Gruber." [*See* 41.09.05C]. *KA*, 3 Sept. 1941, p. 6 [s].

41.09.03B "The Nazi Crusade." [*See* 41.09.05D]. *KA*, 3 Sept. 1941, p. 6 [s].

41.09.05A "Sic Semper Tyrannis." [Assassination attempt on Pierre Laval]. *CJC*, 5 Sept. 1941, p. 3 [i].

41.09.05B "Thyssen Does Us A Favor!" [Fritz Thyssen explains Adolf Hitler's anti-Semitism]. *CJC*, 5 Sept. 1941, p. 3 [u].

41.09.05C "Ibn Sheik-Al-Gruber." [Fascists woo the Muslim world]. *CJC*, 5 Sept. 1941, p. 4 [i].

41.09.05D "The Nazi Crusade." [Resistance to Nazism]. *CJC*, 5 Sept. 1941, p. 4 [i].

41.09.05E "The Fuehrer and the Duce." [Meeting between Adolf Hitler and Benito Mussolini]. *CJC*, 5 Sept. 1941, p. 4 [i].

41.09.09A "Mackenzie King's Address." [*See* 41.09.12E]. *KA*, 9 Sept. 1941, p. 6 [s].

41.09.09B "The Destroyer and the Sub." [*See* 41.09.12F]. *KA*, 9 Sept. 1941, p. 6 [s].

41.09.10A "Kitchener or Berlin?" [*See* 41.09.12D]. *KA*, 10 Sept. 1941, p. 6 [s].

41.09.12A "Reconsecration Week." [Jews reconsecrate their faith]. *CJC*, 12 Sept. 1941, p. 3 [u].

41.09.12B "M. Henri Torres." [Henri Torrès on Vichy France]. *CJC*, 12 Sept. 1941, p. 3 [u].

41.09.12C "The American Zionist Convention." [Forty-fourth American Zionist Convention]. *CJC*, 12 Sept. 1941, p. 3 [u].

41.09.12D "Kitchener or Berlin?" [Desecration of Jewish graves in Kitchener]. *CJC*, 12 Sept. 1941, p. 4 [i].

41.09.12E "Mackenzie King's Address." [Speech of William Lyon Mackenzie King]. *CJC*, 12 Sept. 1941, p. 4 [i].

41.09.12F "The Destroyer and the Sub." [German sub attacks a U.S. destroyer]. *CJC*, 12 Sept. 1941, p. 4 [i].

41.09.19A "The New Year." [Rosh Hashanah]. *CJC*, 19 Sept. 1941, p. 5 [u].

41.09.26A "The Moving Picture Industry." [U.S. senators investigate the American film industry]. *CJC*, 26 Sept. 1941, p. 3 [u].

41.09.26B "Lord Warden of Cinque Ports." [Winston Churchill is appointed Lord Warden of the Cinque Ports]. *CJC*, 26 Sept. 1941, p. 3 [u].

41.09.26C "Shah! Shah!" [Shah disappears with valuable jewels]. *CJC*, 26 Sept. 1941, p. 3 [u].

41.09.26D "He is Not Alone!" [Charles Lindbergh]. *CJC*, 26 Sept. 1941, p. 4 [u].

41.09.26E "The Fall of Kiev." [War in Soviet Union]. *CJC*, 26 Sept. 1941, p. 4 [i].

41.09.30A "The Government of General De Gaulle." [*See* 41.10.03C]. *KA*, 30 Sept. 1941, p. 8 [s].

41.09.30B "Palestine and Russia." [*See* 41.10.03D]. *KA*, 30 Sept. 1941, p. 8 [s].

41.10.03A "Bloodied But Unbowed." [Reinhard Heydrich in occupied Czechoslovakia]. *CJC*, 3 Oct. 1941, p. 3 [u].

41.10.03B "Mutual Life." [Gerald Nye investigates Lewis Douglas]. *CJC*, 3 Oct. 1941, p. 3 [u].

41.10.03C "The Government of General De Gaulle." [Government-in-exile of Charles de Gaulle]. *CJC*, 3 Oct. 1941, p. 4 [i].

41.10.03D "Palestine and Russia." [Soviet Jewry]. *CJC*, 3 Oct. 1941, p. 4 [i].

41.10.03E "The Yellow Badge." [Jews are forced to wear yellow badges]. *CJC*, 3 Oct. 1941, p. 4 [i].

41.10.10A "Menachem Ussishkin." [Death of Menachem Ussishkin]. *CJC*, 10 Oct. 1941, p. 3 [u].

41.10.10B "Mr. Justice Brandeis." [Death of Louis Brandeis]. *CJC*, 10 Oct. 1941, p. 3 [u].

41.10.10C "Streicher's Shabbos Goy." [Germans sympathetic to Jews are dubbed "shabbos goyim"]. *CJC*, 10 Oct. 1941, p. 4 [i].

41.10.10D "Hess Won't Eat!" [Hunger strike of Rudolf Hess]. *CJC*, 10 Oct. 1941, p. 4 [i].

41.10.17A "The Combined Jewish Appeal." [Combined Jewish Appeal]. *CJC*, 17 Oct. 1941, p. 3 [u].

41.10.17B "Hitler's Whistling." [Speech of Adolf Hitler]. *CJC*, 17 Oct. 1941, p. 4 [i].

41.10.17C "The New Canadian Loyalists." [War pamphlet by John Gibbon]. *CJC*, 17 Oct. 1941, p. 4 [i].

41.10.24A "The Montreal Jewish Branch of the Canadian Red Cross." [Work of the Jewish branch of the Canadian Red Cross]. *CJC*, 24 Oct. 1941, p. 3 [u].

41.10.24B "Need There Be Another Lusitania?" [Germans attack U.S. ships]. *CJC*, 24 Oct. 1941, p. 3 [u].

41.10.24C "A Hundred For One." [Nazis execute one hundred French people in revenge for death of one German]. *CJC*, 24 Oct. 1941, p. 3 [u].

41.10.24D "The Morticians Strike." [Morticians demand shorter hours]. *CJC*, 24 Oct. 1941, p. 4 [i].

41.10.24E "Wheeler's War." [Anti-Semitism of Burton Wheeler]. *CJC*, 24 Oct. 1941, p. 4 [i].

41.10.24F "And Wonders Will Not Cease." [British hold a trade conference in Jerusalem]. *CJC*, 24 Oct. 1941, p. 4 [i].

41.10.31A "History Made!" [Fundraising for the Combined Jewish Appeal]. *CJC*, 31 Oct. 1941, p. 3 [u].

41.10.31B "An Academy of Learning." [Refugee yeshiva scholars arrive in Montreal]. *CJC*, 31 Oct. 1941, p. 3 [u].

41.10.31C "The Slippery Mufti." [The Mufti in Rome]. *CJC*, 31 Oct. 1941, p. 3 [u].

41.10.31D " 'That Jewish War'." [Adolf Hitler as a threat to all humanity]. *CJC*, 31 Oct. 1941, p. 4 [i].

41.10.31E "The First Shot — The Last Shot." [Speech of Franklin Delano Roosevelt]. *CJC*, 31 Oct. 1941, p. 4 [i].

41.10.31F "The Doomsday Record." [Governments-in-exile determine to record Nazi war crimes]. *CJC*, 31 Oct. 1941, p. 4 [i].

41.11.07A "The Little Flower." [Re-election of Fiorello La Guardia]. *CJC*, 7 Nov. 1941, p. 3 [u].

41.11.07B "Lo, the Poor Lindyan." [Charles Lindbergh and American isolationism]. *CJC*, 7 Nov. 1941, p. 3 [u].

41.11.07C "German Science." [Science in Nazi Germany]. *CJC*, 7 Nov. 1941, p. 3 [u].

41.11.07D "The Balfour Declaration." [Fate of Jews in WWII]. *CJC*, 7 Nov. 1941, p. 4 [i].

41.11.07E "Stop, Thief!" [Germans accuse U.S. of attacking their U-boats]. *CJC*, 7 Nov. 1941, p. 4 [i].

41.11.07F "The Thorough Sadists." [Jews are forced to wear yellow stars on their nightclothes]. *CJC*, 7 Nov. 1941, p. 4 [i].

41.11.14A "Weizmann's Plea and Protest." [British government's refusal to allow Jewish army in Palestine]. *CJC*, 14 Nov. 1941, p. 3 [i].

41.11.14B "Stalin Speaks." [Speech of Joseph Stalin]. *CJC*, 14 Nov. 1941, p. 4 [i].

41.11.14C "Kultur in the Reich." [Plays of Schiller are banned by the Nazis]. *CJC*, 14 Nov. 1941, p. 4 [i].

41.11.14D "Churchill's Tribute." [Speech of Winston Churchill]. *CJC*, 14 Nov. 1941, p. 4 [i].

41.11.21A "Goebbels' Ten Points." [Nazi ideology and the Jews]. *CJC*, 21 Nov. 1941, p. 3 [u].

41.11.21B "A General Falls." [France during WWII]. *CJC*, 21 Nov. 1941, p. 3 [u].

41.11.21C "Stalin Talks of God." [Joseph Stalin toasts Franklin Delano Roosevelt]. *CJC*, 21 Nov. 1941, p. 3 [u].

41.11.21D "A Blue Print For A Temple of Thor." [Alfred Rosenberg, religion, and Nazism]. *CJC*, 21 Nov. 1941, p. 4 [s].

41.11.28A "Neither a Saint Nor Just." [Anti-Semitic editorial in *Le Canada*]. *CJC*, 28 Nov. 1941, p. 3 [u].

41.11.28B "The Samuel Bronfman Gift to McGill." [Samuel Bronfman endowment to McGill University]. *CJC*, 28 Nov. 1941, p. 3 [u].

41.12.05A "Census of Tragedy." [Jewish casualties in WWII]. *CJC*, 5 Dec. 1941, p. 3 [u].

41.12.05B "Men and Machines." [Britain matches Germany in war machinery]. *CJC*, 5 Dec. 1941, p. 3 [u].

41.12.05C "Roosevelt Talks Turkey." [U.S. foreign policy]. *CJC*, 5 Dec. 1941, p. 3 [u].

41.12.05D "Max Nordau: A Tribune to His People." [Review of *Max Nordau to His People*]. *CJC*, 5 Dec. 1941, p. 4 [s].

41.12.12A "The Maccabean Lesson." [Inspiration of the Chanukah story]. *CJC*, 12 Dec. 1941, p. 3 [u].

41.12.12B "The Sun Comes Up Like Thunder . . ." [Attack on Pearl Harbor]. *CJC*, 12 Dec. 1941, p. 3 [u].

41.12.12C "Notes on a 'Court Jew'." [Jerome Frank and assimilation]. *CJC*, 12 Dec. 1941, pp. 4, 15 [s].

41.12.19A "Hitler's News." [Adolf Hitler takes a rest at Berchtesgaden]. *CJC*, 19 Dec. 1941, p. 3 [u].

41.12.19B "The Anti-Semitic Orgy Continues." [Germans retaliate against U.S. entry into the war]. *CJC*, 19 Dec. 1941, p. 3 [u].

41.12.19C "The Decencies Had Perished with the Stukas." [Review of *Dunkirk* by E.J. Pratt]. *CJC*, 19 Dec. 1941, p. 6 [s].

41.12.26A "The Defense of Hong Kong." [Defence of Hong Kong]. *CJC*, 26 Dec. 1941, p. 3 [u].

41.12.26B "Churchill in America." [Meeting of Winston Churchill and Franklin Delano Roosevelt]. *CJC*, 26 Dec. 1941, p. 3 [u].

41.12.26C "General von Hitler." [Adolf Hitler assumes full military command of the German armed forces]. *CJC*, 26 Dec. 1941, p. 3 [u].

41.12.26D "Arms and the Man." [Humorous reflections on the war]. *CJC*, 26 Dec. 1941, p. 4 [s].

42.01.02A "A Continent Welcomes Churchill." [Winston Churchill visits North America]. *CJC*, 2 Jan. 1942, p. 3 [u].

42.01.02B "Ghandi [*sic*] and Einstein." [Philosophies of Mahatma Gandhi and Albert Einstein]. *CJC*, 2 Jan. 1942, p. 3 [u].

42.01.02C "Of Canadian Unity." [Racism in Canada]. *CJC*, 2 Jan. 1942, p. 3 [u].

42.01.02D "Rabbi Steinberg's Four Principles." [A statement of Jewish principles]. *CJC*, 2 Jan. 1942, p. 4 [s].

42.01.09A "The Canadian Jewish Congress in Plenary Session." [Canadian Jewish Congress, fifth plenary session]. *CJC*, 9 Jan. 1942, p. 3 [u].

42.01.09B "Pinchas Rutenberg." [Death of Pinchas Rutenberg]. *CJC*, 9 Jan. 1942, p. 3 [u].

42.01.09C "The Late Abraham Raginsky." [Death of Abraham Raginsky]. *CJC*, 9 Jan. 1942, p. 3 [u].

42.01.09D "Census of Misunderstanding." [Results of a questionnaire on Judaism]. *CJC*, 9 Jan. 1942, p. 4 [s].

42.01.16A "The Fifth Plenary Session of the Canadian Jewish Congress." [Canadian Jewish Congress, fifth plenary session]. *CJC*, 16 Jan. 1942, p. 3 [u].

42.01.16B "The Talmud Torah Campaign." [Fundraising for Talmud Torahs]. *CJC*, 16 Jan. 1942, p. 3 [u].

42.01.23A "The Canadian Red Cross Russian Appeal." [Fundraising to support the Soviet war effort]. *CJC*, 23 Jan. 1942, p. 3 [u].

42.01.23B "The Sick Generals." [Illness of German generals]. *CJC*, 23 Jan. 1942, p. 3 [u].

42.01.23C "Report from Warsaw." [Religion in the Warsaw Ghetto]. *CJC*, 23 Jan. 1942, p. 3 [u].

42.01.23D "Molotov Speaks Out." [Vyacheslav Molotov notes special mistreatment of Jews by Nazis]. *CJC*, 23 Jan. 1942, p. 3 [u].

42.01.23E "The Recantation of Henry Ford." [Henry Ford recants anti-Semitic statements]. *CJC*, 23 Jan. 1942, pp. 4, 16 [s].

42.01.30A "Behind the New York Times." [Anti-Zionist editorial in the *New York Times*]. *CJC*, 30 Jan. 1942, p. 3 [u].

42.01.30B "A Dubious Ally." [Otto Strasser]. *CJC*, 30 Jan. 1942, p. 3 [u].

42.01.30C "The International Club 'Twenty-One'." [Ninth Pan-American Conference]. *CJC*, 30 Jan. 1942, p. 4 [s].

42.02.06A "Bacteriological Warfare." [Possibility of Germany resorting to germ warfare]. *CJC*, 6 Feb. 1942, p. 3 [u].

42.02.06B "J'Accuse." [Leon Blum]. *CJC*, 6 Feb. 1942, p. 3 [u].

42.02.06C "Hitler's Ninth Year." [Adolf Hitler's ninth year in power]. *CJC*, 6 Feb. 1942, p. 3 [u].

42.02.06D "Robinson Jeffers — Poet-Fascist?" [Review of *Be Angry at the Sun* by Robinson Jeffers]. *CJC*, 6 Feb. 1942, p. 4 [s].

42.02.13A "The Second Victory Loan." [Canada launches a second victory loan]. *CJC*, 13 Feb. 1942, p. 3 [u].

42.02.13B "Peace As An Instrument of War." [Cartel of industrialists favour a negotiated peace between Germany and the Allies]. *CJC*, 13 Feb. 1942, p. 3 [u].

42.02.13C "German Psychological Warfare." [German psychological warfare]. *CJC*, 13 Feb. 1942, p. 4 [s].

42.02.20A "Revenge At Riom." [Trial of deposed French leaders]. *CJC*, 20 Feb. 1942, p. 3 [u].

42.02.20B "Mr. Cameron Recants." [W. J. Cameron recants anti-Semitic statement]. *CJC*, 20 Feb. 1942, p. 3 [u].

42.02.20C "Governor Lehman's Address." [Herbert H. Lehman advocates U.S. involvement in WWII]. *CJC*, 20 Feb. 1942, p. 3 [u].

42.02.27A "The Long Voyage Home — The S.S. Struma." [Plight of Jewish refugees]. *CJC*, 27 Feb. 1942, p. 3 [u].

42.02.27B "Stefan Zweig." [Stefan Zweig]. *CJC*, 27 Feb. 1942, p. 3 [u].

42.02.27C "The Feast of Purim." [Relevance of the Purim story]. *CJC*, 27 Feb. 1942, p. 3 [u].

42.02.27D "The Lesson of Normandy." [Accidental destruction of the Normandie]. *CJC*, 27 Feb. 1942, p. 4 [s].

42.02.27E " 'La Derniere Classe'." [French resistance vs. collaboration]. *CJC*, 27 Feb. 1942, p. 4 [s].

42.02.27F "The Trade in Peace." [Peace advocates congregate in Stockholm]. *CJC*, 27 Feb. 1942, p. 4 [s].

42.02.27G "Munich: Not Only Dead but Buried." [Winston Churchill eliminates "appeasers" from his cabinet]. *CJC*, 27 Feb. 1942, p. 4 [s].

42.03.06A " 'The Nation' Changes Its Policy." [Pro-Zionist articles by Reinhold Niebuhr]. *CJC*, 6 Mar. 1942, p. 3 [u].

42.03.06B "Note on Jewish Hostages." [Anti-Semitism]. *CJC*, 6 Mar. 1942, p. 3 [u].

42.03.06C "Mr. Harvey Golden." [Harvey Golden resigns as director of YMHA]. *CJC*, 6 Mar. 1942, p. 3 [u].

42.03.06D "Zweig's Hail and Farewell." [Review of *Amerigo* by Stefan Zweig]. *CJC*, 6 Mar. 1942, p. 4 [s].

42.03.13A "The Hong Kong Atrocities." [Atrocities perpetrated by the Japanese in Hong Kong]. *CJC*, 13 Mar. 1942, p. 3 [u].

42.03.13B "A Strange Prejudice." [Jean-François Pouliot opposes proposed law to aid returning soldiers]. *CJC*, 13 Mar. 1942, p. 3 [u].

42.03.13C "Lord Cranborn's Answer." [Lord Cranborn on the *S.S. Struma* disaster]. *CJC*, 13 Mar. 1942, p. 3 [u].

42.03.13D "A Great Talmudist." [Rabbi Pinchas Hirshprung]. *CJC*, 13 Mar. 1942, p. 4 [s].

42.03.20A "Interim Report: One Hundred Thousand Dead." [Nazi genocide of Jews]. *CJC*, 20 Mar. 1942, p. 3 [u].

42.03.20B "Arm Chair Critics." [Franklin Delano Roosevelt answers arm-chair critics of Allied strategy]. *CJC*, 20 Mar. 1942, p. 3 [u].

42.03.20C "Interview With A Conscience." [Racism, WWII, and the Jewish refugee problem]. *CJC*, 20 Mar. 1942, p. 4 [s].

42.03.27A "The Fifth Column on Parade!" [League for the Defence of Canada]. *CJC*, 27 Mar. 1942, p. 3 [u].

42.04.01A "Some Passover Reflections." [Reflections on Passover and world events]. *CJC*, 1 Apr. 1942, p. 3 [u].

42.04.01B "The Art of the Passover Haggadah." [Haggadah illustrations]. *CJC*, 1 Apr. 1942, pp. 6–7 [s].

42.04.01C "The S.E.P. Mounts Again." [*Saturday Evening Post* on Jews]. *CJC*, 1 Apr. 1942, p. 11 [s].

42.04.10A "The United Palestine Appeal." [United Palestine Appeal]. *CJC*, 10 Apr. 1942, p. 3 [u].

42.04.10B "Nazism and Fascism." [Italians excluded from a New York music festival]. *CJC*, 10 Apr. 1942, p. 3 [u].

42.04.17A "And High Time Too!" [Fifth column publications in U.S.]. *CJC*, 17 Apr. 1942, p. 3 [u].

42.04.17B "The Hebrew Educational Conference." [Hebrew educational conference in Montreal]. *CJC*, 17 Apr. 1942, p. 3 [u].

42.04.17C "Rabbi Ephraim Levy." [Departure of Rabbi Ephraim Levy from Montreal]. *CJC*, 17 Apr. 1942, p. 3, [u].

42.04.17D "The War Without a Name." [Franklin Delano Roosevelt seeks a name for WWII]. *CJC*, 17 Apr. 1942, p. 4 [s].

42.04.24A "The Plebiscite." [Plebiscite on conscription]. *CJC*, 24 Apr. 1942, p. 3 [u].

42.04.24B "Hitler's Birthday." [Adolf Hitler's fifty-third birthday]. *CJC*, 24 Apr. 1942, p. 3 [u].

42.04.24C "A Symphony of Three Cities." [Vichy, Delhi, and Tokyo]. *CJC*, 24 Apr. 1942, p. 4 [s].

42.05.01A "The Plebiscite Results." [Results of the Canadian plebiscite on conscription]. *CJC*, 1 May 1942, p. 3 [u].

42.05.01B "There Are Two Fronts." [Adolf Hitler is forced to fight on two fronts]. *CJC*, 1 May 1942, p. 3 [u].

42.05.01C "Oil for the Tanks of Serbia." [Serbs trade Italian prisoners for oil]. *CJC*, 1 May 1942, p. 3 [u].

42.05.01D "Ghandi's [*sic*] Pacificism." [Mahatma Gandhi objects to presence of Allied soldiers in India]. *CJC*, 1 May 1942, p. 3 [u].

42.05.01E "The Fuehrer Furioso." [Speech of Adolf Hitler]. *CJC*, 1 May 1942, p. 4 [s].

42.05.08A "Madagascar — The Japs Anticipated." [British occupy Madagascar]. *CJC*, 8 May 1942, p. 3 [u].

42.05.08B "The Hebrew Free Loan Association [Hebrew Free Loan Association]. *CJC*, 8 May 1942, p. 3 [u].

42.05.08C "A Word in its Place." [James Coldwell on Otto Strasser]. *CJC*, 8 May 1942, p. 3 [u].

42.05.08D "That Consular Service." [Prejudice in the granting of visas in Europe]. *CJC*, 8 May 1942, p. 3 [u].

42.05.08E "Non-violent and Non-co-operative Resistance." [Mahatama Gandhi]. *CJC*, 8 May 1942, p. 4 [s].

42.05.08F "Stalin's May Day Speech." [Speech of Joseph Stalin]. *CJC*, 8 May 1942, p. 4 [s].

42.05.08G "Rendezvous at Salzburg." [Adolf Hitler and Benito Mussolini meet at Salzburg]. *CJC*, 8 May 1942, p. 4 [s].

42.05.15A "B'nai B'rith Convention." [Ninetieth B'nai Brith Convention]. *CJC*, 15 May 1942, p. 3 [u].

42.05.15B "The Zionist Conference." [Emergency Zionist conference in New York]. *CJC*, 15 May 1942, p. 3 [u].

42.05.15C "The Last of the Badchonim — Shloime Schmulevitz." [Shloime Schmulevitz]. *CJC*, 15 May 1942, p. 4 [s].

42.05.22A "The Feast of Pentecost." [Shavuoth]. *CJC*, 22 May 1942, p. 3 [u].

42.05.22B "The Appeal of the Yeshivoth." [Yeshivah education]. *CJC*, 22 May 1942, p. 3 [u].

42.05.22C "The Release of Earl Browder." [Release of Earl Browder from prison]. *CJC*, 22 May 1942, p. 3 [u].

42.05.22D "Saadyah Gaon." [Saadyah Gaon]. *CJC*, 22 May 1942, p. 4 [s].

42.05.29A "PM's Timely Campaign." [*PM* Magazine campaigns against racism in U.S.]. *CJC*, 29 May 1942, p. 3 [u].

42.05.29B "Who Will Protect the Protector?" [Assassination attempt on Reinhard Heydrich]. *CJC*, 29 May 1942, p. 3 [u].

42.05.29C "Dr. Mordecai M. Kaplan." [Sixtieth birthday of Mordecai Kaplan]. *CJC*, 29 May 1942, p. 3 [u].

42.05.29D "Vice-President Wallace's Address." [Speech of Henry Wallace]. *CJC*, 29 May 1942, p. 4 [s].

42.05.29E "Bar Cochba in Russia." [Increased tolerance towards Jews in Soviet Union]. *CJC*, 29 May 1942, p. 4 [s].

42.05.29F "Mr. Rene Chaloult." [Speech of René Chaloult]. *CJC*, 29 May 1942, p. 4 [i].

42.05.29G "Paul Robeson and the Berditchever." [Paul Robeson sings the "Kaddish" of Levi Yitschok of Berditchev]. *CJC*, 29 May 1942, p. 4 [s].

42.06.05A "The Air Force Pays a Debt." [Bombing of Cologne and Essen]. *CJC*, 5 June 1942, p. 3 [u].

42.06.05B "The Medines, The Shrybmans, The Zareikins." [Jewish military participation]. *CJC*, 5 June 1942, p. 3 [u].

42.06.05C "Polish-Jewish Relations." [Polish National Council rejects proposal for improved treatment of Jews]. *CJC*, 5 June 1942, p. 3 [u].

42.06.05D "The Flies and the Flypaper." [Review of *The Moon is Down* by John Steinbeck]. *CJC*, 5 June 1942, pp. 4, 16 [s].

42.06.12A "The Reserve Army Campaign." [Recruiting for the Reserve Army]. *CJC*, 12 June 1942, p. 3 [u].

42.06.12B "Lord Wedgwood's Broadcast and its Aftermath." [Lord Wedgwood on British foreign policy on Palestine]. *CJC*, 12 June 1942, p. 3 [u].

42.06.12C "The Late Abraham Goldberg." [Death of Abraham Goldberg]. *CJC*, 12 June 1942, p. 3 [u].

42.06.12D "Your Picture in the Paper." [Objectionable use of photographs by the press]. *CJC*, 12 June 1942, p. 4 [s].

42.06.19A "Goebbels' Threat." [Joseph Goebbels threatens retaliation against Jews for R.A.F. raids]. *CJC*, 19 June 1942, p. 3 [u].

42.06.19B "A New Edition of the MacMahon Letters." [Zionists fear repeat of MacMahon letters incident]. *CJC*, 19 June 1942, p. 3 [u].

42.06.19C "Yellow Anti-Semitism." [Japanese anti-Semitism]. *CJC*, 19 June 1942, p. 3 [u].

42.06.19D "Remember Lidice!" [Nazi destruction of Lidice, Czechoslovakia]. *CJC*, 19 June 1942, p. 4 [s].

42.06.26A "The Canadian Budget." [Wartime budget of James Ilsley]. *CJC*, 26 June 1942, p. 3 [u].

42.06.26B "The Disaster of Tobruk." [German victory at Tobruk]. *CJC*, 26 June 1942, p. 3 [u].

42.06.26C "Pierre von Laval." [Collaboration of Pierre Laval]. *CJC*, 26 June 1942, p. 3 [u].

42.06.26D "The Battle of Armageddon." [Strategic importance of the Near East]. *CJC*, 26 June 1942, p. 4 [s].

42.07.03A "Seventy-Five Years of Confederation." [Seventy-fifth anniversary of Canadian Confederation]. *CJC*, 3 July 1942, p. 3 [u].

42.07.03B "Herzl Day." [Anniversary of the death of Theodor Herzl]. *CJC*, 3 July 1942, p. 3 [u].

42.07.03C "Hitler Diagnosed." [Diagnosis of Adolf Hitler's mental condition]. *CJC*, 3 July 1942, p. 3 [u].

42.07.03D "Is This the Jew the Authors Drew?" [Jews in literature]. *CJC*, 3 July 1942, pp. 4, 16 [s].

42.07.10A "The Nazis Change Their Minds." [Reports of Jews in the German army]. *CJC*, 10 July 1942, p. 3 [u].

42.07.10B "Emil Ludwig's War Objectives." [Emil Ludwig on Allied war objectives]. *CJC*, 10 July 1942, p. 3 [u].

42.07.10C "On the Middle Eastern Front." [Need for a Jewish army in Palestine]. *CJC*, 10 July 1942, p. 3 [u].

42.07.10D "Bialik Thou Shouldst Be Living at This Hour." [Chaim Nachman Bialik as a great Jewish leader]. *CJC*, 10 July 1942, p. 4 [s].

42.07.17A "The Act of Mapmaking." [Columbia University professor designs a projected world map based on Allied victory]. *CJC*, 17 July 1942, p. 3 [u].

42.07.17B "The Chinese Example." [China calls up six million new soldiers]. *CJC*, 17 July 1942, p. 3 [u].

42.07.17C "Bar Hacheim." [Bastille Day is celebrated in Palestine to commemorate French soldiers killed in Lybia]. *CJC*, 17 July 1942, p. 3 [u].

42.07.17D "The Mystery of the Mislaid Conscience." [Need for a voice to speak out for Jews]. *CJC*, 17 July 1942, p. 4 [s].

42.07.24A "Tisha B'Av Sabbath of Consolation." [Tisha B'Av]. *CJC*, 24 July 1942, p. 3 [u].

42.07.24B "A Distinguished Gift." [Samuel Bronfman and Joseph Simard donate a sumbarine chaser to Canada]. *CJC*, 24 July 1942, p. 3 [u].

42.07.24C "The Voice of World Leadership." [Allied rally at Madison Square Gardens]. *CJC*, 24 July 1942, p. 3 [u].

42.07.24D "Nothing to Eat But Food." [Gastronomic themes in Canadian Jewish journalism]. *CJC*, 24 July 1942, p. 4 [s].

42.07.31A "The Notorious Twenty-Eight." [U.S. Dept. of Justice arrests fifth columnists]. *CJC*, 31 July 1942, p. 3 [u].

42.07.31B "A Logical Report." [Canada lifts ban on Communist Party]. *CJC*, 31 July 1942, p. 3 [u].

42.07.31C "Another Expulsion." [Jews are expelled from France]. *CJC*, 31 July 1942, p. 3 [u].

42.08.07A "The Waldo Frank Affair." [Waldo Frank is declared persona non grata in Argentina]. *CJC*, 7 Aug. 1942, p. 3 [u].

42.08.07B "A Voice from the Haunted House." [Nancy Astor criticizes Soviet war effort]. *CJC*, 7 Aug. 1942, p. 3 [u].

42.08.07C "Typical German Barbarism." [German women imprisoned for harbouring Jewish children]. *CJC*, 7 Aug. 1942, p. 3 [u].

42.08.07D "The Moulting Eagle." [Charles Lindbergh testifies at trial of William Pelley]. *CJC*, 7 Aug. 1942, p. 3 [u].

42.08.07E "From One Vegetarian to Another." [Stafford Cripps addresses Mahatma Gandhi's policies]. *CJC*, 7 Aug. 1942, p. 4 [s].

42.08.07F "Bible Stories and Flash Gordon." [Proposal to convert Bible stories into comic strips]. *CJC*, 7 Aug. 1942, p. 4 [s].

42.08.07G " 'The Thunderbolt' — Without Lightning." [Fascist newspaper in Canada]. *CJC*, 7 Aug. 1942, p. 4 [s].

42.08.07H "Dr. Weizmann and Synthetic Rubber." [Chaim Weizmann is rumoured to be at work on inventing synthetic rubber]. *CJC*, 7 Aug. 1942, p. 4 [s].

42.08.14A "From Silver Shirt to Convict Suit." [Conviction of William Dudley Pelley]. *CJC*, 14 Aug. 1942, p. 3 [u].

42.08.14B "On the Other Hand . . ." [Fascism and communism in Canada]. *CJC*, 14 Aug. 1942, p. 3 [u].

42.08.14C "A Wrong Partially Corrected." [Creation of a Jewish-Arab regiment in Palestine]. *CJC*, 14 Aug. 1942, p. 3 [u].

42.08.14D "The Iron Cavalry." [Suggestion to melt down statues for scrap metal]. *CJC*, 14 Aug. 1942, p. 3 [u].

42.08.14E "Shall Never the Twain Meet?" [Nehru's criticism of Western life]. *CJC*, 14 Aug. 1942, p. 4 [s].

42.08.21A "A Historic Meeting: Churchill and Stalin." [Meeting between Winston Churchill and Joseph Stalin]. *CJC*, 21 Aug. 1942, p. 3 [u].

42.08.21B "Is This It?" [Raid on Dieppe]. *CJC*, 21 Aug. 1942, p. 3 [u].

42.08.21C "The Warsaw Ghetto and the New Order." [Death of Adam Czerniakow]. *CJC*, 21 Aug. 1942, p. 3 [u].

42.08.21D "Boake Carter's Religion." [Boake Carter embraces Judaism]. *CJC*, 21 Aug. 1942, p. 3 [u].

42.08.21E "M. Chaloult and the Company He Keeps." [René Chaloult]. *CJC*, 21 Aug. 1942, p. 4 [s].

42.08.28A "The Duke of Kent: A War Casualty." [Death of the Duke of Kent]. *CJC*, 28 Aug. 1942, p. 3 [u].

42.08.28B "The New Naturalization Law." [Canadian naturalization law]. *CJC*, 28 Aug. 1942, p. 3 [u].

42.08.28C "Brazil's War Declaration." [Brazil joins the Allies]. *CJC*, 28 Aug. 1942, p. 3 [u].

42.08.28D "The Japs and Homo Pithecanthropus." [Skulls stolen from a Japanese museum]. *CJC*, 28 Aug. 1942, p. 3 [u].

42.08.28E "The Jewish Unitarian." [Single-minded solutions to Jewish problems]. *CJC*, 28 Aug. 1942, pp. 4, 16 [s].

42.09.04A "Laval Pays With Jews." [Jews in Vichy France]. *CJC*, 4 Sept. 1942, p. 3 [u].

42.09.04B "The Magnanimous Magnes." [Judah Magnes proposes a binational state in Palestine]. *CJC*, 4 Sept. 1942, p. 3 [u].

42.09.04C "Hitler Rants by Proxy." [Someone else reads a speech of Adolf Hitler]. *CJC*, 4 Sept. 1942, p. 3 [u].

42.09.04D "Advertising Declares War." [Advertising exploits the war effort]. *CJC*, 4 Sept. 1942, pp. 4, 16 [s].

42.09.11A "The New Year." [Rosh Hashana]. *CJC*, 11 Sept. 1942, p. 3 [u].

42.09.11B "The Combined Jewish Appeal." [Fund raising for Combined Jewish Appeal]. *CJC*, 11 Sept. 1942, p. 3 [u].

42.09.11C "The Canadian Jewish Daily Eagle." [*Keneder Adler*]. *CJC*, 11 Sept. 1942, pp. 7, 94 [s].

42.09.18A "The Day of Atonement." [Yom Kippur]. *CJC*, 18 Sept. 1942, p. 3 [u].

42.09.18B "A French-Canadian Voice." [Pro-Jewish editorial in *Le Matin*]. *CJC*, 18 Sept. 1942, p. 3 [u].

42.09.25A "An American Tragedy." [Theodore Dreiser in Toronto]. *CJC*, 25 Sept. 1942, p. 3 [u].

42.09.25B "Stout Sweden." [Sweden during WWII]. *CJC*, 25 Sept. 1942, p. 3 [u].

42.09.25C "Nordic First and Second Class." [Nazi race ideology]. *CJC*, 25 Sept. 1942, p. 3 [u].

42.09.25D "The Battle of the Cradles." [Significance of birth rate]. *CJC*, 25 Sept. 1942, p. 4 [s].

42.09.25E " 'Forgive Them Not . . .'." [Germans fear separation of families in event of Allied victory]. *CJC*, 25 Sept. 1942, p. 4 [s].

42.09.25F "The Beer-Cellars of Munich." [R.A.F. raids on Germany]. *CJC*, 25 Sept. 1942, p. 4 [s].

42.09.25G "The Voice of France." [Archbishop of Toulouse on morality of Vichy France]. *CJC*, 25 Sept. 1942, p. 4 [s].

42.10.02A "The Late Chief Justice R.A.E. Greenshields." [Death of R.A.E. Greenshields]. *CJC*, 2 Oct. 1942, p. 3 [u].

42.10.02B "Lord Mayor of London." [Sir Samuel Joseph is elected Lord Mayor of London]. *CJC*, 2 Oct. 1942, p. 3 [u].

42.10.02C "Yiddish Speech in America." [Use of Yiddish language in U.S.]. *CJC*, 2 Oct. 1942, p. 3 [u].

42.10.02D "On Account of a Nail." [Canadian war effort]. *CJC*, 2 Oct. 1942, p. 3 [u].

42.10.02E "Laval Has Headaches." [Pierre Laval]. *CJC*, 2 Oct. 1942, p. 4 [s].

42.10.02F "The Second Front." [Need for the Allies to open a second front]. *CJC*, 2 Oct. 1942, p. 4 [s].

42.10.09A "A Meeting of Protest and Self-Dedication." [Canadian Jewish Congress sponsors meeting on the plight of Jews]. *CJC*, 9 Oct. 1942, p. 3 [u].

42.10.09B "The Jewish Public Library." [Fund raising for the Jewish Public Library]. *CJC*, 9 Oct. 1942, p. 3 [u].

42.10.09C "Hitler vs. Hitler." [Adolf Hitler's nephew is denied admission to U.S. Army]. *CJC*, 9 Oct. 1942, p. 4 [s].

42.10.09D "A Canterbury Tale." [Archbishop of Canterbury on British war aims]. *CJC*, 9 oct. 1942, p. 4 [s].

42.10.09E "Take a Letter: Stalin." [Joseph Stalin on the need for greater Allied assistance to Soviet Union]. *CJC*, 9 Oct. 1942, p. 4 [s].

42.10.09F "Hermann Goering, Chef." [Food shortage in Nazi Germany]. *CJC*, 9 Oct. 1942, p. 4 [s].

42.10.16A " 'Life', and Its Pursuit of Unhappiness." [*Life* Magazine on the British war effort]. *CJC*, 16 Oct. 1942, p. 3 [u].

42.10.16B " 'For Deposit Abroad'." [Signs that Nazis may be fearing defeat]. *CJC*, 16 Oct. 1942, p. 3 [u].

42.10.16C "Down Argentine Way." [Argentine pro-Axis sympathy]. *CJC*, 16 Oct. 1942, p. 3 [u].

42.10.16D "Cosmic Leaders." [Children in Vichy France to be trained as leaders]. *CJC*, 16 Oct. 1942, p. 3 [u].

42.10.16E "An Odyssey of Fire." [Review of *A World In Flames* by J. Weingarten]. *CJC*, 16 Oct. 1942, p. 4 [s].

42.10.23A "The Voice From the Old Guard." [Speech of Jan Christian Smuts]. *CJC*, 23 Oct. 1942, p. 3 [u].

42.10.23B "The American Zionist Conference." [U.S. Zionist conference]. *CJC*, 23 Oct. 1942, p. 3 [u].

42.10.23C " 'Look On This Picture, And On This'." [Nazis threaten to bomb Jerusalem]. *CJC*, 23 Oct. 1942, p. 3 [u].

42.10.23D " 'Spurlos Versunken!' " [Nazi genocide of Jews]. *CJC*, 23 Oct. 1942, p. 3 [u].

42.10.23E "The Nazi War Criminals." [Defining war crimes]. *CJC*, 23 Oct. 1942, pp. 4, 16 [s].

42.10.30A "Mr. Wendell Willkie Makes a Report." [Speech of Wendell Willkie]. *CJC*, 30 Oct. 1942, p. 3 [u].

42.10.30B "A Black Anniversary." [Twentieth anniversary of Benito Mussolini's march on Rome]. *CJC*, 30 Oct. 1942, p. 3 [u].

42.10.30C "The Nazis Keep It Secret." [War in Soviet Union]. *CJC*, 30 Oct. 1942, p. 3 [u].

42.10.30D "Quebec City Passes A By-Law." [Anti-Semitism in Quebec]. *CJC*, 30 Oct. 1942, p. 4 [s].

42.11.06A "Jewry and the New World Order." [Anti-Semitism as a barometer of world climate]. *CJC*, 6 Nov. 1942, p. 3 [u].

42.11.06B "The Town of Krasnia." [Germans destroy Krasnia]. *CJC*, 6 Nov. 1942, p. 3 [u].

42.11.06C "Turkish Neutrality." [Turkey nears a state of war]. *CJC*, 6 Nov. 1942, p. 3 [u].

42.11.06D "The Balfour Declaration; 1917–1942." [Twenty-fifth anniversary of the Balfour Declaration]. *CJC*, 6 Nov. 1942, p. 4 [s].

42.11.13A "The End of 'Collaboration'." [Waning of the Vichy regime]. *CJC*, 13 Oct. 1942, p. 3 [u].

42.11.13B "A Ten Year Plan for Palestine." [Chaim Greenberg's ten-year plan for Palestine]. *CJC*, 13 Nov. 1942, p. 3 [u].

42.11.13C "Some Jewish Consequences of Recent Events." [Defeat of Erwin Rommel prevents German occupation of Palestine]. *CJC*, 13 Nov. 1942, p. 3 [u].

42.11.13D "The Second Phase." [Allies begin aggressive phase of the war]. *CJC*, 13 Nov. 1942, p. 4 [s].

42.11.20A "The Cry of the Wicked." [Nazis condemn Dwight D. Eisenhower's pro-Jewish stand]. *CJC*, 20 Nov. 1942, p. 3 [u].

42.11.20B "Selective Service, Not Discriminatory." [Anti-racist steps taken in Canada]. *CJC*, 20 Nov. 1942, p. 3 [u].

42.11.20C "Three Anniversaries." [Anniversaries of Montreal Jewish leaders]. *CJC*, 20 Nov. 1942, p. 3 [u].

42.11.20D "The Jew Behind the Times." [Arthur Hays Sulzberger]. *CJC*, 20 Nov. 1942, p. 6 [s].

42.11.27A "The Election in Outremont." [L.R. LaFleche]. *CJC*, 27 Nov. 1942, p. 3 [u].

42.11.27B "The Late Dr. Mosensohn." [Death of Ben Zion Mosensohn]. *CJC*, 27 Nov. 1942, p. 3 [u].

42.11.27C "Mr. Willkie and the British Empire." [Wendell Willkie on a remark of Winston Churchill's]. *CJC*, 27 Nov. 1942, p. 3 [u].

42.11.27D "Of Friends and Enemies." [U.S.–French Alliance in North Africa]. *CJC*, 27 Nov. 1942, p. 4 [s].

42.11.27E "The New Order: Murder and Ransom." [Nazi policy towards Jews]. *CJC*, 27 Nov. 1942, p. 4 [s].

42.12.00A "25 Years." [Twenty-five years of Young Judaea]. Judaean, Dec. 1942, pp. 12–13 [s].

42.12.04A "The Feast of Lights." [Chanukah]. *CJC*, 4 Dec. 1942, p. 3 [u].

42.12.04B "The Beveridge Plan." [Beveridge plan for post-war period]. *CJC*, 4 Dec. 1942, p. 3 [u].

42.12.04C "Mussolini's Answer." [Speech of Benito Mussolini]. *CJC*, 4 Dec. 1942, p. 3 [u].

42.12.04D "Churchill's Victory Address." [Speech of Winston Churchill on Allied victory in North Africa]. *CJC*, 4 Dec. 1942, p. 4 [s].

42.12.04E "The Coconut Grove Disaster." [Fire in a Boston nightclub]. *CJC*, 4 Dec. 1942, p. 4 [s].

42.12.11A "Island of Civilization." [Neutrality of Switzerland and Sweden]. *CJC*, 11 Dec. 1942, p. 3 [u].

42.12.11B "Franco Also Runs." [Speech of Francisco Franco]. *CJC*, 11 Dec. 1942, p. 3 [u].

42.12.11C "General Eisenhower's New Order." [Dwight D. Eisenhower revokes anti-Semitic laws in North Africa]. *CJC*, 11 Dec. 1942, p. 3 [u].

42.12.11D "Dr. Magnes of the Hebrew University." [Judah Magnes on Zionism]. *CJC*, 11 Dec. 1942, p. 3 [u].

42.12.11E "Drapeau Holds an Inquest." [Jean Drapeau's racism]. *CJC*, 11 Dec. 1942, p. 4 [s].

42.12.11F "The Double Standard." [Polish anti-Semitism]. *CJC*, 11 Dec. 1942, p. 4 [s].

42.12.11G "The Slaughter of the Children." [Nazi genocide in Poland]. *CJC*, 11 Dec. 1942, p. 4 [s].

42.12.18A "The Grim Poetics." [Bombing of Italy]. *CJC*, 18 Dec. 1942, p. 3 [u].

42.12.18B "Rommel's Flight." [German retreat in North Africa]. *CJC*, 18 Dec. 1942, p. 3 [u].

42.12.18C " 'Protestrabbiner' and Protestants." [Jewish anti-Zionism]. *CJC*, 18 Dec. 1942, p. 3 [u].

42.12.18D "Twenty-five years of Canadian Young Judaea." [Twenty-fifth anniversary of Canadian Young Judaea]. *CJC*, 18 Dec. 1942, p. 4 [s].

42.12.18E "The Progressive-Conservatives." [Conservatives become Progressive Conservatives]. *CJC*, 18 Dec. 1942, p. 4 [s].

42.12.18F "The New Order in Poland." [Adolf Hitler refuses to allow Vatican observers to visit Poland]. *CJC*, 18 Dec. 1942, p. 4 [s].

42.12.25A "Not Merely Sympathy." [Gathering in sympathy for plight of Jews]. *CJC*, 25 Dec. 1942, p. 3 [u].

42.12.25B "General Weygand and His Captors." [Nazis intend to try Maxime Weygand]. 25 Dec. 1942, p. 3 [u].

42.12.25C "Compulsory Education in Quebec." [Quebec institutes compulsory education]. *CJC*, 25 Dec. 1942, p. 4 [s].

42.12.25D "Mussolini's Cancer." [Benito Mussolini's illness]. *CJC*, 25 Dec. 1942, p. 4 [s].

42.12.25E "For Whom the Bell Tolls." [Controversy over film version of *For Whom the Bell Tolls*]. *CJC*, 25 Dec. 1942, p. 4 [s].

42.12.25F "The Anti-Nazi Protest." [Eleven governments condemn Nazi policy toward Jews]. *CJC*, 25 Dec. 1942, p. 4 [s].

43.01.01A "Peter Bercovitch." [Death of Peter Bercovitch]. *CJC*, 1 Jan. 1943, p. 3 [u].

43.01.01B "The Fat Fuehrer." [Adolf Hitler appears to gain weight]. *CJC*, 1 Jan. 1943, p. 3 [u].

43.01.01C "Voice of His People." [Hebrew University establishes a chair in honour of Zvi Hirsch Masliansky]. *CJC*, 1 Jan. 1943, p. 3 [u].

43.01.01D "The Assassination of Darlan." [Assassination of Jean Darlan]. *CJC*, 1 Jan. 1943, p. 4 [s].

43.01.01E "The Boomerang Expulsions." [Distinguished German exiles honoured]. *CJC*, 1 Jan. 1943, p. 4 [s].

43.01.01F "The Seeing Eye." [Henry Wallace on Allied war and post-war aims]. *CJC*, 1 Jan. 1943, p. 4 [s].

43.01.08A "The American White Paper." [White paper on Pearl Harbor]. *CJC*, 8 Jan. 1943, p. 3 [u].

43.01.08B "Restitution of Property." [Allies declare Nazis responsible for post-war reparations and restitution of property]. *CJC*, 8 Jan. 1943, p. 3 [u].

43.01.08C "Professor Franz Boas." [Death of Franz Boas]. *CJC*, 8 Jan. 1943, p. 3 [u].

43.01.08D "A Sculptor, a Singer and a Statistician." [Deaths of Enrico Glicenstein, Shloime Shmulevitz, and Arthur Ruppin]. *CJC*, 8 Jan. 1943, p. 4 [s].

43.01.15A "The United Talmud Torah Campaign." [Fundraising for United Talmud Torahs]. *CJC*, 15 Jan. 1943, p. 3 [u].

43.01.15B "The Ostriches." [American Jewish anti-Zionism]. *CJC*, 15 Jan. 1943, p. 3 [u].

43.01.15C "The Characteristics of Mesozoics." [H.G. Wells goes back to university]. *CJC*, 15 Jan. 1943, p. 3 [u].

43.01.15D "The Politics of Gesticulation." [Symbolism of ideologies in gestures]. *CJC*, 15 Jan. 1943, p. 4 [s].

43.01.15E " '1918'." [German propaganda slogan]. *CJC*, 15 Jan. 1943, p. 4 [s].

43.01.15F " 'Fighting For' and 'Fighting Against'." [Allied war objectives]. *CJC*, 15 Jan. 1943, p. 4 [s].

43.01.22A "Canadian Aid to Russia." [Canadian aid to Soviet Union]. *CJC*, 22 Jan. 1943, p. 3 [u].

43.01.22B "A Word In Its Season." [Selig Brodetsky on plight of Jews]. *CJC*, 22 Jan. 1943, p. 3 [u].

43.01.22C "Willkie on Idolatry." [Wendell Willkie on idolizing political leaders]. *CJC*, 22 Jan. 1943, p. 4 [s].

43.01.22D "Thought Begins at Eighty." [Eightieth birthday of David Lloyd George]. *CJC*, 22 Jan. 1943, p. 4 [s].

43.01.22E "Are the Germans Christians?" [Religion in Nazi Germany]. *CJC*, 22 Jan. 1943, p. 4 [s].

43.01.29A "The End of an Empire." [Allied victory in North Africa]. *CJC*, 29 Jan. 1943, p. 3 [u].

43.01.29B "Casa Blanca: The White House." [Casablanca Conference]. *CJC*, 29 Jan. 1943, p. 3 [u].

43.01.29C "Rev. J.K. Goldbloom." [Birthday of Jacob Goldbloom]. *CJC*, 29 Jan. 1943, p. 3 [u].

43.01.29D "Darkness in Africa." [North Africa after Allied victory]. *CJC*, 29 Jan. 1943, p. 4 [s].

43.01.29E "Abdullah's Arabian Nights Entertainment." [Emir Abdullah on a Jewish homeland in Palestine]. *CJC*, 29 Jan. 1943, p. 4 [s].

43.01.29F "Iraq Discovers the Axis." [Iraq's pro-Axis stance]. *CJC*, 29 Jan. 1943, p. 4 [s].

43.01.29G "A Second Set of McMahon Letters." [Future of Palestine as a Jewish homeland]. *CJC*, 29 Jan. 1943, p. 4 [s].

43.02.05A "The Dark Decade." [Tenth anniversary of Adolf Hitler's coming to power]. *CJC*, 5 Feb. 1943, p. 3 [u].

43.02.12A "Life from the Dead Sea." [Plan to irrigate the Negev]. *CJC*, 12 Feb. 1943, p. 3 [u].

43.02.12B "Israel Rabinovitch." [Israel Rabinovitch]. *CJC*, 12 Feb. 1943, p. 3 [u].

43.02.12C "Another Beveridge Plan." [William Henry Beveridge on relocation of Jewish refugees]. *CJC*, 12 Feb. 1943, p. 3 [u].

43.02.12D "The Curtain Up, and the Moon Down." [Review of dramatisation of *The Moon is Down*]. *CJC*, 12 Feb. 1943, p. 4 [s].

43.02.19A "The American Jewish Committee and Palestine." [American Jewish anti-Zionism]. *CJC*, 19 Feb. 1943, p. 3 [u].

43.02.19B "The North African Legacy." [Jews in North Africa]. *CJC*, 19 Feb. 1943, p. 3 [u].

43.02.19C "A Notable Historical Event." [Review of *Canada: The Foundations of Its Future* by Stephen Leacock]. *CJC*, 19 Feb. 1943, p. 4 [s].

43.02.26A "Stalin's Statement." [American isolationist response to speech of Joseph Stalin]. *CJC*, 26 Feb. 1943 [*misdated* 1942], p. 3 [u].

43.02.26B "Thoughts on a Report." [Work of the Joint Distribution Committee]. *CJC*, 26 Feb. 1943, p. 3 [u].

43.02.26C " 'Globaloney'." [Clare Luce on Anglo-U.S. relations]. *CJC*, 26 Feb. 1943, p. 4 [s].

43.02.26D " 'Es Geht Alles Vorueber'." [Nazi propaganda]. *CJC*, 26 Feb. 1943, p. 4 [s].

43.02.26E "The 'Vernichtungskolonnen'." [Nazi genocide of Jews]. *CJC*, 26 Feb. 1943, p. 4 [s].

43.03.05A "Will the World Accept the Challenge?" [Need for support for Jewish refugees]. *CJC*, 5 Mar. 1943, p. 3 [u].

43.03.05B "Erlich and Alter." [Execution of Henrik Erlich and Victor Alter]. *CJC*, 5 Mar. 1943, p. 3 [u].

43.03.05C "The City of Chelm." [Nazis establish an extermination camp in Chelm]. *CJC*, 5 Mar. 1943, p. 4 [s].

43.03.12A "Moscow and Washington." [U.S.–Soviet relations during WWII]. *CJC*, 12 Mar. 1943, p. 3 [u].

43.03.12B "Many Altars, And Still No Sanctuary." [Jewish refugees]. *CJC*, 12 Mar. 1943, p. 3 [u].

43.03.12C "Nuremberg and Munich." [R.A.F. bombs German cities]. *CJC*, 12 Mar. 1943, p. 3 [u].

43.03.19A "Jewish Unity: A Purim Editorial." [Need for Jewish unity]. *CJC*, 19 Mar. 1943, p. 3 [u].

43.03.26A "The Canadian Jewish Congress and the Challenge of Our Age." [Work of the Canadian Jewish Congress]. *CJC*, 26 Mar. 1943, p. 3 [u].

43.03.26B "Legislation Against Hatred." [Defeat of anti-racism law]. *CJC*, 26 Mar. 1943, p. 3 [u].

43.04.02A "The United Palestine Appeal and Emergency Youth Aliyah." [United Palestine Appeal]. *CJC*, 2 Apr. 1943, p. 3 [u].

43.04.02B "The Tramway Strike." [Tramway strike in Montreal]. *CJC*, 2 Apr. 1943, p. 3 [u].

43.04.09A "The Still-Vexed Bermoothes." [Bermuda Conference]. *CJC*, 9 Apr. 1943, p. 3 [u].

43.04.09B "Absenteeism." [Negation of the Diaspora]. *CJC*, 9 Apr. 1943, p. 3 [u].

43.04.09C "Hostages, Grade 1." [Imprisonment of French leaders]. *CJC*, 9 Apr. 1943, p. 3 [u].

43.04.09D "Italian Tribute." [Italians fear prayers of Jewish prisoners]. *CJC*, 9 Apr. 1943, p. 3 [u].

43.04.16A "And This Too Shall Pass Over." [Passover]. *CJC*, 16 Apr. 1943, p. 3 [u].

43.04.23A "The Bermuda Conference." [The Bermuda Conference on the refugee problem]. *CJC*, 23 Apr. 1943, p. 3 [u].

43.04.23B "Offensive Peace." [Spain appeals for negotiated peace]. *CJC*, 23 Apr. 1943, p. 3 [u].

43.04.30A "Back the Attack." [Canada issues victory bonds]. *CJC*, 30 Apr. 1943, p. 3 [u].

43.04.30B "The Bermuda Results." [Results of the Bermuda Conference]. *CJC*, 30 Apr. 1943, p. 3 [u].

43.04.30C "A Nazi Diplomatic Victory." [Suspension of Polish-Soviet relations]. *CJC*, 30 Apr. 1943, p. 3 [u].

43.05.07A "Control by Starvation." [Germans starve their victims]. *CJC*, 7 May 1943, p. 3 [u].

43.05.07B "Bible Footnote." [Anti-Semitism in the Bible]. *CJC*, 7 May 1943, p. 3 [u].

43.05.07C "The Late Leon Goldman." [Death of Leon Goldman]. *CJC*, 7 May 1943, p. 3 [u].

43.05.14A "The Jewish Immigrant Aid Society." [Fundraising for the Jewish Immigrant Aid Society]. *CJC*, 14 May 1943, p. 3 [u].

43.05.14B "The Late Dr. Chaim Zhitlowsky." [Death of Chaim Zhitlowsky]. *CJC*, 14 May 1943, p. 3 [u].

43.05.14C "The Fall of Tunisia." [Allied victory in Tunisia]. *CJC*, 14 May 1943, [u].

43.05.21A "The Warsaw Ghetto." [Destruction of Warsaw Ghetto]. *CJC*, 21 May 1943, p. 3 [u].

43.05.21B "And Also Earthquakes." [War in Italy]. *CJC*, 21 May 1943, p. 3 [u].

43.05.21C "Apres Nous, le Deluge!" [R.A.F. bombing of German targets]. *CJC*, 21 May 1943, p. 3 [u].

43.05.28A "A Notable Address." [Speech of Samuel Bronfman]. *CJC*, 28 May 1943, p. 3 [u].

43.05.28B "The Rabbinical Seminaries." [Yeshivas]. *CJC*, 28 May 1943, p. 3 [u].

43.05.28C "Stalin the Realist." [Dissolution of the Comintern]. *CJC*, 28 May 1943, p. 3 [u].

43.06.04A "Ibn Saud of Arabia." [Need for a Jewish homeland in Palestine]. *CJC*, 4 June 1943, p. 3 [u].

43.06.04B "Mrs. Samuel Bronfman, O.B.E." [Saidye Bronfman is awarded Order of the British Empire]. *CJC*, 4 June 1943, p. 3 [u].

43.06.11A "Churchill's Address." [Speech of Winston Churchill]. *CJC*, 11 June 1943, p. 3 [u].

43.06.11B "Roosevelt's Warning." [Chemical warfare]. *CJC*, 11 June 1943, p. 3 [u].

43.06.11C "A Labor Zionist House." [Opening of a Labour Zionist Centre]. *CJC*, 11 June 1943, p. 3 [u].

43.06.11D "Castillo's Flight." [Coup in Argentina]. *CJC*, 11 June 1943, p. 3 [u].

43.06.18A "Quebec City Gets Another Park." [Anti-Semitism in Quebec]. *CJC*, 18 June 1943, p. 3 [u].

43.06.18B "The King of Lampedusa." [Italians surrender aircraft carrier to a Jewish soldier]. *CJC*, 18 June 1943, p. 3 [u].

43.06.18C "Harold Laski, Pro-Zionist." [Harold Laski proposes a pro-Zionist resolution to be adopted by the British Labour Party]. *CJC*, 18 June 1943, p. 3 [u].

43.06.25A "Fascism: Made in America." [Race riots in U.S.]. *CJC*, 25 June 1943, p. 3 [u].

43.06.25B "Anti-Semitism of People and of Things . . ." [Anti-Semitism]. *CJC*, 25 June 1943, p. 3 [u].

43.07.02A "The Bundist-in-Exile." [Jewish Bundist denies need for a Jewish homeland in Palestine]. *CJC*, 2 July 1943, p. 3 [u].

43.07.09A "Lessing 'Lackland' Rosenwald." [Anti-Zionism of Lessing Rosenwald]. *CJC*, 9 July 1943, p. 3 [u].

43.07.09B "Mussolini Reads No More." [Benito Mussolini dislikes reading his own speeches in the press]. *CJC*, 9 July 1943, p. 3 [u].

43.07.16A "The Invasion of Sicily." [Allied invasion of Sicily]. *CJC*, 16 July 1943, p. 3 [u].

43.07.16B "Westbrook Pegler's Logic." [Westbrook Pegler opposes anti-discrimination legislation]. *CJC*, 16 July 1943, p. 3 [u].

43.07.16C "British Jewry Revolts." [Board of Deputies of British Jews takes over policy making for British Jews]. *CJC*, 16 July 1943, p. 3 [u].

43.07.23A "Theodor Herzl." [Theodor Herzl]. *CJC*, 23 July 1943, p. 3 [u].

43.07.23B "Franco's Phalanx." [Spanish "neutrality" is threatened by declining Axis power]. *CJC*, 23 July 1943, p. 3 [u].

43.07.23C "The Italian Ultimatum." [Franklin Delano Roosevelt and Winston Churchill issue ultimatum to Italy]. *CJC*, 23 July 1943, p. 3 [u].

43.07.30A "Exit Benito." [Benito Mussolini is removed from power]. *CJC*, 30 July 1943, p. 3 [u].

43.07.30B "New Territories." [Rumoured opening of territories for Jewish settlement]. *CJC*, 30 July 1943, p. 3 [u].

43.08.20A "Arms And The Mandate." [American and British response to Anti-Zionism]. *CJC*, 20 Aug. 1943, p. 3 [u].

43.08.27A "The Quebec Conference." [Allied strategic conference in Quebec]. *CJC*, 27 Aug. 1943, p. 3 [u].

43.08.27B "Kiska, Kharov, Berlin." [Allied victories]. *CJC*, 27 Aug. 1943, p. 3 [u].

43.09.03A "The American Jewish Conference." [American Jewish Conference]. *CJC*, 3 Sept. 1943, p. 3 [u].

43.09.03B "The Russian-Jewish Delegation." [Soviet-Jewish delegation visits Montreal]. *CJC*, 3 Sept. 1943, p. 3 [u].

43.09.03C "The American Council For Judaism Inc." [American Jewish anti-Zionism]. *CJC*, 3 Sept. 1943, p. 3 [u].

43.09.10A "The Capitulation of Italy." [Surrender of Italy to Allies]. *CJC*, 10 Sept. 1943, p. 3 [u].

43.09.10B "The Commonwealth Resolution." [Resolutions of the American Jewish Conference]. *CJC*, 10 Sept. 1943, p. 3 [u].

43.09.10C "The Five Zones." [Clarence Kelland's plan for post-war alliances]. *CJC*, 10 Sept. 1943, p. 3 [u].

43.09.17A "The Combined Jewish Appeal." [Fundraising for the Combined Jewish Appeal]. *CJC*, 17 Sept. 1943, p. 3 [u].

43.09.17B "Why Hitler Saved Mussolini." [Benito Mussolini is saved by the Nazis]. *CJC*, 17 Sept. 1943, p. 3 [u].

43.09.24A "Churchill's Report." [Speech of Winston Churchill]. *CJC*, 24 Sept. 1943, p. 3 [u].

43.09.24B "Turkish Discrimination." [The *New York Times* on Jews in Turkey]. *CJC*, 24 Sept. 1943, p. 3 [u].

43.09.24C "Soviet Realism." [German prisoners call for Adolf Hitler's overthrow]. *CJC*, 24 Sept. 1943, p. 3 [u].

43.09.24D "The Jewish People's Library." [Montreal Jewish Public Library]. *CJC*, 24 Sept. 1943, pp. 8, 16 [s].

43.09.29A "The New Year." [Rosh Hashana]. *CJC*, 29 Sept. 1943, p. 3 [u].

43.10.08A "The Kol Nidre Appeal." [Appeal for aid for Jews overseas]. *CJC*, 8 Oct. 1943, p. 3 [u].

43.10.08B " 'Forget Them Not'." [Fundraising for Quebec Society for Crippled Children]. *CJC*, 8 Oct. 1943, p. 3 [u].

43.10.08C "Sweden Shows the Way." [Sweden shelters Jewish refugees]. *CJC*, 8 Oct. 1943, p. 3 [u].

43.10.13A "The Feast of Tabernacles." [Succoth]. *CJC*, 13 Oct. 1943, p. 3 [u].

43.10.13B "Pilgrimage to the White House." [Franklin Delano Roosevelt refuses to receive demonstrating rabbis]. *CJC*, 13 Oct. 1943, p. 3 [u].

43.10.13C "The Palestine Cause Celebre." [Jews convicted of smuggling arms into Palestine]. *CJC*, 13 Oct. 1943, p. 3 [u].

43.10.20A "Nuremberg of the Argentine." [Anti-Semitism in Argentina]. *CJC*, 20 Oct. 1943, p. 3 [u].

43.10.20B "Saul Tchernichovsky." [Death of Saul Tchernichovsky]. *CJC*, 20 Oct. 1943, p. 3 [u].

43.10.20C "Thomas Mann." [Visit of Thomas Mann to Montreal]. *CJC*, 20 Oct. 1943, p. 3 [u].

43.10.29A "Destroyers of Jewish Unity." [Anti-Zionism of American Jewish Committee]. *CJC*, 29 Oct. 1943, p. 3 [u].

43.10.29B "Badoglio's Statement." [Pietro Badoglio on Italy's involvement in WWII]. *CJC*, 29 Oct. 1943, p. 3 [u].

43.11.05A "The Balfour Declaration." [British foreign policy on Palestine]. *CJC*, 5 Nov. 1943, p. 3 [u].

43.11.05B "Hitlerism On Our Continent." [Anti-Semitism in Argentina]. *CJC*, 5 Nov. 1943, p. 3 [u].

43.11.12A "The Protocols of Zion: Duplessis Edition." [Anti-Semitism in Quebec]. *CJC*, 12 Nov. 1943, p. 3 [u].

43.11.19A "The Massacre at Kiev." [Nazi massacre of Jews at Kiev]. *CJC*, 19 Nov. 1943, p. 3 [u].

43.11.19B "Among the Cedars of Lebanon." [Lebanon seeks independence]. *CJC*, 19 Nov. 1943, p. 3 [u].

43.11.19C "Russia's Secret Weapon." [Equality of all citizens in Soviet Union]. *CJC*, 19 Nov. 1943, p. 3 [u].

43.11.26A "The Mosley Affair." [Release of Oswald Mosley from prison]. *CJC*, 26 Nov. 1943, p. 3 [u].

43.11.26B "Outrage at Ramat Hakovesh." [British officials raid Ramat Hakovesh]. *CJC*, 26 Nov. 1943, p. 3 [u].

43.12.03A "The Doom of Berlin." [R.A.F. bombing of Berlin]. *CJC*, 3 Dec. 1943, p. 3 [u].

43.12.03B "Four Who Are To Meet." [Meeting of Winston Churchill, Joseph Stalin, Franklin Delano Roosevelt, and Chiang Kai-Shek]. *CJC*, 3 Dec. 1943, p. 3 [u].

43.12.03C "Shall Jews Go Back to Germany." [UNRRA states it will aid only refugees returning to the country from which they fled]. *CJC*, 3 Dec. 1943, p. 3 [u].

43.12.10A "The Teheran Talks." [Teheran Conference]. *CJC*, 10 Dec. 1943, p. 3 [u].

43.12.10B "Post-war Germany." [Dorothy Thompson's suggestions for post-war Germany]. *CJC*, 10 Dec. 1943, p. 3 [u].

43.12.17A "The Ezekiel Hart Centenary." [Ezekiel Hart]. *CJC*, 17 Dec. 1943, p. 3 [u].

43.12.17B "Destruction and Construction." [Establishment of a new Jewish settlement in Palestine]. *CJC*, 17 Dec. 1943, p. 3 [u].

43.12.24A "The Feast of Lights." [Chanukah]. *CJC*, 24 Dec. 1943, p. 3 [u].

43.12.24B "Law and Equity." [Jews tried for illegal possession of arms]. *CJC*, 24 Dec. 1943, p. 3 [u].

43.12.24C "The Perfect Man." [Improving man through science and technology]. *CJC*, 24 Dec. 1943, p. 4 [s].

43.12.31A "Support Labor Palestine." [Labour Palestine]. *CJC*, 31 Dec. 1943, p. 3 [u].

43.12.31B "National Anthems." [National anthems]. *CJC*, 31 Dec. 1943, p. 4 [s].

44.01.07A "The Talmud Torah Campaign." [Fundraising for United Talmud Torahs]. *CJC*, 7 Jan. 1944, p. 3 [u].

44.01.07B "Americanism and Antisemitism." [Anti-Semitism in U.S.]. *CJC*, 7 Jan. 1944, p. 3 [u].

44.01.07C "In Memoriam: Rabbi Levi Yitschok of Berdichev." [Rabbi Levi Yitschok of Berditchev remembered as Berditchev liberated from Nazis]. *CJC*, 7 Jan. 1944, p. 4 [s].

44.01.14A "Exit Ciano." [Execution of Galleazo Ciano]. *CJC*, 14 Jan. 1944, p. 3 [u].

44.01.14B "The American Council For Judaism and Realpolitik." [American Jewish anti-Zionism]. *CJC*, 14 Jan. 1944, p. 3 [u].

44.01.14C "1944 — A Year of Increased Red Cross Work." [Work of the Red Cross]. *CJC*, 14 Jan. 1944, p. 3 [u].

44.01.14D "Jewish Self-Hatred." [Review of *Person, Place and Thing* by Karl Shapiro]. *CJC*, 14 Jan. 1944, pp. 4, 15 [s].

44.01.21A "Of Peace and the Rumours of Peace." [Rumours of peace]. *CJC*, 21 Jan. 1944, p. 3 [u].

44.01.21B "Oranges and Bombs." [Shipment of Spanish oranges contains bomb]. *CJC*, 21 Jan. 1944, p. 3 [u].

44.01.21C "Moscow and Jerusalem." [Soviet foreign policy on Jews and Palestine]. *CJC*, 21 Jan. 1944, p. 3 [u].

44.01.21D "Deep in the Heart of Texas." [Reform Judaism]. *CJC*, 21 Jan. 1944, pp. 4, 16 [s].

44.01.28A "The Canadian Zionist Convention." [Twenty-seventh Canadian Zionist Convention]. *CJC*, 28 Jan. 1944, p. 3 [u].

44.01.28B "At Last Sympathy Plus." [Franklin Delano Roosevelt plan to rescue Jews]. *CJC*, 28 Jan. 1944, p. 3 [u].

44.01.28C "Pierre van Paassen: The Remembering Friend." [Review of *The Forgotten Ally* by Pierre van Paassen]. *CJC*, 28 Jan. 1944, pp. 4, 16 [s].

44.02.00A "The Poetry of A.J.M. Smith." [Review of *News of the Phoenix* by A.J.M. Smith]. CF 23 (Feb. 1944), pp. 257–8 [s].

44.02.04A "Weizmann on Partition." [Chaim Weizmann rejects partition of Palestine]. *CJC*, 4 Feb. 1944, p. 3 [u].

44.02.04B "The Captains and the Kings Depart." [Twenty-seventh Canadian Zionist Convention]. *CJC*, 4 Feb. 1944, p. 3 [u].

44.02.04C "Japanese Atrocities." [Japanese war crimes]. *CJC*, 4 Feb. 1944, p. 3 [u].

44.02.04D "The Heart of Europe." [Review of *The Heart of Europe* edited by Klaus Mann and Hermann Kesten]. *CJC*, 4 Feb. 1944, p. 4 [s].

44.02.04E "The Yiddish Encyclopedia." [Review of *The Yiddish Encyclopedia* by S. Petrushka]. *CJC*, 4 Feb. 1944, pp. 4, 15 [s].

44.02.11A "A Friend At Court." [U.S. appeals to Britain for nullification of the 1939 white paper on Palestine]. *CJC*, 11 Feb. 1944, p. 3 [u].

44.02.11B "An Apple A Day." [British foreign policy on Palestine]. *CJC*, 11 Feb. 1944, p. 3 [u].

44.02.11C "The Word of God Out of Zion." [Jewish soldiers bring a Torah scroll to Italy]. *CJC*, 11 Feb. 1944, p. 3 [u].

44.02.11D "Sinai, with Stage Directions." [Review of *The Ten Commandments* ed. Armin L. Robinson]. *CJC*, 11 Feb. 1944, p. 4 [s].

44.02.18A "Roosevelt on Anti-Semitism." [Franklin Delano Roosevelt on Anti-Semitism]. *CJC*, 18 Feb. 1944, p. 3 [u].

44.02.18B "Education at the Andrew Jackson High School." [Anti-Semitism in U.S.]. *CJC*, 18 Feb. 1944, p. 3 [u].

44.02.18C "Explosions in the Holy Land." [Bombing of immigration offices in Palestine]. *CJC*, 18 Feb. 1944, p. 3 [u].

44.02.18D "I.J. Singer." [Death of I.J. Singer]. *CJC*, 18 Feb. 1944, p. 3 [u].

44.02.18E "The Thirteenth Apostle?" [Sholem Asch]. *CJC*, 18 Feb. 1944, p. 4 [s].

44.02.25A "Duplessis, The Postman Who Rings Twice." [Quebec anti-Semitism]. *CJC*, 25 Feb. 1944, p. 3 [u].

44.02.25B "The Ten Lost Tribes." [The British-Israel Federation]. *CJC*, 25 Feb. 1944, p. 3 [u].

44.02.25C "The Clouds of Crying Witnesses." [Sessions of the Foreign Affairs Committee of U.S. House of Representatives]. *CJC*, 25 Feb. 1944, p. 4 [s].

44.03.03A "The Red Cross Campaign." [Work of the Canadian Red Cross]. *CJC*, 3 Mar. 1944, p. 3 [u].

44.03.03B "Let My People Go!" [Egypt opposes resolution of U.S. House of Representatives, Foreign Affairs Committee]. *CJC*, 3 Mar. 1944, p. 3 [u].

44.03.03C "Hitler's Ministers of Jewish Affairs." [Anti-Semitism]. *CJC*, 3 Mar. 1944, p. 3 [u].

44.03.03D "The Last Jew of Danzig." [Jews of Danzig eradicated]. *CJC*, 3 Mar. 1944, p. 4 [s].

44.03.10A "Of the Purim to Be." [Hope for Jewish triumph over Adolf Hitler]. *CJC*, 10 Mar. 1944, p. 3 [u].

44.03.10B "The Bombing of Germany." [Allied opposition to the bombing of Germany]. *CJC*, 10 Mar. 1944, p. 3 [u].

44.03.15A "The Fifth Freedom." [Campaign against the CCF]. *Dos Vort*, 15 Mar. 1944, p. 1 [s].

44.03.17A "President Roosevelt's Palestine Statement." [U.S. foreign policy on Palestine]. *CJC*, 17 Mar. 1944, p. 3 [u].

44.03.17B "Hitler is Silent." [Declining Axis position]. *CJC*, 17 Mar. 1944, p. 3 [u].

44.03.17C "The Duplessis Canard." [Anti-Semitism in Quebec]. *CJC*, 17 Mar. 1944, p. 3 [u].

44.03.17D "Those Blessed Peacemakers." [Review of *Unfinished Business* by Stephen Bonsal]. *CJC*, 17 Mar. 1944, p. 4 [s].

44.03.22A "Americanism and Antisemitism." [*See* 44.01.07B]. *Hillel Scroll* (Queen's University), 22 Mar. 1944, p. 1 [s].

44.03.24A "The United Palestine Appeal." [United Palestine Appeal]. *CJC*, 24 Mar. 1944, p. 3 [u].

44.03.31A "Not This Is The Way!" [Jewish terrorism in Palestine]. *CJC*, 31 Mar. 1944, p. 3 [u].

44.03.31B "Roosevelt's Warning." [Franklin Delano Roosevelt encourages protection of Jewish refugees]. *CJC*, 31 Mar. 1944, p. 3 [u].

44.03.31C "H.M. Caiserman." [Sixtieth birthday of H.M. Caiserman]. *CJC*, 31 Mar. 1944, p. 3 [u].

44.03.31D "Riddle Me This Riddle." [*See* 32.10.28A]. *CJC*, 31 Mar. 1944, p. 4 [s].

44.04.07A "The Feast of Passover." [Hope for Jewish freedom from Nazi enslavement]. *CJC*, 7 Apr. 1944, p. 3 [u].

44.04.07B "Jewish Folk Songs." [*See* 32.06.00B]. *CJC*, 7 Apr. 1944, pp. 9–10 [s].

44.04.13A "Welcome to the Refugees." [Refugees arrive in Canada]. *CJC*, 13 Apr. 1944, p. 3 [u].

44.04.13B "In Memoriam: The Heroes and Martyrs of the Warsaw Ghetto." [Warsaw Ghetto]. *CJC*, 13 Apr. 1944, p. 3 [u].

44.04.13C "Maimonides in Hollywood." [Review of *A Guide to the Bedevilled* by Ben Hecht]. *CJC*, 13 Apr. 1944, p. 6 [s].

44.04.21A "The Dies-Winchell Feud." [Racism in U.S.]. *CJC*, 21 Apr. 1944, p. 3 [u].

44.04.21B "Our Duty as Guardians." [Jewish Commonwealth resolution of U.S. House of Representatives Foreign Affairs Committee]. *CJC*, 21 Apr. 1944, p. 3 [u].

44.04.21C "London Libel." [The *Times of London* on Jewish terrorism in Palestine]. *CJC*, 21 Apr. 1944, p. 3 [u].

44.04.21D " 'Revisionist Fronts'." [Revisionist Zionist organizations]. *CJC*, 21 Apr. 1944, p. 3 [u].

44.04.28A "The Sixth Victory Loan." [Victory Bond Drive]. *CJC*, 28 Apr. 1944, p. 3 [u].

44.04.28B "A Solution to the Palestine Problem?" [British Labour Party proposes a solution to the Palestinian problem]. *CJC*, 28 Apr. 1944, p. 3 [u].

44.04.28C "Le Moraliste." [Anti-Semitism in Quebec newspaper]. *CJC*, 28 Apr. 1944, p. 3 [u].

44.04.28D "The Great Sea." [Review of *The Mediterranean* by Emil Ludwig]. *CJC*, 28 Apr. 1944, p. 4 [s].

44.05.00A "The Fifth Freedom." [*See* 44.03.15A]. *Jewish Observer* 1, 4 (May 1944), p. 11 [s].

44.05.05A "Justice Speaks." [Attempt to halt construction of a synagogue in Quebec City]. *CJC*, 5 May 1944, p. 3 [u].

44.05.05B "The Canadian Legion and Anti-Semitism." [Canadian Legion condemns racism]. *CJC*, 5 May 1944, p. 3 [u].

44.05.05C "The Rabbinical Seminary of Montreal." [Fundraising for Merkaz Hatorah Yeshiva]. *CJC*, 5 May 1944, p. 3 [u].

44.05.05D "A Landmark." [Anglo-Jewish journalism]. *CJC*, 5 May 1944, p. 3 [u].

44.05.05E "The Three-Fold Exile." [Court-martial of Jewish soldiers by Polish army]. *CJC*, 5 May 1944, p. 4 [s].

44.05.12A "The Montreal Jewish General Hospital — The First Decade." [Montreal Jewish General Hospital]. *CJC*, 12 May 1944, p. 3 [u].

44.05.12B "Thirty Years of the Canadian Jewish Chronicle." [Anniversary of the *Canadian Jewish Chronicle*]. *CJC*, 12 May 1944, p. 3 [u].

44.05.12C "The Indigestible 'Reader's Digest'." [Anti-Zionism of Frederick Painton]. *CJC*, 12 May 1944, pp. 4, 14 [s].

44.05.19A "The Course of Polish Antisemitism." [Polish anti-Semitism]. *CJC*, 19 May 1944, p. 3 [u].

44.05.19B "The Fruit of Appeasement." [British foreign policy on Palestine]. *CJC*, 19 May 1944, p. 3 [u].

44.05.19C "The Eleventh Commandment." [Review of *Palestine: Land of Promise* by Walter Clay Lowdermilk]. *CJC*, 19 May 1944, p. 4 [s].

44.05.26A "The Feast of Weeks." [Shavuoth]. *CJC*, 26 May 1944, p. 3 [u].

44.05.26B "Incendiary Anti-Semitism." [Anti-Semitism in Quebec]. 26 May 1944, p. 3 [u].

44.06.02A "The Canadian Friends of the Hebrew University." [Canadian support for the Hebrew University]. *CJC*, 2 June 1944, p. 3 [u].

44.06.02B "The Birth of a Nation." [Hebrew Committee for National Liberation]. *CJC*, 2 June 1944, p. 3 [u].

44.06.09A "The Family Carnovsky." [Review of a performance of *The Family Carnovsky* by I.J. Singer]. *CJC*, 9 June 1944, p. 4 [s].

44.06.16A "Inside Europe." [Weakening of the Axis position]. *CJC*, 16 June 1944, p. 3 [u].

44.06.16B "Pidyan Nefesh." [Aid for Jewish refugees]. *CJC*, 16 June 1944, p. 3 [u].

44.06.16C "Of Cherbourg and Other Ports." [Allied invasion of France]. *CJC*, 16 June 1944, p. 4 [s].

44.06.23A "Again the Hebrew Committee for National Liberation." [Hebrew Committee for National Liberation]. *CJC*, 23 June 1944, p. 3 [u].

44.06.23B "The Pilotless Plane." [Rumours of a pilotless plane]. *CJC*, 23 June 1944, p. 3 [u].

44.06.23C "Schism in Palestine's Labor Party." [Mapai Party]. *CJC*, 23 June 1944, p. 3 [u].

44.06.23D "Of Lowly Things." [Humility]. *CJC*, 23 June 1944, p. 4 [s].

44.06.30A "Prodigal Revisionism." [Revisionist Zionism]. *CJC*, 30 June 1944, p. 3 [u].

44.06.30B "Idealism: A Challenge." [Need for Jewish idealism]. *CJC*, 30 June 1944, p. 3 [u].

44.06.30C "The Generous Heart of the New York 'Times'." [Anti-Semitism of the *New York Times*]. *CJC*, 30 June 1944, p. 3 [u].

44.06.30D "Prayer for a Jewish State." [Prayer for Jewry]. *CJC*, 30 June 1944, p. 3 [u].

44.07.07A "The European Volcano." [Weakening of the Axis]. *CJC*, 7 July 1944, p. 3 [u].

44.07.07B "The Prison of Mauritius." [Jewish refugees]. *CJC*, 7 July 1944, p. 3 [u].

44.07.07C "King David's Minister of Information." [Review of *David* by Duff Cooper]. *CJC*, 7 July 1944, p. 4 [s].

44.07.14A "An International Precedent." [French court declares null and void all sales made by Jews under pressure of Nazi laws]. *CJC*, 14 July 1944, p. 3 [u].

44.07.14B "A Timely Address." [Compassion toward Nazis]. *CJC*, 14 July 1944, p. 3 [u].

44.07.14C "Jewish Cities Without Jews." [Nazi genocide of Jews]. *CJC*, 14 July 1944, p. 3 [u].

44.07.21A "Remembering Theodor Herzl." [Theodor Herzl]. *CJC*, 21 July 1944, p. 3 [u].

44.07.21B "A Dubious Department." [Italian government establishes a department of Jewish affairs]. *CJC*, 21 July 1944, p. 3 [u].

44.07.28A "The Nazi Blood Bank." [Nazis propose to trade Jewish refugees for war vehicles]. *CJC*, 28 July 1944, p. 3 [u].

44.07.28B "The Three Jews of Vilna." [Nazi genocide of Jews]. *CJC*, 28 July 1944, p. 3 [u].

44.07.28C "The Ninth of Ab." [Tisha B'Av]. *CJC*, 28 July 1944, p. 3 [u].

44.07.28D "The Case of the Bungled Bomb." [Assassination attempt on Adolf Hitler]. *CJC*, 28 July 1944, p. 4 [s].

44.08.04A "The Beginning of the End?" [Deteriorating support for Germany]. *CJC*, 4 Aug. 1944, p. 3 [u].

44.08.04B "The Ironies of History." [First Russian into Prussian territory is a Jew]. *CJC*, 4 Aug. 1944, p. 3 [u].

44.08.11A "Sir Ronald Storrs to the Rescue." [Sir Ronald Storrs on U.S. foreign policy on Palestine]. *CJC*, 11 Aug. 1944, p. 3 [u].

44.08.11B "The Last Scapegoat." [Nazis hang their own generals]. *CJC*, 11 Aug. 1944, p. 3 [u].

44.08.11C "The Future of Palestine." [Need for a Jewish homeland in Palestine]. *CJC*, 11 Aug. 1944, p. 4 [s].

44.08.18A "The Lublin Cemetary." [Nazi genocide of Jews]. *CJC*, 18 Aug. 1944, p. 3 [u].

44.08.18B "Another Front." [Allies encircle Axis forces]. *CJC*, 18 Aug. 1944, p. 3 [u].

44.08.18C "A Planetary War?" [Robot bomb]. *CJC*, 18 Aug. 1944, p. 3 [u].

44.08.18D "Berl Katznelson." [Death of Berl Katznelson]. *CJC*, 18 Aug. 1944, p. 3 [u].

44.08.18E "A Jewish Soldier on Vansittartism." [Vansittartism]. *CJC*, 18 Aug. 1944, p. 4 [s].

44.08.25A "The Fall of the Bastille." [Liberation of Paris]. *CJC*, 25 Aug. 1944, p. 3 [u].

44.08.25B "Address Before Sentence." [Statements of Jewish terrorists]. *CJC*, 25 Aug. 1944, p. 3 [u].

44.08.25C "Hugger-Mugger At The Louvre." [Vichy France]. *CJC*, 25 Aug. 1944, p. 4 [s].

44.09.01A "The Artificial Heart." [Dr. Alexis Carrel]. *CJC*, 1 Sept. 1944, p. 3 [u].

44.09.01B "The Writing on the Wall." [Imminent German defeat]. *CJC*, 1 Sept. 1944, p. 3 [u].

44.09.01C "Shape of Things To Come." [Review of *Primer of the Coming World* by Leopold Schwarzschild]. *CJC*, 1 Sept. 1944, p. 4 [s].

44.09.08A "The Lighter Side." [P.G. Wodehouse receives preferential treatment from the Nazis]. *CJC*, 8 Sept. 1944, p. 3 [u].

44.09.08B "Abraham Levin." [Death of Abraham Levin]. *CJC*, 8 Sept. 1944, p. 3 [u].

44.09.08C "Survey of Zionism." [Review of *Harvest in the Desert* by Maurice Samuel]. *CJC*, 8 Sept. 1944, p. 4 [s].

44.09.15A "The Lights Go On Again." [Looking towards rebuilding after the war]. *CJC*, 15 Sept. 1944, p. 3 [u].

44.09.22A "The Combined Jewish Appeal." [Combined Jewish Appeal]. *CJC*, 22 Sept. 1944, p. 3 [u].

44.09.22B "Grand Invective." [Review of *The Tempering of Russia* by Ilya Ehrenburg]. *CJC*, 22 Sept. 1944, p. 4 [s].

44.09.29A "Renegade Ramsay's Release." [Release of Archibald Ramsay from prison]. *CJC*, 29 Sept. 1944, p. 3 [u].

44.09.29B "War Crime Pays." [Allies debate dealing with war crimes]. *CJC*, 29 Sept. 1944, p. 4 [s].

44.10.06A "UNRRA and Jewry." [Policies of the UNRRA]. *CJC*, 6 Oct. 1944, p. 3 [u].

44.10.06B "The Merchant of Venice." [*The Merchant of Venice* banned in Austria]. *CJC*, 6 Oct. 1944, p. 3 [u].

44.10.13A "The Last Card." [Nazi contingency plans for ransoming captured leaders]. *CJC*, 13 Oct. 1944, p. 3 [u].

44.10.13B "A Curious Request." [Nazi war crimes]. *CJC*, 13 Oct. 1944, p. 3 [u].

44.10.13C "Museums of the Future." [Emil Sommerstein proposes preserving death-camps as memorial]. *CJC*, 13 Oct. 1944, p. 3 [u].

44.10.13D "A Jewish Brigade." [Palestinian Jewish brigade]. *CJC*, 13 Oct. 1944, p. 4 [s].

44.10.20A "The State Secret." [Anti-Semitism in Britain]. *CJC*, 20 Oct. 1944, p. 3 [u].

44.10.20B "Some Light for Zion." [U.S. and British foreign policy on Palestine]. *CJC*, 20 Oct. 1944, p. 3 [u].

44.10.20C "Le Moraliste Fights the Jewish Brigade." [Anti-Semitic journalism]. *CJC*, 20 Oct. 1944, p. 3 [u].

44.10.20D "Shaw is Afraid of the Big Bad Wolf." [British administration in Palestine]. *CJC*, 20 Oct. 1944, p. 4 [s].

44.10.27A "The Seventh Victory Loan." [Canada launches a victory loan]. *CJC*, 27 Oct. 1944, p. 3 [u].

44.10.27B "Thirty Nine Steps." [British foreign policy on Palestine]. *CJC*, 27 Oct. 1944, p. 3 [u].

44.10.27C "German Thoroughness." [Majdenek concentration camp]. *CJC*, 27 Oct. 1944, p. 3 [u].

44.10.27D "Oaks and Little Acorns." [Dumbarton Oaks Conference]. *CJC*, 27 Oct. 1944, pp. 4, 15 [s].

44.11.03A "Balfour Day." [British foreign policy on Palestine]. *CJC*, 3 Nov. 1944, p. 3 [u].

44.11.03B "A Voice is Heard in Aachen." [Capture of Aachen]. *CJC*, 3 Nov. 1944, p. 3 [u].

44.11.03C "The Yeshiva Merkaz Hatorah." [Establishment of a yeshiva in Montreal]. *CJC*, 3 Nov. 1944, p. 3 [u].

44.11.10A "The Re-election of Roosevelt." [Re-election of Franklin Delano Roosevelt]. *CJC*, 10 Nov. 1944, p. 3 [u].

44.11.10B "Lord Moyne." [Assassination of Lord Moyne]. *CJC*, 10 Nov. 1944, p. 3 [u].

44.11.17A "Where's Adolf?" [Adolf Hitler]. *CJC*, 17 Nov. 1944, p. 3 [u].

44.11.17B "A Reasonable Offer." [Terrorism in Palestine]. *CJC*, 17 Nov. 1944, p. 3 [u].

44.11.24A "The Smoke of a Pistol." [Winston Churchill's response to assassination of Lord Moyne]. *CJC*, 24 Nov. 1944, p. 3 [u].

44.12.01A "Jewish Book Week." [Jewish Book Week in Montreal]. *CJC*, 1 Dec. 1944, p. 3 [u].

44.12.01B "The World Jewish Congress." [Need for a unified Jewish voice at post-war conferences]. *CJC*, 1 Dec. 1944, p. 3 [u].

44.12.08A "Weizmann at Seventy." [Chaim Weizmann]. *CJC*, 8 Dec. 1944, p. 3 [u].

44.12.08B "Parisian Arabs." [Arabs disrupt Zionist meeting in Paris]. *CJC*, 8 Dec. 1944, p. 3 [u].

44.12.15A "The Palestine Resolution in the American Senate." [U.S. foreign policy on Palestine]. *CJC*, 15 Dec. 1944, p. 3 [u].

44.12.15B "The Jewish Agency Speaks." [Jewish Agency seeks world recognition of Palestine as a Jewish state]. *CJC*, 15 Dec. 1944, p. 3 [u].

44.12.22A "The German Counter-Offensive." [German counter-offensive]. *CJC*, 22 Dec. 1944, p. 3 [u].

44.12.22B "What Democracy Expects of Its Leaders." [Post-war international relations]. *CJC*, 22 Dec. 1944, p. 3 [u].

44.12.29A "The Tactics of Race-Hatred." [Anti-Semitism in Quebec and elsewhere]. *CJC*, 29 Dec. 1944, p. 3 [u].

44.12.29B "The American Council for Judaism, Inc." [American Jewish anti-Zionism]. *CJC*, 29 Dec. 1944, p. 3 [u].

44.12.29C "The Witnesses." [Nazi crimes]. *CJC*, 29 Dec. 1944, p. 3 [u].

45.01.05A "The Voice of the Fuehrer." [Adolf Hitler's oratory]. *CJC*, 5 Jan. 1945, p. 3 [u].

45.01.05B "A Regrettable Incident." [Dissent among American Zionists]. *CJC*, 5 Jan. 1945, p. 3 [u].

45.01.12A "The Sixth Plenary Session of the Canadian Jewish Congress." [Sixth plenary session of the Canadian Jewish Congress]. *CJC*, 12 Jan. 1945, p. 3 [u].

45.01.19A " 'Rededication, Rehabilitation, Relief'." [Sixth plenary session of the Canadian Jewish Congress]. *CJC*, 19 Jan. 1945, p. 3 [u].

45.01.19B "Yiddish Press Anniversary." [Seventy-fifth anniversary of the Yiddish press in America]. *CJC*, 19 Jan. 1945, p. 3 [u].

45.01.26A " 'Save the Children'." [Save the Children Fund]. *CJC*, 26 Jan. 1945, p. 3 [u].

45.01.26B "The War-Criminals." [Debate on Adolf Hitler's status as a war criminal]. *CJC*, 26 Jan. 1945, p. 3 [u].

45.02.02A "The Montreal Jewish General Hospital." [Montreal Jewish General Hospital]. *CJC*, 2 Feb. 1945, p. 3 [u].

45.02.02B "His Last Speech?" [Adolf Hitler's oratory]. *CJC*, 2 Feb. 1945, p. 3 [u].

45.02.09A "The Sinking Ship." [Imminent defeat of the Nazis]. *CJC*, 9 Feb. 1945, p. 3 [u].

45.02.09B "Palestine Moving Pictures." [Film in Palestine]. *CJC*, 9 Feb. 1945, p. 3 [u].

45.02.16A "The Crimea Conference." [Yalta Conference]. *CJC*, 16 Feb. 1945, p. 3 [u].

45.02.16B "The Flirtation of Franco." [Francisco Franco approaches Winston Churchill]. *CJC*, 16 Feb. 1945, p. 3 [u].

45.02.23A "Henrietta Szold." [Death of Henrietta Szold]. *CJC*, 23 Feb. 1945, p. 3 [u].

45.02.23B "U.J.A. Dissolved." [United Jewish Appeal dissolved in U.S.]. *CJC*, 23 Feb. 1945, p. 3 [u].

45.03.02A "Youth Aliyah." [Youth Aliyah]. *CJC*, 2 Mar. 1945, p. 3 [u].

45.03.02B "Query." [Assassination of Ahmed Pasha]. *CJC*, 2 Mar. 1945, p. 3 [u].

45.03.02C "Declarations of War and International Rights." [Representation at the San Francisco Conference]. *CJC*, 2 Mar. 1945, p. 3 [u].

45.03.09A "Poetic Justice." [Jewish retribution]. *CJC*, 9 Mar. 1945, p. 3 [u].

45.03.09B "The Rabbi of Rome." [Chief Rabbi of Rome converts to Roman Catholicism]. *CJC*, 9 Mar. 1945, p. 3 [u].

45.03.09C "Cuza s'accuse." [Trial of a Rumanian fascist]. *CJC*, 9 Mar. 1945, p. 3 [u].

45.03.16A "In Memory of Martyr and Hero." [Remembrance of Jews killed during WWII]. *CJC*, 16 Mar. 1945, p. 3 [u].

45.03.16B "The Arab Compromise." [Arab foreign policy on Palestine]. *CJC*, 16 Mar. 1945, p. 3 [u].

45.03.16C "Rats, Lice and History." [Imminent German defeat]. *CJC*, 16 Mar. 1945, p. 3 [u].

45.03.23A "Mr. Roosevelt's Correction . . ." [U.S. foreign policy on Palestine]. *CJC*, 23 Mar. 1945, p. 3 [u].

45.03.28A "The Feast of Liberation." [Passover]. *CJC*, 28 Mar. 1945, p. 3 [u].

45.04.06A "The United Palestine Appeal." [United Palestine Appeal]. *CJC*, 6 Apr. 1945, p. 3 [u].

45.04.06B "The Werewolves." [Imminent German defeat]. *CJC*, 6 Apr. 1945, p. 3 [u].

45.04.06C "The Jewish Brigade." [Jewish brigade in combat with Nazi troops]. *CJC*, 6 Apr. 1945, p. 3 [u].

45.04.13A "The Murder Cartel." [Nazi war crimes]. *CJC*. 13 Apr. 1945, p. 3 [u].

45.04.13B "The Holding Company." [Nazi war crimes]. *CJC*, 13 Apr. 1945, p. 3 [u].

45.04.13C "The Japs Next?" [Soviet Union declares it will not continue neutrality pact beyond 1946]. *CJC*, 13 Apr. 1945, p. 3 [u].

45.04.20A "Franklin D. Roosevelt." [Death of Franklin Delano Roosevelt]. *CJC*, 20 Apr. 1945, p. 3 [u].

45.04.20B " 'Invest in the Best'." [Victory loan]. *CJC*, 20 Apr. 1945, p. 3 [u].

45.04.20C "Fritz [*sic*] von Papen." [Capture of Franz von Papen]. *CJC*, 20 Apr. 1945, p. 3 [u].

45.04.27A "Hebrew Education." [Hebrew education in Canada]. *CJC*, 27 Apr. 1945, p. 3 [u].

45.04.27B " 'The Golden Gate'." [San Francisco Conference]. *CJC*, 27 Apr. 1945, p. 3 [u].

45.04.27C "Witnessing From Gehenna." [Nazi war crimes]. *CJC*, 27 Apr. 1945, p. 3 [u].

45.04.27D "Israel Rabinovitch (On the Occasion of His Fiftieth Birthday)." [Israel Rabinovitch]. *CJC*, 27 Apr. 1945, p. 14 [s].

45.05.04A "On the Writing of Obituaries." [Deaths of Adolf Hitler and Benito Mussolini]. *CJC*, 4 May 1945, p. 3 [u].

45.05.04B "The Gotterdamerung, The Katzenjammer." [Reports of Adolf Hitler's Death]. *CJC*, 4 May 1945, p. 3 [u].

45.05.04C "Sic Semper Tyrranis [*sic*]." [Execution of Benito Mussolini]. *CJC*, 4 May 1945, p. 3 [u].

45.05.11A "The War Criminals." [Whereabouts of prominent Axis members]. *CJC*, 11 May 1945, p. 3 [u].

45.05.11B "The Jewish Immigrant Aid Society." [Jewish Immigrant Aid Society]. *CJC*, 11 May 1945, p. 3 [u].

45.05.11C "Arcand and Decarie." [Release of French Canadian fascists from prison]. *CJC*, 11 May 1945, p. 3 [u].

45.05.11D "Reflections on V-E Day." [V-E Day]. *CJC*, 11 May 1945, p. 7 [s].

45.05.17A "The Feast of Shevuoth." [Shavuoth]. *CJC*, 17 May 1945, p. 3 [u].

45.05.17B "The Goering Interviews." [Hermann Goering gives a press conference]. *CJC*, 17 May 1945, p. 3 [u].

45.05.17C "Franco's Freedom." [Francisco Franco reinstitutes certain freedoms in Spain]. *CJC*, 17 May 1945, p. 3 [u].

45.05.25A "The San Francisco Conference." [San Francisco Conference]. *CJC*, 25 May 1945, p. 3 [u].

45.05.25B "The Voices." [Lord Haw-Haw and Ezra Pound]. *CJC*, 25 May 1945, p. 3 [u].

45.05.25C "The Warsaw Ghetto." [Germans imprisoned in Warsaw Ghetto]. *CJC*, 25 May 1945, p. 3 [u].

45.05.25D "Denmark and the Jews." [Danish government calls for return of Jews to that country]. *CJC*, 25 May 1945, p. 3 [u].

45.05.25E "Crimes and Punishment." [Review of *Germany's War Crimes and Punishments* by M. H. Myerson]. *CJC*, 25 May 1945, p. 13 [s].

45.06.01A "Mandates and Trusteeships." [Mandates and trusteeships in the Middle East]. *CJC*, 1 June 1945, p. 3 [u].

45.06.01B "The Democracy of the Dead." [WWII casualties]. *CJC*, 1 June 1945, p. 3 [u].

45.06.01C "The Davar." [Twentieth anniversary of *Davar*]. *CJC*, 1 June 1945, p. 3 [u].

45.06.08A "The Nazis Go, The Concentration Camps Remain." [Jews continue to die in concentration camps]. *CJC*, 8 June 1945, p. 3 [u].

45.06.08B "Where Shall They Go?" [Jewish refugees]. *CJC*, 8 June 1945, p. 3 [u].

45.06.08C "Incident in Paris." [Anti-Semitic incident in Paris]. *CJC*, 8 June 1945, p. 3 [u].

45.06.08D "New Writers Series, No. 1." [Review of *Here and Now* by Irving Layton]. *CJC*, 8 June 1945, p. 8 [s].

45.06.15A "Petain's Alibi." [Trial of Henri Pétain]. *CJC*, 15 June 1945, p. 3 [u].

45.06.15B "Is Hitler Alive?" [Search for Adolf Hitler's body]. *CJC*, 15 June 1945, p. 3 [u].

45.06.15C "King Michael Commutes." [King Michael commutes sentences of war criminals]. *CJC*, 15 June 1945, p. 3 [u].

45.06.22A "The Technique of Apologetics." [Nazi war crimes]. *CJC*, 22 June 1945, p. 3 [u].

45.06.22B "The Montreal Jewish General Hospital." [Montreal Jewish General Hospital]. *CJC*, 22 June 1945, p. 3 [u].

45.06.22C "Had Not Thy Torah Been My Delight . . ." [Review of *From the Nazi Vale of Tears* by Rabbi Pinchos Hirschprung]. *CJC*, 22 June 1945, p. 12 [s].

45.06.22D "The Spider." [Review of *The Pan-Germanic Web, Remaking Europe* by Vladimir Grossman]. *CJC*, 22 June 1945, pp. 12–13 [s].

45.06.29A "Rescue or Kidnapping?" [Forced conversion of Jewish child refugees]. *CJC*, 29 June 1945, p. 3 [u].

45.06.29B "Theodor Herzl." [Anniversary of the death of Theodor Herzl]. *CJC*, 29 June 1945, p. 3 [u].

45.06.29C "Sic Transit Nuremberg." [Synagogue service is held in Nueremberg]. *CJC*, 29 June 1945, p. 3 [u].

45.07.06A "The Disappearance of the Nazis." [Nazis deny responsibility for war crimes]. *CJC*, 6 July 1945, p. 3 [u].

45.07.06B "The San Francisco Conference." [San Francisco Conference]. *CJC*, 6 July 1945, p. 3 [u].

45.07.06C "Refugees in Reverse?" [Refugees become political issue]. *CJC*, 6 July 1945, p. 3 [u].

45.07.06D "Some Praise the Lord — Some Pass the Ammunition." [Review of *Sabbath Prayer Book* published by the Jewish Reconstructionist Foundation]. *CJC*, 6 July 1945, pp. 6, 15 [s].

45.07.13A "The Release of Adrien Arcand." [Release of Adrien Arcand from prison]. *CJC*, 13 July 1945, p. 3 [u].

45.07.13B "The Berlin Conference." [Potsdam Conference]. *CJC*, 13 July 1945, p. 3 [u].

45.07.20A "A Superfluous Question." [Anti-Semitism in Britain]. *CJC*, 20 July 1945, p. 3 [u].

45.07.20B "A Jewish State — in Germany!" [Proposal to establish a Jewish state in Germany]. *CJC*, 20 July 1945, p. 3 [u].

45.07.20C "Power Politics and Zionism." [Foreign policy on Palestine]. *CJC*, 20 July 1945, p. 3 [u].

45.07.27A "A Reminder From the Forgotten People." [World Jewish Congress petitions Big Three for improved treatment of Jewish refugees]. *CJC*, 27 July 1939, p. 3 [u].

45.07.27B "Hitler In Palestine." [Rumour that Adolf Hitler is hiding in Palestine]. *CJC*, 27 July 1945, p. 3 [u].

45.07.27C "Tass Blunders." [Anti-Zionist news dispatch]. *CJC*, 27 July 1945, p. 3 [u].

45.08.03A "The British Labour Party." [British foreign policy on Palestine]. *CJC*, 3 Aug. 1945, p. 3 [u].

45.08.03B "The Secret Weapon of the Supermen." [Fall of the Nazis]. *CJC*, 3 Aug. 1945, p. 3 [u].

45.08.03C "The Wandering Laval." [Pierre Laval as fugitive]. *CJC*, 3 Aug. 1945, p. 3 [u].

45.08.03D "The Jews of Europe." [Need for aid to Jewish survivors of WWII]. *CJC*, 3 Aug. 1945, p. 8 [s].

45.08.10A "The London Zionist Conference." [London Zionist Conference]. *CJC*, 10 Aug. 1945, p. 3 [u].

45.08.10B "The Potsdam Decisions." [Potsdam Conference]. *CJC*, 10 Aug. 1945, p. 3 [u].

45.08.10C "Is This the End?" [Soviet Union declares war on Japan]. *CJC*, 10 Aug. 1945, p. 3 [u].

45.08.17A "The Post-War Period Begins." [Post-war period]. *CJC*, 17 Aug. 1945, p. 3 [u].

45.08.24A "The Atomic Bomb." [Atomic bomb and foreign policy on Palestine]. *CJC*, 24 Aug. 1945, p. 3 [u].

45.08.24B "Recalcitrant Refugees?" [Repatriation of refugees]. *CJC*, 24 Aug. 1945, p. 3 [u].

45.08.24C "President Truman's Declaration." [U.S. foreign policy on Palestine]. *CJC*, 24 Aug. 1945, p. 3 [u].

45.08.31A "The Patria." [Arrival of refugees in Palestine]. *CJC*, 31 Aug. 1945, p. 3 [u].

45.08.31B "Shameless Cynicism." [Arab view of U.S. foreign policy on Palestine]. *CJC*, 31 Aug. 1945, p. 3 [u].

45.09.07A "The New Year." [Rosh Hashana]. *CJC*, 7 Sept. 1945, p. 3 [u].

45.09.14A "The Concentration Camps Still Function." [Jewish refugees]. *CJC*, 14 Sept. 1945, p. 3 [u].

45.09.14B "Evil and the Evil-doer." [Retribution for German and Japanese war crimes]. *CJC*, 14 Sept. 1945, p. 3 [u].

45.09.21A "Truman's Amendment." [U.S. foreign policy on Palestine]. *CJC*, 21 Sept. 1945, p. 3 [u].

45.09.21B "Anti-Semitism in Europe." [Continued anti-Semitism in Europe]. *CJC*, 21 Sept. 1945, p. 3 [u].

45.09.21C "Lord Haw Haw." [Conviction of Lord Haw-Haw]. *CJC*, 21 Sept. 1945, p. 3 [u].

45.09.28A "Zionism and the World Conscience." [British foreign policy on Palestine]. *CJC*, 28 Sept. 1945, p. 3 [u].

45.09.28B "Belsen." [Concentration camp at Belsen]. *CJC*, 28 Sept. 1945, p. 3 [u].

45.10.05A "The Combined Jewish Appeal." [Combined Jewish Appeal]. *CJC*, 5 Oct. 1945, p. 3 [u].

45.10.05B "The Snows of Yesteryear." [Review of *My Lexicon* by Melech Ravitch]. *CJC*, 5 Oct. 1945, p. 8 [s].

45.10.12A "The Doubly Broken Promise." [British foreign policy on Palestine]. *CJC*, 12 Oct. 1945, p. 3 [u].

45.10.12B "The Trial of Pierre Laval." [Trial of Pierre Laval]. *CJC*, 12 Oct 1945, p. 3 [u].

45.10.19A "The Last Refuge." [Captive Nazis turn to religion]. *CJC*, 19 Oct. 1945, p. 3 [u].

45.10.19B "The Judicial Process." [Trial of war criminals]. *CJC*, 19 Oct. 1945, p. 3 [u].

45.10.26A "The Ninth Victory Loan." [Canada launches a victory loan]. *CJC*, 26 Oct. 1945, p. 3 [u].

45.10.26B "The Roosevelt Correspondence." [U.S. foreign policy on Palestine]. *CJC*, 26 Oct. 1945, p. 3 [u].

45.10.26C "The Argentine Situation." [Fascism in Argentina]. *CJC*, 26 Oct. 1945, p. 3 [u].

45.11.02A "Balfour Day." [British foreign policy on Palestine]. *CJC*, 2 Nov. 1945, p. 3 [u].

45.11.02B "Ley, the First Minstrel." [Suicide of Robert Ley]. *CJC*, 2 Nov. 1945, p. 3 [u].

45.11.02C "The Poetry Which is Prayer." [Review of *Lider und Loiben* by J.I. Segal]. *CJC*, 2 Nov. 1945, pp. 8, 16 [s].

45.11.09A "In Old Mizraim." [Arab anti-Zionist riots in Egypt]. *CJC*, 9 Nov. 1945, p. 3 [u].

45.11.09B "And Now in Tripoli." [Arab anti-Zionist riots in Tripoli]. *CJC*, 9 Nov. 1945, p. 3 [u].

45.11.09C "The Re-educated Germans." [Germany after WWII]. *CJC*, 9 Nov. 1945, p. 3 [u].

45.11.16A "Le Canada and 'This Hatred'." [Anti-Semitism in Quebec]. *CJC*, 16 Nov. 1945, p. 3 [u].

45.11.16B "Another Commission on Palestine!" [Anglo-American Joint Commission on Palestine]. *CJC*, 16 Nov. 1945, pp. 3, 14 [u].

45.11.16C "An Encyclopedic Work." [Review of *The Mishna* with translation and commentary in Yiddish by Simcha Petrushka]. *CJC*, 16 Nov. 1945, p. 14 [s].

45.11.16D "Those Who Should Have Been Ours." [*See* 46.05.10B]. New Palestine, 16 Nov. 1945, pp. 30–1, 43 [s].

45.11.23A "The Nuerenberg Trial." [Nazi war crimes trials at Nueremberg]. *CJC*, 23 Nov. 1945, p. 3 [u].

45.11.23B " 'Convention Enthusiasm' " [British foreign policy on Palestine]. *CJC*, 23 Nov. 1945, p. 3 [u].

45.11.30A "The Feast of Chanukah." [Relevance of Chanukah story to current events]. *CJC*, 30 Nov. 1945, p. 3 [u].

45.11.30B "Plus Ca Change." [Continued detention of prisoners at Belsen after WWII]. *CJC*, 30 Nov. 1945, p. 3 [u].

45.11.30C "Arms, and the Men." [British shoot Jews in Palestine]. *CJC*, 30 Nov. 1945, p. 3 [u].

45.12.07A "President Truman's Latest Statement." [Harry S. Truman opposes establishment of a Jewish state]. *CJC*, 7 Dec. 1945, p. 3 [u].

45.12.07B "Radar." [Radar is used to detect approach of illegal immigrants to Palestine]. *CJC*, 7 Dec. 1945, p. 3 [u].

45.12.14A "Flight — To Berlin!" [Anti-Semitism in Poland]. *CJC*, 14 Dec. 1945, p. 3 [u].

45.12.14B "Nuerenberg Trials." [Trials at Nueremberg]. *CJC*, 14 Dec. 1945, p. 3 [u].

45.12.14C "The Palestine Commission." [Anglo-American Joint Commission on Palestine]. *CJC*, 14 Dec. 1945, p. 3 [u].

45.12.21A "Allan Bronfman." [Fiftieth birthday of Allan Bronfman]. *CJC*, 21 Dec. 1945, p. 3 [u].

45.12.21B "The Voice Is the Voice of Jacques." [Anti-Semitism of Norman Jacques]. *CJC*, 21 Dec. 1945, p. 3 [u].

45.12.28A "President Truman's Gesture." [Admission of refugees to U.S.]. *CJC*, 28 Dec. 1945, p. 3 [u].

45.12.28B "The Bust of Hitler." [Tolerance of fascism in England]. *CJC*, 28 Dec. 1945, p. 3 [u].

46.01.04A "It's a Conspiracy." [Anti-Zionism]. *CJC*, 4 Jan. 1946, p. 3 [u].

46.01.04B "Exodus and Numbers." [British foreign policy on Palestine]. *CJC*, 4 Jan. 1946, p. 3 [u].

46.01.04C "I Am Become a Not-God." [Hirohito renounces claim to godhood]. *CJC*, 4 Jan. 1946, p. 3 [u].

46.01.04D "The Last Will and Testament of Adolf Hitler." [Publication of Adolf Hitler's will]. *CJC*, 4 Jan. 1946, p. 8 [s].

46.01.11A "The Joint Commmission." [Hearings of the Anglo-American Joint Commission on Palestine]. *CJC*, 11 Jan. 1946, p. 3 [u].

46.01.11B "Morgan on the Reef." [Recalling of Frederick Morgan]. *CJC*, 11 Jan. 1946, p. 3 [u].

46.01.11C "Another Conspiracy." [Anti-Zionist propaganda]. *CJC*, 11 Jan. 1946, p. 3 [u].

46.01.11D "In the Meanwhile." [British foreign policy on the admission of Jewish refugees to Palestine]. *CJC*, 11 Jan. 1946, p. 3 [u].

46.01.18A "The Histadrut." [Importance of the Histadrut in Palestine]. *CJC*, 18 Jan. 1946, p. 3 [u].

46.01.18B "An Injustice All Round." [Commutation of death sentence of Kurt Meyer]. *CJC*, 18 Jan. 1946, p. 3 [u].

46.01.18C "The Racial Gallup." [Racism in Canada]. *CJC*, 18 Jan. 1946, p. 3 [u].

46.01.18D "Queen Mab and Mickey Mouse." [Mickey Mouse and poetry]. *CJC*, 18 Jan. 1946, p. 9 [s].

46.01.25A "The Zionist Convention." [Twenty-eighth Zionist convention]. *CJC*, 25 Jan. 1946, p. 3 [u].

46.01.25B "The Divided Allegiance." [Anti-Zionism of Lessing Rosenwald]. *CJC*, 25 Jan. 1946, p. 3 [u].

46.01.25C "Independence For Transjordan." [Granting of independence to Transjordan]. *CJC*, 25 Jan. 1946, p. 3 [u].

46.01.25D "Of Hebrew Humor." [*See* 35.11.00B]. *CJC*, 25 Jan. 1946, p. 5 [s].

46.02.01A "The Zionist Convention." [Call for Palestine to become the seventh Dominion in the Commonwealth]. *CJC*, 1 Feb. 1946, p. 3 [u].

46.02.01B "The Great Secret." [Anti-Zionist reporting of the flight of Jews from Poland]. *CJC*, 1 Feb. 1946, p. 3 [u].

46.02.01C "To What Lengths?" [British anti-terrorist legislation in Palestine]. *CJC*, 1 Feb. 1946, p. 3 [u].

46.02.01D "Of Hebrew Humor." [*See* 35.11.00B]. *CJC*, 1 Feb. 1946, p. 8 [s].

46.02.08A "Who Won the War?" [Survey of attitudes of U.S. soldiers]. *CJC*, 8 Feb. 1946, p. 3 [u].

46.02.08B "The Pleas Begin." [Nazi war criminals]. *CJC*, 8 Feb. 1946, p. 3 [u].

46.02.08C "Of Hebrew Humor." [*See* 35.11.00B]. *CJC*, 8 Feb. 1946, p. 8 [s].

46.02.15A "An Unworthy Resolution." [Defeat of a proposal to limit aid to refugees]. *CJC*, 15 Feb. 1946, p. 3 [u].

46.02.15B "The Argentine." [U.S. speaks out against Argentine fascism]. *CJC*, 15 Feb. 1946, p. 3 [u].

46.02.15C "Of Hebrew Humor." [*See* 35.11.00B]. *CJC*, 15 Feb. 1946, p. 8 [s].

46.02.22A "Arms and the Spy." [Igor Gouzenko affair]. *CJC*, 22 Feb. 1946, p. 3 [u].

46.02.22B "The Anglo-American Palestine Commission." [Anglo-American Joint Commission on Palestine]. *CJC*, 22 Feb. 1946, p. 3 [u].

46.02.22C "Writing in Canada." [Reply to a questionnaire on writing in Canada (1)]. *CJC*, 22 Feb. 1946, pp. 8, 16 [s].

46.03.01A "Freedom from Fear." [International tension after WWII]. *CJC*, 1 Mar. 1946, p. 3 [u].

46.03.01B "The Nuerenberg Witnesses." [Nazi war crimes trials at Nueremberg]. *CJC*, 1 Mar. 1946, p. 3 [u].

46.03.01C "Franco's End?" [Fascism in Spain]. *CJC*, 1 Mar. 1946, p. 3 [u].

46.03.01D "Writing in Canada." [Reply to a questionnaire on writing in Canada (2)]. *CJC*, 1 Mar. 1946, p. 8 [s].

46.03.08A "Churchill's Speech." [Winston Churchill's speech, "The Sinews of Peace"]. *CJC*, 8 Mar. 1946, p. 3.

46.03.08B "The Slow Process of Reform." [Debate on Zionism among Jews in U.S.]. *CJC*, 8 Mar. 1946, p. 3 [u].

46.03.08C "The Nazis and Gas Warfare." [Nazi use of gas chambers]. *CJC*, 8 Mar. 1946, p. 3 [u].

46.03.15A "The Feast of Purim." [Need for a Jewish homeland]. *CJC*, 15 Mar. 1946, p. 3 [u].

46.03.15B "The Anglo-American Commission on Palestine." [Hearings of Anglo-American Joint Commission on Palestine]. *CJC*, 15 Mar. 1946, p. 3 [u].

46.03.22A "The United Palestine Appeal." [Need for a Jewish homeland in Palestine]. *CJC*, 22 Mar. 1946, p. 3 [u].

46.03.22B "When Jews Are a Minority." [Jews under Arab rule]. *CJC*, 22 Mar. 1946, p. 3 [u].

46.03.22C "Goering Defends Himself." [Hermann Goering's defence at Nueremberg]. *CJC*, 22 Mar. 1946, p. 3 [u].

46.03.22D "Annotation on Shapiro's Essay on Rime." [Review of *Essay on Rime* by Karl Shapiro (1)]. *CJC*, 22 Mar. 1946, p. 8 [s].

46.03.29A "Witnessing in Jerusalem." [Joint Commission hearings in Palestine]. *CJC*, 29 Mar. 1946, p. 3 [u].

46.03.29B "Day But Not Light." [Racist commentary of Jean-Charles Harvey]. *CJC*, 29 Mar. 1946, p. 3 [u].

46.03.29C "A Patron of Yiddish Literature." [Max Grafstein]. *CJC*, 29 Mar. 1946, p. 3 [u].

46.03.29D "Annotation on Shapiro's Essay on Rime." [Review of *Essay on Rime* by Karl Shapiro (2)]. *CJC*, 29 Mar. 1946, pp. 8–9 [s].

46.04.05A "As in 'The Good Old Days'." [Persecution of Jewish refugees in Germany]. *CJC*, 5 Apr. 1946, p. 3 [u].

46.04.05B "The Hebrew University." [Twenty-first anniversary of the founding of the Hebrew University]. *CJC*, 5 Apr. 1946, p. 3 [u].

46.04.12A "The Feast of Passover." [Need for a Jewish homeland]. *CJC*, 12 Apr. 1946, p. 5 [u].

46.04.12B "The Trial Goes On." [Trials at Nueremberg]. *CJC*, 12 Apr. 1946, p. 5 [u].

46.04.19A "The Fast of the Fifteen." [Admission to Palestine of Jewish refugees held at La Spezia, Italy]. *CJC*, 19 Apr. 1946, p. 3 [u].

46.04.19B "Herr Rosenberg is a Philosopher." [Testimony of Alfred Rosenberg at Nueremberg]. *CJC*, 19 Apr. 1946, p. 3 [u].

46.04.19C "A Definition of Poetry." [Impossibility of defining poetry]. *CJC*, 19 Apr. 1946, pp. 8, 12 [s]. See also MS 5073–77.

46.04.26A "The Anglo-American Palestine Report." [Anglo-American Joint Commission on Palestine]. *CJC*, 26 Apr. 1946, p. 3 [u].

46.05.03A "The Herrenvolk." [Nazi war criminals]. *CJC*, 3 May 1946, p. 3 [u].

46.05.03B "The Displaced Persons." [Continued detention of Jewish refugees after WWII]. *CJC*, 3 May 1946, p. 3 [u].

46.05.03C "The Agents-Provocateurs." [Jewish terrorism in Palestine]. *CJC*, 3 May 1946, p. 3 [u].

46.05.10A "An Anniversary." [Anniversary of the end of WWII]. *CJC*, 10 May 1946, p. 3 [u].

46.05.10B "Talents That Should Have Been Ours." [Assimilation of Jewish-American Writers]. *CJC*, 10 May 1946, pp. 6, 15 [s]. See also MS 5269–76.

46.05.17A "The Canadian Arab." [Arab anti-Semitic publication in Canada]. *CJC*, 17 May 1946, p. 3 [u].

46.05.24A "The Fabians." [Handling of the Jewish refugee problem by the Attlee government]. *CJC*, 24 May 1946, p. 3 [u].

46.05.24B "The Habonim Convention." [Zionism in Canada]. *CJC*, 24 May 1946, p. 3 [u].

46.05.24C "Y.M.H.A.'s in Canada." [YMHA's in Canada]. *CJC*, 24 May 1946, p. 3 [u].

46.05.31A "The Feast of Weeks." [State of the world after WWII]. *CJC*, 31 May 1946, p. 3 [u].

46.05.31B "Justice in Germany." [American administration of Germany after WWII]. *CJC*, 31 May 1946, p. 3 [u].

46.05.31C "The Dachau Murderers." [Execution of Nazis]. *CJC*, 31 May 1946, p. 3 [u].

46.06.07A "Canadian Immigration." [Canadian immigration policy]. *CJC*, 7 June 1946, p. 3 [u].

46.06.07B "The Kingdom of Transjordania." [Granting of autonomous statehood to Transjordan]. *CJC*, 7 June 1946, p. 3 [u].

46.06.07C "The Outremont Schools." [Admission of Jewish children to Protestant schools]. *CJC*, 7 June 1946, p. 7 [s].

46.06.07D "Palestine and the Lords Spiritual." [Secularization and modernization of Palestine]. *CJC*, 7 June 1946, pp. 7, 14 [s].

46.06.07E "The Abbe and the Bishop." [Statements limiting Catholic participation in associations outside the Church]. *CJC*, 7 June 1946, p. 14 [s].

46.06.14A "The Labour Party, Mr. Bevin, and Palestine." [British foreign policy on Palestine]. *CJC*, 14 June 1946, p. 3 [u].

46.06.14B "The Disappearing Mufti." [Escape of Haj Ammin al-Husseini from France]. *CJC*, 14 June 1946, p. 6 [s].

46.06.14C "Another Committee." [U.S. State Department Committee on Palestine]. *CJC*, 14 June 1946, pp. 7, 14 [s].

46.06.21A "The Polish-Jewish Delegation." [Meeting of Polish Jews in Canada]. *CJC*, 21 June 1946, p. 3 [u].

46.06.21B "In Defence of the Atom." [Development of atomic technology]. *CJC*, 21 June 1946, p. 3 [u].

46.06.21C "Whom the King Delighteth to Honor." [Decoration of Jews in the Canadian Armed Forces]. *CJC*, 21 June 1946, p. 3 [u].

46.06.28A "Reparations to European Jewry." [Financial reparations to Jews after WWII]. *CJC*, 28 June 1946, p. 3 [u].

46.06.28B "A Fitting Memorial." [Importance of a memorial for Jewish victims of WWII]. *CJC*, 28 June 1946, p. 3 [u].

46.07.05A "Operation Crossroads." [Atomic technology and international relations]. *CJC*, 5 July 1946, p. 3 [u].

46.07.05B "UNRRA and the Jews." [Treatment of Jewish refugees]. *CJC*, 5 July 1946, p. 3 [u].

46.07.05C "When is Kidnapping Legal?" [British arrests of Jewish nationalists in Palestine]. *CJC*, 5 July, 1946, pp. 4–5 [s].

46.07.12A "What the Arab Committee Didn't Write." [Arab Higher Committee letter to Harry S. Truman]. *CJC*, 12 July 1946, p. 3 [u].

46.07.12B "The Polish Paradise." [Persecution of Jews in Poland]. *CJC*, 12 July 1946, p. 3 [u].

46.07.19A "Calling the Bluff." [Delay of admission of Jewish refugees to Palestine]. *CJC*, 19 July 1946, p. 3 [u].

46.07.19B "Another Country." [Substituting a country other than Palestine for a Jewish homeland]. *CJC*, 19 July 1946, p. 3 [u].

46.07.19C "Polish Jewry." [Persecution of Jews in Poland]. *CJC*, 19 July 1946, p. 3 [u].

46.07.19D "Apples of Gold in Pictures of Silver." [Review of *Lexicon of Hebrew Homonyms* by Rabbi Solomon Klonitzke-Kline]. *CJC*, 19 July 1946, p. 8 [s].

46.07.26A "The Attempt on the House of David." [Irgun bombing of the King David Hotel]. *CJC*, 26 July, 1946, p. 3 [u].

46.07.26B "The Voice of Jacques." [Anti-Semitism of Norman Jacques]. *CJC*, 26 July 1946, p. 3 [u].

46.08.02A "The Fast of Tisha B'av." [Mourning the plight of Palestine and the Jews]. *CJC*, 2 Aug. 1946, p. 3 [u].

46.08.02B "The Well-Named Barker." [British anti-Semitism]. *CJC*, 2 Aug. 1946, p. 3 [u].

46.08.02C "Rilke and His Translators." [Review of *Thirty-one Poems* by Rainer Maria Rilke, translated by Ludwig Lewisohn]. *CJC*, 2 Aug. 1946, pp. 8, 13 [s].

46.08.09A "When Ahasveros Imitates Solomon; The Partition Plan." [Plan to divide Palestine]. *CJC*, 9 Aug. 1946, p. 3 [u].

46.08.16A "German Statistics: Politics and Justice." [Post-war Germany]. *CJC*, 16 May 1946, p. 3 [u].

46.08.23A "The British Note on Palestine: Document and Commentary." [Hypocrisy of British foreign policy on Palestine]. *CJC*, 23 Aug. 1946, p. 3 [u].

46.08.30A "Operation Shameful." [British forces raid village of Sedoth Yam]. *CJC*, 30 Aug. 1946, p. 3 [u].

46.08.30B "The Mufti: New Knight of the Round Table." [Nomination of Haj Ammin al-Husseini as a delegate to Palestine Conference]. *CJC*, 30 Aug. 1946, p. 3 [u].

46.08.30C "Literature at Latrun." [Literary activities of interned Jewish nationalists]. *CJC*, 30 Aug. 1946, p. 3 [u].

46.08.30D "Postscript." [U.S. attitude towards Zionism]. *CJC*, 30 Aug. 1946, p. 3 [u].

46.08.30E "On Translating the Yiddish Folk Song." [Translating the Yiddish folk song]. *CJC*, 30 Aug. 1946, p. 6 [s].

46.09.06A "The Four Freedoms on the High Seas." [Jewish refugees denied admission to Palestine]. *CJC*, 6 Sept. 1946, p. 3 [u].

46.09.06B "Memoir at Nueremberg." [Conclusion of the Nueremberg trials]. *CJC*, 6 Sept. 1946, p. 3 [u].

46.09.13A "Jus, Imperium, Pax." [Commemoration of the Roman conquest of Britain]. *CJC*, 13 Sept. 1946, p. 3 [u].

46.09.13B "The Gloomy Dean." [W. R. Inge on justice at Nueremberg]. *CJC*, 13 Sept. 1946, p. 3 [u].

46.09.20A "The No. 1 Anti-Semite" [Soviet anti-Semitism]. *CJC*, 20 Sept. 1946, p. 3 [u].

46.09.20B "Shaw at Ninety." [George Bernard Shaw on the Nueremberg trials]. *CJC*, 20 Sept. 1946, p. 3 [u].

46.09.20C "H. Wolofsky — Septuagenarian." [Tribute to Hirsch Wolofsky]. *CJC*, 20 Sept. 1946, p. 7 [s].

46.09.25A "The New Year." [Reflections on past and future of Jews]. *CJC*, 25 Sept. 1946, p. 3 [u].

46.10.00A "Annotation on Shapiro's 'Essay on Rime'." [*See* 46.03.22D, 46.03.29D]. *Northern Review* 1, 3 (Oct.–Nov. 1946), pp. 30–8 [s].

46.10.04A "The Nuremberg Trial." [Nazi war crimes trials at Nueremberg]. *CJC*, 4 Oct. 1946, p. 3 [u].

46.10.09A "President Truman's Statement." [Harry S. Truman addresses Clement Attlee on the Palestinian question]. *CJC*, 9 Oct. 1946, p. 3 [u].

46.10.09B "The Feast of Tabernacles." [Irony of Succoth for Jewish refugees]. *CJC*, 9 Oct. 1946, p. 3 [u].

46.10.09C "Footnote to Nueremberg." [Verdicts of Nueremberg]. *CJC*, 9 Oct. 1946, p. 3 [u].

46.10.16A "A Reply to Dr. I. M. Rabinowitch." [Reply to anti-Zionist remarks of I. M. Rabinowitch]. *CJC*, 16 Oct. 1946, pp. 3–5 [s]. See also " 'Zionism' — In Reply to Dr. I. M. Rabinowitch," printed pamphlet, n.d.

46.10.25A "The Moslem Brotherhood." [Burning of English books by Arabs]. *CJC*, 25 Oct. 1946, p. 3 [u].

46.10.25B "Another Authority on Palestine." [Dorsey Stevens on Palestine]. *CJC*, 25 Oct. 1946, p. 3 [u].

46.11.01A "The Combined Jewish Appeal." [Combined Jewish Appeal]. *CJC*, 1 Nov. 1946, p. 3 [u].

46.11.08A "Twenty-Nine Years After." [Twenty-ninth anniversary of the Balfour Declaration]. *CJC*, 8 Nov. 1946, p. 3 [u].

46.11.08B "Justice and Politics." [Treatment of Jews by the British administration in Palestine]. *CJC*, 8 Nov. 1946, p. 3 [u].

46.11.08C "The Jewish Agency." [Release of interned members of the Jewish Agency]. *CJC*, 8 Nov. 1946, p. 3 [u].

46.11.15A "Lake Success." [U.N. meetings at Lake Success]. *CJC*, 15 Nov. 1946, p. 3 [u].

46.11.15B "A Kind of Gesture." [Admission of refugees to Palestine]. *CJC*, 15 Nov. 1946, p. 3 [u].

46.11.22A "To Make the Flesh Creep." [Anti-Semitism in the British press]. *CJC*, 22 Nov. 1946, p. 3 [u].

46.11.22B "Reprisals." [British troops attack civilians in Tel Aviv]. *CJC*, 22 Nov. 1946, p. 3 [u].

46.11.22C "A Case And Its Point." [British anti-Semitism]. *CJC*, 22 Nov. 1946, p. 3 [u].

46.11.22D "Departure and Arrival." [Review of *Thieves in the Night* by Arthur Koestler]. *CJC*, 22 Nov. 1946, p. 8 [s].

46.11.29A "Racism — A 'Purely Domestic Affair'?" [South African racism]. *CJC*, 29 Nov. 1946, p. 3 [u].

46.11.29B "The Address of Mr. J.G. MacDonald." [Address of spokesman of the Anglo-American Joint Commission on Palestine]. *CJC*, 29 Nov. 1946, p. 3 [u].

46.11.29C "The Nobel Prize." [Nobel Prize awards for 1946]. *CJC*, 29 Nov. 1946, p. 8 [s].

46.12.06A "The Hagana Issues a Warning." [Haganah speaks out against Jewish terrorism]. *CJC*, 6 Dec. 1946, p. 3 [u].

46.12.06B "The Japanese Deportations." [Deportation of Japanese Canadians]. *CJC*, 6 Dec. 1946, p. 3 [u].

46.12.06C "More Lasting Than Bronze." [Establishment of a colony in Palestine in memory of Jewish Canadian soldiers killed in WWII]. *CJC*, 6 Dec. 1946, p. 3 [u].

46.12.06D "The Snows of Yesteryear." [Review of *Burning Lights* by Bella Chagall]. *CJC*, 6 Dec. 1946, p. 8 [s].

46.12.13A "Dr. Weizmann's Address." [Chaim Weizmann's address to the World Jewish Congress]. *CJC*, 13 Dec. 1946, p. 3 [u].

46.12.13B "Witnesses of Jehovah." [Discrimination against Jehovah's Witnesses in Quebec]. *CJC*, 13 Dec. 1946, p. 3 [u].

46.12.20A "The Feast of Chanukah." [Relevance of Chanukah story to Jews in Palestine]. *CJC*, 20 Dec. 1946, p. 3 [u].

46.12.20B "Happy Days are Here Again." [Racism in U.S.]. *CJC*, 20 Dec. 1946, p. 3 [u].

46.12.27A "Commentary on a Cartoon." [Anti-Zionist cartoon]. *CJC*, 27 Dec. 1946, p. 3 [u].

47.01.03A "The World Zionist Congress." [Twenty-second World Zionist Congress]. *CJC*, 3 Jan. 1947, p. 3 [u].

47.01.03B "This Damnable Terror." [Jewish terrorism in Palestine]. *CJC*, 3 Jan. 1947, p. 3 [u].

47.01.10A "Science and Savagery." [Debate on publication of findings of Nazi experiments]. *CJC*, 10 Jan. 1947, p. 3 [u].

47.01.10B "Chisels and the Man . . ." [Questionable merit of memorials to Winston Churchill and Franklin Delano Roosevelt]. *CJC*, 10 Jan. 1947, p. 8 [s].

47.01.17A "Labour Palestine." [Labour Palestine and Jewish terrorism in Palestine]. *CJC*, 17 Jan. 1947, p. 3 [u].

47.01.17B "The Talmud Torah Campaign." [Talmud Torah and the preservation of Jewish culture]. *CJC*, 17 Jan. 1947, p. 3 [u].

47.01.24A "Canada's Role in International Affairs." [Canadian foreign policy after WWII]. *CJC*, 24 Jan. 1947, p. 3 [u].

47.01.24B "Appeals to the Privy Council." [Canadian law and the Privy Council]. *CJC*, 24 Jan. 1947, p. 3 [u].

47.01.24C "Yerachmiel Weingarten." [Yerachmiel Weingarten]. *CJC*, 24 Jan. 1947, p. 3 [u].

47.01.24D "The World's Conscience." [Public opinion on Jewish refugees]. *CJC*, 24 Jan. 1947, p. 8 [s].

47.01.31A "The Strange Interlude." [Racism]. *CJC*, 31 Jan. 1947, p. 3 [u].

47.01.31B "The Chinese Exclusion Act." [Racism in Canada]. *CJC*, 31 Jan. 1947, p. 3 [u].

47.01.31C "Immigration into Australia." [Australia's alleged offer of sanctuary to Jewish refugees]. *CJC*, 31 Jan. 1947, p. 3 [u].

47.02.07A "Federation-Partition." [Morrison plan for the partition of Palestine]. *CJC*, 7 Feb. 1947, p. 3 [u].

47.02.07B "Churchill and Palestine." [British foreign policy on Palestine]. *CJC*, 7 Feb. 1947, p. 3 [u].

47.02.07C "Senator Bouchard's Plea." [Sectarian education in Canada]. *CJC*, 7 Feb. 1947, p. 3 [u].

47.02.14A "England and the Bible." [Lack of British sympathy for Jewish nationalism]. *CJC*, 14 Feb. 1947, p. 3 [u].

47.02.14B "The Informer." [Jewish terrorism in Palestine]. *CJC*, 14 Feb. 1947, p. 3 [u].

47.02.14C "Who Invented What?" [Soviet claims to American inventions]. *CJC*, 14 Feb. 1947, p. 3 [u].

47.02.21A "Mining and Undermining." [Employment of refugees in British coal mines]. *CJC*, 21 Feb. 1947, p. 3 [u].

47.02.21B "In the Lap of the Demigods." [British foreign policy on Palestine]. *CJC*, 21 Feb. 1947, p. 3 [u].

47.02.21C "Canadian Hadassah Convention." [Zionism in Canada]. *CJC*, 21 Feb. 1947, p. 3 [u].

47.02.28A "Bevin's Latest." [British foreign policy on Palestine]. *CJC*, 28 Feb. 1947, p. 3 [u].

47.02.28B "DGJ's." [Displaced German Jews]. *CJC*, 28 Feb. 1947, p. 3 [u].

47.02.28C "German Intransigence." [Germany after WWII]. *CJC*, 28 Feb. 1947, p. 3 [u].

47.03.07A "The Holy Land and Martial Law." [Jewish terrorism in Palestine]. *CJC*, 7 Mar. 1947, p. 3 [u].

47.03.07B "The Underweight and the Overweight." [U.S. sympathy for postwar Germany]. *CJC*, 7 Mar. 1947, p. 3 [u].

47.03.07C "A British Eccentric." [A British citizen sues Ernest Bevin for breach of promise]. *CJC*, 7 Mar. 1947, p. 3 [u].

47.03.14A "The Change In Geography." [International relations after WWII]. *CJC*, 14 Mar. 1947, p. 3 [u].

47.03.14B "Operation Scuttle." [British foreign policy on Palestine]. *CJC*, 14 Mar. 1947, p. 3 [u].

47.03.14C "The Peace Conference." [Conference of foreign ministers in Moscow]. *CJC*, 14 Mar. 1947, p. 3 [u].

47.03.21A "The United Palestine Appeal." [United Palestine Appeal]. *CJC*, 21 Mar. 1947, p. 3 [u].

47.03.21B "The Shaar Hashomayim Centenary." [Centenary of Shaar Hashomayim Synagogue]. *CJC*, 21 Mar. 1947, p. 3 [u].

47.03.21C "They Fraternize Again." [British administration in Palestine]. *CJC*, 21 Mar. 1947, p. 3 [u].

47.03.28A "The Doctor (Arab) on Zionism." [Anti-Zionism]. *CJC*, 28 Mar. 1947, p. 3 [u].

47.03.28B "Joe Can't Take It Anymore." [Writers in the Soviet Union]. *CJC*, 28 Mar. 1947, p. 3 [u].

47.03.28C "La Chose d'autrui." [British and U.S. foreign policy]. *CJC*, 28 Mar. 1947, p. 3 [u].

47.04.04A "The Feast of Passover." [Comparison of the exodus from Egypt with the plight of Jewish war refugees]. *CJC*, 4 Apr. 1947, p. 3 [u].

47.04.04B "The Moving Ark of the Law." [Fiftieth anniversary of Yeshiva University]. *CJC*, 4 Apr. 1947, p. 3 [u].

47.04.10A "When History is Not Made." [International relations after WWII]. *CJC*, 10 [*misdated* 19] Apr. 1947, p. 3 [u].

47.04.10B "O God! O Montreal!" [Lack of culture in Montreal]. *CJC*, 10 Apr. 1947, p. 3 [u].

47.04.10C "They Protest the Mufti." [Anti-British activity of the Mufti]. *CJC*, 10 Apr. 1947, p. 3 [u].

47.04.18A "It was only 2,000,000!" [Nazi genocide of the Jews]. *CJC*, 18 Apr. 1947, p. 3 [u].

47.04.18B "Photograph herein Enclosed." [Racism in American universities]. *CJC*, 18 Apr. 1947, p. 3 [u].

47.04.18C "German Contribution." [Germany after wwii]. *CJC*, 18 Apr. 1947, p. 3 [u].

47.04.25A "Palestine Prelude." [British administration in Palestine]. *CJC*, 25 Apr. 1947, p. 3 [u].

47.04.25B "The Forthcoming U.N. Session." [Special U.N. session on Palestine]. *CJC*, 25 Apr. 1947, p. 3 [u].

47.04.25C "Wallace on Palestine." [Henry Wallace on Palestine]. *CJC*, 25 Apr. 1947, p. 3 [u].

47.05.02A "The Moscow Conference." [International affairs after wwii]. *CJC*, 2 May 1947, p. 3 [u].

47.05.02B "What this Country Needs." [Chocolate bar boycott in Canada]. *CJC*, 2 May 1947, p. 3 [u].

47.05.02C "The Palestine Debate." [U.N. debate on Palestine]. *CJC*, 2 May 1947, p. 3 [u].

47.05.09A "Hamlet without Hamlet." [U.N. deliberations on Palestine]. *CJC*, 9 May 1947, p. 3 [u].

47.05.09B "The Ambassador of Soccer." [Success of Palestinian soccer team]. *CJC*, 9 May 1947, p. 3 [u].

47.05.09C "Gandhi's Advice." [Passive resistance]. *CJC*, 9 May 1947, p. 3 [u].

47.05.16A "Palestine Independence." [Joint Soviet-Arab stand at U.N.]. *CJC*, 16 May 1947, p. 3 [u].

47.05.16B "The Mufti Unmasked." [Political activities of the Mufti]. *CJC*, 16 May, 1947, p. 3 [u].

47.05.16C "A Book About The People." [Review of *The Jewish People: Past and Present*, Vol. 1 by Central Yiddish Culture Organization, N.Y.]. *CJC*, 16 May 1947, p. 6 [s].

47.05.23A "Gromyko's Palestine Speech." [Soviet anti-Zionism at U.N.]. *CJC*, 23 May 1947, p. 3 [u].

47.05.23B "The Vicarious Heroes." [Jewish terrorism in Palestine]. *CJC*, 23 May 1947, p. 3 [u].

47.05.23C "An Arab Afterthought." [Arab attacks on Jews in Palestine]. *CJC*, 23 May 1947, p. 3 [u].

47.05.30A "The Canadian Jewish Congress." [Canadian Jewish Congress, seventh plenary session]. *CJC*, 30 May 1947, p. 3 [u].

47.05.30B "Public Relations and How Not to Conduct Them." [Jewish public image is damaged]. *CJC*, 30 May 1947, p. 3 [u].

47.06.07A "The Seventh Plenary Session." [Canadian Jewish Congress, seventh plenary session]. *CJC*, 7 June 1947, p. 3 [u].

47.06.07B "A Jewish Civil Service." [Work of the Canadian Jewish Congress]. *CJC*, 7 June 1947, p. 3 [u].

47.06.07C "Dr. Goldman's Address." [Nahum Goldman addresses the Canadian Jewish Congress]. *CJC*, 7 June 1947, p. 3 [u].

47.06.13A "The U.N. Commission on Palestine." [UNSCOP]. *CJC*, 13 June 1947, p. 3 [u].

47.06.13B "Whom the Gods Would Destroy." [Jewish terrorism in Palestine]. *CJC*, 13 June 1947, p. 3 [u].

47.06.13C "Friends of the Court." [Jewish anti-Zionism]. *CJC*, 13 June 1947, p. 3 [u].

47.06.20A "The Commission finds a Welcome Mat." [UNSCOP]. *CJC*, 20 June 1947, p. 3 [u].

47.06.20B "What is a Jew?" [Chaim Weizmann at UNSCOP hearings]. *CJC*, 20 June 1947, p. 3 [u].

47.06.27A "The Central Conference of American Rabbis." [Reform Judaism]. *CJC*, 27 June 1947, p. 3 [u].

47.06.27B "The Arab Boycott." [Arabs boycott hearings of UNSCOP]. *CJC*, 27 June 1947, p. 3 [u].

47.06.27C "True Heroism." [Irgun terrorist activities]. *CJC*, 27 June 1947, p. 3 [u].

47.07.04A "The Octogenarian." [Eightieth anniversary of Confederation]. *CJC*, 4 July 1947, p. 3 [u].

47.07.04B "The Salt of the Earth." [Agriculture in Palestine]. *CJC*, 4 July, 1947, p. 3 [u].

47.07.04C "Another Deadlock." [Conference of foreign ministers at Moscow]. *CJC*, 4 July 1947, p. 3 [u].

47.07.11A "Two Kinds of Justice." [Sentencing of Jewish political offenders in Palestine]. *CJC*, 11 July 1947, p. 3 [u].

47.07.11B "'Rochmanim' and 'bnai-Rochmanim'." [David Ben Gurion at UNSCOP hearings]. *CJC*, 11 July 1947, p. 3 [u].

47.07.18A "Dr. Magnes and the Bi-National State." [Proposal for a bi-national Palestinian state]. *CJC*, 18 July 1947, p. 3 [u].

47.07.18B "International Trusteeship." [Proposal to place Palestine under international trusteeship]. *CJC*, 18 July 1947, p. 3 [u].

47.07.18C "Weizmann and Partition." [Testimony of Chaim Weizmann before UNSCOP]. *CJC*, 18 July 1947, p. 3 [u].

47.07.25A "Exodus 1947." [British foreign policy on admission of refugees to Palestine]. *CJC*, 25 July 1947, p. 3 [u].

47.07.25B "The Surplus." [Jews in Poland]. *CJC*, 25 July 1947, p. 3 [u].

47.08.01A "The Common Responsibililty." [Jewish refugees turned away from Palestine]. *CJC*, 1 Aug. 1947, p. 3 [u].

47.08.01B "The Example of Yemen." [Plight of Yemenite Jews]. *CJC*, 1 Aug. 1947, p. 3 [u].

47.08.08A "Irgun and the Reign of Terror." [Irgun terrorism]. *CJC*, 8 Aug. 1947, p. 3 [u].

47.08.15A "Pakistan." [Establishment of the State of Pakistan]. *CJC* 15 Aug. 1947, p. 3 [u].

47.08.15B "A Seventh Dominion." [Proposal for Palestine to become seventh dominion in the Commonwealth]. *CJC*, 15 Aug. 1947, p. 3 [u].

47.08.22A "Little Nazis." [Amnesty for Nazis]. *CJC*, 22 Aug. 1947, p. 3 [u].

47.08.22B "Urrim and Thummim." [*Fortune* Magazine forecasts U.S. economy]. *CJC*, 22 Aug. 1947, p. 3 [u].

47.08.22C "Look on This Picture and on This . . ." [Review of *A Palestine Picture Book* by Jacob Rosner and Alfred Bernheim and *Polish Jews* by Roman Vishniac]. *CJC*, 22 Aug. 1947, pp. 9, 15 [s].

47.08.29A "Back to Bergen Belsen?" [Return to Europe of refugees aboard *S.S. Exodus 1947*]. *CJC*, 29 Aug. 1947, p. 3 [u].

47.08.29B "The Guessing Game." [Report of UNSCOP]. *CJC*, 29 Aug. 1947, p. 3 [u].

47.08.29C "In Memoriam: Philip Wolofsky" [Obituary for Philip Wolofsky]. *CJC*, 29 Aug. 1947, p. 3 [u].

47.09.05A "German Resurgence." [Germany after WWII]. *CJC*, 5 Sept. 1947, p. 3 [u].

47.09.05B "They Came out of Their Holes." [Resurgence of fascism in Great Britain]. *CJC*, 5 Sept. 1974, p. 3 [u].

47.09.05C "Ben Gurion and the American Zionists." [Jewish terrorism in Palestine]. *CJC*, 5 Sept. 1947, p. 3 [u].

47.09.05D "Palestine and the United Nations." [UNSCOP recommendations]. *CJC*, 5 Sept. 1947, p. 8 [s].

47.09.12A "The New Year and the Old." [Condition of European Jews]. *CJC*, 12 Sept. 1947, p. 3 [u].

47.09.12B "Operation Oasis." [Return to Europe of refugees aboard *S.S. Exodus 1947*]. *CJC*, 12 Sept. 1947, p. 3 [u].

47.10.03A "The End of the Mandate." [British relinquish their mandate over Palestine]. *CJC*, 3 Oct. 1947, p. 3 [u].

47.10.03B "In Memoriam: Rabbi Abramowitz." [Obituary for Rabbi Herman Abramowitz]. *CJC*, 3 Oct. 1947, p. 3 [u].

47.10.10A "Freedom for Fascists." [Fascism in England]. *CJC*, 10 Oct. 1947, p. 3 [u].

47.10.10B "Not News." [Revival of Comintern]. *CJC*, 10 Oct. 1947, p. 3 [u].

47.10.10C "Racialism Inc." [Racism in Canada]. *CJC*, 10 Oct. 1947, p. 3 [u].

47.10.10D "Only Half the Language of Faith." [Review of *The Language of Faith* edited by Nahum N. Glatzer]. *CJC*, 10 Oct. 1947, pp. 6–7 [s].

47.10.17A "America on Palestine" [U.S. Takes pro-Zionist stand]. *CJC*, 17 Oct. 1947, p. 3 [u].

47.10.17B "The Russian Attitude." [Soviets support UNSCOP recommendations]. *CJC*, Oct. 17 1947, p. 3 [u].

47.10.17C "The Arab Answer." [Arab response to UNSCOP report]. *CJC*, 17 Oct. 1947, p. 3 [u].

47.10.17D "In Memoriam: Aaron Wolofsky." [Obituary for Aaron Wolofsky]. *CJC*, 17 Oct. 1947, p. 3 [u].

47.10.24A "The Combined Jewish Appeal." [Combined Jewish Appeal fundraising campaign]. *CJC*, 24 Oct. 1947, p. 3 [u].

47.10.24B "The Partition of the Palestine Plan." [Legality of partition plan is questioned at U.N.]. *CJC*, 24 Oct. 1947, p. 3 [u].

47.10.24C "A Legal Precedent." [Legal conviction on charge of anti-Semitism]. *CJC*, 24 Oct. 1947, p. 3 [u].

47.10.31A "Balfour Day." [Commemorating the issuing of the Balfour Declaration]. *CJC*, 31 Oct. 1947, p. 3 [u].

47.10.31B "They Required of us a Song." [Yehudi Menuhin performs in Germany]. *CJC*, 31 Oct. 1947, p. 3 [u].

47.11.07A "Dead Reckoning." [Casualty figures for WWII]. *CJC*, 7 Nov. 1947, p. 3 [u].

47.11.07B "The Society of Friends." [Nobel Peace Prize awarded to the Quakers]. *CJC*, 7 Nov. 1947, p. 3 [u].

47.11.07C "L'Affaire Turcotte." [Appointment of Edmond Turcotte to a consulship in Chicago]. *CJC*, 7 Nov. 1947, p. 3 [u].

47.11.14A "The Crypto-Fascists." [Adrien Arcand]. *CJC*, 14 Nov. 1947, p. 3 [u].

47.11.14B "Mr. N.S. Fineberg, K.C." [Montreal Hebrew Free Loan Association]. *CJC*, 14 Nov. 1947, p. 3 [u].

47.11.21A "The Royal Wedding." [Marriage of Princess Elizabeth to the Duke of Edinburgh]. *CJC*, 21 Nov. 1947, p. 3 [u].

47.11.21B "King Abdullah of Transjordania." [King Abdullah's views on Palestine]. *CJC*, 21 Nov. 1947, p. 3 [u].

47.11.21C "Problems of Transition." [Partition of Palestine]. *CJC*, 21 Nov. 1947, p. 3 [u].

47.11.28A "The Foreign Ministers." [International relations after WWII]. *CJC*, 28 Nov. 1947, p. 3 [u].

47.11.28B "On the Eve of Partition." [Canada supports the partition of Palestine]. *CJC*, 28 Nov. 1947, p. 3 [u].

47.11.28C "No Sense of Proportion." [British navy prevents refugees from entering Palestine]. *CJC*, 28 Nov. 1947, p. 3 [u].

47.12.05A "The New Judaea." [U.N. sanctions a Jewish state in Palestine]. *CJC*, 5 Dec. 1947, p. 3 [u].

47.12.05B "The Feast of the Maccabees." [Chanukah]. *CJC*, 5 Dec. 1947, p. 3 [u].

47.12.12A "Communique of the Week." [Violent outbreaks in Palestine]. *CJC*, 12 Dec. 1947, p. 3 [u].

47.12.12B "What Will the United Nations Do?" [Arab delegates attempt to reopen debate on Palestine]. *CJC*, 12 Dec. 1947, p. 3 [u].

47.12.12C "The Volunteers." [Foreign recruits join Arab forces]. *CJC*, 12 Dec. 1947, p. 3 [u].

47.12.19A "Doubtful Impartiality." [Use of Arab troops by British forces in Palestine]. *CJC*, 19 Dec. 1947, p. 3 [u].

47.12.19B "Who Is Lipson?" [British anti-Zionism]. *CJC*, 19 Dec. 1947, p. 3 [u].

47.12.19C "The Big Four Deadlock." [International relations after WWII]. *CJC*, 19 Dec. 1947, p. 3 [u].

47.12.26A "A Shameful Dissent." [Racism in U.S.]. *CJC*, 26 Dec. 1947, p. 3 [u].

47.12.26B "Knut Hamsun." [Knut Hamsun is punished for collaborating with the Nazis]. *CJC*, 26 Dec. 1947, p. 3 [u].

47.12.26C "The Irgun's Present Role." [Irgun in Palestine]. *CJC*, 26 Dec. 1947, p. 3 [u].

48.01.02A "Peace on Earth." [Journalism on Palestine]. *CJC*, 2 Jan. 1948, p. 3 [u].

48.01.02B "A Rose is a Rose is a Bomb." [Gertrude Stein on the atomic bomb]. *CJC*, 2 Jan. 1948, p. 3 [u].

48.01.02C "The Irgun Again?" [Jewish terrorism in Palestine]. *CJC*, 2 Jan. 1948, p. 3 [u].

48.01.09A "The Canadian Zionist Convention." [Twenty-ninth Canadian Zionist Convention]. *CJC*, 9 Jan. 1948, p. 3 [u].

48.01.09B "The Canadian Hebrew Culture Organization." [Promotion of Hebrew culture in Canada]. *CJC*, 9 Jan. 1948, p. 3 [u].

48.01.09C "The Talmud Torah Campaign." [Jewish education]. *CJC*, 9 Jan. 1948, p. 3 [u].

48.01.16A "The Imperatives of Self Preservation." [Purchase of arms by Jews in Palestine]. *CJC*, 16 Jan. 1948, p. 3 [u].

48.01.16B "East and West." [International relations and Palestine]. *CJC*, 16 Jan. 1948, p. 3 [u].

48.01.16C "Gandhi's Fast." [Mahatma Gandhi]. *CJC*, 16 Jan. 1948, p. 3 [u].

48.01.23A "Exits Should Be Graceful." [Departure of the British administration from Palestine]. *CJC*, 23 Jan. 1948, p. 3 [u].

48.01.23B "A Successful Fast." [International relations]. *CJC*, 23 Jan. 1948, p. 3 [u].

48.01.23C "Striking in the Ruhr." [German workers' strike]. *CJC*, 23 Jan. 1948, p. 3 [u].

48.01.30A "Learning by Luncheon." [Anti-Zionist speakers at the Canadian Club]. *CJC*, 30 Jan. 1948, p. 3 [u].

48.01.30B "Mr. Issawi's Speech." [Charles Issawi's speech to the Canadian Club]. *CJC*, 30 Jan. 1948, p. 3 [u].

48.01.30C "Inhabited Mars." [Claim that Mars is inhabited]. *CJC*, 30 Jan. 1948, p. 3 [u].

48.02.06A "The Death of Gandhi." [Mahatma Gandhi]. *CJC*, 6 Feb. 1948, p. 3 [u].

48.02.06B "Arrival and Departure." [Terms of the British departure from Palestine]. *CJC*, 6 Feb. 1948, p. 3 [u].

48.02.06C "The Latest Canard." [British turn away Jewish refugees from Palestine]. *CJC*, 6 Feb. 1948, p. 3 [u].

48.02.13A "The United Nations Challenged." [Civil unrest in Palestine]. *CJC*, 13 Feb. 1948, p. 3 [u].

48.02.13B "The War of the Documents." [Release of documents about German-Soviet negotiations 1939–41]. *CJC*, 13 Feb. 1948, p. 3 [u].

48.02.20A "The United Palestine Appeal." [United Palestine Appeal]. *CJC*, 20 Feb. 1948, p. 3 [u].

48.02.20B "Sha! Sha! Shostakovitch." [Artists under Joseph Stalin]. *CJC*, 20 Feb. 1948, p. 3 [u].

48.02.27A "The Arab Threat." [Character of the Arab states]. *CJC*, 27 Feb. 1948, p. 3 [u].

48.02.27B "U.N. Hesitations." [U.N. and U.S. policy on Palestine]. *CJC*, 27 Feb. 1948, p. 3 [u].

48.02.27C "Two Concepts of Justice." [U.S. judge sympathizes with Nazi war criminals]. *CJC*, 27 Feb. 1948, p. 3 [u].

48.03.05A "Croll Presents Zionist Case." [David Croll presents an analysis of the Palestine situation to the House of Commons]. *CJC*, 5 Mar. 1948, p. 3 [u].

48.03.05B "A Bishop Speaks." [Rev. Charles Pilcher speaks out against U.N. and U.S. policy on Palestine]. *CJC*, 5 Mar. 1948, p. 3 [u].

48.03.05C "Genocide Illegal." [Declaration of genocide as illegal]. *CJC*, 5 Mar. 1948, p. 3 [u].

48.03.12A "The Mufti Goes." [Deposing of Haj Ammin al-Husseini]. *CJC*, 12 Mar. 1948, p. 3 [u].

48.03.12B "It Should Have Been Ere This." [Irgun agrees to cooperate with the Haganah]. *CJC*, 12 Mar. 1948, p. 3 [u].

48.03.12C "We Don't Read [*sic*] Them, We Don't Want Them . . ." [Anti-Semite is convicted and deported from Canada]. *CJC*, 12 Mar. 1948, p. 3 [u].

48.03.12D "Daylight Saving Time Illegal." [Government of Alberta prepares to declare Daylight Saving Time illegal]. *CJC*, 12 Mar. 1948, p. 3, [u].

48.03.19A "Plus ca change . . ." [Marshall plan]. *CJC*, 19 Mar. 1949, p. 3 [u].

48.03.19B "In Memoriam: Leib Yaffe." [Death of Leib Yaffe]. *CJC*, 19 Mar. 1948, p. 3 [u].

48.03.19C "The Jewish State in Process of Becoming." [The Jewish Agency prevents men from leaving Palestine]. *CJC*, 19 Mar. 1948, p. 3 [u].

48.03.19D "On Bernard Lazare." [Review of *Job's Dungheap* by Bernard Lazare]. *CJC*, 19 Mar. 1948, p. 8.[s].

48.03.26A "The Feast of Purim." [Purim]. *CJC*, 26 Mar. 1948, p. 3 [u].

48.03.26B "The Little Man Who Was Not There." [Anti-Semitism in Quebec]. *CJC*, 26 Mar. 1949, p. 3 [u].

48.03.26C "Short-changed Again." [U.S. foreign policy on Palestine]. *CJC*, 26 Mar. 1948, p. 3 [u].

48.04.02A "Life and Eternity." [Anti-Zionist journalism]. *CJC*, 2 Apr. 1948, pp. 3, 15 [u].

48.04.09A "The U.S. Trusteeship Plan for Palestine." [U.S. trusteeship plan for Palestine]. *CJC*, 9 Apr. 1948, p. 3 [u].

48.04.09B "The Policeman's Lot." [British administration in Palestine]. *CJC*, 9 Apr. 1948, p. 3 [u].

48.04.16A "A Canadian Bill of Rights." [Social Credit opposes a proposed Canadian bill of rights]. *CJC*, 16 Apr. 1948, p. 3 [u].

48.04.16B "The Anti-Nazi Trials." [Trials of Nazi war criminals]. *CJC*, 16 Apr. 1948, p. 3 [u].

48.04.16C "Baedeker: Kasrilivke." [Review of *Inside Kasrilivke* by Sholom Aleichem, translated by Isidore Goldstick]. *CJC*, 16 Apr. 1948, pp. 6, 14.

48.04.23A "The Passover Haggadah." [Passover story and Jewish statehood]. *CJC*, 23 Apr. 1948, p. 3 [u].

48.04.23B "Rome and Jerusalem." [International relations affect Palestine]. *CJC*, 23 Apr. 1949, p. 3 [u].

48.04.29A "The Capture of Haifa." [Jewish capture of Haifa]. *CJC*, 29 Apr. 1948, p. 3 [u].

48.04.29B "Goebbels Diaries." [Diaries of Joseph Goebbels]. *CJC*, 29 Apr. 1948, p. 3 [u].

48.05.07A "The Doctrine of Sanctuary." [Pro-Zionist speech at U.N.]. *CJC*, 7 May 1948, p. 3 [u].

48.05.07B " 'David, King of Israel'." [Palestine]. *CJC*, 7 May 1948, p. 3 [u].

48.05.07C "Two Changes." [U.S. and British foreign policy on Palestine]. *CJC*, 7 May 1948, p. 3 [u].

48.05.14A "On the Eve of Geulah." [Anticipation of events following the proclamation of the State of Israel]. *CJC*, 14 May 1948, p. 3 [u].

48.05.14B "The New Jewish State." [Proclamation of State of Israel]. *CJC*, 14 May 1948, pp. 5, 16 [s].

48.05.21A "The First Week." [Events in the first week of Israel's statehood]. *CJC*, 21 May 1948, p. 3 [u].

48.05.21B "Recognition for the State of Israel." [Recognition of the State of Israel]. *CJC*, 21 May 1948, p. 3 [u].

48.05.21C "Mrs. Blanche Dugdale." [Death of Blanche Dugdale]. *CJC*, 21 May 1948, p. 3 [u].

48.05.28A "The Dangers of Divided Loyalty." [Reply to anti-Zionist editorial]. *CJC*, 28 May 1948, p. 3 [u].

48.06.04A " 'Buzz' Beurling." [Death of George (Buzz) Beurling]. *CJC*, 4 June 1948, p. 3 [u].

48.06.04B "While there's 'Life'." [Anti-Zionist editorial in *Life* Magazine]. *CJC*, 4 June 1948, p. 3 [u].

48.06.11A "The Feast of Weeks." [Celebration of Shavuoth in the new State of Israel]. *CJC*, 11 June 1948, p. 3 [u].

48.06.11B "The South African Elections." [Election of Daniel Malan]. *CJC*, 11 June 1948, p. 3 [u].

48.06.11C "Casablanca." [Killing of Jews in Casablanca]. *CJC*, 11 June 1948, p. 3 [u].

48.06.11D "Marginalia." [Nature of Poetry, Browning]. *CJC*, 11 June 1948, pp. 8–9 [s]. See also MS 5090–95, 5173–5249.

48.06.18A "That Famous Bill of Rights." [Need for a Canadian bill of rights]. *CJC*, 18 June 1948, p. 3 [u].

48.06.18B " 'The Said Land Not to be Sold to Jews.' " [Anti-Semitic contract clause upheld in court]. *CJC*, 18 June 1948, p. 3 [u].

48.06.18C "Jonathan and David." [Major-General Orde-Wingate]. *CJC*, 18 June 1948, p. 3 [u].

48.06.25A "Collossus of Rhodes." [Palestine and the United Nations]. *CJC*, 25 June 1948, p. 3 [u].

48.06.25B "The Civil War Within the Civil Truce." [Irgun and the Haganah]. *CJC*, 25 June 1948, p. 3 [u].

48.06.25C "Marginalia. [Robert Frost]. *CJC*, 25 June 1948, p. 8 [s].

48.07.02A "The American DP Bill." [U.S. legislation on refugees]. *CJC*, 2 July 1948, p. 3 [u].

48.07.02B "The Irgun Goes Underground." [Irgun attempt to establish rule over Israel]. *CJC*, 2 July 1948, p. 3 [u].

48.07.02C "New Mizraim." [Egypt aggression against Israel]. *CJC*, 2 July 1948, p. 3 [u].

48.07.09A "The Bernadotte Plan." [Bernadotte peace plan]. *CJC*, 9 July 1948, p. 3 [u].

48.07.09B "German Antisemitism." [German anti-Semitism after wwii]. *CJC*, 9 July 1948, p. 3 [u].

48.07.09C " 'Truly Democratic'." [Conflict of political ideology at World Jewish Congress]. *CJC*, 9 July 1948, p. 3 [u].

48.07.16A "Unnecessary Polemic . . ." [Religious argument]. *CJC*, 16 July 1948, p. 3 [u].

48.07.16B "The Gesture of the Bible." [Language in the Bible]. *CJC*, 16 July 1948, p. 9 [s].

48.07.23A "The Palestine Truce." [Attempt to negotiate a truce in Palestine]. *CJC*, 23 July 1948, p. 3 [u].

48.07.23B "The Homing Pigeons." [Jewish refugees]. *CJC*, 23 July 1948, p. 3 [u].

48.07.23C "The Dybbuk." [Anski's *The Dybbuk* (1)]. *CJC*, 23 July 1948, p. 9 [s].

48.07.30A "Theodor Herzl." [Anniversary of the death of Theodor Herzl]. *CJC*, 30 July 1948, p. 3 [u].

48.07.30B "The Arab's Last Resort — Justice." [Syrian bid to have Palestine question decided by international court]. *CJC*, 30 July 1948, p. 3 [u].

48.07.30C "Look on This Picture and on This." [Capture of Nazareth by Jewish soldiers]. *CJC*, 30 July 1948, p. 3 [u].

48.07.30D "The Dybbuk." [Anski's *The Dybbuk* (2)]. *CJC*, 30 July 1948, p. 13 [s].

48.08.06A "Canadian Recognition of Israel." [Urging Canadian recognition of State of Israel]. *CJC*, 6 Aug. 1948, p. 3 [u].

48.08.06B "The Jews of Cyprus." [Calling for release of refugees interned in Cyprus]. *CJC*, 6 Aug. 1948, p. 3 [u].

48.08.06C "The Krupp Verdict." [Trial of German industrialists and financiers for war crimes]. *CJC*, 6 Aug. 1948, p. 3 [u].

48.08.13A "A Great Career." [Retirement of William Lyon Mackenzie King]. *CJC*, 13 Aug. 1948, p. 3 [u].

48.08.13B "The Hon. Louis St. Laurent." [Louis St. Laurent assumes leadership of the Liberal party]. *CJC*, 13 Aug. 1948, p. 3 [u].

48.08.13C "Arabs Reject Peace." [Arabs refuse invitation to peace talks]. *CJC*, 13 Aug. 1948, p. 3 [u].

48.08.20A "$20,000 an Hour!" [Israel's economy]. *CJC*, 20 Aug. 1948, p. 3 [u].

48.08.20B "The 'Native Sons' and Israeli Trade." [Anti-Semitism in Canada]. *CJC*, 20 Aug. 1948, p. 3 [u].

48.08.27A "The State of Israel and the United Nations." [Need for Israel to become a member of U.N.]. *CJC*, 27 Aug. 1948, p. 3 [u].

48.08.27B "Ben Gurion's Internal Policy." [David Ben Gurion's handling of internal opposition from the Irgun]. *CJC*, 27 Aug. 1948, p. 3 [u].

48.08.27C "Jerusalem the Golden." [Jerusalem]. *CJC*, 27 Aug. 1948, p. 4 [s].

48.09.00A "Cantabile." [Review of *The Cantos of Ezra Pound* I–LXXX]. *Northern Review* 2, 3 (Sept.–Oct. 1948), pp. 30–31 [s].

48.09.03A "Samuel Bronfman Honoured." [Samuel Bronfman receives honorary degree from Université de Montréal]. *CJC*, 3 Sept. 1948, p. 3 [u].

48.09.03B "God and the Jewish State." [Religion and government in Israel]. *CJC*, 3 Sept. 1948, p. 3 [u].

48.09.10A "The Jewish Agency and the Jewish State." [Role of the Jewish Agency in the new State of Israel]. *CJC*, 10 Sept. 1948, p. 3 [u].

48.09.10B "The Handclasp that Hurts." [Pro-Jewish statement made at the World Council of Churches]. *CJC*, 10 Sept. 1948, p. 3 [u].

48.09.10C "Against Mendel and Menachem Mendel." [Science in the Soviet Union]. *CJC*, 10 Sept. 1948, p. 3 [u].

48.09.10D "Isaak Babel." [Review of *Benya Krik the Gangster* by Isaak Babel]. *CJC*, 10 Sept. 1948, pp. 8, 13 [s].

48.09.17A "The Hon. Lester B. Pearson." [Lester Pearson assumes External Affairs portfolio]. *CJC*, 17 Sept. 1948, p. 3 [u].

48.09.17B "A Classic Judgement." [Judgment in an assault case]. *CJC*, 17 Sept. 1948, p. 3 [u].

48.09.17C "Leaflets Bring Casualties." [Need for American public opinion to reach Soviet Union]. *CJC*, 17 Sept. 1948, p. 3 [u].

48.09.17D "German Indoctrination." [Cultural values in post-war Germany]. *CJC*, 17 Sept. 1948, p. 3 [u].

48.09.17E "That Rank Picture." [Anti-Semitism in the movie version of *Oliver Twist*]. *CJC*, 17 Sept. 1948, p. 8 [s].

48.09.24A "And into the Scandinavian." [Assassination of Count Bernadotte]. *CJC*, 24 Sept. 1948, p. 3 [u].

48.10.01A "The New Year." [Reviewing Jewish history at the New Year]. *CJC*, 1 Oct. 1948, p. 3 [u].

48.10.08A "The Day of Atonement." [Jewish refugees]. *CJC*, 8 Oct. 1948, p. 3 [u].

48.10.08B "Of Genocide." [Debate over legality of genocide]. *CJC*, 8 Oct. 1948, p. 3 [u].

48.10.08C "Mickey Mouski." [Art in the Soviet Union]. *CJC*, 8 Oct. 1943, p. 3 [u].

48.10.08D "A Lady with a Lamp." [Early release of Ilse Koch from prison]. *CJC*, 8 Oct. 1948, p. 8 [u].

48.10.15A "The Feast of Booths." [Succoth]. *CJC*, 15 Oct. 1948, p. 3 [u].

48.10.15B "Is it Imminent?" [Cold War]. *CJC*, 15 Oct. 1948, p. 3 [u].

48.10.15C "The Pity Propaganda." [Wave of journalism sympathetic to post-war Germany]. *CJC*, 15 Oct. 1948, p. 3 [u].

48.10.22A "War in the Negev." [Arab-Israeli war]. *CJC*, 22 Oct. 1948, p. 3 [u].

48.10.22B "Collaborationist and D.P." [Admission of former French collaborationists to Canada]. *CJC*, 22 Oct. 1948, p. 3 [u].

48.10.29A " 'German Coolies'." [Growing Western sympathy for post-war Germany]. *CJC*, 29 Oct. 1948, p. 3 [u].

48.10.29B "Simchas Torah in Palestine." [First celebration of Simchas Torah in the new State of Israel]. *CJC*, 29 Oct. 1948, p. 3 [u].

48.11.05A "The American Elections." [U.S. presidential election]. *CJC*, 5 Nov. 1948, p. 3 [u].

48.11.05B "Of Jewish Existentialism." [Review of *Antisemite and Jew* by Jean-Paul Sartre]. *CJC*, 5 Nov. 1948, p. 8 [s].

48.11.12A "The Combined Jewish Appeal." [Combined Jewish Appeal]. *CJC*, 12 Nov. 1948, p. 3 [u].

48.11.12B "The All too Human." [German behaviour during WWII]. *CJC*, 12 Nov. 1948, p. 3 [u].

48.11.12C "T.S. Eliot and the Nobel Prize." [Nobel Prize for literature awarded to T.S. Eliot (1)]. *CJC*, 12 Nov. 1948, p. 8 [s].

48.11.19A "Of Public Opinion Polls." [Public opinion polls]. *CJC*, 19 Nov. 1948, p. 3 [u].

48.11.19B "Religion in Palestine." [Laxity of religious observance in Israel]. *CJC*, 19 Nov. 1948, p. 3 [u].

48.11.19C "King and the Prince." [Retirement of William Lyon Mackenzie King]. *CJC*, 19 Nov. 1948, p. 3 [u].

48.11.19D "T.S. Eliot and the Nobel Prize." [Nobel Prize for literature awarded to T.S. Eliot (2)]. *CJC*, 19 Nov. 1948, p. 8 [s].

48.11.26A "Canadian Recognition of Israel." [Canadian recognition of Israel]. *CJC*, 26 Nov. 1948, p. 3 [u].

48.11.26B " 'Back Numbers'." [Adrien Arcand]. *CJC*, 26 Nov. 1948, p. 3 [u].

48.11.26C "The Generals and Their Memoirs." [Military memoirs]. *CJC*, 26 Nov. 1948, p. 3 [u].

48.11.26D "T.S. Eliot and the Nobel Prize." [Nobel Prize for literature awarded to T.S. Eliot (3)]. *CJC*, 26 Nov. 1948, p. 8 [s].

48.12.03A "The Partition Anniversary." [Anniversary of U.N. decision to partition Palestine]. *CJC*, 3 Dec. 1948, p. 3 [u].

48.12.03B " 'The Untouchables'." [Outlawing of caste system in India]. *CJC*, 3 Dec. 1948, p. 3 [u].

48.12.03C "The Prime Minister and His Housing Problem." [Need for an official residence for the Prime Minister of Canada]. *CJC*, 3 Dec. 1948, p. 3 [u].

48.12.03D "A Chassidic Anthology." [Review of *Tales of the Hasidim: The Later Masters* by Martin Buber]. *CJC*, 3 Dec. 1948, p. 12 [s].

48.12.10A "The Zionist Order Habonim." [Habonim]. *CJC*, 10 Dec. 1948, p. 3 [u].

48.12.10B "Whodunit?" [Espionage affair in U.S.]. *CJC*, 10 Dec. 1948, p. 3 [u].

48.12.10C "Israel's Admission to U.N." [Israel's admission to U.N.]. *CJC*, 10 Dec. 1948, p. 3 [u].

48.12.10D "Book Reviewing; In Seven Easy Lessons." [Book reviewing]. *CJC*, 10 Dec. 1948, p. 8 [s].

48.12.17A "Churchill Speaks Out." [Pro-Israeli speech of Winston Churchill]. *CJC*, 17 Dec. 1948, p. 3 [u].

48.12.17B "Declaration of Human Rights." [U.N. Declaration of Human Rights]. *CJC*, 17 Dec. 1948, p. 3 [u].

48.12.17c "Hemlock and Marijuana." [Review of *In the Penal Colony: Stories and Short Pieces* by Franz Kafka]. *CJC*, 17 Dec. 1948, p. 8 [s].

48.12.24A "The Feast of Chanukah." [Chanukah]. *CJC*, 24 Dec. 1948, p. 3 [u].

48.12.24B "Exit the Mufti Weeping." [Replacement of the Mufti]. *CJC*, 24 Dec. 1948, p. 3 [u].

48.12.24c "Marginalia." [Japanese poetry; sentimental poetry; poetic form]. *CJC*, 24 Dec. 1948, p. 6 [s].

48.12.31A "Canadian Recognition of Israel." [Canadian recognition of State of Israel]. *CJC*, 31 Dec. 1948, p. 3 [u].

48.12.31B "The Diplomatic Twins." [Recognition of the State of Israel]. *CJC*, 31 Dec. 1948, p. 3 [u].

48.12.31c "Judaism Incorporated and Rosenwald." [Anti-Zionism of Lessing Rosenwald]. *CJC*, 31 Dec. 1948, p. 3 [u].

49.01.07A "Pharaoh in Reverse." [Egyptian retreat from Israel]. *CJC*, 7 Jan. 1949, p. 3 [u].

49.01.07B "U.N. Lyrics Hit the Spot." [Radio station broadcasts songs about U.N.]. *CJC*, 7 Jan 1949, p. 3 [u].

49.01.07c "Weizmann's Biography." [Serialized biography of Chaim Weizmann to appear in the *Canadian Jewish Chronicle*]. *CJC*, 7 Jan. 1949, p. 3 [u].

49.01.14A "The Talmud Torah Campaign." [Talmud Torah Campaign]. *CJC*, 14 Jan. 1949, p. 3 [u].

49.01.14B "British-Israel." [British foreign policy on Middle East]. *CJC*, 14 Jan. 1949, p. 3 [u].

49.01.14c "Franco's Invitation." [Francisco Franco invites Jews to return to Spain]. *CJC*, 14 Jan. 1949, p. 3 [u].

49.01.14D "The Usurper." [Poets and copywriters]. *CJC*, 14 Jan. 1949, p. 4 [s].

49.01.21A "The Hadassah Convention." [Thirtieth Hadassah Convention]. *CJC*, 21 Jan. 1949, p. 3 [u].

49.01.21B "The South African Race Riots." [Racism in South Africa]. *CJC*, 21 Jan, 1949, p. 3 [u].

49.01.21c "Melech Grafstein's Sholom Aleichem." [Review of *Sholom Aleichem Panorama* ed. by Melech Grafstein]. *CJC*, 21 Jan. 1949, pp. 8, 16 [s].

49.01.28A "The United Israel Appeal." [United Israel Appeal]. *CJC*, 28 Jan. 1949, p. 3 [u].

49.01.28B "The Palestine Elections." [Israeli elections]. *CJC*, 28 Jan. 1949, p. 3 [u].

49.01.28C "German Musicians." [Nazi musicians refused entrance to U.S.]. *CJC*, 28 Jan. 1949, p. 3 [u].

49.01.28D "Marginalia." [Modern poetry]. *CJC*, 28 Jan. 1949, p. 6 [s].

49.02.04A "British Recognition of Israel." [Britain recognizes the State of Israel]. *CJC*, 4 Feb. 1949, p. 3 [u].

49.02.04B "The Next Step." [Need for Jewish representation at U.N.]. *CJC*, 4 Feb. 1949, p. 3 [u].

49.02.11A "The Roads from Rhodes." [Arab-Jewish Peace negotiations at Rhodes]. *CJC*, 11 Feb. 1949, p. 3 [u].

49.02.11B " 'A Sincere Man'." [Death of Norman Jacques]. *CJC*, 11 Feb. 1949, p. 3 [u].

49.02.11C "The Israeli Budget." [Distribution of financial aid received from abroad]. *CJC*, 11 Feb. 1949, p. 3 [u].

49.02.11D "What's in a Name." [Anti-Semitism in Quebec]. *CJC*, 11 Feb. 1949, p. 3 [u].

49.02.11E "The Draft Constitution of Israel." [Draft constitution of Israel (1)]. *CJC*, 11 Feb. 1949, p. 4 [s].

49.02.18A "The Parliament of Israel." [Convening of the first session of the Knesseth]. *CJC*, 18 Feb. 1949, p. 3 [u].

49.02.18B "Exit from Cyprus." [Last refugees are released from camps on Cyprus]. *CJC*, 18 Feb. 1949, p. 3 [u].

49.02.18C "In Memoriam: Menachem Boraisha." [Death of Menachem Boraisha]. *CJC*, 18 Feb. 1949, p. 3 [u].

49.02.18D "The Draft Constitution of Israel." [Draft constitution of Israel (2)]. *CJC*, 18 Feb. 1949, p. 4 [s].

49.02.25A "Another Twist to Oliver." [Movie version of *Oliver Twist* shown in Berlin]. *CJC*, 25 Feb. 1949, p. 3 [u].

49.02.25B "And in the American Zone." [Anti-Semitism among Americans in Germany]. *CJC*, 25 Feb. 1949, p. 3 [u].

49.02.25C "Farewell to Mr. Petrushka." [Simcha Petrushka leaves Canada for Israel]. *CJC*, 25 Feb. 1949, p. 3 [u].

49.02.25D "The Draft Constitution of Israel." [Draft constitution of Israel (3)]. *CJC*, 25 Feb. 1949, p. 3 [u].

49.03.04A "The De Bernonville Debate." [Debate over admission of Jacques de Bernonville to Canada]. *CJC*, 4 Mar. 1949, p. 3 [u].

49.03.04B "Some Recent Legislation." [Education in Quebec]. *CJC*, 4 Mar. 1949, p. 3 [u].

49.03.04C "Old Ez and His Blankets." [Bollingen Prize awarded to Ezra Pound]. *CJC*, 4 Mar. 1949, pp. 4, 13 [s].

49.03.11A "A Million Jews." [Jews under Arab rule]. *CJC*, 11 Mar. 1949, p. 3 [u].

49.03.11B "Celebration in Cairo." [Egyptian victory celebration]. *CJC*, 11 Mar. 1949, p. 3 [u].

49.03.11C "Israel Lazare." [Death of Israel Lazare]. *CJC*, 11 Mar. 1949, p. 3 [u].

49.03.18A "Judaism Inc. and Islam Ltd." [Pro-Arab work of Lessing Rosenwald]. *CJC*, 18 Mar. 1949, p. 3 [u].

49.03.18B "Pity or Proganda." [Germany after WWII]. *CJC*, 18 Mar. 1949, p. 3 [u].

49.03.18C "Isaac Gold." [Death of Isaac Gold]. *CJC*, 18 Mar. 1949, p. 3 [u].

49.03.18D "The Dangers of Success." [Israeli chauvinism]. *CJC*, 18 Mar. 1949, p. 4 [s].

49.03.25A "Abdullah Hitler." [Arabs threaten revenge against Jews]. *CJC*, 25 Mar. 1949, p. 3 [u].

49.03.25B "The Coat of Arms." [Israeli coat of arms]. *CJC*, 25 Mar. 1949, p. 3 [u].

49.03.25C "Nathaniel S. Fineberg." [Death of Nathaniel Fineberg]. *CJC*, 25 Mar. 1949, p. 3 [u].

49.04.01A "Peace Conference or Staged Trial?" [United Nations Cultural and Scientific Conference for World Peace]. *CJC*, 1 Apr. 1949, p. 3 [u].

49.04.01B "The Still-Vexed Bermoothes." [Suggestion for Bermuda to join Canada]. *CJC*, 1 Apr. 1949, p. 3 [u].

49.04.01C "A Memorable Ceremony." [U.S. sends first ambassador to Israel]. *CJC*, 1 Apr. 1949, p. 3 [u].

49.04.08A "Communists Revile Zion." [Communists attack Zionism]. *CJC*, 8 Apr. 1949, p. 3 [u].

49.04.08B "Wolsey on Service." [U.S. rabbi criticizes aid to Jews overseas]. *CJC*, 8 Apr. 1949, p. 3 [u].

49.04.08C "Turkey Recognizes Israel." [Turkey recognizes State of Israel]. *CJC*, 8 Apr. 1949, p. 3 [u].

49.04.13A "The New Haggadah." [Inclusion of recent Jewish history in the Haggadah]. *CJC*, 13 Apr. 1949, p. 3 [u].

49.04.22A "Leniency or Expediency." [U.S. judge delivers lenient sentences on Nazis]. *CJC*, 22 Apr. 1949, p. 3 [u].

49.04.22B "Rabbi Meyer Berlin." [Death of Rabbi Meyer Berlin]. *CJC*, 22 Apr. 1949, p. 3 [u].

49.04.22C "A Chair in Yiddish." [Chair of Yiddish language and literature is established at the Hebrew University]. *CJC*, 22 Apr. 1949, p. 3 [u].

49.04.22D "Of Hebrew Names." [Adoption of Hebrew names by Jews in Israel]. *CJC*, 22 Apr. 1949, p. 6 [s].

49.04.29A "Arab Leaders Plan for 'Der Tag'." [Arabs plan economic boycott of Israel]. *CJC*, 29 Apr. 1949, p. 3 [u].

49.04.29B "A Controlled Economy in Israel." [Israel's economy]. *CJC*, 29 Apr. 1949, p. 3 [u].

49.04.29C "The Late Rabbi Stephen Wise." [Death of Rabbi Stephen Wise]. *CJC*, 29 Apr. 1949, p. 3 [u].

49.05.06A "The State of Israel: First Anniversary." [First anniversary of State of Israel]. *CJC*, 6 May 1949, p. 3 [u].

49.05.06B "The Jewish General Hospital Drive." [Fundraising for the Jewish General Hospital]. *CJC*, 6 May 1949, p. 3 [u].

49.05.13A "Back to Earth." [Suspension of the Berlin blockade]. *CJC*, 13 May 1949, p. 3 [u].

49.05.13B "Glubb the Glib." [Glubb Pasha on the Jerusalem question]. *CJC*, 13 May 1949, p. 3 [u].

49.05.13C "Of Jewish Culture." [Desirability of synthesis of Diaspora and Israeli culture]. *CJC*, 13 May 1949, p. 3 [u].

49.05.20A "Israel Among the United Nations." [Israel is admitted to U.N.]. *CJC*, 20 May 1949, p. 3 [u].

49.05.20B "The Vote on Spain." [Vote on the admission of Spain to U.N.]. *CJC*, 20 May 1949, p. 3 [u].

49.05.27A "Israel Recognized De Jure." [Canada recognizes State of Israel]. *CJC*, 27 May 1949, p. 3 [u].

49.05.27B "The Late Harry Vechsler." [Death of Harry Vechsler]. *CJC*, 27 May 1949, p. 3 [u].

49.05.27C "The East Shanghai'd." [Capture of Shanghai by communist forces]. *CJC*, 27 May 1949, p. 3 [u].

49.06.02A "The Feast of Pentecost." [Shavuoth in light of the Cold War]. *CJC*, 2 June 1949, p. 3 [u].

49.06.02B "The New Orientation." [Zionism in U.S.]. *CJC*, 2 June 1949, p. 3 [u].

49.06.02C "The Electric Brain." [Science and technology]. *CJC*, 2 June 1949, p. 3 [u].

49.06.10A "The Literature of Israel." [New Hebrew mentality]. *CJC*, 10 June 1949, p. 3 [u].

49.06.10B "The Beast of Buchenwald." [U.S. leniency toward Ilse Koch]. *CJC*, 10 June 1949, p. 3 [u].

49.06.17A "The Discriminatory Clause." [Racist law in Ontario]. *CJC*, 17 June 1949, p. 3 [u].

49.06.17B "Arcand Rides Again." [Adrien Arcand runs for federal office]. *CJC*, 17 June 1949, p. 3 [u].

49.06.17C "Resolutions to be Implemented." [Quebec Federation of Labour speaks out against racism]. *CJC*, 17 June 1949, p. 3 [u].

49.06.17D "Arms to the Arabs?" [British supply weapons to the Arab states]. *CJC*, 17 June 1949, p. 3 [u].

49.06.24A "Zionism Behind the Iron Curtain." [Anti-Zionism in the Soviet bloc]. *CJC*, 24 June 1949, p. 3 [u].

49.06.24B "Compulsory Education in Israel." [Compulsory education instituted in Israel]. *CJC*, 24 June 1949, p. 3 [u].

49.06.24C "Arcand's Campaign." [Adrien Arcand]. *CJC*, 24 June 1949, p. 3 [u].

49.06.24D "A Plebiscite in Palestine." [Plebiscite on the fate of Arab Palestine]. *CJC*, 24 June 1949, p. 3 [u].

49.07.01A "The Liberal Landslide." [Liberal election victory]. *CJC*, 1 July 1949, p. 3 [u].

49.07.01B "A Unified Arab Command." [Lebanon proposes an Arab military command]. *CJC*, 1 July 1949, p. 3 [u].

49.07.01C " 'Let My People Go'." [Jews in the Soviet bloc]. *CJC*, 1 July 1949, p. 3 [u].

49.07.08A "Swords and Ploughshares." [Israeli internal policy]. *CJC*, 8 July 1949, p. 3 [u].

49.07.08B "Dr. Bernard Joseph." [Bernard Joseph]. *CJC*, 8 July 1949, p. 3 [u].

49.07.08C "A Renascent Fascism?" [Resurgent fascism in Germany]. *CJC*, 8 July 1949, p. 3 [u].

49.07.08D "Tovarisch or Gospodin." [Soviet-Yugoslavian relations]. *CJC*, 8 July 1949, p. 3 [u].

49.07.15A "The British Crisis." [British economic crisis]. *CJC*, 15 July 1949, p. 3 [u].

49.07.15B "They Don't Laugh Enough." [Russian humour]. *CJC*, 15 July 1949, p. 3 [u].

49.07.15C "The Wingless Chicken." [Science seeks to develop the wingless chicken]. *CJC*, 15 July 1949, p. 3 [u].

49.07.22A "The Heidelberg Talmud." [Publication of a new edition of the Talmud in Germany]. *CJC*, 22 July 1949, p. 3 [u].

49.07.22B "The Tobiansky Case." [Vindication of Meyer Tobiansky]. *CJC*, 22 July 1949, p. 3 [u].

49.07.29A "Regrettable Regrets." [World leaders regret decisions made during wwii]. *CJC*, 29 July 1949, p. 3 [u].

49.07.29B "Glib Glubb." [Glubb Pasha]. *CJC*, 29 July 1949, p. 3, [u].

49.08.05A " 'Notebook of a Journey'." [Announcing forthcoming series of articles on trip to Israel]. *CJC*, 5 Aug. 1949, p. 3 [u].

49.08.05B "An Israeli Consul at Montreal." [Establishment of an Israeli consulate in Montreal]. *CJC*, 5 Aug. 1949, p. 3 [u].

49.08.05C " 'Work and Bread.' " [Mass unemployment in Israel]. *CJC*, 5 Aug. 1949, p. 3 [u].

49.08.12A "Notebook of a Journey." [Departure for Israel]. *CJC*, 12 Aug. 1949, pp. 3, 6 [s].

49.08.19A "Notebook of a Journey." [Travelling to Israel]. *CJC*, 19 Aug. 1949, p. 5 [s].

49.08.26A "Notebook of a Journey." [Travelling to Israel]. *CJC*, 26 Aug. 1949, p. 5 [s].

49.09.02A "Notebook of a Journey." [Tel Aviv]. *CJC*, 2 Sept. 1949, pp. 5, 16 [s].

49.09.09A "Notebook of a Journey." [Remains of Theodor Herzl are brought to Israel]. *CJC*, 9 Sept. 1949, pp. 5, 16.

49.09.16A "Back at the Old Stand." [Klein resumes editorial duties at the *Canadian Jewish Chronicle*]. *CJC*, 16 Sept. 1949, p. 3 [u].

49.09.16B "New British Policy." [British foreign policy on Palestine]. *CJC*, 16 Sept. 1949, p. 3 [u].

49.09.16C "Notebook of a Journey." [Casablanca]. *CJC*, 16 Sept. 1949, p. 7 [s].

49.09.23A "The New Year." [International relations]. *CJC*, 23 Sept. 1949, p. 3 [u].

49.09.23B "The Future of Jerusalem." [Plan to internationalize Jerusalem]. *CJC*, 23 Sept. 1949, p. 3 [u].

49.09.23C "Mass Deportations." [Forced migration of minority groups to Siberia]. *CJC*, 23 Sept. 1949, p. 3 [u].

49.09.23D "Notebook of a Journey." [Casablanca]. *CJC*, 23 Sept. 1949, p. 5 [s].

49.09.30A "The Day of Atonement." [Abuse of atomic technology]. *CJC*, 30 Sept. 1949, p. 3 [u].

49.09.30B "Devaluation of the Pound." [Devaluation of the British pound]. *CJC*, 30 Sept. 1949, p. 3 [u].

49.09.30C "Jerusalem and the High Holydays." [Plan to internationalize Jerusalem]. *CJC*, 30 Sept. 1949, p. 3 [u].

49.09.30D "Notebook of a Journey." [Jews of North Africa and Yemen]. *CJC*, 30 Sept. 1949, p. 8 [s].

49.10.07A "The Feast of Booths." [Jewish refugees continue to seek permanent homes]. *CJC*, 7 Oct. 1949, p. 3 [u].

49.10.07B "Mr. Churchill on the Warpath." [Winston Churchill challenges the Attlee government]. *CJC*, 7 Oct. 1949, p. 3 [u].

49.10.07C "A Typical Championship." [International relations]. *CJC*, 7 Oct. 1949, p. 3 [u].

49.10.07D "Notebook of a Journey." [Safed]. *CJC*, 7 Oct. 1949, p. 8 [s].

49.10.14A "Israel's Immigration Crisis." [Mass immigration to Israel]. *CJC*, 14 Oct. 1949, p. 3 [u].

49.10.14B "Hebrew Broadcasts." [BBC starts broadcasting to Israel]. *CJC*, 14 Oct. 1949, p. 3 [u].

49.10.14C "Notebook of a Journey." ["Miracles" in Israel]. *CJC*, 14 Oct 1949, p. 5 [s].

49.10.21A "The Eighth Plenary Session." [Eighth plenary session of the Canadian Jewish Congress]. *CJC*, 21 Oct. 1949, p. 3 [u].

49.10.21B "A Decade of Canadian Jewish Leadership." [Samuel Bronfman]. *CJC*, 21 Oct. 1949, p. 3 [u].

49.10.21C "Israel and Polygamy." [David Ben Gurion bans polygamy]. *CJC*, 21 Oct. 1949, p. 3 [u].

49.10.21D "Notebook of a Journey." [Sabras]. *CJC*, 21 Oct. 1949, p. 6 [s].

49.10.28A "Israeli Immigration." [Problems of mass immigration to Israel]. *CJC*, 28 Oct. 1949, p. 3 [u].

49.10.28B "German Resurgence." [Germany after WWII]. *CJC*, 28 Oct. 1949, p. 3 [u].

49.10.28C " 'Oliver Twist' Banned in Quebec." [Movie version of *Oliver Twist* is banned in Quebec]. *CJC*, 28 Oct. 1949, p. 3 [u].

49.10.28D "Notebook of a Journey." [Israeli politics]. *CJC*, 28 Oct. 1949, p. 6 [s].

49.11.04A "The Combined Jewish Appeal." [Combined Jewish Appeal]. *CJC*, 4 Nov. 1949, p. 3 [u].

49.11.04B "Israeli Peace Negotiations." [Israel ceases negotiations with the Arab states]. *CJC*, 4 Nov. 1949, p. 3 [u].

49.11.11A "Isaac Harry Wolofsky." [Death of Hirsch Wolofsky]. *CJC*, 11 Nov. 1949, p. 3 [u].

49.11.11B "The Hard Core." [Need for continued financial support for Zionist causes]. *CJC*, 11 Nov. 1949, p. 3 [u].

49.11.11C "Notebook of a Journey." [Israeli politics]. *CJC*, 11 Nov. 1949, p. 8 [s].

49.11.18A "Wavell's Warning." [Resurgence of German fascism]. *CJC*, 18 Nov. 1949, p. 3 [u].

49.11.18B "Bible Pictures." [Religious art]. *CJC*, 18 Nov. 1949, p. 3 [u].

49.11.25A "If I Forget Thee, O Jerusalem . . . ." [U.N. plan to internationalize Jerusalem]. *CJC*, 25 Nov. 1949, p. 3 [u].

49.11.25B "The Unregenerate Nazis." [Religion and Nazism]. *CJC*, 25 Nov. 1949, p. 3 [u].

49.11.25C "Notebook of a Journey." [Israeli literature]. *CJC*, 25 Nov. 1949, p. 8 [s].

49.12.02A "In Memoriam: H. Wolofsky." [Death of Hirsch Wolofsky]. *CJC*, 2 Dec. 1949, pp. 3, 15 [s].

49.12.09A "In Tribute to Talmud Torah Governors." [Dinner in honour of Talmud Torah governors]. *CJC*, 9 Dec. 1949, p. 3 [u].

49.12.09B "And Again Jerusalem!" [U.N. plan to internationalize Jerusalem]. *CJC*, 9 Dec. 1949, p. 3 [u].

49.12.09C "But — Look!" [U.N. plan to internationalize Jerusalem]. *CJC*, 9 Dec. 1949, p. 3 [u].

49.12.09D "Uncle Tom's Cabin." [Anti-black racism in Dresden, Ontario]. *CJC*, 9 Dec. 1949, p. 3 [u].

49.12.09E "Notebook of a Journey." [Rome: Michelangelo's Moses]. *CJC*, 9 Dec. 1949, p. 8 [s].

49.12.16A "The Feast of Lights." [Chanukah in Israel]. *CJC*, 16 Dec. 1949, p. 3 [u].

49.12.16B "Jerusalem, the Capital." [Jerusalem is declared capital of Israel]. *CJC*, 16 Dec. 1949, p. 3 [u].

49.12.16C "Arab Refugees." [Arab refugees return to Israel]. *CJC*, 16 Dec. 1949, p. 3 [u].

49.12.16D "Notebook of a Journey." [Rome: Arch of Titus]. *CJC*, 16 Dec. 1949, p. 5 [s].

49.12.23A "Let My People Go!" [Arrests of Jews in Iron Curtain countries]. *CJC*, 23 Dec. 1949, p. 3 [u].

49.12.23B "Back to the Old Stand." [Soviet foreign policy on Israel]. *CJC*, 23 Dec. 1949, p. 3 [u].

49.12.23C "The First Million." [Israeli census lists first million in population]. *CJC*, 23 Dec. 1949, p. 3 [u].

49.12.23D "The Last Trial." [Last trial of Nazi war criminals]. *CJC*, 23 Dec. 1949, p. 3 [u].

49.12.23E "Notebook of a Journey." [Klein reviews his trip to Israel]. *CJC*, 23 Dec. 1949, p. 8 [s].

49.12.30A "The Knesseth in Jerusalem." [Knesseth meets in Jerusalem for the first time]. *CJC*, 30 Dec. 1949, p. 3 [u].

49.12.30B "Einstein's New Theory." [Albert Einstein's theory of gravitation]. *CJC*, 30 Dec. 1949, p. 3 [u].

49.12.30C "And the Rains Came." [Housing shortage in Israel]. *CJC*, 30 Dec. 1949, p. 3 [u].

50.01.06A "All is Forgiven." [Amnesty for Nazis declared in West Germany]. *CJC*, 6 Jan. 1950, p. 3 [u].

50.01.06B "Abdullah's Grab." [King Abdullah annexes part of Palestine]. *CJC*, 6 Jan. 1950, p. 3 [u].

50.01.06C "The Psalms of David." [Lecture series on the Psalms]. *CJC*, 6 Jan. 1950, p. 3 [u].

50.01.13A "The Canadian Constitution." [Constitutional conference]. *CJC*, 13 Jan. 1950, p. 3 [u].

50.01.13B "Capital Punishment in Israel." [Capital punishment in Israel]. *CJC*, 13 Jan. 1950, p. 3 [u].

50.01.13C "The Speaker in a Yarmulka." [The Speaker of the House of Commons inquires about synagogue decorum]. *CJC*, 13 Jan. 1950, p. 3 [u].

50.01.20A "The Zionist Convention." [Thirtieth convention of the Zionist Organization of Canada]. *CJC*, 20 Jan. 1950, p. 3 [u].

50.01.20B "Vice-President Barkley on Israel." [Pro-Zionist speech of Alben Barkley]. *CJC*, 20 Jan. 1950, p. 3 [u].

50.01.20C "No Antisemitism at U.N." [Charges of anti-Semitism directed at U.N.]. *CJC*, 20 Jan. 1950, p. 3 [u].

50.01.27A "The Zionist Convention." [Thirtieth Convention of the Zionist Organization of Canada]. *CJC*, 27 Jan. 1950, p. 3 [u].

50.01.27B "And Add Quhissling." [Conviction of Alger Hiss for perjury]. *CJC*, 27 Jan. 1950, p. 3 [u].

50.02.03A "The Hydrogen Bomb." [U.S. announces it will manufacture a hydrogen bomb]. *CJC*, 3 Feb. 1950, p. 3 [u].

50.02.03B "Arms and the Arabs." [Britain supplies arms to the Arabs]. *CJC*, 3 Feb. 1950, p. 3 [u].

50.02.03C "The Israeli Economy." [The Israeli economy]. *CJC*, 3 Feb. 1950, p. 3 [u].

50.02.10A "Einstein and the Hebrew University." [Albert Einstein becomes chairman of the Joint Council of the Hebrew University]. *CJC*, 10 Feb. 1950, p. 3 [u].

50.02.10B "Of Reynard the Fuchs." [Klaus Fuchs passes western nuclear technology to the Soviets]. *CJC*, 10 Feb. 1950, p. 3 [u].

50.02.10C "The Six Changes." [World affairs as reported by the *World Almanac and Book of Facts*]. *CJC*, 10 Feb. 1950, p. 3 [u].

50.02.17A "Egyptian Peace Terms." [Egypt proposes terms for peace with Israel]. *CJC*, 17 Feb. 1950, p. 3 [u].

50.02.17B "The Scientific Mind." [Albert Einstein makes a plea for an end to the arms race]. *CJC*, 17 Feb. 1950, p. 3 [u].

50.02.17C "The Hon. Mr. Justice Batshaw." [Harry Batshaw appointed to the bench of the Superior Court of Quebec]. *CJC*, 17 Feb 1950, p. 3 [u].

50.02.24A "The Israeli School System." [Education in Israel]. *CJC*, 24 Feb. 1950, p. 3 [u].

50.02.24B "Thanks to Norway." [Thanks to Norway for assisting Jewish refugees]. *CJC*, 24 Feb. 1950, p. 3 [u].

50.03.03A "Marriage Laws in Israel." [Knesseth debate on prohibiting marriage of girls under 18]. *CJC*, 3 Mar. 1950, p. 3 [u].

50.03.03B "Compensation to Nazis?" [U.S. delegate to the U.N. moves that Israeli government return confiscated Nazi property]. *CJC*, 3 Mar. 1950, p. 3 [u].

50.03.03C "An Imminent Peace." [Imminent peace between Israel and Transjordan]. *CJC*, 3 Mar. 1950, p. 3 [u].

50.03.03D "The Purimplicity of Survival." [Jewish survival]. *CJC*, 3 Mar. 1950, p. 7 [s]; See also MS 7447–49.

50.03.10A "The United Israel Appeal." [Need for continued support for the State of Israel]. *CJC*, 10 Mar. 1950, p. 3 [u].

50.03.10B "A New Exodus." [Jews remaining in Germany flee to Paris]. *CJC*, 10 Mar. 1950, p. 3 [u].

50.03.17A " 'Zionist Imperialism'." [Soviets accuse Jews of imperialism]. *CJC*, 17 Mar. 1950, p. 3 [u].

50.03.17B " 'Mercy Killing'." [Euthanasia]. *CJC*, 17 Mar. 1950, p. 3 [u].

50.03.17C "Politics, Ideals and Expediency." [British racism]. *CJC*, 17 Mar. 1950, p. 3 [u].

50.03.24A "Ben Gurion on the Future of Israel." [David Ben Gurion on the future of Israel]. *CJC*, 24 Mar. 1950, p. 3 [u].

50.03.24B "Also An Election." [Re-election of Joseph Stalin]. *CJC*, 24 Mar. 1950, p. 3 [u].

50.03.24C "The Zoomites." [Man prepares for end of the world]. *CJC*, 24 Mar. 1950, p. 3 [s].

50.03.24D "Holy Land Pilgrimages." [Review of *Israel Diary* by Bernard M. Bloomfield]. *CJC*, 24 Mar. 1950, p. 5 [s].

50.03.31A "A New Haggadah." [Modernization of the Haggadah]. *CJC*, 31 Mar. 1950, p. 3 [u].

50.03.31B "The Marshalleise." [Controversy over Marshall Plan]. *CJC*, 31 Mar. 1950, p. 3 [u].

50.04.07A "Ulcer in Gaza." [Israelis attacked by terrorists]. *CJC*, 7 Apr. 1950, p. 3 [u].

50.04.07B "Bevin's Geography." [Ernest Bevin says Haifa should belong to Arabs]. *CJC*, 7 Apr. 1950, p. 3 [u].

50.04.07C "The Chernicovsky Prizes." [Negation of Diaspora culture]. *CJC*, 7 Apr. 1950, p. 3 [u].

50.04.14A "The Lukewarm War." [The Cold War]. *CJC*, 14 Apr. 1950, p. 3 [u].

50.04.14B "The Practical Ben Gurion." [David Ben Gurion urges acceptance of all immigrants to kibbutzim]. *CJC*, 14 Apr. 1950, p. 3 [u].

50.04.14C "Menuhin's Apology." [Yehudi Menuhin apologizes for performing in Germany]. *CJC*, 14 Apr. 1950, p. 3 [u].

50.04.14D "The Late Simcha Petrushka." [Death of Simcha Petrushka]. *CJC*, 14 Apr. 1950, p. 3 [u].

50.04.21A "The Second Anniversary." [Second anniversary of the State of Israel]. *CJC*, 21 Apr. 1950, p. 3 [u].

50.04.21B "Freedom of Religion." [Religious sect attacked in Quebec]. *CJC*, 21 Apr. 1950, p. 3 [u].

50.04.21C "Democratic Exdoctrination." [Anti-Semitism in Germany]. *CJC*, 21 Apr. 1950, p. 3 [u].

50.04.21D "Mr. Bevin's Ailment." [Ernest Bevin suffers from hemorrhoids]. *CJC*, 21 Apr. 1950, p. 3 [u].

50.04.28A "The Arms Race." [Britain supplies arms to Arabs but refuses Jews]. *CJC*, 28 Apr. 1950, p. 3 [u].

50.04.28B "Not the Real McCloy." [Reports of anti-Semitism in Germany]. *CJC*, 28 Apr. 1950, p. 3 [u].

50.04.28C "A Jew in the Sistine Chapel." [Sistine Chapel as an allegory of recent Jewish history (1)]. *CJC*, 28 Apr. 1950, p. 5 [u]. See also *SS*, pp. 135–150.

50.05.05A "The Nazi Renaissance." [Anti-Semitism in Germany]. *CJC*, 5 May 1950, p. 3 [u].

50.05.05B "The Russians on Jerusalem." [Soviet position on the sovereignty of Jerusalem]. *CJC*, 5 May 1950, p. 3 [u].

50.05.05C " 'Worlds in Collision'." [Review of *Worlds in Collision* by Immanuel Velikovsky]. *CJC*, 5 May 1950, p. 3 [u].

50.05.05D "A Jew in the Sistine Chapel." [Sistine Chapel as an allegory of recent Jewish history (2)]. *CJC*, 5 May 1950, p. 5 [u].

50.05.12A "The Semi-United Nations." [Herbert Hoover suggests exclusion of communist countries from U.N.]. *CJC*, 12 May 1950, p. 3 [u].

50.05.12B "Social Credit." [Social Credit dissociates itself from the Union of Quebec Electors because of the Union's anti-Semitism]. *CJC*, 12 May 1950, p. 3 [u].

50.05.12C "The Doukhobors." [Doukhobor problem in Canada]. *CJC*, 12 May 1950, p. 3 [u].

50.05.12D "A Jew in the Sistine Chapel." [Sistine Chapel as an allegory of recent Jewish history (3)]. *CJC*, 12 May 1950, p. 5 [u].

50.05.19A "The Feast of Shevuoth." [Shavuoth]. *CJC*, 19 May 1950, p. 3 [u].

50.05.19B "The Rimouski Fire." [Tragic fire in Rimouski]. *CJC*, 19 May 1950, p. 3 [u].

50.05.19C "Urgent Need." [Appeal for donations to the Joint Distribution Committee]. *CJC*, 19 May 1950, p. 3 [u].

50.05.26A "The Persistent Blasphemy." [Nazism in post-war Germany]. *CJC*, 26 May 1950, p. 3 [u].

50.05.26B "Teheran." [Jewish refugees gather in Teheran]. *CJC*, 26 May 1950, p. 3 [u].

50.05.26C "The Technique of Potiphar's Wife." [King Farouk refuses to recognize the marriage of his sister to a Christian]. *CJC*, 26 May 1950, p. 3 [u].

50.05.26D "The Dismal Decade." [Review of *Martyrdom and Miracle* by Harry J. Stern]. *CJC*, 26 May 1950, p. 5 [u].

50.06.00A "The Masked Yeats." [Review of several books on Yeats]. Northern Review 3, 5 (June-July 1950), pp. 43–5 [s].

50.06.02A "The Buttenweiser Affair." [Jewish aide to U.S. High Commissioner in Germany denies existence of Nazi activities]. *CJC*, 2 June 1950, p. 3 [u].

50.06.02B "The Chinese Puzzle." [Debate on admission of China to U.N.]. *CJC*, 2 June 1950, p. 3 [u].

50.06.02C "Transjordan and Syria." [State of affairs in Syria]. *CJC*, 2 June 1950, p. 3 [u].

50.06.09A "Operation Ali Baba." [Jews to leave Iraq]. *CJC*, 9 June 1950, p. 3 [u].

50.06.09B "The Third Force." [International relations after WWII]. *CJC*, 9 June 1950, p. 3 [u].

50.06.09C "Poet of a World Passed By." [Review of *Sefer Yiddish* by J. I. Segal]. *CJC*, 9 June 1950, p. 5 [s].

50.06.16A "Exodus from Rumania." [Jews leave Rumania]. *CJC*, 16 June 1950, p. 3 [u].

50.06.16B "The Little Fuhrers [*sic*]." [Prominent former Nazi is elected in Germany]. *CJC*, 16 June 1950, p. 3 [u].

50.06.16C "The Cold War." [Comment on suggestion that Cold War could be stopped if Joseph Stalin got a new suit]. *CJC*, 16 June 1950, p. 3 [u].

50.06.23A "The Sixth Column." [Ubiquitousness of fifth column]. *CJC*, 23 June 1950, p. 3 [u].

50.06.30A "The New Koreagraphy." [Impending war in Korea]. *CJC*, 30 June 1950, p. 3 [u].

50.06.30B "Abdullah Called to Account." [Negotiating terms of peace between Israel and Transjordan]. *CJC*, 30 June 1950, p. 3 [u].

50.06.30C "Who Nose?" [Doctor disproves stereotype of Jews' having hooked noses]. *CJC*, 30 June 1950, p. 3 [u].

50.07.07A "The Youth of Israel." [Character of Israeli youth]. *CJC*, 7 July, 1950, p. 3 [u].

50.07.07B "Perfumed Newspapers." [*Le Soleil* issues a perfumed edition]. *CJC*, 7 July 1950, p. 3 [u].

50.07.07C "The Cold War." [Soviets accuse U.S. of dropping potato bugs on East German fields]. *CJC*, 7 July 1950, p. 3 [u].

50.07.14A "A Sign of the Times." [British admiral flies an Israeli flag]. *CJC*, 14 July 1950, p. 3 [u].

50.07.14B "The Korean War." [Outbreak of the Korean War]. *CJC*, 14 July 1950, p. 3 [u].

50.07.14C "Israeli Immigration." [Israel has difficulties absorbing large numbers of immigrants]. *CJC*, 14 July 1950, p. 3 [u].

50.07.21A "The Korean Setback." [U.S. setbacks in Korean War]. *CJC*, 21 July 1950, p. 3 [u].

50.07.21B "In Memoriam: Vladimir Jabotinsky." [Tenth anniversary of the death of Vladimir Jabotinsky]. *CJC*, 21 July 1950, p. 3 [u].

50.07.21C "With Wallace Bled." [Henry Wallace abandons communist sympathies]. *CJC*, 21 July 1950, p. 3 [u].

50.07.28A "In Memoriam: Mackenzie King." [Death of William Lyon Mackenzie King]. *CJC*, 28 July 1950, p. 3 [u].

50.07.28B "Freedom of Speech." [British allow Ilya Ehrenberg into England]. *CJC*, 28 July 1950, p. 3 [u].

50.07.28C "Austerity in Israel." [Israeli economy]. *CJC*, 28 July 1950, p. 3 [u].

50.08.04A "Walk-Out and Return." [Soviet behaviour at U.N.]. *CJC*, 4 Aug. 1950, p. 3 [u].

50.08.04B "They Protest Too Much." [Arabs accuse Israel of acts of aggression]. *CJC*, 4 Aug. 1950, p. 3 [u].

50.08.04C "An Almost-Abdication." [King Leopold of Belgium promises to abdicate after marrying a commoner]. *CJC*, 4 Aug. 1950, p. 3 [u].

50.08.11A "Canada's or Germany's 'Native Sons'." [Cold War hostilities]. *CJC*, 11 Aug. 1950, p. 3 [u].

50.08.11B "Sought Horizon." [Chinese move against Tibet]. *CJC*, 11 Aug. 1950, p. 3 [u].

50.08.11C "An Israeli Loan." [Need to shift support for Israel from philanthropy to financial investment]. *CJC*, 11 Aug. 1950, p. 3 [u].

50.08.18A "The Stockholm Petition." [Soviet pacifist propaganda]. *CJC*, 18 Aug. 1950, p. 3 [u].

50.08.18B "Soviet Propaganda." [Soviet anti-American propaganda]. *CJC*, 18 Aug. 1950, p. 3 [u].

50.08.18C "The New Stuermer." [Revival of *Der Stuermer*]. *CJC*, 18 Aug. 1950, p. 3 [u].

50.08.25A "The Israeli Constitution." [Abandonment of the idea of an Israeli constitution]. *CJC*, 25 Aug. 1950, p. 3 [u].

50.08.25B "The P.E.N. Club." [PEN Club and communism]. *CJC*, 25 Aug. 1950, p. 3 [u].

50.08.25C "Melting Pot and Pressure Cooker." [Strain of mass immigration on Israeli economy]. *CJC*, 25 Aug. 1950, p. 3 [u].

50.09.01A " 'Bury the Dead'." [Futility of pacifism]. *CJC*, 1 Sept. 1950, p. 3 [u].

50.09.01B "For Good Behaviour." [Clemency to be granted to interned Nazis]. *CJC*, 1 Sept. 1950, p. 3 [u].

50.09.08A "Of Hope and Premonition." [International relations on eve of New Year]. *CJC*, 8 Sept. 1950, p. 3 [u].

50.09.08B "What Are Free Elections?" [Soviet propaganda]. *CJC*, 8 Sept. 1950, p. 3 [u].

50.09.15A "The Contemporary Pharaoh." [King Faud of Egypt]. *CJC*, 15 Sept. 1950, p. 3 [u].

50.09.15B "The Billion Dollar Loan." [Proposal to launch a billion dollar loan to Israel]. *CJC*, 15 Sept. 1950, p. 3 [u].

50.09.15C "Sign of the Times." [Philosophical society discontinues meetings due to apathy of its members]. *CJC*, 15 Sept. 1950, p. 3 [u].

50.09.22A "German Rearmament." [Debate on possible re-armament of West Germany]. *CJC*, 22 Sept. 1950, p. 3 [u].

50.09.22B "Jan Christian Smuts." [Death of Jan Christian Smuts]. *CJC*, 22 Sept. 1950, p. 3 [u].

50.09.22C "The Books but not the People." [Survival of Jewish books]. *CJC*, 22 Sept. 1950, p. 3 [u].

50.09.29A "The Nobel Peace Prize." [Nobel Peace Prize awarded to Ralph Bunche]. *CJC*, 29 Sept. 1950, p. 3 [u].

50.09.29B "The Last Salient." [Israel's strained economy]. *CJC*, 29 Sept. 1950, p. 3 [u].

50.09.29C "A Question of Manners." [Thomas Dewey insults Russians]. *CJC*, 29 Sept. 1950, p. 3 [u].

50.10.06A "Sharett on Germany." [Moshe Sharett speaks at U.N. about the appeasement of Germany]. *CJC*, 6 Oct. 1950, p. 3 [u].

50.10.06B "Citizen of the World." [Gary Davis declares himself a citizen of the world]. *CJC*, 6 Oct. 1950, p. 3 [u].

50.10.13A "Dr. Goldman's Address." [Need for Zionist activity after the establishment of the State of Israel]. *CJC*, 13 Oct. 1950, p. 3 [u].

50.10.13B "The Maccabiad." [1950 Maccabiad]. *CJC*, 13 Oct. 1950, p. 3 [u].

50.10.20A "The Israeli Crisis." [Political deadlock in Israel]. *CJC*, 20 Oct. 1950, p. 3 [u].

50.10.20B "Hippocratic or Hippocritic?" [World Medical Association admits German doctors]. *CJC*, 20 Oct. 1950, p. 3 [u].

50.10.27A "In Memoriam: H. Wolofsky." [In memory of Hirsch Wolofsky]. *CJC*, 27 Oct. 1950, p. 3 [u].

50.10.27B "Truman's True Peace Plan." [Harry S. Truman proposes a disarmament plan]. *CJC*, 27 Oct. 1950, p. 3 [u].

50.11.03A "The Combined Jewish Appeal." [Fundraising campaign for Combined Jewish Appeal]. *CJC*, 3 Nov. 1950, p. 3 [u].

50.11.03B "The Washington Conference." [Eliezer Kaplan speaks on Israeli economy]. *CJC*, 3 Nov. 1950, p. 3 [u].

50.11.03C "The Israeli Crisis Resolved." [Resolution of Israeli cabinet crisis]. *CJC*, 3 Nov. 1950, p. 3 [u].

50.11.10A "Shangrila." [Chinese occupation of Tibet]. *CJC*, 10 Nov. 1950, p. 3 [u].

50.11.10B "The Unrepenting Nazis." [Persistence of Nazi ideology in Germany]. *CJC*, 10 Nov. 1950, p. 3 [u].

50.11.10C "The Israeli Truce." [Uncertainty of continued peace between Arabs and Jews]. *CJC*, 10 Nov. 1950, p. 3 [u].

50.11.10D "One-Eyed Recognition." [Admission of Spain to U.N.]. *CJC*, 10 Nov. 1950, p. 3 [u].

50.11.17A "The Arab Refugee." [Plight of Arab refugees]. *CJC*, 17 Nov. 1950, p. 3 [u].

50.11.17B "Two War Ministers." [Views of British and French politicians]. *CJC*, 17 Nov. 1950, p. 3 [u].

50.11.24A "In Memoriam: The Venerable Rabbi Zvi Hirsch Cohen." [Death of Rabbi Zvi Hirsch Cohen]. *CJC*, 24 Nov. 1950, p. 3 [u].

50.12.01A "The Feast of Chanukah." [Relevance of Chanukah story to contemporary Israel]. *CJC*, 1 Dec. 1950, p. 3 [u].

50.12.01B "The Notorious Restrictive Clause." [Anti-Semitism in Canada]. *CJC*, 1 Dec. 1950, p. 3 [u].

50.12.08A "No Atomic Bomb." [U.S. says it will not use atomic bomb in Korea]. *CJC*, 8 Dec. 1950, p. 3 [u].

50.12.08B "A Protest Vindicated." [Egypt accumulates arms]. *CJC*, 8 Dec. 1950, p. 3 [u].

50.12.15A "Truth or Parable." [Arab-Israeli relations]. *CJC*, 15 Dec. 1950, p. 3 [u].

50.12.15B "Truman: The Critic's Critic." [Harry S. Truman defends his daughter's singing against critic]. *CJC*, 15 Dec. 1950, p. 3 [u].

50.12.15C "Situation Really Serious." [Baseball commissioner declares sport will be suspended in the event of war]. *CJC*, 15 Dec. 1950, p. 3 [u].

50.12.22A "To Whom Honour is Due: Samuel Bronfman." [Tribute to Samuel Bronfman]. *CJC*, 22 Dec. 1950, p. 3 [u].

50.12.29A "In Memoriam: H.M. Caiserman." [Tribute to H. M. Caiserman]. *CJC*, 29 Dec. 1950, p. 3 [i].

51.01.05A "Peace; It's Wonderful!" [Cold War and international relations]. *CJC*, 5 Jan. 1951, p. 3 [u].

51.01.05B "The Burning Bush." [Moishe Sneh on German rearmament]. *CJC*, 5 Jan. 1951, p. 3 [u].

51.01.12A "In Memoriam: Alexander Bercovitch." [Death of Alexander Bercovitch]. *CJC*, 12 Jan. 1951, p. 3 [u].

51.01.12B "Israel at the United Nations." [Israel proposes a peace plan for Korea at U.N.]. *CJC*, 12 Jan. 1951, p. 3 [u].

51.01.19A "Welcome to the Israel Philharmonic Orchestra." [Israel Philharmonic Orchestra performs in Montreal]. *CJC*, 19 Jan. 1951, p. 3 [u].

51.01.19B "The End of a Hoax." [Hoax of Biro-Bidjan]. *CJC*, 19 Jan. 1951, p. 3 [u].

51.01.19C "The Thieves of Baghdad." [Synagogue bombed in Baghdad]. *CJC*, 19 Jan. 1951, p. 3 [u].

51.01.26A "The Jewish National Fund." [Fundraising for the Jewish National Fund]. *CJC*, 26 Jan. 1951, p. 3 [u].

51.01.26B "Let My People Go." [Jews are permitted to leave Iraq]. *CJC*, 26 Jan. 1951, p. 3 [u].

51.01.26C "British Israel Relations." [Improving British-Israeli relations]. *CJC*, 26 Jan. 1951, p. 3 [u].

51.01.26D "American-Israel Cultural Relations." [Cultural exchange between Israel and U.S.]. *CJC*, 26 Jan. 1951, p. 3 [u].

51.02.02A "Trade Relations With Israel." [Canadian-Israeli trade relations]. *CJC*, 2 Feb. 1950, p. 3 [u].

51.02.02B "The Qualifications of a Plenipotentiary." [Soviets refuse to accept Israeli ambassador]. *CJC*, 2 Feb. 1951, p. 3 [u].

51.02.09A "The Value of the Bible." [Purchase of a Gutenberg Bible]. *CJC*, 9 Feb. 1951, p. 3 [u].

51.02.09B "The Hurried Amnesties." [Pardoning of Nazi war criminals]. *CJC*, 9 Feb. 1951, p. 3 [u].

51.02.09C "Investment Possibilities in Israel." [Investment possibilities in Israel]. *CJC*, 9 Feb. 1951, p. 3 [u].

51.02.16A "The De Bernonville Case." [Jacques de Bernonville denied sanctuary in Canada]. *CJC*, 16 Feb. 1950, p. 3 [u].

51.02.16B "The Case of Fritz Thyssen." [Fate of Fritz Thyssen]. *CJC*, 16 Feb. 1951, p. 3 [u].

51.02.16C "Turkey and Israel." [Improved relations between Turkey and Israel]. *CJC*, 16 Feb. 1951, p. 3 [u].

51.02.23A "Education in Israel." [Need for a national school system in Israel]. *CJC*, 23 Feb. 1951, p. 3 [u].

51.03.02A "Varieties of Genocide." [Cultural genocide in the Soviet Union]. *CJC*, 2 Mar. 1951, p. 3 [u].

51.03.02B "Dewey on Isolationism." [Herbert Hoover and Robert Taft advocate U.S. isolationism]. *CJC*, 2 Mar. 1951, p. 3 [s].

51.03.09A "Samuel Bronfman: — Yet Another Benefaction." [Samuel Bronfman establishes a fund for the humanities]. *CJC*, 9 Mar. 1951, p. 3 [u].

51.03.09B "Conscription in Israel." [Conscription of both men and women in Israel]. *CJC*, 9 Mar. 1951, p. 3 [u].

51.03.16A "The Thieves of Bagdad." [Plight of Iraqi Jews]. *CJC*, 16 Mar. 1951, p. 3 [u].

51.03.16B "The Feast of Purim." [Purim as a parable for recent Jewish history]. *CJC*, 16 Mar. 1951, p. 3 [u].

51.03.23A "Israel and Jewish Rehabilitation." [National conference on Israel and Jewish rehabilitation]. *CJC*, 23 Mar. 1951, p. 3 [u].

51.03.23B "Iraqi Plunder." [Persecution of Iraqi Jews]. *CJC*, 23 Mar. 1951, p. 3 [u].

51.03.23C "The Diplomats." [Disappearance of two British diplomats]. *CJC*, 23 Mar. 1951, p. 3 [u].

51.03.30A "A Symbol of the Times." [Continued Arab-Israeli hostility despite peace treaty]. *CJC*, 30 Mar. 1951, p. 3 [u].

51.03.30B "German Reparations." [German reparations to Jews after WWII]. *CJC*, 30 Mar. 1951, p. 3 [u].

51.03.30C "A Thousand a Night." [Flight of Jews from Iraq]. *CJC*, 30 Mar. 1951, p. 3 [u].

51.04.06A "The Pit and the Pendulum." [Poe's "The Pit and the Pendulum" as a parable for recent Jewish history]. *CJC*, 6 Apr. 1951, p. 3 [u].

51.04.13A "The Stalin Peace Prize." [Stalin Peace Prize]. *CJC*, 13 Apr. 1951, p. 3 [u].

51.04.13B "Menace on the Syrian Frontier." [Syria attacks Israeli settlers on its border]. *CJC*, 13 Apr. 1951, p. 3 [u].

51.04.20A "Joseph and His Brethren." [The story of Joseph as a parable for recent Jewish history]. *CJC*, 20 Apr. 1951, p. 3 [u].

51.04.27A "The Council for Judaism, Inc." [Jewish American anti-Zionism]. *CJC*, 27 Apr. 1951, p. 3 [u].

51.05.04A "What! No Drama?" [Waning of Zionism in North America]. *CJC*, 4 May 1951, p. 3 [u].

51.05.04B "The Altered Jewish Scene." [Jewish history since the death of Theodor Herzl]. *CJC*, 4 May 1951, p. 3 [u].

51.05.11A "Israel's Independence Day." [Celebration of Israeli independence in light of continued Arab hostility]. *CJC*, 11 May 1951, p. 3 [u].

51.05.11B "New Canadians." [Students graduate from Jewish Immigrant Aid Society night school]. *CJC*, 11 May 1951, p. 3 [u].

51.05.18A "Religious Fire." [Religious extremists try to burn down the Knesseth]. *CJC*, 18 May 1951, p. 3 [u].

51.05.18B "Neo-Nazism." [Neo-Nazism in Germany]. *CJC*, 18 May 1951, p. 3 [u].

51.05.25A "Ben Gurion's Triumphal Progress." [David Ben Gurion tours U.S.]. *CJC*, 25 May 1951, p. 3 [u].

51.05.25B "Abba Eban on the Arab Refugee." [Abba Eban on the Arab refugee problem]. *CJC*, 25 May 1951, p. 3 [u].

51.06.01A "The Seven Who Were Not Hanged." [Amnesty for Nazi war criminals]. *CJC*, 1 June 1951, p. 3 [u].

51.06.01B "Peron's Bomb." [Juan Peron announces a cheaper way of generating atomic energy]. *CJC*, 1 June 1951, p. 3 [u].

51.06.01C "The Bang That Became a Whimper." [Declining reputation of Douglas MacArthur]. *CJC*, 1 June 1951, p. 3 [u].

51.06.08A "Shevuoth." [Immorality of nations]. *CJC*, 8 June 1951, p. 3 [u].

51.06.08B "Required: A New Orientation." [Need to redefine Zionism]. *CJC*, 8 June 1951, p. 3 [u].

51.06.15A "The Shadow of the Mushroom." [Atomic bomb]. *CJC*, 15 June 1951, p. 3 [u].

51.06.22A "Diversion in Baghdad." [Scapegoating of Jews in Iraq]. *CJC*, 22 June 1951, p. 3 [u].

51.06.22B "The Budapest Expulsions." [Expulsion of Jews from Budapest]. *CJC*, 22 June 1951, p. 3 [u].

51.06.29A "Malik's Peace Proposals." [Malik's peace proposal for Korea]. *CJC*, 29 June 1951, p. 3 [u].

51.06.29B "The Iran Oil Dispute." [Iran-Israeli oil dispute]. *CJC*, 29 June 1951, p. 3 [u].

51.06.29C "Israel and Switzerland." [Israeli-Swiss relations]. *CJC*, 29 June 1951, p. 3 [u].

51.07.06A "The Laws of the Medes and the Persians." [Iranian oil and international relations]. *CJC*, 6 July 1951, p. 3 [u].

51.07.06B "A Statue for the Seven?" [Neo-Nazism in Germany]. *CJC*, 6 July 1951, p. 3 [u].

51.07.13A "Peace with Germany." [U.N.'s reconciliation with Germany]. *CJC*, 13 July 1951, p. 3 [u].

51.07.13B "Not a Dove — a Canard." [False announcement of reconciliation between Israel and Germany]. *CJC*, 13 July 1951, p. 3 [u].

51.07.20A "The Hosts of Pharaoh." [Mid-eastern oil and international relations]. *CJC*, 20 July 1951, p. 3 [u].

51.07.20B "Mapam Has a Conference." [Mapam party's political demands to the Ben Gurion government]. *CJC*, 20 July 1951, p. 3 [u].

51.07.27A "The Assassination of King Abdullah." [The assassination of King Abdullah of Transjordan]. *CJC*, 27 July 1951, p. 3 [u].

51.08.03A "The Elections in Israel." [Israeli elections]. *CJC*, 3 Aug. 1951, p. 3 [u].

51.08.03B "New Times, New Approaches." [Improving Anglo-Jewish relations]. *CJC*, 3 Aug. 1951, p. 3 [u].

51.08.03C "Oil in the Negev." [Probability of oil in the Negev]. *CJC*, 3 Aug. 1951, p. 3 [u].

51.08.10A "Egypt and Britain." [Egyptian and British policy on the Suez Canal]. *CJC*, 10 Aug. 1951, p. 3 [u].

51.08.10B "The Disc Jockey." [Soviet president sends letter of peace to U.S.]. *CJC*, 10 Aug. 1951, p. 3 [u].

51.08.10C "Peron Sings Hatikvah." [Juan Peron sings Hatikvah]. *CJC*, 10 Aug. 1951, p. 3 [u].

51.08.17A "The Zionist Congress." [Debate over role of the Jewish Agency]. *CJC*, 17 Aug. 1951, p. 3 [u].

51.08.17B "Is McCarthy a Communist Agent?" [McCarthyism]. *CJC*, 17 Aug. 1951, p. 3 [u].

51.08.24A "The Mufti's Schemes." [Activities of the Mufti]. *CJC*, 24 Aug. 1951, p. 3 [u].

51.08.24B "A Long Farewell." [Jacques de Bernonville flees to Brazil]. *CJC*, 24 Aug. 1951, p. 3 [u].

51.08.31A "The Men Who Were Not There." [Egyptian and Syrian acts of aggression despite peace treaty]. *CJC*, 31 Aug. 1951, p. 3 [u].

51.08.31B "The Plane That Was Not There." [Communists claim Korean peace negotiations are disrupted by U.S. bombing]. *CJC*, 31 Aug. 1951, p. 3 [u].

51.08.31C "The Place That Was Not There." [Soviets announce dissolution of Biro-Bidjan]. *CJC*, 31 Aug. 1951, p. 3 [u].

51.09.07A "The Japanese Treaty." [Impending peace treaty with Japan]. *CJC*, 7 Sept. 1951, p. 3 [u].

51.09.07B "The Case of the Unburied Indian." [American Indian killed in Korea is denied burial in a white cemetery]. *CJC*, 7 Sept. 1951, p. 3 [u].

51.09.07C "Abraham Cahan." [Death of Abraham Cahan]. *CJC*, 7 Sept. 1951, p. 3 [u].

51.09.14A "Austerity in Israel." [Israel's struggling economy]. *CJC*, 14 Sept. 1951, p. 3 [u].

51.09.14B "And Now, With Germany." [Possibility of a treaty of reconciliation with Germany]. *CJC*, 14 Sept. 1951, p. 3 [u].

51.09.14C "There Should be a Law." [Objection to having pets as beneficiaries]. *CJC*, 14 Sept. 1951, p. 3 [u].

51.09.21A "The Arab Refugees." [Arab refugees and Arab-Israeli relations]. *CJC*, 21 Sept. 1951, p. 3 [u].

51.09.28A "The New Year." [Hope for improved international relations in New Year]. *CJC*, 28 Sept. 1951, p. 3 [u].

51.09.28B "A Kind of Repentance." [Suggestion to destroy all records of Nazi activity]. *CJC*, 28 Sept. 1951, p. 3 [u].

51.09.28C "The Russian Encyclopedia." [The *Soviet Encyclopedia* makes no mention of Jewish culture]. *CJC*, 28 Sept. 1951, p. 3 [u].

51.09.28D "The Bible Manuscripts." [The Bible manuscripts (1)]. *CJC*, 28 Sept. 1958, p. 9 [s].

51.10.05A "Germany's Contribution." [Konrad Adenauer declares Germany is ready to make restitution]. *CJC*, 5 Oct. 1951, p. 3 [u].

51.10.05B "Eve in the Garden." [Attempted coup in Argentina]. *CJC*, 5 May 1951, p. 3 [u].

51.10.05C "— And it Isn't Because I Wasn't Invited." [Decadence of Don Carlos de Beistegui]. *CJC*, 5 Oct. 1951, p. 3 [u].

51.10.05D "The Bible Manuscripts." [The Bible manuscripts (2)]. *CJC*, 5 Oct. 1951, p. 10 [s].

51.10.12A "The Feast of Tabernacles." [Relevance of Jewish holidays to contemporary Jewish history]. *CJC*, 12 Oct. 1951, p. 3 [u].

51.10.12B "Good For You, Keenleyside." [Hugh Keenleyside refuses to shake hands with Hjalmar Schacht]. *CJC*, 12 Oct. 1951, p. 3 [u].

51.10.12C "The Bible Manuscripts." [The Bible manuscripts (3)]. *CJC*, 12 Oct. 1951, p. 10 [s].

51.10.19A "The Smouldering Middle East." [Middle East oil and international relations]. *CJC*, 19 Oct. 1951, p. 3 [u].

51.10.19B "The Bible Manuscripts." [The Bible manuscripts (4)]. *CJC*, 19 Oct. 1959, p. 8 [s].

51.10.26A "Welcome the Royal Visitors!" [Royal visit to Canada]. *CJC*, 26 Oct. 1951, p. 3 [u].

51.10.26B "Representation at the Vatican." [Harry S. Truman appoints an ambassador to the Vatican]. *CJC*, 26 Oct. 1951, p. 3 [u].

51.10.26C "A Stupid By-Law." [By-law restricting religious worship in private homes]. *CJC*, 26 Oct. 1951, p. 3 [u].

51.10.26D "The Bible Manuscripts." [The Bible manuscripts (5)]. 26 Oct. 1951, p. 9 [s].

51.11.02A "The Congress Plenary Session." [Ninth plenary session of the Canadian Jewish Congress]. *CJC*, 2 Nov. 1951, p. 3 [u].

51.11.02B "The First Joint Campaign." [Fundraising for Jewish philanthropic organizations]. *CJC*, 2 Nov. 1951, p. 3 [u].

51.11.09A "The Proposed Middle Eastern Pact." [Proposed peace agreement for the Middle East]. *CJC*, 9 Nov. 1951, p. 3 [u].

51.11.09B "German Reparations." [German reparations to Jews after WWII]. *CJC*, 9 Nov. 1951, p. 3 [u].

51.11.16A "The Nobel Peace Prize." [Nobel Peace Prize awarded to Leon Jouhaux]. *CJC*, 16 Nov. 1951, p. 3 [u].

51.11.16B "The Magic Carpet Lands." [Evacuation of Jews from Yemen]. *CJC*, 16 Nov. 1951, p. 3 [u].

51.11.23A "The Laughing Vishinsky." [Vishinsky laughs at possibility of world peace]. *CJC*, 23 Nov. 1951, p. 3 [u].

51.11.23B "Limitation of Immigration." [Possibility of limiting immigration to Israel]. *CJC*, 23 Nov. 1951, p. 3 [u].

51.11.23C "Canadian Radio Broadcasts." [MP's seek to limit freedom of the CBC]. *CJC*, 23 Nov. 1951, p. 3 [u].

51.11.30A "The Case of Kurt Meyer." [Kurt Meyer receives special treatment in prison]. *CJC*, 30 Nov. 1951, p. 3 [u].

51.11.30B "In Memoriam: Samuel Talpis." [Death of Samuel Talpis]. *CJC*, 30 Nov. 1951, p. 3 [u].

51.12.07A "German Renazification." [German dissatisfaction with boundaries assigned after WWII]. *CJC*, 7 Dec. 1951, p. 3 [u].

51.12.07B "Call me Mayer [*sic*]!" [Rumours of possible freeing of Kurt Meyer]. *CJC*, 7 Dec. 1951, p. 3 [u].

51.12.14A "The Egyptian Audacity." [Israeli-Egyptian relations]. *CJC*, 14 Dec. 1951, p. 3 [u].

51.12.21A "Chanukah." [Chanukah story and contemporary Jewish history]. *CJC*, 21 Dec. 1951, p. 3 [u].

51.12.21B "Buber's Prize" [Goethe Prize awarded to Martin Buber]. *CJC*, 21 Dec. 1951, p. 3 [u].

51.12.28A "European Federation." [Western European nations form a federation]. 28 Dec. 1951, p. 3 [u].

52.01.04A "Death of a Salesman." [Death of Maxim Litvinov]. *CJC*, 4 Jan. 1952, p. 3 [u].

52.01.04B "Congratulations to Rabbi Herschorn." [Rabbi S. Herschorn is elevated to head of the Montreal Council of the Rabbinate]. *CJC*, 4 Jan. 1952, p. 3 [u].

52.01.11A "Mr. Barre and His Bargains." [Anti-Semitism of Laurent Barré]. *CJC*, 11 Jan. 1952, p. 3 [u].

52.01.11B "The Zionist Convention." [Thirty-first convention of Zionist Organization of Canada]. *CJC*, 11 Jan. 1952, p. 3 [u].

52.01.18A "German Reparations." [German offer of reparations to surviving victims of Nazism]. *CJC*, 18 Jan. 1952, p. 3 [u].

52.01.18B "The Adath Israel Academy." [Opening of new Adath Israel Academy]. *CJC*, 18 Jan. 1952, p. 3 [u].

52.01.25A "Churchill and the Middle East." [Speech of Winston Churchill on the Middle East]. *CJC*, 25 Jan. 1952, p. 3 [u].

52.01.25B "The Quebec Legislature." [Inappropriate behaviour of Quebec MNA's]. *CJC*, 25 Jan. 1952, p. 3 [u].

52.01.25C "Legislature Bargains." [Fee for official name change refunded to Jewish organization]. *CJC*, 25 Jan. 1952, p. 3 [u].

52.02.01A "Without the Prince of Denmark." [Communist rewriting of the Bible in Israel]. *CJC*, 1 Feb. 1952, p. 3 [u].

52.02.01B "Mr. Duplessis' Explanation." [Maurice Duplessis comments on anti-Semitic remark of Laurent Barré]. *CJC*, 1 Feb. 1952, p. 3 [u].

52.02.08A "Canada Mourns." [Death of King George VI]. *CJC*, 8 Feb. 1952, p. 3 [u].

52.02.08B "Long Live the Queen!" [Elizabeth II becomes Queen of England]. *CJC*, 8 Feb. 1952, p. 3 [u].

52.02.15A "The Middle Eastern Pact." [Middle East and international affairs]. *CJC*, 15 Feb. 1952, p. 3 [u].

52.02.15B "Yet Another Party." [Sternist party proposes program for Israel]. *CJC*, 15 Feb. 1952, p. 3 [u].

52.02.22A "The Egyptian Army." [Growing Egyptian army is a potential threat to Israel]. *CJC*, 22 Feb. 1952, p. 3 [u].

52.02.22B "The West German Army." [Americans train West German army]. *CJC*, 22 Feb. 1952, p. 3 [u].

52.02.22C "Canadian Young Judaea." [Thirty-fifth anniversary of Young Judaea]. *CJC*, 22 Feb. 1952, p. 3 [u].

52.02.29A "Youth Aliyah." [Work of Youth Aliyah Organization]. *CJC*, 29 Feb. 1952, p. 3 [u].

52.02.29B "Concessions Breed Impudence." [Germany tries to reclaim territory lost during WWII]. *CJC*, 29 Feb. 1952, p. 3 [u].

52.02.29C "Let My People Go." [Zionist leaders purged in Rumania]. *CJC*, 29 Feb. 1952, p. 3 [u].

52.03.07A "The Feast of Purim." [Relative calm of Jewish world situation]. *CJC*, 7 Mar. 1952, p. 3 [u].

52.03.07B "A Game of Chess." [Soviets consider chess an imperialist game]. *CJC*, 7 Mar. 1952, p. 3 [u].

52.03.07C "The Foot and Mouth Disease." [Admission of pro-Nazi German immigrants to Canada]. *CJC*, 7 Mar. 1952, p. 3 [u].

52.03.14A "The Budget for 'Peace'." [Soviet military expenditures]. *CJC*, 14 Mar. 1952, p. 3 [u].

52.03.14B "The Czechs Double-Checked." [Anti-Semitism in Czechoslovakia]. *CJC*, 14 Mar. 1952, p. 3 [u].

52.03.14C "The Late Joseph Schubert." [Death of Joseph Schubert]. *CJC*, 14 Mar. 1952, p. 3 [u].

52.03.21A "The Histadruth." [Work of the Histadrut]. *CJC*, 21 Mar. 1952, p. 3 [u].

52.03.21B "The Mink, Its Decline and Fall?" [Jews and mink coats]. *CJC*, 21 Mar. 1952, p. 3 [u].

52.03.28A "Racism in South Africa." [Racist legislation in South Africa]. *CJC*, 28 Mar. 1952, p. 3 [u].

52.03.28B "A Unique Position." [Jews in the Soviet Union]. *CJC*, 28 Mar. 1952, p. 3 [u].

52.04.04A "Sharett visits the Pope." [Moshe Sharett visits the Pope]. *CJC*, 4 Apr. 1952, p. 3 [u].

52.04.04B "Those German-Jewish Reparation Talks." [Negotiations over German reparations to Jews]. *CJC*, 4 Apr. 1952, p. 3 [u].

52.04.04C "The Art of Hertz Grosbard." [Hertz Grosbard]. *CJC*, 4 Apr. 1952, pp. 4, 9 [s].

52.04.09A "The Feast of Passover." [Need for emancipation of the oppressed]. *CJC*, 9 Apr. 1952, p. 3 [u].

52.04.09B "How do you know? Einstein is wrong!" [Soviet magazine declares Albert Einstein to be wrong about relativity]. *CJC*, 9 Apr. 1952, p. 3 [u].

52.04.18A "Who Wants to Build Up Germany?" [Germany and East-West relations]. *CJC*, 18 Apr. 1952, p. 3 [u].

52.04.18B "The Council for Judaism, Inc." [Jewish anti-Zionism]. *CJC*, 18 Apr. 1952, p. 3 [u].

52.04.25A "The Fourth Anniversary." [Fourth anniversary of the State of Israel]. *CJC*, 25 Apr. 1952, p. 3 [u].

52.04.25B "Farewell, Moshe Yuval." [Israeli consul general leaves Montreal posting]. *CJC*, 25 Apr. 1952, p. 3 [u].

52.05.02A "Racism in South Africa." [Jewish MP speaks out against racism in South Africa]. *CJC*, 2 May 1952, p. 3 [u].

52.05.02B "German Reparations." [Negotiations over German reparations to Jews]. *CJC*, 2 May 1952, p. 3 [u].

52.05.09A "The Jewish Agency." [Status of the Jewish Agency]. *CJC*, 9 May 1952, p. 3 [u].

52.05.09B "The Arab Refugee." [Arab refugee problem]. *CJC*, 9 May. 1952, p. 3 [u].

52.05.16A "The Genocide Convention." [Genocide to be debated in Canadian House of Commons]. *CJC*, 16 May 1952, p. 3 [u].

52.05.16B "The Moscow Synagogue." [Soviets claim that Judaism flourishing in Soviet Union]. *CJC*, 16 May 1952, p. 3 [u].

52.05.23A "The Jewish Public Library." [New Montreal Jewish Public Library]. *CJC*, 23 May 1952, p. 3 [u].

52.05.23B "Tribute to Michael Garber." [Sixtieth birthday of Michael Garber]. *CJC*, 23 May 1952, p. 3 [u].

52.05.29A "Homage to Ludwig Lewisohn." [Ludwig Lewisohn's seventieth birthday]. *CJC*, 29 May 1952, p. 3 [u].

52.05.29B "The Feast of Shevuoth." [Wish for world-wide observance of the ten commandments]. *CJC*, 29 May 1952, p. 3 [u].

52.06.06A "Israel and Germany." [Israeli government refuses to participate in reconciliation of Germany with U.N.]. *CJC*, 6 June 1952, p. 3 [u].

52.06.06B "The Closing of Pardess Hannah." [Closing of an immigration reception centre in Israel]. *CJC*, 6 June 1952, p. 3 [u].

52.06.13A "Israel's Drastic Economic Measures." [Drastic economic measures taken in Israel]. *CJC*, 13 June 1952, p. 3 [u].

52.06.20A "Welcome to Moshe Sharett!" [Moshe Sharett visits Canada]. *CJC*, 20 June 1952, p. 3 [u].

52.06.20B "They Have Them, Too." [Israeli communists]. *CJC*, 20 June 1952, p. 3 [u].

52.06.27A "Israel." [Issues raised by Moshe Sharett during visit to Canada]. *CJC*, 27 June 1952, p. 3 [u].

52.06.27B "Canaan." [Jewish terrorists bomb home of Israeli cabinet minister]. *CJC*, 27 June 1952, p. 3 [u].

52.06.27C "Philistia." [Plan to rebuild Ashkelon]. *CJC*, 27 June 1952, p. 3 [u].

52.07.04A "Definitions." [Definition of "chutzpah"]. *CJC*, 4 July 1952, p. 3 [u].

52.07.04B "Moslem Green." [Arabs ask that German reparations promised to Jews be given to Arab refugees]. *CJC*, 4 July 1952, p. 3 [u].

52.07.04C "German Brown." [Germany demands possession of Saar Basin]. *CJC*, 4 July 1952, p. 3 [u].

52.07.04D "Commie Red." [Anti-Americanism of Canadian communists]. *CJC*, 4 July 1952, p. 3 [u].

52.07.11A "The Red Dean." [Hewlett Johnson]. *CJC*, 11 July 1952, p. 3 [u].

52.07.11B "Conventions in the Republic." [U.S. anti-Semitism]. *CJC* 11 July 1952 p. 3 [u].

52.07.18A "Eliezer Kaplan." [Death of Eliezer Kaplan]. *CJC* 18 July 1952 p. 3 [u].

52.07.18B "The Laws of the Medes and the Persians." [Anti-Semitism in Iran]. *CJC*, 18 July 1952, p. 3 [u].

52.07.25A "Austria Gemutlich." [Austria grants amnesty to Nazis]. *CJC*, 25 July 1952, p. 3 [u].

52.07.25B "The Red Magen David." [Israel is refused membership in World Red Cross]. *CJC*, 25 July 1952, p. 3 [u].

52.07.25C "Rewards for the Prolific." [Bursaries for prolific mothers in Israel]. *CJC*, 25 July 1952, p. 3 [u].

52.08.01A "Farouk: Ex Marks the Spot." [Political divisiveness in Egypt]. *CJC*, 1 Aug. 1952, p. 3 [u].

52.08.08A "A Fable." [Satire on U.N.]. *CJC*, 8 Aug. 1952, p. 3 [u].

52.08.15A "Of Armorial Bearings." [Inappropriateness of heraldic symbols]. *CJC*, 15 Aug. 1952, p. 3 [u].

52.08.22A "Industrial Development in Israel." [Industrial development in Israel]. *CJC*, 22 Aug. 1952, p. 3 [u].

52.08.29A "The Canadian Association for Labor Israel." [Third National Histadrut Conference]. *CJC*, 29 Aug. 1952, p. 3 [u].

52.08.29B "The World is Getting Smaller." [New record set for two-way transatlantic flight]. *CJC*, 29 Aug. 1952, p. 3 [u].

52.09.05A "Racism in South Africa." [Racism in South Africa]. *CJC*, 5 Sept. 1952, p. 3 [u].

52.09.12A "The Jewish People's Schools." [Fundraising for Jewish People's Schools]. *CJC*, 12 Sept. 1952, p. 3 [u].

52.09.12B "The Jewish Scene." [Need for Jewish solidarity]. *CJC*, 12 Sept. 1952, p. 3 [u].

52.09.12C "Is Hitler Dead?" [Doubt about Adolf Hitler's death]. *CJC*, 12 Sept. 1952, p. 3 [u].

52.09.19A "The New Year." [Uncertainty of the future]. *CJC*, 19 Sept. 1952, p. 3 [u].

52.09.19B "Naguib and Shishakley." [Rule of new Egyptian leaders]. *CJC*, 19 Sept. 1952, p. 3 [u].

52.09.26A "The Day of Atonement." [Yom Kippur]. *CJC*, 26 Sept. 1952, p. 3 [u].

52.09.26B "The Case of Hjalmar Schacht." [Influence of Hjalmar Schacht]. *CJC*, 26 Sept. 1952, p. 3 [u].

52.09.26C "Poems of Yehoash." [Review of *Poems of Yehoash* selected and translated by Isidore Goldstick]. *CJC*, 26 Sept. 1952, p. 4 [s].

52.10.03A "The Feast of Tabernacles." [Succoth]. *CJC*, 3 Oct. 1952, p. 3 [u].

52.10.03B "Arab Freedom." [Speech of Abba Eban on Arab-Israeli relations]. *CJC*, 3 Oct. 1952, p. 3 [u].

52.10.03C "Politics." [U.S. presidential politics]. *CJC*, 3 Oct. 1952, p. 3 [u].

52.10.10A "The Jewish Community Grows." [Growing Jewish community of Montreal]. *CJC*, 10 Oct. 1952, p. 3 [u].

52.10.10B "Yeshiva — An International University." [Yeshiva University]. *CJC*, 10 Oct. 1952, p. 3 [u].

52.10.17A "Stalin's New Line." [Soviet foreign policy]. *CJC*, 17 Oct. 1952, p. 3 [u].

52.10.17B "The Jewish People's Library." [Laying the cornerstone for the new Montreal Jewish Public Library]. *CJC*, 17 Oct. 1952, p. 3 [u].

52.10.24A "The Combined Jewish Appeal." [Fundraising for Combined Jewish Appeal]. *CJC*, 24 Oct. 1952, p. 3 [u].

52.10.24B "An Experiment Worth Continuing." [Reception held at Israeli consulate]. *CJC*, 24 Oct. 1952, p. 3 [u].

52.10.31A "The Mufti Speaks." [Interview with the Mufti]. *CJC*, 31 Oct. 1952, p. 3 [u].

52.10.31B "The Old Guard." [Honouring of former Nazis]. *CJC*, 31 Oct. 1952, p. 3 [u].

52.11.07A "Mizrachi Organization of Canada." [Work of the Mizrachi Organization of Canada]. *CJC*, 7 Nov. 1952, p. 3 [u].

52.11.07B "A New Era for the U.S.A." [Dwight D. Eisenhower wins U.S. presidential election]. *CJC*, 7 Nov. 1952, p. 3 [u].

52.11.14A "Chaim Weizmann." [Death of Chaim Weizmann]. *CJC*, 14 Nov. 1952, p. 3 [u].

52.11.21A "The Case of Regina O'Hara." [Request of a woman convert to Judaism to undertake rabbinical studies]. *CJC*, 21 Nov. 1952, p. 3 [u].

52.11.21B "The New TN Weapon." [Development of the hydrogen bomb]. *CJC*, 21 Nov. 1952, p. 3 [u].

52.11.28A "The Golems of Prague." [Prague purge trials]. *CJC*, 28 Nov. 1952, p. 8 [u].

52.11.28B "The Yiddish Proverb." [The Yiddish proverb (1)]. *CJC*, 28 Nov. 1952, p. 4 [s].

52.12.05A "The Czech-Off System." [Soviet anti-Zionism]. *CJC*, 5 Dec. 1952, p. 3 [u].

52.12.05B "Ben Beutel." [Fiftieth birthday of Ben Beutel]. *CJC*, 5 Dec. 1952, p. 3 [u].

52.12.05C "Witness: Einstein." [Albert Einstein appears in court]. *CJC*, 5 Dec. 1952, p. 3 [u].

52.12.05D "In Memoriam: Jack Klein." [Death of Jack Klein]. *CJC*, 5 Dec. 1952, p. 3 [u].

52.12.05E "The Yiddish Proverb." [The Yiddish proverb (2)]. *CJC*, 5 Dec. 1952, p. 4 [s].

52.12.12A "The Feast of Chanukah." [The Book of the Maccabees]. *CJC*, 12 Dec. 1952, p. 3 [u].

52.12.12B "The Yiddish Proverb." [The Yiddish proverb (3)]. *CJC*, 12 Dec. 1952, p. 4 [s].

52.12.19A "The Jewish Community Council of Montreal." [Work of Vaad Ha'ir in Montreal]. *CJC*, 19 Dec. 1952, p. 3 [u].

52.12.19B " 'Grieven'." [Searching for an English equivalent for "grieven"]. *CJC*, 19 Dec. 1952, p. 3 [u].

52.12.19C "The Yiddish Proverb." [The Yiddish proverb (4)]. *CJC*, 19 Dec. 1952, p. 4 [s].

52.12.26A "Youth Aliyah." [Hadassah Youth Aliyah program]. *CJC*, 26 Dec. 1952, p. 3 [u].

52.12.26B "Nothing Personal." [Soviet anti-Semitism]. *CJC*, 26 Dec. 1952, p. 3 [u].

52.12.26C "The Yiddish Proverb." [The Yiddish proverb (5)]. *CJC*, 26 Dec. 1952, p. 4 [s].

53.01.02A "The Stalin Perennial." [Joseph Stalin offers to discuss peace with Dwight D. Eisenhower]. *CJC*, 2 Jan. 1953, p. 3 [u].

53.01.02B "The McCarran Act." [American anti-communism]. *CJC*, 2 Jan. 1953, p. 3 [u].

53.01.02C "The Yiddish Proverb." [The Yiddish proverb (6)]. *CJC*, 2 Jan. 1952, p. 4 [s].

53.01.09A "Hjalmar Schacht, Banker." [Hjalmar Schacht opens a bank]. *CJC*, 9 Jan. 1953, p. 3 [u].

53.01.09B "Kingdom for a Horse!" [Anecdotes about horses]. *CJC*, 9 Jan. 1953, p. 3 [u].

53.01.09C "In Praise of the Diaspora." [Achievements of the Diaspora (1)]. *CJC*, 9 Jan. 1953, p. 4 [u].

53.01.16A "Stalin Purges Doctors!" [Communist purge trials]. *CJC*, 16 Jan. 1953, p. 3 [u].

53.01.16B "In Praise of the Diaspora." [Achievements of the Diaspora (2)]. *CJC*, 16 Jan. 1953, p. 4 [u].

53.01.23A "The Canadian Israel Bond Drive." [The Canadian Israel Bond Drive]. *CJC*, 23 Jan. 1953, p. 3 [u].

53.01.23B "The Soviet Attack on the Joint Distribution Committee [Soviets attack work of the American Jewish Joint Distribution Committee]. *CJC*, 23 Jan. 1953, p. 3 [u].

53.01.23C "In Praise of the Diaspora." [Achievements of the Diaspora (3)]. *CJC*, 23 Jan. 1953, p. 4 [u].

53.01.30A "A Friend is Dead." [Death of Louis Athanase David]. *CJC*, 30 Jan. 1953, p. 3 [u].

53.01.30B "Mo'ess Chittim." [Mo'ess Chittim Campaign]. *CJC*, 30 Jan. 1953, p. 3 [u].

53.01.30C "Rabbi Abba Hillel Silver at Sixty." [Sixtieth birthday of Rabbi Abba Hillel Silver]. *CJC*, 30 Jan. 1953, p. 3 [u].

53.02.06A "Soviet Antisemitism: The Beginning of the End." [Rise of anti-Semitism in the Soviet bloc countries]. *CJC*, 6 Feb. 1953 [u].

53.02.06B "In Praise of the Diaspora." [Achievements of the Diaspora (4)]. *CJC*, 6 Feb. 1953, p. 4 [u].

53.02.13A "Incident in Tel Aviv." [Bombing of the Soviet legation in Tel Aviv]. *CJC*, 13 Feb. 1953, p. 3 [u].

53.02.13B "Naguib: 'A Loan? . . . A Gift? . . . Anything?' " [Naguib demands reparation for Arabs]. *CJC*, 13 Feb. 1953, p. 3 [u].

53.02.13C "In Praise of the Diaspora." [Achievements of the Diaspora (5)]. *CJC*, 13 Feb. 1953, p. 4 [u].

53.02.20A "The Israel Bond Drive." [Israel Bond Drive]. *CJC*, 20 Feb. 1953, p. 3 [u].

53.02.20B "In Praise of the Diaspora." [Achievements of the Diaspora (6)]. *CJC*, 20 Feb. 1953, p. 4 [u].

53.02.27A "The Feast of Purim." [Purim story and growing Soviet anti-Semitism]. *CJC*, 27 Feb. 1953, p. 3 [u].

53.02.27B "Welcome to Dov Joseph." [Bernard Joseph visits Canada]. *CJC*, 27 Feb. 1953, p. 3 [u].

53.02.27C "The Budget." [Reduced tariffs on imported religious objects in Canada]. *CJC*, 27 Feb. 1953, p. 3 [u].

53.02.27D "In Praise of the Diaspora." [Achievements of the Diaspora (7)]. *CJC*, 27 Feb. 1953, p. 4 [u].

53.03.06A "A Rabbi Passes." [Death of Rabbi Julius Berger]. *CJC*, 6 Mar. 1953, p. 3 [u].

53.03.06B "Bring a Neighbour." [Montreal Jews protest Soviet anti-Semitism]. *CJC*, 6 Mar. 1953, p. 3 [u].

53.03.06C "Hebrew Writers' Week." [Hebrew Writers' Week in Canada]. *CJC*, 6 Mar. 1953, p. 3 [u].

53.03.06D "The Bible's Archetypical Poet." [Joseph as an allegory of the poet (1)]. *CJC*, 6 Mar. 1953, p. 7 [s]. See also MS 5062–66 [notes].

53.03.13A "Joseph Stalin: An Appraisal." [Leon Trotsky's appraisal of Joseph Stalin]. *CJC*, 13 Mar. 1953, p. 3 [u].

53.03.13B "The Bible's Archetypical Poet." [Joseph as an allegory of the poet (2)]. *CJC*, 13 Mar. 1953, p. 4 [s].

53.03.20A "The Bible's Archetypical Poet." [Joseph as an allegory of the poet (3)]. *CJC*, 20 Mar. 1953, p. 4 [s].

53.03.27A "The Feast of Passover." [Passover story and continued oppression of Jews behind the Iron Curtain]. *CJC*, 27 Mar. 1953, p. 3 [u].

53.04.03A "Queen Mary." [Death of Queen Mary]. *CJC*, 3 Apr. 1953, p. 3 [u].

53.04.03B "Poor Pablo Picasso." [Pablo Picasso's portrait of Joseph Stalin]. *CJC*, 3 Apr. 1953, p. 3 [u].

53.04.10A "Reversal in the Kremlin." [Apparent reversal of Soviet policy]. *CJC*, 10 Apr. 1953, p. 3 [u].

53.04.17A "The Jewish National Fund." [Jewish National Fund National Conference]. *CJC*, 17 Apr. 1953, p. 3 [u].

53.04.17B "Against Discrimination." [Anti-discrimination legislation passed in Canada]. *CJC*, 17 Apr. 1953, p. 3 [u].

53.04.24A "Israel's Fifth Anniversary." [Fifth anniversary of Israeli independence]. *CJC*, 24 Apr. 1953, p. 3 [u].

53.05.01A "The Case of Jascha Heifetz." [Heifetz performs Richard Strauss in Israel]. *CJC*, 1 May 1953, p. 3 [u].

53.05.01B "U.S. Jewry Honours Samuel Bronfman." [U.S. Jewry honours Samuel Bronfman]. *CJC*, 1 May 1953, p. 3 [u].

53.05.08A "Einstein and Non-Conformism." [Lord and Taylor Awards for non-conformity]. *CJC*, 8 May 1953, p. 3 [u].

53.05.08B "To Sam Schwisberg — A Well-Deserved Tribute." [Dinner honouring Sam Schwisberg]. *CJC*, 8 May 1953, p. 3 [u].

53.05.08C "Of Hebrew Calligraphy." [Review of *The Israel Art Haggadah* by Jacob Zim]. *CJC*, 8 May 1953, p. 4 [s].

53.05.15A "The Feast of the Giving of the Law." [Shavuoth]. *CJC*, 15 May 1953, p. 3 [u].

53.05.15B "The Spanish and Portuguese Synagogue." [One hundred and eighty-fifth anniversary of the Spanish and Portuguese Synagogue]. *CJC*, 15 May 1953, p. 3 [u].

53.05.15C "The Decline and Fall of the Gibbons." [Apartheid]. *CJC*, 15 May 1953, p. 4 [s].

53.05.22A "Dulles Learns About Khayyam." [U.S. involvement in Middle-East peace negotiations]. *CJC*, 22 May 1953, p. 3 [u].

53.05.22B "The Yizkor Bond Appeal." [Israel Bond drive]. *CJC*, 22 May 1953, p. 3 [u].

53.05.29A "Her Majesty Queen Elizabeth, Long May She Reign." [Coronation of Elizabeth II]. *CJC*, 29 May 1953, p. 3 [u].

53.06.05A "The Scaling of Mount Everest." [First ascent of Mount Everest]. *CJC*, 5 June 1953, p. 3 [u].

53.06.12A "The Coronation Album." [Photograph of Commonwealth leaders]. *CJC*, 12 June 1953, p. 3 [u].

53.06.12B "The BIG Show for Israel Bonds." [Fund raising show for Israel]. *CJC*, 12 June 1953, p. 3 [u].

53.06.12C "In Memoriam: Michael Hirsch." [Death of Michael Hirsch]. *CJC*, 12 June 1953, p. 3 [u].

53.06.19A "The Budget of Humanitarianism." [Work of the Joint Distribution Committee]. *CJC*, 19 June 1953, p. 3 [u].

53.06.19B "Malan and Ben-Gurion." [Daniel Malan meets with David Ben Gurion]. *CJC*, 19 June 1953, p. 3 [u].

53.06.19C "Champagne, Vodka, Whiskey." [Anecdotes about prominent figures and alcohol]. *CJC*, 19 June 1953, p. 3 [u].

53.06.26A "The Riddle of the Sphinx." [Egypt is declared a republic]. *CJC*, 26 June 1953, p. 3 [u].

53.06.26B "The Eskimo Vote." [Canadian Inuit are granted the vote]. *CJC*, 26 June 1953, p. 3 [u].

53.07.03A "The Jewish Community Grows." [Growth of the Montreal Jewish community]. *CJC*, 3 July 1953, p. 3 [u].

53.07.03B "Jewish Camping." [Jewish summer camps]. *CJC*, 3 July 1953, p. 3 [u].

53.07.03C "Israel's Redemption Month." [Fundraising for Israel]. *CJC*, 3 July 1953, p. 3 [u].

53.07.10A "Herzl and Bialik." [Theodor Herzl and Chaim Nachman Bialik]. *CJC*, 10 July 1953, p. 3 [u].

53.07.10B "The Wonders That Do Not Cease." [Egyptian military tribunal institutes proceedings against King Farouk]. *CJC*, 10 July 1953, p. 3 [u].

53.07.10C "Israel Bond Drive Branches Out." [Israel Bond Drive]. *CJC*, 10 July 1953, p. 3 [u].

53.07.17A "A Policeman's Lot is Not a Happy One." [Head of Soviet secret police falls into disfavour]. *CJC*, 17 July 1953, p. 3 [u].

53.07.17B "The Reservoir of Jewish Leadership More Productive Than Ever." [New graduates from Yeshiva University]. *CJC*, 17 July 1953, p. 3 [u].

53.07.24A "In Front of the Iron Curtain." [Soviet foreign policy]. *CJC*, 24 July 1953, p. 3 [u].

53.07.24B "Israel and Uganda." [Uganda as a Jewish homeland]. *CJC*, 24 July 1953, p. 3 [u].

53.07.31A "Lessons of Korea." [Truce signed in Korean War]. *CJC*, 31 July 1953, p. 3 [u].

53.07.31B "The Federal Elections." [Canadian federal election]. *CJC*, 31 July 1953, p. 3 [u].

53.07.31C "Prohibited Food." [Food shortage in East Germany]. *CJC*, 31 July 1953, p. 3 [u].

53.08.07A "Statistics for Heaven." [Religious poll taken in U.S.]. *CJC*, 7 Aug. 1953, p. 3 [u].

53.08.07B "The Federal Elections." [*See* 53.07.31B]. *CJC*, 7 Aug. 1953, p. 3 [u].

53.08.14A "The Federal Elections." [Results of Canadian federal election]. *CJC*, 14 Aug. 1953, p. 3 [u].

53.08.14B "Malenkov's Speech." [Speech of Georgi Malenkov]. *CJC*, 14 Aug. 1953, p. 3 [u].

53.08.21A "Holy Land, U.S.A." [Suggestion to build a replica of Jerusalem in U.S.]. *CJC*, 21 Aug. 1953, p. 3 [u].

53.08.21B "Say A-H! . . . says the doctor." [Soviets announce they have the H-bomb]. *CJC*, 21 Aug. 1953, p. 3 [u].

53.10.09A "The Threatening Horizons." [Worsening Arab-Israeli relations]. *CJC*, 9 Oct. 1953, p. 3 [u].

53.10.09B "The Isaac Elchanan Yeshivah." [Yeshiva University]. *CJC*, 9 Oct. 1953, p. 3 [u].

53.10.16A "Sir Wilfrid Laurier." [Unveiling of statue of Sir Wilfrid Laurier]. *CJC*, 16 Oct. 1953, p. 3 [u].

53.10.23A "The Jordan flows into the Nile." [Jordan accuses Israel of attacking a village]. *CJC*, 23 Oct. 1953, p. 3 [u].

53.10.30A "The Combined Jewish Appeal." [Fund raising for Combined Jewish Appeal]. *CJC*, 30 Oct. 1953, p. 3 [u].

53.10.30B "The Hadassah Convention." [Hadassah Convention, Montreal]. *CJC*, 30 Oct. 1953, p. 3 [u].

53.10.30C "Winston Churchill and the Nobel Prize." [Nobel Prize for literature awarded to Winston Churchill]. *CJC*, 30 Oct. 1953, p. 3 [u].

53.11.06A "A Jordan Valley Authority?" [Proposed joint Arab-Israeli development of the Jordan Valley]. *CJC*, 6 Nov. 1953, p. 3 [u].

53.11.13A "The Changing Middle East." [Western romanticization of Arabs]. *CJC*, 13 Nov. 1953, p. 3 [u].

53.11.20A "Where the Cap Fits." [Canadian politics]. *CJC*, 20 Nov. 1953, p. 3 [u].

53.11.20B "Munchausen of the North." [Canadian deceives journalist with phony espionage story]. *CJC*, 20 Nov. 1953, p. 3 [u].

53.11.27A "The Undefended Frontier." [McCarthy Committee demands that Canada extradite Igor Gouzenko]. *CJC*, 27 Nov. 1953, p. 3 [u].

53.12.04A "The Festival of Lights." [Chanukah and Middle East situation]. *CJC*, 4 Dec. 1953, p. 3 [u].

53.12.04B "The Resolution of Censure." [U.N. holds Israel responsible for incident at Kibya]. *CJC*, 4 Dec. 1953, p. 3 [u].

53.12.11A "The Choice." [Atomic technology]. *CJC*, 11 Dec. 1953, p. 3 [u].

53.12.18A "The Missing Link." [Threat of the atomic bomb]. *CJC*, 18 Dec. 1953, p. 3 [u].

53.12.18B "David ben Gurion." [Retirement of David Ben Gurion]. *CJC*, 18 Dec. 1953, p. 3 [u].

54.01.15A "Unholy War Against Israel." [U.S. plans to supply arms to Arab nations]. *CJC*, 15 Jan. 1954, p. 3 [u].

54.01.15B "The United Talmud Torahs." [Fundraising for United Talmud Torahs]. *CJC*, 15 Jan. 1954, p. 3 [u].

54.01.22A "Freedom of Worship." [Freedom of worship legislation in Quebec]. *CJC*, 22 Jan. 1954, p. 3 [u].

54.01.29A "The Zionist Convention." [Thirty-second National Convention of the Zionist Organization of Canada]. *CJC*, 29 Jan. 1954, p. 3 [u].

54.02.05A "Gibraltar and Suez." [Francisco Franco's attempts to end British control of Gibraltar and the Suez Canal]. *CJC*, 5 Feb. 1954, p. 3 [u].

54.02.12A "The Myth of Arab Unity." [Lack of Arab unity]. *CJC*, 12 Feb. 1954, p. 3 [u].

54.02.12B "Racial Harmony a la carte." [Suggestion to cure anti-Semitism with Jewish food]. *CJC*, 12 Feb. 1954, p. 3 [u].

54.02.19A "The Egyptian Blockade Against Israel." [Egyptian blockade of the Suez Canal]. *CJC*, 19 Feb. 1954, p. 3 [u].

54.02.26A "Israel Abolishes Capital Punishment." [Debate on the abolition of capital punishment in Israel]. *CJC*, 26 Feb. 1954, p. 3 [u].

54.03.12A "In Memoriam: J.I. Segal." [Death of J. I. Segal]. *CJC*, 12 Mar. 1954, pp. 3, 6 [i].

54.03.19A "The Book of Esther." [The Book of Esther]. *CJC*, 19 Mar. 1954, p. 3 [u].

54.03.19B "Has Anybody Here Seen Kelly?" [Similarities between the Irish and the Jews]. *CJC*, 19 Mar. 1954, p. 3 [u].

54.03.26A "Outrage in the Negev." [Arabs attack a busload of Israelis]. *CJC*, 26 Mar. 1954, p. 3 [u].

54.05.07A "American Judaism, Inc." [American Jewish anti-Zionism]. *CJC*, 7 May 1954, p. 3 [u].

54.06.04A "Hollywood and Holy Writ." [Film adaptations of the Bible]. *CJC*, 4 June 1954, p. 3 [u].

54.06.18A "The Bronfman Collection of Jewish Canadiana." [Dedication of Bronfman Collection of Jewish Canadiana at the Montreal Jewish Public Library]. *CJC*, 18 June 1954, p. 3 [u].

54.10.15A "Espionage in Egypt?" [Egypt claims it is infiltrated by spies]. *CJC*, 15 Oct. 1954, p. 3 [u].

54.10.22A "Peace in the Middle East." [Arab-Israeli relations]. *CJC*, 22 Oct. 1954, p. 3 [u].

54.10.22B "The New Canadian Currency." [Objections to design of Canadian currency]. *CJC*, 22 Oct. 1954, p. 3 [u].

54.10.29A "Herzl Year." [Celebration of Herzl Year]. *CJC*, 29 Oct. 1954, p. 3 [u].

54.10.29B "The Burlap Curtain." [Israelis erect a burlap curtain along the Jordanian border]. *CJC*, 29 Oct. 1954, p. 3 [u].

54.11.12A "The American Jewish Tercentenary." [Jews in U.S.]. *CJC*, 12 Nov. 1954, p. 3 [u].

54.11.19A "Einstein: His Eternal Verities and His Relative Conveniences." [Albert Einstein complains of the ethical dilemmas of science]. *CJC*, 19 Nov. 1951, p. 3 [u].

55.03.11A "Gaza and Good Neighborhood." [Western opinion on Israeli military action in Gaza]. *CJC*, 11 Mar. 1955, p. 3 [u].

55.03.18A "Jingoism and Jive." [Arab-Israeli tensions]. *CJC*, 18 Mar. 1955, p. 3 [u].

55.03.18B "Rabbinical College of Canada [[Rabbinical College of Canada]. *CJC*, 18 Mar. 1955, p. 3 [u].

55.03.25A "A Wizard out of Egypt." [Egypt proposes that Israel hand over the Gaza Strip and the Negev]. *CJC*, 25 Mar. 1955, p. 3 [u].

55.04.01A "The Uninvited Guests." [Egyptians attack Israeli settlement in the Negev]. *CJC*, 1 Apr. 1955, p. 3 [u].

55.04.06A "The Feast of Freedom." [Passover story and the continuing struggle of Jews for freedom in Israel]. *CJC*, 6 Apr. 1955, p. 3 [u].

55.04.15A "Sir Winston Churchill." [Winston Churchill]. *CJC*, 15 Apr. 1955, p. 3 [u].

55.04.22A "Albert Einstein." [Albert Einstein]. *CJC*, 22 Apr. 1955, p. 3 [u].

55.04.29A "Seven Years of Statehood." [Founding and first seven years of the State of Israel]. *CJC*, 29 Apr. 1955, pp. 3, 7 [u].

55.05.06A "The Power of the Slogan." [Cold War]. *CJC*, 6 May 1955, p. 3 [u].

55.05.13A "Canada Hall." [Hadassah sponsors the construction of an auditorium at the Hebrew University]. *CJC*, 13 May 1955, p. 3 [u].

55.05.20A "Neutralism." [Neutrality and the Cold War]. *CJC*, 20 May 1955, p. 3 [u].

55.06.03A "Tito and the Kremlin." [Moscow attempts a reconciliation with Yugoslavia]. *CJC*, 3 June 1955, p. 3 [u].

55.06.10A "From a Position of Strength." [Moral superiority of the West]. *CJC*, 10 June 1955, p. 3 [u].

2

Works on A.M. Klein

C Books and Special Issues of Periodicals, Articles and Sections of Books, Theses and Dissertations, Interview, Audio-Visual Material, and Awards and Honours

Books and Special Issues of Periodicals

C1 Marshall, T.A., ed. and introd. *A.M. Klein*. Critical Views on Canadian Writers, No. 4. Toronto: Ryerson, 1970. vi–xxv, 165 pp.

Since this is a collection of previously published articles and reviews, each entry is listed in the appropriate section under its original publication date.

C2 Waddington, Miriam. *A.M. Klein*. Studies in Canadian Literature. Toronto: Copp Clark, 1970. 147 pp.

Waddington has "put Klein's language and diction at the critical centre" of her study. Klein is a humanist owing more to the secular tradition of Yiddish culture than to religious orthodoxy. *Hath Not a Jew . . .* contains few, if any, religious poems. It "mythologizes the traditional customs of eastern European Chassidic life." Its language is inventive, combining elements from Hebrew, Yiddish, English, and French. *Poems* is a spiritually bankrupt attempt to retreat from the modern world, reflected stylistically by Klein's use of archaism. *The Hitleriad* is, in contrast, an affirmative "act of hope" and is more vigorous in language than *Poems*. Klein's last and best works, *The Second Scroll* and *The Rocking Chair*, elaborate the humanist concerns of his earlier work. In *The Rocking Chair* religious content is finally discarded in favour of a real sense of here and now. Klein's deepest commitment is to the power of language to discover and possess the world. *The Rocking Chair* shares the themes of Klein's earlier works, but stylistically it is marked by an abandonment of archaism, which is directed toward the past, for metaphor, which is a form of discovery directed toward the future. Klein's attitude to language as a means "whereby new forces are liberated must always be dangerous for the writer" and may have contributed to his final breakdown. See "Signs on a White Field: Klein's *The Second Scroll*" (C56) and "The Cloudless Day: The Radical Poems of A.M. Klein" (C62) for annotations on these two chapters.

C3 *Jewish Di'al-og*, [A.M. Klein – A Tribute]. Ed. Joseph Rosenblatt. Passover 1973. 64 pp.

A special issue on A.M. Klein. Each item has been listed separately in Section C of this bibliography. See C87–C95.

C4 Fischer, G.K. *In Search of Jerusalem: Religion and Ethics in the Writings of A.M. Klein*. Introd. G.K. Fischer. Montreal: McGill-Queen's Univ. Press, 1975. 1–7, 256 pp.

Klein is essentially religious in his outlook and has an "ardent concern with religious systems that conceive of divinity in the natural universe." He was interested "in a wide spectrum of creeds," all of which had in common a view of God as immanent in the universe rather than transcending it. The most important event in Klein's religious development, after his abandonment of traditional orthodoxy, was his discovery of Spinoza, who equated God and nature. When Spinoza's austere disregard of the individual began to trouble Klein, he turned to the joyfulness of Chassidism and the poetic mythologizing of the Kabbalah, without, however, completely abandoning Spinoza. Fischer discusses Klein's works with special emphasis on *The Second Scroll* and argues that, despite appearances, from the time of Klein's discovery of Spinoza he always continued to believe in God and that his frequent bouts of despair arose, not from any loss of faith in God's existence, but from doubts about His concern with the fate of humanity. Even these doubts were laid to rest by the founding of the State of Israel which reassured Klein that the creation is good. This book is based on Fischer's dissertation (C243).

C5 Mayne, Seymour, ed. and introd. *The A.M. Klein Symposium*. Reappraisals: Canadian Writers, No. 2. Ottawa: Univ. of Ottawa Press, 1975. ix–xi, 123 pp.

This is a record of the A.M. Klein Symposium held at the University of Ottawa in 1974, with an introduction by the editor and a bibliography and index to manuscripts by Usher Caplan. Letters from Klein to A.J.M. Smith, 1941–51 are included. A letter from Colman Klein to Seymour Mayne is also included. Individual items are listed under the names of their authors. See C101–C108.

C6 *Viewpoints*, [A Tribute to A.M. Klein]. Ed. William Abrams *et al.* 11, No. 4 (Spring 1981). 56 pp.

A special issue on A.M. Klein. Each item has been listed separately in Section C of this bibliography. See C153–C157.

C7 Caplan, Usher. *Like One That Dreamed: A Portrait of A.M. Klein.* Foreword Leon Edel. Pref. Usher Caplan. Toronto: McGraw-Hill Ryerson, 1982. 13–15, 224 pp.

Caplan provides an introduction to Klein's life, milieu, and development as a writer. He makes extensive use of unpublished material from the Klein papers in the National Archives, and draws on interviews with many who knew Klein. The book is aimed at a general rather than a strictly scholarly audience and lacks the documentation of the dissertation upon which it is based (C247). The text is supplemented by photographs and by excerpts from Klein's works, many previously unpublished. Caplan cites the political, social, and cultural forces that went into Klein's formation as a man and artist, with special emphasis on the Montreal he knew as a child and young man. The final phase of Klein's literary career, when he produced a considerable body of works which have not yet been published, is discussed along with the years of silence which followed his breakdown.

C8 Spiro, Solomon J. *Tapestry for Designs: Judaic Allusions in* The Second Scroll *and the* Collected Poems of A.M. Klein. Pref. and Introd. Solomon J. Spiro. Vancouver: Univ. of British Columbia Press, 1984. vii–ix, 1–11, 236 pp.

Spiro places Klein in the Jewish tradition of *Haskalah*, or Enlightenment, whose aim was to create a modern Jewish culture, rich in Jewish allusions, but modelled on European forms. The bulk of the book consists of annotations to *The Second Scroll* and the poems collected in Miriam Waddington's edition (A12). There are also several Appendices concerning various aspects of *The Second Scroll.* The book is based on the author's dissertation (C251).

C9 *Journal of Canadian Studies/Revue d'études canadiennes*, [A.M. Klein's Montreal/A.M. Klein à Montréal]. Ed. Zailig Pollock. 19 (Summer 1984). 172 pp.

A special issue on A.M. Klein. Each item has been entered separately in Sections C and D of this bibliography. See C178–C187, C268, D91, D100.

C10 Brenner, Rachel Feldhay. *A.M. Klein, the Father of Canadian Jewish Literature: Essays in the Poetics of Humanistic Passion.* Lewiston, N.Y.: Edwin Mellen Press, 1990. i-ix, 144 pp.

Brenner focuses on the connection between Klein's rootedness in Jewish tradition and his commitment to broader humanistic values: Klein's Jewishness is "the window to the world of art in service of humanism rather than a locked room of ethnic idiosyncrasies." The two opening chapters of the book explore the psychological and historical context of Klein's career and of the breakdown and silence which brought it to an end. In the following four chapters, Brenner "explores the refractions of Klein's humanistic passion," arguing that "it seems possible to understand Klein's silence as the yet 'unvoiced' anticipation of moral revival.

C11 Golfman, Noreen. *A.M. Klein and His Works.* Toronto: ECW PRESS, [1991]. 47 pp.

Golfman surveys Klein's life, times, and works, arguing that "the more closely and the more often his work continues to be read, the more it will reveal the modernist's struggle to locate order in a rapidly changing world." This struggle is reflected in Klein's attempt, throughout his career, and especially in its later stages, "to accommodate a committed dependence on traditional forms to a world undergoing radical upheaval." Golfman illustrates her argument with a number of close readings of Klein's poetry.

Articles and Sections of Books

C12 Edel, Leon. "Abraham M. Klein." *The Canadian Forum*, May 1932, pp. 300–02.

Klein's voice is "of an uncompromising youth." His Jewish poems are rich, exotic, and varied in tone and technique. His lyric gift is particularly important. Edel approves of Klein's developing interest in political poetry, as evidenced in "Soirée of Velvel Kleinburger" and "Diary of Abraham Segal, Poet." Klein is the most original poet writing in Canada, and he is just beginning to find himself.

C13 Brown, E.K. "The Immediate Present in Canadian Literature." *Sewanee Review* [Univ. of the South, Sewanee, Tenn.], 41 (Jan.–March 1933), 436–39.

Brown refers to Klein as a "significant" poet on the contemporary scene. "His culture seems broader and more intense than that of any other Canadian poet." The two most important elements in his vision are his Jewishness and his experience of the city, the former finding its best expression in "Out of the Pulver and the Polished Lens," the latter in "Diary of Abraham Segal, Poet" and "Soirée of Velvel Kleinburger." Klein "is in full revolt from Canadian life."

C14 Kennedy, Leo. "Orpheus in a Caftan." *Jewish Standard*, 14 April 1933, pp. 170, 207–08.

A sketch of the young A.M. Klein and his poetry. Kennedy emphasizes Klein's energy and versatility and refers to some works planned or in progress which were either never completed or have not survived. Klein is not orthodox, but has a deep knowledge of Judaism and is romantically attracted to the culture and tradition of Old Jewry. His poetry "curiously combines keen intellectual and deep emotional qualities." Klein has a "sturdy temperament" and wants to create genuine Jewish poetry which will not be "soaked with maudlin Jewish tears."

C15 Caiserman-Vital, H.M. "A.M. Klein." In *Yiddishe Dichter in Kanada* [*Jewish Poets in Canada*]. Montreal: Eagle Publishing, 1934, pp. 167–74.

This article is written in Yiddish. Caiserman-Vital reprints a number of Klein's poems on Jewish themes with free Yiddish translations and commentary. Klein is the most important young Jewish-English poet in Canada. Caiserman-Vital praises Klein's knowledge of Jewish life, the high level of his culture, and his passion and humour. However, Klein has a tendency to over-intellectualize and to slip into didacticism. Klein has accomplished much for a man of his years, and he gives promise of greater achievements in the future.

C16 Collin, W.E. "The Spirit's Palestine." In his *The White Savannahs*. Toronto: Macmillan, 1936, pp. 207–31. Rpt. (abridged) in *A.M. Klein*. Ed. T.A. Marshall. Critical Views on Canadian Writers, No. 4. Toronto: Ryerson, 1970, pp. 1–11. Rpt. in *The White Savannahs*. By W.E. Collin. Literature of Canada: Poetry and Prose in Reprint, No. 15. Toronto: Univ. of Toronto Press, 1975, pp. 207–31.

Klein's poetry is an expression of the spiritual rebirth of the Jewish people, but also draws on European roots. The sonnets are the best statement of Klein's vision and will outlast the prophetic and satiric works. There is a poignancy in Klein's poetry arising from the conflict between Zionist aspirations and the lure of Western culture.

C17 Callaghan, Morley. "A Criticism." *New Frontier*, 1, No. 1 (April 1936), 24.

An evaluation of three short stories appearing in the first issue of *New Frontier* including Klein's "Friends, Romans, Hungrymen." "A.M. Klein knows how to use words sharply, and in this piece he often gets a sharp and vigorous feeling." Its effectiveness is limited by Klein's "very great determination to pull off striking effects." Callaghan laments the lack of passion in all three stories.

C18 Abramson, Samuel H. "Abe Klein – in Person." *Jewish Standard*, Sept. 1936, p. 23.

Abramson provides a biographical sketch based on conversations with Klein. It contains some information not available elsewhere about his early years and his literary interests.

C19 Lewisohn, Ludwig. "Concerning a Jewish Poet." *Jewish Standard*, Sept. 1936, pp. 8, 39. Rpt. (Foreword) in *Hath Not a Jew . . .* Rpt. (Appendix) in *Collected Works*. pp. 350–52. Rpt. ("Foreword to *Hath Not a Jew . . .*") in *A.M. Klein*. Ed. T.A. Marshall. Critical Views on Canadian Writers, No. 4. Toronto: Ryerson, 1970, pp. 12–14.

Klein is "the first Jew to contribute authentic poetry to the literatures of English speech." Other Jewish poets have abandoned their Jewishness and slavishly imitated non-Jewish models. Klein, however, by drawing on Jewish traditions, has created poetry which is both original and universal in its appeal.

C20   Brown, E.K. *On Canadian Poetry.* Toronto: Ryerson, 1943, pp. 70, 73–74.

Klein "always writes as a Jew." The influence of T.S. Eliot on "Soirée of Velvel Kleinburger" is obvious, but it is transformed into something "richly and vigorously Jewish." In *Hath Not a Jew* . . . Klein turns from the cosmopolitan world around him to the world of his own people. He is able to universalize Jewish themes, but most of the volume falls short of "Out of the Pulver and the Polished Lens," which contains "some of the best passages in our poetry between the wars." Klein appears to be moving beyond *Hath Not a Jew* . . . , and it is reasonable to hope that in later works the promise of his beginnings will be realized. That promise is "as high as any Canadian poet has ever given."

C21   Robertson, Duncan. "A.M. Klein and the National Element in Canadian Poetry." *The Undergrad* [Univ. of Toronto], 1946, pp. 29–31.

"Klein is one of the most vigorous poets that Canada has produced." His poetry reflects little of the Canadian environment and has its deepest roots in Jewish and European culture. This lack of interest in Canadian nationalism is justifiable since Canada lacks "a richness of tradition."

C22   Smith, A.J.M. "Abraham Moses Klein." Trans. Guy Sylvestre. *Gants du ciel,* 11 (printemps 1946), 67–81. Rpt. in *A.M. Klein.* Ed. T.A. Marshall. Critical Views on Canadian Writers, No. 4. Toronto: Ryerson, 1970, pp. 26–40.

Klein is the most important Canadian poet of his generation. His poetry, though modern, grows out of tradition, rather than rejecting it, and is the expression of an intellectual humanism with deep emotional roots. The most intense emotions expressed in Klein's poetry are love and anger. His best works lyrically affirm the divine dignity of mankind, while fiercely attacking those who deny it. Klein's later poetry is innovative, not only in technique but in subject matter as well; it moves beyond Klein's Jewish milieu to celebrate the people of Quebec who are seen as sharing the same basic aspirations as the Jews. Throughout his poetry, Klein's values remain unchanged, "traditionnels, essentiellement conservateurs et fondamentallement classiques."

C23   Sutherland, John. "The Poetry of A.M. Klein." *Index,* 1 (Aug. 1946), 8–12, 20–21. Rpt. in *A.M. Klein.* Ed. T.A. Marshall. Critical Views on Canadian Writers, No. 4. Toronto: Ryerson, 1970, pp. 41–54. Rpt. in *Essays, Controversies and Poems.* By John Sutherland. Ed. and introd. Miriam Waddington. New Canadian Library, No. 81. Toronto: McClelland and Stewart, 1972, pp. 128–38.

"Klein is not the poet to express a serious idea or even a serious emotion."

Hath Not a Jew . . . is an escape into a world of romance. Its sentimental ideal of tolerance is unconvincing, and the solemn poems expressing this ideal are inferior to the poems for children and fanciful caricatures. Klein's later poetry is an unsuccessful attempt to adopt a more serious stance. His role of prophet, adopted in *Poems* and *The Hitleriad,* is compromised by a simplistic view of good and evil. The greater technical complexity and intellectuality of this poetry fail to disguise the fact that Klein has "very little or nothing to say." Despite appearances, Klein's later poetry is not really modern but is weakly imitative of eighteenth-century models. His most important work remains the caricatures in *Hath Not a Jew . . .*

C24 Smith, A.J.M. Introduction. In *The Book of Canadian Poetry: A Critical and Historical Anthology.* Ed. A.J.M. Smith. 2nd ed. Toronto: Gage, 1948, pp. 30–31. Rev. ed., 1957, pp. 28–29.

". . . Klein's poetry has a richness and power, a surging emotional drive, and a dry scholastic (we should say talmudic) wit." His Jewish background has given him insight into French Canada and his French-Canadian poems make "the attempts of any other writer in English look pale and thin."

C25 Wells, Henry W. *Where Poetry Stands Now.* Toronto: Ryerson, 1948, pp. 54–55.

Klein's poetry attempts and, to a certain degree, achieves a synthesis of the one and the many, self and society. He is a "modernistic traditionalist" who "writes specifically as a Jew" and shows the "advantage of an inherited viewpoint." His finest work to date consists of the psalms in *Poems* in which "Israelite and Israel are one." "Klein is in a measure defeated by his own romantic enthusiasm," which is not under complete control. "He is not as yet a great poet, but . . . a highly significant one."

C26 Warhaft, Sid. "Universality in the Poetry of Klein." *Creative Campus* [Univ. of Manitoba], Spring 1950, pp. 37–43.

Klein, unlike most modern poets, is heir to a rich tradition with which he feels at home. He is not, therefore, forced by "an aridity of culture . . . to turn inward or to please himself by the use of esoteric reference, form and language." In expressing traditional Jewish values, Klein inevitably expresses universal human values as well. "His vision of emancipation, his portrayal of the wanderer in search of a homeland, his humane and metaphysical view of mankind, his fine humour and understanding pity, above all, his hatred of oppression – all these are universal."

C27 Dudek, Louis. "A.M. Klein." *The Canadian Forum,* April 1950, pp. 10–12. Rpt. (revised) in *A.M. Klein.* Ed. T.A. Marshall. Critical Views on Canadian Writers, No. 4. Toronto: Ryerson, 1970, pp. 66–74. Rpt. in *Selected Essays and*

Criticism. By Louis Dudek. Ottawa: Tecumseh, 1978, pp. 4–10.

Dudek traces Klein's development through three stages. The poetry of the first stage is religious, idealistic, and romantic in attitude and archaic in diction. In his second stage, Klein responds to the Depression and the rise of Hitler with Marxist satires, which unsuccessfully ape T.S. Eliot, and with *The Hitleriad*, which is technically crude and lacking in density or weight of thought. The poetry of the third stage, represented by *The Rocking Chair*, shows greater technical skill and sophistication of attitude. The poems are vital and stimulating, but not completely satisfying. Klein suffers from working in a provincial milieu which is incapable of offering him sound criticism. His development has consequently been slow and uneven, but his recent work gives hope of greater things to come.

C28 Phelps, Arthur L. "Two Poets: Klein and Birney." In his *Canadian Writers*. Toronto: McClelland and Stewart, 1951, pp. 111, 116–19.

Klein's poetry shows "the comprehensive catholicity of human understanding which gives its authority to noble verse. This does not mean softness and easy tolerance. Klein's wit can be a rapier-thrust against pretensions and cruelty and the intricate evil in man."

C29 Pacey, Desmond. *Creative Writing in Canada: A Short History of English-Canadian Literature*. Toronto: Ryerson, 1952, pp. 131–33. Rev. ed., 1961, pp. 142–44.

Klein's poetry exhibits "audacity, energy, and richness." He is a master of "brilliant technical effects" and expresses praise or blame in "strong and vigorous" words. His frankness is a great strength in his poetry, but he sometimes falls into sentimentality or invective.

C30 Dehler, Charles Ronald. "Canada's English Poetry since Thirty-nine." *Culture*, 14 (1953), 247–55.

Klein is the best poet of the Montreal Group. His work is "consistently good, marked with high intelligence, superb technique, and a wisdom all his own." Klein's deep roots in Jewish tradition have made it possible for him to become "the surest recorder of French-Canadian spirit today."

C31 "The Elegy Concerning Our Holocaust." *Izkor-Buj. Ratne. Libra en Homenajes a Nuestros Hermanos Masacrados por la Barbarie Nazi en Nuestro Pueblo Natal*. Buenos Aires: Sociedad Residentes de Ratne y Aldredores en la Argentina, 1954, pp. 713–14.

In this Yiddish introduction to Klein's "Elegy," included in a volume in memory of the Jews of Ratno who died in the Holocaust, the writer says that the poem is "the most powerful lament for the Holocaust not written in Yiddish." The power comes from the way in which the speaker begins with the tragedy of his own family and moves from the particular to a "general lament" (Pollock's translation).

C32 "A Something Possible." *The Times Literary Supplement* [London], 5 Nov. 1954, p. 704.

Klein's poetry "is among the most impressive of recent years." *The Rocking Chair* is his best work, and his "highly intelligent and vigorous verse is of the greatest importance: a portent of what may yet be achieved, and an example of how the theme of the people can be treated."

C33 Frye, Northrop. "English Canadian Literature, 1929–1954." *Books Abroad* [Univ. of Oklahoma, Norman], 29 (1955), 271–72.

Hath Not a Jew . . . and *The Hitleriad* "are full of the Rabbinical spirit of erudition, humor, kindliness, and charity under pathological and meaningless hatred." *The Rocking Chair* "is full of brilliant and sympathetic studies of French Canada, some of them written in a curious bilingual vocabulary which is one of the liveliest poetic experiments yet made in this country." *The Second Scroll* is "a strange symbolic novel."

C34 "Canadian Writers Come into Their Own." *The Times Literary Supplement* [London], 5 Aug. 1955, p. iii.

"Mr. A.M. Klein's *The Rocking Chair* still remains the best interpretation of French Canada by an English poet. His awkward use of language well fits his subject matter."

C35 Whalley, George, ed. *Writing in Canada: Proceedings of the Canadian Writer's Conference, Queen's University, 28–31 July, 1955.* Introd. F.R. Scott. Toronto: Macmillan, 1956, pp. 13–15.

A.J.M. Smith discusses the reception of poetry in society and Klein's treatment of this subject in "Portrait of the Poet as Landscape."

C36 Daniells, Roy. "Literature: Poetry and the Novel." In *The Culture of Contemporary Canada.* Ed. Julian Park. Ithaca, N.Y.: Cornell Univ. Press, 1957, pp. 59, 72–73.

Klein's poetry is wide-ranging in mood and theme, "but the centre from which all radiates is the love of one tradition." *The Second Scroll* demonstrates "an incandescent honesty of purpose" and "an accomplished and highly individual style." Klein examines "religious issues in an almost patriarchal fashion of knowledge and authority."

C37 Steinberg, M.W. "The Stature of A.M. Klein." *Reconstructionist* [New York], 29 Nov. 1957, pp. 13–18. Rpt. ("Poet of a Living Past") *Canadian Literature*, No. 25 (Summer 1965), pp. 5–20. Rpt. in *A Choice of Critics: Selections from Canadian Literature.* Ed. George Woodcock. Toronto: Oxford Univ. Press, 1966, pp. 203–20. Rpt. in *A.M. Klein*. Ed. T.A. Marshall. Critical Views on Canadian Writers, No. 4. Toronto: Ryerson, 1970, pp. 99–118.

"Probably no other major Canadian writer so deliberately and consistently wrote within a tradition." At the heart of Klein's work is a religious commitment which persists through his career despite moments of doubt. Even his radical poems are rooted in the religious tradition of the Hebrew prophets, rather than in Marxism. Klein's early poetry, from *Hath Not a Jew . . .* to *The Hitleriad*, is concerned with celebrating the Jewish tradition and attacking anti-Semitism. His Zionism, as expressed in *The Second Scroll* and elsewhere, is part of this and is essentially a "religious yearning." After the defeat of Hitler, Klein's concerns broadened, and in *The Rocking Chair* he recognizes parallels between French-Canadian society and the Jewish tradition which "shaped and directed his creative powers."

C38 Frye, Northrop. "Poetry." In *The Arts in Canada: Stocktaking at Mid-century*. Ed. Malcolm Ross. Toronto: Macmillan, 1958, pp. 88–89.

Klein "is perhaps the most distinguished single poet of the generation following Pratt, though none of his poetry equals the passion and fire of his prose romance *The Second Scroll*, which for sheer intensity has little if anything to rival it in Canadian fiction." In his earlier poetry he "exploit[s] the special knowledge and sensitivity which his religious and ethical affinities gave him." The poems of *The Rocking Chair* "show how understanding of one community may develop an understanding of another . . . ." Klein's "linguistic experiments" are influenced by James Joyce. "Portrait of the Poet as Landscape" is "one of the most searching studies of the modern poet in Canadian literature."

C39 Pacey, Desmond. "A.M. Klein." In his *Ten Canadian Poets: A Group of Biographical and Critical Essays*. Toronto: Ryerson, 1958, pp. 254–92.

Klein is "a psalmist among poets." His poetry recalls the Psalms of David in its themes of praise, lamentation, and invective against the enemies of the Jewish people. Like the Psalms, Klein's poetry has a "rhetorical splendour" that sets it apart from most Canadian verse. Pacey traces Klein's development, emphasizing the "familiar pattern of doubt, despair, and final affirmation . . . tinctured with irony."

C40 Rashley, R.E. *Poetry in Canada: The First Three Steps*. Toronto: Ryerson, 1958, p. 128.

Klein's "content is neither new nor original, and his Jewish material is a limitation rather than an enrichment of the Canadian tradition. His style is loose-textured, imitative, and rhetorical rather than poetic, but it has striking images and is in all of these respects very reminiscent of Charles Heavysege."

C41 Wilson, Milton. "Recent Canadian Verse: Selected and Edited with a General Introduction." *Queen's Quarterly*, 66 (Summer 1959), 271, 273.

"Among our older living poets, Pratt and Klein are the only ones with any appreciable influence on their young successors." The "School of Klein," including Eli Mandel, Miriam Waddington, Irving Layton, and Leonard Cohen, contributes a "Hebraic strand" to Canadian poetry, which is the source of "most of its vitality." From the classical and Christian "School of Pratt" "Canadian poetry gets most of its brilliance and organization."

C42 Steinberg, M.W. "A Twentieth Century Pentateuch." *Canadian Literature*, No. 2 (Autumn 1959), pp. 37–46. Rpt. in *Masks of Fiction: Canadian Critics on Canadian Prose*. Ed. A.J.M. Smith. New Canadian Library Original, No. 2 Toronto: McClelland and Stewart, 1961, pp. 151–61. Rpt. (revised) in *The Second Scroll*. By A.M. Klein. New Canadian Library No. 22. Toronto: McClelland and Stewart, 1961, pp. vii–xvi.

Steinberg sees *The Second Scroll* as religious rather than just Zionist in essence. The character Uncle Melech embodies the Jewish people, as well as the Messiah (with whom the Jewish people are traditionally identified). The miraculous creation of the State of Israel out of the experience of the Holocaust suggests that, through God's will, evil can lead to a greater good. Klein's solution to the problem of good and evil and of God's relationship to man reflects "the traditional Jewish position, an optimistic view which does not regard reason or will as fixed and final, but as a dynamic force capable of expansion to the point where man, by his efforts, aided by Divine Law and the occasional intervention of a loving God, approaches a Messianic condition."

C43 Wilson, Milton. "Klein's Drowned Poet: Canadian Variations on an Old Theme." *Canadian Literature*, No. 6 (Autumn 1960), pp. 11–15, 17. Rpt. (abridged) in *A.M. Klein*. Ed. T.A. Marshall. Critical Views on Canadian Writers, No. 4. Toronto: Ryerson, 1970, pp. 92–98.

Wilson discusses the metaphor of the drowned poet in Canadian poetry and focuses on "Portrait of the Poet as Landscape." He argues that the " 'stark infelicity' " which the poem describes has deeper roots than Klein's dissatisfaction with the poet's role in society. Wilson emphasizes the tentativeness of the final section of the poem, although he sees it as "still fundamentally affirmative" and very close in its vision to "Out of the Pulver and the Polished Lens." Wilson also comments on Klein's relation to other writers and on the "interpenetration of worlds and images" among Klein's works.

C44 [Ó Broin, Pádraig.] "Fire-Drake." [Interview with Irving Layton.] *Teangadóir*, Ser. 2, 5, No. 2 [No. 38] (Nov. 1961), 73–80.

This informally written interview relies heavily on paraphrase. In Layton's discussion of Jewish-Canadian writing, he notes that Klein is more conscious of his Jewish heritage than any other Jewish-Canadian writer. His weakness is that he is backward-looking and retreats from modern life. In *The Second Scroll* he took refuge in "the messianic vision." The book is brilliant and beautiful poetry, but "doesn't convince." Klein's later silence is evidence that ". . . he hasn't found the spiritual, aesthetic, moral values to sustain him as a writer in either the Gentile or Jewish world."

C45 Rome, David. "A.M. Klein." In *Jews in Canadian Literature: A Bibliography.* Montreal: Jewish Public Library and Canadian Jewish Congress, 1962, pp. 24–105. Rev. ed., 1964, pp. 24–105A.

The pioneering bibliography of A.M. Klein, somewhat marred by misprints and inconsistent format. Still useful, especially for entries on Klein's Jewish predecessors and contemporaries.

C46 Tallman, Warren. "Creation Beyond Perception." *Canadian Literature*, No. 11 (Winter 1962), pp. 72–73.

Klein's "central attempt in [*The Second Scroll*] is to make a stylistic adjustment, responding to the magnitude of his subject by a kind of ironic opulence in the style . . . . There can be no doubt of the skill, but there is much reason to feel in the often pointless and cloying language-play a serious discrepancy between the artist's perceptions and his creation."

C47 Feshbach, Sidney. "Klein's Perception." *Canadian Literature*, No. 13 (Summer 1962), pp. 87–88.

In an exchange of letters occasioned by Warren Tallman's "Creation Beyond Perception" (C46), Feshbach criticizes Tallman's lack of clarity in his use of the terms "creation" and "perception." "Much of Klein's genius has been used to construct a language. More of his genius has been used in applying that language to realizing his extraordinary perceptions. . . . Klein's formal conception (the imposition of the Hebrew Bible on a Modern Instance) is made valid by his brilliant realization."

C48 Tallman, Warren. "Klein's Perception: Mr. Tallman Replies." *Canadian Literature*, No. 13 (Summer 1962), p. 88.

Tallman reasserts his claim that the "portentousness" of Klein's style fails because Klein does not "perceive (know) the portentous." He acknowledges, however, that the fault may be the reader's, not the writer's.

C49 Kayfetz, B.G. "Immigrant Reaction as Reflected in Jewish Literature." *Congress Bulletin*, Oct. 1962, pp. 4–5.

Klein is "the best example of the influences of the Shtetl being exerted upon a Canadian-born writer." He is "essentially in harmony with his environment." His writing combines Jewish and Canadian elements in harmony, "a very rare kind of phenomenon, for it is generally the very conflict and turmoil that makes for creativity."

C50 Hierano, Keiichi. "Abraham M. Klein." *Studies in English Literature* [Tokyo] (1964), pp. 71–103.

An introductory survey of Klein's life and works with special emphasis on the early Jewish poetry and the political poetry. *The Rocking Chair* is barely alluded to. Hierano sees Klein as going through a process of spiritual and political development parallel to Uncle Melech's in *The Second Scroll*, where disillusionment, first with naïve faith and then with equally naïve politics, eventually leads to a mature synthesis of the two.

C51 Sylvestre, Guy, Brandon Conron, and Carl F. Klinck, eds. *Ecrivains Canadiens/Canadian Writers: A Biographical Dictionary*. Toronto: Ryerson, 1964, pp. 72–73. Rev. ed. 1966, pp. 81–82.

Bio-bibliographical data.

C52 Beattie, Munro. "Poetry: 1920–1935." In *Literary History of Canada: Canadian Literature in English*. Gen. ed. Carl F. Klinck. Toronto: Univ. of Toronto Press, 1965, pp. 735–37. 2nd ed., 1976. Vol. 11, pp. 246–49.

Klein is "by far the most gifted of the Montreal poets, and one of Canada's four or five finest." Beattie briefly surveys Klein's earlier poetry with its "almost Wordsworthian note of piety and remembered bliss." Beattie focuses in most detail on *The Rocking Chair*, in which the "exquisitely wrought structures" of the poems "interpret a broad vision of a way of life. . . . Those qualities which might be thought of as peculiarly Jewish – a sombre sort of wit, a mellowed scepticism, a resignation that is never flaccid – are just the qualities that have best served A.M. Klein in his dealing with the world of his poems, even where his subjects have been least Jewish."

C53 McPherson, Hugo. "Fiction: 1940–1960." In *Literary History of Canada: Canadian Literature in English*. Gen. ed. Carl F. Klinck. Toronto: Univ. of Toronto Press, 1965, pp. 710–11. 2nd ed., 1976. Vol. 11, pp. 222–23.

"*The Second Scroll* draws near one of the limits of the novel's range in the direction of the 'anatomy,' and near another in the direction of poetry." It has the power and exuberance of the best of Klein's poems, but remains "an exotic in the Canadian field."

C54 Livesay, Dorothy. "The Polished Lens: Poetic Techniques of Pratt and Klein." *Canadian Literature*, No. 25 (Summer 1965), pp. 34–42. Rpt. in *A.M. Klein*. Ed. T.A. Marshall. Critical Views on Canadian Writers, No. 4. Toronto: Ryerson, 1970, pp. 119–31.

Livesay compares Klein's development with that of E.J. Pratt. Klein's work shows an increasing mastery, especially in diction and rhythm, in contrast to a disappointing lack of real growth in Pratt's work. Pratt is a "self-made" poet, a skilful story-teller who does not commit "his deeper self." Klein's poetry benefitted from a triple tradition – English, French, and Jewish. He was also a "natural" poet, who "probed inwards to the human soul, revealing its possibilities for creative joy as well as its predilections for darkness, madness."

C55 Marshall, T.A. "Theorems Made Flesh: Klein's Poetic Universe." *Canadian Literature*, No. 25 (Summer 1965), pp. 43–52. Rpt. in *A.M. Klein*. Ed. T.A. Marshall. Critical Views on Canadian Writers, No. 4. Toronto: Ryerson, 1970, pp. 151–62.

Klein believes "that the order in the universe can be grasped by the intellect." He is influenced in this belief by the Kabbalah, especially by the Kabbalistic concept of a God who manifests himself through the act of creation. This parallels Klein's own concept of the poet who "must create in order 'to be.'" Marshall outlines some of the major metaphors unifying Klein's work. In the early poetry, the Jew is seen as dwarf or clown, martyr or wanderer. He is in quest of Zion, which represents spiritual wholeness and is linked with natural imagery pointing to an eternal unchanging order. In the 1930s Klein is disillusioned and tends to see the world as materialistic and mechanical, dominated by golem figures, especially Hitler. In the 1940s he recovers his faith and the earlier imagery returns with an important difference: the Jew is no longer seen as a dwarf or clown, but as a martyr seeking perfection. He blends into a solitary and creative everyman figure who both perceives and recreates the universe.

C56 Waddington, Miriam. "Signs on a White Field: Klein's *The Second Scroll*." *Canadian Literature*, No. 25 (Summer 1965), pp. 21–32. Rpt. in *A Choice of Critics: Selections from* Canadian Literature. Ed. George Woodcock. Toronto: Oxford Univ. Press, 1966, pp. 142–55. Rpt. ("Signs on a White Field: *The Second Scroll*") in *A.M. Klein*. By Miriam Waddington. Studies in Canadian Literature. Toronto: Copp Clark, 1970, pp. 99–108.

The narrative of *The Second Scroll* celebrates the secular miracle of language and Uncle Melech embodies "the humanist resolution" of communism and religion "which combines devotion to God with an equal devotion to man."

C57 Fisch, Harold. "Nathaniel Tarn and A.M. Klein: Poets of the Hebraic Consciousness." *Judaism* [New York], 14 (Fall 1965), 485–90.

Unlike most Jewish writers, Klein is at home in his traditions. His major achievement is *The Second Scroll*, a long poem with "the grander sweep of invention which makes the longer poem possible." Klein "brings us back to the august tradition of public poetry, the poetry of shared values and images of an enclosing framework which makes possible the broad and massive design."

C58 Gotlieb, Phyllis. "Klein's Sources." *Canadian Literature*, No. 26 (Autumn 1965), pp. 82–84.

The story of the journey of Rabbi Nachman of Bratzlav to Palestine as recounted by Martin Buber in *Tales of Rabbi Nachman* is an important source for the structure of *The Second Scroll* and the character of Uncle Melech.

C59 Matthews, John. "Abraham Klein and the Problem of Synthesis." *Journal of Commonwealth Literature*, No. 1 (Sept. 1965), pp. 149–63. Rpt. in *A.M. Klein*. Ed. T.A. Marshall. Critical Views on Canadian Writers, No. 4. Toronto: Ryerson, 1970, pp. 132–50.

Klein's Jewishness is only part of the complex "mosaic" that makes up his background, but it is to Jewish culture with "its own intellectual and moral discipline" and "ethical absolutes" that he looks for his basic values. Matthews traces the development of these values through five stages, paralleled by the five chapters of *The Second Scroll*. By the end of this process of development, Klein is as committed to Jewish values as ever, but has come to see them as "only one way of stating the universal truth."

C60 Klinck, Carl F., and Reginald Watters, eds. and preface. *Canadian Anthology*. Toronto: Gage, 1966, pp. 328–52, 582. Rev. 3rd ed. 1974, pp. 335–49, 677.

Works by and about Klein. Bio-bibliographical data and criticism.

C61 Story, Norah. "Klein, A.M. (1909–)." In her *The Oxford Companion to Canadian History and Literature*. Toronto: Oxford Univ. Press, 1967, p. 407.

Story emphasizes the influence of Joyce and of Klein's Jewish background on his writing. "His poetry is distinguished by its range of erudition and vocabulary, its vigour, and its biblical rhythms."

C62 Waddington, Miriam. "The Cloudless Day: The Radical Poems of A.M. Klein." *The Tamarack Review*, No. 45 (Autumn 1967), pp. 65–92. Rpt. ("The Cloudless Day: The Radical Poems") in *A.M. Klein*. By Miriam Waddington. Studies in Canadian Literature. Toronto: Copp Clark, 1970, pp. 30–59.

The radical poems of the 1930s have been undervalued and their debt to T.S. Eliot overstated. They are more complex in diction, ideas, and metaphor than generally acknowledged and offer an active humanist response to poverty and inequality which remains constant throughout Klein's career.

C63 Van Tieghem, Philippe and Pierre Josserand. "Klein (Abraham Moses), 1909–." *Dictionnaire des Littératures*. Vol. 2. Paris: Presses Univ. de France, 1968, p. 2146.

Bio-bibliographical data. "Ses recueils de poèmes en font un des meilleurs poètes canadiens, sinon le plus grand de tous."

C64 Sutherland, Ronald. "The Body-Odour of Race." *Canadian Literature*, No. 37 (Summer 1968), p. 48.

Sutherland discusses the treatment of English-French conflicts in Canadian literature. Sutherland quotes part of "Political Meeting" and comments on "the power and detailed accuracy of Klein's description" to convey the subtle nature of Canadian racism.

C65 Pacey, Desmond. *Essays in Canadian Criticism 1938–1968*. Preface Michael Gnarowski. Toronto: Ryerson, 1969, p. 105.

A.M. Klein is "the chief rival [of E.J. Pratt] for the position of Canada's greatest living poet." Pacey emphasizes Klein's sympathy for ordinary people and his concern with social justice. The "combination of anger and delight [in Klein's poetry] together with the audacity of his images, the strength and richness of his diction, and the variety of his rhythms, has made his poetry fresh and distinctive."

C66 Dudek, Louis. "The Poetry of the City." *English Quarterly*, 2, No. 2 (June 1969), 75–77. Rpt. in his *Selected Essays and Criticism*. Ottawa: Tecumseh, 1978, pp. 245–47.

Dudek discusses "the dialectic of good and evil, heaven and hell" in three of Klein's poems on urban themes: "Autobiographical," "Filling Station," and "Frigidaire."

C67 Marshall, T.A. Bibliography. In *A.M. Klein*. Ed. T.A. Marshall. Critical Views on Canadian Writers, No. 4. Toronto: Ryerson, 1970, pp. 163–65.

Bibliography of works by Klein.

C68 Marshall, T.A. "Introduction: Canada's A.M. Klein." In *A.M. Klein*. Ed. T.A. Marshall. Critical Views on Canadian Writers, No. 4. Toronto: Ryerson, 1970, pp. vi–xxv.

Klein's vision of "unity in diversity," especially as expressed in *The Second Scroll*, is essentially Canadian. Marshall traces the development of this vision from the archaic and parochial early poetry to the later work with its "greater awareness of the facts of life." Even in the later work, however, Klein lacks a real understanding of evil, in particular how "man's wish to be the One" can be a source of evil as well as good. Klein is the outstanding Canadian example of a poet who begins in dream rather than observation and who seeks to enrich the language rather than purify it. Whatever his faults, Klein "is the man who has come closer than any other Canadian poet to greatness."

C69 Fischer, G.K. "A.M. Klein's Forgotten Play." *Canadian Literature*, No. 43 (Winter 1970), pp. 42–53.

Fischer gives a detailed account of the play *Hershel of Ostropol* and argues that its main character, the jester Hershel, embodies Chassidic values which have universal validity. "A.M. Klein has always been a writer with a mission . . . ." This is evident "in his effort to wake in the Canadian reader a sympathetic understanding of the world of the Shtetl of Eastern Europe which lives on in the memory and basic attitudes of Yiddish immigrants."

C70 Fisch, Harold. *The Dual Image*. New York: Ktav, 1971, pp. 139–41.

Klein "gazes upon the amazing contradictions of Jewish history and sees them blending and dissolving into some new vision of purposive unity." *The Second Scroll* is Klein's major work, and attempts to present the Jew as "an integrated moral being."

C71 Reference Division, McPherson Library, University of Victoria, B.C., comp. *Creative Canada: A Biographical Dictionary of Twentieth-Century Creative and Performing Artists*. Vol. 1. Toronto: Univ. of Toronto Press, 1971, p. 177.

Bio-bibliographical data.

C72 Thomson, Peter. "Klein, Abraham (1909–)." In *British Commonwealth Literature*. Vol. 1 of *The Penguin Companion to Literature*. Ed. David Daiches. Harmondsworth, Eng.: Penguin, 1971, p. 296.

"Klein's often humorous poetry is erudite without becoming obscure or verbose. The conflict between rejection and celebration of life is reflected in a presiding irony."

C73 Stephen, S.J. "Adam in Exile: A.M. Klein's 'Portrait of the Poet as Landscape.'" *Dalhousie Review*, 51 (Winter 1971–72), 553–58.

Stephen provides a reading of "Portrait of the Poet as Landscape" in terms of Lurianic Kabbalah. The poet is Adam in exile and his task is to perform the act of *tikkun*, or redemption of the fallen fragmented world. His method of doing so is through poetry which recalls "the mystic arrangement of word and symbol which is central to the Kabbalistic doctrine of man working with God in the process of Creation."

C74 Thomas, Clara. "Abraham Klein." In *Our Nature – Our Voices: A Guidebook to English-Canadian Literature*. Vol. 1 of *Our Nature – Our Voices*. Toronto: New, 1972, pp. 132–34.

Thomas gives a brief overview of Klein's work, but curiously omits *Hath Not a Jew . . .* and *Poems* and incorrectly identifies "Portrait of the Poet as Landscape" as an "early . . . apprentice work to Klein's major works."

C75 Waddington, Miriam. "Klein, Abraham Moses (1909–)." *Encyclopaedia Judaica*. Vol. 10. Jerusalem: Keter, 1972, p. 1098.

Bio-bibliographical data. Klein is "one of the most original creative writers in Canada." Waddington emphasizes Klein's Jewish roots and his progress towards an understanding of the complexities of Canada's many-sided culture. "Whatever his theme, his writing always retains social significance."

C76 Nadel, Ira Bruce. "The Absent Prophet in Canadian Jewish Fiction." *The English Quarterly*, 5 (Spring–Summer 1972), 83–92.

Nadel compares *The Second Scroll* with Mordecai Richler's *St. Urbain's Horse-*

man (and, briefly, Adele Wiseman's *The Sacrifice* and Leonard Cohen's *The Favorite Game*) in relation to the myth of "the absent prophet . . . whose reported but unseen actions lead the protagonist to a new religious and psychological affirmation of the self." Nadel discusses this central Jewish myth in terms derived from Martin Buber. He argues that its presence distinguishes Canadian-Jewish from American-Jewish literature which, in comparison, is "post-European" and "assimilative."

C77 Marshall, T.A. "Portrait of a People: Some Afterthoughts about the Landscape of A.M. Klein." *Jewish Di'al-og* [Toronto], Rosh Hashanah 1972, pp. 32–33.

For a fuller version see C136.

C78 Levi, S. Gershon. "A.M. Klein, a Memoir." *Conservative Judaism* [New York], 27, No. 1 (Fall 1972), 50–55.

Klein was "a warm gregarious man with a bubbling sharp wit." The environment in which he grew up allowed a cross-fertilization of Jewish and non-Jewish culture which is probably no longer possible. Klein was recognized by French-Canadian critics as the first English-language writer to understand the Québécois.

C79 Ravitch, Melech. "A.M. Klein – in Memoriam" [Pollock's trans.]. *Keneder Adler* [Montreal], 29 Sept. 1972, p. 7.

This reminiscence of A.M. Klein is written in Yiddish. Ravitch emphasizes the tensions Klein was under in trying to express one culture in the language of another. He recounts a number of anecdotes, including ones from Klein's later years, and appeals for an edition of Klein's selected poems to be translated into Yiddish and Hebrew.

C80 Waddington, Miriam. "The Late Poet A.M. Klein." *Canadian Jewish Outlook*, Oct. 1972, p. 9.

"To Klein the essence of art was love; love of country with its landscapes, traditions and people. And love of the world despite its contradictions and cruelties." His background, drawing on Jewish, English, and French elements, made him "a typical Canadian . . . always in the centre of one culture and at the edge of another." This mixture contributed to Klein's greatest achievement, *The Rocking Chair*, in which his recognition of the similarities between the French and the Jews allows him to enter the "French-Canadian psyche" and to "bridge the gap between the French and English cultures."

C81 Waddington, Miriam. "On A.M. Klein." *The Canadian Forum*, Oct.–Nov. 1972, pp. 4–5. Rpt. in *Jewish Di'al-og* [A.M. Klein – A Tribute], Passover 1973, p. 30.

"The force which most consistently informs [Klein's] work is love. It begins with a passion for justice and love for the Jews, and expands to become a conscious love for this country, its people and history." The other side of this love was bitter anger, as expressed in the satires of the 1930s. Klein was the first poet of the "new Canada," the Canada of the cultural mosaic. He was a "great provincial in the same way that Flaubert, Arnold Bennett, and Gogol were provincials."

C82 Laub, Morris. "A.M. Klein: A Recollection." *Congress Bi-weekly*, 22 Dec. 1972, pp. 20–21.

Laub, who was Director for North African Operations for the American Jewish Joint Distribution Committee, recalls meeting Klein in Casablanca and showing him around the Jewish quarter. Klein "was charming, witty, eloquent, erudite, a bit of a bon vivant and an unparalleled prober of Jewish values." He reproduces two letters from Klein. In the first, Klein explains the Messianic significance of Uncle Melech and the "implication of the tale . . . that the contemporary Messiah is the totality of Israel, the latter day élan vital of our people." In the second, he expresses pleasure at the generally favourable reception of *The Second Scroll*, but regrets that it is "far, far indeed from a best-seller."

C83 Rome, David. "A.M. Klein (1909–1972)." *JIAS* [Jewish Immigrant Aid Society] *News*, Dec. 1972, p. 6.

"From Day One the community knew him as the prodigy-spokesman for the new Canadian Jewry, the wonder example of Judaism becoming so Canadian that the world which speaks English will learn to call him its conscience and its voice." Rome emphasizes Klein's openness to a wide range of experience, linguistic and social, and his ability to bring everything together in "oneness." His work "is the greatest gift which Canadian Jewry has thus far made to the total culture of Canada and to the English language world."

C84 Seymour-Smith, Martin. *Funk and Wagnall's Guide to Modern World Literature*. New York: Funk and Wagnall, 1973, p. 333. Rpt. in *American, Australian, British, Canadian, South African, New Zealand*. Vol. 1 of *Guide to Modern World Literature*. London: Hodder and Stoughton, 1975, p. 333.

"Klein is Canada's most original poet, and perhaps the only one of his generation who . . . was entirely unsatisfied with the poetic procedures of the nineteenth century." His late work is reminiscent of John Berryman in its "mixture of heroic poesy, old high manner, archaism and quaintness."

C85 Toye, William. "Klein, A.M. (1909–72)." In *Supplement to The Oxford Companion to Canadian History and Literature*. Ed. William Toye. Toronto: Oxford Univ. Press, 1973, pp. 175–76.

Klein was "a poet of the minorities," whether writing on Jewish or non-Jewish themes. *The Rocking Chair* is his most important book and contains "enduring images of the Canadian experience."

C86 Walsh, William. "Canada." *Commonwealth Literature*. London: Oxford Univ. Press, 1973, pp. 85, 87–88, 90, 91. Rpt. (expanded, "Klein, A[braham]. M[oses].") in *Commonwealth Literature*. Ed. William Walsh. Great Writers Student Library. London: Macmillan, 1979, pp. 123–25.

"The condition of being Jewish . . . [is the] substantial experience of all A.M. Klein's best poetry," including *The Rocking Chair*. This condition includes three aspects: "the consciousness of the divine as totally other . . . the absolute ground of being"; "the enjoyment of a rich immediacy of life"; "the vital sense of a continuous tradition." The poems of *Hath Not a Jew . . .* are "the product of a rarely civilised mind in possession of a marvellously humane tradition." Klein's ". . . marriage of a suffering but essential serenity with a nervous and accurate response make for a poetry which is altogether independent but also splendidly central." This is especially true of *The Rocking Chair*, which, despite its flaws, is perhaps "the best single book of verse ever to be published in Canada and of the best in English anywhere since the war." A biography, a list of Klein's published works, and a selected list of published bibliographies and critical studies on Klein are included.

C87 Gibbs, Jean. "Klein's Fabled City." *Jewish Di'al-og* [Toronto], Passover 1973, pp. 50–57.

Klein is a personal poet; his work forms a unified whole, recording a "struggle between doubt and affirmation" eventually leading to self-realization. In *Hath Not a Jew . . .* , Klein is essentially a spokesman for his people, with the exception of a few poems, notably "Out of the Pulver and the Polished Lens" where ". . . there is the sense that the persona of the poem and Klein are most nearly one." The psalms of *Poems* provide a much more explicit account of Klein's difficult achievement of an "uneasy peace between doubt and belief." In "Portrait of the Poet as Landscape," Klein's inner struggles are most vividly presented and they lead to his most powerful account of the power of poetry and of the poet's discovery of himself. In *The Second Scroll*, Klein brings together his concerns with religion and art. The ending is unresolved but optimistic, as the search for self-realization continues.

C88 Marshall, T.A. " 'Another Planet': Caricature and Perspective in the Work of A.M. Klein." *Jewish Di'al-og* [Toronto], Passover 1973, pp. 32–35.

Klein has a gift for caricature which expresses itself in the creation of diminutive worlds peopled by smaller-than-life characters. This is not escapist, as some have claimed, but a way of reducing the world to a manageable size so that it can be grasped by the imagination. Klein is typical of many Canadian writers in the shifting perspective on reality which he tries to achieve. In his best work Klein tempers criticism with sympathy, and limited individuals are seen as part of "the ongoing process of natural and human life."

C89 Nadel, Ira Bruce. "Portraits and the Artist: The Poetry of A.M. Klein." *Jewish Di'al-og* [Toronto], Passover 1973, pp. 20–25.

Klein's poetry reveals a "fascination with portraits" which reaches a climax in "Portrait of the Poet as Landscape." The portraits by the satirists William Hogarth and Honoré Daumier are probably closest to Klein's verbal portraits.

C90 Page, P.K. "The Sense of Angels." *Jewish Di'al-og* [Toronto], Passover 1973, pp. 18–19.

Page's memoir of Klein in the 1940s emphasizes his relationship to the *Preview* group. Klein has an ability to examine "the immediate world," yet "to reach beyond . . . to a larger reality." Klein's work, which reaches its climax in *The Second Scroll*, is an attempt "to reverse the fragmentation of contemporary consciousness, to make whole."

C91 Siebrasse, Glen. "A.M. Klein: A Bibliography." *Jewish Di'al-og* [Toronto], Passover 1973, pp. 60–64.

Bibliographical data.

C92 Steinberg, M.W. and Seymour Mayne. "A Dialogue on A.M. Klein." *Jewish Di'al-og* [Toronto], Passover 1973, pp. 10–16.

Steinberg sees *The Second Scroll* as essentially religious, exploring man's relationship to God; Mayne emphasizes the theme of the poet's relationship to language. Klein is a "poet's poet." His broader influence and reputation are limited because of the content of his work, which appeals mostly to those who share his Jewish-Canadian background, and because of the richness of its language, which the current generation of writers and readers is incapable of appreciating. Mayne also notes that *The Rocking Chair* contains suggestions that Klein was "caught within a poetic circle of diminishing returns and circumferences" and that he had not much more to say that was "crucial or urgent." Steinberg disagrees, claiming that Klein's "expansion of interests" would have continued and that "his resources as a writer" were far from exhausted at the time of his final breakdown.

C93 Stevens, Peter. "Radicalism and Jewishness in the Poetry of A.M. Klein." *Jewish Di'al-og* [Toronto], Passover 1973, pp. 40–46.

Klein's political poems of the 1930s, especially "Of Daumiers a Portfolio" and "Barricade Smith: His Speeches," rise above propaganda because of their ironic control. "The ironic tone of the poems creates an ambivalence that militates against dogmatism," with Klein attacking not only unjust oppressors, but also the oppressed, who passively accept their lot. This is true as well in the Jewish poems of the 1930s collected in *Hath Not a Jew . . .*, especially "Childe Harold's Pilgrimage" and "Design for Mediaeval Tapestry." The medieval setting of many of these poems is Klein's way of achieving an objective distance from which to view the social and political situation of modern Jews.

C94 Woodcock, George. "On A.M. Klein: A Tentative Note." *Jewish Di'al-og* [Toronto], Passover 1973, pp. 58–59. Rpt. (revised) in *The World of Canadian Writing: Critiques & Recollections*. By George Woodcock. Vancouver: Douglas & McIntyre, 1980, pp. 270–76.

A mythology has grown up around Klein which interferes with our response to his poetry. He wrote "a handful of poems as good as the best any Canadian poet has written." He reflected the events of his time and did so in poetry which drew on traditions, European and Jewish, but transformed them into something new. His poetry is marked by richness rather than purity, and is sometimes over-elaborate and sentimental. But, at his best, particularly in the poems set in the urban world of Montreal, Klein wrote "remarkably fine poetry," the work of "a good man and . . . a good poet."

C95 Gustafson, Ralph. "A.M. Klein." *Jewish Di'al-og* [Toronto], Summer 1973, p. 6.

A.M. Klein has "surety of permanence" because of his passionate love of language, his mastery of form, and the richness of personality which his work expresses.

C96 Steinbach, A. Alan. "A.M. Klein (1909–1972): A Memorial Tribute." *Jewish Book Annual*, 31 (1973–74), 71–77.

Steinbach gives a eulogistic account of Klein's life and works. Klein "was never even remotely vexed by the conflict between tradition and assimilation." He remains true to his Jewish roots but, at the same time, achieves "a vision of unity" which makes his work universal. Klein is seen as "affirming Judaism's invincible optimism."

C97 Colombo, John Robert. *Colombo's Canadian Quotations*. Edmonton: Hurtig, 1974, p. 312.

Quotes passages from *Poems, The Hitleriad, The Rocking Chair,* and Klein's letters.

C98 Duran, Gillian. "A.M. Klein and Working-Class Poetry." *Literature and Ideology* [Toronto], No. 17 (1974), pp. 25–30.

Duran discusses "Soirée of Velvel Kleinburger" and argues that Klein "was a bourgeois poet writing about the working class from a bourgeois point of view."

C99 Waddington, Miriam. Introduction. In *The Collected Poems of A.M. Klein*. Toronto: McGraw-Hill Ryerson, 1974, pp. vi–x.

"Klein's poetry shows how a poet's use of cultural tradition . . . moves from the general and literary to the specific and individual, and how the cultural experience of the group finds expression in what is ultimately the local life and voice of the poet." Klein's rich language background contributed to his linguistic virtuosity and also made him "aware of some of the dangerous and chaotic forces that might be hidden in language." Throughout his career, Klein dealt simultaneously with Jewish issues and broader secular ones. He celebrated the poet's ability to create new forms and point to the future. He also understood "the paradox that the poet's self must always remain submerged and anonymous in his community . . . before he can speak for it."

C100 Kaufman, David. "The Poet as Nobody." *Present Tense* [New York], 1 (Spring 1974), 65–68.

Kaufman outlines Klein's life and work and the Montreal milieu that shaped him. Klein's breakdown is discussed, and Kaufman suggests that Klein's financial difficulties may have played a role. "Klein was among the most integrated Jewish writers in the Diaspora."

C101 Caplan, Usher. "The A.M. Klein Papers." The A.M. Klein Symposium, Univ. of Ottawa, Ottawa, 4 May 1974. Printed in *The A.M. Klein Symposium*. Ed. Seymour Mayne. Reappraisals: Canadian Writers, No. 2. Ottawa: Univ. of Ottawa Press, 1975, pp. 31–36.

Caplan surveys the A.M. Klein papers in the National Archives of Canada. The collection consists mostly of working papers containing a large number of both unfinished and unpublished manuscripts of the late 1940s and early 1950s. Caplan gives a brief account of letters, diaries, poetry, fiction, drama, criticism, translations, speeches and lectures, and miscellaneous notes, and suggests that the next important task facing researchers is to establish an accurate chronology.

C102 Edel, Leon. "Marginal *Keri* and Textual *Chetiv*: The Mythic Novel of A.M. Klein." The A.M. Klein Symposium, Univ. of Ottawa, Ottawa, 4 May 1974. Printed in *The A.M. Klein Symposium*. Ed. Seymour Mayne. Reappraisals: Canadian Writers, No. 2. Ottawa: Univ. of Ottawa Press, 1975, pp. 15–29.

Edel provides a memoir of Klein and his Montreal with special emphasis on the writing of *The Second Scroll*. Material on the novel is quoted directly and indirectly from Klein's letters. Edel emphasizes "the astonishing directness and sincerity" underlying the novel's complexities. Despite the great influence of Joyce, "*The Second Scroll* is really pure Klein."

C103 Fiamengo, Marya. "Catholic Resonances in the Poetry of A.M. Klein." The A.M. Klein Symposium, Univ. of Ottawa, Ottawa, 5 May 1974. Printed in *The A.M. Klein Symposium*. Ed. Seymour Mayne. Reappraisals: Canadian Writers, No. 2. Ottawa: Univ. of Ottawa Press, 1975, pp. 65–71.

Klein's writings often have Catholic resonances which arise out of the close links between Jewish and Christian theology. In *The Rocking Chair*, Catholic allusions are sometimes explicit, but they are also "startlingly apparent" in *Hath*

Not a Jew . . . , where they are not deliberate, and in *The Second Scroll* "whose resonances are not only Catholic, but catholic."

C104 Fischer, G.K. "Religious Philosophy in the Writings of A.M. Klein." The A.M. Klein Symposium, Univ. of Ottawa, Ottawa, 5 May 1974. Printed in *The A.M. Klein Symposium*. Ed. Seymour Mayne. Reappraisals: Canadian Writers, No. 2. Ottawa: Univ. of Ottawa Press, 1975, pp. 37–45.

Fischer discusses "Klein's effort to rejuvenate in his writings the faith into which he was born, to adapt it, to fuse it with the experience of twentieth-century man." At an early age Klein became dissatisfied with his traditional orthodox faith and adopted Spinoza's pantheistic philosophy, which sees divinity in all things. He was sometimes discouraged by the apparent indifference of Spinoza's God to the fate of individuals, but Spinoza remained the great influence. In later years he was also influenced by the Kabbalah, whose theory of divine emanations is consistent with Spinoza. "The idea of the essential oneness and divinity of the universe" helped Klein develop his vision of "all people and all things [as] equal in the great design," a vision of real importance to contemporary Canadians.

C105 Gotlieb, Phyllis. "Hassidic Influences in the Poetry of A.M. Klein." The A.M. Klein Symposium, Univ. of Ottawa, Ottawa, 5 May 1974. Printed in *The A.M. Klein Symposium*. Ed. Seymour Mayne. Reappraisals: Canadian Writers, No. 2. Ottawa: Univ. of Ottawa Press, 1975, pp. 47–64.

Gotlieb traces the mystical populist Hassidic tradition and places special emphasis on Rabbi Nachman of Bratzlav, a "visionary and depressive [who] seems to be the personal angel of Abraham Klein." *Hath Not a Jew . . .* shows a superficial use of Hassidism; in *Poems* and *The Second Scroll*, Hassidism is a more serious influence. Uncle Melech's story, in *The Second Scroll*, is largely based on the journey of Rabbi Nachman to the Holy Land. Gotlieb explicates a number of passages from *The Second Scroll* in the light of Hassidic traditions. She concludes that the novel is a record of Klein's unsuccessful search for God. It achieves no epiphany or mystic unity and, because of its lack of "true joyfulness," it is not satisfying, although it does communicate Klein's "enormous passion for learning, and the sweetness and loving-kindness of his nature."

C106 Gustafson, Ralph. "Informal Reflections on the Klein Symposium." The A.M. Klein Symposium, Univ. of Ottawa, Ottawa, 5 May 1974. Printed in *The A.M. Klein Symposium*. Ed. Seymour Mayne. Reappraisals: Canadian Writers, No. 2. Ottawa: Univ. of Ottawa Press, 1975, pp. 81–84.

Gustafson provides a response to the Klein symposium, pointing out the danger of concentrating too much on Klein's ideas and forgetting that he was "a wordsmith making out of experience (his and no one else's) verbal *poems*."

C107 Steinberg, M.W. "A.M. Klein and the Canadian Mosaic." The A.M. Klein Symposium, Univ. of Ottawa, Ottawa, 5 May 1974. Printed in *The A.M. Klein Symposium*. Ed. Seymour Mayne. Reappraisals: Canadian Writers, No. 2. Ottawa: Univ. of Ottawa Press, 1975, pp. 73–76.

Klein was a product of three distinctive components of the Canadian mosaic, Jewish, French, and English, the latter mostly in terms of the English literary tradition. His major contribution to the Canadian mosaic is his presentation of Jewish experience. In presenting French Canadians in *The Rocking Chair*, he is responding to parallels between their culture and that of the Jews. It is "the interaction of ethnic groups and cultures" that especially fascinates Klein.

C108 Steinberg, M.W. "The Achievement of A.M. Klein." The A.M. Klein Symposium, Univ. of Ottawa, Ottawa, 5 May 1974. Printed in *The A.M. Klein Symposium*. Ed. Seymour Mayne. Reappraisals: Canadian Writers, No. 2. Ottawa: Univ. of Ottawa Press, 1975, pp. 77–80.

Klein "is probably first major writer of authentic Jewish poetry in the English language," and his treatment of French-Canadian society is almost as important. Technically, he showed mastery of a wide range of verse forms; his poetry is varied in tone; it blends intellect, passion, and lyric beauty; it expresses the personal in universal terms. The most remarkable quality of the poetry is its diction, which ranges from the colloquial to the esoteric. Klein's greatest literary achievement is *The Second Scroll*. Apart from his achievements as a writer, he made important contributions to the Canadian literary milieu of the 1940s and 1950s and was a leader in the Canadian Jewish community.

C109 Feshbach, Sidney. "Pilgrimage to the Center: About A.M. Klein." *Jewish Arts Quarterly*, 1 (Fall 1974), 1–12.

This introduction to Klein's work is aimed especially at American readers. "The fusion or confusion of nationalities, languages, and allusions [in Klein's work] reflects Klein's constant attempts to achieve a single powerful perspective by which he could understand both the history of the Jews and the theology of Judaism." Klein suffers from a "dilemma of identity," being torn between his local condition as a Canadian Jew and the greater European tradition of Judaism. This issue is explored most fully in *The Second Scroll* which Feshbach discusses in some detail, with special attention to sources. He sees the narrator's relationship to Uncle Melech as analogous to Martin Buber's account of the relationship between "I" and "Thou." Yet there is another way to understand this relationship. Uncle Melech can be seen as an intense "religious" figure with immediate knowledge of the central spiritual experiences of the age. The narrator can be seen as a less intense, "pious" commentator, more distanced from these central experiences, attempting to make imaginative sense of them.

C110 Mayne, Seymour. "A Conversation with Patrick Anderson." *Inscape* [Ottawa], 11, No. 3 (Fall 1974), 56–57.

Anderson recalls Klein as "a prickly man . . . rather inclined to quarrel. . . . there was a kind of dangerous sparkle or kind of anticipation of possible difference and difficulty in the way Abe Klein approached people outside, so to speak, Cartier and the ghetto of those days." *Preview* was instrumental in helping Klein to widen his interests.

C111 Nadel, Ira Bruce. "A.M. Klein on Literature." *Jewish Di'al-og*, Hanukah 1974, pp. 4–7.

Klein's "most important critical essays are those that focus on literary form, the writing scene in Canada, and James Joyce." They "combine cultural analysis with textual detail" and show a familiarity with European literature and the history of literary forms unparalleled by any other Canadian critic. Nadel summarizes and quotes extensively from essays in *The Canadian Jewish Chronicle* and Klein's three articles on Joyce.

C112 Nadel, Ira Bruce. "The Prose and Poetry of A.M. Klein: An Introduction." *Midstream* [New York], Dec. 1974, pp. 36–48.

Nadel provides a survey of Klein's life and work, arguing that Klein "celebrates the spirituality of the past within the immediacy of the present" throughout his work. "In style, theme, and awareness of the Jewish past, Klein has shaped an important group of succeeding Canadian poets."

C113 Edel, Leon. "When McGill Modernized Canadian Literature. Literary Revolution: The 'Montreal Group.' " In *The McGill You Knew: An Anthology of Memories 1920–1960*. Ed. Edgar Andrew Collard. Don Mills, Ont.: Longman, 1975, pp. 118–19, 121.

Edel provides a detailed description of the McGill Group, with a brief account of "the vigorous, troubled, incisive spirit of A.M. Klein" and his first encounter with the group.

C114 "Klein, A.M." *Encyclopedia Canadiana*. 1975 ed.

"Klein's poetry is distinguished by its richness of colour and texture, its exuberance of diction, imagery and rhythm, and its emotional warmth . . . he abounds in intellectual vigour and subtlety, and in wit and humour."

C115 Mayne, Seymour. Introduction. In *The A.M. Klein Symposium*. Ed. Seymour Mayne. Reappraisals: Canadian Writers, No. 2. Ottawa: Univ. of Ottawa Press, 1975, pp. ix–xi.

Mayne gives an account of the proceedings of The A.M. Klein Symposium held 3–5 May 1974 by the Department of English at the University of Ottawa. The most important issue raised in the discussions was Klein's silence, "a crucial 'secret' of our literature that must be plumbed by biographers and critics."

C116 Middlebro', T. "Yet Another Gloss on A.M. Klein's *The Second Scroll*." *Journal of Canadian Fiction*, 4, No. 3, (1975), 117–22.

The Second Scroll shows the influence of James Joyce's *Ulysses*, T.S. Eliot's *The Wasteland*, and the Kabbalah. However, its main organizing principle is the life of Moses, the author of the first scroll, the Pentateuch. The Pentateuch is "the spiritual autobiography of a leader who, in the course of his journey from bondage and exile to freedom and homeland, was granted the vision of man's lost original home in free communion with God and the revelation of His laws which continue to operate in a world to which His back seems turned." Uncle Melech recalls many other Jewish questers in exile, all "subsumed under the archetype of Moses."

C117 Russell, Kenneth C. "The Religious Poetry of A.M. Klein." *Chelsea Journal* [Saskatoon], 1, No. 3 (1975), 126–30.

A survey of Klein's career from the perspective of his religious convictions. Klein "is a religious poet because he writes out of an awareness of the covenant relationship which should exist between a just God and fragile man. He is aware of the covenant but he is not mutely content within it nor, least of all, does he find it a pleasant refuge from reality. On the contrary, this frame of reference sharpens his anguish and God's silence is his burden."

C118 Beattie, Munro. "Poetry 1920–1935." In *Literary History of Canada*. Ed. Carl F. Klinck *et al.* 2nd edition. Toronto: Univ. of Toronto Press, 1976. II, 246–49.

Klein is "by far the most gifted of the Montreal poets, and one of Canada's four or five finest." Beattie briefly surveys Klein's earlier poetry with its "almost Wordsworthian note of piety and remembered bliss" but focuses in most detail on *The Rocking Chair* in which the "exquisitely wrought structures" of the poems "interpret a broad vision of a way of life." "Those qualities which might be thought of as peculiarly Jewish – a sombre sort of wit, a mellowed scepticism, a resignation that is never flaccid – are just the qualities that have best served A.M. Klein in his dealing with the world of his poems, even where his subjects have been least Jewish."

C119 Colombo, John Robert. *Colombo's Canadian References*. Toronto: Oxford Univ. Press, 1976, p. 277.

Brief bio-bibliographical data and list of works by Klein.

C120 Farley, T.E. *Exiles and Pioneers: Two Visions of Canada's Future*. Ottawa: Borealis, 1976, pp. 137–39.

The Rocking Chair represents "a withdrawal from life." It describes a world which "has a present and a past – but no future." In *The Second Scroll* the "withdrawal from the Canadian scene" is "complete."

C121 Fee, Margery, and Ruth Cawker. *Canadian Fiction: An Annotated Bibliography.* Toronto: Peter Martin, 1976, pp. 62–63.

Biographical data and bibliographical data related to *The Second Scroll.*

C122 McPherson, Hugo. "Fiction 1940–1960." In *Literary History of Canada.* Ed. Carl F. Klinck *et al.* 2nd edition. Toronto: Univ. of Toronto Press, 1976. II, 222–23.

"*The Second Scroll* draws near one of the limits of the novel's range in the direction of the 'anatomy,' and near another in the direction of poetry." It has the power and exuberance of the best of Klein's poems, but remains "an exotic in the Canadian field."

C123 Pinsker, Sanford. "On Abraham Klein." *The Jewish Spectator* [New York], Spring 1976, pp. 24–26.

Klein's work survives "as both a model of what Jewish poetry written in English *can* be and on its own terms." Pinsker supports this claim with a brief survey illustrated by numerous quotations from Klein's work. He emphasizes the doubleness of Klein's poetry, which "speaks lyrically in one voice and with darkling whispers in another."

C124 Frye, Northrop. "Haunted by Lack of Ghosts." In *The Canadian Imagination: Dimensions of a Literary Culture.* Ed. and introd. David Staines. Cambridge, Mass.: Harvard Univ. Press, 1977, p. 42.

Frye cites the closing lines of "Portrait of the Poet as Landscape," comparing them to T.S. Eliot's comments on the poet as catalyst and Keats's on the poet's lack of identity. "But the final phrase ['At the bottom of the sea.'] comes out of the belly of the Canadian leviathan, for the leviathan, as no one knew better than Klein, is a sea monster."

C125 Mandel, Eli. "The City in Canadian Poetry." In his *Another Time.* Three Solitudes: Contemporary Literary Criticism in Canada, No. 3. Erin, Ont.: Porcépic, 1977, pp. 118–19.

Mandel discusses Klein's "Autobiographical" as a "double image" combining the Montreal of Klein's childhood memories and the image of the New Jerusalem. "The magical city of boyhood thus becomes the possibility of God's city promised in scripture . . . . Therefore the past validates the future."

C126 "Klein, Abraham Moses (1909–1972)." In *Modern Commonwealth Literature: A Library of Literary Criticism.* Ed. John H. Ferres and Martin Tucker. New York: Frederick Ungar, 1977, pp. 288–93.

Reprints excerpts from C16, C19, C23, C55, D13, D59, D62, D72.

C127 Russell, Kenneth C. "The Blasphemies of A.M. Klein." *Canadian Literature,* No. 72 (Spring 1977), pp. 59–66.

Miriam Waddington's claim that Klein is not a religious poet is a result of a biassed view of religion as escapism, and of a mistaken "neat dichotomy between faith and doubt." Klein's poetry traces a spiritual evolution from "the naive faith of the child" through "the adult's faith-in-tension" to "the mature faith that says its amen in the darkness of unconditional acceptance." Some of Klein's poems may "seem to overstep the boundaries of religious propriety," but, as a whole, they reflect "without veneer the bitter tensions of a soul that takes God seriously."

C128   Gnarowski, Michael. "Klein, Abraham Moses, 1909–." In his *A Concise Bibliography of English Canadian Literature*. Toronto: McClelland and Stewart, 1978, pp. 66–67.
Bibliographical data.

C129   Steinberg, M.W. "The Conscience of Art: A.M. Klein on Poets and Poetry." In *A Political Art: Essays and Images in Honour of George Woodcock*. Ed. W.H. New. Vancouver: Univ. of British Columbia Press, 1978, pp. 82–94.

In his critical writings, Klein consistently argues that a writer must be rooted in a culture and a tradition without being limited by them. The writer must be original, but he must also have a sense of moral responsibility, which to a certain extent may put a restraint on his art; Klein is aware of the dangers of self-censorship and propaganda. The most elaborate statement of Klein's literary creed is "The Bible's Archetypical Poet," a reading of the story of Joseph as an allegory of the poet's relationship to his society. This piece, written late in Klein's career, contains "a rather bitter note" in its account of the poet's rejection by his fellow men.

C130   Fisher, Esther Safer. "A.M. Klein: Portrait of the Poet as Jew." *Canadian Literature*, No. 79 (Winter 1978), pp. 121–27.

Klein is a sceptic who questions all values but is attracted to the religion he doubts. His Jewish heritage is central to him, and he is particularly fascinated by the Jewish Middle Ages which he sees as a period of "independence, intellectual ferment and growing culture." Many of his best poems use "his Jewish heritage . . . in a way that makes these poems particularly Canadian and entirely universal." Klein's vision is messianic, "not only for his own people, but for all mankind."

C131   Popham, E.A. "A.M. Klein: The Impulse to Define." *Canadian Literature*, No. 79 (Winter 1978), pp. 5–17.

Underlying the variety of theme and technique in Klein's work is "his attempt simultaneously to present and to define his subject. While the early poems take a tradition and create around it a defining situation, the later poems take an object and create for it a defining tradition." This process of development is traced in *The Second Scroll*, "an autobiographical survey of poetic technique," climaxing with the discovery of poetry as a "miracle" with the power of creative definition. Klein's poetry achieves this power in *The Rocking Chair*, in which he no longer feels the need to reaffirm a threatened identity but is free to create a new one. In "Portrait of the Poet as Landscape," the "ideal poets" are the "definers/creators" rather than the "definers/preservers." Klein has "moved from close adherence to tradition and traditional modes of expression to the consideration of new areas, and a culture which was in need of creative definition."

C132 Greenstein, Michael. "History in *The Second Scroll*." *Canadian Literature*, No. 76 (Spring 1978), pp. 37–46. Rpt. (revised as "Doublecrossing the Atlantic in A.M. Klein's *The Second Scroll*") in *Third Solitudes: Tradition and Discontinuity in Jewish-Canadian Literature*. Montreal: McGill-Queen's Univ. Press, 1989, pp. 18–34.

There are two theories of history simultaneously at work in *The Second Scroll*, the cyclical, deriving from Giambattista Vico, and the dialectical, deriving from Hegel, Marx and Talmudic *pilpul*. History is "a double exposure with the present second scroll superimposed on the original past in a cycle of recurrence." Klein's poetics of process demands of readers that they participate imaginatively in the completion and transformation of history.

C133 Weir, Lorraine. "Portrait of the Poet as Joyce Scholar: An Approach to A.M. Klein." *Canadian Literature*, No. 76 (Spring 1978), pp. 47–55.

In Weir's discussion of Klein's criticism of James Joyce she places special emphasis on two of his articles on *Ulysses* "Oxen of the Sun" and "The Black Panther." Klein's criticism raises larger issues about the evolution of Joyce's aesthetic and its relationship to Klein's own. Weir compares the structures of *Ulysses* and *The Second Scroll* and the role of epiphany in these structures. The way in which Klein has "fused the logos with topography" in "Portrait of the Poet as Landscape" recalls a similar process in *Finnegans Wake*.

C134 Marchessou, Hélène. "Identité et méconnaisance ou reconnaisance de l'altérité chez Margaret Laurence, Leonard Cohen, Joe Rosenblatt et A.M. Klein: pluralité ethnique canadienne et littérature." *Etudes canadiennes/Canadian Studies* [Univ. de Bordeaux III], No. 4 (juin 1978), pp. 69, 76.

Canadian society and literature provide a more complex response than that of the United States to the issue of ethnic plurality, of how an ethnic group can maintain its own identity without being alienated from the majority culture. Klein is the best example of a fruitful cultural synthesis of English, French, and Jewish elements. *The Second Scroll*, and particularly "Gloss Gimel," go beyond even this to a vision of a universal synthesis. "La littérature ici, avec le canadien Klein, remplit sa fonction civilisatrice, qui consiste à faire dialoguer toutes les voix, sans en taire une seule, et à montrer que rien n'est fixé une fois pour toutes, mais qu'il nous incombre de construire le monde que nous voulons."

C135 Kertzer, J.M. "A.M. Klein's Meditation on Life." *Journal of Commonwealth Literature*, 13, No. 1 (1978), 1–19.

"A.M. Klein's meditation on life is a debate about faith and despair." Kertzer traces three stages in this debate: a debate between "youthful faith and crippling despair"; a debate between "despair and reason"; and "despair and reason as given voice by language." The climax of this process is *The Second Scroll*, Klein's fullest exploration of language, in which there is a progression in the nature of language, from dogma and curses, to philosophy, to theology, to prayer until "Both reason and faith triumph in the assurance that there is a rational explanation though man has not yet found it, which will be revealed at the dawn of the Messianic age."

C136 Marshall, T.A. "The nth Adam: A.M. Klein." In his *Harsh and Lovely Land: The Major Canadian Poets and the Making of a Canadian Tradition.* Vancouver: Univ. of British Columbia Press, 1979, pp. 55–60.

Klein's best poetry, contained in *The Rocking Chair*, "expresses what must become the collective Canadian consciousness, a tapestry of minority groups, each in its own cultural garrison or ghetto and surrounded by a vast and forbidding landscape." Klein emphasizes the need to overcome the Canadian sense of exile through communication among "the numerous Canadian garrisons." This would lead to an awareness of "ultimate unity." Communication is the poet's task, but, tragically for Klein, the poet is ignored by the society he seeks to heal. Ideally, the poet will be able to reconcile the "immersion" of his individual ego and the "transcendence" of the unifying vision which he experiences, and which perhaps someday his society will share.

C137 Rome, David, Judith Nefsky, Paule Oberheimer. "A.M. Klein." In *Les Juifs du Québec: Bibliographie retrospective annotée.* Québec: Institut québecois de recherche sur la culture, 1979, pp. 195–96.

Bibliographical data.

C138 Pollock, Zailig. "The Myth of Exile and Redemption in 'Gloss Gimel.'" *Studies in Canadian Literature*, 4, No. 1 (Winter 1979), 26–42.

Pollock's analysis of "Gloss Gimel" places emphasis on its complex linguistic texture and Kabbalistic structure. Pollock argues that "Gloss Gimel" exemplifies, and was probably influenced by, Gershom Scholem's discussion of the way in which myth evolves in response to historical pressures, as especially seen in Lurianic Kabbalah. Charles de Tolnay's analysis of Michelangelo's paintings on the ceiling of the Sistine Chapel, as illustrations of Neoplatonic doctrines that parallel doctrines of the Kabbalah, also influenced Klein.

C139   Walsh, William. "The Shape of Canadian Poetry." *Sewanee Review* [Univ. of the South, Sewanee, Tenn.], 87 (Winter 1979), 74–75, 85–90.

Walsh examines Klein's concerns and achievement. "Klein's passion for English literature was second only to his love for Judaism, and in each the feeling was supported by a refined and extensive scholarship." " '*In Re* Solomon Warshawer' . . . is in no respect inferior to the liveliest of Browning's productions in this mode." *The Rocking Chair* may be "the best single book of verse ever to be published in Canada." "Klein's creative generosity . . . works first to establish the being of the object, event, place, or experience at the center of the poem, and then to enlarge its significance." "Portrait of the Poet as Landscape" explores ". . . the truth . . . that the making of these creative connections, the articulation of our human experience, is the business of someone who has been dismissed from real society, the poet."

C140   Kage, Allan B. "A.M. Klein's Coat of Arms" *JIAS* [Jewish Immigrant Aid Society] *News*, Spring 1979, p. 3.

Klein's work was influenced by three main currents of Jewish thought: orthodoxy, Hassidism, and Zionism, although none of these provided him with satisfactory answers to the problems of persecution and inequality which always troubled him.

C141   Hutcheon, Linda, and Alain Goldschlager. " 'Out of the Pulver and the Polished Lens': A.M. Klein as Wordsmith." *Canadian Poetry: Studies, Documents, Reviews*, No. 4 (Spring–Summer 1979), pp. 52–58.

"Out of the Pulver and the Polished Lens" is Klein's "way of reconciling his religious beliefs and the dictates of his intellect." The poem's structure can be seen as both circular and linear, in each case with the fifth and central section playing a key role. Analyzed in circular terms, sections I, II, III, and IV are paired with sections IX, VIII, VII, and VI, respectively, which answer the questions they raise. Analyzed linearly, the poem moves from the "suppose" of "institutionalized dogmatic religion" in sections I–IV to the "fact" of Spinoza's philosophy of Nature and God in sections VI–IX.

C142   Waddington, Miriam. "The Function of Folklore in the Poetry of A.M. Klein." *Ariel* [Univ. of Calgary], 10, No. 3 (July 1979), 5–19.

"While the lore of the folk embodies everyone's fears, values, and aspirations, it is left to the literary artist to identify them, reveal their psychological implications and to interpret them." The Jewish folklore motifs of the dwarf and the goat are symbolic means of exploring "the Jewish tendency towards inconspicuousness in the social life of the larger out-group and towards humility in the moral and religious life of the small in-group." The motif of evil spirits "hints at certain unconscious fears in both the poet and his special group." In

Klein's use of French folk objects and customs in *The Rocking Chair* we see "the beginnings of the long slow process through which the future will transform the elements of the present into the symbols of the past."

C143 Kreisel, Henry. "The 'Ethnic' Writer in Canada." Identifications: Ethnicity and the Writer in Canada, Univ. of Alberta, Edmonton. Sept. 1979. Printed in *Identifications: Ethnicity and the Writer in Canada*. Ed. Jars Balan. The Alberta Library in Ukrainian Canadian Studies. Edmonton: Canadian Institute of Ukrainian Studies, Univ. of Alberta, 1982, pp. 2, 8, 11–12, 13. Rpt. ("Language and Identity: A Personal Essay") in *Another Country: Writings by and about Henry Kreisel*. Ed. Shirley Neuman. Edmonton: NeWest, 1985, pp. 109–18. Rpt. in *Jewish Life and Times* [Winnipeg] 5 (1988), 16–27.

Kreisel describes the importance Klein's example had for his own attempts to write, in English and in Canada, about "material that came from a specifically European and Jewish experience." Klein "intermingled Jewish, English and French culture and experience . . . to give each element its proper and unique weight, to observe and render people other than his own with sensitivity and seriousness. . . . Klein demonstrated in his work the creative uses of multiculturalism, and showed how the heirs of one cultural tradition could transmit the values of that tradition and at the same time bring a uniquely valuable perspective to the exploration of other themes and other realities of the Canadian experience so that a new level of understanding could be reached."

C144 Pollock, Zailig. "Sunflower Seeds: A.M. Klein's Hero and Demagogue." *Canadian Literature*, No. 82 (Autumn 1979), pp. 48–58.

Pollock places "Political Meeting" in the context of Klein's work as a whole and emphasizes Klein's concern with the opposing figures of Hero and Demagogue. Pollock focuses on the phrase "a country uncle with sunflower seeds in his pocket" and links it with the concept of the "One in the many," which dominates all aspects of Klein's work. The Hero reunites the dismembered body of his people – "re-members" it – by drawing on an essential underlying principle of unity. The Demagogue, an evil parody of the Hero, creates a false unity by playing on anxieties and exacerbating fears of outsiders. The Orator in "Political Meeting" is fascinating because, while genuinely sympathetic to the concerns of his people, concerns which Klein himself shares, he has manipulated them and "perverted what should have been a ritual of re-membering into one of dismembering."

C145 Steinberg, M.W. "A.M. Klein as Journalist." *Canadian Literature*, No. 82 (Autumn 1979), pp. 21–30. Rpt. (revised as Introduction) in *Beyond Sambation: Selected Essays and Editorials, 1928–1955*. By A.M. Klein. Ed. M.W. Steinberg and Usher Caplan. Toronto: Univ. of Toronto Press, 1982, pp. xiii–xxi.

The editorials, articles, and book reviews which Klein wrote over many years for *The Judaean*, *The Canadian Zionist*, and *The Canadian Jewish Chronicle* "constitute, in effect, an intellectual and to some extent literary autobiography." Most of the pieces deal with Jewish subjects, but a number also reflect his interest in literature. As a journalist, Klein was committed rather than disinterested. His journalistic pieces are stylistically varied, but they all reflect his love of words. They were often dictated hastily and contain flaws of structure and grammar, but they also gain in effectiveness by giving the impression of the spoken word. Apart from its literary merit, the journalism is important for the insight it gives into Klein's poetry.

C146 Broad, Margaret I. "Art and the Artist: Klein's Unpublished Novella." *Journal of Canadian Fiction*, No. 30 (1980), pp. 114–31.

Broad discusses "The Bells of Sobor Spasitula" in relation to "Portrait of the Poet as Landscape" and *The Second Scroll*. She argues for a gradual development of Klein's view of the artist and his role. "In his 'Portrait,' *The Second Scroll*, and *The Bells*, Klein moves from the personal to the national to the universal concerns of art." The composer Vladimir Sergeivich Terpetoff refuses to compromise his commitment to humanity and universal harmony in the face of totalitarian oppression. He sacrifices himself, but, in so doing, leaves a mark and proves himself "the sole bulwark of society against those who would destroy tradition and suppress creativity." Terpetoff's story clearly reflects the pressures Klein felt himself under towards the end of his literary career.

C147 Heidenreich, Rosmarin. "A.M. Klein's *The Second Scroll* and Joyce's *Ulysses*: Some Allusive Relationships." *Leaflets of a Surfacing Response*. 1st Symposium Canadian Literature in Germany. Ed. Jürgen Martini. Bremen: Univ. of Bremen Press, 1980, pp. 31–41. Rpt. (expanded) ("Epic Allusion as Narrative Strategy in A.M. Klein's *Second Scroll*") in *The Postwar Novel in Canada: Narrative Patterns and Reader Response*. Waterloo: Wilfrid Laurier Univ. Press, 1989, pp. 226–42.

Heidenreich examines the series of allusions in *The Second Scroll* to the Pentateuch and to Joyce's *Ulysses* whose "significance . . . rests not on the similarities between text and model, but on the deviations of the text from the model . . . omissions, additions, displacements, extension or other deformations of the reality or 'world' of the model." The allusions perform "communicatory functions," calling attention to the "communicatory structures" of the novel.

C148 Karfilis, Peggie. "A.M. Klein." In *Profiles in Canadian Literature*. Ed. Jeffrey M. Heath. Vol. 1. Toronto: Dundurn, 1980, pp. 97–104.

"The artistic evolution of A.M. Klein . . . [is] from doubt to despair to a final affirmation tinged with and troubled by irony." Although he achieves greater mastery as he develops, his basic themes remain the same: the Jewish experience, the essence of religious faith, love, death, madness, and artistic creation. Klein's treatment of these themes is marked by a tension between "seemingly opposed points of view." Underlying the complexity of his vision is a belief in an underlying unity in diversity and a commitment to the artist's "crucial task of imaginatively re-creating the whole of God's creation."

C149 Merivale, Patricia. "The Biographical Compulsion: Elegiac Romance and Canadian Fiction." *Journal of Modern Literature* [Temple Univ.], 8 (Feb. 1980), 139–43, 147–49, 151.

The Second Scroll is an example of elegiac romance, in which a self-effacing "first person narrator is under a sort of biographical compulsion to tell us the story of a person now dead . . . [who] is a little larger and more splendid than the conventions of psychological realism encourage." The "hero" comes to be seen as a mythological projection of the narrator's own search for self-knowledge, and the biographical compulsion comes to be seen as autobiographical. In *The Second Scroll*, the narrator's search leads to a successful conclusion: "establishing and integrating his own identity" as "a Jewish Canadian who has accepted Israel." Parallels are drawn with Dante, Joseph Conrad, and, especially, the self-reflexive fiction of Vladimir Nabokov.

C150 Wisse, Ruth R. "Reading about Jews." *Commentary*, March 1980, pp. 45–46.

Klein is the most successful of those North American Jewish writers who have sought to "forge new links between the inherited teachings and the amorphous claims of the present." His struggle, not always successful, to combine the perspectives of artist and Jew produced "a fine body of poetry and a novel, *The Second Scroll*, that are as close as modern Jewish readers have come to an English-language high culture addressed directly to their collective imagination."

C151 Nadel, Ira Bruce. "Abraham Moses Klein, 1909–72." *Jewish Writers of North America: A Guide to Information Sources*. Detroit: Gale Research, 1981, pp. 151–53.

Bio-bibliographical data.

C152 Spriet, Pierre. "Les Poètes Juifs de Montréal et le Christianisme." *Apocalypse et Autres Travails. Le Facteur Réligeux en Amérique du Nord*. No. 2. Actes du Colloque des 10 et 11 Octobre 1980. Ed. Jean Béranger. Bordeaux: Maison des Sciences de l'Homme d'Aquitaine, 1981, pp. 177–91.

A comparison of the responses of Klein and Irving Layton to the Christian milieu of Quebec and, especially, to anti-Semitism. Klein is critical of all religious institutions, whether Jewish or Christian, which serve as means of oppression, but he remains committed to what he sees as eternal Jewish values.

He is dismayed at the disappearance of these values among his own people but finds them still vital among the French-Canadians: "Klein s'émerveille de trouver chez eux les mêmes vertus qu'il exalte chez ses pères et qui ont disparu chez ses contemporains juifs: le Canadien-français n'est pas l'oppresseur, mais le frère du Juif, on pourrait dire son double."

C153   Caplan, Usher. "The Making of *The Second Scroll.*" *Viewpoints*, [A Tribute to A.M. Klein], 11, No. 4 (Spring 1981), 38–45. Rpt. in *Like One That Dreamed: A Portrait of A.M. Klein.* By Usher Caplan. Toronto: McGraw-Hill Ryerson, 1982, pp. 167–77.

An account of the events leading up to and immediately following the writing of *The Second Scroll.* Caplan discusses Klein's experiences during a fact-finding mission to Israel, Europe, and North Africa which he undertook for the Canadian Jewish Congress. These experiences formed the basis of "Notebook of a Journey," which appeared in several instalments in *The Canadian Jewish Chronicle*, and of a series of lectures which he gave after his return. Caplan traces the development of the novel from the "Notebook" material and the lectures, and he discusses the various symbolic implications of the novel's central character, Uncle Melech. He suggests that the artistic and popular success of the novel significantly altered Klein's concept of himself as a writer.

C154   Lappin, Ben. "The Receding World of Abraham Klein." *Viewpoints*, [A Tribute to A.M. Klein], 11, No. 4 (Spring 1981), 16–29.

Klein was the poet of Jewish Montreal when it was the organizational and cultural heart of Canadian Jewry. The nature of the Jewish community in Montreal and the rest of Canada changed after the Second World War when the tightly-knit Jewish community scattered to the suburbs and Yiddish culture began to die out. Unlike younger Jewish Montreal writers like Irving Layton, Mordecai Richler and Leonard Cohen, Klein was unable to come to terms with his changing audience or to find "a way of coping with the iron law of universalism and relevance demanded from the Jewish writer seeking a way into the mainstream of literature in the West." His tragic realization of his situation drove him to retreat into himself and silence.

C155   Layton, Irving. "A Personal Memoir." *Viewpoints*, [A Tribute to A.M. Klein], 11, No. 4 (Spring 1981), 3–4.

Klein was Layton's "first literary mentor" and a continuing influence on his work. He was the best poet of his generation in the English-speaking world. He was aware of "radical evil, human perversity," though his basic optimism kept him from fully entering into them as an artist. Until his breakdown, he addressed himself to the "punishing moral and psychological issues of his time" and did so with "a keen mind, a cultivated sensibility and a compassionate heart."

C156 Lester, Roslyn. "A.M. Klein: Poet of Kith and Kin." *Viewpoints*, [A Tribute to A.M. Klein], 11, No. 4 (Spring 1981), 5–13.

Lester provides a brief biographical sketch of Klein, drawing largely on Usher Caplan's dissertation (C247). Although Klein always remained rooted in his Jewish background, he "embodied the Canadian mosaic" and was more alive to the social and historical issues of his time than any other Canadian poet.

C157 Steinberg, M.W. "A.M. Klein as Critic: Towards a Definition of Poetry." *Viewpoints*, [A Tribute to A.M. Klein], 11, No. 4 (Spring 1981), 31–37.

Klein is not a major critic, but his criticism is often witty and illuminating and provides insights into his own poetry. Although he mistrusted deliberate attempts to define poetry, his writings over the years imply a coherent viewpoint. In the tradition of William Wordsworth and Samuel Taylor Coleridge, he emphasized the miraculous aspect of poetry, its capacity to perceive wonder in the everyday and to make the supernatural seem natural. The unique pleasures of poetry stem from a response to the fashioning imagination at work. Klein was particularly concerned with fitness of language: he admired the "coiled phrase," in which the impact is all the greater because of the depth of meanings. Language can fail if it is overelaborate or lacks imagination. In considering other elements of poetic form, Klein praises simplicity when it is appropriate to the artist's vision, but he is especially attracted to complex craftsmanship as represented by James Joyce. Poetry, at its best, must reconcile logic and intuition, reason and faith, the "apocalyptic" and the "mystical."

C158 Fuerstenberg, Adam G. "The Poet and the Tycoon: The Relationship Between A.M. Klein and Samuel Bronfman." *Canadian Jewish Historical Society Journal*, 5 (Fall 1981), 49–69.

Fuerstenberg rejects Irving Layton's claim that Klein's relationship with Samuel Bronfman contributed to his breakdown. Rather, the tensions that eventually overwhelmed Klein preceded the relationship and had relatively little to do with it. Klein sometimes felt uncomfortable about his role as Bronfman's adviser, speechwriter, and public relations man and resented the lack of public acknowledgement. The two men, despite their differences, respected each other and together made a major contribution to Canadian Jewish unity and self-respect.

C159 Golfman, Noreen. "Semantics and Semitics: The Early Poetry of A.M. Klein." *University of Toronto Quarterly*, 51 (Winter 1981–82), 175–91.

Golfman gives an account of the Jewish traditions underlying Klein's conception of the poet, drawing heavily on unpublished material, especially the early poetry and the late unfinished novel "The Golem." Klein's obsession with words recalls the Midrash, the Talmud, and, especially, the Kabbalah. Creation is seen as the expression of God's hidden name and, as such, is a puzzle to be solved or a code to be cracked. Klein's Jewish poetry and *The Second Scroll*, with their arcane allusions and symbolism, are conceived in similar terms. The poet, like God, is the creator of an essentially verbal universe which demands interpretation. The parallel between God and the poet is presented in its fullest form in "The Golem," which is strongly influenced by the Kabbalah. Klein's fascination with James Joyce arises out of the fact that both he and Joyce sought to create, through language, a universe which would preserve, in timeless form, the essences of their communities.

C160 Brown, Russell, and Donna Bennett. "Klein, Abraham Moses 1909–1972." In *An Anthology of Canadian Literature in English*. Ed. Russell Brown and Donna Bennett. Vol. 1. Toronto: Oxford Univ. Press, 1982, pp. 492–93, 494–509.
Bio-bibliographical data.

C161 Caplan, Usher. "Introduction to 'The Bible's Archetypical Poet.'" *Prooftexts*, 2 (1982), 123–24.
An introduction to a reprint of Klein's essay "The Bible's Archetypical Poet." Caplan discusses the essay as "Klein's central statement on the subject of Jewish tradition and the individual talent" which explores the tension he felt as an artist between his "impulse towards privacy and individualism" and his desire to speak for his people. The essay expresses Klein's own increasing frustrations as a writer and gives evidence of his "incipient paranoia."

C162 Edel, Leon. Foreword. In *Like One That Dreamed: A Portrait of A.M. Klein*. By Usher Caplan. Toronto: McGraw-Hill Ryerson, 1982, pp. 7–12.
Edel gives an account of Klein's career and some personal memories of him. "Klein embraced the ingrained wit of the human animal and showed himself master of a polyglot keyboard that yielded him endless ironies." His poetry "possesses a splendid stance," but "in the end he was trapped between the heroic and the mundane, plagued, like Herman Melville, with dollars."

C163 Fuerstenberg, Adam G. "Yiddish Influence in the Work of A.M. Klein: Folk Character in *Hershel of Ostropol*." *Yiddish*, No. 4 (Winter 1982), pp. 74–85.
Klein's Jewishness, defined as "his ability to give his poetry the verbal nuances of Yiddish speech" and "to recreate the emotional range of Jewish experience" is a pervasive element in his work. This is especially true of his verse play, *Hershel of Ostropol*, which has many parallels with the traditional Purim Shpil, especially in its emphasis on the optimistic Purim fool and the theme of "rescue and redemption." Klein underlined this theme by publishing the play in *The Canadian Jewish Chronicle* in 1939, as a response to Nazi persecution of the Jews. The specific date of publication of the play, in the Passover and the High Holidays issues of *The Canadian Jewish Chronicle*, further underlines this theme.

C164 Pollock, Zailig. "Errors in *The Collected Poems of A.M. Klein.*" *Canadian Poetry: Studies, Documents, Reviews*, No. 10 (Spring–Summer 1982), pp. 91–99.

Pollock lists four categories of errors in *The Collected Poems of A.M. Klein*: some of Klein's published poems are omitted; some poems are wrongly dated; in the case of many of the previously uncollected poems, the copy-text used is not the first published version, as claimed; and many errors are either reproduced from faulty copy-texts or are introduced.

C165 Hoy, Helen. "Klein, A.M. (1909–72)." In her *Modern English-Canadian Prose.* Vol. 38 of *American Literature, English Literature and World Literatures in English.* An Information Guide Series. Detroit: Gale, 1983, pp. 216–23.

Bio-bibliographical data, with a list of works by and about Klein.

C166 Madoff, Mark. " 'B'ir Ha-harégāh' – 'In the City of Slaughter': Sources of Rhetorical Tension in A.M. Klein's *Hitleriad.*" In *Translation in Canadian Literature.* Ed. and introd. Camille La Bossière. Ottawa: Univ. of Ottawa Press, 1983, pp. 83–100.

Klein's several translations of Chaim Nachman Bialik's "In the City of Slaughter," commemorating the Kishinev pogrom, provide an instructive comparison with *The Hitleriad*, which was much less successful. Bialik's poem exhibits great mastery of tone, which Klein's translations successfully reproduce, and its final effect is ironic. The poem is aimed less at those responsible for the pogrom than at the passive self-pitying response of its victims. It is, in the end, a call to action, which, historically, proved very effective. In the face of the much greater horrors of the Holocaust, Klein cannot allow in *The Hitleriad* the subtleties of "self-reflective ironies." It is "an indictment of master-slaughterers, not arousal of the survivors through dialectics." Klein is unable to achieve Bialik's control, and his rage and ridicule tend to work against each other.

C167 Nardi, Shulamit. "Canada." In *The Place of Israel in Three English-Speaking Communities: Australia, South Africa and Canada.* Jerusalem: Hebrew Univ. of Jerusalem, 1983, pp. 23–26.

In this article, which is written in Hebrew, Nardi notes that Jewish writers form an unusually strong presence in Canadian literature, and a large proportion of them are concerned with their Jewish roots and their relationship to Israel. Klein's lasting influence is, in part, responsible for this. Nardi gives a brief account of Klein's work, with emphasis on *The Second Scroll*, and traces Klein's influence on such writers as Mordecai Richler, Irving Layton, and Seymour Mayne.

C168 Pollock, Zailig. "Klein, A.M." In *The Oxford Companion to Canadian Literature.* Ed. William Toye. Toronto: Oxford Univ. Press, 1983, pp. 411–13.

Klein's relationship to his Jewish heritage and his need to feel part of a larger community are at the heart of his work. In his early poetry, he affirms this relationship in terms of the essentially optimistic concept of the "One in the many." Later, as his view of man and history becomes more troubled, Klein develops a dialectical vision that allows him to come to terms with the darker aspects of experience. This vision underlies his finest works, but it eventually proves inadequate to stave off a growing sense of despair. Pollock also provides bio-bibliographical material.

C169　Pollock, Zailig. "A Source for A.M. Klein's 'Out of the Pulver and the Polished Lens.'" *Canadian Poetry: Studies, Documents, Reviews*, No. 12 (1983), pp. 34–39.

Pollock identifies the Modern Library *Philosophy of Spinoza Selected from His Chief Works*, edited by Joseph Ratner (1927), as the major source for "Out of the Pulver and the Polished Lens" (1931). Klein owned a copy in which he heavily annotated Ratner's introductory essays on Spinoza's life and philosophy, but not the actual selections from Spinoza's writings. Pollock argues that the poem was probably occasioned by the approaching centenary of Spinoza's birth in 1932, and that Klein had little genuine knowledge of or interest in Spinoza's philosophy.

C170　Steinberg, M.W. Introduction. In *The Collected Short Stories of A.M. Klein*. By A.M. Klein. Toronto: Univ. of Toronto Press, 1983, pp. vii–xix.

Klein's short stories span more than a quarter of a century and are extremely varied in theme and style. They include essentially realistic portrayals of Jewish urban life, fables, Kafkaesque parables, fantasies, political satires, parodies. The early stories are on Jewish themes. Their tone is generally romantic, though undercut by a "sense of play" as well as by Klein's "acute realism." Some of these stories contain "the suggestion of the presence of a malignant fate," and this dark note tends to intensify in the later works, especially those dealing with the role of the artist in society and the effect of totalitarianism on the individual.

C171　Valente, Francesca. "A.M. Klein: l'Arpa ammutolita." In *Canada: Testi e Contesti*. Ed. Alfredo Rizzardi. Saggi e Ricerche di Lingue e Letterature Straniere, No. 11. Albano Terme: Piovan, 1983, pp. 243–60.

In this article, which is written in Italian, Valente notes that the richness and complexity of Klein's achievement suggest that, at the time of his breakdown, he still had the potential for further development. His breakdown seems to have been the result of tensions that were present in his work from the very beginning, but which eventually became intolerable. Valente examines "i paradossi sociali, religiosi, razziali, e in ultima analisi esistenziali che egli tentò di affrontare in maniera logica e allo stesso tempo appassionata, ma che non fu mai capace di risolvere." Klein was torn between a desire for the solitude and independence necessary for the development of his art and his sense of social commitment. It was his growing sense of isolation and impotence that resulted in his final silence:

"Egli si sentirà solo in adirata costernazione di fronte alla indecifrabilità e all'incomunicabilità dell'universo e del suo Artefice."

C172 Melançon, Robert. "Un écrivain à venir: A.M. Klein." *Nuit Blanche* [Québec], No. 11 (Dec.–Jan. 1983–84), pp. 54–55.

Klein is perhaps the greatest poet whom Canada has yet produced. He demands much from his readers, but the rewards are great. "Klein est non seulement un écrivain profond, complexe et savant, il est aussi un superbe artisan de la langue, un *charmeur* si l'on veut bien se rappeler l'étymologie: 'poème' en latin se dit à peu pres 'charme.' "

C173 Anctil, Pierre. "Les écrivains juifs de Montréal." In *Juifs et réalités juives au Québec*. Ed. Pierre Anctil et Gary Caldwell. Quebec: Institut québécois de recherche sur la culture, 1984, pp. 216–27.

"L'oeuvre de Klein représente dans la littérature canadienne un sommet insurpassé quant à la qualité littéraire de son interprétation du fait juif, et quant à la profondeur du sentiment mystique qui s'y révèle." Anctil surveys Klein's work, placing it in the social context of the Jewish Montreal of his day, with special reference to its rich Yiddish culture.

C174 Di Stefano, Mariantonietta. Afterword. *A.M. Klein: Poesie.* Trans. Mariantonietta di Stefano. Rome: Bulzoni, 1984, pp. 203–13.

A biographical and critical examination of Klein, emphasizing his search for a substitute for his lost religious faith, and commenting on the richness and boldness of his language.

C175 Gorlier, Claudio. Introduction. *A.M. Klein: Poesie.* Trans. Mariantonietta di Stefano. Rome: Bulzoni, 1984, pp. 5–14.

A discussion of "il modernismo kleiniano," situating Klein's work in relation to the two poles of "Out of the Pulver and the Polished Lens" and "Portrait of the Poet as Landscape." Klein attempts to use language to reconstruct the sense of unity destroyed by industrialization and the mechanization of life. He draws on all of the "inventorio" of language to do this, using "le risorse inesauribili dell'artista *trickster*, del poeta irresistibile e religioso giocatore."

C176 Bentley, D.M.R. "A Nightmare Ordered: A.M. Klein's 'Portrait of the Poet as Landscape.' " *Essays on Canadian Writing*, No. 28 (Spring 1984), pp. 1–45.

Bentley examines "Portrait of the Poet as Landscape," and provides a stanza-by-stanza explication, aiming at a "fully comprehensive and correctly nuanced understanding . . . of Klein's extraordinarily rich and complex poem." Bentley considers a number of issues, including some never touched on before in the criticism: stanzaic structure, numerological symbolism, narrative technique, and the poem's dense texture of allusion, especially to Dante. He makes use of notes which Klein himself provided for a school edition of the poem.

C177 Spira, Ruth. "Havilah al hagav [With a Back-Pack On]." Interview with Seymour Mayne. *Maariv* [Tel Aviv], 23 March 1984, pp. 39–40.

In this interview, written in Hebrew, Mayne discusses Klein's influence on Canadian literature as a whole. "Klein, who was the most important Canadian poet between the two World Wars, was a Jew who wrote in English about the French, and served as a bridge that eventually helped to bring about Canada's great national awakening" (Pollock's translation).

C178 Anctil, Pierre. "A.M. Klein: Du poète et de ses rapports avec le Québec français." *Journal of Canadian Studies/Revue d'études canadiennes* [Trent Univ.], [A.M. Klein's Montreal/A.M. Klein à Montréal] 19, No. 2 (Summer 1984), 114–31.

Klein's last book of poems, *The Rocking Chair*, marks an encounter between the poet's Judaic upbringing and the Franco-Catholic environment that surrounded him. Klein's effort at *rapprochement* between these two cultures coincided with a global reorientation of the Jewish community that took place immediately after the end of World War II. In this sense Klein can be shown to have been at the very edge of a movement of goodwill towards francophones that broke with the growing tension that had been the hallmark of inter-ethnic relations in the twenties and thirties in Quebec, and that is still gaining momentum today.

C179 Bentley, D.M.R. "Klein, Montreal, and Mankind." *Journal of Canadian Studies/Revue d'études canadiennes* [Trent Univ.], [A.M. Klein's Montreal/A.M. Klein à Montréal] 19, No. 2 (Summer 1984), 34–57.

The Rocking Chair is a manifestation of A.M. Klein's profound humanism. Revealing a consciousness of human values and human limitations, the poems in the volume constitute a search for balance between the demands of the individual and the demands of the collectivity. Dialectical in structure, *The Rocking Chair* contains several groups of related poems, for example the personal poems of the Mount Royal group and the empathetic series of French-Canadian character portraits near the end of the collection. Such groupings are also interrelated in a volume that reveals many unities, including a unity of technique, a unity of theme, and a unity of place (Montreal). When seen as a whole, *The Rocking Chair* permits a recognition of the depths, complexity, and coherence of Klein's humanistic concerns.

C180 Edel, Leon. "The Klein-Joyce Enigma." *Journal of Canadian Studies/Revue d'études canadiennes* [Trent Univ.], [A.M. Klein's Montreal/A.M. Klein à Montréal] 19, No. 2 (Summer 1984), 27–33.

This article is partly based on Klein's 1940s letters to Edel, which are read in the light of Usher Caplan's biography of Klein (C7). The article explores the poet's obsession with James Joyce and his other extra-poetic activities – public relations, journalism, Zionist lectures, and politics. The article suggests that beyond his struggle for a livelihood, Klein had a marked ambivalence towards his mother, who was critical of his bookishness and his failure to adhere to the bourgeois side of life, as well as towards his law practice. Klein's plan to produce a gloss to all of *Ulysses* and his 'transference' to Joyce are discussed in the light of their Judaeo-Catholic and Montreal-Dublin affinities.

C181 Ferguson, Linda Luft. "*The Rocking Chair*: Portrait of the Poet as Province." *Journal of Canadian Studies/Revue d'études canadiennes* [Trent Univ.], [A.M. Klein's Montreal/A.M. Klein à Montréal] 19, No. 2 (Summer 1984), 58–65.

The Quebec depicted in *The Rocking Chair* provides a medium through which Klein communicates concerns which are central to himself and which dominate his poetic *oeuvre*: religion and tradition, the joys of childhood and youth, the life of the community as it both nourishes and alienates the poet. Klein's portrait of Quebec is, as a result, a very personal one, and one which differs significantly from the portraits we find in the writings of Klein's Québécois contemporaries; however, Klein does show a keen awareness of many aspects of the people of Quebec as their society moved through a period of rapid and difficult transition.

C182 Fuerstenberg, Adam G. "From Yiddish to 'Yiddishkeit': A.M. Klein and the Attempt to Preserve Montreal's Yiddish Culture." *Journal of Canadian Studies/Revue d'études canadiennes* [Trent Univ.], [A.M. Klein's Montreal/A.M. Klein à Montréal] 19, No. 2 (Summer 1984), 66–81.

Klein matured in a Jewish Montreal which was largely Yiddish-speaking, and he knew its prominent Yiddish writers and communal leaders, especially the poet J.I. Segal with whom he shared a nostalgia and love for the values and traditions of Eastern European 'shtetl' life. Klein's roots in Yiddish Montreal and his identification with Segal were a major source of inspiration in his attempt to synthesize Yiddish and English culture in a futile desire to arrest Jewish assimilation in North America. Unfortunately, his sense of failure at being ignored by the Jewish public on whose behalf he had attempted this synthesis likely aggravated his growing alienation in his last years and contributed to his tragic silence after 1954.

C183 Horn, Michiel. "Lost Causes: The League for Social Reconstruction and the Co-Operative Commonwealth Federation in Quebec in the 1930s and 1940s." *Journal of Canadian Studies/Revue d'études canadiennes* [Trent Univ.], [A.M. Klein's Montreal/A.M. Klein à Montréal] 19, No. 2 (Summer 1984), 132–56.

Horn explains that the failure of the LSR and the CCF to move beyond a narrow base in anglophone Montreal establishes a historical context for Klein's unsuccessful attempt to win the Cartier riding for the CCF in 1949. By that date, whatever hopes the party had of capturing Quebec were already dead.

C184   Kattan, Naïm. "A.M. Klein: Modernité et Loyauté." *Journal of Canadian Studies/Revue d'études canadiennes* [Trent Univ.], [A.M. Klein's Montreal/A.M. Klein à Montréal] 19, No. 2 (Summer 1984), 22–26. Rpt. as "A.M. Klein" in *Le repos et l'oubli: essais.* By Naïm Kattan. Montreal: Hurtubise, 1986, pp. 169–75.

Klein was deeply involved in the life of Jewish Montreal and in the destiny of the Jewish people after the Holocaust and the founding of the State of Israel. But he was also an English writer in the modernist tradition, especially as expressed in the works of James Joyce. *The Second Scroll* is his finest work. As a commentary on and celebration of the Bible, it is one of the outstanding modernist works in English-Canadian literature. For Klein, Judaism is a way of reading the world which is not contradicted by the religions which developed out of Judaism, namely Christianity and Islam.

C185   Pollock, Zailig. "A.M. Klein and His Montreal." *Journal of Canadian Studies/Revue d'études canadiennes* [Trent Univ.], [A.M. Klein's Montreal/A.M. Klein à Montréal] 19, No. 2 (Summer 1984), 3–4.

An introduction to the issue of the *Journal of Canadian Studies* marking the seventy-fifth anniversary of Klein's birth. Pollock briefly outlines the major developments in Klein scholarship in the ten years since the Klein Symposium and the publication of the *Collected Poems.*

C186   Tulchinsky, Gerald. "The Third Solitude: A.M. Klein's Montreal, 1910–1950." *Journal of Canadian Studies/Revue d'études canadiennes* [Trent Univ.], [A.M. Klein's Montreal/A.M. Klein à Montréal] 19, No. 2 (Summer 1984), 96–112.

A survey of Klein's Montreal, the world of Montreal Jewry from about 1910 to 1950, which formed a kind of "third solitude" between the dominant French and English solitudes. Although united by certain common concerns and by a common language – Yiddish – the community was an extremely varied one politically, economically, and culturally. By the end of this period, the community came to assume a certain order and structure, adapting to, as well as contributing to, the social development of Montreal.

C187   Walsh, William. "A.M. Klein and the Condition of Being Jewish." *Journal of Canadian Studies/Revue d'études canadiennes* [Trent Univ.], [A.M. Klein's Montreal/A.M. Klein à Montréal] 19, No. 2 (Summer 1984), 9–21.

"Klein's sensibility and creative achievement were shaped by the fact of his being Jewish, and this is as true of *The Rocking Chair* as it is of his explicitly Jewish works. Klein's Jewishness has little to do with his faith or lack of it; it is more a matter of feeling part of a complex tradition which is at once brimming with life and threatened by external hostility. Klein's characteristic notes of tenderness and toughness grow out of his relationship with this tradition, as does his ability, especially in *The Rocking Chair*, to evoke a rich social and cultural context out of precisely delineated objects and individuals."

C188 Kertzer, J.M. "Personality and Authority: A.M. Klein's Self-Portrait." *Canadian Poetry: Studies, Documents, Reviews*, No. 15 (Fall–Winter 1984), pp. 31–47.

Klein "fails to define an authoritative, authentic, poetic self because he cannot accept the traditional religious, romantic or existential assurances of personality." Klein attempts to define himself "in relation to the legacy and tragedy of his own people, and in relation to his own confused loneliness." Kertzer examines a number of traditional concepts which Klein draws on: the Kabbalistic vision of an unequivocal but mysterious Divine authority behind endlessly equivocal texts; Ahad Ha'-Am's idealistic account of the poet as part of the national self; the effacement of self as a means of approaching God. However, in the end Klein is unable to overcome his sense of alienation and the "vacuum or absence within the work and within the poetic self that it creates."

C189 Shohet, Linda. "A.M. Klein – In Memoriam." *Viewpoints* [Montreal]. [Supplement to the *Canadian Jewish News*.] 13, No. 3 (Nov. 1984), 8.

Klein was the only poet writing in English to deal with the Holocaust as it was occurring. A number of his poems seem to anticipate the horrors to come, and throughout the War he spoke up for the victims of Hitler in his poetry and in his journalism. After the War he wrote works that show signs of "survivor guilt," and *The Second Scroll* is his final attempt to come to terms with the experience of the Holocaust, before he lapsed into silence. Klein "challenged other Canadian Jewish writers, who, without necessarily sharing Klein's convictions or visions, were forced to make their own personal responses."

C190 Cavell, Richard. "The Nth Adam: Dante and Klein's *Second Scroll*." *Canadian Literature*, No. 106 (1985), pp. 45–53. Rpt. ("L'Esempio di Dante in *The Second Scroll* di A.M. Klein") in *Canada: the verbal creation/la creazione verbale*. Ed. Alfredo Rizzardi. Albano Terme: Piovane, 1985, pp. 143–55.

Like many modernists, Klein was influenced by Dante. There are numerous references to Dante scattered throughout Klein's poetry, but the most sustained and significant example of Dante's influence is *The Second Scroll*. The narrator undertakes a Dantean journey through the hell of the Holocaust, culminating in a vision of Paradise, the new state of Israel. In this journey, the narrator's guide is Uncle Melech, who, like Dante's guide, Vergil, points the poet towards a new language, drawing on the past but "refashioned to accommodate contemporary usage."

C191 Di Stefano, Mariantonietta. "A.M. Klein tra Israele e Montreal: *The Second Scroll* e i suoi generi testuali." In *Canada: the verbal creation/la creazione* *verbale*. Ed. Alfredo Rizzardi. Albano Terme: Piovane, 1985, pp. 157–66.

An introduction to Klein in general and *The Second Scroll* in particular, based on the author's dissertation (C252).

C192 Keith, W.J. *Canadian Literature in English*. London: Longman, 1985, pp. 66–70, 155.

Klein is among the first and most distinguished poets from neither an English nor a French background to contribute to Canadian literature. The power of his poetry arises from "the creative collision within his mind between the vast collection of stories, customs, and learning that make up the Jewish heritage and a developed and flexible language that had never been used to contain them." Although he was influenced by modernism the "basis of his personality" is "essentially Romantic." His "love of language" and "acute sense of a culture" are as evident in his later Québécois poems as in his earlier ones on Jewish themes. *The Second Scroll* is a "brilliant allegorical narrative . . . one of the supremely idiosyncratic books in Canadian literature."

C193 Kreisel, Henry. *Another Country: Writings by and about Henry Kreisel*. Ed. Shirley Neuman. Edmonton: NeWest, 1985.

This collection contains numerous references to Klein's importance for Kreisel as an example of an artist making full use, within a Canadian context, of his Jewish and European background.

C194 Mayne, Seymour. Introduction. *The Essential Words: An Anthology of Jewish Canadian Poetry*. Ed. Seymour Mayne. Ottawa: Oberon, 1985, pp. 11–12.

Klein was Canada's first major Jewish poet. Beginning with his own Jewish heritage, he explored by analogy the world of French Canada and played a crucial role in shaping Canadian self-awareness. "As a Canadian and a Jewish poet, he grows in stature, and what he may not have pursued to completion in his own *oeuvre* may come to fruition in a generation of poets who were too young to have known him personally."

C195 Feshbach, Sidney. "Introducing A.M. Klein, Canadian Jewish Poet, Novelist, Editor." *Jewish Currents* [New York], 40, No. 8 (September 1985), 16–19.

An introduction to Klein's work, especially *The Second Scroll*, for American readers. *The Second Scroll* is "a masterwork of subdued power, like sabbath cooking, simmering steadily, never brought to a boil, in potential a familiar feast." Reprinted, in slightly revised form, as the introduction to the Marlborough Press reprint (A8).

C196 Healy, J.J. "Auschwitz, Hiroshima, and the Shaping of A.M. Klein." *SPAN: Newsletter of the South Pacific Association for Commonwealth Literature and Language Studies*, No. 22 (1986), pp. 4–23.

Klein was a "*lieur*, a tier-together" who tried to unify the various strands of his experience. The central *Erlebnis* of his greatest creative period was the Holocaust which "unified [his] dispersed affiliations, like a tragic explosion *imploding* into the fragile and Judaic/gentile compartments of his articulated affirmations." Klein's attempt to confront the Holocaust eventually led to his final silence, but he was "better and more tragically equipped than most men of his time to handle [the] two catastrophes of the Holocaust and Hiroshima . . . which reduced the best to silence."

C197 Davies, Robin Edwards. " 'A Game's Stances': Questions of Language and Unity in 'The Provinces.' " *Canadian Poetry: Studies, Documents, Reviews*, No. 19 (Fall–Winter 1986), pp. 49–56.

A close reading of "The Provinces" as a poem pointing to a unity which is suggested but never defined for the reader. "The poet's indirection and, hence, the reader's sense of an absence which must be found and made present, allows the universal and the specific to interpenetrate, bringing Klein's vision of unity to life." Davies places the poem in the context of Klein's work as a whole and argues for a numerological symbolism influenced by the Kabbalah.

C198 Gingell, Susan. "Prosodic Significance in the Longer Poems of Klein's *Hath Not a Jew*." *Canadian Poetry: Studies, Documents, Reviews*, No. 19 (Fall–Winter 1986), pp. 11–25.

A detailed prosodic analysis of six major poems from *Hath Not a Jew . . .* , demonstrating how Klein's "awareness of prosodic history enables him to employ meter and form allusively to establish tone or context, and [how] his skill is evident in the ways he uses prosody to delineate the character or the nature of various parts of his poetic world."

C199 Brenner, Rachel Feldhay. "The Canadian Jew and the State of Israel: Explorations in Canadian Jewish Writing." *Viewpoints* [Supplement to *Canadian Jewish News*] [Montreal] 15, No. 5 (1987), 1–2.

Brenner examines the conflict between a commitment to, on the one hand, universal humanistic ideals and, on the other, loyalty to Jewish ideals and to the State of Israel in the works of Klein, Mordecai Richler, Irving Layton, and Leonard Cohen. Klein "succeeds, to some extent, in reconciling these polarized notions," arguing that the recognition of the State of Israel "validate[s] the humanist ideal of justice for all." But as "Israel's perennial struggle against the hostile world has undermined the validity" of this ideal, the later writers have found the two notions more difficult to reconcile.

C200 Caplan, Usher. Introduction. In *Literary Essays and Reviews*. By A.M. Klein. Ed. by Usher Caplan and M.W. Steinberg. Toronto: Univ. of Toronto Press, 1987. pp. xi–xxiii.

Much of Klein's writings on literary and cultural topics was ephemeral journalism, often uneven in quality, but "the pieces gathered [in *Literary Essays and Reviews*] form a rich body of material, sparkling with insight and wit and of immeasurable value to anyone seeking a deeper understanding of Klein's own aims as a creative writer." A wide range of topics is discussed: Jewish literature, culture, and folklore; the Bible; literature and the arts; Canadian, American, British, and European literature; and, most ambitiously, Joyce's *Ulysses*. Throughout there is evidence of the tension Klein felt between a desire for artistic independence and a sense of social responsibility.

C201 May, Cedric. "Dire l'exode: l'oeuvre d' A.M. Klein." *Ellipse* 37 (1987), 57–69.

An introduction to a selection of poems by Klein in French translation. May emphasizes Klein's obsession with language: "Le vrai culte de Klein est celui qu'il entretient pour la langue, en particulier pour la langue littéraire." He compares Klein to Saint-Denys Garneau, arguing that, despite their many differences, they were "tous les deux des âmes secrètes et farouches, se réfugiant dans la poésie et dans l'écriture."

C202 Greenstein, Michael. "Canadian Poetry after Auschwitz." *Canadian Poetry: Studies, Documents, Reviews*, No. 20 (Spring–Summer 1987), pp. 1–16.

An examination of the response to the Holocaust in the works of Klein – especially *The Hitleriad* and *The Second Scroll* – and of his successors, Irving Layton, Leonard Cohen, and Eli Mandel. Greenstein argues that Klein "lacks the necessary historical distance for coping with the enormity of the Holocaust." The later poets were more successful in achieving such a distance, but "by the time Klein had grasped the historical perspective, he succumbed to silence."

C203 Feshbach, Sidney. "About A.M. Klein." *Jewish Studies Network* [New York], 1, No. 2 (Fall 1987), 1–3.

A brief introductory survey, aimed at Jewish-American readers, of the life and works of A.M. Klein, focusing on *The Second Scroll* and recommending it as "supremely suited to a class in Jewish studies."

C204 Brenner, Rachel Feldhay. "The Almost Meeting: The Quest for the Holocaust in Canadian Jewish Literature." *Methodology in the Academic Teaching of the Holocaust*. Ed. Zev Garber, Alan L. Berger, and Richard Libowitz. Lanham, Md.: Univ. Press of America, 1988, pp. 191–211.

Brenner discusses Henry Kreisel's *The Rich Man*, Klein's *The Second Scroll*, and Mordecai Richler's *St. Urbain's Horseman* as examples of Jewish-Canadian responses to the Holocaust. In all three the "motif of the protagonist's search for a lost relative in Europe reveals the emotional need to 'meet' history." This search is, in each case, a failure since the "novelists can view the tragedy only through an intermediating metaphor of the quest for the irrevocably lost heritage." By presenting the Holocaust as part of a historical pattern leading to the development of the State of Israel, Klein "displaces the Holocaust's unutterable horror and fear with a sweeping vision of spiritual and physical rebirth."

C205 Caplan, Usher. "Klein, Abraham Moses." *The Canadian Encyclopedia.* 1988 ed.

Bio-bibliographical data. "Klein's work is remarkable for its linguistic exuberance, wit, learning, and moral fervour."

C206 Melançon, Robert. "Le poète est un traducteur." *Canadian Literature,* No. 117 (1988), pp. 108–12.

Melançon discusses the aims and challenges of translation and how they have affected his own poetry. He cites his experience in translating "Lone Bather": "Il faut le traduire en français pour feuilleter toute son épaisseur." He also discusses the difficulty of translating *The Second Scroll* with its complex "espace intertextuel" and its "traits de virtuosité stylistique éblouissants mais jamais gratuits."

C207 Rozmovits, Linda. "A.M. Klein's Translation of Moyshe Leib Halpern: A Problem of Jewish Modernism." *Canadian Poetry: Studies, Documents, Reviews,* No. 22 (1988), pp. 1–9.

An analysis of a set of poems by the modern Yiddish poet Moyshe Leib Halpern, which Klein produced in the early thirties. Rozmovits demonstrates how the translations consistently subvert the elements of modernism in Halpern's work, and argues that Klein's uneasiness about poetry that is both Yiddish and modernist reflects the tensions between his own modernism and Jewishness.

C208 Steinberg, M.W. "A.M. Klein." *Dictionary of Literary Biography: Canadian Writers 1920–1959.* Vol. 68. First Series, ed. W.H. New. Detroit: Bruccoli Clark Lyman, 1988. pp. 194–205.

A detailed survey of the entire range of Klein's work, placing it in the context of the Montreal Jewish milieu which shaped his imagination. Klein is a many-faceted writer of broad human sympathies who remains "basically a romantic," despite the modernist elements in his work. He is probably "the single most important English-language Canadian writer of the first half of the twentieth century."

C209 Stouck, David. "A.M. Klein." *Major Canadian Authors: A Critical Introduction to Canadian Literature in English.* 2nd ed. Lincoln: Univ. of Nebraska Press, 1988, pp. 163–78.

Klein is "essentially a pastoral poet in search of a lost Eden." He draws on three cultures – Jewish, English, and French – but is alienated from all three. All of his work is "marked by the voice of an alien." In "Portrait of the Poet as

Landscape," which is "often regarded as the most accomplished single poem by a Canadian," he portrays "the artist as an introvert, an alien and ghostly creature." It foreshadows his final complete breakdown.

C210 Wieland, James. *The Ensphering Mind: History, Myth, and Fictions in the Poetry of Allen Curnow, Nissim Ezekiel, A.D. Hope, A.M. Klein, Christopher Okigbo, and Derek Walcott.* Washington, D.C.: Three Continents Press, 1988, pp. 32–46, 115–22.

Wieland discusses Klein in the context of the "quarrels with history" of a number of Commonwealth poets who all "seek in myth and fictions the order and coherence they believe is missing from history." Klein views history through three "powerful lenses": religion, literary tradition, and Marxism. There is an increasing multiplicity of perspectives in Klein's later works and a tension between irony and affirmation.

C211 Butovsky, Mervin. "A.M. Klein: A Jewish Poet in the Modern World." *Jewish Book Annual* 46 (1988–89), 20–32.

An introductory survey of Klein's life and work, with special attention to the *Collected Works.* Butovsky emphasizes Klein's struggle to synthesize his Jewish heritage and his concerns with contemporary society. "No modern Jewish writer since the Enlightenment has been unaffected by the psychic strain of having to live simultaneously in two worlds. In the writing of A.M. Klein we have a dramatic example of how enriching and costly that process could be."

C212 Brenner, Rachel Feldhay. "Klein, Abraham Moses." *Blackwell Companion to Jewish Culture from the 18th Century to the Present.* Oxford: Blackwell's, 1989, pp. 415–16.

Bio-bibliographical data. Brenner emphasizes Klein's "sensitivity to the multicultural aspects of his environment" and his "need to reconcile humanistic universalism and Zionist particularism."

C213 Brenner, Rachel Feldhay. "A.M. Klein and Mordecai Richler: Canadian Responses to the Holocaust." *Journal of Canadian Studies*, No. 2 (1989), pp. 65–77.

Brenner discusses the responses of Klein and Mordecai Richler to the recent history of the Jewish people, and especially to the Holocaust and to the birth of the Jewish state, arguing that they were shaped by the writers' personal experiences of fascism and anti-Semitism in Quebec. These responses are best seen "not in terms of divergence and contradiction but rather in terms of continuum and process." Both writers share the same basic humanist liberal ideals, but Richler is more sceptical about the effectiveness of such ideals.

C214 Greenstein, Michael. *Third Solitudes: Tradition and Discontinuity in Jewish-Canadian Literature.* Montreal: McGill-Queen's Univ. Press, 1989.

Greenstein sees A.M. Klein, and, especially, *The Second Scroll*, as crucial to the development of Jewish-Canadian literature. In his introduction (pp. 3–17), he links Klein to a Jewish tradition of "a subversive resistance to closure," citing the Talmud, Maimonides, Freud, Buber, Kafka, Adorno, Hartman, Bloom, and Derrida. "Mediation, displacement, deferment, exile, absence, equivocal meaning – these are the themes . . . of Jewish writing in Canada from Klein to the present." Greenstein's chapter on *The Second Scroll*, "Doublecrossing the Atlantic in A.M. Klein's *The Second Scroll*" (pp. 18–34) is a revised version of C132.

C215 Heidenreich, Rosmarin. *The Postwar Novel in Canada: Narrative Patterns and Reader Response*. Waterloo: Wilfrid Laurier Univ. Press, 1989.

Chapter 5, "Epic Allusion as Narrative Strategy in A.M. Klein's *Second Scroll*" (pp. 226–42), is an expanded version of C147.

C216 New, W.H. *A History of Canadian Literature*. London: Macmillan, 1989, pp. 169–72.

"Klein made language his subject as well as his medium of expression" through which he "orchestrate[d] a dialectic of multiple identities." He sought through his art a "deliberate connection with the world," but at the same time he struggled to remain true to his own personal vision. In his later years Klein's faith in his art was undermined by the "temptations of solipsism" and he fell silent.

C217 Waddington, Miriam. *Apartment Seven: Essays Selected and New*. Toronto: Oxford Univ. Press, 1989.

Reprints two articles, "The Cloudless Day: Klein's Radical Poems" (pp. 120–38), and "Alone: Klein's *Rocking Chair*" (pp. 139–56), which are also included as chapters in *A.M. Klein* (C2).

C218 Brenner, Rachel Feldhay. "A.M. Klein's *Hath Not a Jew*: in Search of Vision." *Canadian Poetry: Studies, Documents, Reviews*, No. 26 (1990), pp. 54–69.

Brenner traces a development in Klein's view of "man and his works" in *Hath Not a Jew* . . . In the earliest stage, Klein presents a hopeful vision of moral regeneration; his Zionism is seen as "the materialization of the universal ideals of brotherhood and peace." In response to the rise of fascism, Klein's vision darkens, and he uses the legend of the golem to present a "nihilistic notion of the world." Eventually he comes to suggest the possibility of redemption through the active confrontation of the forces of brutality and oppression. In *The Hitleriad* Klein "actualizes [this] vision of mankind ready to defend the humanist ideal."

C219 Brenner, Rachel Feldhay. "A.M. Klein's *The Rocking Chair*: Toward the Redefinition or the Poet's Function." *Studies in Canadian Literature*, 15, No. 1 (1990), 94–116.

Brenner criticizes the view of *The Rocking Chair* as a "product" expressing an ideologically coherent and static point of view. Instead, she argues, it is a "production" which "defies the stasis of an ideological signification." As such, it is consistent with the view of the poet as presented in "Portrait of the Poet as Landscape," which is critical of the "stasis of a finalized 'meaning'." "The poems in *The Rocking Chair* enact "the poet's progression toward self-definition through the exploration and exposure of the 'forgotten' layer of social consciousness." There is an increasing sense of disillusionment with reassuring social myths, as the text acknowledges "its own anxiety, 'nervousness,' and disorientation."

C220 Melançon, Robert. Préface. In *Le Second Rouleau*. By A.M. Klein. Translated by Charlotte and Robert Melançon. Montréal: Boréal, 1990, pp. 9–20.

The Second Scroll is a complex work which draws on the conventions of many different genres: the detective novel, the *Bildungsroman*, the historical novel, the novel of initiation. It is a kind of *midrash*, expanding on the meaning of the first scroll, the Pentateuch, and its glosses provide a further level of *midrashic* commentary on the main narrative. Klein is a stylistic virtuoso, but all aspects of the novel contribute to the larger whole of "un livre total, encyclopédique . . . . Comme tous les grands livres, *Le Second Rouleau* échappe aux classifications parce qu'il crée sa propre forme."

C221 Pollock, Zailig. Introduction. In *The Complete Poems*. By A.M. Klein. Ed. by Zailig Pollock. Toronto: Univ. of Toronto Press, 1990. pp. xi–xxx.

Klein's poetry represents a relatively small proportion of his writings but it is by far the most important. His career as a poet is characterized by short periods of intense creativity interspersed with periods of silence. This pattern seems to reflect Klein's struggle to create a vision of his relationship as a poet to his community which forms the central theme of his poetry. Pollock discusses this vision and its development in response to changing historical circumstances. He emphasizes the conflict between Klein's desire for artistic independence and sense of commitment to community, a conflict which led to Klein's finest achievements as a poet in the mid-forties but which he eventually found impossible to maintain.

C222 Rozmovits, Linda. "History and the Poetic Construct: The Modernism of A.M. Klein." *Canadian Literature*, No. 126 (1990), pp. 87–102.

Rozmovits argues that "Portrait of the Poet as Landscape" represents "not modernism at the height of triumphant defiance, but rather modernism tottering on the brink," and that Klein's work as a whole moves towards "the increasingly unsettled borders of the post-modern." She contrasts Klein with Ezra Pound, who saw the artist's role as restoring value, which had disappeared from mass society, through the autonomy of art. For Klein art has no autonomy; value, as embodied in a community and its traditions of which he still feels a part, is being assailed by the undeniable forces of history. Rozmovits demonstrates how Klein dramatizes the assault of history in a number of his major poems through the disruption of traditional poetic forms.

C223 Melançon, Robert. "Réédifier Jérusalem." *Montréal: l'invention juive.* Actes du Colloque tenu le 2 mars 1990 à l'Université de Montréal. Montréal: Département d'études françaises. Univ. de Montréal, 1991. pp. 25–49.

Klein's view of the world was profoundly shaped by his experience of Montreal: "le monde s'est présenté à lui sous la forme de sa ville . . . . Klein est un homme habité. Il porte en lui la form d'une ville, de sa ville, Montréal." Although Klein was aware of ethnic conflict and anti-Semitism in Montreal, for him the city represented an ideal of harmony in diversity, an ideal which combined with his vision of the universal city of Jerusalem "qui serait le lieu d'une humanité réconcilié aves ses différences."

C224 Bentley, D.M.R. " 'The Notes Suggested by Klein Himself' to 'Portrait of the Poet as Landscape.' " *Essays on Canadian Writing*, No. 40 (Spring, 1990), pp. 153–55.

Bentley reproduces, with a brief introduction, fourteen notes to "Portrait of the Poet as Landscape" from *Longer Poems for Upper-School, 1955–56*, ed. Roy Allin and Alan F. Meikeljohn (Toronto: Ryerson Press, 1955), which, according to Allin, were "suggested by Klein himself."

C225 Davies, Robin Edwards. "Re: Reading Klein's 'Krieghoff: Calligrammes.' " *Canadian Poetry: Studies, Documents, Reviews*, No. 27 (Fall-Winter 1990), pp. 30–39.

In a detailed explication of "Krieghoff: Calligrammes," Davies argues that the theme of the poem "would seem to be the multiplicity of language," a theme which "emerges as much from the language that gives the poem its form as from the celebration of language that becomes part of its content." She reads the poem from a wide range of perspectives, and demonstrates how Klein's use of language, here and elsewhere in his works, invites multiple, open-ended readings.

C226 Lemm, Richard. "Klein's Zionist Poetry and the Palestinian Conflict." *Studies in Canadian Literature*, 16, No. 2 (1991), 54–78.

Lemm surveys Klein's Zionism and his attitudes to Arabs, as expressed in his poetry, his journalism, and *The Second Scroll*, placing it in the context of the development of Zionism from the nineteenth century to the present day. At times, Klein expresses a genuine sense of fellow-feeling for the plight of the Palestinians, as in the conclusion of "Greeting on This Day," but, in general, his concern with the fate of the Jewish people leads him to accept stereotypes of the Arab as the other, and to adopt, in an uncritical manner, the self-serving Zionist account of the development of the Jewish state. Klein always, however, retained a hope that a genuine harmony between Arabs and Jews could be achieved, once the Jews were secure in their own state.

C227   Marrus, Michael R. *Mr. Sam: The Life and Times of Samuel Bronfman.* New York: Viking, 1991. pp. 222, 266, 273–78, 281, 284, 291–95, 304–05, 360, 366, 380–81, 387, 408, 424-28, 469, 519.

Marrus presents a sympathetic account of Klein's relationship with Samuel Bronfman. Although Marrus acknowledges that Klein at times experienced "loathing" for the kind of tasks he was called upon to perform as Bronfman's speechwriter and PR man, he argues that there was genuine affection and mutual respect between the two men.

C228   Rozmovits, Linda. "A Narrative Messiah: The Redemptive Historiography of A.M. Klein's *The Second Scroll.*" *Prooftexts*, 11 (1991), pp. 25–39.

Rozmovits places *The Second Scroll* in the context of the struggle faced by Jewish modernists who are attracted to the claims of modernism to transcend history through art yet, at the same time, are sceptical of this claim. *The Second Scroll* "is deeply engaged in history," but "it is not a historical novel," since its subject is not history itself but the attempt to construct a Messianic narrative which has the power to redeem history. Rozmovits focuses on three aspects of this attempt to create "aught from naught": Uncle Melech's in "Gloss Gimel," the narrator's in "Deuteronomy," and Klein's own attempt in the two epigraphs to the novel. In each case the redemption of history through language is seen to be precarious at best.

C229   Richler, Mordecai. "Speak Easy of Sam Bronfman." *Saturday Night,* July-August 1992, p. 15.

In a response to *Mr. Sam* (C227), Richler presents a very negative account of Klein's relationship to Samuel Bronfman, accusing him of "degrading himself" by "fill[ing] the humiliating office of Sam's poet laureate."

Theses and Dissertations

C230   Scullion, John. "Abraham Moses Klein, Poet and Novelist." M.A. Thesis Montréal 1953.

The Second Scroll is a limited success, but the poetry is accomplished in its technique and seriousness of thought. This thesis was written before Klein's breakdown, and Scullion predicts "a fuller and riper poetry in the future."

C231   Schultz, Gregory Peter. "The Periodical Poetry of A.J.M. Smith, F.R. Scott, Leo Kennedy, A.M. Klein and Dorothy Livesay, 1925–1950." M.A. Thesis Western Ontario 1957.

Schultz provides an account of the Canadian periodicals in which much of

Klein's early poetry appeared. The influence of metaphysical poetry, Freudian psychology, J.G. Frazer's *The Golden Bough*, and social issues are discussed in relation to Klein and the other poets who published in these periodicals. Lists of all of Klein's periodical poetry are provided and some examples are reproduced.

C232 Watt, F.W. "Radicalism in English Canadian Literature since Confederation." Diss. Toronto 1957.

"Radicalism acted as a dialectical thrust in [Klein's] thinking and his attitudes against the tendency to an introverted, parochial, exclusive Jewishness, and helped to turn Klein's interest towards social problems and other areas of experience he formerly ignored." Although the political poems of the 1930s turn away from Jewish themes, they are imbued with the spirit of the Old Testament prophets.

C233 Palnick, E.E. "A.M. Klein: A Biographical Study." M.A. Thesis Hebrew Union 1959.

Palnick draws on personal interviews with Klein in this biography. He is critical of Klein's inability to break free of the restraints of his background and sees this as central to his decline.

C234 Marshall, T.A. "The Poetry of A.M. Klein: A Thematic Analysis of the Poetry of Abraham Moses Klein in the Light of the Major Themes of *The Second Scroll*." M.A. Thesis Queen's 1964.

Marshall traces the development of Klein's vision, which remains essentially the same throughout his career. Central to this vision is "the imaginative re-creation of the order inherent in the world" that allows one to "define and realize oneself in it." When man exercises this power of re-creation through poetry or love he achieves a kind of divinity and becomes part of the One. Klein's vision gradually becomes more mature and inclusive as he moves away from the dream world of the early verse and achieves a fuller cognizance of the world around him and of the material aspects of man's existence. The climax of this process of development is *The Rocking Chair* and *The Second Scroll*. Klein's vision is finally limited, however, by his inability or unwillingness to confront the fact of evil.

C235 Lyons, Roberta. "Jewish Poets from Montreal: Concepts of History in the Poetry of A.M. Klein, Irving Layton, and Leonard Cohen." M.A. Thesis Carleton 1966.

Chapter III of the thesis discusses "the development of an increasingly comprehensive and mature concept of history" in Klein's work. Throughout his career, Klein expresses "faith in the value of human endeavour." *Hath Not a Jew* . . . focuses on the past and criticizes the passivity of the Jews in the face of suffering. The satires of the 1930s and *Poems* represent a shift to the present and view history as a recurrent series of events over which people have some control. *The Rocking Chair* celebrates the values of the past, but warns against overwhelming the present with the past. *The Second Scroll* is the "final and most complete stage" of Klein's view of history. The future as well as the past and the present are seen as part of an Eternal Now in which both people and God control human affairs.

C236 Bell, Merirose. "The Image of French Canada in the Poetry of William Henry Drummond, Emile Coderre and A.M. Klein." M.A. Thesis McGill 1967.

Klein's attitude to French Canada is more complex than William Henry Drummond's sentimentality or Emile Coderre's satirical bitterness. He is primarily interested in the psychology of the French Canadians as a minority group, similar in many ways to the Jews. He explores the conflict between tradition and progress and the ways in which potentials are realized or go to waste.

C237 Djwa, Sandra. "Metaphor, World View and the Continuity of Canadian Poetry: A Study of the Major English Canadian Poets with a Computer Concordance to Metaphor." Diss. British Columbia 1968.

Djwa places Klein in the third stage of a four-stage model of the development of Canadian poetry: the building up of community; a Romantic transcending of the land which overlaps evil; acknowledgment of evil in man and nature; and a concentrated inquiry into the evil of human nature. Klein demonstrates an "eschatological" concern in his poetry, a concern with "a definition of man and his end." He is deeply affected by "the human evil released by world war." [Note: Klein is not one of the poets included in the concordance to metaphor.]

C238 Stevens, Peter. "The Development of Canadian Poetry between the Wars and Its Reflection of Social Awareness." Diss. Saskatchewan 1968.

Chapters VII and VIII contain some close readings of Klein's political poems of the 1930s and of the poems of social comment collected in *Hath Not a Jew* . . . For Stevens' general argument see C93.

C239 Bitton, Janet. "The Canadian 'Ethnic' Novel: The Protagonists' Search for Self Definition." M.A. Thesis Montréal 1971.

Bitton examines the struggle of immigrants to gain a sense of a unified self in the face of a new environment, as it is portrayed in several Canadian novels. In *The Second Scroll*, unlike some later Canadian novels, traditional myth is still the dominating force. "The protagonist of *The Second Scroll* evolves a vision of mankind's eventual union into the One through social interaction stemming from a creative involvement with language."

C240 Spiro, Solomon J. "The Second Gloss: An Exegesis of *The Second Scroll* by A.M. Klein." M.A. Thesis Sir George Williams 1971.

This is a study of the literary, religious, and philosophical background of *The*

Second Scroll. Spiro examines Klein's Jewish sources and models. There is a particularly extensive treatment of parallels between each of the five chapters of the novel and its corresponding book in the Pentateuch.

C241 Tisdall, Douglas Michael. "The Not Unsimilar Face: A Comparative Study of the Influence of Culture, Religion and Locale in French-Canadian and English-Canadian Poetry." Diss. Toronto 1971.

Klein is free of the Jansenist-Calvinist dualism which dominates Canadian poetry. "His unified world view, which asserts life at all levels, has an immense restorative capacity for Canadian poetry and Canadian culture at large, for it stands against that current which harbours thoughts of death and morbidity and which is almost the strongest characteristic of Canadian life." However, Klein's affirmative vision is eventually shattered by the harsh realities of Jewish suffering and of what he sees as his own rejection as a poet.

C242 Barrie, Brian. "The Structure and Genre of A.M. Klein's *The Second Scroll.*" M.A. Thesis New Brunswick 1972.

Barrie examines the Jewish content of *The Second Scroll* and the form through which it is expressed. The glosses comment on the main narrative, just as the Talmud comments on the Pentateuch. The novel as a whole draws on a wide range of Jewish literature and culture, especially the Kabbalah. The genre of the novel is essentially epic, as is much of the Old Testament, and is based on the myth of the quest adapted to the situation of modern Jews.

C243 Fischer, G.K. "A.M. Klein: Religious Philosophy and Ethics in His Writings." Diss. McGill 1972.

This dissertation was revised and published as a book. See C4.

C244 Staskevicius, Arunas. "The Quest for Identity Theme in the Works of A.M. Klein and Mordecai Richler." M.A. Thesis McMaster 1972.

Staskevicius compares A.M. Klein's and Mordecai Richler's attitudes to the Jewish community and Israel. Klein is more at home with Jewish traditions than is the largely assimilated Richler, and he celebrates them while Richler tends to view them satirically. Klein presents the Jewish ghetto as a tightly knit community united and nourished by a common set of beliefs; Richler condemns the ghetto as a spiritual prison. Klein idealizes Israel as the miraculous reunion of the exiled Israelites; Richler presents it as an uneasy alliance among differing and even hostile groups.

C245 Esco, Helen Esther. "Judaic Tradition and the Poetry of A.M. Klein." M.A. Thesis Queen's 1973.

At the core of Klein's poetry is an intense religious commitment to the God of his forefathers. His Jewish background is not constricting but provides an integrated view of the universe which allows him to look at all life, Jewish or not, as a totality. Klein's political poems arise not out of "secular humanism" but out of the Jewish tradition which demands that every man share in the process of divine creation by furthering social justice on earth. Klein sees the poet's role as the glorifying of God through praising His creation.

C246 Still, Robert Ernest. "The Early Poetry of A.M. Klein." M.A. Thesis Western Ontario 1974.

Still explores Klein's poetry of the 1920s and 1930s, placing special emphasis on *Hath Not a Jew . . .* and the political satires. Klein's work shows a movement from an autobiographical emphasis in the earliest poetry through a growing concern with Jewish traditions, in *Hath Not a Jew . . .*, to "a more cosmopolitan view of human society" in the political satires, which point, ultimately, to *The Rocking Chair* and *The Second Scroll.* A good discussion of the organization of *Hath Not a Jew . . .*

C247 Caplan, Usher. "A.M. Klein: An Introduction." Diss. State Univ. of New York at Stony Brook 1976.

This dissertation was revised and published as a book. See C7.

C248 Berck, Brenda. "Marginality and Detachment in the Poetry of A.M. Klein." M.A. Thesis McMaster 1977.

"Klein is marginal to the religious traditions of his ancestors, to many aspects of his life in Montreal, to Palestine, and to many of the expressions of contemporary Judaism." He uses various literary devices to emphasize that what he is portraying is outside his own immediate experience. In this way he distances himself from areas of life with which he feels uncomfortable.

C249 Campbell, Sandra. "Jewish Tradition in the Journalism of A.M. Klein." M.A. Thesis Carleton 1978.

Campbell examines Klein's journalism devoted to Zionism and to literary criticism. Both aspects of the journalism reflect Klein's commitment to a Jewish tradition which is defined in ethical rather than specifically religious terms.

C250 Lehman, Victoria Evelyn. "The Poet as Isolated Visionary in the Work of Margaret Avison and A.M. Klein." M.A. Thesis Queen's 1980.

Margaret Avison and A.M. Klein explore the problematic role of the poet in modern industrial society. Both condemn the "sacrifice of creative potential at the altar of technology." Avison's poetry expresses moral and religious certainty, while Klein, especially in "Portrait of the Poet as Landscape," is sceptical of such certainties; he locates the source of the poet's strength in "inner courage" rather than in "some supreme figure of faith." However, both share a "sense of the importance of a personal vision of which society must take cognizance or perish as a whole."

C251 Spiro, Solomon J. "A Study and Interpretation of the Judaic Allusions in

The Second Scroll and *The Collected Poems of A.M. Klein*: Annotations and Commentary." Diss. McGill 1980.

This dissertation was revised and published as a book. See C8.

C252 Di Stefano, Mariantonietta. "A.M. Klein: *The Second Scroll*: Testo e intertesto." Tesi Pisa 1981.

In this thesis, which is written in Italian, di Stefano presents a detailed analysis of *The Second Scroll*. The novel is seen as a "summa" which includes many literary genres. The complex relationships between these genres, as well as the dense web of allusions to ancient and modern literature and culture, echo Klein's sense of the tension between the multifariousness of the Jewish people and its desire for unity with "lo Spirito puro." With the help of diagrams, di Stefano outlines the network of parallels linking the narrator's story, Uncle Melech's story, and the glosses, and she relates these parallels to their underlying biblical model. She concludes with an analysis, based on medieval rhetoric, which distinguishes five different levels of meaning, or "isotopie testuali," in the text: narrative (the narrator's search for his uncle); allegorical (the exile and return of a people); pedagogical (the search for truth); anagogical (the spiritual voyage of two souls); analogical (the divinity of people). She also includes a detailed diagram of the Sistine Chapel ceiling, keyed to the relevant passages in "Gloss Gimel."

C253 Munton, Margaret Ann. "The Paradox of Silence in Modern Canadian Poetry: Creativity or Sterility?" Diss. Dalhousie 1981.

The silence which ended Klein's career is only one aspect of a concern which is central to his writing. As a subject it is reflected in his treatment of voiceless minority groups, the silence of nature and lovers, and the golem. God's silence, whether as a symbol of His ineffable essence or as a reflection of the poet's own despair in the face of apparently meaningless suffering, is also important. Political silence, and the need to speak out against evil, eventually became central issues, especially during the war years. Toward the end of his career Klein became increasingly concerned with the struggle to recreate a new language in response to the chaos of his age. The experimental writing of this period can be viewed as an "esthetic of silence." The imaginative energy and tension involved in this struggle may have contributed to his final collapse into silence.

C254 Lester, Roslyn. "Of Kith and Kin: A Biographical and Critical Study of Cultural Influence on the Prose of A.M. Klein." M.A. Thesis Concordia 1984.

A study of Klein's journalism and short fiction in the context of his Jewish heritage and Montreal background. "Klein's writing projected his ethical idealism as he stressed the necessary unity between artist and society."

C255 Golfman, Noreen. "The Poetry of A.M. Klein." Diss. Western Ontario 1986.

A "full explication of the poetry of A.M. Klein," arguing that "Klein's poetry consistently and masterfully represents the central conflict of modernism: the struggle to find order in a fragmented universe." Golfman gives special attention to Klein's relationship with Jewish culture and history. In addition to the poetry, she discusses Klein's journalism and his unfinished novel, *The Golem*.

C256 Lemm, Richard. "Polished Lens and Improved Binoculars: Moral Vision in the Poetry of A.M. Klein and Irving Layton." Diss. Dalhousie 1986.

A study of moral vision in the poetry of A.M. Klein and Irving Layton. Lemm surveys the work of both poets, examining their "various aesthetic, emotional and intellectual strategies for containing evil and envisioning good." He sees "tensions in [Klein's] moral vision between his longing for unity and his awareness of division, conflict and suffering."

C257 Finkelstein, Mark. "The Style of A.M. Klein." Diss. Toronto 1988.

An eclectic approach to Klein's literary style, "concentrating on major issues and topics, while at the same time trying to stay as close as possible to the actual technical methods of his work." Finkelstein discusses Klein's peculiar relation to language in general, his devotion to linguistic grandeur and his attempt to achieve a synthesis between his Jewish themes and the English language in which he wrote. Finkelstein also examines the evolution of Klein's style, presenting his "modernist (or modernizing) style as a fulfilment of his early archaizing style."

C258 Rozmovits, Linda. "A.M. Klein and Modernism." M.A. Thesis McGill 1988.

Klein's work is dominated by historical imperatives. This study "resituate[s] Klein, his Jewishness, and his modernity," by considering the historical dynamic which informs both his attraction to modernism and his enduring commitment to Jewish traditionalism. Although Klein is attracted to the artistic independence of modernism he is repelled by its authoritarian tendencies, so that even at the height of his modernity it is difficult for him to sustain a modernist position.

Interview

C259 Spurgeon, D.C. "Whither Green Haired Poet?". *Saturday Night*, 23 May 1950, pp. 12, 46.

This is the only interview with Klein. Klein rejects the idea that a poet "must be somewhat cracked," which originated with the French symbolist poets. He claims to be "extremely well adjusted." He mentions T.S. Eliot and W.H. Auden as two major influences on contemporary poetry and refers to his project to annotate James Joyce's *Ulysses*, which he expects to complete in two years.

C260   Rabbi Solomon Spiro Collection
       Sound Archives
       National Archives of Canada
       Ottawa, Ontario

The Rabbi Solomon Spiro Collection contains interviews with Max Garmaise, 26 April 1970 (1 hr., 4 min.); Rabbi Bender, 24 June 1970 (47 min.); and Joseph Frank, 26 June 1970 (1 hr., 2 min.).

C261   David Kaufman Collection
       Sound Archives
       National Archives of Canada
       Ottawa, Ontario

The David Kaufman Collection contains interviews with Irving Layton, April 1973 (54 min.) and Sharon Klein, April 1973 (1 hr.).

C262   The Jewish Public Library Collection
       Sound Archives
       National Archives of Canada
       Ottawa, Ontario

The Jewish Public Library Collection contains speeches by Shulamit Yelin (45 min.) and David Lewis (50 min.) delivered at the A.M. Klein Memorial Evening in the Jewish Public Library Auditorium, 4 Nov. 1973.

C263   University of Ottawa Department of English Collection
       Sound Archives
       National Archives of Canada
       Ottawa, Ontario

The University of Ottawa Department of English Collection contains the proceedings of the A.M. Klein Symposium, University of Ottawa, 4–5 May 1974 (approx. 12 hr.).

C264   Usher Caplan Collection
       Sound Archives
       National Archives of Canada
       Ottawa, Ontario

The Usher Caplan Collection contains an interview with David Rome, 12 Feb. 1975 (1 hr., 25 min.).

C265 Mayne, Seymour. "A.M. Klein: A Portrait of the Poet." *CBC Tuesday Night*. CBC Radio, 6 and 8 Nov. 1973 (AM and FM networks), 1 hr., 40 min.).

This radio documentary on the life and work of A.M. Klein includes readings of his own poetry by Klein, interviews with those who knew him, and commentary by Mayne.

C266 Kaufman, David. *A.M. Klein: The Poet as Landscape*. 1978. (Colour; 58 min.).

This independently produced film is a documentary on Klein with excerpts from his poetry, interviews with those who knew him, and scenes of the areas of Montreal in which he lived.

C267 Marchand, Jacques, and Konyves, Tom. *Les années trente et quarante: A.M. Klein et Louis Dudek*. Les poetes québécois de langue anglaise, cahier no. 2. Radio Canada, 26 nov. 1982.

A discussion of Klein's role in the development of English poetry in Quebec. Louis Dudek comments on Klein's relationship to the Jewish and French communities of Quebec and his lack of relationship to the English community.

C268 Kaufman, David. "A.M. Klein and His Montreal: A Photographic Essay." *Journal of Canadian Studies/Revue d'études canadiennes* [Trent Univ.], [A.M. Klein's Montreal/A.M. Klein à Montréal] 19, No. 2 (Summer 1984), 82–95.

This is a collection of photographs of Klein and the Montreal he knew and celebrated in his poetry.

Awards and Honours

C269 First prize in the Zionist Organization of America contest for the best poem on Yehuda Halevi, for "Yehuda Halevi, His Pilgrimage" (1941).

C270 Edward Bland Prize for "Seven Poems" (1947).

C271 Governor-General's Literary Award for Poetry for *The Rocking Chair and Other Poems* (1949).

C272 National Jewish Book Award in English Poetry (1951).

C273 Lorne Pierce Medal of the Royal Society of Canada for outstanding contribution to Canadian literature (1957).

D Selected Book Reviews

D1 Benedict, Libby. "Hail Poet!" *Menorah Journal*, 28, No. 2 (Summer 1940), 218–20.

Klein writes out of a sense of Jewish history at a time when many Jews are trying to deny their history. He is a Spinozist whose "humility . . . is not humble at all because it merges with the cosmos and is therefore at once the apotheosis of pride." His language is occasionally too complex but, at his best, he is capable of "a clear lyricism in which the Jewishness . . . is but an adumbration enhancing the thought."

D2 Levi, S. Gershon. "Jewish Poet Enriches English Literature." *Canadian Zionist* [Montreal], June 1940, p. 5.

Klein's poetry is "a strikingly successful coming-together of the richness of the English tongue with the depth and color of Jewish tradition and experience." Klein draws on Chaucer, Shakespeare, Byron, Auden, as well as Isaiah, Halevi, Gabirol, Gordon, Bialik. His English has some of "the terse, chiselled quality of Hebrew speech." Levi especially praises the poems written for children.

D3 Wiseman, Shloime. Rev. of *Hath Not a Jew . . . The Canadian Jewish Chronicle* [Montreal], 14 June 1940, pp. 6, 14.

Hath Not a Jew . . . "is one of the most Jewish books of poetry . . . in Hebrew and Yiddish literature within the last decade." Klein is steeped in Jewish lore and tradition, and, unlike many other young Jewish writers, he confidently asserts his Jewishness. He is "an able master of several poetic forms and categories," especially character sketches and children's verse, and will no doubt produce many other important books of poetry.

D4 Bernstein, Edgar. "The Poetry of Jewish Life." *South African Jewish Times* [Johannesburg], 2 Aug. 1940, p. 10.

"Ranging the gamut of Jewish life, . . . [Klein] picks up the subdued note of its soft music, the thunder of its wrath, the grandeur of its pride." His most impressive poems are those, like "Design for Mediaeval Tapestry," in which "the rage of centuries, Bialik's rage, finds its expression." Klein can be playful as well, but in a few of his poems the playfulness degenerates into mere cleverness.

D5 Kennedy, Leo. Rev. of *Hath Not a Jew . . . Canadian Poetry Magazine*, 5, No. 1 (Sept. 1940), 39–40.

Klein "has easily been the most interesting younger Canadian poet since about 1930," and *Hath Not a Jew . . .* "will probably prove to be the major literary event in Canada of 1940. . . . Klein is at all times the Jew and the poet who learned from Shakespeare and Keats."

D6 Benjamin, L.M. Rev. of *Hath Not a Jew . . . Canadian Jewish Year Book*, 2 (1940–41), 160–63.

Klein is the foremost Canadian-Jewish poet writing in English, but his achievement is limited by his nostalgia for the simpler world of the medieval ghetto. He does not confront the complex problems facing modern Jews, and his retreat from the twentieth century is reflected in "his unwillingness to grasp the poetry of simple modern speech, a reversion to what seem archaic forms of speech which, to some, are wholly inadequate in the light of modern demands."

D7 Birney, Earle. "Canadian-Jewish Poet." *The Canadian Forum*, Feb. 1941, pp. 354–55.

Hath Not a Jew . . . "is one of the finest volumes of verse ever written by a Canadian." Praise such as Ludwig Lewisohn's (C19) for the Jewishness of Klein's poetry misses the point; Klein is least impressive when he tries to be most Jewish and falls into obscurantism. The real strength of the book is its "polished and mordant satire, dancing wit, metrical versatility and originality of metaphor . . . ."

D8 Brown, E.K. "Letters in Canada: 1940. Poetry." *University of Toronto Quarterly*, 10 (April 1941), 283, 286–87.

Hath Not a Jew . . . is a work "of great importance and astonishing originality." Klein would have done better to include local, immediate, and secular poems such as "Soirée of Velvel Kleinburger" among those which deal with Jewish life in religious or universal terms. Many of the poems present a "charming, homely, and wholly human picture of Jewish religious life." Others strike a "loftier and even stern note." The erudition of the poems may put some readers off, but it is fully justified.

D9 Edel, Leon. "Poetry and the Jewish Tradition." *Poetry* [Chicago], 58 (April 1941), 51–53. Rpt. in *A.M. Klein*. Ed. T.A. Marshall. Critical Views on Canadian Writers, No. 4. Toronto: Ryerson, 1970, pp. 15–17.

Klein's language is "exciting and exotic," in the Jewish tradition, "but runs the risk of surfeiting the reader." The satirical poems avoid this risk because they are "close to life" and mix "the real and the fantastic." The poems of *Hath Not a Jew . . .*, though vital and important, mark a retreat from reality. The language, for all its strengths, is often quaint and lacking in discipline. The note of "eloquent rebellion" is missing.

D10 Lesser, Allen. Rev. of *Hath Not a Jew . . . Contemporary Jewish Record* [New York], 5 (June 1942), 333.

The poems in *Hath Not a Jew . . .* "attempt to depict East European Jews for the most part and achieve a certain old-world atmosphere almost in spite of the poet . . . [who] shows little sensitiveness to the value of words or their meaning." Lesser objects to Klein's "phony coinings" and "poetic licence" and to his "constant qualification" of Jews as little.

D11   Kissin, I. Rev. of *Hath Not a Jew . . . . Forward* [New York], 28 Feb. 1943, p. 5.

Writing in Yiddish, Kissin observes that Klein has a profound knowledge of all aspects of Jewish culture and draws successfully on English as well as Jewish poetic traditions in dealing with "Jewish history and the hopes and despairs of the Jewish present" (Pollock's translation). Ludwig Lewisohn's Foreword (C19) is quoted at some length.

THE HITLERIAD

D12   Woodhead, W.D. Rev. of *The Hitleriad. The Gazette* [Montreal], 1 Sept. 1944, p. 9.

"Here is a subject which has attracted many a writer, but nothing resembling this poem has appeared, and it should be read and welcomed by all who appreciate wit, power, and sincerity clothed in racy and vigorous verse."

D13   Flint, F. Cudworth. Rev. of *The Hitleriad. The New York Times Book Review*, 3 Sept. 1944, p. 4. Rpt. in *A.M. Klein*. Ed. T.A. Marshall. Critical Views on Canadian Writers, No. 4. Toronto: Ryerson, 1970, p. 22.

The attempt to ridicule Hitler fails because Klein "has not enough ingenuity or verbal dexterity or malice — as distinguished from rage."

D14   Brown, E.K. "Satirical Verse." *Poetry* [Chicago], 65 (Oct. 1944), 54–56.

The Hitleriad exhibits "sharp simplification of emotion, easy mastery of learning, subtle suggestions which offer a special pleasure to the alert reader without putting the simple reader at a loss to the main effect intended." The poem "abounds in vigorous and brilliant passages, and is always lively," but it suffers from the defect of "making a goose of Hitler," with the result that "the subject is robbed of much of its intrinsic import."

D15   Pratt, E.J. Rev. of *The Hitleriad. The Canadian Forum*, Oct. 1944, p. 164. Rpt. in *A.M. Klein*. Ed. T.A. Marshall. Critical Views on Canadian Writers, No. 4. Toronto: Ryerson, 1970, pp. 18–24.

The Hitleriad develops from Klein's recent satiric verse and "extends Klein's range both in material and treatment." The poem is Drydenian in its militant denunciation. While it lacks delicacy and urbanity and is sometimes strident and excessive, ". . . few will deny the drive of the masculine thrust against the foes of humanity."

D16 Layton, Irving. Rev. of *The Hitleriad*. *First Statement*, 2, No. 9 (Oct.–Nov. 1944), 17–20.

The Hitleriad is a technically masterful and eloquent work, "fresh, audacious and exciting." It does not wholly succeed, however, because ". . . satire intends to ridicule the follies of mankind, and not its beastlier perversions" as represented by the Nazis. Klein must humanize the Nazis if he is to satirize them, and this is impossible to do successfully.

D17 Brown, E.K. "Letters in Canada: 1944. Poetry." *University of Toronto Quarterly*, 14 (April 1945), 261.

The mixture of satire and burlesque in *The Hitleriad* is not successful; the two elements do not reinforce each other. The verse gives the impression of haste. The advantages of "spontaneity, intensity, conviction . . . are bought at the high price of more than occasional carelessness."

D18 Sylvestre, Guy. Rev. of *The Hitleriad*. *Revue dominicaine*, 51 (juin 1945), 369–73.

Sylvestre places *The Hitleriad* in the context of the response of English-Canadians to World War II (and the lack of response of French-Canadians). The poem is summarized and quoted from at some length. Despite some weaknesses, it is an interesting work with some fine passages. It is original and personal, ". . . une nouvelle réussite d'un grand poète."

POEMS

D19 Teller, I.L. "A Book of Pure Jewish Poems Written in English" [Pollock's trans.]. *Der Morgen Zhurnal* [New York], 6 Feb. 1945, p. 7.

Writing in Yiddish, Teller assesses *Poems* and the work leading up to it in light of the Jewish poetic tradition. This tradition has two sources, the Yiddish folk-song and the ancient Hebrew poetry of the Bible. *Hath Not a Jew . . .* draws largely on the folk-song tradition, but Klein, who is essentially serious-minded, lacks the humour and wit to succeed fully in this mode. In *The Hitleriad*, Klein "continues his struggle to create a Jewish style which reaches its fulfilment in the psalms of *Poems*. These poems achieve a synthesis of folk-song, traditional liturgy, and modern poetic form. The explicitly satirical parts of *Poems* are less impressive. Klein "may not be a great poet, but he manages to unite the 'otherness' of his own culture with the English poetic tradition" (Pollock's translation).

D20 Lewisohn, Ludwig. "The Jew as Poet." *The Canadian Jewish Chronicle* [Montreal], 2 March 1945, p. 6. Rpt. in *Jewish Book Annual*, 4 (1945–46), p. 99. Rpt. in *The New Palestine News Reporter*, 16 Feb. 1948, pp. 122–23.

Klein neither denies his Jewishness nor insists upon it in a rhetorical or ironic manner; he writes "out of his self which was and is, of course, a Jewish self." His best work to date is the sequence, "The Psalter of Avram Haktani" in *Poems*. In the poems of this sequence, Klein "stands at the very centre of his Jewishness and, therefore, at the centre of his *kind* of humanity and so of *all* humanity and is, by rigid consequence, one of the few living poets of *any* kind who can write of beautiful deep human things according to their proper sanctity and vestiture."

D21 Kreymborg, Alfred. "The Shadow of Mars." *Saturday Review of Literature* [New York], 24 March 1945, p. 35.

"This dynamic tour de force lapses at times into careless workmanship or facile expression but is on the whole robust, affecting, and effective."

D22 Brown, E.K. "Letters in Canada: 1944. Poetry." *University of Toronto Quarterly*, 14 (April 1945), 261–62.

Klein's work in *Poems*, especially in the psalms, is "more careful than it has ever been." The psalms form the most successful section of the book. They are "remarkably varied both in topic and feeling, and . . . [Klein] has usually found appropriate forms." Most of the psalms strike a new note of "sobriety and tranquillity." The other poems are more in the manner of *Hath Not a Jew . . .* The least successful of these is "Yehuda Ha-Levi, His Pilgrimage," which lacks "finish and aptness" of details.

D23 Layton, Irving. Rev. of *Poems. First Statement*, 2, No. 12 (April–May 1945), 35–36. Rpt. in *A.M. Klein*. Ed. T.A. Marshall. Critical Views on Canadian Writers, No. 4. Toronto: Ryerson, 1970, pp. 23–25.

The thirty-six psalms of *Poems* continue Klein's "passionate debate with the Deity" first begun in *Hath Not a Jew . . .* Although they are limited by Klein's lack of a sense of evil, and are occasionally "noisy and unconvincing," at their best they have "gusto, warmth, eloquence and imagination."

D24 Nims, J.F. "Tares and Wheat." *Poetry* [Chicago], 66 (May 1945), 104–05.

Poems is an uneven volume and only Part 1, "The Psalter of Avram Haktani," contains poetry of value. For the most part, the psalms are "spontaneous and free from special pleading." They express a wide range of emotion, and the "materials are generally deployed with force and ingenuity." The rest of the volume suffers from excessive rhetoric.

D25 Glatstein, Jacob. "The English-Jewish Poet A.M. Klein" [Pollock's trans.]. *Yiddisher Kemfer* [New York], 4 May 1945, pp. 15–17. Rpt. trans. in Hebrew in *Davar* [Tel Aviv], 13 July 1945, p. 2, and in English in Rome (C45), p. 6.

Writing in Yiddish, Glatstein praises *Poems* and Klein's work as a whole. He surveys the contemporary Jewish writers who have either abandoned their Jewish background or treat it satirically and sees in Klein a new voice and the beginning of a new culture that will synthesize English and Jewish culture. In the psalms of *Poems*, Klein shows profound knowledge of Yiddish and Hebrew classics as well as the work of contemporary English poets, particularly T.S. Eliot and W.H. Auden.

D26 Levy, Amelia. "The Roots of Tradition: The Poetry of A.M. Klein." *Jewish Affairs*, July 1945, p. 9.

In *Poems*, Klein has found himself after the failure of *The Hitleriad*. The poems are unselfconscious and avoid preachiness and sloganeering.

D27 Frank, M. Tz. Rev. of *Poems*. *Forward* [New York], 2 Sept. 1945, p. 4.

In this review, which is written in Yiddish, Frank notes that "The Psalter of Avram Haktani" is Klein's best work to date. In his psalms, the characteristic richness of his style is mature and disciplined. "Klein's work is a ray of light and love in the thick darkness of our American Jews' ignorance of and indifference to the treasures of Jewish culture" (Pollock's translation).

D28 Goldstick, Isidore. Rev. of *Poems*. *Canadian Zionist* [Montreal], 14 Sept. 1945, p. 7.

In his highly laudatory review of *Poems*, Goldstick says the work "is wrought of pure and beautiful thoughts and words, set with many an epigram of gemmy lustre." Goldstick praises "The Psalter of Avram Haktani" in particular, which he sees as "reverentially pious in tone."

D29 Jarrell, Randall. "These Are Not Psalms." *Commentary*, Nov. 1945, pp. 88–90.

Poems is "academic, semi-religious verse," which fails in what it sets out to do. Klein is "a pleasant, 'well-adjusted,' civilized man, as unconsciously secular as he is consciously religious." He is, therefore, incapable of rising to his subject — Hitler's destruction of the Jews — which is "not only uncongenial to but completely beyond the scope of his gentle talents." For "the particular reality of the language of a successful poem," Klein substitutes a trivializing "stagey" rhetoric.

D30 Goldstick, Isidore. "Demurrer to Jarrell." *Commentary*, Jan. 1946, pp. 88–89.

Goldstick disagrees with Randall Jarrell's review of *Poems* (D29) and questions Jarrell's understanding of the Jewish traditions that inform Klein's psalms. Goldstick cites a number of passages to support his claim that the psalms "stand out . . . as Canada's sublimest poetic expression."

POEMS OF FRENCH CANADA and SEVEN POEMS

D31 Poirier, Jean-Marie. "Poète juif parmi nous." *La presse* [Montreal], 21 nov. 1947, p. 33. Rpt. in *Huit poèmes canadiens (en englais)*, pp. 5–7.

Klein is one of the very few writers, English or French, who have been able to understand the people of Quebec and record essential aspects of the Quebec mentality. His Jewish, English, and French backgrounds "offrent une matière extrêmement riche à l'inspiration, tour à tour émue, fantaisiste, puissante, voire épique." "Grain Elevator," "The Cripples," "For the Sisters of the Hôtel Dieu," and "The Break-up" are singled out for special praise.

D32 Rev. of *Poems of French Canada. Les carnets viatoriens*, 13 (jan. 1948), 62–63.

"Son accent sobre et ému, tendre et pourtant viril, intéressé humblement à tout l'objet de la vision circonvoisine, son sens de l'aspect poétique et du mot qui l'exprime, tout cela touche l'âme et réjouit l'esprit." "Grain Elevator" and "For the Sisters of the Hôtel Dieu" are praised.

D33 Shaw, J.G. Rev. of *Seven Poems. The Canadian Register* [Toronto], 27 March 1948, p. 4.

Klein's poems show genuine spiritual sensitivity. He has penetrated into the soul of Quebec. The poetry occasionally suffers from unassimilated influences, but, on the whole, Klein has made excellent use of his models, especially Walt Whitman and Gerard Manley Hopkins.

D34 Brown, E.K. "Letters in Canada: 1947. Poetry." *University of Toronto Quarterly*, 17 (April 1948), 262–63.

"*Seven Poems* is outstanding." The poems "touch on aspects of the national life in extraordinarily illuminating fashion, and in a language which if less rich in texture than Mr. Klein once employed is firm and imaginative."

D35 Regimbal, A. "Artistes israélites au Canada français." *Relations*, 8 (juin 1948), 184–85.

Klein's Jewish background has not prevented him from being deeply sympathetic to the French-Canadian milieu. He possesses ". . . une âme qui vibre à l'unisson de la nôtre, soit devant la piété émouvante des pélerins de l'Oratoire, la pédanterie choquante des M. Bertrand, ou la coquetterie des villages laurentiens."

HUIT POÈMES CANADIENS (en anglais)

D36 Dufresne, Henri. "Un poète juif au pays de Québec." *La patrie* [Montréal], 16 jan. 1949, p. 62.

"Réalisme et coloris, joints à une très vive sensibilité, donne à cette poésie un charme pénétrant." Klein is modern in style, but not excessively so. Sometimes he recalls Victor Hugo, sometimes Baudelaire, but he is difficult to classify: "Il est à la fois primitif, romantique, impressioniste, naturaliste, moderniste et vous pouvez en ajouter." "For the Sisters of the Hôtel Dieu" is praised for its "naïveté charmante" and its "légerté." "Parade of St. Jean Baptiste" is "un essai amusant de *langage bilingue*." Klein shows an astonishing virtuosity in vocabulary and imagery.

THE ROCKING CHAIR AND OTHER POEMS

D37 Rome, David. Rev. of *The Rocking Chair and Other Poems. Congress Bulletin* [Montreal], 7 Sept. 1948, p. 10.

The Rocking Chair, in its sympathetic portrayal of French Canada, demonstrates that Klein's deep roots in Jewish tradition have not had an isolating effect on him. Klein's art has reached a new height and, if his writing is occasionally open to the charge of artificiality and preciosity, these elements arise from genuine learning and breadth of culture. "Portrait of the Poet as Landscape" is one of the less successful poems in the volume. It suffers from "a certain coldness and impersonality" and is not a true portrait of Klein.

D38 Avison, Margaret. Rev. of *The Rocking Chair and Other Poems. The Canadian Forum*, Nov. 1948, p. 191. Rpt. in *A.M. Klein.* Ed. T.A. Marshall. Critical Views on Canadian Writers, No. 4. Toronto: Ryerson, 1970, pp. 55–58.

Klein's writing in *The Rocking Chair* is characterized by "precision"; his purpose is to "discipline speech into clarity." Klein's tone is "dispassionate and forceful," and he speaks of himself as "simply and accurately" as he does of any other part of experience. The best poems of the collection translate their Canadian context through metaphor into something universal.

D39 MacKay, L.A. "Klein's Latest Verse Collection an Event in Canadian Literature." *Saturday Night*, 6 Nov. 1948, p. 17.

The Rocking Chair displays "a mature understanding of present strains and traditional influences" in French Canada. Klein is more outward-looking than he has been in his earlier poetry, displaying "a faculty of observation at once intimate and objective." The lyric and satiric strains are more assured than ever. "Portrait of the Poet as Landscape" "combines balance of judgement with resolute intensity of conviction."

D40 Humphries, Rolphe. Rev. of *The Rocking Chair and Other Poems. The Nation* [New York], 13 Nov. 1948, pp. 556–57.

"Mr. Klein has grown tremendously, out of a rather heavy, rather self-conscious, rather morbid and wilfully alien idiom into full stature." Klein "can give even our Mr. Auden a lesson or two" in the unobtrusive mastery of technique. "Les Filles Majeures" puts him in Rilke's company, "The Green Old Age" in

Baudelaire's. Many poems are praised, especially "Portrait of the Poet as Landscape."

D41 Bruce, Charles. Rev. of *The Rocking Chair and Other Poems. Canadian Poetry Magazine*, 12, No. 2 (Dec. 1948), 32–33.

Klein is best when dealing in concrete terms with what he knows. When he turns to philosophical abstraction, he is less impressive. His poetry is of high quality, but "somehow puzzles and disturbs, while it seldom stirs." Like most modern poetry, it lacks warmth.

D42 Hamel, Charles. "Images du Canada français." *Le Canada*, 24 Dec. 1948, p. 7.

In *The Rocking Chair* there is "une vive comprehension, une connaissance du Canada français qui vient davantage encore du coeur que de l'esprit." Klein does not limit himself to vignettes of traditional Quebec, but also writes about the contemporary scene. "For the Sisters of the Hôtel Dieu" is quoted and praised.

D43 Sergeant, Howard. Rev. of *The Rocking Chair and Other Poems. Poetry Commonwealth* [London], 4 (Spring 1949), 15–16.

Klein is "original in thought" and "adventurous in imagination," but lacks a "sense of discrimination" and "mature craftsmanship." The satirical tone of many of the poems shows the influence of T.S. Eliot, but its effect is undercut by Klein's boisterousness. Klein has "remarkable powers of association and . . . felicity for selecting the commonplace, yet eminently suitable, objects as his symbols."

D44 Brown, E.K. "Letters in Canada: 1948. Poetry." *University of Toronto Quarterly*, 18 (April 1949), 255–57.

Klein's ability to enter into the spirit of French Canada "is an important political fact." Apart from its political importance, *The Rocking Chair* is a work of "poetic force and beauty . . . . In the best poems there is a bold, full utterance and a fine profusion of imagery, depending on a buoyancy and force of temperament very rare . . . in the poetry of this age, wherever written." The only false note is the occasional "irony and self-distrust," which seems to be a reflection of current fashion, rather than an expression of Klein's true nature.

D45 Duhamel, Roger. Rev. of *The Rocking Chair and Other Poems. L'Action universitaire* [Univ. de Montréal], 15 (avril 1949), 82–83.

Duhamel praises Klein's "don de sympathie, visible dans chacun de ses poèmes" and his "tendance à l'observation à la fois ironique et amusée qui lui permet la reconstitution de tableautins charmants, ou le trait frôle parfois la caricature, sans jamais aucune trace d'aigreur ou de moquerie." The best poems in the collection are the shorter ones, in which Klein seems to be inspired by his immediate experience of particular people and objects. His talent is "beaucoup plus descriptif que créateur." The best poem in the collection is "Les Filles

Majeures." Klein occupies "un rang enviable dans la cohorte des poètes mineurs et intimistes."

D46 Anderson, Violet. "Page and Pattern." *Food for Thought*, May 1949, pp. 43–44.

"Mr. Klein appeals most when he deals with the manifold sensations of things and the inside feel of them." Klein's real achievement is in the use of metaphor, especially in "Grain Elevator," "Les Filles Majeures," and "For the Sisters of the Hôtel Dieu."

D47 Crawley, Alan. "Notes after Reading *The Rocking Chair*." *Contemporary Verse*, No. 28 (Summer 1949), pp. 20–23.

Klein is a romantic and a regional poet. The source of his poetry is "in the child's security in that surpassing love and in the warm intimacy of family affection" as described in the poem "Autobiographical." *The Rocking Chair* as a whole can be seen as an enlargement and expansion of this vision.

D48 Sutherland, John. "Canadian Comment." *Northern Review*, 2, No. 6 (Aug.–Sept. 1949), 30–34. Rpt. in *A.M. Klein*. Ed. T.A. Marshall. Critical Views on Canadian Writers, No. 4. Toronto: Ryerson, 1970, pp. 59–65. Rpt. ("A.M. Klein: The Laughter of Seriousness") in *Essays, Controversies and Poems*. By John Sutherland. Ed. and introd. Miriam Waddington. New Canadian Library, No. 81. Toronto: McClelland and Stewart, 1972, pp. 139–44.

The Rocking Chair is Klein's best book, characterized by "subtle analysis" and "contemporary technique." The two greatest influences on his poetry, W.H. Auden and Dylan Thomas, are successfully absorbed, helping Klein to bring together the intellectual and sensuous aspects of his work. In the works of Klein's first period, represented by *Hath Not a Jew . . .* and *Poems*, sensuousness dominated in the form of a lyrical irony which tended towards sentimentality. In the works of the second period, represented by *The Hitleriad* and poems like "Pawnshop," intellectuality dominated in the form of satire which showed a greater social consciousness, but which was often "dull and directionless." *The Rocking Chair* brings these strands together in a "more intense lyricism fortified by sophistication and tough logic." Klein "is writing out of a tradition and defending himself against it." He is not fully aware of this tension, but it is the source of his poetry's vitality.

D49 Poster, William. Rev. of *The Rocking Chair and Other Poems*, by A.M. Klein; *Mr. Whittier and Other Poems*, by Stanfield Townley Scott. *Poetry* [Chicago], 75 (Nov. 1949), 105–06.

Klein's poetry has matured since *The Hitleriad*. However, he has still not completely found his voice and betrays the influence of poets like Karl Shapiro, often to the detriment of his own "very substantial gifts, his fertility, fluency, powers of observation, and unforced human sympathy." The best poems in the volume "have a cheerful acceptance of life and humanity" and promise finer things to come.

D50 Weiss, Neil. Rev. of *The Rocking Chair and Other Poems. Commentary*, Dec. 1949, pp. 610–11.

Klein's best poems are "'observations' . . . and proceed from a blend of modernism and regionalism." Klein's regional roots save him from the "dead-end" of subjectivity and alienation. Weiss sees parallels in the poems with the Joycean epiphany, singling out "Lone Bather" as a particularly good example.

THE SECOND SCROLL

D51 Edel, Leon. "Beautiful Tale of a 20th Century Wandering Jew." *Compass* [Kutztown State College, Kutztown, Pa.], 23 Sept. 1951, p. 29. Rpt. in *The Canadian Jewish Chronicle* [Montreal], 5 Oct. 1951, p. 4.

The Second Scroll is written "in an extraordinarily rich and fanciful prose . . . yet ever lucid and swift-moving." The book encompasses a wide range of feeling and has "a sardonic humor and sense of irony that makes for a kind of bubbling laughter as a cloak of tragedy." Klein is a "born story-teller, a supreme verbal artist."

D52 Kerwin, Roy. Rev. of *The Second Scroll. The Gazette* [Montreal], 29 Sept. 1951, p. 28.

"Mr. Klein would do his people and all Canadians more good if he wrote more as a Canadian and less as a Zionist . . . . [His] talent is of world-wide value, but he aims at such a narrow field."

D53 Scott, James. "The Eternal Search for the Promised Land." *The Telegram* [Toronto], 6 Oct. 1951, p. 30.

The Second Scroll is an impressive poetic achievement, but it is flawed as a novel. Klein's eloquence appeals to the ear, rather than "to the intelligence and understanding . . . through the eye." The example of James Joyce has misled Klein. The book is "a magnificent statement of profound belief," but "as a piece of writing . . . it has widely missed the mark."

D54 Sandwell, B.K. "About Eternal Murder." *Saturday Night*, 13 Oct. 1951, p. 27.

The Second Scroll is a richly rewarding experience. It is "wrought with the scrupulous care of high art, and employed for a purpose nobler . . . than any other tale that resembles it in English literature, although Blake and Joyce come to mind. The evil of Nazism has never been better characterized.

D55 Davies, Robertson. "Bibliomania." Rev. of *The Second Scroll*, by A.M. Klein; and *The Blessing*, by Nancy Mitford. *Peterborough Examiner*, 20 Oct. 1951, p. 4.

The Second Scroll is "probably the most remarkable novel ever to be written in Canada . . . because of the richness of the prose which clothes it." The novel is "an exposition of the inveterate and ingrained nature of Judaism and of the role of the Jew as the Suffering Servant and scapegoat of mankind." Klein handles his theme "nobly and eloquently," and, although the novel presents some difficulties for non-Jewish readers, it is "by no means beyond the comprehension of any reader who is attentive."

D56 Deacon, William Arthur. "One Mercurial Jew Reveals Complexity of Race's Fate." *The Globe and Mail* [Toronto], 27 Oct. 1951, p. 14.

"Original in all respects, profoundly important and certainly a work of genius, A.M. Klein's first novel is a bold attempt at appraisal, within the narrow framework of an extended fable, of the essence of the Jewish racial soul." *The Second Scroll* is not really a novel. It "falls into no known category. It is a *Pilgrim's Progress* in miniature." It is the most important Jewish contribution to Canadian literature.

D57 Samuel, Maurice. "The Book of the Miracle." *Jewish Frontier* [New York], Nov. 1951, pp. 11–15. Rpt. in *The Canadian Jewish Chronicle* [Montreal], 14 Dec. 1951, pp. 10–11, 15. Rpt. in *A.M. Klein*. Ed. T.A. Marshall. Critical Views on Canadian Writers, No. 4. Toronto: Ryerson, 1970, pp. 79–88.

Apart from its great intrinsic merit as a work of literature, *The Second Scroll* has a "non-literary importance" for Jews. Klein is the first writer to have found "commensurate utterance" for the Jewish experience of the Holocaust and of the establishment of the State of Israel. His language is "Judaeo-English," drawing fully on the resources of Jewish culture and the English language, and marks the beginning of the process through which ". . . the literary idiom of . . . Jewish culture in the West is yet to be created."

D58 Ravitch, Melech. "A New Genre in Jewish Literature?" [Pollock's trans.]. *Keneder Adler* [Montreal], 2 Nov. 1951, pp. 4, 6.

Writing in Yiddish, Ravitch comments that Klein is one of the "almost born in America" who serve as a kind of bridge between Jews of the Old World and the New. In *The Second Scroll*, he has created a rich work deserving of long and careful study. Uncle Melech is a complex character representing the sum of Jewish experience. The book is "kaleidoscopic" in its effect and may point to a new genre in Jewish literature written in a kind of "super English" drawing on Hebrew and Yiddish as well as other languages. (Pollock's translation.)

D59 Swados, Harvey. "A Work of Splendor." *The Nation* [New York], 3 Nov. 1951, pp. 379–80.

The Second Scroll is "the most profoundly creative summation of the Jewish condition by a Jewish man of letters since the European catastrophe." Swados singles out "Gloss Gimmel" for special praise: "Intricate, beautiful, and passionate, it is surely one of the greatest pieces of 'art appreciation' of our time — and it is much more than that."

D60 Sylvester, Harry. "Pathway to Israel." *The New York Times Book Review*, 25 Nov. 1951, p. 58.

The Second Scroll contains "some good verse, some moving and unsentimental prayers." It is, however, "an unsatisfying non-novel."

D61 Segal, J.I. "A.M. Klein's *The Second Scroll*" [Pollock's trans.]. *Keneder Adler* [Montreal], 26 Nov. 1951, pp. 5–6.

Writing in Yiddish, Segal views *The Second Scroll* as an attempt to bridge the gap between the experiences of Jews in the Old World and the New, and Uncle Melech's story illustrates this process against the background of the most testing period in Jewish history. Through Klein, Jewish culture and values will be passed on to the younger generation.

D62 Mandelbaum, Allen. "Everyman on Babylon's Shore." *Commentary*, Dec. 1951, pp. 602–04. Rpt. (abridged) in *A.M. Klein*. Ed. T.A. Marshall. Critical Views on Canadian Writers, No. 4. Toronto: Ryerson, 1970, pp. 75–78.

"No other Jewish writer in English has attempted to give symbolic — as against episodic — form to so much Jewish experience. And where Klein fails, his failures are themselves significant, for in casting up before us experimental images of the Jew, Klein — even in nostalgia, fuzziness, or inadequacy of insight — is everyman on Babylon's shore." Mandelbaum discusses the influence of James Joyce's *Ulysses*, especially the "Cyclops" and "Sirens" episodes, but points out that Klein lacks Joyce's "remorselessness." The book is "deficient in drama" because the narrator "is, essentially, always at one with his Fathers." The book would have been improved by "less celebration, more dramatic precision and self-examination," but it remains "a uniquely rich document in the library of Jewish literature in English, one of the few works in this tradition that belong also to modern literature."

D63 Slonim, Reuben. Rev. of *The Second Scroll*. *Canadian Zionist* [Montreal], Dec. 1951, p. 8.

The Second Scroll is not a novel, since it lacks "psychological analysis," but a poem in which the poet reveals himself, allowing the reader to share in his experience. Klein is "a fine artist who has achieved harmony and wholeness in his life as a Jew and human being"; he shows that his Jewishness is "not a problem but a privilege." The most valuable parts of the book are the glosses, especially "Gloss Gimel" and "Gloss Hai," which is one of the few valuable modern contributions to Jewish liturgy.

D64 Sugrue, Thomas. "A Modern Search for Faith." *New York Herald Tribune*, 2 Dec. 1951, p. 42.

The Second Scroll is based on a "sound" concept. Klein has "the intellectual and stylistic talents necessary for its proper development, but he seems to have tired of it too soon." Uncle Melech is killed off "just as the reader is about to meet him and share in his experiences and thinking," and this prevents the book from "grow[ing] into something of stature and meaning."

D65 Bonenfant, Jean-Charles. "La seconde Thora." *La revue de l'Université de Laval*, 6 (jan. 1952), 403–05.

A.M. Klein is one of the most remarkable figures in Canadian intellectual life. In *The Second Scroll*, he emulates James Joyce, and his book bears comparison with Joyce in its inspiration and verbal beauty, which even those without a Jewish background can appreciate.

D66 Ross, Malcolm. Rev. of *The Second Scroll*. *The Canadian Forum*, Jan. 1952, p. 234. Rpt. in *A.M. Klein*. Ed. T.A. Marshall. Critical Views on Canadian Writers, No. 4. Toronto: Ryerson, 1970, pp. 89–91.

Ross places *The Second Scroll* in the "inescapably cosmopolitan" Canadian tradition that reflects "a uniquely structured people with multi-dimensional cultural possibilities." *The Second Scroll* both exemplifies and extends this tradition. "The method is that of analogy and is therefore of a piece with the patterning of diverse and seemingly discontinuous facts of experience characteristic of Klein's best poetry." The book is sometimes "overcompressed," and "purple passages" sometimes clash with more "cerebral" ones. But it is a "compelling," "adult" book and a major contribution to the "fruitful collision and interpretation of many inheritances," which is the Canadian pattern.

D67 Stern, Harry. "Far More Than I Have Read Is in That Scroll." *Canadian Jewish Chronicle* [Montreal], 25 Jan. 1952, p. 12.

The Second Scroll "is the most impressive piece of writing that has come to us since the creation of the State of Israel, and it is the only work that has come to match in literary skill and symbolism this greatest event of modern times in the life of Jewry."

D68 Rome, David. "Our Generation Is Hero of Klein's Novel." *Congress Bulletin* [Montreal], Feb. 1952, pp. 17–18.

The Second Scroll "is among the premier classics of the literature of Canadian Jewry." The journey Klein describes is essentially an internal one "evok[ing] from him various aspects of himself, his relationships to the different segments of his Jewish psyche." Klein is not a preacher or an original thinker; "He articulates and elevates the silent thoughts of the inarticulate Jew."

D69   Bissell, Claude T. "Letters in Canada: 1951. Fiction." *University of Toronto Quarterly*, 21 (Apr. 1952), 264–65.

The Second Scroll is not a typical novel: Klein "prefers the compression of rhetoric and poetry to the discursiveness of fiction." But its "narrative outline is clear and firm," and "it will commend itself to readers as a rare and skilfully fashioned work of art."

THE COLLECTED POEMS OF A.M. KLEIN

D70   Geddes, Gary. Rev. of *The Collected Poems of A.M. Klein*. *The Globe and Mail* [Toronto], 3 Aug. 1974, p. 29.

Geddes describes the A.M. Klein Symposium in Ottawa and discusses the relationship between Klein's art and life and the kinds of tensions that may have contributed to his breakdown. Klein shows great range, and his failings "are those of excess rather than poverty of genius."

D71   Warkentin, Germaine. Rev. of *The Collected Poems of A.M. Klein*. *Quill & Quire*, Oct. 1974, p. 24.

Next to E.J. Pratt, Klein is English Canada's best poet. Miriam Waddington's collection, though admirable, does not add much to our sense of Klein, since the poetry he chose to publish in book form was his best.

D72   Lewis, David. "Oscillations of Integrity." *Books in Canada*, Nov. 1974, p. 20.

Klein's is a poetry of contradictions; its oscillations between "conviction and doubt, between hope and despair" are signs of his thoughtfulness and sensitivity. Klein's breakdown, foreshadowed in his poetry, has its source in the persecution and destruction of the Jews by the Nazis. But as the "social poetry of the 1930s" and *The Rocking Chair* show, his poetry "reaches far beyond his feelings of personal tragedy." *The Collected Poems of A.M. Klein* makes it possible to see Klein's development more clearly.

D73   Watt, F.W. "Fruits of Stifled Genius." *The Canadian Forum*, Nov.–Dec. 1974, p. 18.

The Collected Poems of A.M. Klein does not change our sense of Klein. The previously uncollected poems are lesser, though interesting work, and no unpublished poems are included. There is probably nothing in the unpublished work to explain the stifling of Klein's genius. He was never a confessional poet, and his inability to deal "poetically with the depths of his own inwardness" places him "on the other side of a great divide" from present-day writers who are searching for forms to "hold together private and public realities." There "seems to be a blank, a silence" in the heart of Klein's poetry.

D74 Marshall, T.A. "Klein's Poet Surfacing." *Canadian Literature*, No. 63 (Winter 1975), pp. 81–85.

The Collected Poems of A.M. Klein suffers from not including Klein's unpublished poems and from the misleading order in which some of the poems are printed. However, it is an "important publication" and makes available "one of the most ambitious and fascinating testimonies of creative achievement that we have had." Marshall surveys Klein's career, characterizing his work as Canadian "insofar as it proposes an ultimate unity while retaining respect for the individual categories, cultures, boundaries and creatures that make up the whole."

D75 Steinberg, M.W. Rev. of *The Collected Poems of A.M. Klein*. *Queen's Quarterly*, 82 (Winter 1975), 648–49.

The Collected Poems of A.M. Klein performs a valuable task in making previously uncollected poems available and providing a better context for Klein's published collections. However, the edition is seriously flawed. The ordering of the poems by publication date of the separate volumes is often misleading. The titling and indexing of poems in sequences are inconsistent. There are many typographical errors, some reproduced from bad texts, others introduced by the editor. The editor has chosen not to publish unpublished poems and has not taken into account variants of published poems.

D76 Dudek, Louis. Rev. of *The Collected Poems of A.M. Klein*. *Canadian Review*, 2 (Jan.–Feb. 1975), 26–27.

Miriam Waddington's edition is seriously flawed, particularly in its arrangement, which is basically chronological, but inconsistent for no apparent reason. Klein, as is clear from the collection, is much overrated. His writing is often bombastic, barbaric, crude, and nonsensical and he is torn by "a profound unresolved conflict" between a reality which repels him and "the unreality of the Judaic historical fantasies and religious invocations."

D77 Edel, Leon. "Mirrorings of A.M. Klein." *The Tamarack Review*, No. 66 (June 1975), pp. 94–98.

The Collected Poems of A.M. Klein shows for the first time the shape of Klein's career; in addition, it "makes clear for us Klein's gifts — but also his limitations." Although Klein was, from the first, gifted with "a great verbal exuberance, a skilful inventiveness and a cunning ear for the styles of other poets, . . . he lacked the supreme self-discipline of poetry." His late work shows "a capacity for renewal and enlargement," but it also suggests "deep anguish and a spiritual crisis." Klein's final collapse seems to have been linked to "a faltering of self-esteem."

D78 Kabakoff, Jacob. Rev. of *The Collected Poems of A.M. Klein*. *Judaism* [New York], 25 (Winter 1976), 115–20.

Kabakoff's survey of Klein's work emphasizes its Jewish aspects. Kabakoff comments on Klein's interest in Yiddish and Hebrew poetry, especially the poetry of Chaim Nachman Bialik. Klein's "quarter of a century of creative accomplishment will stand out as a high point of Jewish-American writing in our century."

D79 Rosenthal, Helene. "Of Frolicks, Jousts, and Wailing Walls." *West Coast Review* [Simon Fraser Univ., Burnaby, B.C.], 11, No. 2 (Oct. 1976), 34–36.

Klein's "poetic pilgrimage [is] childhood-regressive advancing to objective-perceptive." His earlier poetry, despite its passion and virtuosity, is marred by "simplistic" thought. Klein, "the breast-beater, vengeful in his lamentations," is an unattractive figure. His radical poems are less concerned with "the workers of the world, the common poor," than with a "desire to recapture the family closeness of the Jewish quarter existing in an alien midst." It is only in *The Rocking Chair* that Klein is able to "perceive that he lives among neighbours" who possess "a humanity analogous to his own."

D80 Still, Robert Ernest. Rev. of *The Collected Poems of A.M. Klein. Canadian Poetry: Studies, Documents, Reviews*, No. 1 (Fall–Winter 1977), pp. 91–92.

Klein is a subjective poet who eventually, in *The Rocking Chair*, discovers a "oneness among all men in his society." He "exalts mankind and the creative energy at work within him." Miriam Waddington's edition is marred by typographical errors and inconsistencies and "does not do justice to the achievement of Klein as a poet of stature."

BEYOND SAMBATION: SELECTED ESSAYS AND EDITORIALS, 1928–1955

D81 Morley, Patricia. "Late Montreal Poet's Fine Essays Excellently Presented by Co-Editors." *The Citizen* [Ottawa], 14 Aug. 1982, p. 34.

Beyond Sambation shows that Klein was "a major writer of prose" as well as verse. He believed that the journalist "was to be not merely the eyes and ears of the world but also the sensitive conscience. This role he fulfilled brilliantly."

D82 Russell, Judith. "Rage Impervious to Time." *The Whig-Standard* [Kingston], 28 Aug. 1982, p. 21.

In his editorials, Klein "rages as no one has raged in Canada since." He has a "gift for the vivid, the startling, the unexpectedly beautiful twist of word or phrase." *Beyond Sambation* is of more than academic interest: it is "as much an ethical history of Canada as it is the plea of one man for world humanitarianism."

D83 Dorland, Michael. "Downhill from *The Second Scroll*." *Herald Weekend* [*The Calgary Herald*], 11 Sept. 1982, p. 15.

Beyond Sambation exposes the reader "to the beneficial effects of a man who represents the very best of centre-left classical humanism." However, his vision is now out of date, and the material collected in this book is of little value in itself, "the detritus of the daily life of the working writer."

D84 Livesay, Dorothy. "A.M. Klein: Politics Distilled in Poetry." *The Vancouver Sun*, 17 Sept. 1982, p. L27.

° "*Beyond Sambation* is a valuable document, not only for historians, Jewish scholars and sociologists, but also for Canadian writers and literary critics." It reflects Klein's "humanity, his wit, his utter commitment to the joy and pain of living; and . . . his loyalty to Canada."

D85 Sherman, Kenneth. "Burnt Angel." Rev. of *Like One That Dreamed: A Portrait of A.M. Klein*, by Usher Caplan; and *Beyond Sambation: Selected Essays and Editorials, 1928–1955*, ed. M.W. Steinberg and Usher Caplan. *Waves*, 11, No. 1 (Fall 1982), 83–87.

Unlike most modern poets, Klein tried to see himself as integral to his community, not peripheral to it. This caused a tension in him between the creative individual and the public spokesman, a tension reflected in the public voice of his editorials for the *The Canadian Jewish Chronicle*. On the whole, they are forced and inauthentic; language is used as "an avoidance tactic," and the results are "far below what one expects from a creative writer of Klein's talent."

D86 Finkelstein, Mark. "Preaching to the Converted." *The Canadian Forum*, Nov. 1982, p. 33.

In *Beyond Sambation*, we see Klein as spokesman for the Montreal and Canadian Jewish community. The volume illustrates Klein's "savage Yiddish sarcasm" and "strange forensic majesty." It is also a sourcebook for students of Klein's thought and style. However, it is sometimes boring, suffering from the effects of "the cultural isolation in which Klein, the editor, worked."

D87 Mathews, Robin. "Songs of Zion." *Books in Canada*, Dec. 1982, pp. 21–22.

Klein's journalism, like his poetry, reflects "a continual tension between the moral basis of his demands upon the world and the actual behaviour he saw on the smallest and largest stages of action." The tension Klein felt as a "tragically idealistic artist and man of ideas" provided the source of "rich dynamism . . . insight and cutting irony." Sometimes, however, Klein seems "naïve, uncomprehending, and even petulant."

D88 Melançon, Robert. "Abraham Moses Klein, Poète." *Liberté* [Montréal], 25, No. 2 [No. 146] (April 1983), 86–90.

Klein was probably the greatest Canadian poet. He was a complex figure whose work was addressed to a number of different publics, none of which could fully appreciate it. His final silence may have resulted from this fragmentation, which is reflected in his journalism. In *Beyond Sambation* ". . . on ne trouve pas . . . une penseé abstraite ni l'exposé de quelque système philosophique mais la vie intérieure d'un homme d'une grande noblesse, sensible et intelligent, qui reçoit comme des affronts personnels, des blessures intimes, la cruauté de l'histoire, la stupidité des hommes, le grouillement nauséeux des préjugés."

D89 Watt, F.W. "Uneasy in Zion: Klein as Journalist." *Canadian Poetry: Studies, Documents, Reviews*, No. 12 (Spring–Summer 1983), pp. 87–90.

In his journalism, Klein was a teacher of traditional Jewish values, which he saw as "the vital fuel of a modern drive for self-realization, and even survival," and a preacher in the cause of Zionism, especially cultural Zionism. "To read through this book page by page is to recognize how fully Klein exposed himself to the raw flow of events during two decades and more in which the plight of European Jews dreadfully worsened, how fully he entered into and became identified with that fate in the way a genuine writer must who chooses to pitch his imaginative energy into the daily task of finding words to cope with a reality dreadful beyond words." Watt criticizes the editors for not providing a complete bibliography of the journalism, for not discussing the newspapers for which Klein wrote and the nature of his readership, and for misrepresenting, in the Introduction, Klein's views on the relationship between Israel and the Diaspora.

D90 Golfman, Noreen. "Will the World Accept the Challenge?" *Essays on Canadian Writing*, No. 28 (Spring 1984), pp. 46–56.

The dominant note of Klein's editorials is the "anxiety of hope." Klein insists again and again on the need for commitment in both art and journalism, and he himself "is energetically committed to stalking morality and justice in a world going increasingly mad." The collection provides valuable insights into Klein's world and into his better known works.

D91 Walden, Keith. Rev. of *Beyond Sambation: Selected Essays and Editorials, 1928–1955. Journal of Canadian Studies/Revue d'études canadiennes*, 19, No. 2 (Summer 1984), 158–60.

Klein is an eloquent writer, and many of the pieces in the collection, such as "In Praise of the Diaspora" and "Notebook of a Journey," are powerful. However, the collection lacks "an on-going development of new insights which would prevent the emotions from becoming monotonous." This is probably the result of the day-to-day conditions under which the editorials were written, which precluded deeper analysis. Walden questions the choice of editorials; a more selective volume, including editorials on literary and cultural matters, would have been more attractive. The notes are inconsistent and inconveniently located at the back of the book. The editors could have located Klein more precisely in his social and cultural context.

D92 Drache, Sharon. "A Dark Vision from a Silenced Voice." *The Globe and Mail* [Toronto], 11 June 1983, p. E3.

Klein is an important writer of short fiction. The Jewish stories "render Jewish tradition and lore immediate." Other important stories explore Klein's "dark vision" of the artist's role, of the forces that conspire against his freedom to say what he wants to say.

D93 Adachi, Ken. "Poet Klein's Short Stories Heavy-Handed." *The Toronto Star*, 18 June 1983, p. H10.

Klein is a powerful poet, but ". . . the short-story form doesn't suit [his] imagination. He does not have the delicately inquisitive sensibility, the natural inclination towards writing about people brought to the moments of white-hot awareness. He won't allow his fictional accidents to *happen*." The stories are forced and over-rhetorical; they are "in the tradition of the sermon, the lecture, the essay, the prayer — not in the tradition of narrative fiction."

D94 Mathews, Robin. "Klein Stories Worth Preserving." *The Citizen* [Ottawa], 18 June 1983, p. 46.

Klein's short stories are occasionally joyful or amusing, but their dominant tone is dark: "Klein seems to hold out little hope for individual fulfillment in a just society." The stories often suffer from over-elaborate diction and wooden characterization. As the work of a major poet, they deserve to be gathered together, but they are "a minor strain in the production of a major author."

D95 Templeton, Wayne. "A.M. Klein: Graphic Portrayal of a Lost Life." *The Vancouver Sun*, 8 July 1983, p. L28.

"The best of Klein's short fiction is that in which human attributes, frailties, and the complexity and enigma of relationships are dramatized. These stories often extend slightly beyond the realistic in their attempt to capture, in the style of the Old Testament, or more recently, of writers like Gabriel Garcia Marquez, the marvellous, the awesome, the frightening and the unexplainable through fanciful, often lyrical language and image combined with an irony that objectifies and thus serves to minimize the threat of excessive sentimentality."

D96 Garvie, Maureen McCallum. "Back into the Light." *The Whig-Standard* [Kingston], 3 Sept. 1983, p. 19.

The themes and styles of Klein's stories are wide-ranging, though running through many of them is "the theme of the grief and anger of the artist whose gift is always under threat." Klein's "poet's ear" is impeccable in dialogue, but he is not gifted at creating characters, and many of the stories seem dated.

D97 Wisse, Ruth R. "Klein: Portrait of an Emerging Writer." *The Montreal Gazette*, 10 Sept. 1983, p. 13.

Klein's short stories are the "record . . . of someone continually trying out new voices and testing his hand at different kinds of material, of a perpetually restless imagination that has not yet found its true centre. Reading this book through from start to finish is like watching a writer in the process of becoming a writer." Klein is a "stylistic virtuoso . . . who finds it hard to settle down in any single personal literary sphere." The best stories are those like "A Myriad-Minded Man," which are rooted in Klein's personal experience. The collection is uneven, and Klein's reputation might have been better served by a selected volume, but "the entire opus . . . constitutes a rich social document."

D98 Marshall, T.A. "Thirty Years of Solitude." *Books in Canada*, Dec. 1983, pp. 21–23.

"Klein's fictional bent seems to have been in the direction of the metaphysical and the fantastic"; he writes fables rather than stories, which recall James Joyce, Jorge Luis Borges, Vladimir Nabokov, and the South American fabulists. Most of the pieces in the book are not among his best work and will be of interest primarily to Klein scholars. However, there are several outstanding exceptions. "The Bells of Sobor Spasitula" is "Klein's subtlest and most resonant fable."

D99 Melançon, Robert. "Les nouvelles de A.M. Klein." *Liberté* [Montréal], 26, No. 1 [No. 151] (Feb. 1984), 102.

Klein's short stories can, to a certain extent, be seen as a preparation for the "narrative somptueuse" of *The Second Scroll*. But ". . . ces nouvelles font plus qu'un appendice à l'oeuvre de Klein: plusieurs suffiraient à lui assurer une enviable réputation d'écrivain."

D100 Kreisel, Henry. Rev. of *The Short Stories of A.M. Klein*. *Journal of Canadian Studies/Revue d'études canadiennes*, 19, No. 2 (Summer 1984), 160–62.

"Klein was not really a natural short story writer. His short prose is at its best when he presents what are essentially meditations and reflections cast into dramatic form." Many of the stories in the collection are parables and fables, and it is in these that ". . . the full power of Klein's art is to be found." Klein's stories present "a dark world, yet paradoxically a world that is full of zest . . . [where] there is nothing to do but to strive, to endure, to err, and, once in a while, if only for a moment, to be triumphant."

LITERARY ESSAYS AND REVIEWS

D101 Butovsky, Mervin. Rev. of *Literary Essays and Reviews*. *Choice* (1987), 622.

The volume testifies to Klein's "keen intelligence and incomparable linguistic erudition." The essays show Klein "determined to mediate between his profound cultural awareness and the more limited understanding of his readers."

D102 Healy, J.J. " 'Exploded Book' from Essayist in Seascape of Drowned Isolation." *The Citizen* [Ottawa], 25 Apr. 1987, p. C5.

Literary Essays and Reviews is an "exploded book" in which "we meet fragmented, sculpted conversations." The volume reflects the wide range of Klein's reading and thinking. "Nothing that Klein touches with his appetite to understand/calibrate/cauterize remains the same."

D103 Groening, Laura. "Klein's Essays." *Canadian Literature*, No. 119 (1988), pp. 131–33.

Klein's essays on Jewish themes, in which his aim is to educate his readers, are "serious and earnest," but less immediately appealing than the other essays, in which "we see Klein wrestling with the poles of aestheticism and morality." The volume as a whole is essential reading for readers who wish to come to terms with the "exotic difference" of Klein's poetry.

D104 Keith, W.J. Rev. of *Literary Essays and Reviews*. *Canadian Book Review Annual* (1988), 215–16.

Although many of the items in the volume were produced under less than ideal conditions as weekly journalism, they "convey the extraordinary range of Klein's mind and the diversity of his interests." The volume is "a model of good editing."

D105 Kertzer, J.M. of *Literary Essays and Reviews*. *Ariel*, 19, No. 1 (1988), 99–101.

Klein's literary essays display "an intellectual ebullience" and a conviction "that literature is inescapably moral." In some of the essays, however, there is evidence of "a radical doubt that corrodes the optimism of his intellectual and moral faith." The editorial standards of the volume are high, but Klein's allusiveness makes completely satisfactory annotation almost impossible.

D106 Rozmovits, Linda. Rev. of *Literary Essays and Reviews*. *American Review of Canadian Studies*, 18, No. 4 (1988), 494–95.

The "hybrid nature" of the volume testifies to the paradoxical nature of Klein's work. Torn between his obligations as a journalist and public spokesman and his impulses as a creative writer, Klein experienced "the intolerable and conflicting pressures of [his] age: the competing claims of artistic independence and social responsibility, the relentless dialectic of politics and art."

COMPLETE POEMS

D107 Beaton, Belinda. "The Potency of Symbols." *Books in Canada*, 20, No. 5 (June-July, 1991), 52–53.

Klein's "poems capture our country, our culture, and our history in language so passioante that it soars." Klein's most important poems are those collected in *The Rocking Chair*, which reflect an astounding capacity for synthesis.

D108 Dudek, Louis. "Studying Klein." *Ottawa Citizen*, 17 Aug. 1991, p. B11.

"Klein has always been the most troubling, and the most troubled, of the modern Canadian poets." His poetry "is always puzzling and deeply moving." It is limited, however, by Klein's nostalgia for a vanished past and fear of change, and for this reason "very little of it is entirely satisfying." Dudek praises the edition for its fine introduction and for the "superlative fasion" in which it, and the other volumes in the *Complete Works*, have presented Klein's writings, but he queries "whether such exhaustive publication is really necessary or useful."

D109 Bentley, D.M.R. "The Book Becomes a Living Thing." *Canadian Poetry: Studies, Documents, Reviews*, No. 28 (Spring-Summer 1991), pp. 85–92.

Bentley provides a detailed discussion of the editorial principles and procedures of the *Collected Poems*, which he characterizes as "a highly important contribution to Canadian scholarship and a very worthy addition to the existing volumes of *The Collected Works of A.M. Klein*." He argues, however, that the Klein's own arrangement of his poems in the published volumes is an important aspect of his work that is obscured by Pollock's decision to arrange the poems chronologically.

D110 Middlebro', T. "Klein's Poetry." *The Canadian Forum*, Sept. 1991, pp. 27–28.

The edition has been prepared "with exemplary thoroughness and care." The chronological arrangement "allows the reader to trace [Klein's] poetic development. What is lost is the cumulative aesthetic effect of the careful grouping of poems made by the poet in individual volumes." Klein's poetry shows an awareness of dualities; for Klein, "all facets of existence met in God." He "was a gentle and complex man" whose "great spiritual courage" took him eventually "to the frontier and beyond, into the years of tragic seclusion during which . . . he paid the price for having cared too much."

INDEX TO "ESSAYS, ARTICLES, AND REVIEWS"

Aaron 51.04.20A

Abbott, Douglas Charles 53.02.27C,
53.08.14A

Abdullah, King of Jordan 39.06.02A,
47.11.21B, 48.05.14A, 48.07.23A,
48.12.24B, 49.12.16B, 50.01.06B,
50.02.17A, 50.03.03C, 50.04.07A,
50.06.02C, 50.06.30B, 51.07.27A,
51.08.24A, 53.11.13A

Abner 50.05.05D

Abraham Yaakov, Rabbi of Sadagora
48.12.03D

Abraham of Bristol 32.03.00A

Abramson, Samuel 39.02.17G, 41.01.17C

Achad Ha-am (Asher Ginsberg) 28.11.00A,
31.11.00A, 36.10.00D, 37.05.00B,
37.06.00A, 44.03.31A, 48.09.24A

Acheson, Dean 50.02.03B, 52.06.06A

Adenauer, Konrad 50.05.05A, 50.11.17B,
51.09.28B, 51.10.05A, 52.01.18A,
52.02.29B, 52.04.04B, 52.06.06A,
52.06.20B

Adler, Cyrus 39.06.23C, 40.04.12B

Advertising 39.09.22D, 42.09.04D,
44.11.17A, 49.01.14D. *See also* journalism; propaganda.

Aestheticism 42.07.10D. *See also* art for art's
sake.

Ahasuerus 29.12.00A, 39.03.05A, 42.02.27C,
45.05.11D, 46.08.09A, 51.03.16B,
53.02.27A, 54.03.19A

Akavyah ben Mahalalel 31.00.00A

Akiba, Rabbi 29.12.00A, 34.02.00A,
35.11.00B, 39.03.31A, 42.04.01A

Alexander I, Czar of Russia 39.09.22G

Alfonso XIII, King of Spain 43.07.23B,
52.09.19B

Alkabez, Solomon Halevi 49.10.07D

Alter, Victor 43.03.05B

Alterman, Nathan 49.11.25C

American Council for Judaism 43.01.15B,
43.09.03C, 44.01.14B, 44.02.25C,
44.12.29B, 45.12.07A, 46.01.11A,
46.01.25B, 46.03.08B, 48.12.31C,
49.03.18A, 49.06.02B, 50.01.27A,
51.04.27A, 52.04.18B, 54.05.07A

American Jewish Committee 40.04.12B,
42.01.02D, 43.02.19A, 43.03.19A,
43.09.10B, 43.10.29A, 52.06.20B

American Jewish Conference 43.09.03A,
43.09.10B, 43.10.29A, 44.01.14B,
45.01.19A, 50.11.03B

American Jewish Congress 39.01.08A,
40.03.01C, 40.03.15D, 42.01.09B,
43.02.19B, 43.03.19A, 43.05.07A,
43.08.20A, 53.05.01B, 53.07.17B

American Jewish Joint Distribution
Committee 38.12.09A, 39.01.06B,
39.11.24A, 39.12.15E, 40.04.12B,
40.12.06A, 41.08.29A, 42.03.13D,
43.02.26B, 43.03.19A, 45.01.19A,
45.02.23B, 46.01.11A, 49.07.22A,
49.11.11B, 49.12.23A, 50.05.19C,
50.05.26B, 50.06.09A, 50.12.22A,
51.11.16B, 53.01.23B, 53.04.10A, 53.06.19A

Anan ben David 42.05.22D

Anders, Wladyslaw 40.05.10F, 46.07.26A

Andreyev, Andrei Andreyevich 39.03.28B

Anglo-American Joint Commission on
Palestine 45.11.16B, 45.12.14C, 46.01.11A,
46.01.11D, 46.01.18A, 46.01.25B,
46.02.22B, 46.03.15B, 46.03.29A,
46.04.26A, 46.05.24A, 46.06.07D,
46.06.14C, 46.07.12B, 46.07.19A,
46.08.09A, 46.11.29B, 47.02.28A,
47.04.25C, 47.06.13A, 47.07.04B

Anski, S. (Solomon Rapaport) 48.07.23C, 48.07.30D

Anti-comintern 39.05.26B, 39.08.25A, 39.10.20I, 41.06.27F, 43.05.28C. *See also* anti-communism.

Anti-communism. *See also* anti-comintern.
fascist 39.09.27F
Nazi 39.10.20I, 40.05.05B, 41.05.16C
Quebec 39.07.07C, 39.09.13C, 39.12.22A
United States 40.02.09B, 41.07.04A, 50.11.10B, 51.08.17B, 53.01.02B, 53.11.27A. *See also* McCarthyism.
Vichy France 41.09.05C

Anti-Defamation League 42.01.23E, 52.07.11B

Anti-Intellectualism 27.11.26A

Anti-Semitism 27.11.19A, 27.12.03A, 31.00.00A, 31.06.00A, 32.07.08J, 32.08.12A, 34.10.00A, 34.12.00A, 37.06.00C, 38.12.23A, 38.12.23B, 39.01.13A, 39.02.19A, 39.02.24G, 39.03.05A, 39.05.26A, 39.06.09D, 39.07.14C, 39.08.18F, 39.10.13A, 39.12.29B, 40.01.05G, 40.01.12D, 40.02.16C, 40.03.29F, 40.04.19A, 40.07.26B, 40.11.01D, 41.03.14D, 41.12.19B, 42.02.27C, 42.03.06B, 42.04.10B, 42.05.08D, 42.07.03D, 42.09.25A, 42.10.23E, 42.11.06A, 43.01.15D, 43.02.05A, 43.03.19A, 43.05.07B, 43.06.25B, 44.02.18A, 44.02.25B, 44.03.03C, 44.03.10A, 44.03.24A, 44.04.07A, 44.07.14A, 44.07.21A, 44.10.06B, 44.10.13D, 45.07.20B, 46.02.01D, 47.05.16C, 48.01.30B, 48.03.12C, 48.03.19D, 48.09.10B, 48.11.05B, 49.01.14C, 49.02.25A, 49.02.25B, 49.10.21D, 49.10.28B, 54.02.12B. *See also* anti-Zionism; Christian Front; fascism; Nazism; pogroms.
accusations of ritual murder 32.07.29A
and Roman Catholic Church 40.08.16C
Arab countries 42.12.11C, 43.02.19B
Argentina 42.10.16C, 43.10.20A, 43.11.05B, 44.01.07B, 45.10.26C, 46.02.15B

Bolivia 44.01.07B
Brazil 36.12.00F
Britain 31.12.00A, 32.08.12C, 39.07.28G, 39.11.10E, 40.03.29D, 40.04.12E, 41.08.08G, 42.06.12B, 44.09.29A, 44.10.20A, 45.07.20A, 46.06.14A, 46.07.05C, 46.08.02B, 46.11.22C, 46.12.27A, 47.01.03B, 47.10.24C, 48.09.17E
Canada 29.04.00B, 32.08.12C, 32.08.12G, 32.08.26A, 39.01.08A, 39.02.03D, 39.03.05A, 39.04.28B, 39.07.21B, 39.12.01A, 40.02.23D, 40.09.27A, 41.06.13C, 41.06.13G, 41.06.20D, 41.07.18E, 41.09.12D, 41.11.28A, 42.08.07G, 42.08.21E, 44.10.20C, 45.12.21B, 46.01.18C, 46.05.17A, 46.07.26B, 47.01.31A, 47.10.24C, 48.06.18B, 48.08.20B, 49.02.11B, 49.03.04A, 49.07.01A, 50.08.11A, 50.12.01B
causes of 42.01.02D
control of 42.01.02D, 42.04.01C
Czechoslovakia 38.12.30L, 39.01.20D, 39.01.27B, 39.08.18B, 42.10.30D, 43.06.25B, 52.11.28A
Europe 45.06.29A, 46.03.15A, 47.01.31A, 47.04.04A
France 39.04.28B, 40.07.12C, 40.08.30C, 40.08.30E, 40.10.23A, 40.10.23C, 40.12.13C, 41.05.23F, 42.09.04A, 42.09.18B, 42.10.02E, 42.11.20A, 45.06.08C
Germany 32.07.08C, 32.07.08E, 32.08.12E, 34.05.00A, 35.07.19A, 35.07.26A, 37.07.16A, 38.12.09D, 38.12.30B, 39.01.17A, 39.03.03E, 39.05.03A, 39.09.07A, 39.09.13A, 39.09.22C, 39.10.13D, 39.10.20I, 39.11.28A, 40.12.13C, 41.01.03B, 41.05.16E, 41.12.12C, 42.01.09D, 42.06.19A, 42.06.26D, 47.01.31A, 48.07.09B, 50.03.10B, 50.04.21C, 50.04.28B, 50.05.05A, 50.06.02A, 50.08.11A, 53.02.20B
Hungary 38.12.30B, 39.06.16C, 40.11.22B, 45.09.21B, 50.03.17A,

318

39.02.03F, 39.02.10A, 39.02.24A,
39.03.10C, 39.03.10G, 39.03.31D,
39.04.21C, 39.04.28F, 39.05.05H,
39.06.18A, 39.08.11C, 39.08.18D,
40.02.09G, 40.03.01B, 40.03.08A,
40.05.03F, 40.07.19A, 40.09.27B,
40.11.29A, 42.05.15B, 42.06.19B,
43.06.04A, 43.11.26B, 43.12.24B,
44.02.04A, 44.02.25C, 44.03.03B,
44.03.31A, 44.04.21C, 44.04.28B,
44.05.12C, 45.03.16B, 45.11.09A,
45.11.23B, 46.01.11D, 46.03.15B,
46.04.26A, 46.05.24A, 46.06.07D,
46.07.12A, 46.08.09A, 46.10.09A,
46.12.06A, 47.02.07A, 47.03.28A,
47.04.25C, 47.05.23A, 47.05.23C,
47.06.20A, 47.06.20B, 47.07.04B,
47.07.11B, 47.08.15A, 47.08.15B,
47.09.05D, 47.10.03A, 48.01.16A,
48.01.23A, 48.01.30B, 48.02.06B,
48.02.13A, 48.02.27A, 48.03.05A,
48.03.05B, 48.03.12A, 48.04.02A,
48.04.09A, 48.04.09B, 48.07.09A,
48.07.23A, 48.08.13C, 48.09.03B,
48.12.03A, 48.12.17A, 49.01.28B,
49.03.18A, 49.03.25A, 49.04.08A,
49.05.06A, 49.09.16B, 49.12.16C,
50.11.17A, 51.03.23B. *See also* Palestine, Arab riots.
western romanticization of 53.11.13A
western support for 55.03.11A
Arcand, Adrien 32.07.08A, 32.07.22A,
32.07.29A, 32.08.12G, 32.08.26A,
35.07.19A, 35.08.02F, 39.02.10B,
39.03.10F, 39.06.09A, 39.06.23B,
39.07.21B, 39.07.21E, 39.07.21G,
39.07.28I, 39.08.04A, 39.09.06B,
39.09.13C, 39.12.01A, 39.12.22A,
40.01.05C, 40.01.19G, 40.05.31A,
40.06.02A, 40.06.07E, 40.06.14H,
40.06.21B, 40.06.28B, 40.06.28F,
40.07.05B, 40.08.09B, 40.11.01C,
41.11.28A, 42.03.27A, 42.08.14B,
45.04.27D, 45.05.11C, 45.07.13A,
47.11.14A, 48.11.26B, 49.06.17B,
49.06.17C, 49.06.24C, 49.07.01A,
53.08.14A

Arch of Titus 49.12.16D
Arendt, Hannah 48.03.19D
Argentina 39.01.06G, 43.11.05B, 46.02.15B,
46.10.16A, 51.06.01B, 51.08.24B,
51.10.05B. *See also* anti-Semitism; fascism; Jews; racism; World War II.
Aristophanes 39.02.24E, 39.03.17C,
41.05.23C, 41.12.26D
Aristotle 31.06.00A, 39.07.21H, 40.10.02A,
41.05.02B, 42.06.05D, 44.01.28C
Armistice Day 38.11.18F, 39.08.04I, 39.11.10A
Arnold, Matthew 30.04.00A, 37.06.00A,
41.03.07A, 41.08.29E, 46.04.19C
Art. *See also* communism; cubism; dadaism; Nazism.
and religion 49.11.18B
Soviet Union 48.10.08C
Art for art's sake 32.08.05E, 33.01.00A,
37.06.00A, 41.12.05D, 45.07.06D. *See
also* aestheticism.
Artists and society 51.01.12A, 53.04.03B
Asch, Sholem 36.10.00E, 44.01.14D,
44.02.18E, 46.02.22C, 46.05.10B
Assyrians 39.02.17A, 48.01.30B
Astor, Lady Nancy 39.09.20A, 39.09.22F,
42.08.07B
Ataturk, Kemal 38.11.18C, 52.09.19B
Atlantic Charter 41.08.22C, 41.08.22D,
41.08.29E, 41.09.05E, 41.11.14A,
41.12.26B, 42.01.30A, 42.03.13C,
42.03.20C, 42.04.01A, 42.07.17A,
42.07.17D, 42.10.23B, 42.10.30A,
42.11.06D, 42.11.20D, 42.12.11E,
43.05.28A, 43.08.20A, 43.11.19B,
43.11.26B, 44.01.28A, 44.04.21B,
44.08.11C, 44.10.27D, 44.12.22B,
45.02.16A, 45.07.06B, 45.08.17A,
46.03.01A, 46.09.06A, 46.09.25A,
50.07.28B, 50.09.22A
Atomic era 45.08.10C, 45.08.17A, 45.08.24A,
45.09.07A, 45.11.09C, 45.11.30C,
46.01.11A, 46.03.01A, 46.05.10A,
46.06.21B, 46.07.05A, 46.09.20B,
46.09.25A, 47.01.10A, 48.01.02B,
49.01.28D, 49.04.01A, 49.06.02A,
49.09.30A, 49.10.07B, 50.02.03A,
50.02.10B, 50.02.17B, 50.03.24C,

50.10.27B, 50.12.08A, 51.04.13A,
51.06.01B, 51.06.08A, 51.06.15A,
51.08.10B, 52.04.09B, 52.08.08A,
52.11.21B, 53.07.31A, 53.08.14B, 53.08.21B,
53.12.11A, 53.12.18A, 54.11.19A, 55.04.22A.
See also international politics, post-
World War II; science and technology;
World War II, Nagasaki; warfare, modern.

Attlee, Clement 45.08.10A, 40.05.10A,
40.05.17E, 41.08.08B, 45.08.03A,
45.09.21A, 45.09.28A, 45.10.12A,
45.11.16B, 45.11.23B, 45.11.30C, 45.12.07A,
45.12.14C, 46.01.11C, 46.01.11D,
46.04.26A, 46.05.24A, 46.06.14C,
46.08.09A, 46.08.23A, 46.08.30B,
46.09.20A, 46.10.09A, 46.10.16A,
47.02.07B, 47.02.21A, 47.03.07C,
47.03.14A, 47.03.14B, 47.03.21C,
47.04.10C, 47.04.25C, 47.08.15B,
47.08.29A, 47.09.05B, 47.09.05D,
47.09.12A, 47.09.12B, 47.10.03A,
47.11.28C, 47.12.19B, 48.07.23A,
48.08.27A, 49.02.04A, 49.06.17D,
49.09.30B, 49.10.07B, 51.03.23C,
51.08.10A, 51.10.19A

Auden, Wystan Hugh 46.02.22C,
46.03.22D, 49.01.28D

Austin, Warren Robinson 48.03.26C

Australia 43.03.12B, 43.07.30B, 46.10.16A,
47.01.31C

Austria, Anschluss 38.12.02F, 38.12.09C,
39.01.13B, 39.01.17A, 39.02.03C,
39.03.17A, 39.03.24F, 39.05.05C,
39.07.28F, 39.08.04B, 39.09.08E,
39.09.27H, 39.11.24E, 40.03.22F

Ave-Lallemant, Robert Christian Berthold
41.01.03E

Baal Shem Tov, Israel 30.11.14A, 41.10.10C,
45.07.06D, 45.11.02C, 48.12.03D,
54.03.12A

Babel, Isaak Emmanuilovich 48.09.10D

Badoglio, Pietro 43.07.30A, 43.09.10A,
43.09.17B, 43.09.24A, 43.10.29B

Bailey, William Louis 39.02.10C

Balbo, Italo 38.11.11F, 40.07.05E

Balch, Emily Green 46.11.29C

Baldwin, Stanley 38.12.27B, 39.02.05B,
39.03.24G, 39.08.18F, 40.05.24E,
41.01.03D

Balfour, Arthur James 36.11.00A,
37.07.09A, 39.05.26A, 39.09.01G,
41.05.09A, 41.11.07D, 42.07.17D,
42.11.06D, 44.03.17D, 44.11.03A,
46.01.04A, 46.02.01B, 46.07.05C,
46.10.16A, 47.02.14A, 48.05.21C,
49.12.09B, 50.07.14A, 55.05.13A

Balfour Declaration 31.11.00A, 32.07.08I,
32.07.15C, 32.07.22D, 36.11.00A,
36.11.00B, 36.12.00C, 37.05.00A,
37.07.09A, 37.07.23A, 37.07.30D,
38.11.11G, 39.02.17A, 39.02.17E,
39.03.03A, 39.03.10G, 39.03.24C,
39.03.24E, 39.05.12A, 39.05.26A,
39.06.02H, 39.06.18A, 39.06.23A,
39.06.23G, 39.06.30E, 39.07.14E,
39.07.21A, 39.10.06B, 39.12.22F,
40.03.08A, 41.01.17A, 41.01.24B,
41.02.07A, 41.03.14A, 41.06.06D,
41.08.08E, 41.10.10A, 41.11.07D,
42.06.12B, 42.06.19B, 42.07.17D,
42.08.07H, 42.09.04B, 42.11.06A,
42.11.06D, 42.12.18D, 43.01.29G,
43.02.19A, 43.07.23A, 43.08.20A,
43.11.05A, 43.11.12A, 43.11.26B, 44.02.11A,
44.02.25B, 44.03.24A, 44.03.31A,
44.07.07B, 44.08.11C, 44.09.08C,
44.11.03A, 44.12.08A, 44.12.15A,
44.12.15B, 45.03.16B, 45.07.20C,
45.10.12A, 45.10.26B, 45.11.02A,
46.01.04B, 46.02.01A, 46.02.01B,
46.04.26A, 46.05.24B, 46.06.14A,
46.07.05C, 46.07.12A, 46.07.19B,
46.08.09A, 46.08.23A, 46.09.13A,
46.10.16A, 46.11.08A, 46.11.15A,
46.12.13A, 46.12.27A, 47.01.03A,
47.02.21A, 47.02.21C, 47.03.14B,
47.03.21A, 47.06.13A, 47.06.20B,
47.07.25A, 47.08.15A, 47.09.05D,
47.09.12A, 47.10.17A, 47.10.31A,
47.11.28B, 47.12.05A, 48.01.23A,
48.05.21C, 48.07.09A, 48.12.31B,
49.01.07A, 49.01.14B, 49.02.18D,

49.09.16B, 49.10.14B, 50.04.07B,
52.02.22C, 52.11.14A, 55.04.15A
Bar Kamza 51.10.05D
Bar Kochba 29.12.00A, 34.10.00A,
42.05.29E, 42.06.05B, 43.10.20B
Bar-Ilan University 52.11.07A
Barker, Evelyn 46.08.02B, 47.03.21C
Barkley, Alben W. 50.01.20B, 53.06.12B
Barré, Laurent 48.03.26B, 52.01.11A,
52.01.25B, 52.01.25C, 52.02.01B
Barrymore, John 40.09.13G
Baruch, Isaac Loeb 50.04.07C
Baruch, Rabbi of Mayence 43.10.20B
Basle Program 31.00.00A, 33.01.00A
Bastille Day 40.07.19D, 41.04.25F,
41.07.18F, 42.07.17C
Batshaw, Harry 31.00.00A, 40.04.05A,
41.02.07A, 41.03.14A, 42.04.10A,
50.02.17C
Baudelaire, Charles 33.01.00A, 34.01.05A
Baxter, Beverly 38.12.30H, 41.10.24E,
42.03.06B
Beaverbrook, Lord 40.04.12E, 40.05.17B,
41.11.14B
Beck, Jozef 39.03.29A, 39.05.12E, 40.05.10F
Beecher, Henry Ward 50.05.26D
Beersheba 49.12.23E
Begin, Menachem 47.08.08A, 48.01.02C,
48.07.02B, 48.08.27B
Belkin, Samuel 47.04.04B, 53.07.17B
Ben Asher, Moshe 51.10.05D, 51.10.19B
Ben Avi, Ittamar 32.07.08D, 37.05.00A,
37.07.30B
Ben Bag-Bag 39.12.01G, 50.06.09C
Ben Chasdai 32.10.07A
Ben Gurion, David 37.07.23C, 38.12.23B,
39.09.01G, 40.04.05A, 41.01.31A,
41.03.14A, 42.05.15B, 43.02.12A,
43.08.20A, 46.03.15B, 46.06.14A,
46.07.26A, 46.10.16A, 47.07.11B,
47.07.18B, 47.09.05C, 47.10.03A,
48.05.28A, 48.07.23A, 48.08.27B,
48.10.29B, 48.11.19B, 48.12.31C,
49.01.28B, 49.02.11E, 49.04.08A,
49.04.29B, 49.07.22B, 49.09.02A,
49.09.16B, 49.10.21C, 49.10.28A,
49.10.28D, 49.11.11C, 49.12.16B,

49.12.16C, 49.12.30A, 50.02.03C,
50.03.24A, 50.03.31B, 50.04.14B,
50.08.25A, 50.10.13B, 50.10.20A,
50.11.03C, 51.01.05B, 51.02.02B,
51.02.23A, 51.05.25A, 51.06.08B,
51.07.20B, 51.07.27A, 51.08.03A,
51.08.17A, 52.02.01A, 52.03.28B,
52.05.09A, 52.06.20A, 52.07.25C,
52.09.19B, 52.12.05A, 53.04.24A,
53.06.19B, 53.12.18B
Ben Israel, Menasseh 32.03.00A,
37.04.00B, 47.02.14A, 48.10.01A
Ben Yochai, Simeon 32.10.07A, 49.10.07D
Ben Zakkai, Jochanan 34.02.00A,
35.11.00B, 40.01.05A, 40.05.31B,
42.05.22B, 43.05.28B, 47.04.04B
Ben Zvi, Isaac 39.02.10A, 41.10.03D
Beneš, Edouard 32.07.29C, 38.12.30L,
39.01.04A, 39.04.28H, 39.06.02G,
40.07.26D, 40.11.15C, 41.05.09B,
42.05.08C, 42.06.19D, 43.06.25B
Benjamin of Tudela 35.11.00B, 50.03.24D
Bennett, Archibald B. 41.01.17C, 41.02.28B,
42.06.12D, 42.07.24D
Bension, Ariel 32.10.07A
Bercovici, Konrad 35.08.09A, 42.09.11C
Bercovitch, Alexander 51.01.12A
Bercovitch, Peter 32.07.08J, 38.11.11C,
40.03.15C, 40.03.29A, 43.01.01A
Berditchev 44.01.07C
Bergen, Carl-Ludwig Diego von 39.03.10A
Bergson, Henri 40.12.13C, 41.01.10E,
42.02.13C, 46.02.01D, 48.07.16B
Bergson, Peter 44.06.02B, 44.06.23A,
44.06.30A, 48.07.02B, 48.08.27B
Beria, Lavrenti Pavlovich 53.04.10A,
53.07.17A, 53.07.24A, 53.08.14B,
55.06.03A
Berlin crisis 48.10.15B, 49.05.13A,
49.05.27C, 51.07.06A
Berlin Zeitung 40.10.11E
Berlin, Meyer 49.04.22B
Bernadotte, Folke 48.06.25A, 48.07.02C,
48.07.09A, 48.07.23A, 48.08.13C,
48.08.27A, 48.09.24A, 48.10.22A
Bernadotte Peace Plan 48.07.09A
Bernheim, Alfred 47.08.22C

Bernonville, Jacques de 49.03.04A,
51.02.16A, 51.08.24B
Bernstein, Leonard 51.01.19ABess, Demaree
41.01.17D, 41.04.04A
Beurling, George (Buzz) 48.06.04A
Beutel, Ben 48.01.09C, 49.12.09A,
52.12.05B, 54.01.15B
Beveridge, William Henry 42.12.04B,
43.02.12C, 43.03.05A, 46.08.16A
Bevin, Ernest 40.10.16B, 41.12.19C,
45.11.16B, 45.11.23B, 46.01.25A,
46.01.25C, 46.02.01A, 46.02.01C,
46.06.14A, 46.06.28A, 46.07.05C,
46.07.12B, 46.07.26A, 46.08.02B,
46.08.30A, 46.08.30D, 46.11.08A,
46.12.06A, 46.12.27A, 47.02.07B,
47.02.14A, 47.02.21B, 47.02.28A,
47.03.07C, 47.03.14B, 47.03.21C,
47.04.25A, 47.04.25B, 47.05.02A,
47.07.25A, 47.08.15B, 47.08.29A,
47.09.05B, 47.09.05D, 47.09.12A,
47.09.12B, 47.11.28C, 47.12.19A,
47.12.19B, 47.12.19C, 48.02.06C,
48.05.21C, 48.06.04B, 48.07.23A,
48.07.23B, 48.08.06B, 48.08.27A,
48.12.17A, 49.01.14B, 49.02.04A,
49.02.25A, 49.06.17D, 49.07.29A,
49.09.16B, 50.03.17C, 50.04.07B,
50.04.21D, 50.04.28A, 51.07.13B,
51.08.03B
Bialik, Chaim Nachman 36.09.00A,
37.01.00D, 37.05.00B, 37.06.00A,
37.06.00B, 37.06.00C, 40.07.26A,
40.08.09A, 42.07.10D, 42.12.18D,
43.10.20B, 43.12.24A, 44.01.14D,
44.03.03D, 44.04.13C, 44.05.19C,
49.05.13C, 49.06.10A, 49.08.19A,
51.07.13A, 53.07.10A
Bible 32.09.23A, 38.12.23B, 39.06.02A,
39.08.25C, 39.12.01G, 41.01.17A,
41.01.31E, 41.05.23B, 41.05.30C,
42.08.07F, 43.05.07B, 44.02.11C,
45.11.02C, 48.09.24A, 49.01.28D,
51.10.12C, 52.02.01A, 53.11.13A, 55.04.15A.
See also decalogue; poetry; Torah.
and British society 47.02.14A
as literature 29.02.00A, 38.04.15A,

41.04.11C
books of, Chronicles 29.02.00A,
41.04.11C
books of, Daniel 40.06.14F
books of, Deuteronomy 30.09.19A,
32.08.12G, 44.09.22B, 46.01.04B,
53.12.11A
books of, Ecclesiastes 29.02.00A,
29.05.00A, 37.01.00B, 41.04.11C,
53.01.23C
books of, Esther 39.03.05A, 41.01.17C,
41.03.14D, 44.03.10A, 45.03.09A,
48.03.26A, 51.03.16B, 52.03.07A,
52.12.12A, 52.12.19C, 53.02.27A,
54.03.19A, 54.03.19B
books of, Exodus 29.02.00A, 41.04.11C,
42.04.01A, 44.04.07A, 45.10.19A,
46.01.04B, 51.07.20A, 51.09.28D,
53.02.06B, 53.05.15A, 54.06.04A
books of, Ezekiel 29.02.00A, 41.04.11C,
46.04.12A
books of, Genesis 32.08.12G, 34.02.00A,
41.04.11C, 43.05.21C, 46.01.04B,
46.03.29D, 48.06.11D, 49.02.11E,
50.04.28C, 51.04.20A, 53.03.06D,
53.03.13B, 53.03.20A
books of, Hosea 37.06.00A
books of, Isaiah 34.02.00A, 37.05.00C,
39.07.21D, 41.04.11C, 42.07.24A,
43.02.12A, 45.05.11D
books of, Jeremiah 40.03.08A, 53.08.07A
books of, Job 29.02.00A, 34.02.00A,
41.04.11C, 41.09.05A, 41.12.19C,
53.08.07A
books of, Jonah 52.12.12A
books of, Joshua 38.11.18E, 44.06.16C
books of, Judges 29.02.00A, 34.02.00A,
41.04.11C, 44.04.07C
books of, Kings 29.02.00A, 41.04.11C,
44.07.07C, 51.09.28D
books of, Lamentations 29.02.00A,
39.07.21D, 41.04.11C, 42.03.13D,
44.01.07C, 45.05.04A, 46.08.02A,
53.01.09C
books of, Leviticus 32.08.12G,
46.01.04B, 51.10.19B
books of, Numbers 44.02.25C,

44.II.17A, 46.01.04B

books of, Pentateuch 44.07.07C

books of, Proverbs 29.02.00A,
  40.02.04A, 41.04.IIC, 41.08.15A,
  53.04.03A

books of, Psalms 29.02.00A, 37.06.00A,
  41.02.07H, 41.04.IIC, 44.02.25C,
  44.03.03D, 46.10.16A, 48.05.07B,
  49.04.13A, 50.01.06C, 53.01.16B,
  53.01.23C, 53.05.22B

books of, Romans 40.02.04A

books of, Ruth 29.02.00A, 41.04.IIC,
  46.07.05C, 52.12.12A

books of, Samuel 32.08.12G, 37.07.30E,
  39.01.17A, 44.07.07C, 50.04.21D

books of, Song of Songs 28.II.00A,
  32.05.00A, 40.10.IIF, 41.02.28D,
  41.04.IIC, 44.06.16C, 48.06.25C,
  53.03.27A

Gutenberg 40.05.24D, 51.02.09A

humour in 35.II.00B, 46.01.25D

in film 54.06.04A

language of 39.02.10C, 46.03.22D,
  48.07.16B, 49.II.IIB

manuscripts 35.07.26B, 51.10.05D,
  53.02.06B

poetry in 29.02.00A, 41.04.IIC,
  46.03.29D

translations of 29.05.00A, 39.02.10C,
  42.05.22D, 51.10.26D

translations of, King James 29.02.00A,
  29.05.00A, 32.03.00A, 41.04.IIC,
  52.09.26C

translations of, Septuagint 29.02.00A,
  37.06.00B, 41.04.IIC, 42.05.22D,
  51.10.26D, 52.09.26C

Bidault, Georges 46.06.14B, 47.05.02A,
  47.12.19C

Biro-Bidjan 51.01.19B, 51.08.31C, 51.09.28C,
  52.03.28B

Bismarck, Otto von 32.07.29B, 40.02.27A,
  40.03.01F, 40.II.22F, 41.12.05D,
  43.01.22E

Blake, William 32.03.00A, 32.10.07A,
  40.12.06A, 46.04.19C, 54.03.12A

Blitzstein, Mark 40.04.12C

Blok, Alexander 48.09.10D

Bloomfield, Bernard 50.01.20B, 50.03.24D

Blum, Leon 38.12.02E, 40.07.26H,
  40.09.20D, 40.10.23A, 41.01.10E,
  41.08.15A, 42.02.06B, 42.02.20A,
  43.04.09C, 44.10.13A

B'nai-Brak, sages of 49.04.13A

B'nai Brith 36.II.00B, 37.02.00C,
  39.01.20A, 39.01.27C, 40.03.15D,
  42.05.15A, 43.03.19A, 50.06.02A

Board of Deputies of British Jews
  32.07.08A, 39.12.22F, 40.02.16D,
  43.07.16C, 45.01.19A, 50.05.05A

Boas, Franz 43.01.08C

Bollingen Prize 49.03.04C

Bonaparte, Napoleon 39.05.09A,
  39.07.02A, 39.09.22G, 39.12.15F,
  44.09.29B, 45.01.26B, 48.08.27C,
  48.10.01A, 51.12.28A, 54.02.05A

Book reviewing 47.05.16C, 48.12.10D

Borah, William 39.03.29A, 39.04.07D,
  39.04.21F, 39.09.20A, 39.09.22F

Boraisha, Menachem 49.02.18C

Borgese, Giuseppe Antonio 44.02.04D

Bormann, Martin 45.II.23A

Borne, Lucien 39.07.21E, 42.10.30D

Bouillon, Godfrey de 48.08.27C

Bourassa, Henri 42.03.27A

Bracken, Brendan 39.08.04H, 44.07.14B

Bradley, Omar Nelson 51.06.01C

Brainin, Reuben 39.12.08B, 42.09.IIC,
  43.09.24D

Brandeis, Louis Dembitz 32.07.22E,
  36.10.00D, 39.01.13C, 39.02.17B,
  41.10.10B, 41.12.12C, 42.01.30A,
  44.12.08A, 46.01.25B

Brauchitsch, Heinrich Alfred von
  39.09.22A, 41.12.26C, 42.01.23B

Brecht, Berthold 44.08.25A

Britain. *See also* anti-Semitism; anti-Zionism; communism; fascism; Israel; Jews;
  journalism; racism; refugees; socialism;
  World War II; Zionism.
  conscription 39.04.28A, 39.04.28K
  economy 49.07.15A, 49.09.30B,
    49.10.07B
  foreign policy 39.01.13F, 39.03.03E,
    39.04.07E, 39.10.13A, 47.03.14A,

325

47.03.28C, 47.04.25C, 47.05.09C,
47.05.23A, 47.08.15B, 48.12.17A,
50.02.03B, 50.11.17B, 51.03.23C. *See
also* Israel; Middle East; Palestine.
politics 43.06.18C, 44.04.28B,
44.09.29A, 45.07.20A, 45.08.03A,
45.08.10A, 45.09.28A, 45.10.12A,
46.06.14A, 50.03.17C
British Broadcasting Corporation
41.02.07C, 49.10.14B
British Commonwealth 40.05.24A,
40.08.02A, 47.01.24B, 52.03.28A,
52.09.05A, 53.06.12A
British Empire, decline of 50.02.10C
British North America Act 42.07.03A,
47.02.07C, 47.07.04A, 48.04.16A,
48.06.18A, 50.01.13A
Brodetsky, Selig 39.12.22F, 42.12.25A,
43.01.22B
Bronfman, Allan 39.05.19A, 40.03.22A,
41.02.21A, 41.08.29A, 41.10.17A,
41.10.31A, 43.01.22A, 44.05.12A,
45.06.22B, 45.12.21A, 46.04.05B,
49.05.06B, 54.10.29A
Bronfman, Saidye 38.12.30C, 39.11.10B,
40.06.14C, 41.10.24A, 43.06.04B,
45.01.26A, 45.03.02A
Bronfman, Samuel 39.01.13A, 39.01.27A,
39.08.11A, 39.11.10B, 39.11.24A,
40.02.23A, 40.07.12A, 40.10.02B,
40.12.06A, 41.03.07A, 41.07.04B,
41.08.29A, 41.10.31A, 41.11.28B,
42.01.09A, 42.01.16A, 42.07.24B,
42.10.09A, 43.02.05A, 43.02.19C,
43.03.26A, 43.05.14A, 43.05.28A,
44.04.13A, 44.10.06A, 45.01.12A,
45.01.19A, 45.02.02A, 45.04.27B,
47.03.21A, 47.04.30A, 47.06.07A,
48.08.06A, 48.09.03A, 49.02.04A,
49.10.21B, 50.05.19B, 50.12.22A,
51.02.02A, 51.03.09A, 51.03.23A,
51.11.02A, 51.11.09B, 52.06.27A,
52.10.17B, 53.05.01B, 53.07.03C,
54.06.18A
Bronfman Collection of Jewish Canadiana
54.06.18A
Brontë, Emily 39.04.14F

Brooke, Rupert 32.05.00A, 37.06.00A,
41.12.19C
Browder, Earl 39.12.15H, 39.12.22B,
40.03.01D, 40.04.26B, 40.08.28B,
40.11.22G, 42.05.22C
Brown, E.K. 46.03.01D
Browning, Robert 30.04.00A, 32.03.00A,
39.01.06A, 40.04.26E, 40.08.09A,
41.07.25A, 42.09.11A, 47.10.10D,
48.06.11D, 49.01.28D, 53.05.01A
Buber, Martin 42.09.04B, 48.12.03D,
51.12.21B
Buchan, John (Lord Tweedsmuir)
40.02.16A, 46.02.22A, 46.10.16A
Bullitt, William Christian 40.04.05E,
40.08.23C, 40.09.06F
Bunche, Ralph 50.09.29A
Bundism 40.03.22B, 43.07.02A, 49.03.18D,
52.10.24A
Burns, Robert 40.04.12D, 40.07.26B
Butler, Samuel 47.04.10B
Buttenwieser, Benjamin J. 50.06.02A
Byron, George Noel Gordon 27.10.29A,
27.11.05A, 32.03.00A, 37.06.00A,
40.08.23D, 40.11.01D, 41.02.14F,
41.02.28D, 41.05.02B, 41.07.18D,
44.01.28C, 49.08.19A

Caesar, Julius 39.03.15A, 40.11.22E,
41.02.14F, 46.01.04D, 46.09.13A,
51.12.28A, 52.12.12A, 53.02.13C
Cagoulards 40.07.26H, 40.10.23A, 41.01.10E
Cahan, Abraham 51.09.07C
Caiserman, H.M. 38.11.18D, 39.05.12C,
44.03.31C, 47.06.07B, 50.12.29A
Cameron, William John 42.01.23E,
42.02.20B, 42.08.21D
Canada. *See also* anti-Semitism; anti-Zionism; Arabs; censorship; communism;
fascism; Germans; Israel; Jews; journalism; nationalism; Quebec; racism; refugees; religion; World War I; World War
II; Zionism; Zionist Organization of
Canada.
confederation 42.07.03A
conscription 42.03.27A, 42.04.24A,
42.05.01A, 42.12.11E

326

constitution 50.01.13A

currency 54.10.22B

economy 39.06.09E, 40.01.12A,
40.09.13C, 41.05.02A, 42.02.13A,
42.06.26A, 42.10.02D, 43.04.30A,
44.03.15A, 44.04.28A, 44.10.27A,
45.04.20B, 45.10.26A, 47.05.02B,
49.09.30B, 53.02.27C

education 47.02.07C

federal elections 40.03.15C, 40.03.29A,
49.07.01A, 53.07.31B, 53.08.14A

federal-provincial relations 41.01.17B,
50.01.13A

foreign policy 38.11.25C, 39.09.13D,
47.01.24A, 48.12.31A, 49.05.20B,
49.05.27A, 49.06.17D, 49.12.09C

House of Commons 52.05.16A

human rights 48.04.16A, 48.06.18A,
53.04.17B

identity 48.09.17B

Japanese deportations 46.12.06B

labour 32.07.22C

native peoples 38.11.25C, 53.06.26B

politics 44.03.15A, 53.07.31B, 53.11.20A

politics, Co-operative Commonwealth
Federation 39.09.13D, 40.03.29A,
42.03.13B, 42.05.08C, 42.08.07G,
44.03.15A, 47.01.24B, 53.08.14A

politics, Liberal Party 40.03.15C,
40.03.29A, 41.11.28A, 49.07.01A,
53.08.14A

politics, Progressive Conservative Party
40.03.15C, 42.12.18E

politics, Social Credit Party 40.03.29A,
45.12.21B, 47.01.31A, 47.10.10C,
47.10.24C, 48.03.05A, 48.04.16A,
48.06.18A, 49.02.11B, 49.05.27A,
49.07.01A, 50.05.12B, 53.08.14A

prisoners of war 46.01.18B

privy council 47.01.24B, 47.02.07C

provincialism 46.03.01D

Roman Catholic Church 46.06.07E

Canada-American relations 52.11.07B,
53.11.27A

Canadian Broadcasting Commission
39.01.13E, 39.09.22B, 39.12.22A,
40.08.30F, 51.11.23C

Canadian Club 40.09.27D, 48.01.30A,
48.01.30B

Canadian Forum, The 46.03.01D, 47.01.24B

Canadian Jewish Chronicle, The 39.01.05A,
39.01.20C, 39.08.25C, 40.06.21B,
40.06.28C, 41.01.03E, 41.07.18E,
42.05.08B, 42.11.20C, 44.05.12B,
46.09.20C, 46.10.16A, 49.05.27B,
49.06.10A, 49.07.22A, 49.08.05A,
49.11.11A, 50.10.27A, 53.03.13A

Canadian Jewish Committee 32.07.08A,
32.07.22A

Canadian Jewish Congress 37.07.09B,
37.07.16A, 37.08.06C, 38.11.18D,
39.01.04C, 39.01.08A, 39.01.20A,
39.01.27A, 39.01.27B, 39.03.24B,
39.08.04A, 39.08.11A, 39.11.10B,
40.02.23A, 40.02.23D, 40.07.12A,
40.10.02B, 40.12.06A, 41.01.17C,
41.02.07B, 41.02.28B, 41.03.07A,
41.04.17B, 41.08.22A, 41.11.28B,
42.01.09A, 42.01.16A, 42.04.17B,
42.04.24A, 42.05.01A, 42.06.12A,
42.07.24B, 42.09.11B, 42.10.09A,
42.11.20B, 43.02.05A, 43.02.19C,
43.03.26A, 43.05.28A, 43.07.16B,
43.09.17A, 43.12.17A, 44.03.17C,
44.03.31C, 44.06.02A, 44.06.16B,
44.09.22A, 44.10.06A, 45.01.12A,
45.01.19A, 45.10.05A, 45.12.21A,
45.12.28A, 46.05.24C, 46.11.01A,
47.05.30A, 47.05.30B, 47.06.07A,
47.06.07B, 47.06.07C, 47.10.03B,
48.08.06A, 48.09.03A, 49.02.04A,
49.08.05A, 49.10.21A, 49.10.21B,
49.10.28B, 49.11.04A, 49.12.02A,
50.09.22C, 50.11.24A, 50.12.01B,
50.12.22A, 50.12.29A, 51.03.09A,
51.03.23A, 51.11.02A, 51.11.09B,
52.02.01B, 52.06.27A, 52.10.17B,
52.10.24A, 52.12.19A, 53.03.06B,
53.05.01B, 53.10.30A

*Canadian Jewish Eagle, The. See Keneder
Adler.*

Canadian Legion 44.05.05B

Canadian Youth Congress 40.07.12D,
40.08.09B

Canadian Zionist, The 36.10.00B

Čapek, Karel 39.01.04A, 44.02.04D, 52.11.28A

Capitalism 39.10.13F, 40.05.17F

Caplan, Rupert 48.07.23C, 48.07.30D

Capone, Al 39.01.06D, 39.12.08G, 39.12.15I, 40.03.01D, 45.10.19A

Cardozo, Benjamin 32.07.22E

Carlyle, Thomas 27.12.10A, 39.04.28G, 42.07.10D

Carman, Bliss 41.01.10C

Caro, Rabbi Joseph 41.12.26D, 49.10.07D

Carol, King of Rumania 38.12.09C, 38.12.30B, 38.12.30E, 39.10.13E, 39.12.08E, 40.01.24A, 40.03.22F, 40.06.28D, 40.07.05A, 40.07.05F, 40.08.09E, 40.08.16D, 40.09.06D, 40.09.13F, 40.09.20H, 40.10.11C

Carrel, Alexis 39.10.20G, 42.10.16D, 44.09.01A

Casablanca 48.06.11C, 49.09.16C, 49.09.23D. *See also* World War II, Casablanca conference.

Catullus 39.02.17G

Celtic Revival 37.06.00A, 42.07.10D

Censorship. *See also* freedom of speech; journalism; propaganda.
    Canada 40.11.29D, 51.11.23C
    Italy 38.11.25A
    Palestine 44.10.20D
    Quebec 39.04.14F, 40.01.05G, 40.04.28A
    Soviet Union 37.07.30C, 40.09.27G

Chabad, Motka 34.02.00A, 53.01.02C, 53.01.23C

Chagall, Bella 46.12.06D

Chagall, Marc 46.12.06D, 50.06.09C

Chaloult, René 42.05.29F, 42.08.21E

Chamberlain, Houston Stewart 41.12.05D

Chamberlain, Joseph 39.06.30E, 43.04.16A, 43.04.30B

Chamberlain, Neville 39.05.19D, 38.11.11I, 38.11.18F, 38.11.25E, 38.11.25F, 38.12.02A, 38.12.02C, 38.12.02F, 38.12.09F, 38.12.16E, 38.12.27B, 38.12.30F, 38.12.30G, 38.12.30H, 39.01.06A, 39.01.15B, 39.01.22B, 39.01.27B, 39.01.27F, 39.02.03C, 39.02.10A,
39.02.10G, 39.02.21C, 39.03.03A, 39.03.05A, 39.03.15C, 39.03.17A, 39.03.17C, 39.03.17D, 39.03.24F, 39.03.24G, 39.03.29A, 39.03.31F, 39.04.07A, 39.04.07D, 39.04.07E, 39.04.21F, 39.04.28A, 39.05.09A, 39.05.19G, 39.05.26A, 39.06.09F, 39.06.16B, 39.06.23H, 39.07.07B, 39.07.14G, 39.07.21F, 39.07.21G, 39.07.21H, 39.07.28B, 39.07.28E, 39.07.28G, 39.08.04G, 39.08.18F, 39.08.25A, 39.08.25D, 39.09.08A, 39.09.08E, 39.09.13D, 39.09.27E, 39.10.06C, 39.10.13A, 39.10.15A, 39.11.24C, 39.11.24D, 39.11.24E, 40.01.19A, 40.02.02A, 40.03.01F, 40.04.12A, 40.04.12E, 40.05.10I, 40.05.17E, 40.07.24A, 40.11.15G, 41.06.27D, 41.07.25C, 41.08.15B, 41.11.14A, 42.02.27G, 42.06.05A, 42.07.03C, 42.08.21A, 44.01.28A, 44.03.24A, 44.05.19B, 44.08.11C, 44.10.20B, 44.10.20D, 44.11.03A, 45.03.23A, 45.08.17A, 45.09.28A, 45.10.12A, 46.07.26A, 46.11.08A, 47.10.31A, 49.07.29A, 55.04.15A. *See also* oratory.

Chambers, Whittaker 50.02.10B, 50.07.28B

Chanukah 29.12.00A, 38.12.23A, 39.12.08A, 40.12.27A, 41.12.12A, 42.12.04A, 43.12.24A, 45.11.30A, 46.12.20A, 47.12.05B, 48.12.24A, 49.12.16A, 50.12.01A, 51.12.21A, 52.05.29B, 52.12.12A, 53.12.04A

Chaplin, Charlie 38.11.11H, 41.07.25D, 49.06.02C

Chassidism 32.006.00A, 35.11.00B, 44.01.07C, 45.11.02C, 46.08.30E, 48.12.03D. *See also* Jewish folksongs; messianism.

Chaucer, Geoffrey 32.03.00A, 36.10.00E

Chelm 35.11.00B, 39.09.08F, 43.03.05C, 46.02.15C, 53.01.02C

Chesterton, G.K. 27.11.05A, 27.11.19A

Chiang Kai-shek 39.06.30C, 41.02.28D, 41.03.21F, 42.08.14E, 43.01.22C, 43.01.29B, 43.12.03B

Chmelnitzki, Bogdan 32.03.00A,
39.07.21G, 43.12.31B, 45.05.11D,
45.08.03D, 48.10.01A

Chovevei Zion 31.06.00A, 31.11.00A,
32.05.00A, 36.10.00D, 43.05.07C,
48.05.14B, 48.07.30A, 53.12.18B

Christian Front 40.01.19F, 40.01.26D,
40.02.02F, 40.02.09B, 40.03.15D,
40.04.05B, 44.02.18A

Church, Samuel Harden 40.05.03A,
40.05.03D

Churchill, Winston 37.07.30A, 38.12.30H,
39.06.09F, 39.07.28G, 39.08.18F,
39.09.22B, 39.10.06E, 40.01.24A,
40.01.26A, 40.02.02A, 40.03.01A,
40.05.10I, 40.05.15A, 40.05.17E,
40.06.07B, 40.06.21A, 40.06.28E,
40.07.12E, 40.07.19E, 40.08.23A,
40.08.30G, 40.09.06I, 40.09.13A,
40.10.16B, 40.10.23A, 40.11.15B,
40.11.29A, 40.11.29H, 40.11.29I,
40.12.13B, 41.01.03A, 41.02.14D,
41.02.14E, 41.03.14A, 41.03.21E,
41.03.28A, 41.04.17D, 41.05.02D,
41.05.09B, 41.05.09C, 41.05.16E,
41.05.30A, 41.06.13A, 41.06.27A,
41.06.27D, 41.07.18C, 41.08.01B,
41.08.22C, 41.08.22D, 41.08.22F,
41.08.29E, 41.09.05E, 41.09.12C,
41.09.26B, 41.10.10D, 41.11.07D,
41.11.14A, 41.11.14D, 41.12.05B, 41.12.26B,
42.01.02A, 42.01.16A, 42.02.06A,
42.02.27G, 42.05.08F, 42.06.26B,
42.07.10C, 42.07.17D, 42.07.24C,
42.08.14C, 42.08.21A, 42.08.21B,
42.09.25A, 42.10.09D, 42.10.30A,
42.11.13A, 42.11.27C, 42.12.04C,
42.12.04D, 42.12.18B, 43.01.22C,
43.01.29A, 43.01.29B, 43.03.12A,
43.05.14C, 43.06.11A, 43.07.23C,
43.08.27A, 43.09.10A, 43.09.24A,
43.09.29A, 43.11.05A, 43.12.03A,
43.12.03B, 43.12.10A, 44.01.28A,
44.02.11A, 44.02.11B, 44.03.10B,
44.05.05E, 44.08.11A, 44.08.11C,
44.08.25C, 44.09.01C, 44.09.22B,
44.10.13D, 44.10.20A, 44.10.20B,

44.10.20C, 44.10.27D, 44.11.03A,
44.11.10B, 44.11.24A, 44.12.22B,
45.01.05A, 45.02.02B, 45.02.16A,
45.02.16B, 45.03.02B, 45.03.02C,
45.03.16C, 45.03.23A, 45.04.06B,
45.04.20B, 45.06.15A, 45.08.03A,
45.08.17A, 45.10.12A, 46.02.22C,
46.03.01B, 46.03.08A, 46.08.02A,
46.09.06A, 46.10.16A, 46.11.29C,
47.01.10B, 47.02.07B, 47.02.21A,
47.03.14A, 47.03.14B, 48.04.29B,
48.06.11B, 48.12.17A, 48.12.24A,
49.03.25A, 49.07.15A, 49.07.29A,
49.09.16B, 49.09.23D, 49.09.30B,
51.07.13A, 51.08.10A, 51.10.05C, 51.12.14A,
52.01.25A, 52.02.08A, 52.09.05A,
53.06.12A, 53.06.19C, 53.07.31A,
53.10.30C, 53.12.11A, 54.02.05A,
54.02.05A, 55.04.15A, 55.05.06A. *See also*
oratory.

Chutzpah 52.07.04A

Ciano, Galeazzo 38.12.09D, 39.08.18E,
39.11.03H, 40.03.22E, 40.09.27E,
41.01.24C, 44.01.14A

Cicero, Marcus Tullius 32.08.05B,
46.03.29D

Clausewitz, Karl von 44.09.01C, 48.06.25A,
49.04.01A, 49.05.13B, 49.07.29B,
51.10.19A

Clemenceau, Georges 32.07.29C,
35.07.19B, 36.10.00E, 39.03.24E,
39.06.30A, 40.06.28E, 41.07.04E,
41.08.22D, 42.11.13A, 42.11.27D,
42.12.11C, 43.01.22D, 44.03.17D,
48.04.09A, 48.04.23A

Clichés 49.01.28D

Clough, Arthur Hugh 39.05.19B, 41.05.02D

Cocteau, Jean 44.02.04D

Cohen, Elliot 37.05.00C

Cohen, Florence Friedlander 41.06.20E

Cohen, Zvi Hirsch 40.05.03B, 50.11.24A,
52.01.04B, 52.12.19A

Cold War 48.10.15B, 49.05.13A, 49.05.27C,
49.06.02A, 49.09.23A, 50.02.17B,
50.03.24C, 50.04.14A, 50.05.12A,
50.06.02B, 50.06.09B, 50.06.16C,
50.07.07C, 50.07.14B, 50.08.11A,

50.08.18A, 50.10.27B, 50.12.08A,
51.01.05A, 51.06.15A, 51.08.10B, 51.11.16A,
52.04.18A, 52.08.08A, 52.09.05A,
52.09.12B, 52.10.17A, 53.01.02A,
53.08.14B, 53.08.21B, 53.12.11A, 55.03.11A,
55.05.06A, 55.05.20A, 55.06.10A. *See also*
anti-communism; atomic era;
McCarthyism.

Coldwell, James William 41.06.20D,
42.05.08C, 42.08.07G, 47.05.02B,
49.02.11B

Coleridge, Samuel Taylor 32.03.00A,
39.06.16G, 45.07.06D, 46.04.19C

Colette 41.09.05A

College diplomas 41.06.20B

Combined Jewish Appeal 41.10.17A,
41.10.31A, 42.09.11B, 43.09.17A,
44.09.22A, 45.10.05A, 46.11.01A,
47.10.24A, 48.11.12A, 49.11.04A,
50.11.03A, 51.11.02B, 52.10.24A,
52.12.05D, 53.10.30A

Comic strips 42.08.07F

Comintern 41.06.27D, 41.07.04A,
43.05.28C, 43.12.31B, 47.10.10B. *See also*
anti-comintern.

Communism 30.01.24A, 39.02.24B,
39.03.17B, 39.09.01F, 39.09.22E,
39.09.27F, 39.10.06D, 39.10.13F,
39.10.20E, 39.12.22A, 40.01.05D,
40.01.05G, 40.01.19D, 40.02.16B,
40.05.17F, 40.12.20F, 43.05.28C,
44.01.07B, 44.09.22B, 47.07.04C,
47.10.10B, 47.10.24C, 48.02.06C,
49.03.04A, 49.04.01A, 49.04.29A,
49.05.27C, 49.07.15B, 50.12.01B,
52.11.28A. *See also* anti-comintern; anti-
communism;
comintern; dialectic; propaganda; Russian Revolution (1917); Soviet Union;
totalitarianism; United Nations; Young
Communist League.
and art 30.11.14A, 32.08.05E, 48.02.20B,
50.08.25B
Britain 39.08.25A, 43.06.18C, 45.07.20C,
52.07.11A
Canada 40.03.08C, 40.03.29A,
40.08.09B, 40.12.27B, 42.07.31B,

42.08.07G, 42.08.14B, 52.07.04D,
53.08.14A. *See also* The Red Martlet.
China 49.05.27C, 50.11.10A
France 40.07.26H, 40.09.13H
Germany 32.07.08C, 32.07.29B,
32.08.05B
Israel 49.11.11C, 49.12.23B, 50.08.25A,
51.01.05B, 51.07.20B, 51.08.03A,
51.12.14A, 52.02.01A, 52.06.20B
Italy 48.04.23B
Jewish 39.12.22D, 39.12.29E, 41.12.12C,
49.04.08A, 50.05.05B, 52.06.20B,
52.12.05A, 52.12.26B
purge trials 39.03.28B, 39.09.01F,
40.08.23B, 43.03.05B, 49.04.01A,
51.11.23A, 52.03.14B, 52.06.20B,
52.11.28A, 52.12.05A, 52.12.26B,
53.01.16A, 53.04.10A
United States 39.12.01E, 39.12.15H,
39.12.22B, 40.03.01D, 40.08.28B,
40.11.08F, 40.11.22F, 40.11.22G,
41.06.27A, 42.05.22C, 50.07.21C

Computers 49.06.02C

Conscientious objectors 40.02.02G,
51.03.09B

Contemporary Jewish Record 42.01.02D

Cooper, Duff 38.12.27B, 39.10.06C,
44.07.07C

Coppard, A.E. 46.03.29D

Coughlin, Charles 38.11.18B, 39.07.21C,
39.07.28A, 39.08.25C, 39.12.22A,
40.01.19F, 40.01.26D, 40.02.02F,
40.02.09B, 40.03.15D, 40.08.30D,
41.11.07B, 42.02.06D, 42.04.17A,
44.02.18A

Cowper, William 46.04.19C

Crane, Hart 46.03.29D

Creech-Jones, Arthur 47.08.01B, 47.10.03A

Crestohl, Leon 48.12.10A, 51.05.25A,
53.02.27C, 53.08.14A

Cripps, Stafford 39.03.21B, 42.02.27G,
42.03.20C, 42.04.24C, 42.04.24D,
42.05.08C, 42.08.07E, 49.07.15A,
49.09.30B, 49.10.07BCroce, Benedetto
44.02.04D

Croll, David 39.10.13B, 40.08.16F,
46.12.06C, 48.03.05A, 50.01.27A,

53.08.14A

Cromwell, Oliver 32.03.00A, 40.07.24A,
    41.02.14F, 41.10.31D, 44.06.16C,
    45.10.26A, 47.02.14A, 48.10.01A
Cruikshank, George 48.09.17E
Cubism 27.12.03A
Cudahy, John 40.08.16E
Cummings, E.E. 46.03.22D
Cuppy, Will 41.12.12C
Czechoslovakia. *See also* anti-Semitism;
    Munich agreement; World War II.
    German cession of the Sudetenland
        38.11.11D, 38.12.02F, 38.12.30E,
        39.01.02B, 39.01.06G, 39.01.17A,
        39.02.03C, 39.03.03A, 39.03.17A,
        39.03.24A, 39.03.24F, 39.03.29A,
        39.03.31E, 39.05.12E, 39.07.28B,
        39.09.19A, 39.11.24D, 40.03.22F,
        41.10.03A
    post-World War II 52.12.05A, 52.12.26B
Czerniakow, Adam 42.08.21C

Dadaism 48.11.05B
Daladier, Edouard 38.11.11I, 38.12.02E,
    38.12.09D, 39.01.06A, 39.01.27A,
    39.01.27B, 39.02.10G, 39.03.17C,
    39.03.21B, 39.03.24F, 39.03.28A,
    39.04.07D, 39.05.12E, 39.05.19G,
    39.07.14D, 39.07.28E, 39.08.11B,
    39.08.18D, 39.09.08A, 39.10.20A,
    40.02.02A, 40.08.02E, 40.08.16C,
    40.09.20D, 41.01.10E, 42.02.06B,
    42.02.20A, 43.04.09C
Dalton, Hugh 40.12.06B, 46.06.14A,
    48.07.23A
Dante Alighieri 32.07.08A, 39.01.06E,
    39.06.16G, 40.08.09A, 46.02.22C,
    49.01.28D
Darlan, Jean Louis François 41.03.21C,
    41.03.21F, 41.04.04C, 41.05.16B,
    41.05.23E, 41.05.30E, 41.05.30G,
    41.06.06C, 41.08.15A, 41.08.15B,
    41.08.29D, 41.10.24C, 41.11.21B,
    42.02.27E, 42.11.13D, 42.11.27D,
    42.12.11C, 43.01.01D, 43.09.10A
Darwin, Charles 46.01.18D, 50.05.05C
Davar 44.08.18D, 45.06.01C, 46.08.30C,

49.12.23E
David, Athanase 32.07.08J, 53.01.30A
David, King of Israel 29.12.00A, 37.06.00A,
    39.01.17A, 44.06.23D, 48.05.07B,
    50.05.12D, 53.01.16B, 53.03.06D
Dead Sea 43.02.12A, 44.05.19C, 52.08.22A
Dearborn Independent, The 38.12.09H,
    41.02.21F, 42.01.23E, 42.02.20B,
    45.11.02B
Deborah 29.12.00A, 49.10.14C, 52.11.21A
Decalogue 32.10.07A, 39.05.19B, 40.06.07A,
    41.05.30C, 41.10.31D, 42.04.01B,
    44.02.11C, 44.02.11D, 44.05.26A,
    45.05.17A, 45.11.16D, 46.05.31A,
    48.07.16C, 51.06.08A, 51.09.28D,
    52.05.29B, 53.02.20B, 53.05.15A,
    54.06.04A
De Gaulle, Charles 40.08.30I, 40.06.28E,
    40.11.01F, 41.01.10E, 41.06.06C,
    41.10.03C, 43.01.01D, 43.01.29B,
    43.01.29D, 44.08.25A, 45.06.15A
De Haas, Jacob 34.12.00C, 37.04.00B
Demagoguery 40.11.22E, 41.09.26D,
    42.03.27A, 42.12.11E, 43.01.22C,
    44.05.26B
De Mille, Cecil B. 54.06.04A
Democracy 39.01.13B, 39.03.24D,
    39.10.06C, 40.01.19D, 40.02.02E,
    40.02.09E, 41.01.24E, 43.09.24D,
    44.11.10A, 44.12.22B, 49.06.24B
Der Angriff 39.06.16A, 39.07.28G, 39.08.04C
Der Forvertz 36.10.00E, 40.02.09B,
    45.01.19B, 45.03.23A
Der Stuermer 40.03.15F, 40.03.22B,
    40.08.07A, 40.09.13H, 41.10.10C,
    45.11.16A, 48.11.05B, 50.08.18C
Der Tog 40.02.07B, 41.07.25A, 47.09.05A
Dewey, Thomas E. 39.02.28B, 39.07.25J,
    44.10.20B, 48.11.05A, 48.11.19A,
    50.09.29C, 51.03.02B, 52.11.07B
Dialectic 39.03.17B, 39.10.13F, 39.12.22B,
    40.11.22F, 40.11.22G, 43.05.28C,
    43.12.31B, 44.09.22B, 46.03.29D,
    49.01.28D, 49.04.08A
Diaspora 28.11.00A, 29.05.00A, 29.11.00A,
    29.12.00A, 31.06.00A, 32.05.00A,
    32.07.08J, 32.09.23A, 33.01.00A,

34.05.00A, 36.10.00A, 36.12.00B,
37.02.00A, 38.12.16C, 39.03.31A,
39.04.14A, 39.07.21A, 40.01.05B,
40.01.19B, 40.12.20F, 41.01.31A,
41.03.14A, 41.05.09A, 42.11.06D,
42.11.20D, 42.12.18D, 43.04.09B,
43.07.09A, 43.10.17B, 44.07.28C,
46.03.22A, 46.08.02A, 47.04.04B,
48.01.09B, 48.01.09C, 48.04.23A,
48.04.29A, 48.05.14B, 48.07.30A,
48.09.24A, 48.10.01A, 49.02.11E,
49.05.13C, 49.08.05B, 49.08.19A,
49.09.02A, 49.09.09A, 49.09.30C,
49.10.21D, 49.11.11C, 50.03.24D,
50.10.13B, 51.02.23A, 51.04.20A,
51.05.11A, 52.01.11B, 52.09.12B, 52.11.28A,
52.11.28B, 54.01.29A, 55.04.06A
achievements of 50.04.07C, 53.01.09C,
53.01.16B, 53.02.06B, 53.02.13C,
53.02.20B, 53.02.27D
negation of 31.00.00A, 49.03.18D,
49.04.22D, 49.06.10A, 50.04.07C,
50.04.07C, 51.11.02A, 53.01.09C,
53.01.16B, 53.02.06B
Dickens, Charles 40.11.01F, 48.09.17E,
48.12.10C, 49.02.25A
Dickinson, Emily 46.04.19C
Dictatorship 38.11.18C, 38.11.18F, 39.02.03I,
39.03.17A, 39.03.17B, 39.05.05D,
39.05.19G, 39.10.06C, 39.10.27H,
39.11.24C, 39.12.22C, 40.01.19D,
40.02.02E, 40.04.05D, 40.08.09C,
41.05.16E. See also communism; Nazism; totalitarianism.
Dictionary of National Biography, The
47.03.07C
Dies, Martin 39.12.08F, 40.02.02F,
40.04.05B, 40.08.28B, 40.11.22D,
44.04.21A
Dilling, Elizabeth 42.07.31A
Disney, Walt 46.01.18D
Disraeli, Benjamin 27.11.05A, 31.00.00A,
31.12.00A, 32.05.00A, 32.08.12A,
34.05.00A, 39.03.24G, 40.02.27A,
40.03.01F, 44.07.28D, 44.08.25B,
45.07.20A, 46.07.19A, 46.08.23A,
46.09.13A, 47.07.25A, 49.02 18B,

51.10.19A, 51.12.14A, 53.02.20B, 53.04.03A
Dizengoff, Meier 36.10.00D
Doenitz, Karl 44.03.17B, 46.10.04A,
52.06.06A
Dollfuss, Engelbert 39.08.04B, 41.09.05B
Donne, John 44.02.00A, 44.02.25A,
45.08.17A, 46.03.29D, 50.05.26D
Doré, Gustave 49.09.16C
Doriot, Jacques 40.08.02E, 40.09.13H,
42.10.02E, 44.08.25C
Dostoyevsky, Fyodor 49.07.15B
Doughty, Charles Montagu 50.03.24D
Douglas, Lewis 41.10.03B
Doukhobors 50.05.12C
Draft dodgers 41.05.02F
Drake, Francis 40.07.19E
Drapeau, Jean 42.12.11E
Dreiser, Theodore 35.07.19B, 42.09.25A
Drew, George Alexander 42.08.07G,
49.07.01A, 53.08.14A, 53.11.20A
Dreyfus, Alfred 31.06.00A, 35.02.00A,
35.07.19B, 39.04.28B, 40.08.16C,
40.08.30I, 42.07.17D, 44.07.21A,
48.03.19D
Dryden, John 27.10.29A, 32.03.00A
Dudek, Louis 45.06.08D
Duke of Edinburgh 47.11.21A, 51.10.26A,
53.06.19C
Dulles, John Foster 50.04.14A, 53.05.22A,
53.06.26A, 53.11.06A, 54.02.19A,
55.05.06A
Dunkelman, Ben 48.07.30C, 49.11.25A
Duplessis, Maurice 37.08.06C, 39.05.05A,
39.06.09A, 39.07.11A, 39.07.28I,
39.10.27B, 40.04.14B, 40.04.28A,
40.06.02A, 43.11.12A, 44.03.17C,
44.04.28C, 44.10.20C, 46.06.07C,
46.12.13B, 47.01.24B, 47.05.30B,
48.03.26B, 49.10.28C, 52.01.11A,
52.01.25B, 52.02.01B, 54.01.22A
Dybbuk 48.07.23C

Eban, Abba 49.01.28A, 49.05.20B,
49.06.17D, 49.11.04B, 50.03.03B,
50.08.25C, 51.05.25B, 51.07.20A,
51.08.10A, 51.08.10A, 52.10.03B,
54.02.19A, 54.10.22A, 55.04.01A

paganda.
and religion 39.03.10A, 39.08.11D
and Roman Catholic Church
38.12.09G, 38.12.16D, 40.05.10D,
40.05.10G
Arab 39.07.14D, 39.07.21H, 39.10.27F,
40.11.08B, 41.09.05C
Argentina 45.10.26C, 46.02.15B
Belgium 39.04.07C
Britain 36.11.00B, 39.07.28G, 39.08.11B,
39.11.10E, 40.01.12D, 40.02.02A,
40.03.29D, 41.08.08G, 43.11.26A,
44.09.29A, 45.12.28B, 46.11.22A,
47.09.05B, 47.10.10A
Canada 39.01.13E, 39.03.10F, 39.04.28J,
39.09.06B, 42.08.07G, 42.08.14B
Denmark 39.04.07C
economics 39.02.03I
Germany 38.12.09D, 49.07.08C
Hungary 39.06.16C
Italy 38.12.09D, 39.05.05F, 39.05.19G,
40.09.13B, 42.10.30B
Latin America 39.02.03B
Mexico 43.01.15D
Quebec 35.08.09B, 39.02.10B,
39.02.24F, 39.04.28E, 39.05.05A,
39.05.12D, 39.06.02D, 39.06.09A,
39.06.23B, 39.07.11A, 39.07.21E,
39.07.21G, 39.08.04A, 39.08.04F,
40.05.31A, 40.06.02A, 40.06.14H,
40.06.21B, 40.06.28B, 40.06.28F,
40.07.05B, 42.03.27A, 44.04.28C,
45.05.11C, 45.07.13A
rise of 32.08.05D, 39.09.01D
South Africa 41.02.07F
Spain 39.02.24D, 40.04.05C, 42.12.11B,
42.12.25E, 45.10.26C, 46.03.01C
Sweden 42.09.25B
Switzerland 39.03.31G
United States 39.03.03B, 39.07.28A,
39.09.20A, 39.11.12A, 39.12.01I,
39.12.22A, 40.01.19F, 40.01.26D,
40.02.02F, 40.02.09B, 40.04.05B,
40.08.16B, 40.08.23G, 40.08.28B,
40.11.08F, 41.11.07B, 42.04.17A
Fast, Howard 46.05.10B
Faulhaber, Michael von 38.11.18A,

38.12.16D, 39.04.21A, 40.07.05B
Federal Bureau of Investigation 40.01.19F
Federation of Jewish Community Services
52.01.25C, 52.10.24A, 53.10.30A
Federation of Jewish Philanthropies
39.06.30B, 39.10.27A, 40.11.01A,
40.12.20B, 41.03.07A, 41.07.04B,
41.08.29A, 41.10.17A, 41.10.31A,
42.09.11B, 42.09.11C, 43.09.17A,
44.03.17C, 44.09.22A, 45.10.05A,
46.11.01A, 49.12.02A, 50.11.24A,
50.12.22A, 52.01.25C, 52.12.05D
Federation of Polish Jews 39.09.07A,
39.11.24A, 40.10.11A, 40.12.06A,
41.10.31B, 42.03.13D, 52.12.19A
Feffer, Itzik 43.09.03B, 51.09.28C
Feifer, Shaika 34.02.00A, 53.01.23C
Ferdinand II, King of Spain 40.07.26G
Feuchtwanger, Lion 31.01.00A, 40.05.15B,
40.07.12F, 40.12.20F, 44.02.04D
Fifth column 40.05.03E, 40.05.10C,
40.05.24A, 40.05.24G, 40.05.31A,
40.06.28B, 40.07.05B, 40.07.19E,
40.07.19F, 40.08.02C, 40.08.09D,
40.08.16H, 40.08.23G, 40.08.28B,
40.09.06F, 40.09.13E, 40.09.13H,
40.11.29D, 40.12.13D, 41.01.17D,
41.01.24B, 41.01.31F, 41.02.07F,
41.02.28E, 41.04.25C, 41.05.02F,
41.06.20A, 41.07.11A, 41.09.26A,
41.10.31D, 42.03.27A, 42.04.17A,
42.04.24A, 42.05.08E, 42.08.07G,
42.08.14B, 42.09.25A, 43.06.25A,
43.11.26A, 50.06.23A, 51.09.21A
Film 39.07.16B, 39.07.16J, 39.12.29G,
40.07.12B, 40.09.13G, 41.09.26A,
41.10.03B, 41.10.24E, 44.04.13C,
45.02.09B, 46.01.18D, 48.09.17E,
54.06.04A. See also anti-Semitism; Bible.
Fineberg, Nathaniel S. 39.04.14C,
40.05.03G, 47.11.14B, 49.03.25C
Fineberg, Zigmond 39.04.14C, 41.05.23A,
49.03.25C
First Statement 45.06.08D
Fitch, Louis 39.01.20B, 39.05.05A, 39.07.28I
Fitzgerald, Edward 29.05.00A
Flandin, Pierre-Etienne 40.12.20D,

41.01.10E

Flaubert, Gustave 48.09.10D

Forbes, Rosita 40.02.16C, 40.02.23D

Ford, Henry 32.07.08J, 40.06.28A,
  40.08.16H, 40.08.30F, 41.02.21F,
  41.03.14C, 41.04.17E, 41.06.27A,
  41.07.11B, 42.01.23E, 42.02.20B,
  43.02.19C, 45.11.02B, 46.11.29C

Foster, William Zebulon 39.12.22B,
  41.06.27A

Four Freedoms 41.01.10D, 41.03.28A,
  41.06.06D, 42.04.01A, 42.07.17D,
  42.10.09D, 43.01.15F, 43.02.26B,
  43.03.26B, 43.04.16A, 43.05.28A,
  43.06.18A, 44.04.21B, 44.08.11A,
  44.08.11C, 44.10.27D, 44.12.22B,
  46.09.06A, 46.09.25A, 47.04.04A,
  49.09.23D

Fourteen Points 36.10.00E, 38.11.18F,
  39.03.24E, 39.06.30A, 39.08.18F,
  39.11.05A, 39.11.24E, 41.08.22C,
  41.08.22D, 43.04.23A, 43.08.27A,
  44.03.17D, 44.09.29B, 45.02.16A,
  48.04.09A

France, Anatole 35.07.19B, 42.10.30D

France. See also anti-Semitism; Arabs;
  French Revolution; Front Populaire;
  Jews; journalism; nationalism; racism;
  World War I; World War II.
  foreign policy 39.02.21C, 39.03.21B,
    39.03.28A, 39.06.30E, 39.08.18D,
    39.10.13A, 40.04.12G, 45.06.01A,
    50.09.22A, 50.11.17B
  Vichy 40.06.28E, 40.07.09A, 40.07.12C,
    40.07.12E, 40.07.19B, 40.07.19D,
    40.07.19F, 40.08.02E, 40.08.16C,
    40.08.23F, 40.08.30C, 40.08.30E,
    40.08.30I, 40.09.06F, 40.09.06G,
    40.09.06H, 40.09.13H, 40.09.20D,
    40.10.11E, 40.10.23A, 40.10.23B,
    40.10.23C, 40.11.01F, 40.11.22E,
    40.11.22F, 40.12.13C, 40.12.20D,
    41.01.10B, 41.01.10E, 41.02.07E,
    41.03.21C, 41.03.28B, 41.04.04C,
    41.04.25F, 41.05.16B, 41.05.23E,
    41.05.23F, 41.06.06C, 41.06.13F,
    41.07.04E, 41.07.18F, 41.08.01C,

41.08.01D, 41.08.08A, 41.08.15A,
    41.08.15B, 41.08.29D, 41.09.05A,
    41.09.12B, 41.10.03C, 41.10.24C,
    41.11.21B, 42.01.02A, 42.02.20A,
    42.02.27E, 42.04.24C, 42.04.24D,
    42.05.08A, 42.06.26C, 42.07.31C,
    42.09.04A, 42.09.18B, 42.09.25G,
    42.10.02E, 42.10.16D, 42.11.13A,
    42.11.27D, 42.12.11C, 43.01.01D,
    43.02.19B, 43.04.09C, 43.05.14C,
    44.03.03C, 44.03.17B, 44.08.25A,
    44.08.25C, 45.06.15A, 45.08.03C,
    49.03.04A. See also anti-commu-
    nism; Arabs.

Franco, Francisco 37.07.23B, 38.12.30F,
  38.12.30G, 39.01.27F, 39.02.03G,
  39.02.17B, 39.02.24D, 39.03.03D,
  39.05.26B, 39.05.26C, 39.08.25D,
  40.04.05C, 40.07.19F, 40.07.26G,
  40.08.02A, 40.09.06F, 41.04.11B,
  42.12.11B, 42.12.25E, 43.07.23B,
  44.01.21B, 44.08.04A, 45.02.16B,
  45.05.11A, 45.05.17C, 45.06.15B,
  45.08.03C, 45.10.26C, 46.02.15B,
  48.03.19A, 48.04.16B, 49.01.14C,
  49.05.20B, 50.11.10D, 54.02.05A,
  54.02.05A, 54.02.19A. See also oratory.

Frank, Jacob 41.12.12C

Frank, Jerome 41.12.12C, 42.01.30A,
  42.04.01C, 43.07.09A, 43.07.16C

Frank, Joseph N. 54.01.29A

Frank, Waldo 42.04.01C, 42.08.07A

Frankfurter, Felix 32.07.22E, 39.01.13C,
  39.02.17B

Freedom of speech 39.03.03B, 39.07.21E,
  39.11.24C, 42.04.17A, 42.05.29F,
  44.01.07B, 47.10.10A, 50.12.15B,
  51.11.23C. See also censorship.

Freeman-Mitford, Unity 39.11.03D,
  40.01.12E

Freiman, Archibald 36.10.00E, 39.09.01B,
  40.01.12A, 40.06.21C, 41.01.17A,
  41.01.24A, 41.10.10A, 44.02.04B,
  44.09.08B, 53.05.08B

Freiman, Lillian 36.10.00E, 40.01.12B,
  40.06.21C, 40.11.08A, 40.11.29C,
  41.01.24A, 41.10.10A, 49.01.21A, 53.01.30A

French Revolution 40.07.09A, 40.07.19D,
41.04.25F, 41.09.05A
Freud, Sigmund 39.06.16E, 39.09.27C,
42.02.13C, 46.02.01D, 46.03.29D,
48.07.16B, 49.01.28D, 53.02.20B
Fritsch, Werner von 39.09.27J, 40.07.05E,
41.05.16E, 42.01.23B, 46.05.03A,
46.10.09C
Front Populaire 39.08.25A, 40.07.26H,
40.09.13H, 40.09.20D
Frost, Robert 48.06.25C
Fuchs, Klaus 50.02.10B
Funk, Walther 45.11.02B, 52.06.06A
Furtwangler, Wilhelm 41.02.07D

Galileo 40.10.11D
Gamelin, Maurice Gustave 39.09.10B,
40.08.23F, 41.11.21B, 42.02.06B,
42.02.20A, 43.04.09C
Gandhi, Mahatma 35.08.09G, 36.10.00A,
38.12.16G, 39.01.22D, 39.03.15C,
39.10.20A, 40.02.07B, 40.06.14E,
40.07.26C, 40.09.20E, 41.01.03B,
41.08.08F, 42.01.02B, 42.03.20C,
42.05.01D, 42.05.08E, 42.08.07E,
42.08.14E, 43.11.26A, 44.08.18E,
46.04.19A, 46.11.29C, 47.05.09C,
48.01.16C, 48.01.23B, 48.02.06A,
48.04.02A, 48.12.03B, 50.09.01A
Garber, Michael 44.02.04B, 50.12.22A,
52.05.23B, 54.01.29A
Garber, Rabbi Simcha 42.03.13D
Gayda, Virginio 39.04.14E, 39.09.01A,
40.05.10D, 40.08.02A, 40.09.20B,
40.11.08E, 41.01.10F, 41.02.28F, 41.05.23D
Gaza 51.09.21A, 55.03.11A, 55.03.25A
Gelber, Edward E. 50.01.27A, 53.01.23A,
53.07.03C, 54.01.29A
Genocide 52.05.16A. *See also* Nazism; Soviet
Union.
George V, King of England 53.04.03A
George VI, King of England 37.08.06E,
39.05.12A, 39.06.02C, 39.06.02D,
41.09.26B, 51.10.26A, 52.02.08A
Germ warfare 47.02.28C
German-American Bund 39.06.16B,
39.07.25J, 39.07.28A, 39.12.01I,

39.12.15G, 40.06.28F, 40.08.23G,
40.08.28B, 40.11.08F
German-Soviet non-aggression pact
39.09.01A, 39.09.01D, 39.09.01F,
39.09.08C, 39.09.13C, 39.09.17A,
39.09.19A, 39.09.22E, 39.09.22G,
39.09.27D, 39.09.27F, 39.10.06G,
39.11.03B, 39.11.17C, 39.12.15K,
40.01.05D, 40.01.19D, 40.02.16B,
40.03.15E, 40.03.22H, 40.04.17A,
40.09.13H, 40.10.16C, 40.11.01E,
41.04.17D, 41.06.20F, 41.06.27A,
41.06.27D, 41.07.18B, 41.08.08F,
46.01.04D, 48.02.13B, 52.01.04A,
53.01.16A
Germans
Canada 39.03.03E, 39.07.28C
Palestine 37.07.23F
Germany. *See also* anti-Semitism; communism; fascism; Israel; Jewish homeland;
Jews; journalism; Nazism; socialism;
United Nations; World War I; World
War II.
national character 40.02.23F
overeating 39.07.21I
post-World War I 37.07.16A, 40.02.16C,
47.02.28C, 51.12.07A
post-World War II 43.12.10B, 45.08.10B,
45.11.09C, 46.05.31B, 46.08.16A,
47.02.28C, 47.03.07B, 47.04.18C,
47.08.22A, 47.09.05A, 48.01.23C,
48.03.19A, 48.07.09B, 48.09.17D,
48.10.15C, 48.10.29A, 49.01.28C,
49.02.25A, 49.02.25B, 49.03.18B,
49.07.08C, 49.10.28B, 49.11.18A,
50.01.06A, 50.03.03B, 50.03.10B,
50.04.28B, 50.05.05A, 50.06.16B,
50.09.01B, 50.09.22A, 50.10.06A,
50.11.10B, 50.11.17B, 51.01.05B,
51.07.06B, 51.07.13A, 51.07.13B,
51.09.07A, 51.09.14B, 52.02.22B,
52.02.29B, 52.03.07A, 52.04.04B,
52.07.04C, 52.10.31B, 53.01.09A,
53.07.31C
post-World War II, denazification
50.04.21C, 50.05.26A, 50.06.02A,
50.08.11A, 51.05.18B, 51.09.28B,

336

43.10.20C, 44.02.04D, 47.12.26B

Handel, George Frideric 36.12.00F

Hannah 29.12.00A, 40.12.27A, 48.12.24A, 49.12.16A, 52.12.12A

Hanson, Richard Burpee 41.06.13C, 41.07.18E

Harrison, Earl Gray 45.10.05A, 45.10.12A, 45.11.16B, 46.01.11A

Hart, Ezekiel 43.12.17A

Hart, Liddell 39.09.10B

Hartt, Maurice 39.10.27B, 40.01.12C, 43.09.24D, 44.03.17C, 44.04.28C, 47.05.30B

Harvey, Jean-Charles 39.03.03C, 40.01.19G, 40.07.05B, 46.03.29B

Haskala 42.03.13D

Hasmoneans 29.12.00A, 32.05.00A, 34.10.00A, 35.02.00A, 38.12.23A, 39.12.08A, 40.12.27A, 41.12.12A, 43.12.24A, 45.04.06C, 45.09.07A, 45.11.30A, 46.12.20A, 47.01.17A, 47.12.05B, 48.12.24A, 49.12.16A, 50.10.13B, 50.12.01A, 51.10.19B, 51.12.21A, 52.05.29B, 52.12.12A, 53.01.16B, 53.02.27B, 53.12.04A

Hauptmann, Gerhart 35.07.19B, 39.05.19F, 39.07.21H, 40.05.10F, 41.02.07D, 43.10.20C

Haushofer, Karl 40.02.09H, 41.05.23G, 42.02.13C, 42.07.17A, 43.01.08A

Hayes, Saul 43.03.26A, 44.03.17C, 44.04.13A, 44.10.06A, 45.01.19A, 47.06.07B

Hebrew alphabet 32.07.08D, 51.10.12C

Hebrew calligraphy 53.05.08C

Hebrew Committee for National Liberation 44.06.02B, 44.06.23A, 44.06.30A

Hebrew culture 36.12.00E, 48.01.09B, 49.03.18C, 53.03.06C

Hebrew education 32.07.22F, 39.01.13A, 39.12.01G, 42.04.17B, 45.04.27A, 49.03.18C

Hebrew Free Loan Association 39.04.14C, 40.05.03G, 41.05.23A, 42.05.08B, 47.11.14B, 49.03.25C

Hebrew grammar 46.07.19D

Hebrew language 29.11.00A, 31.11.00A, 32.07.08D, 32.08.12F, 36.10.00E, 37.02.00D, 37.06.00A, 38.12.23B, 40.08.09A, 42.05.22D, 44.01.21D, 46.07.19D, 47.08.15A, 48.01.09B, 48.01.09C, 49.02.18D, 49.03.18C, 49.04.13A, 49.04.22C, 49.06.10A, 49.10.14B, 49.11.25C, 53.02.20B

Hebrew literature 37.06.00A, 37.06.00B, 39.12.08B, 40.01.19B, 40.08.09A, 42.07.10D, 43.10.20B, 44.12.01A, 49.06.10A, 46.03.22D, 46.07.19D, 51.11.02A, 53.07.10A. *See also* Hebrew Renaissance.

Hebrew Renaissance 29.11.00A, 37.06.00A, 42.07.10D, 43.10.20B

Hebrew scholarship 47.01.24C, 49.06.10A

Hebrew University 34.12.00C, 36.11.00B, 37.07.23C, 39.10.06B, 42.09.04B, 42.12.18D, 43.01.01C, 44.06.02A, 46.04.05B, 47.07.18A, 49.04.22C, 50.02.10A, 50.06.30B, 51.09.21A, 55.05.13A

Hecht, Ben 44.04.13C, 47.01.17A

Hegel, Georg Wilhelm Friedrich 39.03.17B, 40.04.26A, 43.11.19B, 49.04.08A

Heifetz, Jascha 53.05.01A

Heine, Heinrich 31.00.00A, 31.03.00A, 34.02.00A, 35.11.00B, 37.05.00D, 39.02.24E, 39.03.10D, 39.06.09B, 40.01.12F, 40.01.19E, 40.09.20F, 41.03.07E, 41.04.11C, 41.06.27D, 41.11.14C, 42.05.22D, 42.08.28E, 44.07.28D, 46.02.08C, 48.12.31A, 51.02.02A, 53.02.20B

Hellenism 32.05.00A, 40.11.01D, 45.11.30A

Hemingway, Ernest 42.12.25E, 44.02.00A, 45.08.17A, 49.06.10A

Hepburn, Mitchell 40.01.26F, 40.02.02E, 40.03.08G, 40.03.29C, 41.01.17B

Heraldry 52.08.15A

Heredia Jose-Maria de 48.06.11D

Herodotus 48.07.23C

Hershel of Ostropol 34.02.00A, 42.05.15C, 53.01.02C, 53.01.23C

Hertzog, James Barry 41.02.07F, 40.02.09E, 40.11.22A

Herzl, Theodor 30.01.00A, 31.00.00A,
  31.06.00A, 31.11.00A, 32.05.00A,
  32.07.22B, 33.01.00A, 34.10.00A,
  35.02.00A, 35.07.19B, 35.08.09F,
  36.10.00E, 36.11.00B, 37.01.00A,
  37.04.00B, 37.05.00B, 37.08.06A,
  39.01.06C, 39.04.07A, 39.06.30D,
  39.06.30E, 39.10.13D, 40.08.09A,
  41.05.09A, 41.07.18A, 41.10.10A,
  41.12.05D, 42.05.15B, 42.07.03B,
  42.12.18C, 43.04.16A, 43.04.30B,
  43.07.23A, 44.12.08A, 45.06.29B,
  46.10.16A, 47.06.27A, 48.05.14B,
  48.07.30A, 49.01.14C, 49.09.09A,
  50.03.24D, 51.05.04B, 52.05.29A,
  52.11.14A, 53.07.10A, 53.07.24B,
  54.06.04A, 54.10.29A
Herzog, Isaac Halevi 42.07.03B, 42.07.10C,
  42.07.24A, 44.06.30D
Heschel, Abraham J. 47.08.22C
Hess, Moses 31.06.00A, 37.05.00B,
  46.10.16A
Hess, Rudolf 39.09.27E, 39.11.101,
  39.12.27C, 41.05.16A, 41.05.16C,
  41.05.16E, 41.05.23G, 41.06.13B,
  41.07.25E, 41.08.01C, 41.10.10D,
  42.12.18B, 42.12.25B, 43.02.26D,
  43.03.12B, 43.04.09C, 43.09.17B,
  44.09.29A, 45.12.14B, 46.09.06B,
  47.04.18A, 47.04.18C, 52.06.06A
Hesse, Hermann 46.10.04A, 46.11.29C,
  48.11.12C
Heydrich, Reinhard 41.10.03A, 41.10.31F,
  42.03.20A, 42.05.29B, 42.06.19D
Hillel 46.11.01A, 52.10.24A, 53.10.30A
Hillman, Sidney 41.07.11B, 44.12.29A
Himmler, Heinrich 39.09.27E, 40.01.191,
  40.08.02C, 40.08.16A, 40.09.20E,
  40.11.22C, 41.01.17D, 41.08.01C,
  41.10.03A, 41.10.31F, 41.11.21D,
  42.02.13C, 42.03.20A, 42.05.29B,
  42.06.19D, 42.11.27E, 43.01.01D,
  43.10.08C, 44.03.03D, 44.08.25C,
  44.09.29B, 44.11.10A, 44.11.17A,
  45.08.03D, 47.08.01B, 47.08.22A,
  51.02.16B
Hindenburg, Paul von 32.07.29B, 39.08.27B

Hirohito, Emperor of Japan 38.12.02D,
  39.02.17B, 39.08.25D, 39.08.27B,
  42.06.19C, 43.08.27B, 44.02.04C,
  45.04.13C, 45.06.15B, 46.01.04C
Hirsch, Baron Maurice de 31.06.00A,
  39.12.08H
Hirschprung, Pinchos 42.03.13D, 45.06.22C
Hiss, Alger 50.01.27B, 50.02.10B
Histadrut 34.12.00C, 39.02.03A, 40.02.02B,
  41.01.31A, 43.06.11C, 43.12.31A,
  44.04.21D, 44.08.18D, 45.06.01C,
  46.01.18A, 47.01.17A, 50.01.20B,
  52.03.21A, 52.08.29A, 53.12.18B
Hitler, Adolf 34.05.00A, 35.07.26A,
  36.10.00E, 36.10.00G, 38.11.11D,
  38.11.11H, 38.11.25D, 38.12.02A,
  38.12.02D, 38.12.09C, 38.12.16G,
  38.12.30E, 39.01.02B, 39.01.06A,
  39.01.06D, 39.01.06F, 39.01.13E,
  39.01.13G, 39.01.27G, 39.02.03C,
  39.02.03D, 39.02.10A, 39.02.10D,
  39.02.10E, 39.02.10G, 39.02.17B,
  39.02.24E, 39.03.03B, 39.03.03D,
  39.03.05A, 39.03.10D, 39.03.15C,
  39.03.17A, 39.03.17B, 39.03.17C,
  39.03.24A, 39.03.24F, 39.03.28A,
  39.03.31A, 39.03.31C, 39.03.31F,
  39.04.07A, 39.04.07D, 39.04.21F,
  39.04.28E, 39.04.28F, 39.04.28G,
  39.05.05B, 39.05.05C, 39.05.09A,
  39.05.12E, 39.05.12F, 39.05.19D,
  39.06.02A, 39.06.02C, 39.06.07A,
  39.06.16F, 39.06.23H, 39.07.02A,
  39.07.07D, 39.07.14D, 39.07.14H,
  39.07.21F, 39.07.28B, 39.07.28D,
  39.07.28E, 39.07.28F, 39.07.28G,
  39.07.28H, 39.08.041, 39.08.18E,
  39.08.18F, 39.08.25A, 39.08.25D,
  39.08.27B, 39.09.01C, 39.09.01D,
  39.09.01F, 39.09.08A, 39.09.08C,
  39.09.08E, 39.09.08F, 39.09.13C,
  39.09.13E, 39.09.13J, 39.09.22B,
  39.09.22E, 39.09.22G, 39.09.27C,
  39.09.27E, 39.09.27H, 39.09.271,
  39.10.04A, 39.10.04B, 39.10.06D,
  39.10.13A, 39.10.13C, 39.10.13D,
  39.10.13E, 39.10.13F, 39.10.15A,

340

Jacob 29.12.00A, 39.06.30D, 53.03.06D,
53.03.13B, 53.03.20A
Jacobs, Samuel William 32.07.15A,
38.11.11C, 40.03.15C
Jacques, Norman 45.12.21B, 46.07.26B,
47.01.31A, 47.05.30B, 49.02.11B
Jaffe, Leib 36.12.00D, 48.03.19B
James, F. Cyril 40.02.16C, 41.11.28B
Jammes, Francis 45.11.02C
Japan 39.06.27A, 41.05.16D. *See also* anti-
Semitism; World War II.
foreign policy 39.08.25D, 40.07.09B,
41.02.21D, 41.02.28D
post-World War II 51.09.07A
Jeffers, Robinson 42.02.06D
Jehovah's Witnesses 46.12.13B, 54.01.22A
Jeremiah 31.00.00A, 33.01.00A, 53.01.09C
Jerusalem 40.05.31B, 40.06.07G, 41.10.24F,
42.10.23C, 44.08.11C, 47.09.05D,
48.07.30C, 48.08.27C, 48.12.24A,
49.05.13B, 49.09.09A, 49.09.30C,
49.11.25A, 49.12.09B, 49.12.09C,
49.12.09E, 49.12.16B, 49.12.30A,
50.04.07B, 51.09.21A, 53.01.23C
internationalization 49.09.23B,
50.05.05B
Jesus 44.02.18E, 48.07.16A
Jewish Agency 31.11.00A, 32.05.00A,
34.12.00C, 36.12.00A, 37.07.09A,
38.11.11B, 39.02.17E, 39.03.03A,
39.04.14A, 39.06.30D, 39.09.07A,
39.10.27D, 39.12.22F, 40.09.06B,
40.09.27A, 41.01.24B, 41.05.09A,
42.02.27A, 42.07.10C, 42.11.13B,
43.02.12A, 43.08.20A, 43.10.13C,
43.11.26B, 44.03.24A, 44.05.12C,
44.06.23C, 44.10.20D, 44.11.17B,
44.11.24A, 44.12.15B, 45.07.27C,
46.03.15B, 46.04.26A, 46.05.03C,
46.07.05C, 46.07.26A, 46.08.02B,
46.08.09A, 46.08.30C, 46.09.13A,
46.10.09A, 46.10.16A, 46.11.08C,
46.12.06A, 47.02.07A, 47.02.14B,
47.02.21B, 47.02.28A, 47.05.16A,
47.05.23A, 47.06.07C, 47.06.20B,
47.07.18C, 47.08.08A, 47.10.03A,
47.11.28B, 47.12.19A, 47.12.19B,

47.12.26C, 48.01.16B, 48.01.23A,
48.02.06C, 48.03.05A, 48.03.05B,
48.03.19C, 48.03.26C, 48.05.28A,
48.09.10A, 49.10.28A, 49.11.11B,
49.12.30A, 50.01.20A, 51.06.08B,
51.08.17A, 51.11.16B, 51.11.23B, 52.01.18A,
52.05.09A, 52.07.18A, 52.11.14A,
53.12.18B, 54.01.29A. *See also* World
Zionist Organization.
Jewish art 42.04.01B, 43.01.08D
Jewish assimilation 28.11.00A, 29.11.00A,
30.01.24A, 31.00.00A, 31.06.00A,
32.05.00A, 32.07.08J, 32.08.05B,
33.01.00A, 35.07.19E, 35.08.09A,
36.10.00D, 37.05.00C, 37.06.00A,
38.12.23B, 39.06.09B, 39.07.07C,
39.07.14C, 39.08.25C, 40.02.16C,
40.04.12B, 41.01.17A, 41.12.12C,
42.01.02D, 42.01.23C, 42.04.01B,
42.05.22D, 42.07.10D, 42.11.20D,
43.07.02A, 43.07.09A, 43.07.16C,
44.01.14B, 44.01.21D, 44.02.25C,
44.04.13C, 44.10.13D, 45.11.16A,
46.05.10B, 47.01.17A, 48.03.19D,
48.07.30A, 48.11.05B, 49.10.21D,
52.05.29A. *See also* anti-Semitism, Jewish.
Jewish athletics 32.07.08G, 50.10.13B,
52.12.05D
Jewish contributions to medicine 53.02.20B
Jewish culture 31.00.00A, 32.08.12B,
35.05.00A, 40.01.19C, 40.02.23B,
40.08.02D, 40.08.09A, 41.01.17C,
42.03.13D, 42.05.22B, 43.05.14B,
47.01.17B, 47.05.16C, 48.09.24A,
49.05.13C, 50.01.06C, 50.04.07C,
50.09.22C, 50.11.24A, 51.03.02A,
51.09.28C, 52.03.28B, 53.02.20B,
53.07.10A, 54.03.19B
Jewish education 31.00.00A, 32.07.22F,
32.11.04A, 39.01.13A, 39.09.08D,
39.12.01G, 40.01.05A, 40.06.14D,
41.01.10A, 41.06.06B, 41.06.27C,
41.10.31B, 42.01.16B, 42.11.27B,
43.01.15A, 43.05.28B, 44.01.07A,
44.11.03C, 46.05.24C, 48.01.09C,
49.01.14A, 52.10.10B, 53.06.12C,

53.07.17B, 53.10.09B, 55.05.13A. *See also*
Bar-Ilan University; Hebrew University; Israel; Jewish Theological Seminary; Talmud Torahs; Yeshiva University; Yeshivas.

Canada 32.08.12F, 37.07.09B,
  39.01.04C, 47.10.03B, 50.11.24A,
  52.01.18B, 52.02.22C, 52.09.12A,
  52.10.10A, 52.12.05B, 52.12.19A,
  53.01.30A, 54.01.15B, 55.03.18B. *See also* Jewish Radical School; Jewish Schools Question; Talmud Torahs; yeshivas.

Jewish exodus from Egypt 40.02.09A,
  41.04.11A, 46.03.15A, 46.04.12A,
  47.04.04A, 47.07.25A, 48.04.23A,
  49.04.13A, 51.04.20A, 51.10.12A,
  53.02.06B, 54.06.04A

Jewish expulsion from Spain 40.04.05C,
  40.07.26G, 40.08.23A, 48.10.01A

Jewish folklore 32.09.23A, 35.11.00B,
  43.03.05C. *See also* Jewish humour.

Jewish folksongs 32.06.00B, 42.05.15C,
  43.01.08D, 46.08.30E, 53.01.02C. *See also* Chassidism.

Jewish food 54.02.12B

Jewish General Hospital 39.05.19A,
  40.03.22A, 41.02.21A, 41.03.07A,
  41.08.29A, 41.10.17A, 41.10.31A,
  42.09.11B, 43.09.17A, 44.05.12A,
  44.06.02A, 45.02.02A, 45.06.22B,
  45.10.05A, 45.12.21A, 45.12.21A,
  46.11.01A, 49.05.06B, 49.12.02A,
  52.10.10A, 52.10.24A, 52.12.05D,
  53.07.03A, 53.10.30A

Jewish ghettos 31.00.00A. *See also* Lodz ghetto; Vilna ghetto; Warsaw ghetto.

Jewish heroism 29.12.00A

Jewish history 28.11.00A, 31.00.00A,
  31.06.00A, 34.12.00A, 39.03.31A,
  40.01.05A, 40.10.02A, 47.04.04B,
  47.05.16C, 48.04.29A, 48.05.14B,
  48.10.01A, 48.12.24A, 49.02.18A,
  49.04.22D, 49.08.19A, 49.10.14C,
  50.03.03D, 50.05.26D, 50.09.08A,
  51.04.06A, 51.05.04B, 52.04.09A,
  54.03.19B, 55.04.29A

Jewish holidays 30.09.19A, 31.11.00A,
  39.08.18G, 45.03.16A, 45.11.30A,
  53.05.15A. *See also* Chanukah; Jewish liturgy; Purim; Rosh Hashanah; Sabbath; Shavuoth; Simchas Torah; Succoth; Tisha B'Av; Yom Kippur.

Jewish homeland. *See also* Biro-Bidjan.

British Guiana 39.06.30C

China 39.06.30C

Egypt 54.06.04A

Ethiopia 39.10.27E, 39.11.17D, 40.03.05A

Germany 45.07.20B

Madagascar 37.02.00A, 40.07.26B

North Africa 43.07.30B

Palestine 28.11.00A, 32.05.00A,
  33.01.00A, 34.05.00A, 34.10.00A,
  36.10.00A, 36.12.00C, 37.02.00A,
  37.07.09A, 38.12.23B, 39.03.24C,
  39.06.16A, 39.06.30C, 39.07.14E,
  39.07.21A, 39.08.18D, 39.10.27E,
  39.11.03G, 40.03.08A, 40.04.05A,
  40.12.20F, 41.01.24B, 41.04.04B,
  41.05.09A, 41.07.18A, 41.09.12C,
  41.10.10A, 42.01.30A, 42.04.10A,
  42.05.15B, 42.06.12B, 42.08.07H,
  42.08.28E, 42.11.06A, 42.11.06D,
  42.12.18C, 43.01.15B, 43.01.29A,
  43.01.29G, 43.02.05A, 43.02.12C,
  43.02.19A, 43.04.02A, 43.04.09A,
  43.04.09B, 43.04.30B, 43.05.28A,
  43.06.04A, 43.07.02A, 43.07.09A,
  43.07.30B, 43.09.10B, 43.09.29A,
  43.10.29A, 43.11.05A, 44.01.28A,
  44.02.25C, 44.03.24A, 44.04.28B,
  44.07.21A, 44.07.28C, 44.08.11C,
  45.02.23B, 45.06.08B, 45.06.29B,
  45.07.13B, 45.07.20B, 45.08.03D,
  45.08.10A, 45.08.17A, 45.08.24A,
  45.08.24B, 45.09.14A, 45.09.28A,
  45.10.12A, 45.11.09A, 45.12.07A,
  46.01.04A, 46.01.11A, 46.01.25A,
  46.01.25C, 46.02.01A, 46.03.08B,
  46.03.15A, 46.03.22A, 46.04.12A,
  46.04.26A, 46.06.28B, 46.07.19B,
  46.08.09A, 46.09.25A, 46.11.08A,
  46.12.13A, 47.01.24D, 47.05.02C,
  47.05.09B, 47.05.16A, 47.05.23A,

47.06.13A, 48.07.23B, 49.02.18D
San Domingo 37.02.00A
Uganda 37.07.09A, 53.07.24B
Jewish humour 34.02.00A, 35.11.00B,
37.05.00D, 40.01.19B, 43.03.05C,
46.01.25D, 46.02.01D, 46.02.08C,
46.02.15C. *See also* Bible; Talmud.
Jewish identity 28.11.00A, 30.01.24A,
32.05.00A, 32.08.05B, 38.12.23B,
39.06.16E, 44.01.21D, 47.06.20B,
49.02.11E, 49.04.22D
Jewish Immigrant Aid Society 40.11.29B,
43.05.14A, 44.03.17C, 44.04.13A,
45.05.11B, 51.05.11B, 53.10.30A
Jewish intellectualism 30.01.24A
Jewish journalism 41.01.03C, 44.02.18E,
45.01.19B, 51.11.30B
    Britain 41.03.21A, 44.05.05D. *See also*
    The London Jewish Chronicle.
    Canada 39.05.19C, 40.05.03B,
    41.06.20E, 42.06.12D, 42.07.24D,
    42.09.11C, 43.02.12B, 44.03.31C,
    44.05.12B, 44.08.18E, 45.04.27D,
    47.08.29C, 49.11.11A, 49.12.02A,
    51.11.02A, 52.05.23B, 53.03.06B. *See*
    also The Canadian Jewish Chronicle;
    The Canadian Zionist; The Judaean;
    Keneder Adler.
    Poland 40.08.02F
    United States 45.03.23A, 51.09.07C. *See*
    also Contemporary Jewish Record;
    Der Forvertz; Der Tog; The Menorah
    Journal.
Jewish labour 41.04.17E
    Montreal 42.09.11C
Jewish Labour Committee 40.03.22B,
42.10.09A, 43.03.19A, 43.09.10B,
49.06.17C, 53.03.06B
Jewish law 47.04.04B, 50.01.13B, 50.05.19A,
52.05.29B
Jewish Legion 40.08.09A, 41.11.14A,
46.07.05C
Jewish liturgy 29.04.00A, 40.10.11A,
41.09.19A, 42.07.24A, 42.08.28E,
44.01.07C, 45.09.07A, 48.10.01A,
50.03.31A, 51.11.02A, 53.05.22B. *See also*
Jewish holidays.

Kaddish 32.06.00B, 32.08.05A,
    34.05.00A, 39.09.13A, 39.10.04A,
    40.01.19C, 41.10.10A, 42.06.12D,
    45.02.23A, 48.04.02A, 50.06.09C
Maariv 40.12.20C, 41.02.21A, 46.02.08C
Machzor 35.08.09D, 39.08.18G,
    39.09.13A, 40.10.02A, 41.09.19A,
    49.08.19A, 51.10.05D
Mincha 40.12.20C, 41.02.21A,
    46.02.08C, 52.12.19C
Ne'ilah 42.09.18A, 43.09.29A, 44.01.07C
Shachrith 40.12.20C, 49.08.26A
Shma 42.04.01A, 51.10.05D, 53.02.27D
Shofar 30.01.00A, 32.08.05A, 35.08.02A,
    37.06.00A, 37.07.30B, 41.09.19A,
    43.09.29A, 44.01.07C, 48.10.01A,
    49.12.16D, 50.05.12D, 51.11.02A,
    53.02.27C
Siddur 31.06.00A, 42.05.22D,
    45.07.06D, 45.11.02C
Un'saneh Toikef 39.08.18G, 39.09.13A,
    40.10.02A, 43.10.08A, 45.09.07A
Jewish music 40.10.11F, 45.04.27D, 51.01.19A
Jewish National Fund 36.11.00B,
    37.04.00A, 37.04.00C, 37.05.00B,
    39.04.14A, 40.01.05B, 40.04.04A,
    40.04.05A, 40.05.31B, 41.03.14A,
    41.10.10A, 43.04.02A, 44.03.24A,
    46.01.18A, 46.12.06C, 47.03.21A,
    48.03.19B, 49.11.11B, 51.01.26A,
    52.12.19A, 53.04.17A, 53.05.08B
Jewish nationalism 28.11.00A, 30.01.24A,
    31.00.00A, 32.05.00A, 33.01.00A. *See also*
    Zionism.
Jewish People's Library 39.12.08B
Jewish People's Schools 39.01.04C,
    40.06.14D, 41.06.06B, 50.12.29A,
    52.09.12A, 52.10.10A, 53.07.03A
Jewish philanthropy 28.11.00A, 30.09.19A,
    31.00.00A, 31.06.00A, 31.11.00A,
    32.11.04A, 33.01.00A, 38.11.11A,
    39.10.27A, 42.08.28E, 42.09.11C,
    43.06.04B, 45.01.19A, 51.02.09C,
    51.03.09A, 53.01.23B. *See also* Combined
    Jewish Appeal; Federation of Jewish
    Community Services; Federation of
    Jewish Philanthropies; Jewish National

40.03.15D, 40.03.22B, 40.04.12B,
40.04.26D, 40.09.20G, 40.09.27A,
40.09.27D, 41.04.04A, 41.09.12C,
41.09.26A, 41.10.10B, 41.10.31B,
41.11.07D, 41.12.12C, 42.01.02D,
42.01.09D, 42.01.23E, 42.02.06C,
42.04.01C, 42.04.10B, 42.05.15B,
42.10.02C, 42.10.23B, 43.01.15B,
43.03.19A, 43.07.16C, 43.09.03A,
43.09.03B, 43.09.03C, 43.09.10B,
43.10.13B, 43.10.13C, 43.10.29A,
44.01.14B, 44.01.21D, 44.02.25C,
44.04.21B, 44.04.21D, 44.05.05D,
44.05.12C, 44.06.02B, 44.06.23A,
44.09.22A, 44.12.08A, 45.02.23A,
45.02.23B, 45.06.22C, 45.12.07A,
46.06.14A, 46.07.19A, 46.12.20B,
47.01.17A, 47.04.04B, 47.05.23B,
47.06.13C, 48.01.30B, 49.04.08B,
49.04.22A, 49.04.29C, 49.06.02B,
50.11.10C, 51.03.23A, 51.04.27A,
51.09.07C, 51.11.02A, 52.01.11B,
52.09.12A, 52.09.12B, 52.11.21A,
53.01.23B, 53.07.17B, 53.10.09B,
54.11.12A
world distribution of 39.06.25C
Jinnah, Mohammed Ali 47.08.15A
Johnson Act 42.11.20D, 44.01.14B,
44.02.11A, 45.12.07A, 45.12.28A
Johnson, Hewlett 50.07.28B, 51.04.13A,
52.07.11A, 53.06.19C
Johnson, Samuel 27.11.12A, 28.11.00A,
45.10.19A, 46.03.29D, 46.04.19C
Jonah 50.05.12D
Jonson, Ben 48.12.24C
Jordan 34.12.00C, 36.11.00A, 36.12.00C,
37.07.09A, 40.03.08A, 42.11.13B,
44.08.11C, 45.10.12A, 46.01.25C,
46.02.01A, 46.06.07B, 46.08.09A,
47.10.03A, 47.11.21B, 48.05.14A,
48.07.09A, 48.08.13C, 49.07.29B,
49.12.16B, 50.01.06B, 50.02.17A,
50.06.02C, 51.09.21A, 55.04.15A
Joseph, Bernard 36.12.00A, 46.07.26A,
46.08.30C, 48.08.27C, 49.04.29B,
49.07.08B, 49.08.05C, 49.09.02A,
49.10.28D, 49.12.16A, 50.07.28C,

52.02.22C, 53.02.20A, 53.02.27B
Joseph 50.05.26C, 51.04.20A, 53.03.06D,
53.03.13B, 53.03.20A
Journalism 34.05.00A, 39.01.05A, 39.05.19D,
39.09.01D, 39.09.13C, 40.01.26E,
43.08.27A, 44.01.28C. See also advertising; editorial writing; anti-Semitism;
anti-Zionism; Jewish journalism; propa-
ganda; racism.
and world affairs 39.08.22A
Britain 49.07.08C. See also The Manches-
ter Guardian; The Times of London.
Canada 39.01.20C, 39.10.20B, 39.12.08C,
44.03.15A. See also The Globe and
Mail.
Fascist 39.01.13C
France 39.04.28B
Italy 37.07.30C
Quebec 32.07.08A, 35.08.09B,
38.12.02A, 39.03.03C, 39.12.01A,
40.06.02A, 40.10.23A, 41.11.28A,
42.09.18B, 44.04.28C. See also La
Presse; Le Canada; Le Chameau; Le
Devoir; Le Goglu; Le Jour; Le
Matin; Le Miroir; Le Moraliste; Le
Patriote; Le Soleil; The Montreal
Daily Star; The Montreal Gazette.
Soviet Union 37.07.30C, 40.03.15E,
49.07.15A, 50.03.31B. See also
Izvestia; Pravda; Soviet Union,
purge of journalists; Tass.
United States 40.11.29G, 49.07.08C. See
also The Dearborn Independent; Lib-
erty Magazine; Life Magazine; The
Nation; The New Republic; The
New York Times; The New York Her-
ald Tribune; The Reader's Digest;
The Saturday Evening Post; Time
Magazine.
Joyce, James 32.10.07A, 41.08.15C,
44.02.04D, 46.03.01D, 47.08.22C,
48.06.11D, 48.07.23C, 48.09.00A,
48.11.12C, 48.12.24C, 49.01.28D,
49.11.18B, 49.12.09E, 52.03.07C
Joyce, William (Lord Haw-Haw)
40.03.29A, 41.07.18D, 41.08.08G,
44.09.08A, 44.09.29A, 45.05.25B,

45.09.21C, 45.10.19B

Judaean, The 30.09.19A, 31.00.00A

Judah Loew ben Bezalel, Rabbi of Prague 39.01.20D, 52.11.28A

Judah Maccabee 48.08.27C, 48.12.24A, 52.12.12A

Judaism 28.11.00A, 32.05.00A, 39.01.06A, 39.08.18G, 39.08.25C, 39.09.08D, 42.05.22D, 42.08.28E, 44.01.07C, 45.07.06D, 46.10.16A, 48.08.27C, 49.04.08B, 53.02.06B. *See also* Bible; decalogue; Jewish education; Jewish holidays; Jewish liturgy; Jewish philosophy; Kabbalah; synagogues; Talmud.
  bar mitzvah 40.01.19C, 45.04.27D, 49.09.23D
  dietary laws 32.11.04A, 52.12.19A
  orthodox 41.12.12C
  reconstructionist 42.04.01B, 42.05.29C, 42.08.28E, 45.07.06D, 48.11.05B
  reform 31.11.00A, 42.01.09D, 43.09.03C, 44.01.21D, 46.03.08B, 47.06.27A, 52.11.21A
  Shulchan Aruch 30.04.18A, 32.08.12A, 42.01.02D, 48.11.19B, 49.10.07D, 49.11.11C, 49.12.16D, 52.05.16B
  women 52.11.21A

Judith 29.12.00A, 50.05.12D

Kabbalah 30.01.00A, 32.10.07A, 39.03.10D, 47.05.16C, 48.07.23C, 48.07.30D, 49.10.07D, 50.04.28C, 52.11.28A, 53.01.16B. *See also* golem; Safed.

Kafka, Franz 44.02.04D, 48.12.17C, 49.10.28D

Kahana 34.02.00A

Kalinin, Mikhail Ivanovich 39.03.28B, 39.11.05A

Kalonymus ben Kalonymus 34.02.00A

Kant, Immanuel 27.11.26A, 39.01.06D, 39.02.17F, 39.02.24C, 39.03.17C, 40.04.26A, 41.08.08D, 42.09.11A, 46.05.31C, 55.04.22A

Kaplan, Eliezer 39.06.30D, 48.09.10A, 49.02.11C, 50.02.03C, 50.11.03B, 51.08.03A, 52.07.18A

Kaplan, Mordecai M. 42.04.01B, 42.05.29C, 42.08.28E, 45.07.06D, 48.11.05B

Karaism 42.05.22D

Katznelson, Berl 41.10.03D, 44.08.18D

Keats, John 30.11.14A, 32.03.00A, 32.10.07A, 34.01.05A, 37.01.00B, 37.06.00A, 40.04.26E, 41.02.21C, 41.04.11C, 43.12.24C, 44.01.14D, 48.06.11D, 48.06.25C

Keenleyside, Hugh 51.10.12B, 52.09.26B, 53.01.09A

Keith-Roache, E. 39.02.17E, 43.11.26B, 44.01.28C

Keneder Adler 32.07.08A, 32.07.15A, 35.08.09A, 37.07.23A, 37.07.30A, 38.12.18A, 39.01.05A, 39.01.15B, 39.01.20C, 39.02.17F, 39.05.19C, 39.06.02D, 39.08.04F, 39.11.28A, 39.12.01H, 39.12.08B, 40.01.12D, 40.06.07D, 40.08.23F, 40.10.11F, 41.02.07H, 41.12.26C, 42.05.22B, 42.07.10C, 42.09.11C, 42.10.16E, 43.02.12B, 43.03.05B, 43.09.24D, 44.06.23B, 45.04.27D, 46.09.20C, 46.10.16A, 47.08.29C, 47.10.17D, 48.02.20B, 49.11.11A, 49.12.02A, 50.01.13C, 50.10.27A, 51.11.30B

Kennedy, Leo 34.01.05A

Keren Hayesod 37.04.00A, 39.04.14A, 39.10.06B, 40.04.05A, 44.03.24A, 44.09.08B, 46.01.18A, 47.03.21A, 49.11.11B

Kerensky, Alexander Feodorovich 39.12.22A, 42.01.09B

Khazars 35.02.00A

Khrushchev, Nikita 55.06.03A

Kierkegaard, Soren 43.02.19C, 48.11.19D

Kipling, Rudyard 42.03.20C, 42.12.04D, 46.02.22C, 48.11.26D

Kishinev 33.01.00A, 36.09.00A, 37.06.00A, 40.12.06C, 41.01.31B, 42.07.10D, 51.07.13A

Kleiber, Erich 39.01.06F

Klonitzki-Kline, Solomon 46.07.19D

Knox, Frank 42.01.30A, 43.01.08A

Koch, Ilse 48.10.08D, 49.06.10B

Koestler, Arthur 42.06.05D, 46.11.22D
Kohn, Eugene 45.07.06D
Korean War 50.06.30A, 50.07.14B,
    50.07.21A, 50.07.21C, 50.08.04A,
    50.08.11A, 50.11.10A, 50.12.08A,
    51.01.12B, 51.06.29A, 51.07.06A,
    51.08.31B, 52.07.11A, 52.10.17A,
    53.01.02A, 53.04.10A, 53.07.24A, 53.07.31A
Koussevitzky, Serge 51.01.19A
Krafft-Ebbing Report 45.06.22A,
    45.09.28B, 48.11.12B
Kristallnacht 38.11.18A, 39.06.25B, 39.11.03A
Krupp, Gustav 39.01.20G, 39.03.17A,
    39.05.05C, 40.02.16C, 40.05.17F,
    48.08.06C, 51.02.09B
Ku Klux Klan 40.08.23G, 40.11.29G,
    41.11.07B, 43.06.25A, 46.12.20B,
    47.01.31A
Kuhn, Fritz 39.03.03B, 39.07.25J, 39.11.12A,
    39.11.17F, 39.12.01I, 39.12.15G, 39.12.22A,
    40.06.28F, 40.08.23G
Kun, Bela 44.03.17D

La Guardia, Fiorello 35.08.02B, 39.03.03B,
    40.03.15D, 41.06.27B, 41.11.07A,
    42.01.09D, 42.07.31A
La Presse 39.12.22A, 40.06.02A
La Rochefoucauld, Duc François de
    38.12.16G, 40.09.27C
Labour relations 39.08.11. *See also* Canada;
    Quebec; United States.
Ladino 29.11.00A
Lafleche, Leo R. 41.05.02F, 42.11.27A,
    42.12.11E
Lakish, Resh 35.11.00B
Lamed Vovnik 30.04.18A, 45.11.02C,
    48.07.23C, 50.12.29A, 53.01.23C,
    54.03.12A
Landor, Walter Savage 37.06.00A
Lang, Andrew 36.11.00B, 46.03.29D
Language 27.11.12A, 28.11.00A, 32.05.00A,
    39.06.23A, 40.05.03H, 41.04.04A,
    43.01.15D, 46.03.22D, 50.09.08B,
    51.06.15A. *See also* Bible; Hebrew lan-
    guage; Jewish use of language; poetry;
    Yiddish language.
    and cultural identity 29.11.00A,

    32.05.00A
    and religion 50.03.31A
    and war 39.09.22D
Lanier, Sidney 46.03.29D
Lapointe, Ernest 39.02.10B, 39.04.21A,
    39.10.27B, 40.06.28B, 40.07.05B,
    40.12.13E, 41.11.28A, 43.03.26B
Laroche, François 39.12.22A, 39.12.29E
Laski, Harold 43.06.18C, 45.07.20A,
    45.08.10A, 45.09.28A
Laurier, Wilfrid 31.00.00A, 32.08.12G,
    39.03.03C, 39.10.27B, 41.11.28A,
    42.09.11C, 44.04.13A, 46.03.01D,
    46.06.07A, 47.01.24A, 47.07.04A,
    48.08.13A, 48.08.13B, 50.07.28A,
    52.07.04D, 53.01.30A, 53.10.16A
Laval, Pierre 40.07.09A, 40.07.19B,
    40.07.26H, 40.08.02E, 40.08.23F,
    40.09.06G, 40.10.23A, 40.10.23C,
    40.11.01F, 40.11.22F, 40.12.13C,
    40.12.20D, 41.01.10E, 41.02.07E,
    41.05.23F, 41.05.30E, 41.08.29D,
    41.09.05A, 42.04.24C, 42.04.24D,
    42.05.08A, 42.06.26C, 42.07.31C,
    42.09.04A, 42.09.18B, 42.09.25G,
    42.10.02E, 42.11.13A, 43.01.01D,
    43.02.19B, 43.09.17B, 44.03.17B,
    44.05.05E, 44.08.25C, 45.05.11A,
    45.08.03C, 45.10.12B, 45.10.19B
Lavergne, Armand 32.07.29A, 32.08.12G,
    32.08.26A
Lavery, Salluste 40.06.14H, 40.06.21B,
    40.06.28B, 42.08.14B
Lawrence, D.H. 27.10.29A
Lawrence, T.E. 39.02.17A, 39.04.21G,
    48.06.18C, 50.03.24D
Layton, Irving 45.06.08D
Lazare, Bernard 48.03.19D
Lazare, Israel 49.03.11C
Lazaron, Morris Samuel 42.11.20D,
    42.12.11D, 42.12.18C, 54.05.07A
Leacock, Stephen 43.02.19C
League for the Defence of Canada
    42.03.27A, 42.11.27A, 42.12.11E
League of Nations 34.05.00A, 35.07.19C,
    35.08.02B, 37.05.00A, 37.07.23B,
    37.08.06B, 39.01.20F, 39.02.17A,

39.03.24E, 39.04.19B, 39.05.19D,
39.06.18A, 39.06.23A, 39.08.11C,
39.08.22A, 39.08.25D, 39.09.01G,
39.10.27D, 39.12.08E, 40.03.08A,
40.04.26C, 40.05.03A, 40.05.10B,
41.01.24B, 41.03.14B, 41.08.22C,
42.10.23E, 43.01.22D, 43.02.26A,
44.03.17D, 44.10.27D, 45.07.06B,
46.07.12A, 46.10.09A, 46.11.15A,
47.02.21B, 47.07.25A, 48.02.13A,
48.03.26C, 48.08.06B

Le Canada 39.08.06A, 39.12.01A, 40.01.05E,
40.04.28A, 40.09.27A, 40.10.23A,
41.11.28A, 45.11.16A, 47.11.07C

Le Chameau 32.07.08A, 32.07.22A,
32.07.29A, 40.06.02A, 40.06.14H,
44.04.28C, 45.05.11C

Le Devoir 32.07.08B, 37.07.16A, 38.12.02A,
39.02.03H, 39.07.07C, 39.08.18H,
40.01.19D, 40.01.26B, 40.02.02D,
40.10.23A, 41.01.24B, 42.08.21E,
42.11.27A

Le Goglu 32.07.08A, 32.07.08B, 32.07.08J,
32.07.22A, 32.07.29A, 44.04.28C

Le Jour 39.01.27D, 39.03.03C, 40.01.19G,
40.07.05B, 46.03.29B

Le Matin 39.07.21B

Le Miroir 32.07.08A, 32.07.08B, 32.07.22A,
32.07.29A, 32.08.26A, 40.06.02A,
40.06.14H

Le Moraliste 44.04.28C, 44.10.20C

Le Patriote 35.07.19A

Le Soleil 40.01.19E, 50.07.07B

Leftwich, Joseph 41.01.03E

Lebanon 43.11.19B, 48.05.14A, 49.07.01B,
50.01.06B

Lehman, Herbert H. 42.02.20C, 42.04.10B,
46.01.04A

Leib, Mani 45.11.02C

Leishmann, J.B. 46.08.02C

Leivick (Leivick Halpern) 39.04.16A,
39.04.28D, 41.07.25A, 43.09.24D,
46.07.05B

Lenin, Nikolai 39.07.07C, 39.11.03B,
39.12.22A, 40.04.05D, 40.08.23B,
40.11.15F, 41.02.14C, 41.11.14B,
49.10.28D, 50.08.18A, 52.10.17A,

53.07.31A

Leon, Moses de 32.10.07A, 35.02.00A

Leopold, King of Belgium 40.05.31C,
40.06.07F, 44.10.13A, 50.08.04C

Letter writing 37.05.00B

Levi, Gershon 41.04.17B, 44.08.18E,
46.06.21C

Levi Yitschok, Rabbi of Berditchev
30.11.14A, 32.06.00A, 39.02.03B,
42.05.29G, 44.01.07C, 45.11.02C,
53.01.02C

Levin, Shmaryahu 36.11.00B, 37.05.00C,
37.06.00B, 39.06.09F, 39.09.27C,
40.10.02A, 44.04.13C, 44.12.08A,
52.05.29A, 54.01.29A

Lewis, C. Day 46.03.22D

Lewis, David 35.08.09C, 40.07.12D,
44.03.15A

Lewis, John L. 40.11.01E, 40.11.08F,
41.03.14C, 41.07.11B, 43.07.16B, 48.11.05A

Lewis, Sinclair 39.07.16J, 40.01.19F,
41.07.04A, 41.07.18D, 41.09.26D,
42.07.31A, 45.05.25B

Lewisohn, Ludwig 46.05.10C, 46.08.02C,
52.05.29A

Ley, Robert 39.09.27E, 45.05.11A, 45.05.11D,
45.08.03B, 45.11.02B

Liberty Magazine 37.07.23A, 38.12.23B,
39.03.10F, 39.12.15C, 40.01.19D,
40.02.09H, 40.04.05B, 40.07.26C,
41.06.20F, 41.09.05B

Libya 38.11.11F

Lidice 42.06.19D, 42.07.17D, 42.11.06B,
43.03.05C

Lie, Trygve 50.01.20C, 50.05.05B,
50.06.02B, 50.09.29C, 52.07.04B

Lieberman, Abraham 35.08.09E

Life Magazine 39.06.02D, 40.05.10H,
40.08.16B, 40.09.13E, 41.01.10E,
41.01.31B, 41.08.15B, 42.04.17A,
42.10.16A, 43.07.09A, 43.12.10B,
44.01.14B, 48.04.02A, 48.06.04B,
48.10.15C, 48.10.29A, 49.03.18B,
52.10.31A, 53.01.09B

Lincoln, Abraham 39.01.13B, 39.02.05B,
41.09.26D

Lindbergh, Anne Morrow 41.01.31F,

356

40.11.22D, 41.02.14C, 44.04.21A, 51.08.17B, 53.11.27A. *See also* anti-Semitism; Cold War.

McDiarmid, Hugh 50.08.25B

McGill University 39.01.04B, 40.04.12C, 40.12.27B, 41.11.28B, 45.06.22B, 51.03.09A, 53.03.06A

McGilliad, The 27.11.26A, 27.12.17A

Medres, Israel 39.08.04F, 40.03.22A, 42.09.11C

Meek, Theophile James 36.12.00E

Meighen, Arthur 44.03.15A

Meir, Golda 51.02.02B

Meir, Rabbi of Rothenberg 38.12.23D

Ménard, Joseph 32.07.08A, 32.07.22A, 32.07.29A, 32.08.12G, 35.07.19A, 35.08.02F, 40.06.02A

Mencken, H.L. 30.04.00A, 42.07.03D

Mendelssohn, Moses 31.03.00A, 42.05.22D, 52.09.26C, 53.02.20B

Menorah Journal, The 37.05.00C, 42.01.02D

Menuhin, Yehudi 47.10.31B, 50.04.14C

Menzies, Robert Gordon 41.04.25A, 53.06.12A

Messianism 30.01.00A, 31.00.00A, 31.06.00A, 32.05.00A, 32.08.05B, 41.12.12C, 46.08.02A, 47.02.14A, 47.05.16C, 49.08.19A, 53.01.23C

Metaxas, Ioannis 40.08.23D, 40.08.30A, 40.11.22E

Meyer, Kurt 46.01.18B, 51.11.30A, 51.12.07A, 51.12.07B

Michael, King of Rumania 40.09.13F, 45.06.15C

Michelangelo 49.11.18B, 49.12.09E, 50.04.28C, 50.05.05D, 50.05.12D

Mickey Mouse 38.11.25A, 46.01.18D, 48.10.08C

Middle East. *See also* Arabs; Israel; Palestine; United Nations; World War I; World War II.
American foreign policy on 50.12.08B, 51.10.19A, 53.05.22A, 53.10.09A, 54.01.15A, 54.02.12A, 54.02.19A, 54.10.22A
British foreign policy on 49.01.07A, 49.06.17D, 50.04.07B, 50.04.21D,

50.04.28A, 50.12.08B, 51.01.26C, 51.07.20A, 51.08.03B, 51.08.10A, 51.10.19A, 51.12.14A, 52.01.25A, 54.10.22A
post-World War II 51.11.09A, 52.02.15A

Mifal Bitzaron 37.04.00A, 40.04.05A, 43.04.02A, 44.03.24A

Military memoirs 48.11.26C

Millay, Edna St. Vincent 40.06.17A, 42.02.06D

Miller, Salem 37.05.00D

Milton, John 32.03.00A, 39.05.05G, 40.01.26D, 40.04.28B, 40.09.06A, 41.04.11A, 41.05.09B, 45.04.13B, 45.10.26A, 46.02.22C, 47.02.14A, 48.12.24C, 52.09.26C

Miracles 27.12.10A, 41.05.23B, 49.10.14C

Mishna 45.11.16C, 49.02.25C. *See also* Talmud; Tosfoth.

Mizrachi 37.07.23C, 40.06.07D, 44.03.24A, 49.04.22B, 49.11.11C, 50.01.06C, 50.10.20A, 50.11.24A, 52.11.07A, 54.02.26A

Modena, Leon de 32.10.07A

Moicher Sforim, Mendele (Shalom Jacob Abramovitsch) 40.06.28C

Molière 32.07.08J

Molotov, Vyacheslav Mikhailovich 39.08.27B, 39.09.01F, 39.09.19A, 39.09.22A, 39.09.22E, 39.10.04A, 39.10.06D, 39.10.06G, 39.10.27G, 39.10.27H, 39.11.03A, 39.11.03B, 39.11.05A, 39.11.10C, 39.12.01B, 39.12.13A, 39.12.15F, 39.12.22B, 40.01.21C, 40.02.16B, 40.04.26B, 40.08.09C, 40.11.15D, 41.02.14D, 41.04.17D, 41.05.16D, 41.06.20F, 41.06.27D, 42.01.23D, 46.06.14A, 46.07.05C, 47.02.14C, 47.07.04C, 47.11.28A, 47.12.19C, 48.01.16C, 48.01.23B, 49.04.08A, 49.09.23C, 50.04.14A, 52.03.07B, 53.01.16A, 53.07.24A, 55.03.11A, 55.05.06A. *See also* oratory.

Montaigne, Michel de 53.02.20B

Montefiore, Moses 31.11.00A, 44.09.08C, 49.03.11A

Montgomery, Bernard 43.04.16A,

41.02.28F, 41.03.07C, 41.04.04E,
41.04.11B, 41.05.02D, 41.05.09B,
41.06.13A, 41.06.13B, 41.07.04E,
41.07.25D, 41.08.01D, 41.08.08C,
41.08.15C, 41.09.05E, 42.04.10B,
42.05.01C, 42.05.08G, 42.08.28C,
42.10.30B, 42.11.13D, 42.12.04C,
42.12.04D, 42.12.11B, 42.12.18A,
42.12.25D, 43.01.01B, 43.01.15D,
43.01.29A, 43.05.14C, 43.05.21B,
43.07.16A, 43.07.30A, 43.09.10A,
43.09.17B, 43.09.24A, 43.10.29B,
44.01.14A, 44.07.07A, 44.07.28D,
44.08.04A, 45.05.04A, 45.05.04C,
46.06.14B, 48.01.06A, 50.08.04A,
54.02.05A, 54.02.05A. *See also* oratory.
Mussolini, Bruno 40.07.05E, 40.11.08C,
41.08.15C
Mussolini, Vittorio 40.07.05E, 40.11.08C,
41.08.15C, 42.12.18A, 46.04.19C
Myerson, M. H. 45.05.25E
Nachman, Rabbi of Bratzlav 30.11.14A,
40.11.08A, 45.11.02C, 47.10.10D,
54.03.12A
Naguib, Mohammed 52.09.19B, 52.10.03B,
53.02.13B, 53.04.24A, 53.05.22A,
53.06.26A, 53.07.10B, 54.02.19A,
54.06.04A
Names 39.07.07C, 40.03.01G, 42.04.17D,
50.02.10B
Hebrew 49.04.22D
Nathan 50.05.05D
Nation, The 34.05.00A, 37.02.00C,
39.07.28A, 40.09.06F, 42.03.06A,
42.05.08D, 43.06.18C, 45.08.10A,
45.09.28A
National anthems 35.08.02A, 39.01.02B,
43.12.31B
**National Conference for Israel and Jewish
Rehabilitation** 51.03.23A, 52.06.27A,
53.01.23A, 53.02.20A
Nationalism 32.05.00A, 37.07.30E,
39.08.25C, 40.08.09A, 43.12.31B,
45.10.19A, 46.01.25B, 46.11.22D,
48.01.30B, 48.04.02A, 49.11.25A. *See also*
Jewish nationalism.
Arab 39.07.14B, 41.06.06D, 43.08.20A,

44.05.19B, 45.06.01A, 48.03.12A
Canada 40.01.19G
France 41.09.05A
in literature 46.02.22C, 46.03.01D
Ireland 37.08.06E, 46.02.01C, 46.11.22A,
49.08.26A, 54.03.19B. *See also* Celtic
Revival.
Poland 39.10.04A
post-World War II 50.02.10C
Quebec 37.08.06G, 38.11.18D, 39.10.27B,
42.08.21E, 47.10.10C, 50.01.13A. *See
also* St. Jean Baptiste Society.
Soviet Union 38.12.30E, 44.09.22B
Ukraine 38.12.30E
United States 44.01.07B
NATO 53.05.08A
Nazism 32.07.08C, 32.07.08E, 35.07.19D,
37.03.00B, 39.01.06B, 39.01.06D,
39.01.20G, 39.01.27G, 39.02.03D,
39.02.03E, 39.02.10D, 39.02.17F,
39.02.24B, 39.02.24C, 39.03.10B,
39.03.10H, 39.03.17C, 39.07.14A,
39.09.01C, 39.09.27E, 39.10.20E,
39.11.03A, 39.12.22E, 39.12.29A,
40.03.15F, 40.04.12G, 40.06.07A,
40.10.11D, 41.06.27D, 42.04.10B,
42.08.07C, 42.09.11A, 42.09.25F,
43.01.15D, 44.02.11D, 44.09.22B,
52.07.25A, 53.02.20B, 55.04.22A. *See also*
anti-communism; Austria, Anschluss;
Kristallnacht; Lidice; propaganda.
aggression in Europe, pre-World War II
38.12.02F, 38.12.30E, 39.01.02B,
39.02.03C, 39.02.10G, 39.03.24A,
39.03.24C, 39.03.24F, 39.03.31C,
39.04.07C, 39.04.07D, 39.05.12E,
39.06.16C, 39.06.23F, 39.07.28B,
39.07.28E, 39.09.01A, 39.09.01D,
39.09.08A, 39.09.27G, 39.10.13A,
39.10.13E, 39.10.20A, 39.11.10A,
39.11.17A, 39.11.24F, 39.12.08G,
40.01.05D, 40.02.26B, 40.03.22E,
40.11.08B
and art 39.02.24E, 39.06.07A, 41.11.14C,
43.10.20C, 47.12.26B
and intellectuals 41.02.07D
and religion 35.07.19A, 35.08.02F,

35.08.09B, 38.11.25D, 38.12.02B,
38.12.09G, 38.12.16D, 38.12.16F,
39.01.13H, 39.06.02A, 39.08.11D,
39.09.08C, 40.01.19I, 40.03.29F,
41.01.31D, 41.07.11D, 41.10.24E,
41.11.21D, 43.01.22E, 45.10.19A,
49.11.25B
and Roman Catholic Church
35.07.19A, 35.07.26A, 39.02.24H,
39.04.28E
and science 41.11.07C
book burning 40.03.08D
Canada 39.01.27E
concentration camps 39.05.19D,
39.11.01A, 40.02.09A, 44.10.27C,
45.04.13A, 45.04.13B, 45.04.27C,
45.05.25E, 45.06.08A, 45.06.22A,
45.07.06A, 45.07.27A, 45.09.07A,
45.09.14A, 45.09.28B, 45.11.30B,
46.03.08C, 46.05.31C, 47.04.18A,
48.10.08D, 49.06.10B, 50.04.28C,
52.09.26B, 52.12.26B
confiscation of Jewish property
39.06.25B
culture 40.03.08D, 41.08.08D, 46.08.02C
economy 37.07.16A, 38.11.11E, 38.12.26B,
39.01.22A, 39.02.03I
foreign policy 39.06.16F, 39.08.25D
genocide of Jews 39.09.08E, 42.03.20A,
42.07.17D, 42.10.23D, 42.11.27E,
42.12.11G, 42.12.25F, 43.01.22B,
43.02.05A, 43.02.26E, 43.03.05A,
43.03.19A, 43.04.02A, 43.05.07A,
43.06.04A, 43.09.29A, 43.11.19A,
44.01.28A, 44.03.03D, 44.07.14C,
44.07.28B, 44.08.18A, 45.06.01B,
45.06.22C, 45.08.03D, 45.09.07A,
45.10.12A, 45.11.16C, 45.12.14A,
46.01.04D, 46.03.08C, 46.04.19B,
46.05.10A, 46.08.30B, 46.09.25A,
46.12.13A, 46.12.27A, 47.01.17B,
47.04.18A, 47.07.25B, 48.03.05C,
48.10.08B, 50.04.28C, 50.05.05D,
50.05.12D, 51.03.02A, 53.01.09C
genocide of Slavs 46.04.19B
Gestapo 39.07.28H, 41.01.31D, 42.05.08E
ideology 36.11.00B, 39.03.24D,

39.06.02B, 39.06.16D, 39.10.20I,
40.01.05C, 40.01.05G, 40.01.19I,
40.01.26E, 40.01.26F, 40.01.31A,
40.02.09A, 40.02.23D, 40.03.08F,
40.04.26A, 40.07.05C, 40.08.16G,
40.09.27C, 40.11.22C, 41.05.23G,
41.11.21A, 41.11.21D, 42.02.13C,
42.03.20A, 42.07.10A, 42.09.25C,
42.10.09A, 42.11.06A, 43.05.28B,
43.09.24D, 44.08.11B, 44.10.13D,
46.05.03A, 47.01.10A
medical experiments 47.01.10A
Mein Kampf 36.12.00F, 38.12.30E,
39.01.22B, 39.01.27A, 39.02.03C,
39.02.24F, 39.03.17B, 39.03.31A,
39.04.28F, 39.04.28I, 39.06.02A,
39.08.25A, 39.09.01F, 39.10.20A,
39.10.29B, 40.02.16C, 40.03.01E,
40.04.12D, 40.05.03H, 40.06.10B,
40.07.05F, 40.11.15F, 41.03.07E,
41.05.16C, 41.05.16E, 41.05.30G,
41.09.05C, 41.11.21D, 42.08.14A,
43.01.08A, 44.03.10A, 44.07.07A,
46.01.04D, 46.12.20B
Nueremberg laws 38.12.02D, 39.06.02A,
39.09.01F, 39.10.13D, 40.05.05B,
40.12.13C
Reichstag fire 39.11.17E
rise of 32.08.05B, 36.10.00E, 38.12.30E,
39.03.03B, 39.03.31B, 44.10.20D
United States 39.03.03B, 39.07.25J,
39.12.15G, 40.01.05C. *See also* German-American Bund.
women 39.01.13G, 40.01.12E
Nebuchadnezzar 39.07.21D, 39.09.13A
Negev 43.02.12A, 44.02.04A, 44.05.19C,
48.10.22A, 55.03.25A, 55.04.01A
Nehru, Jawaharlal 40.05.24A, 42.08.14E
Nelson, William Henry 40.06.14B
Neo-Nazism 51.05.18B, 51.07.06B, 51.10.05A
Nero 40.03.15F, 41.03.14D
Neumann, Ernst 34.01.05A, 43.02.19C
Neurath, Konstantin von 39.06.25B,
40.01.12E, 41.10.03A, 42.05.29B,
46.10.04A, 52.06.06A
New Deal 39.01.13C, 40.11.01E, 40.11.08F,
40.12.06B, 41.12.12C

New Republic, The 43.03.19A, 43.06.18C, 47.04.25C

New York Herald Tribune, The 40.08.09D, 40.08.30G, 41.09.05E, 44.06.30C, 47.04.18C

New York Times, The 40.05.03A, 40.07.26H, 41.08.08G, 42.01.30A, 42.03.06A, 42.11.20D, 43.09.24B, 44.06.30C, 45.10.05A, 47.01.17A, 49.09.23C

New Zionist Organization 40.09.27A, 43.03.19A, 44.06.30A. *See also* Zionism, revisionist.

Niebuhr, Reinhold 42.03.06A

Niemoller, Martin 38.12.16D, 39.04.21A, 39.04.28E, 39.08.11D, 39.09.27J, 40.07.05B, 41.10.24E, 41.11.21D, 43.01.22E, 45.06.22A

Nietzsche, Friedrich Wilhelm 27.11.26A, 33.01.00A, 40.04.26A, 40.10.11D, 41.05.23G, 42.02.06D, 42.09.25E, 44.02.11D, 51.06.15A

Niger, Shmuel 32.08.05E, 35.08.09E

Noah 50.05.05D

Nobel Prize 38.11.25F, 39.12.01F, 43.01.01E, 46.11.29C, 47.11.07B, 48.11.12C, 48.11.19D, 48.11.26D, 50.09.29A, 51.11.16A, 53.10.30C

Nordau, Max 31.06.00A, 33.01.00A, 37.05.00B, 39.01.27B, 39.10.27E, 40.08.02D, 41.10.10A, 41.12.05D, 42.01.30A, 42.07.24D, 43.04.30B, 44.02.18A, 53.07.24B

Nye, Gerald P. 41.09.26D, 41.10.03B, 44.11.10A

Obituaries 45.05.04A

Odets, Clifford 39.04.16A

O'Hara, Regina 52.11.21A

Olgin, Moussaye 39.12.01E

Olympic games 35.08.02B, 39.12.15K

Omar Khayyam 29.05.00A

Optimism 27.11.05A

Oratory 39.05.05C, 39.05.12E, 39.05.12F, 39.05.19G, 39.06.23A, 39.07.21C, 39.08.18F, 40.02.02A, 40.04.08A, 40.08.09A, 41.02.14F, 41.05.02B,

44.12.08A, 46.03.08A, 49.11.18A

Neville Chamberlain 40.02.02A, 40.02.27A, 40.03.01F, 40.04.08A

Winston Churchill 39.08.18F, 40.02.02A, 40.06.07B, 40.07.19E, 40.08.23A, 40.08.30G, 40.09.13A, 41.01.03A, 41.02.14F, 41.03.21E, 41.05.02D, 41.07.18C, 41.08.29E, 41.11.14D, 41.12.19C, 43.06.11A, 44.09.22B, 45.01.05A, 45.02.02B, 45.04.06B, 49.10.07B

Francisco Franco 39.03.03D

Joseph Goebbels 41.03.07C

Adolf Hitler 38.12.02F, 39.02.03C, 39.02.24E, 39.05.03A, 39.05.05C, 39.09.22B, 39.09.22E, 39.10.13D, 39.10.13E, 39.10.27H, 40.02.02A, 40.02.27A, 40.03.01F, 40.03.15G, 40.04.08A, 40.07.26F, 40.11.15E, 40.12.13A, 41.01.03B, 41.02.28C, 41.03.21D, 41.06.27E, 41.10.17B, 41.12.19B, 42.05.01E, 42.09.04C, 42.10.16B, 44.03.17B, 44.07.07A, 45.01.05A, 45.02.02B, 46.08.02C

David Lloyd George 39.08.18F, 40.02.02A, 40.08.23A

William Lyon Mackenzie King 41.09.12E

Vyacheslav Mikhailov Molotov 39.09.22E

Benito Mussolini 39.03.28A, 39.05.19G, 41.02.28F, 42.12.04C, 43.07.09B

Franklin Delano Roosevelt 40.09.06E, 41.01.03D, 41.03.21D, 41.03.21F, 41.04.04F, 41.05.30A, 41.10.31E

Joseph Stalin 41.11.14B, 42.05.08F, 44.09.22B

Orbeli, Leon Abgarovich 48.09.10C

ORT 38.12.09A, 39.11.24A, 40.12.06A, 52.06.27C

Ossietsky, Karl von 41.08.08G, 48.11.12C

Paassen, Pierre van 40.02.09H, 40.11.29C, 42.04.10A, 42.06.26D, 43.11.26B, 44.01.28C

Pacifism 29.12.00A, 39.03.24F, 39.04.14D, 39.10.20A, 39.11.03A, 40.05.10B,

40.05.24E, 40.06.14E, 40.08.02D,
40.11.08B, 41.04.17E, 41.08.08F,
42.01.02B, 42.05.01D, 42.05.08E,
46.11.29C, 47.07.18A, 49.10.14C,
50.08.18A, 50.09.01A

Paderewski, Ignace 39.03.10E, 40.04.12F,
42.01.09D

Paine, Thomas 31.00.00A, 44.04.21A

Palestine 29.12.00A, 32.05.00A, 32.08.05B,
34.12.00C, 37.01.00B, 37.01.00C,
37.02.00C, 39.02.03A, 39.02.17F,
40.01.12B, 42.01.09B, 42.06.26D,
42.11.13B, 43.12.31A, 44.06.30D,
45.03.02A, 45.12.14C, 46.09.20A,
46.10.16A, 47.05.09A, 47.10.17C,
47.12.12B, 47.12.19B, 48.01.30A,
48.04.23A, 48.07.30B, 48.08.27C. *See
also* Arabs; censorship; Germans; Israel;
Jewish homeland; Jews; socialism;
United Nations; World War II; Zionism.
 agriculture 37.01.00D, 37.04.00C,
  39.08.25E, 43.02.12A, 44.05.19C,
  46.03.29A, 47.07.04B
 American foreign policy on 43.01.08A,
  43.08.20A, 44.02.11A, 44.02.25C,
  44.03.03B, 44.03.17A, 44.04.21B,
  44.08.11A, 44.10.20B, 44.10.20D,
  44.12.15A, 45.01.05B, 45.03.23A,
  45.07.20C, 45.08.24C, 45.08.31B,
  45.09.21A, 45.10.26B, 45.12.07A,
  46.06.14C, 47.08.01A, 48.02.13B,
  48.03.05B, 48.03.26C, 48.04.02A,
  48.05.07C, 52.03.14A. *See also* Anglo-
  American Joint Commission on
  Palestine.
 Arab riots 32.07.08I, 39.04.28D,
  39.05.26A, 39.10.27F, 39.12.29I,
  40.03.15E, 40.08.30H, 40.11.08B,
  43.08.20A, 44.02.18C, 44.05.19B,
  46.05.17A, 46.06.14B, 46.07.05C,
  47.12.05B, 47.12.12A, 48.05.14A,
  49.04.08A, 51.08.24A, 51.12.14A,
  52.06.20B, 52.10.31A, 52.12.05A
 bi-national state 42.09.04B, 42.10.23B,
  47.07.18A, 47.09.05D
 British foreign policy on 32.07.08I,

32.07.15C, 32.07.22D, 35.08.02A,
  36.11.00B, 36.12.00C, 37.05.00A,
  37.07.30D, 38.12.30C, 39.02.10A,
  39.02.17A, 39.02.17E, 39.03.03A,
  39.03.10C, 39.03.24E, 39.03.31D,
  39.04.21C, 39.04.26A, 39.05.19G,
  39.06.02F, 39.06.09D, 39.07.14E,
  40.03.15B, 40.03.15E, 40.04.05A,
  40.04.12E, 40.05.03F, 40.09.27A,
  40.11.29A, 41.05.30B, 41.07.18A,
  42.02.27A, 42.03.13C, 42.03.20C,
  42.06.12B, 42.07.10C, 42.08.14C,
  42.10.23B, 43.01.29G, 43.02.12A,
  43.03.05A, 43.04.23A, 43.07.09A,
  43.09.10B, 43.11.26A, 43.11.26B,
  44.01.28C, 44.02.04A, 44.04.28B,
  44.07.07B, 44.11.24A, 45.03.02B,
  45.03.02C, 45.09.21A, 45.11.16B,
  45.11.30C, 45.12.07B, 45.12.14C,
  46.01.11D, 46.01.25A, 46.02.01A,
  46.02.01B, 46.04.19A, 46.05.03C,
  46.06.07B, 46.07.12B, 46.08.23A,
  46.08.30A, 46.08.30D, 46.09.06A,
  46.09.13A, 46.11.15B, 46.11.22D,
  46.12.20A, 47.02.14A, 47.02.21A,
  47.02.28A, 47.03.07C, 47.03.14B,
  47.03.21C, 47.03.28C, 47.04.25A,
  47.04.25B, 47.05.23B, 47.08.01A,
  47.08.15B, 47.10.03A, 47.10.31A,
  47.12.19A, 48.01.02A, 48.01.23A,
  48.02.06B, 48.02.06C, 48.04.09A,
  48.07.23B, 48.09.17E, 48.12.17A,
  49.01.14B, 49.02.04A, 49.06.17D,
  49.09.16B, 49.10.14B, 49.12.09B,
  49.12.09C, 49.12.16B. *See also* Anglo-
  American Joint Commission on
  Palestine.
 British foreign policy on, Passfield
  white paper 32.07.08H, 37.07.30A,
  39.06.23G, 42.11.06D
 British foreign policy on, Peel Commission 36.11.00A, 36.12.00A,
  36.12.00C, 36.12.00F, 37.07.09A,
  37.07.23A, 37.07.23C, 37.07.23F,
  37.07.30A, 37.07.30B, 37.07.30E,
  37.08.06B, 38.11.11B, 38.11.11G,
  39.06.23G, 46.08.09A, 47.02.07A,

Poe, Edgar Allen 44.03.03D, 44.08.25C,
46.04.19C, 48.12.17C, 51.04.06A

Poetry 27.12.10A, 41.12.19C, 42.02.06D,
46.01.18D, 48.07.16B. *See also* Bible;
Hebrew literature; Yiddish literature.
and creative process 48.06.11D
and Jewishness 45.06.08D
bad 48.12.24C
Canada 34.01.05A, 44.02.00A. *See also*
First Statement.
centrifugal, centripetal, and static
48.06.11D
definition of 32.10.07A, 37.06.00A,
46.04.19C
free verse 27.10.29A, 29.05.00A,
32.08.05E, 41.04.11C, 49.01.28D
Imagism 27.10.29A
Japan 48.12.24C
metaphysical 44.02.00A
modern 27.10.29A, 46.03.22D,
46.03.29D, 48.09.00A, 48.12.24C,
49.01.28D, 49.03.04C, 50.06.00A
proletarian 32.08.05E

Poetry Magazine 45.11.16D, 46.03.01D

Poets 34.01.05A, 42.07.10D, 44.01.14D,
46.04.19C, 48.12.24C, 49.01.14D,
53.03.20A
and society 53.03.06D, 53.03.13B
definition of 31.06.00A

Pogroms 38.11.18A, 40.03.15E, 45.08.03D,
46.01.04A, 46.02.01B, 46.04.05A,
46.06.21A, 46.07.12B, 46.07.19C,
46.08.23A, 46.09.20A, 47.04.18A,
48.10.01A. *See also* anti-Semitism;
Kishinev.

Polygamy 39.03.31D, 49.10.21C

Pope, Alexander 27.10.29A, 32.03.00A,
46.03.29D

Pope Pius XI 35.07.19A, 38.11.18B,
38.12.09G, 38.12.16D, 39.01.27D,
39.02.17D, 39.04.21A, 39.07.14C,
40.01.26D, 40.05.10G, 52.04.04A

Pope Pius XII 39.02.24H, 39.03.10A,
39.03.15A, 39.06.02B, 39.07.14C,
39.10.04A, 40.01.26B, 40.03.08E,
40.03.29F, 40.05.10G, 41.07.04F,
41.07.11D, 42.09.04A, 51.10.26B,

52.04.04A

Postage stamps 37.05.00B, 40.05.08A

Pouliot, Jean-François 42.03.13B,
42.03.27A, 48.04.16A

Pound, Ezra 27.10.29A, 44.02.00A,
45.05.25B, 48.09.00A, 48.11.19D,
49.03.04C

Pratt, E.J. 41.12.19C

Pravda 37.07.30C, 39.09.13H, 39.12.01D,
40.09.20H, 41.04.25B, 41.05.02C,
41.06.20F, 41.06.27A, 41.08.08F,
42.10.16E, 44.01.21A, 45.07.27C,
47.03.28B, 48.02.13B, 49.06.24A,
53.01.16A, 53.07.17A

Prokofiev, Sergei 48.02.20B

Propaganda 39.09.27G, 40.05.03H,
40.11.08B, 51.06.15A. *See also* advertising; anti-Semitism; journalism.
and journalism 37.08.06D, 39.07.28D
anti-British 47.04.10C
anti-Soviet 43.03.12A
communist 39.10.13F, 39.11.03B,
39.11.10C, 39.12.01B, 39.12.01D,
39.12.15F, 39.12.15H, 39.12.22B,
39.12.29G, 40.01.26C, 40.03.15A,
40.11.08D, 43.03.05B, 50.07.28B,
50.08.18A, 50.08.18B, 50.09.08B,
52.07.11A, 55.05.20A
fascist 38.12.16B, 40.05.24C, 40.11.08E
in World War I 40.04.05E
Nazi 35.08.02E, 36.12.00F, 38.11.25C,
38.11.25E, 38.12.02F, 38.12.16F,
39.04.28F, 39.05.12D, 39.05.19F,
39.06.09C, 39.06.16A, 39.06.16B,
39.08.04G, 39.08.11B, 39.08.11D,
39.08.18F, 39.09.22B, 39.09.27F,
39.10.13A, 39.10.13C, 39.10.20A,
39.11.10D, 39.11.17E, 39.12.20B,
40.01.12D, 40.01.26A, 40.03.22B,
40.04.05E, 40.04.12D, 40.05.10A,
41.02.28E, 41.03.07C, 41.07.04F,
41.08.01E, 41.09.05C, 41.10.24F,
41.11.07E, 41.11.21A, 41.12.19B,
42.01.30C, 42.03.20A, 42.06.19A,
42.10.16C, 42.12.11A, 43.01.15E,
43.02.26D, 43.03.12A, 43.09.17B,
45.02.16A, 45.09.14B, 46.01.04D,

50.08.18A. *See also Der Angriff; Der Stuermer; Voelkischer Beobachter.*

Protocols of the Elders of Zion 32.07.08A, 32.07.08J, 32.08.12C, 38.11.18B, 38.12.09H, 40.01.12D, 40.02.16C, 40.03.15D, 40.04.05E, 40.05.31A, 43.03.19A, 43.11.12A, 44.02.25B, 45.12.21B, 47.10.10C

Proust, Marcel 53.02.20B

Public opinion polls 48.11.19A

Purim 29.04.00A, 34.02.00A, 39.03.05A, 41.03.14D, 41.12.12A, 42.02.27C, 42.12.04A, 44.03.10A, 44.04.07A, 45.03.28A, 45.09.07A, 46.03.15A, 48.03.26A, 50.03.03D, 51.03.16B, 51.10.12A, 52.03.07A, 52.05.29B, 52.12.12A, 53.02.27A, 54.03.19B

Pythagoras 48.07.23C

Quakers 38.12.16F, 39.11.17A, 39.11.24A, 39.11.24B

Quebec. *See also* anti-communism; anti-Semitism; censorship; fascism; Jews; journalism; Montreal; nationalism; racism; religion; World War II.
 conscription 39.10.27B
 education 32.07.15A, 38.12.23E, 39.01.04B, 42.12.25C, 47.02.07C, 49.03.04B
 labour 49.06.17C
 law 38.12.16A, 40.01.05G, 40.04.14B, 47.03.28C
 politics 38.12.23C, 40.03.15C, 40.03.29A, 44.04.28C. *See also* Jewish schools question.
 politics, Action Liberale Nationale 37.08.06G, 39.10.27B
 politics, Liberal Party 39.10.27B, 44.02.25A
 politics, Union Nationale 39.06.09A, 39.06.23B, 39.07.21G, 40.05.31A, 40.06.14H, 40.06.28B, 40.06.28F, 40.07.05B, 43.11.12A, 44.02.25A, 47.01.24B, 52.01.11A
 Roman Catholic Church 46.06.07E
 women 40.04.14B

Quisling, Vidkun 40.05.03E, 40.05.10C,

40.07.05B, 40.07.26H, 41.01.17D, 41.01.31D, 41.03.28D, 42.12.11A, 43.02.19B, 44.05.05E

Rabelais, François 41.04.23C

Rabinovitch, Israel 37.07.23A, 37.07.30A, 39.01.05A, 39.01.13H, 39.02.17F, 39.04.07D, 39.06.02D, 39.07.28I, 39.09.08F, 39.11.28A, 39.12.01H, 40.01.12D, 40.01.26E, 40.03.01E, 40.08.23F, 40.10.11F, 41.01.17C, 41.02.07H, 41.12.26C, 42.07.10C, 42.09.11C, 43.02.12B, 43.03.05B, 43.09.24D, 44.06.23B, 45.04.27D, 46.09.20C, 46.10.16A, 48.01.30A, 48.02.20B

Racism 38.12.23B, 39.02.24F, 39.06.02B, 41.03.28C, 42.05.29A, 42.11.06A, 42.12.11E, 46.11.29A, 47.01.31B. *See also* anti-Semitism; fascism; Nazism; South Africa.
 Argentina 47.01.31A
 Britain 50.03.17C
 Canada 40.01.19G, 41.01.24B, 42.01.02C, 42.08.21E, 42.11.20B, 43.03.26B, 44.05.05B, 46.01.18C, 46.03.29B, 46.07.26B, 46.12.06B, 47.01.31A, 47.05.30B, 47.10.10C, 49.06.17A, 49.06.17B, 49.12.09D
 France 40.08.30C
 in journalism 39.06.02D
 Quebec 32.07.08B, 49.06.17C
 United States 32.07.29D, 39.10.20G, 39.11.17G, 39.12.08F, 42.03.20C, 43.06.25A, 46.12.20B, 47.01.31A, 47.04.18B, 47.12.26A, 48.07.02A, 51.09.07B. *See also* Ku Klux Klan.

Radar 45.12.07B

Raeder, Erich 40.05.10B, 41.05.30A, 41.05.30D, 44.03.17B, 46.10.04A, 52.06.06A

Raginsky, Abraham 39.08.18G, 42.01.09C

Ramsay, Archibald 41.08.08G, 44.09.29A, 44.10.20A

Rand, Ivan 48.12.31A, 50.12.01B, 53.11.06A

Rand, Sally 39.10.20H

Rank, Arthur J. 48.09.17E, 49.02.25A,

40.08.23B, 41.01.24E, 41.05.16E
Romains, Jules 44.02.11D
Roman Catholic Church 32.08.12G,
39.03.10A, 49.11.25A, 51.10.26B. *See also*
anti-Semitism; Canada; fascism; Nazism; Quebec; Spanish Inquisition.
Roman Empire 40.03.15F, 46.01.04C,
49.12.16D
Romanticism 27.12.10A, 49.08.19A
Rome 40.06.07G, 40.09.13B, 42.10.23C,
49.12.09E, 49.12.16D
Rome, David 47.06.07B
Rommel, Erwin 42.06.26B, 42.06.26D,
42.07.10C, 42.07.24A, 42.11.06C,
42.11.13A, 42.11.13D, 42.12.18B,
43.01.29A, 43.01.29F, 43.02.26D,
44.03.03B, 44.04.13B, 44.06.16C,
44.06.23C, 44.08.04A, 44.08.11C,
45.07.27B, 45.11.09B, 46.05.17A,
46.07.26A, 48.06.18C, 48.07.02C,
51.11.09A, 52.02.22A, 53.02.13B
Roosevelt, Eleanor 39.12.08F, 43.01.22A,
46.02.15A, 46.07.05B
Roosevelt, Franklin Delano 35.08.02B,
38.11.18A, 38.11.18B, 38.12.16B, 38.12.27B,
39.01.13B, 39.01.13C, 39.02.05B,
39.02.07A, 39.02.19A, 39.03.03B,
39.04.21F, 39.05.05B, 39.05.05C,
39.05.12E, 39.05.12F, 39.07.14D,
39.07.28A, 39.09.07A, 39.09.08B,
39.11.03E, 39.11.03G, 39.11.05A, 39.11.10G,
39.11.17D, 40.02.16B, 40.03.01A,
40.03.01C, 40.03.15F, 40.03.29E,
40.04.05E, 40.05.03A, 40.05.17D,
40.05.24E, 40.05.24G, 40.06.14A,
40.07.26E, 40.07.26F, 40.08.23E,
40.08.30D, 40.09.06E, 40.11.01D,
40.11.01E, 40.11.08F, 40.11.22E,
40.11.29G, 40.12.06B, 40.12.20A,
41.01.03D, 41.01.10B, 41.01.10D,
41.01.24E, 41.02.14F, 41.02.28E,
41.03.14B, 41.03.14C, 41.03.21D,
41.03.21F, 41.03.28A, 41.03.28D,
41.04.04F, 41.04.25A, 41.05.02E,
41.05.09D, 41.05.30A, 41.05.30E,
41.05.30F, 41.06.13B, 41.07.11B,
41.07.11E, 41.07.25B, 41.08.01A,

41.08.01E, 41.08.08H, 41.08.22C,
41.08.22D, 41.08.29E, 41.09.05E,
41.09.26A, 41.09.26D, 41.10.31E,
41.11.07A, 41.11.07B, 41.11.07D,
41.11.07E, 41.11.21C, 41.11.21D, 41.12.05C,
41.12.19B, 41.12.26B, 42.01.09D,
42.01.16A, 42.01.30C, 42.02.20C,
42.03.20B, 42.04.01A, 42.04.17D,
42.05.08F, 42.05.29D, 42.07.17D,
42.07.24C, 42.10.02B, 42.10.09A,
42.10.09D, 42.10.30A, 42.11.27D,
43.01.01B, 43.01.01D, 43.01.01F,
43.01.15F, 43.01.22C, 43.01.29B,
43.02.19B, 43.03.05A, 43.03.12A,
43.03.19A, 43.04.23B, 43.06.11B,
43.07.23C, 43.08.27A, 43.10.13B,
43.10.20A, 43.11.05B, 43.12.03B,
43.12.10A, 44.01.28B, 44.02.18A,
44.02.18B, 44.03.17A, 44.03.31B,
44.04.21B, 44.05.19B, 44.06.23A,
44.08.11A, 44.08.11C, 44.10.20B,
44.10.27D, 44.11.10A, 44.12.22B,
45.02.09A, 45.02.16A, 45.03.23A,
45.04.20A, 45.04.27B, 45.05.25A,
45.05.25B, 45.08.17A, 45.08.24C,
45.08.31B, 45.10.26B, 46.08.02A,
46.08.30D, 46.09.06A, 47.01.10B,
47.08.01A, 48.04.29B, 48.09.17C,
48.11.05A, 49.07.29A, 49.09.23D,
50.08.11B, 50.11.10A, 51.07.13A,
52.11.07B. *See also* oratory.
Roosevelt, Theodore 38.12.16B, 47.05.02B
Rose, Fred 50.02.10B
Rosenberg, Alfred 38.12.02D, 39.02.17F,
39.02.24C, 39.11.17G, 41.01.31D,
41.07.11D, 41.07.18F, 41.11.21A, 41.11.21D,
42.02.13C, 42.09.11A, 42.09.25C,
43.03.05C, 45.05.11A, 46.04.12B,
46.04.19B
Rosenberg, Isaac 41.12.19C
Rosenberg, Louis 36.12.00F, 40.02.23A,
41.07.18E, 42.07.24D, 46.01.18A,
47.06.07B
Rosenwald, Lessing 43.07.09A, 43.07.16C,
43.08.20A, 44.01.14B, 44.02.25C,
44.10.13D, 45.12.07A, 46.01.25B,
47.06.13C, 48.03.19D, 48.12.31C,

Sneh, Moishe 48.01.16B, 48.02.06C,
48.09.03B, 49.11.11C, 51.01.05B,
51.12.14A, 52.02.01A
Socialism 39.10.13F, 41.06.27A, 44.03.15A,
48.11.05B
Britain 43.06.18C, 46.05.24A
Germany 32.07.29B
Jewish 30.01.24A, 42.08.28E, 43.06.18C
Palestine 40.02.02B
United States 41.04.17E
Socrates 27.11.26A
Sokolow, Nahum 31.06.00A, 32.03.00A,
32.07.29B, 32.08.05B, 34.05.00A,
41.03.14D
Solomon, King of Israel 37.06.00A,
40.02.04A, 46.08.09A, 53.03.06D
Souster, Raymond 46.02.22C
South Africa 40.05.24A, 40.11.22A,
41.02.07F, 46.11.15A. *See also* anti-Semi-
tism; fascism; United Nations.
Apartheid 40.02.09E, 46.11.29A,
48.06.11B, 49.01.21B, 50.03.17C,
52.03.28A, 52.05.02A, 52.09.05A,
53.05.15C, 53.06.12A, 53.06.19B
Soviet Encyclopedia, The 51.09.28C
Soviet Union 39.02.10G, 39.02.24B,
48.09.17C. *See also* anti-Semitism; anti-
Zionism; art; censorship; Jews; journalism; nationalism; religion; Russia, czar-
ist; Russian humour; Russian
Orthodox Church; Russian Revolution
(1905); Russian Revolution (1917); *The
Soviet Encyclopedia*; White Russians;
World War II; Zionism.
cultural genocide of Jews 51.03.02A. *See
also* Biro-Bidjan; Yevsektzia.
economy 52.03.14A
exoneration of Jewish doctors
53.04.10A, 53.07.17A
forced migrations 49.09.23C
foreign policy 39.05.05C, 39.09.01A,
39.09.01F, 39.09.22A, 39.09.22E,
39.10.06F, 39.11.03B, 39.11.10C,
39.12.01B, 39.12.01D, 39.12.22B,
40.01.19D, 40.05.17F, 40.05.24C,
40.08.09C, 43.02.26A, 44.01.21C,
45.07.06B, 46.03.01A, 46.03.08A,

47.04.25C, 47.05.16A, 47.05.23A,
47.07.18B, 47.10.17B, 49.04.08A,
49.06.24A, 49.07.01C, 49.07.08D,
49.07.29B, 49.12.23B, 50.10.27B,
50.11.17B, 51.01.05A, 51.07.06A,
51.08.10B, 51.12.28A, 52.01.04A,
52.03.07B, 52.03.14A, 52.10.17A,
53.01.02A, 53.07.24A, 53.08.14B,
55.03.11A, 55.05.06A, 55.05.20A,
55.06.03A, 55.06.10A. *See also* Israel;
Palestine.
ideology 43.11.19C, 52.03.07B
politics 40.08.09C, 50.03.24B,
52.03.07B, 53.07.17A
purge of journalists 37.07.30C
science in 48.09.10C, 52.04.09B
writers 47.03.28B
Spain 39.05.26B, 39.05.26C, 40.04.05C,
49.05.20B, 54.02.05A, 54.02.05A. *See
also* anti-Semitism; fascism; Jewish
expulsion from Spain; Jews; Spanish
Civil War; Spanish Inquisition; United
Nations; World War I; World War II.
foreign policy 39.08.25D
human rights 45.05.17C
Spanish Civil War 37.07.23B, 38.12.30F,
39.01.24A, 39.02.03G, 39.02.24D,
39.03.03D, 39.03.28A, 39.05.26B,
39.06.16F, 39.06.23H, 39.10.13A,
39.10.13F, 40.04.05C, 40.08.16B,
40.09.20D, 41.08.08C, 53.07.31A
Mackenzie-Papineau battalion
39.02.10B, 39.02.17G
Spanish Inquisition 39.03.10D, 40.04.05C,
45.08.03D, 49.01.14C
Speer, Albert 46.10.04A, 52.06.06A
Spender, Stephen 46.03.29D, 50.12.29A
Spengler, Oswald 41.05.23G, 42.02.13C,
44.02.04D, 49.01.28D
Spinoza, Benedict 48.07.16B
Spiritualism of East 42.08.14E
St. Jean Baptiste Society 39.01.27D,
39.02.03D, 39.04.21A, 39.09.10A
St. Laurent, Louis 42.08.07G, 46.11.29A,
47.01.24B, 48.08.06A, 48.08.13B,
48.12.03C, 48.12.31A, 49.02.11B,
49.07.01A, 53.06.12A, 53.08.14A, 53.11.20A

Thailand 41.08.08B
theft of art treasures 40.07.19C
Turkey 41.02.21E, 41.06.27F, 41.12.05C,
    42.11.06C, 42.12.25A, 44.08.04A
second front 42.10.02F, 43.07.16A,
    43.09.24A
United States 39.10.04A, 39.11.03C,
    39.11.10G, 40.04.05E, 40.05.24E,
    40.06.17A, 40.08.23A, 40.12.06B,
    40.12.20A, 41.01.10B, 41.01.10D,
    41.03.14B, 41.03.21E, 41.03.21F,
    41.03.28D, 41.04.17A, 41.05.30A,
    41.06.20A, 41.07.11E, 41.08.01A,
    41.08.01B, 41.08.22C, 41.08.22D,
    41.08.22F, 41.10.24B, 41.10.31E,
    41.11.07E, 41.12.05C, 41.12.12B,
    41.12.19B, 42.04.24A, 42.05.29D,
    42.07.31A, 43.01.08A, 43.02.26C,
    43.03.12A, 46.02.08A
V-E Day 45.05.11D, 45.05.25E,
    45.08.17A, 45.09.07A
V-J Day 45.09.07A
war at sea 39.10.06E, 39.12.22G,
    40.02.23C, 40.04.12A, 40.04.26B,
    40.04.26H, 40.07.05D, 40.12.06B,
    41.01.10B, 41.01.10B, 41.02.28C,
    41.03.21C, 41.03.21E, 41.04.04C,
    41.05.02D, 41.05.30D, 41.07.11E,
    41.09.12F, 41.09.26B, 41.10.24B,
    41.11.07E
war in the air 40.08.30G, 40.10.16B,
    40.11.08E, 41.01.31E, 41.02.28C,
    41.07.18C, 42.05.01B, 42.06.05A,
    42.06.19A, 42.09.25F, 42.12.18A,
    43.03.12C
war in the Pacific 41.02.28D, 41.12.12B,
    42.03.20C, 42.05.08A, 43.08.27B
Yalta conference 45.02.16A, 45.03.23A,
    55.05.06A
Yugoslavia 39.08.13D, 41.03.28E,
    41.04.04D, 41.04.11B, 41.05.02D,
    41.05.16D, 41.06.20F, 41.08.29D,
    41.10.24C
World Zionist Organization 31.06.00A,
    33.01.00A, 34.05.00A, 34.12.00C,
    37.01.00A, 37.01.00C, 37.07.09A,
    37.08.06A, 39.02.17A, 39.07.28H,

39.08.18A, 39.08.22A, 39.08.25B,
    39.08.25D, 39.09.01G, 40.04.05A,
    41.02.07A, 41.05.09A, 41.08.08E,
    41.11.14A, 41.12.05D, 42.06.19B,
    42.08.07H, 43.03.19A, 43.04.02A,
    43.10.13C, 44.02.04A, 44.06.30A,
    44.12.01B, 44.12.08A, 44.12.15B,
    45.08.10A, 46.01.25A, 46.02.01A,
    46.04.26A, 46.08.23A, 46.10.16A,
    46.12.06A, 46.12.13A, 46.12.20A,
    47.01.03A, 47.01.03B, 47.06.27A,
    48.09.10A, 49.12.02A, 51.06.29C,
    51.08.17A, 52.11.07A, 52.11.14A,
    53.07.24B. *See also* Jewish Agency;
    Keren Hayesod; United Israel Appeal;
    United Palestine Appeal.
Wren, Christopher 45.06.08D, 46.06.28B
Wylie, Elinor 40.08.09A

Xenophobia 49.03.18D

Yarmolinsky, Avraham 48.09.10D
Yeats, William Butler 37.06.00A,
    44.01.28C, 46.03.29D, 48.07.30D,
    50.06.00A
Yehoash (Yehoash Solomon Bloomgarden)
    48.04.16C, 52.09.26C
Yesenin, Sergei 41.07.25A
Yeshiva University 47.04.04B, 52.10.10B,
    53.07.17B, 53.10.09B
Yeshivas 40.01.05A, 40.05.31B, 40.10.11A,
    41.01.10A, 41.10.31B, 42.03.13D,
    43.05.28B, 55.05.13A
    Montreal 42.05.22B, 44.05.05C,
        44.11.03C, 55.03.18B
Yevsektzia 39.10.06A, 39.12.22D, 39.12.29E,
    41.10.03D, 42.05.29E, 43.12.31B
Yiddish Encyclopedia, The 32.08.12B
Yiddish language 28.11.00A, 29.05.00A,
    29.11.00A, 30.11.14A, 31.00.00A,
    32.07.08D, 32.08.12B, 32.08.12F,
    39.07.04A, 42.10.02C, 45.04.27D,
    45.11.02C, 49.04.22C, 50.06.09C,
    52.11.28B, 52.12.05E, 54.03.12A
Yiddish literature 32.08.05E, 37.07.23D,
    39.04.28D, 40.06.28C, 41.01.03E,
    41.05.23C, 41.07.25A, 42.07.10D,

44.02.18D, 44.12.01A, 45.04.27D,
45.10.05B, 45.11.02C, 46.03.29C,
49.01.21C, 49.02.18C, 49.04.22C,
50.04.14D, 50.06.09C, 51.09.07C,
51.09.28C, 51.11.02A, 53.01.02C, 54.03.12A

Young, Edward 53.08.07A

Yom Kippur 40.10.11A, 42.09.18A,
43.10.08A, 45.09.14A, 46.10.09A,
48.10.08A, 49.09.30A, 51.11.02A,
52.09.26A, 53.03.27A

Young Communist League 40.12.27B,
47.02.14C

Young Judaea 28.11.00A, 30.01.24A,
30.09.19A, 31.00.00A, 32.06.00A,
34.10.00A, 34.12.00A, 36.12.00A,
39.10.06B, 40.04.12C, 41.02.07A,
42.01.09D, 42.12.00A, 42.12.18D,
49.07.08B, 52.02.22C, 53.02.27B,
53.05.08B, 54.01.29A

**Young Men's-Young Women's Hebrew
Association** 39.05.12B, 39.10.20D,
42.03.06C, 43.02.12D, 44.12.01A,
46.05.24C, 52.10.10A, 53.07.03B

Youth Aliyah 38.12.30C, 40.01.12B,
43.04.02A, 44.03.24A, 45.02.23A,
45.03.02A, 52.02.29A, 52.12.26A,
53.10.30B, 55.05.13A

Zadoc, Rabbi 48.05.14A

Zangwill, Israel 31.06.00A, 36.11.00B,
39.06.27B, 41.03.14D, 41.12.05D,
46.03.22A, 52.07.04A

Zelea-Codreanu, Corneliu 38.12.09C,
38.12.30B, 40.12.06C

Zhitlovsky, Chaim 40.02.07B, 40.02.23F,
40.08.02D, 43.05.14C, 43.09.24D

Zim, Jacob 53.05.08C

Zinoviev, Grigori Evseyevich 39.12.22A,
53.01.16A

Zionism 30.01.00A, 31.06.00A, 31.11.00A,
32.05.00A, 32.07.22B, 32.08.05B,
34.05.00A, 36.10.00A, 36.10.00D,
36.12.00B, 37.01.00A, 37.02.00C,
37.05.00A, 37.05.00B, 37.07.23A,
37.07.23C, 37.07.30A, 37.07.30E,
37.08.06A, 38.12.23B, 39.03.03A,
39.03.31D, 39.05.26A, 39.06.02F,

39.07.28H, 39.08.18A, 39.08.22A,
39.08.25C, 39.08.25D, 39.08.25E,
39.12.22D, 40.02.16A, 40.03.22B,
40.04.05A, 40.04.12C, 40.08.09A,
40.12.20F, 41.01.24B, 41.03.14A,
41.07.18A, 41.10.10A, 41.10.10B,
41.12.05D, 42.06.12B, 42.06.12C,
42.06.19B, 42.07.03B, 42.08.28E,
42.09.04B, 42.09.11C, 42.11.13B,
42.11.20D, 42.11.27B, 42.12.11D,
42.12.18C, 43.01.15B, 43.01.29C,
43.01.29E, 43.01.29G, 43.02.19A,
43.03.19A, 43.06.18C, 43.07.09A,
43.07.23A, 43.08.20A, 43.12.31A,
43.12.31B, 44.01.14B, 44.01.21C,
44.01.21D, 44.02.04A, 44.02.25C,
44.08.11C, 44.09.08C, 44.11.24A,
44.12.01B, 44.12.08A, 44.12.15B,
44.12.29B, 45.01.12A, 45.03.02C,
45.03.16B, 45.06.29B, 45.08.10A,
45.08.31B, 45.09.28A, 45.10.26B,
46.01.11A, 46.01.18A, 46.01.25B,
46.04.19A, 46.05.03C, 46.06.07D,
46.06.14A, 46.07.26A, 46.10.16A,
46.10.25A, 46.11.29B, 46.12.13A,
46.12.20A, 47.01.03A, 47.01.17A,
47.02.21B, 47.02.21C, 47.02.28B,
47.03.07A, 47.03.21A, 47.03.28A,
47.05.09A, 47.05.16A, 47.05.16C,
47.05.23A, 47.06.13A, 47.06.27A,
47.07.11B, 47.07.18C, 47.08.08A,
47.10.03B, 47.10.17A, 47.10.24B,
47.11.28B, 48.01.30A, 48.01.30B,
48.02.06C, 48.03.12B, 48.03.19B,
48.03.26C, 48.04.02A, 48.05.07A,
48.05.14B, 48.05.21B, 48.07.30A,
48.12.10A, 49.03.18D, 49.04.01C,
49.04.22B, 49.06.24A, 49.11.11B,
50.07.21B, 51.08.17A, 52.02.29A,
52.05.29A, 52.11.07A, 52.11.14A, 52.11.28A,
53.04.17A, 53.07.10A, 54.01.29A,
54.03.19B, 54.10.29A, 55.04.15A,
55.04.22A, 55.05.13A. *See also* anti-
Zionism; Balfour Declaration; Basle
Program; Chovevei Zion; Habonim;
Histadrut; Israel; Jewish homeland; Jewish nationalism; Palestine; refugees; ter-

rorism; Youth Aliyah.

Britain 39.12.22F, 43.01.22B

Canada 30.09.19A, 31.00.00A,
32.06.00A, 32.07.15B, 34.10.00A,
34.12.00A, 36.10.00B, 36.10.00C,
36.12.00A, 37.01.00A, 37.04.00B,
39.10.06B, 40.06.21C, 40.11.01B,
40.11.08A, 40.11.29C, 40.12.20B,
41.01.17A, 41.01.24A, 41.01.31A,
41.02.07A, 41.05.09A, 42.10.09A,
42.12.18D, 43.04.02A, 43.05.07C,
43.06.11C, 44.01.28A, 44.02.04B,
44.03.24A, 44.09.08B, 45.01.19A,
46.02.01A, 46.05.17A, 46.05.24B,
46.07.26B, 47.02.21C, 47.05.30B,
48.01.09A, 48.02.20A, 49.01.21A,
50.01.20A, 50.01.20B, 50.01.27A,
50.11.24A, 50.12.22A, 50.12.29A,
51.01.26A, 51.11.30B, 52.01.11B,
52.02.22C, 52.10.10A, 53.02.27B,
53.05.08B, 54.01.29A. *See also The
Canadian Zionist*; United Zionist
Council of Canada; Young Judaea;
Zionist Organization of Canada.

cultural 28.11.00A, 48.09.24A

North America 50.10.13A, 51.05.04A

revisionist 34.05.00A, 37.04.00B,
37.07.23C, 40.08.09A, 40.09.06B,
44.04.21D, 44.06.30A, 49.10.28D.
See also Irgun; New Zionist Organization; Stern Group.

Soviet Union 33.01.00A, 41.10.03D

United States 32.07.15B, 39.02.17B,
41.01.31E, 41.09.12C, 41.12.12C,
42.05.15B, 42.10.23B, 45.01.05B,
45.02.23A, 45.02.23B, 46.03.08B,
46.06.14C, 46.08.30D, 47.09.05C,
49.06.02B, 49.09.02A, 51.06.08B,
53.01.30C

Zionist Organization of America
32.07.15B, 41.09.12C, 42.10.23B,
45.01.05B, 45.03.23A, 49.06.02B,
53.01.30C

Zionist Organization of Canada
39.09.01B, 40.06.21C, 40.11.01B,
40.12.20B, 41.01.17A, 41.01.24A,
42.11.20C, 43.05.07C, 43.11.12A,
44.01.28A, 44.02.04B, 44.03.17C,
46.01.25A, 46.02.01B, 48.01.09A,
50.01.20A, 50.01.27A, 50.02.17C,
50.12.22A, 52.01.11B, 53.01.23A, 54.01.29A

Zlotnik, Judah Leib 29.05.00A, 32.09.23A,
37.05.00D, 40.01.19C, 48.12.10A

Zog, King of Albania 39.06.02E

Zola, Émile 35.07.19B, 42.02.06B,
42.07.17D, 44.01.28C, 48.06.25C

Zunz, Leopold 30.01.00A, 46.02.08C

Zweig, Stefan 42.02.27B, 42.03.06D,
44.02.04D

INDEX TO CRITICS LISTED
IN THE BIBLIOGRAPHY